The Ultimate Guide to Deer Hunting Skills, Tactics, and Techniques

The Ultimate Guide to Deer Hunting Skills, Tactics, and Techniques

Edited by **Jay Cassell**

Skyhorse Publishing

Skyhorse Publishing books may be purchased in bulk at special discounts for sales promotion, corporate gifts, fund-raising, or educational purposes. Special editions can also be created to specifications. For details, contact the Special Sales Department, Skyhorse Publishing, 307 West 36th Street, 11th Floor, New York, NY 10018 or HYPERLINK "mailto: info@skyhorsepublishing.com"info@skyhorsepublishing.com.

Skyhorse® and Skyhorse Publishing® are registered trademarks of Skyhorse Publishing, Inc.®, a Delaware corporation.

Visit our website at www.skyhorsepublishing.com.

10 9 8 7 6 5 4 3 2 1

Library of Congress Cataloging-in-Publication Data is available on file.

Cover design by Owen Corrigan
All images courtesy of Thinkstock unless otherwise noted.

Print ISBN: 978-1-62914-464-1
Ebook ISBN: 978-1-63220-235-2

Printed in Canada

Table of Contents

Introduction

JAY CASSELL

While putting this book together, I have to admit that I've been sneaking into my television room to watch the World Cup. Today, I saw two different types of soccer matches: Argentina convincingly beat Nigeria 3-1, and France and Ecuador played to a grueling 0-0 tie. In the first game, Argentine star Lionel Messi pounded in two goals in the first half – one, a penalty shot, the other a shot that careened off a teammate's leg. His first goal came early, the second late in the first half – suddenly, seemingly out of nowhere. The rest of the game went back and forth, with each team getting one goal.

The France – Ecuador game (don't worry, this is not a soccer book, please bear with me) was a hard-fought battle, with neither side scoring. Each team probed and shot and was rejected, only to try again, to be rejected again. Neither team was fulfilled at the end of the game (although France did advance into the next round, based on prior victories).

Why do I bring this up? Because, as I watched the games, it was clear that deer hunting is actually quite similar to soccer – or, in a sense, to a hard-fought football game, or a day of bass fishing. You try and you try and you try, and you come up empty again and again. But you keep trying. And sooner or later you score – a goal if soccer, a good-sized bass if fishing, a buck if deer hunting. It's all about being persistent.

Think about this. How many days have you sat in a treestand and seen nothing – nothing in the morning, nothing in the late afternoon, nothing in the middle of the day should you choose to hunt at that time. The weather changes, the season changes, the hunting pressure shift, and you sit there, not seeing anything. I sure have my long list of deerless days. You do too, I'm certain. But…BUT…you pay your dues, spend your time, and you know…YOU KNOW…that eventually something is going to come walking down the trail you're watching. It might be a doe or a spike or a forkhorn…or, it could be a monster 10-pointer. It will happen—maybe not this season, or next, but in your hunting days, it's going to occur. Just as a chance at shooting a goal in soccer will happen if you stick to it, if you keep trying. And, when you get that chance, are you up for the task? Will your shot be true? If you're a bowhunter, will you draw back your bow quietly, unseen by the approaching buck? And, when you release the arrow, will your shot be on the mark? Will all those days and weeks of practice finally pay off? Or, will you blow it? Will buck fever get the better of you? Or, perhaps, will an unseen twig deflect your arrow (or bullet) just enough to make you miss?

This is deer hunting. It's the ultimate challenge. You practice, you study your quarry, you study the terrain of your hunting area, then you give it your best shot. Sometimes you win, sometimes you don't. But when your time comes, when the moment of truth arrives, when a buck comes out of that thicket and presents a shot and your adrenaline is pumping so hard you can't even think, that's what we live for. That's why we do it. That's why we put in the time. Fill the freezer? Absolutely? But what a way to do it, if you are able to.

In this book, you're going to find solid information that you can use to help you get a deer this year. Be it information on using deer calls, properly placing a treestand, still-hunting, hunting different phases of the rut, trailing deer, cooking venison --- it's all here, with chapters from many experts, including Peter Fiduccia, John Trout, Dr. Leonard Lee Rue III, Hal Blood, J. Wayne Fears, and more. I've even included a few chapters of my own in here – tactics I've learned from hunting the highly pressured Catskill Mountains of New York. I also included a story I wrote about hunting blacktail deer on Alaska's Kodiak Island – an incredibly beautiful island that just happens to be home to some of the largest bears in the world. If you want to know what an adrenaline rush is really about, step foot on the shores of Kodiak. When you see a pawprint in the sand that's twice as long as your boot, when you realize that you are no longer the number one predator in the area, you'll suddenly be humbled in ways that words can't describe. All that is because deer hunting brought you there.

I hope you enjoy this book. It's taken a long time to put together, because there is so much information out there. Sifting through it all, picking just the right stories, took much hard work. But if you can you use some of this information to your advantage, if you can get a deer with it, then my job has been worth it.

Good hunting!

Jay Cassell
Katonah, New York
June 24, 2014

The Ultimate Guide to Deer Hunting Skills, Tactics, and Techniques

Part 1

Tactics and Techniques

Introduction

JAY CASSELL

The first section of this book is the largest, and for good reason. There are so many conceivable tactics and techniques in deer hunting that you could easily fill up a book on them alone. Much depends on where you hunt. Do you hunt in the mountains? Farmlands? Suburbs? Over food plots?

Much of your hunting should depend on what you know about the deer in your area. Study them, know what they do and where they go, understand how they use their senses, learn how to read their sign. Then you can make informed decisions on hunting your favorite areas.

The next question is, when do you hunt? Before the rut? During the rut? After it's over? And what about hunting in hot weather or cold weather? Rain or snow? Wind? Early or late in the day? Midafternoon?.

As far as gear is concerned, do you hunt with a rifle? Bow? Muzzleloader? Handgun? All or some of the above?

How about hunting from a treestand – is that your preference? You get a good view of the land, and if the wind is right, your scent is blowing away from where deer are likely to come from. On the other hand, you aren't exactly mobile in a treestand, and if you hunt a stand too often, the deer are going to figure out that there is a human being in the area, and they're going to avoid that stand site.

Me, I like to still-hunt when it makes sense, because I can creep along ever so slowly and check out likely areas. I don't do it when the leaves are dry and crackly, or the snow is encrusted with ice, because then I sound like a freight train in the woods. That's when I go climb a tree.

And if you get something – well, we've got techniques for butchering your deer here as well, courtesy of hunting expert John Weiss.

So spend some time with this section. No, it's not all-knowing, all-seeing, but it cover a lot of ground. Some of the tactics in here are going to be just what are looking for. You just have to figure out when and where to use them to your advantage!

The Five Senses

DR. LEONARD LEE RUE

Formerly, when I was asked in my lectures which of the deer's five senses was the most important, I unequivocally championed the sense of smell. Now I qualify that by saying that would be true only when conditions are favorable. What caused me to qualify my statement?

Hearing

It is true that deer can detect danger for a longer distance using their sense of smell, but only if the wind is blowing that scent toward them. If the wind is blowing away from them, the deer cannot smell danger even if it is close. In view of that reassessment, I now say that, under most conditions, the deer's hearing is its most important sense, because even if the wind is not favorable, there is the chance that the deer will hear something. In addition, there are times when a deer simply isn't using its other senses but is always using its hearing. A deer can be in a deep sleep, but its ears never stop moving, winnowing its surroundings for the slightest sound of danger. What is more remarkable is that even while a deer is sleeping, its brain is analyzing and filteringout sounds that don't represent danger. A deer's brain remembers a huge file of nonthreatening sounds, such as tree limbs rubbing gently against one another; dried leaves and nuts falling; mice, voles, and shrews scampering in the forest duff. Even the noisy sound of a squirrel

While there are times when a deer is not using its other senses, it is always using its hearing.

A deer's sense of hearing may be its most important one. It's large ears help funnel the slightest sound to auditory nerves.

A deer can turn its ears to the rear to listen behind. It also pivots its ears rearward so they don't impair vision in that direction.

scurrying in nearby leaves will not cause the deer to awaken. Yet the distant footfall of a human, a twig snapping, or hard-surfaced clothing scraping against brush will waken that deer in an instant. That's why wool and fleeces are better materials for hunting clothing. Their soft-napped surfaces aren't nearly as noisy as denim, canvas, and Gore-Tex.

When we humans want to hear something better, we often cup a hand behind our ear so that more sound waves are directed into the auditory canal. The deer's large ears do that same thing, but they do it better.

The average whitetail's ear is about seven inches in length and about four and a half inches in width, giving it approximately twenty-four square inches of receptive surface. Deer have a further advantage over humans because their ears are movable and can pivot in all directions. Much of the time a deer will have one ear turned forward and the other pivoted to the rear so it can listen for sounds in each direction. They also pivot their ears backward so they don't block their vision when they want to see to the rear.

We have to turn our head to hear best from a given direction. But we can usually sense the direction when the sound enters equally in both ears, guiding our eyes toward the source.

Mr. Andrews, my high school principal, liked to ask such theoretical questions as, "If a tree fell in the forest and no one were there to hear it, would it make noise when it fell?" Of course it would, because the crash would create sound waves. Noise, or sound, waves are created whether or not creatures hear them. Hearing becomes involved only if some creature's auditory nerves are stimulated.

Sound is a form of energy that reaches the ear as cyclic vibrations. With low-pitched sounds, the waves are fairly shallow and wide spaced. High-pitched sounds compress the width of the wave, forcing them into high peaks, or frequencies. The adult human ear can hear in the range of forty to sixteen thousand cycles per second. Deer have a greater hearing range. I can attest to the fact that they can hear frequencies higher than thirty thousand cycles. As a wildlife photographer, I occasionally use a "silent" dog whistle to get some creature's attention. The human ear cannot hear this very high-pitched whistle, which was calibrated by machine, but dogs and deer respond to it readily.

Despite the difference in the size of the external ears of humans and deer, the auditory canal opening is the same in both: about one-third inch. The sound waves entering the auditory canal are compressed and directed to the "tympanic membrane," or eardrum, causing the membrane to vibrate. These vibrations activate the three tiny bones of the inner ear, which in turn amplify the incoming sound as much as ninety times. These vibrations also cause the thousands of tiny hairs in the "endolymph" fluid to be stimulated, allowing them to turn a mechanical motion into an electrical impulse that activates the auditory nerve. The nerve impulses are then transmitted to the temporal lobe of the brain, which deciphers what is being heard.

The volume of sound is measured in decibels. Here again, deer have the advantage. They do not wear iPods, use jackhammers, or stand close to jet engines, all of which gradually destroy the tiny hairs that make hearing possible. Most of the current generation of young people will suffer tremendous hearing loss as they age because of the destruction they've done to their ears by playing music at high volume.

Deer become extremely nervous during periods of high wind, when the crashing of branches drowns out other sounds. Many hunters have noticed that deer leave the area, when a flock of wild turkeys comes feeding through the woods. It's not that the deer are afraid of the turkeys; instead, the deer may sense that the turkeys' constant scratching in the leaves would mask sounds of potential danger.

I have found that a gunshot does not represent danger to deer. It will alert the deer, but if there

Fog will hold all types of scents close to the ground where deer will more easily detect it.

is only a single shot the deer may not be able to ascertain the direction of the shot any better than we humans do. Deer can even become habituated to gunshots; in fact, they can get used to almost all types of noise that does not represent danger to them. On many army bases, deer are not hunted because of the military facility. Such deer often feed on artillery practice ranges, where even the constant booming of the big guns does not disturb them because it's not a threat. Everyone has seen deer feeding alongside highways, with huge tractor-trailers roaring by, yet if no vehicle stops, the deer don't even look up.

I have also noticed that sound often stimulates the deer's "bump of curiosity." The old saying that "curiosity killed the cat" can also be the undoing of a deer. Curiosity is a sign of intelligence, and deer are intelligent creatures. I know that deer do dumb things at times, but at times, so do humans. Sometimes when a deer hears a sound and can't confirm the source by scent, it decides to check it out. The deer will either circle around to get the wind in its favor or advance very cautiously, directly toward the sound. At such times, a deer is as fully alert as it will ever be. It walks stifflegged in the direction of the sound, with its head bobbing up and down or side to side and both ears swept forward. A deer may snort in the attempt to startle the unknown something into betraying its location. But such curiosity may get it into trouble.

Scent

At what distance can a deer detect danger by scent? How can a person eliminate human odor? For answers, let's go back to basics.

Almost all odors in the natural world are of organic composition and are released as molecules of gas. For gases to be smelled, and there are some odorless gases, they must be mixed with or dissolved in liquid. Many variables affect a deer's ability to smell, such as barometric pressure, humidity, temperature, rain, snow, and wind direction and velocity. Ideal scenting conditions exist at sixty to seventy degrees Fahrenheit, with a humidity of 60 to 70 percent. High temperatures will waft scent aloft; low temperatures keep the scent molecules close to the ground, but they make it harder for creatures to smell the scents because low temperatures dry out the lining of their nostrils. Rain and snow drive scent molecules to the earth and dilute them. And wind disperses them—the stronger the wind, the faster and farther they are dispersed.

I recall a very graphic example of my scent diffusing outward. I had a permanent photographic blind set up on Helen Whittemore's estate. Helen had fed the deer every day for years and my blind had been in place for years, built right into her fence. The deer were accustomed to feeding in safety, and my blind was a part of their environment.

That day, I was in the blind and the scenting conditions for the deer were ideal; there was not a breath of a breeze. My scent diffused outward from the blind in a circle, and although the deer couldn't see me, it was if a barrier was physically pushing the deer backward as my scent moved outward, and they refused to cross that scent barrier. This explains why a hunter's stand can be fantastic one day and useless at another. If the hunter goes into his tree stand on a fabulous October afternoon when the air is crisp, the sun warm, and the sky cobalt blue, his chances for success are high. The sun, warming the earth, will create thermals, lifting his scent almost directly upward so no matter what direction a deer approaches the area from, it is not likely to detect the hunter's scent. If, early the next morning, the hunter goes back to the same stand, while the ground is shrouded with light fog, his chances of being successful are almost nil. That's because his scent is dropping to the ground and rolling outward toward the deer.

Especially in no-hunting areas, deer have learned that human scent does not necessarily mean danger.

How far can a deer detect a scent? Under those ideal conditions of sixty to seventy degrees Fahrenheit and 60 to 70 percent humidity I just described, if the scent is pushed along by a moderate breeze, I am sure a deer can detect human scent at half a mile if not farther.

Can you eliminate human scent? no. Wearing charcoal-impregnated clothing will help because the charcoal will filter out body odor caused by bacterial action on our sweat glands. Keeping your hunting or photography clothes in a clean plastic bag with cedar branches when not in use will help, because it will prevent their absorbing human or other household odors. Using cover scents, such as fox or deer urine, will help, because they can mask human odor. Using chlorophyll tablets to cleanse your breath does not help, because goats eat lots of grass filled with chlorophyll, and I can verify that chlorophyll doesn't mask a goat's breath or odor. Your breath is going to be your undoing every time because as long as you are alive you have to breathe, and every time you exhale you are pouring out body odor. If you stop breathing, you will smell even worse in a very short time.

I want to bring up an aspect of human odor on which I do not have an answer but will state my views. I have read articles, corroborated by very successful deer hunters who urinate from their tree stands when they need to empty their bladders. They claim that deer are attracted to urine no matter what the source. Some professional hunters have written that they've used regular household ammonia as a deer attractant, with results as good as using the deer's own urine. All I can say is that all of those methods contradict everything I have experienced and learned over a lifetime of studying, observing, trapping, hunting, and photographing wildlife. I stick by my statement, "The scent of man, in any form, means danger to deer, under most circumstances."

Deer continually lick their nose because the moisture helps trap scent molecules.

It is true that urban and suburban deer are not as alarmed by the odor of man as their ancestors were, because they are exposed to human scent in "safe areas" where man does not represent danger. Where deer are hunted, the odor of humans still means danger.

I know several dairy farmers who have collected, and successfully used, urine from their cows in estrus as an attractant for whitetail bucks. It wasn't the ammonia that attracted the bucks; it was the pheromones in the cow's urine.

In hopes of rerouting deer to my stand, I sometimes urinated on a trail that I did not want the deer to use, basically saying "deer detour." If you are going to urinate on the ground around your stand, why bother to do any of the things that increase your chances of success? Why use a cover scent; why put your stand downwind of where you hope the deer will come; why keep your clothing and body as scent free as possible; why use the wisdom employed by hunters forever? The Indians would stand in smudge fires of sweet grass or evergreen boughs to help overcome their body odor.

They always took advantage of the wind direction to make sure the deer were not aware of their presence. I bet they didn't urinate in the spot they were standing while waiting for a deer, and I advise you not to do it either.

The sense of smell is the response to "chemoreception" by the limbic system, found on the base of cerebrum, the front portion of the brain. The olfactory bulb then transmits an electrical impulse directly to the brain stem where the odor is classified. This area of the brain also controls appetite, digestion, and emotions, linking the sense of smell closely to all three.

The "rhinarium," the hairless skin covering on the front of the deer's nostrils, is moist from subcutaneous glands, but the deer increases the amount of moisture by frequent licking with its tongue. The moose and caribou, being northern animals, have hair covering their rhinarium to protect it from freezing. The deer's long muzzle also aids in the collecting of scent molecules because its extra length has a greater "epithelial" surface for the scent molecules to adhere to.

We know that the deer's sense of smell is far superior to that of a human and may not be as good as that of the average dog. A human can detect skunk odor, "mercaptar" even when it is dissolved to one to twenty-five hundred thousand part of one milligram. On a foggy night, you can walk a quarter mile through an unpleasant fog of skunk scent, even though the skunk released only a few drops of its musk. Most of us can identify hundreds of odors, while the trained noses of professional "perfumers" can identify thousands. It is claimed that dogs can detect odors one hundred million times better than we humans can. Unfortunately, we don't know what deer can smell because they do not lend themselves to testing. Deer just aren't as interested in pleasing humans as dogs are.

I find it very interesting, and puzzling, that a mother deer cannot recognize the voice of her own fawn. A doe will respond to the distress call of any fawn but will not allow any fawn to nurse, until she has first proven to herself that it is her own by smelling it.

Deer live in a world rich with scents that we humans can't even imagine.

Vision

There is nothing that moves within a deer's range of vision that deer do not detect. Yet, if a person stands motionless, detection is unlikely. However, unless you blend into your surroundings, the deer may become suspicious, even if it does not recognize you as a human. Deer are so thoroughly familiar with everything in their home range that any

The deer has a much larger eye than we humans. And its elongated pupil helps give wide-angle viewing.

unfamiliar object is cause for suspicion. In an effort to blend in with my outdoor surroundings, I always wear camouflage clothing, which might not always blend with my background, but it does break up my human outline.

We humans have eyes in the front of our heads, as do most predators, which provides us with binocular vision and greater acuity of sight—both factors helping us gauge distances. We have a range of vision between 170 to 180 degrees of a circle— roughly a half circle. Deer have eyes on the sides of their heads, as do most prey species, and their eyes protrude beyond the skull, which allows them to see almost a full circle around themselves, roughly 310 degrees, except for a small wedge behind the skull of about fifty degrees.

The human eye has a round pupil that is of different color, primarily according to race. The deer has a brown rectangular pupil that enhances its wide-angle view of its world. I have seen photographs of a local deer that had blue eye pigment instead of the normal brown—the so-called watch-eye that is fairly common in horses. The blue or white pigment does not seem to affect the horse's vision. This is a genetic condition, and all of the Catahoula hounds, the state dog of Louisiana, have the watch-eye. The condition is also quite common in husky dogs.

Deer have much larger eyes than humans do, and this adaptation enables them to move about after dark. The larger eye allows more transmittal of light. In addition, deer see better in the dark because they do not have the yellow filter in the lens of their eyes that humans have. Because humans are basically "diurnal" creatures (sleeping at night), the yellow filter helps to shield our eyes from the sun's harmful ultraviolet rays. By contrast, deer are "crepuscular," moving about primarily at dawn, dusk, or at night. Not having the yellow filter allows deer to see in the

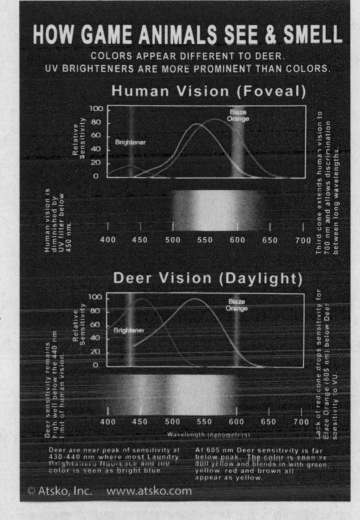

cold or blue range of the light spectrum which is a tremendous advantage in low-light situations.

As to color vision, it was long thought that deer and most mammals except primates see everything in shades of gray. That seemed to partially explain why there are no brightly colored mammals. We now know that deer have "dichromatic vision" and can see through the violet, blue, green, and yellow region of the light spectrum. They cannot see color in the orange and red range as we humans do. This is why the blaze orange color that hunters are required to wear in most states has been so effective. The use of blaze orange has dramatically reduced hunting accidents but has not reduced hunting success because the deer don't see that color; they see it as a shade of light yellow. Wherever legal to do so, I recommend that hunters wear blaze-orange camo to break up what would otherwise be a large, blaze-orange block of light yellow.

The eye works along the same basic principle as a camera. The cornea acts as filter to protect the lens, much as I use a skylight filter on my camera lens. The lens allows for the transmission of light. But, whereas the pupil of our eye opens or closes according to the intensity of the light, that of the deer does not. The lens focuses the image seen on the retina at the back of the eye, which is comparable to the film in the back of a camera. The retina, the photoreceptive surface at the back of the eye, is composed of rods and cones. Sharpness of vision and sensitivity to color depend on the cone cells. The rod cells are used primarily for night vision, and deer have more rods, while we humans have more cones. We do have a circle of rod cells that we can

A deer's eyes reflect light shined on them because they have a mirrored surface at the rear of the retina called the "tapetum lucidum."

use at night if we do not look directly at what we want to see, but rather look slightly off to the side of it. Behind the deer's rod cells—as in many animals, but not primates, including humans—is a reflective layer known as the "tapetum lucidum," which reflects the light back through the rods, doubling the amount of light that the optic nerves receive. This produces the "eye shine" that deer show when a light is directed in their eyes at night.

Under the cover of darkness, deer will often bed in the open area they are feeding in, something they would not do during daylight hours. Many times when driving into these open fields at night to census the deer, I would see dozens of eyes reflecting my headlight like scattered diamonds. Scientists have calculated that deer can see at least one thousand times better than humans in low-light situations. The optic nerves receive the image and generate the neural impulses that send the image to the occipital lobes of the brain where the images from the two optic nerves are coordinated into one.

Grooming and Bonding

The bonding, done through touch, is as important to deer and other creatures as it is to humans. From the moment of birth, the doe spends hours licking the amniotic fluids from her fawns, cleansing their bodies but also creating the bond that will unite them until they become adults and even beyond. Fawns at a very young age will reciprocate by licking their mother in what is known as "mutual grooming." This no longer serves a cleansing function; rather, it reinforces recognition and reassurance, important in the relationship. Each time the doe returns to nurse her fawns, she will lick their anal region, while they nurse, to stimulate their bowels. She then consumes both feces and urine that is voided. This helps protect the fawns by eliminating

A doe licks her fawn's anal region while it nurses, and this stimulates its bowels. She consumes the waste as it's voided.

the potential odor of their waste. After the nursing is completed, the grooming continues until the fawns wander off to seek a place of concealment.

Deer live in a matriarchal society, and the female fawns may stay in their mother's family group until they are two and a half to three and a half years old, and mutual grooming continues to knit the family together. At dispersal time, one and a half years of age, young bucks leave their mothers to form juvenile bachelor groups or join a group of adult bucks. Mutual grooming also bonds these male groups together, which are rent by the increasing competitiveness of bucks, young and old, as the rutting season begins. In the bachelor groups, all bucks mutual-groom one another, but the subordinate bucks usually initiate the grooming. Grooming may be done to all parts of the body but is most often concentrated on the head

and neck areas where deer can't groom themselves. Frequently, the grooming concentrates in licking each other's forehead scent glands.

Touch

Quite often when a doe and her fawns lie down they will bed close enough so their bodies touch.

Touch is also very important during the breeding season and is engaged in much more by the sexually experienced adult bucks than by the yearlings. Even at the peak of a doe's estrus period, she will usually run off a short distance before allowing the buck to breed her again. To shorten the distance involved in chasing, the experienced, older buck will rub his body against the doe; he will groom her head, neck, and body and lick her vulva.

There are times when the doe will not only reciprocate but actually initiates sexual grooming. Young bucks that haven't learned the proper courtship proceedings chase does all over the place before they can get them to stand. The chaos created in a herd from which all of the adult bucks have been removed is one of the big drawbacks to the emphasis by state game departments on trophy buck

Bucks and does mutually groom each other during courtship, which is a form of foreplay.

management. Does that have been run ragged during the rutting season by inexperienced young bucks may have a hard time surviving a severe winter.

Tactile sensations are also important when deer stomp a front hoof to signal that they detect something that might prove dangerous. Such a message is often received by deer that can't even see the sender. They feel hoof-stomp vibrations through the earth.

Taste

I often think that taste should be considered in combination with smell. Have you ever noticed that you can't really taste many things until you exhale the odor past the scent receptors in your nose, which are ten thousand times more discerning than your taste buds? We know that deer are usually able to distinguish between poisonous and nonpoisonous plants, but we don't know if they do so by taste or smell.

I recently learned from Dr. James Kroll that some of the deer in the hill country of Texas eat a plant that effectively emasculates the bucks. The toxins in the plant cause the buck's testicles to shrink to the size of marbles and the resulting lack of testosterone prevents the full antler cycle from occurring. We don't know if the same plant prevents the does from becoming pregnant. And we don't know which plant is the culprit and why the deer don't avoid eating it.

Deer love to eat both mushrooms and lichens.

In September, the woodlands in my area produce untold numbers of the deadly amanita mushroom, yet the deer never eat them.

Deer also discriminate among the acorns they eat, always eating the white oak acorns first, because they have the least amount of the

Deer eat many kinds of lichen, which are high in protein.

bitter tannic acid. Deer will eat the chestnut oak acorn only when they have to, because of its comparatively high tannic-acid content. Research lists over seven hundred different plants that the deer will eat in my area of northeastern United States, but circumstances and season often determine when they eat many of those plants. In some areas, the deer will eat daylilies; but they seldom do near my home in New Jersey. A list of deer foods for Massachusetts includes spicebush, but in New Jersey I have seen it eaten by deer on only three occasions, and only when all other foods were in short supply. In the fall of 2004, when the acorn crop was very poor, deer ate spicebush even though the volatile aromatic oil in the plant inhibits the bacterial fermentation in the deer's rumen.

Terrain Aerial Photos Tell All

JOHN WEISS

Because the definition of scouting is "an attempt to find something by conducting a search," the deer hunter who does not make use of aerial photos cannot possibly hope to take home big bucks on a regular basis.

One exception to this rule is an acquaintance of mine by the name of Mule Morris, who lives in central Tennessee. Morris, 65, has taken a nice buck every year he has hunted. The reason for his success is that he hunts exclusively upon the 520-acre homestead farm where he was born and has lived all his life. As a result, if you know him well, and are able to gain permission to hunt his acreage, there's no need to do any scouting. Mule will simply point out any number of places where you can go sit on opening morning, and no matter which place you select, he'll bet a dollar your buck will be hanging in his barn by sundown. To the best of my knowledge, he's never had to reach for his wallet.

In virtually every other circumstance, however, aerial photos are essential to a hunter's success.

My regular hunting partner Al Wolter seconds that scouting axiom. For more than 20 years, Wolter worked for the U.S. Forest Service, managing hundreds of thousands of acres of national forest lands in several states.

"In fact," Wolter says, "the topographical maps we deer hunters have used for many years yield only a fraction of the information aerial photos do."

Taking a Closer Look

A dedicated whitetail hunter with more than 100 bucks to his credit, Wolter religiously uses aerial photos every hunting season. He's puzzled as to why others do not utilize this invaluable tool as well.

"I can remember sitting in my office studying aerial photos to compile a new forest management plan for a given region," he recently recalled, "and it was often difficult to pay attention to my work. I began spotting generation-worn deer trails leading to and from food plots such as mast-bearing oak trees, and this tempted me to begin evaluating how animals were living and moving in that specific area. After that. I'd sometimes even begin daydreaming where I'd place a stand to have the best chance at bushwhacking a nice buck."

Aerial photographs came into widespread use in the early 1930s when Congress passed the Agricultural Adjustment Act. This was during the Depression, and the goal of the AAA was to assist farmers in establishing and maintaining a balance between crop and livestock production and national food-consumption needs. It quickly became apparent that virtually any landform could be measured and studied in only a fraction of the time with aerial photos than by actually walking the ground, dragging surveyor's chains, and then drawing maps.

Since then, three other agencies of the U.S. Department of Agriculture—the Farm Service Agency (FSA), U.S. Forest Service (USFS), and Soil Conservation Service (SCS)—have come to rely upon the precise visual information provided by aerial photos. Those photos are now used to assist in conservation practices, forest management, urban development, pollution studies, drainage programs, boundary determinations, watershed planning, road construction, and even tax assessment. The combined aerial photography files they maintain presently cover about 90 percent of the nation.

How to Obtain Aerial Photos

USDA offices generally maintain photo files only for their specific county-by-county regions. In most instances, these photos are in 12x12-inch black & white format and in scales ranging from one inch = 4,833 feet to one inch = 200 feet, each at a cost of about $6 apiece. There are variations ranging in size up to 38x38 inches, and in some regions such photos are even available in color.

If the particular photos you're interested in are not on file in the county seat where you plan to hunt, agency officials will help you fill out the necessary order form, which is then mailed to the Aerial Photography Field Office, P.O. Box 30010, Salt Lake City, UT 84130. Your photos will arrive, rolled up and in a tube, in approximately three weeks.

It's important to note that although you can look at and study an aerial photo, just as you would a common photo that you might take yourself, an aerial photo is not like a one-dimensional topographic map. Far from it. Most aerial photos are taken with the intention of being viewed in

stereo pairs with a handy little device known as a stereoscope (photo below). Compact models of stereoscopes intended for field use are available for less than $20 through stores that sell engineering supplies and surveying equipment.

A stereoscope gives you a three-dimensional look at the landscape, which is critical if you want to really learn about the terrain structure. In so doing, it's like watching a 3-D movie in which you can see deep into valleys and riverbottoms while the higher elevations literally jump out into the forefield of view. There is simply no comparison between looking at an ordinary topo map comprised of an artist's contour lines and having an intimate, first-hand look at the environment as it really is through a stereoscopic examination of an aerial photo. Another advantage to using a stereoscope is that the device magnifies what you're looking at by 2 ½ to five times

Aerial photos come in standard twelve-inch-square format and are designed to be viewed with a stereoscope.

what the naked eye would see in studying the same photo. This provides a wealth of insight because, just like fish, deer use terrain contours in their travels, and even ten-foot changes in elevation may have a pronounced influence upon their directional movements.

Scouting From Your Living Room

In my own pursuit of whitetails, I use aerial photos in two distinctly different ways, and both have vastly enhanced my understanding of the habitat I'll be hunting. This, in turn, has helped me better understand the behavior patterns of resident animals.

When I first start studying unfamiliar terrain, I look at 12x12-inch photos in stereo pairs with a stereoscope (photo above). This tells me more about the area in less than one hour than I could learn in several days of hiking around on foot. Scouting, then, need only be undertaken in a minimum amount of time, at a later date -- and this only to confirm what I already basically know, plus to look for smaller, recent sign that obviously would not be present on the photos, such as rubbed saplings and scrapes.

Next, I bring into play a much larger aerial photo of the same tract of land. Mine is 24x24 inches (cost — $12) and I have mounted it in a sturdy picture frame. The frame protects the photo from wear and tear but, more important, the glass front allows me to write on the photo with a grease pencil (see photo on page 16). This lets me mark the exact locations of physical sign that I discovered while scouting, property-line boundaries, where stands have been placed, or even logistics for staging drives. This is invaluable, especially when I'm hunting with friends who are unfamiliar with the region and need a visual reference as to where stands are located, what routes they should take as drivers, or even how to negotiate the terrain when participating in cooperative still-hunts.

Small-format photos are supposed to be studied in pairs. This yields an in-depth stereo effect that's similar to the view one would have in flying over the landscape.

Conducting the Search

Any tract of good deer hunting habitat may reveal slight changes from one season to the next. Consequently, the glass covering my aerial photo allows me to erase last year's information and draw in the types and locations of this year's crops, the whereabouts of any ponds which may have recently been built, areas where logging may have been undertaken, perhaps where a forest fire ravaged the landscape, and, of course, any new scrapes, rubs, and other deer sign that I have discovered.

To provide an example of the wealth of insight that can be gleaned from an aerial photo, consider the trees and how the following, quick-identification procedure can tell you what hunting tactics might be in order even months before you actually set foot in the woods (photo on page 16).

On aerial photos, large, mature trees always appear as big dots to the naked eye, while immature trees appear as small dots; with a close-up look through a stereoscope, you'll next be able to see the crowns and branches.

If those big dots are relatively light-colored, they are mature hardwoods that should be producing

Obtain a large-format aerial photo and put it in a picture frame. This allows you to write on the glass with a grease pencil to indicate recent scouting finds.

mast crops such as acorns, beechnuts, hickory nuts, or the seed-fruits of maples or poplars, to name a few. This tells you where a prime fall/winter food source is located—a source that animals are sure to visit regularly. Yet, from your previous hunting experience, you also know that such mature trees create a high, overhead canopy that prevents sunlight from bathing the ground; this, in turn, means there shouldn't be much ground-level cover for midday bedding purposes or for deer to hide in when hunting pressure begins to intensify.

Conversely, if you see light-colored, small dots thickly saturating a tract of real estate, those are immature hardwood saplings not yet bearing annual mast crops. Deer may be able to browse here upon the occasional buds and branchtips that are within their reach, but any prolonged activity will probably consist of bedding in nearby regenerative brush cover. Major feeding will occur elsewhere, so use your stereoscope to look for trails entering and exiting this bedding area. The trails will appear on the photo as thin, white, threadlike lines.

On aerial photos, dark-colored large dots indicate the presence of mature conifer species. Since you know that spruces, pines, firs, and other

With a panoramic look at the terrain, a hunter cuts his scouting time in half. He can study ridges, clearings, and even deer trails and potential bedding areas.

evergreen species constitute only starvation rations for deer when they cannot find more desirable foods, and since such species likewise shade out vegetative understory growth, you know in advance that these areas are not likely to be used by deer for much of anything.

If those dark-colored dots are small, however, you know it's an immature conifer plantation; since such trees have dense whorls of branches close to the ground, they provide ideal security cover for deer, either for bedding or for hiding shortly after opening-day hunting action begins to heat up.

Moreover, if your aerial photo shows trees that appear as large, light-colored dots, and if they are systematically laid out in evenly spaced rows and tree-to-tree intervals, you know what that means. You've found an orchard! (photo on page

17) If the trees in question are bearing apples, peaches, or plums, they'll be magnets for deer. Now scrutinize the perimeters of the orchard for thick concentrations of small, dark-colored dots indicating bedding cover in the form of immature, dense pines, and the bulk of your scouting of that area may nearly be finished, right from the comfort of your living room! Later, all you have to do is hike to that specific edge where the security cover borders the orchard to ascertain exactly where to place your stand.

In the Game

One year, while hunting in Alabama, we used an aerial photo to help us take three nice bucks in as many days. The photo revealed a ten-acre clearcut that wasn't visible from any of the back roads winding through the region. Beginning about three or four years after an area has been logged-off, regenerative growth affords deer with splendid browsing opportunities. Finding this particular clearcut would have been a stroke of luck or required extensive scouting on foot.

Aerial photos are so precise that even the species of individual trees and their ages can be identified. This old orchard was first found by studying a photo and then later double-checking it on foot for deer activity.

Yet once we were aware of the clearcut's existence and its exact dimensions—all of this having been ascertained while still at home in Ohio—we actually were able to pick out specific trees that would be likely candidates for portable stands, even though we had never actually visited the region!

After studying an aerial photo of your intended hunting grounds, it seems logical that finding and interpreting deer sign would mostly be a matter of visually seeing and examining it during scouting missions. That is true to some extent, but you also must be able to relate sign found in one area to sign found in another, in order to figure out how the animals are using the topography.

This brings us back to our earlier mention of the value of using a grease pencil to mark each and every find on your aerial photo; if you don't make use of an elaborate, framed photo with a glass front, at least paste your photo to a board and cover it with a clear plastic overlay. In this manner, various discoveries that may otherwise seem to be happenstance may suddenly, when viewed in conjunction with other located sign, begin to bear clear relevance, with a pattern emerging. For example, what you initially thought was an incidental scrape may actually be one of many in a rather straight line between a feeding and distant bedding area.

The bottom line is that through the use of aerial photos, you'll learn far more about your hunting grounds than you ever imagined possible. And when you know almost as much about the terrain as the deer themselves, your accumulated knowledge and insight will begin translating into a higher level of hunting success.

Scouting and Track Analysis

JOHN WEISS

For generations, books, magazine articles, and seminars by hunting experts have addressed various methods for patterning trophy bucks. Unfortunately, most have involved generalities instead of practical methods or specific details that an average hunter can put to use in the field.

One thing we're recognizing more each year is that big-buck success hinges not only upon outsmarting the animals themselves, but also on dealing with hunting pressure in a specific area. This greatly complicates the scouting process. Aerial photos used in conjunction with topo maps can be especially valuable for this. Here is the game-plan most experts adopt.

Always consider the effect other hunters will have upon deer behavior. Roadside pull-offs where day hunters park and others camp will become hubs of activity that deer will retreat from.

Scout the De-Militarized Zones

On a table, lay out the topo map of the area under consideration for this year's hunting. Next, use a felt-tipped marking pen containing see-through ink (such as yellow or light blue) to color in all the terrain within 1500 feet of either side of every road or trail a vehicle or four-wheeler can be driven upon; this is easily done by keeping in mind that on standard 7.5-minute series topo maps, three quarters of an inch equals 1500 feet. You can eliminate this ground from any consideration because the chances of taking a nice buck there are between slim and none.

Studies of hunter pressure on deer have shown that most hunters do not venturi farther than a quarter of a mile from some type of road or trail, and a quarter of a mile just happens to equal 1500 feet on a topo map. Some of these hunters are simply lazy, but most of the others don't make use of maps because they probably fear becoming lost. As a result, these zones of hunter influence constitute hubs of human activity the deer won't tolerate for more than a day or so, especially during the firearms season.

Since most hunters don't hike far from roads, use a topo map and a pen with see-through ink to indicate these areas of hunter influence. Scout beyond those zones of hunter activity and you'll find twice as many deer.

If you therefore work somewhat farther back into the woods, you'll actually double your chances of seeing deer. Not only will you encounter the resident trophy deer that prefer such undisturbed habitat in the first place, but as the days pass you should also begin seeing immigrants that have retreated from the hunter influence zones bordering each road.

It is at this point that aerial photos should be brought into use to further narrow the search, as described in the previous chapter, whereupon actual scouting for sign can begin. Keep in mind that the techniques we've just described apply to public hunting areas only. On a large tract of private land, where only a select few have hunting permission, or in a sparsely populated region where hunting pressure is minimal, you may wish to rely exclusively upon aerial photos.

Once afield, tracks, droppings, and beds can yield a wealth of information, but only if they're interpreted properly.

New Insights on Tracks

In past decades, biologists attempted to solve the riddle of distinguishing between buck and doe tracks. Among them were Dr. Fredrick Weston in 1956, D.R. McCullough in 1965, and J.L. Roseberry in 1975. Their findings were largely futile and gave birth to the notion that the only way to be sure a set of tracks were made by a buck is to see the deer actually standing in the tracks!

Then along came Wayne Laroche, a research biologist from Vermont, who has turned the deer hunter's world upside-down.

"Like most hunters, I used to tell tales about big deer tracks and using rifle car-tridges to gauge their size for as long as I can remember," Laroche recalled. "But this really isn't a very scientific—or accurate—way to home-in upon a big buck. Yet since it is common knowledge among biologists that dimensions of an animal's body typically increase as an animal increases in weight, I decided to find out if there is any relationship between the weight of whitetail bucks and their track dimensions that can be accurately measured in the field."

One of the startling things Wayne Laroche discovered is that the width of a track more accurately describes a buck's size than the length of the track does.

By artificially making tracks using hooves removed from deer carcasses, Laroche found that the natural shape of whitetail hooves causes the length of tracks from each hoof to vary considerably depending upon the hardness of the ground. Understandably, as ground hardness increases, less and less of the raised pad at the rear of the hoof is imprinted in the tracks. As a result, tracks on hard ground provide clear impressions of only the front part of the hoof.

Conversely, under soft ground conditions (mud, snow, loam, sand), the hoof sinks farther into the surface, with increasingly more of the raised rear pad of the hoof, and even the dewclaws, included in the print, thus making the track longer. "Dewclaw imprints in particular can greatly mislead hunters

Hunters once believed the length of a deer track indicated the animal's sex and age. Biologists now tell us it's the hoof width, which slowly increases with age and body growth, that distinguish bucks and does.

into thinking a given set of tracks were left by a buck," says naturalist Dr. Leonard Lee Rue III. "Since both bucks and does have dewclaws, the fact that they show in the tracks does not indicate the deer's sex. The only thing it indicates is that the ground was soft when the animal left the tracks."

Additionally, the toenails of deer grow and wear constantly, as do those of all hooved animals. This abrasive wear, to greater or lesser degrees, hinges upon the predominant nature of the animal's home range, which lends truth to the old adage that mountain bucks tend to have rounded hooves and swamp bucks tend to have sharp, pointed hooves.

All of this is precisely why the length of a deer track isn't reliable in evaluating the animal that made the track. The ground conditions under which a track are made may be so variable that a given buck may actually leave a large number of tracks of different lengths, depending upon the route he takes over and across different terrain conditions.

"It's an altogether different story with hoof width," Laroche explained "Maximum hoof width occurs just in front of the rear margin of the hoofs toenail near the middle of the hoof. Since the bottom of the toenail contacts the ground a: a more or less flat surface, a deer leaves its maximum track width regardless of the degree of ground hardness."

While it's true that hoof width may vary slightly depending upon whether or no the animal has splayed its toes—as a deer does for increased stability when runninig across mud or other soft or slippery terrain—Laroche's field observations have revealed that the average toe spread of a deer walking normally is about one quarter inch. As we'll see later, it's important to keep this in mind when actually measuring tracks.

"Beginning in the fall of 1990, I took hundreds of measurements of white-tailed buck hooves with known, dressed weights ranging from ninety-seven to 244 pounds," Laroche described. "To make sure my data base was as accurate as possible, these measurements were made of bucks taken from the pre-rut, rut, and post-rut periods in order to reflect the differences in body weights that bucks experience throughout the fall/winter seasons of the year."

After performing a statistical evaluation known as "regression analysis" on the maximum hoof width and dressed weight data, Laroche found very strong relationships confirming that hoof width is a solid indicator of a buck's body weight. It naturally follows that bucks with the heaviest body weights are the most likely to be mature animals with the largest trophy racks.

"Now that I had developed equations that could be used to accurately estimate the weight of whitetailed bucks by measuring the width of their tracks, another problem arose," Laroche explained. "I knew it would be awkward for a hunter to make calculations or refer to tables while in the field. So I designed a lightweight plastic caliper that I named the 'Trackometer'. It's completely weatherproof and conveniently fits into one's pocket. When the caliper is adjusted to span the inside width of a particular deer track, it automatically indicates on a printed scale the body weight of the animal." (To obtain the Trackometer and Wayne Laroche's 85-page tracking guidebook, contact Stonefish Environmental, Box 839, Enosburg Falls, VT 05450.)

With a tool for measuring deer tracks, still another hurdle had to be contended with. Namely, how does a hunter looking at tracks distinguish between those from the front feet and rear feet?

This is important because still another of Laroche's stunning findings is that in the case of mature bucks, their front hooves are larger than their rear hooves!

"Since the front and rear hooves of mature bucks differ in maximum width, it's necessary to first be able to tell which is which before using the Trackometer to determine the animal's true body weight," Laroche said.

"Keep in mind that walking and slowly trotting whitetails place their rear hooves directly into the tracks of their front hooves. For this reason, all clear tracks left behind by unalarmed, slowly moving deer are tracks of the rear hoofs. On the other hand, running deer swing their rear legs ahead of the front tracks. Therefore, tracks made by both the front and rear hoofs are clearly visible."

Body Weights Are the Key

In going back to the subject of body weights being the most likely indicators of mature animals, it has long been documented that big-bodied does are extremely rare; in fact, according to data gathered by the Vermont Department of Natural Resources, only twelve does in 1000 exceed 140 pounds in weight.

What this means is that if a hunter measures a deer track with a Trackometer and discovers that the body weight of the animal that left the track exceeds the 140-pound mark, there is a 98.8 percent chance the animal is a buck!

Moreover, according to the Vermont data, only one doe in 1000 exceeds 160 pounds in weight. As a result, a measured deer track that indicates an animal exceeding 160 pounds means there is a 99.9 percent degree of certainty the animal is a buck!

Why don't does grow as heavy as bucks? Although genetics probably play a role, the most logical explanation is that lactating does expend a great deal of energy rearing fawns. An average whitetail doe begins bearing twins and heavily lactating at about three years of age, whereupon annual growth remains essentially flat. According to studies published by the Wildlife Management Institute (in its book White-tailed Deer; Ecology and Management, 1984), the body weight of a doe at three years of age is the approximate body weight she'll carry for the rest of her life, or until she becomes barren and ceases bearing offspring. Yet just the opposite is true with bucks. They continue to grow and steadily put on weight until they are at least seven or eight years old, whereupon tooth wear begins to limit food intake and the animals, and their racks, begin to degenerate.

This is invaluable insight. When using a Trackometer, and determining that a given track represents an animal exceeding 170 pounds in body weight, it is virtually guaranteed that not only is the animal a buck but that it is at least four and one-half years of age.

The reason this is so crucial to a hunter's scouting is because the magic figure of four and one-half years of age is the turning point in which a buck has grown from a teen-ager into a mature adult

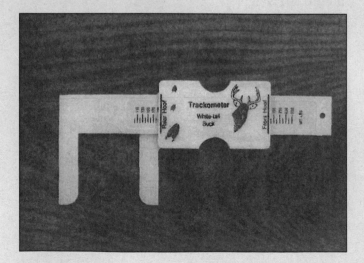

The Trackometer tool can tell a hunter to within ninety-eight-percent accuracy if a track was made by a mature buck.

that is beginning to achieve the largest antlers he will grow in his lifetime. And, likely as not, he's the dominant buck inhabiting your hunting grounds.

Even more eye-opening, if the track-width measurement indicates a deer exceeding 190 pounds, the buck is probably at least five and one-half years of age and may be a potential candidate for the record book.

Of course, keep in mind that average whitetail body weights and track sizes may vary slightly around the country in accordance with the particular subspecies living in each locale; as a result, the very largest-bodied animals are far more likely to inhabit the northern border states and Midwest than the deep South. In time, however, a hunter who incorporates track-measuring strategies into his regular scouting routines can easily determine what constitutes tracks made by big bucks in his own region.

Although the Trackometer is a new and important tool that enables hunters to evaluate a buck's age and body weight by measuring its track width, it is by no means the only clue for distinguishing buck tracks from doe tracks.

Although it is probably impossible to tell the difference between tracks of mature does and small, immature bucks, most hunters who have spent any amount of time tracking whitetails will agree that the tracks of mature bucks reveal certain definable characteristics. Careful observation reveals daily activities that provide direct evidence of the many behavioral differences between the sexes.

Again according to naturalist Leonard Lee Rue, "big bucks, especially during the rut, tend to walk with a stiff-legged gait which causes an outward arcing of their feet. In other words, the tracks often appear to toe out. Conversely, small bucks and does tend to lift their feet higher and swing them forward in a straight line when walking, due to their relatively narrow body width and more even distribution of weight over the front and hind legs.

"As with the presence of dewclaw imprints lying to you, the presence of drag marks in snow supposedly indicating the track of a buck is yet another wive's tale," Rue continued. "Drag marks are made by bucks and does alike by the tips of the toes as they begin to straighten up so that their bearing surface is brought horizon-tal to the ground just before the next step is made. As the deer continues to walk, the front of the toes leave just a slight forward 'slice' in the snow as they leave the track to take the next step."

Another feature of walking tracks of big bucks is a distinctive staggered pattern that suggests a spraddle-legged gait caused by the increase in body width, which accompanies the increase in body mass of big bucks.

Laroche also notes that should the deer you are tracking urinate, more clues to sex will be visible. A doe's tracks will show that she has hunched back on her hind legs and urinated in her tracks, leaving a wide spray pattern. Bucks don't hunch back. They urinate straight down, leaving a narrow slot-like pattern that sometimes continues to drip as the buck moves on.

Studying deer sign is important to understanding their whereabouts and activities. Hunters with advanced knowledge can examine such sign and accurately predict the age and sex of the animal that left it.

Deer Pellets and Beds

Deer droppings can tell a hunter a lot more than where a deer left the remains of last night's dinner. Recent biological studies have revealed that deer pellets can be analyzed by the casual hunter afield, allowing him to make a highly accurate guess as to the sex of the animal, how old it is, and even what the deer was eating.

"The story of man's preoccupation with deer droppings in this century starts with the flashes of insight of Ernest Thompson Seton and his classic deer scatology illustrations," explains biologist Dr. Rob Wegner in his popular book Deer & Deer Hunting (Stackpole Books, 1984).

"By the late 1930s, deer researchers began to use droppings as an index to deer populations, thus going well beyond Seton's descriptions and illustrations. By the 1960s, scientists refined their survey method to the point where they could determine the species (plant composition) of the droppings by pH analysis. By the mid-1970s, they were baking the droppings at sixty degrees C in forced-air ovens and measuring their weights to determine the eating habits of their makers via microscopic identification. Today's statistical and computerized analysis of deer droppings, with their complex mathematical equations, simply overwhelm the mind of the deer hunter, if not the mind of the deer biologist as well. In central Utah, researchers now statistically analyze deer droppings

An observant hunter can study deer droppings and accurately determine the age and sex of the animal that left them.

with range-area data extracted from Landsat satellite imagery."

How Many Deer?

Much of this new information has been filtering down to hunters in the know, enabling them to devise hunting strategies their fathers and grandfathers never dreamed of.

Examining individual piles of pellet droppings, for example, is a good way to gauge the size of a deer herd in a given area. After intensive field studies, biologists Creed, Haberland, Kohn, and McCaffery of the Wisconsin Department of Natural Resources have determined that whitetails defecate an average of thirteen times every twenty-four hours. With this insight, it's now possible for a hunting party to determine whether a prospective new hunting region is worth their time.

The most difficult aspect of this is recruiting the help of your hunting partners on a weekend to thoroughly scour one square mile of the real estate you might be interested in hunting come fall; studying only one square mile is sufficient, even though the actual size of the tract of land may be considerably larger. On the first day, line up as if you were beginning a deer drive, but with your "drivers" much closer together than usual. Then, systematically hike the length or breadth of the terrain back and forth as many times as is necessary to cover the entire 640 acres; with five hunters participating, this should take the better part of the day. Additionally, each "hunter" should be armed with a can of biodegradable, yellow spray paint.

Each time one of you discovers a pile of deer pellets, give the pile a quick spray of paint, regardless of how old or fresh the droppings seem to be. Naturally, performing this type of deer census is much easier and far more accurate if done in February or March when there is either a very light skiff of snow on the ground or an absence of vegetation; this makes spotting the pellets easy from a distance, as compared to summertime scouting when plant life will obscure many pellet piles from view.

Your party of hunters should hike the same terrain the very next day. This time, each participant should carry a can of red spray paint, a notepad, and a pencil. Each unmarked pile of droppings discovered on this second day will be less than twentyfour hours old and will be easily distinguished from those droppings with the yellow paint, which are more than twenty-four hours old. The purpose of the red paint is to identify the fresh droppings so that they are not inadvertently counted a second time when you later sweep back through the same general area from the opposite direction. Each hunter should also record the number of new piles of droppings he discovers.

Finally, at day's end, add total up the number of new piles of fresh droppings discovered by the entire party and divide that figure by thirteen to determine the number of deer present.

According to the Wisconsin DNR, a region possessing five deer or less per square mile should probably be discounted from consideration because it is unlikely that more than one of those deer would be a mature buck. In this case, it would be wise to scout another location at least several miles away, hoping for a pellet count to reveal at least fifteen to twenty-five deer per square mile.

Keep in mind that the Law of Diminishing Returns eventually kicks in with deer population densities; too many deer (more than thirty-five per square mile) is just as indicative of poor trophy buck production as too few deer.

In going back to the above example, if you and your partners counted a total of 247 fresh piles of droppings, that means there are approximately nineteen deer using that 640-acre tract of land you've just scouted, a clear indication you could expect reasonably good hunting in that region.

Admittedly, doing weekend pellet counts like this takes time and effort. But many hunting parties I know combine this activity with searching for shed antlers, which provides yet more valuable information pertaining to bucks that survived the hunting season and still are in the vicinity.

Taking a Closer Look

"The type of food eaten determines the shape and consistency of deer excrement," says Dr. Leonard Lee Rue III. "This is valuable to hunters because it can furnish a clue to where deer have been browsing or grazing. If a deer has been feeding upon grasses, forbs, or fruit, its feces is usually in the form of a loose mass of very soft pellets. When the deer has been browsing upon drier material such as woody twigs and dead leaves, the feces will be in the form of elongated pellets that are quite hard."

"In the spring and summer," Wegner adds, "fresh pellets acquire a greenish or bronze hue, they tend to glisten, and they're very soft inside. Yet later in the fall and winter months, pellet coloration may range from shades of brown to dark mahogany or almost black."

But don't allow the effects of weather to fool you into thinking that pellets are fresher than they really are. Obviously, pellets will dry quicker in direct sunlight, in windy weather, or in low humidity than in shade, on still days, or in high humidity.

Moreover, old, dry pellets may appear shiny and fresh if subjected to rain, fog, or early morning dew. To determine whether this is the case, simply crush several droppings. Deer pellets always dry from the outside in. Therefore, pellets that glisten on the outside but crumble when squeezed are at least several days old. Conversely, pellets that shine on the outside but have the consistency of modeling clay inside may be only hours old.

Pellet Sizes Tell All

Perhaps of greatest value to hunters who learn how to analyze deer excrement is the possibility of determining the approximate age of the animal in question and whether the pellets were left by a buck or doe.

All of this boils down to the simple fact that, within a given species, older and more mature animals leave larger-size calling cards than young, immature animals. Also, within the same age category of animals of the same species, males always give off larger-size excrement than females simply because of their larger body sizes and larger internal anatomy.

Therefore, during the course of pellet-count surveys or any other scouting mission, an important tool hunters should make use of is a simple tape measure and notebook. Then, when pellet piles are discovered, record the average size of the individual pellets comprising those piles.

Keep in mind there are thirty different whitetail subspecies across the continent, and they vary greatly in body size and therefore the sizes of pellets they drop. In the region I hunt most often (the upper Midwest), the whitetail species is Odocoileus virginianus borealis, also known as the northern woodland deer, which is the largest whitetail subspecies.

My hunting buddies and I have learned that droppings which are one-half inch or less in length indicate a doe, yearling, or fawn; droppings that are five-eighths inch in length indicate a buck approaching maturity, probably a two and one-half year old; while droppings that are three-quarters to one and one-quarter inches in length indicate a trophy buck that's three and one-half years or older.

Conversely, in South Carolina, where O.v. virginianus resides, which also is known as the Virginia deer, average body sizes are considerably smaller; as a result, pellet sizes of all age groups and sexes will likewise be smaller. In other words, while pellets measuring one and one-quarter inches in length indicate trophy bucks in Ohio, Illinois, and Wisconsin, pellets measuring only three-quarters of an inch the Palmetto State may very well represent the presence of mature bucks.

Buck or Doe?

Aside from pellet sizes, an even more intriguing way of determining whether a deer's calling card is from a buck or doe is presently under investigation.

Some researchers believe that, in most instances, doe excrement piles are in the form of individual, loose pellets ranging in number from twenty-five to sometimes more than fifty. They are also of the opinion that buck droppings are not only individually larger but are evacuated in greater quantity. Maryland deer biologist C.J. Winand's studies have concluded, for example, that bucks can be ascertained by dropping piles in which there are seventy-five or more pellets. Additionally, buck droppings are often clumped together in amorphous, walnut-sized or larger

Biologists have learned that a deer defecates thirteen times a day. A mature buck's pellet pile contains an average of seventy-five droppings that average one and a quarter inches in length.

globs. This is especially the case when the animal's diet consists largely of succulent vegetation. Yet when killing frosts cause whitetails to make a transition from grazing to browsing, buck excrement becomes somewhat less mucous and adhesive and may be found in smaller, looser clumps that sometimes break apart from the impact of hitting the ground.

An area of speculation currently being debated by biologists is that although a deer's diet largely influences the shape, color, and consistency of its feces, another factor may be involved to explain the "clumping" tendency of buck droppings. Nutritional studies conducted by biologist Charles Ruth of Clemson University with penned deer during the non-rutting period have shown that bucks have a higher body metabolism than does, due to their need to achieve body weight more quickly. This suggests that previously ingested food passes through a buck's intestinal tract more quickly, causing it to become consolidated and compacted.

In referring back to the situation in which we described hypothetically finding 247 piles of pellets indicating the presence of nineteen deer, it's now clear that adding pellet-size information and pellet-clumping characteristics of bucks to the picture can broaden your insight immensely. An astute hunting party may actually come to the conclusion, again hypothetically, that of those nineteen resident animals, fourteen are does, yearlings or fawns; four are mature two-and-one-half-yearold bucks; and one is three and one-half years or older and must undoubtedly have a very impressive rack.

As a result, while many hunters often become preoccupied with finding big tracks, large scrapes, and rubbed saplings, the most encouraging scouting reports are those in which members of our party describe finding clumped droppings with individual pellets averaging one inch or longer.

The Bedding Connection

Conducting a diligent search for droppings during the course of scouting missions can, in still another way, greatly assist in piecing together the puzzling lives of deer in a given region. While whitetails may defecate almost anytime or anywhere, which explains the occasional finding of droppings on a trail or in a meadow where they have been feeding, the most pellets are found in an altogether different location.

According to Dr. Wegner's research, there is irrefutable evidence that most whitetails defecate shortly after rising from their beds. Moreover, the quantity of pellets around the periphery of the bed indicates the length of time that a deer remained in that particular spot.

This is important insight when it comes to deciding upon a strategic stand location. Perennial advice given to deer hunters is to situate a stand somewhere between the deer's feeding and bedding areas in order to ambush them as they go back and forth. Well, ascertaining feeding areas is not difficult, especially in farm country, but finding bedding areas can be a exercise in frustration.

The reason is because whitetails—especially bucks—rarely bed in the same spot each day. Rather, they have general bedding "areas" and, therefore, each bedding episode seldom leaves a well-pronounced, matted oval to be easily detected by the hunter's searching eyes. The two exceptions to this are the presence of snow or damp leaves.

Always take the time to evaluate beds found under such conditions. Beds measuring forty inches or less in length indicate a doe, yearling or fawn. Beds fortyfive inches in length indicate two and one-half-year-old bucks, while beds that are fifty to fifty-six inches in length indicate three and one-half- to six and one-halfyear-old bucks. (Again, these figures will have to be adjusted slightly downward in regions where specific, small-bodied whitetail subspecies exist). Furthermore, look at how the beds relate to each other. Two or three small beds accompanied by one large bed usually represent a doe with her current offspring. A lone bed, especially if it's located on higher ground, is nearly always that of a mature buck.

In the absence of visible beds in snow or damp leaves, many individual piles of both old and fresh pellets in a relatively small area saturated with dense cover is a sure indication of a bedding area. Closer examination of the pellets should next offer clues to the ages and sexes of the animals and, following this, it should not be difficult to determine the most probable route the animals are using when they travel to nearby feeding areas.

Finding concentrated numbers of droppings, which reveal bedding areas, is important in two other ways. Within the home range of each whitetail is an approximate forty-acre "core area" where the animal spends up to ninety percent of its time. This core area offers the best combination of desirable attributes to be found within the animal's much larger home range. There will be easy access to water and a prime food source, to be sure, but of even greater concern to deer, and especially mature bucks, is that the core area will be virtually free of human disturbance. In short, a core area offers a buck a greater sense of security than anywhere else with in his home range.

Consequently, when hunting pressure begins to mount and the biggest bucks in a given region become almost exclusively nocturnal in their feeding, drinking, and other activities, you know exactly where they'll be sequestered during the daylight hours. They'll be hunkered down in their beds, somewhere in their core areas. Because you've already determined the location of those bedding regions by

When scouting, take a small tape measure. Beds you find that are fifty to fifty-six-inches in length are those of mature bucks.

finding and analyzing their droppings, staging an effective drive or cooperative stillhunt with a partner should give you a good chance for success.

If you prefer to hunt solo, keep in mind that bedded whitetails always lay with their legs splayed to the left, facing downwind; in this manner, the animal can scent-monitor anything that might attempt to approach from directly behind him where he cannot see, and he can see very well in the other directions in which he cannot smell.

The fact that deer always lay on their right side, facing downwind, is important to keep in mind. If the wind is from the south, for example, a careful stalk from the east, advancing toward the bedded deer's blind side, would be more likely to succeed than a stalk from the north, west, or south.

By the same token, even when hunting pressure is light or nonexistent, these safe bedding areas are the places to check when storm fronts move through the region, assaulting the landscape with severe weather and causing deer to seek seclusion.

Studies with radio-collared deer have shown they rarely bed in the same exact spot every day. Rather, they have general bedding areas in high security regions seldom penetrated by humans.

Antler Rubs: Communication Signposts

JOHN WEISS

I came upon the huge rub while hunting squirrels, not while scouting for deer. And an unusual discovery it was, because this was in early September, a full six weeks before Ohio's bowhunting season opened and more than two months before the rut. Moreover, I'd never seen a pine tree so ravaged. It was entirely stripped of all its bark to a height of about five feet off the ground, and its former branches had been reduced to an array of sorry looking, broken stubs.

This happened twenty years ago, and I was destined to hunt many additional years before I'd look back and appreciate the significance of that particular rub. I'm also confident that I know the very buck that made it. The animal undoubtedly was the huge 12-pointer old man Harley Wilkes killed on this, his farm property, and it was the biggest deer he'd seen there since his father homesteaded the place during the Great Depression.

Two decades later, I was an avid student of noted whitetail biologists Larry Marchington, John Ozoga, James Kroll, and other university luminaries, all of whom earned PhDs in large part from engaging in research projects dealing with antler rubs and the complex method of communication among both male and female deer.

We still do not fully understand every aspect pertaining to rubbing behavior, and even among the most respected scientists there is occasional disagreement on certain fine points. Nevertheless, every year new information surfaces. The astute hunter who keeps abreast of these findings is sure to refine his knowledge of whitetails, and it is this very educational process which translates directly into more and bigger bucks hanging on the meatpole.

But first, let's dispel a few long-held wives tales. To begin with, antler rubs do not indicate places where bucks have removed their velvet and then polished and sharpened their tines.

When a whitetail's maximum annual antler growth has been attained, the skin-like velvet dies, dries, and begins falling away in shreds, mostly of its own accord; the entire shedding process is often completed in less than eight hours. About the only time a buck hastens its removal is when an annoying, stringy remnant hangs down and impairs his vision, whereupon he briefly thrashes his antlers on a nearby shrub.

Once the underlying antlers are fully exposed, the main beams are already smooth, and the tine tips are pointed. There is no need for the buck to hone them like a gladiator readying his swords for battle.

The height of the rub is also not of any importance, which is yet another myth that supposedly indicates the size of the buck that made it. After all, deer sometimes stand on their hind legs when making a rub, and it is not unusual for a very limber sapling to bend all the way over, enabling even a young buck to straddle the trunk and rake it all the way to its uppermost crown of branches.

Scientists tell us bucks do not rub trees to remove their antler velvet. The velvet naturally dries and peels away, and the underlying tines are already smooth and sharp at their tips.

On the other hand, the diameter of the rubbed tree is indeed significant, with the largest diameter trees indicating large bucks and smaller diameter trees representing the work of younger males. But here again, you must be careful in your analysis of rubbed trees and not simply restrict your search to large rubs. The rule of thumb is that big bucks sometimes rub small trees as well as large trees, yet it is very rare for small bucks to rub large trees.

The occurrence of a big buck rubbing both large and small trees is undoubtedly a combination of happenstance and planning. As we'll discuss in a moment, the deer wants to leave numerous calling cards, in the form of olfactory signposts, to alert as many does as possible to his presence, so he rubs all manner of trees. But he will also specifically target a number of unusually large diameter trees to rub, to create visual signposts, in order to warn other mature males that this is his breeding territory.

As to the exact significance of individual antler rubs, most biologists believe they serve the purpose

Antler rubs are signposts bucks use to communicate visual and olfactory information to other deer. The diameter of the tree rubbed indicates the buck's approximate age.

of enabling each buck to establish a breeding territory of sorts. It should be emphasized that whitetails are not territorial in the true sense of the word, as it would be quite impossible for even a dominant buck to drive all other male deer out of his several-square-mile home range. As a result, in most regions, several or perhaps many bucks must share the same turf.

Still, despite the fact that whitetails are not territorial, they must nevertheless acquire a breeding area where they feel secure, while simultaneously obtaining a social status that gives them breeding privileges over subordinate or lower-ranked animals.

Timing the Rub

There are two distinct periods when most antler rubs are created. The first rubbing activity usually occurs during the first three weeks of September, when bucks are still in their bachelor groupings. Now is when they are developing their herd rankings. This is when they decide, within their local society, which are the superior "alpha" deer and which are the subordinate "beta" deer. Moreover, the very first rubs are made by the dominant bucks in the region, due to their anxiety to get on with the business of firmly establishing the herd pecking order. How many rubs does a mature buck make? According to deer biologist Marchington, who has stud-ied the subject intensively, a mature buck makes anywhere from sixty-nine to 538 rubs in any given year, with each buck making an overall average of 300 rubs! With the peak rubbing period of mature males being the first three weeks in September, this means a dominant buck can be expected to make at least fourteen rubs per day.

Insightful hunters should therefore mark on their aerial photos or topo maps the exact locations of the first rubs they discover during early scouting missions, as they were likely made by the largest deer in the immediate area. Confirmation of this suspicion, of course, comes in the form of noting the sizes of the rubs; they should be at least two and one-half inches or larger in diameter.

The second flurry of rubbing activity takes place during the first week of October. This is when the other, lesser deer in the region instinctively engage in their rubbing.

The Mast Connection

Another revealing thing we've learned about whitetails is that a buck's antler-rubbing behavior is directly tied to seasonal mast production. When there is a bountiful mast crop, a hunter can expect to find a much higher number of rubs than usual. Conversely, in years when mast production is low, rub densities may be thirty to sixty percent less than that of the previous year.

The reason is that a buck's physical health is dependent upon mast. Acorns, in particular, but other types of mast as well, are transition foods that deer utilize shortly after hard frosts kill the lush vegetation they've been feeding upon during spring and summer but before they've fully switched to browsing upon twigs and branch tips. As a result, when there is a poor or virtually nonexistent mast crop, the midfall physical condition of the animals deteriorates just enough to reduce the vigor and intensity with which they engage in pre-rut rubbing.

Keep this in mind when you are scouting, and if you are not finding as many rubs as you'd expect, don't automatically conclude there aren't many bucks around. Take the time to check a number of oak ridges or hardwood forests to evaluate the mast crop. If you find little mast, bucks are most likely in the area, but they are simply rubbing less that year. On the other hand, if mast is plentiful, but rubs seem markedly absent, chances are the buck population is indeed quite low.

Timing the Rut

Interestingly enough, biologists now have reason to believe that the peak of the rut may change slightly from year to year as a result of bucks having the ability to influence the estrus cycles of does.

Essentially, what happens is this. When there is a greater number of buck rubs in a given area than normal, it's quite likely that an earlier than usual estrus will take place among local does because of so-called "priming pheromones" deposited on trees by bucks. These scents, when deposited in greater quantity than usual, have been found to induce early ovulation in does, pushing the peak of the rut forward.

For example, in one Michigan study, the average peak rutting date in an area with only a marginal number of bucks was determined to be November 11. Yet five years later, when there were more and older bucks in the same area, the peak of the rut had advanced to October 23.

Therefore, while hunters in past years commonly asked their local wildlife officials when the peak of the rut occurred in their state, and then intensely hunted during that time, such a practice is no longer recommended, since the advice may be off by as much as two weeks in either direction.

Instead, hunters can now more accurately determine when local rutting activity is destined to occur by diligently scouting for rubs.

In my home state of Ohio, for example, I had long accepted the Division of Wildlife's proclamation that the peak of the rut is November 15. But I now know this is only a statistical average of the past 25 years, and that the coming deer season may see frenzied rutting activity as early as November 1. This was exactly what happened during the 1994 deer season, and I knew about it in advance, because as soon as autumn leaves began to fall, innumerable antler rubs appeared almost overnight. Conversely, during Ohio's 1998 deer season, we found only a random rub here and there--far fewer than any other year I could remember--and, as we expected, this delayed rutting activity. In fact, we were seeing bucks chasing does as late in the year as December 10.

The priming pheromones deposited on rubs by alpha bucks not only induce early ovulation in does, but also have the effect of suppressing the already lower testos-terone levels in young bucks. This well-ordered plan causes a region's subordinate bucks to not begin engaging in rubbing behavior until October and November, anc thereby effectively reduces their aggressiveness and competition for breeding privileges.

In nature's mysterious way, this well-planned scheme is designed to benefit the herd. Young bucks, which are chemically induced into a low position in the breed ing hierarchy, engage in minimum reproductive effort and therefore experience les: late-season weight loss. They are thus better able to make it through the upcoming harsh winter months and are more likely to grow to larger and healthier sizes thi following year, when they are destined to become dominant breeding animals them selves.

Pinning Down Your Buck

When a buck leaves his bedding area, heading in the direction of a known food source or making his rounds to check scrapes, he occasionally rubs saplings adjacent to the trail he's traveling. In time, distinct rub lines are created. Savvy hunters can interpret these signs and, with a high level of accuracy, ascertain the direction the animal was traveling and even the time of day the buck made the rub. With this information at hand, being in the right place at the right time come hunting season becomes much easier.

But first, one must have a general idea where to begin conducting his search for rubbed trees. Again according to biologist Marchington and his research, twenty-six percent of all rubs are found along deer trails, ten percent along old logging trails, and fifteen percent along stream banks in valleys. The remaining forty-nine percent are random rubs created along field edges, woodlot clearings, in the vicinity of thickets, and throughout forested regions.

Because of this, it makes a lot of sense to investigate such locations, especially where there are pockets of terrain known to have aromatic trees such as cedars, pines, spruces, shining sumac, cherry, and dogwood. However, according to biologists at the University of Georgia, a whitetail buck's No. 1 choice of species to rub upon is the sassafras. Despite the fact that sassafras comprises an extremely small percentage of trees in most forests east of the Mississippi, more than eighty percent of the largest rubs discovered in study areas were found on sassafras.

In the absence of these species, bucks will create rubs on virtually any species, but they distinctly like the ones listed above. The most commonly accepted explanation for this preference is that the oily, resinous cambiums of these species will retain the buck's forehead gland scent longer. In the case of non-aromatic species, much of the scent deposited during rubbing activity is likely to wash off during the next rainstorm, thereby making the rub less effective as an olfactory signpost.

Taking a Closer Look

As mentioned earlier, hunters should take a topo map or aerial photo of their hunting area, and mark the locations of each rub they find, especially the season's first rubs, which are indicative of the largest bucks in the region. If this isn't done, each discovery may seem totally happenstance. But when you can study large numbers of individual rubs on a map, your perspective broadens, and a pattern can often be discerned that reveals distinct rub lines and thereby the trails a buck is using.

With this accomplished, it's time for a closer investigation of the individual rubs comprising the overall rub line.

If the tree is rubbed on the downhill side, you can bet that it was made in the morning when the buck was ascending to his midday bedding area; hence, you've found a trail worth watching during the morning hours. Conversely, if the rub is on the uphill side of the tree, the deer was invariably coming downhill in the evening to feed or search for ready does in the lower elevations; this trail calls for an evening stand.

A similar situation takes place in flat terrain, with rubs found in open feeding areas and around the perimeters of woodlots generally having been made during the night hours and rubs deep in heavy cover generally having been made during midday.

During the course of his scouting, a hunter may chance upon an area of intense rubbing activity where it seems like virtually every tree within fifty square yards has been ravaged. Upon seeing this, the hunter's first thought is usually that a monster buck's pent-up anxiety and sexual frustration caused him to go berserk.

To be sure, anything is possible in the world of whitetails, but according to biologists, what the hunter most probably found was a rub concentration that is not overly significant, at least in terms of pegging the whereabouts of a mature buck.

Rub concentrations are created early in the season when bucks are still in their bachelor groups. If there are two or three bucks keeping company, and they are all of the same age-class and carrying antlers of roughly equivalent size, chances are they're having difficulty sorting out their hierarchal rankings and determining who's who on the totem pole. This is especially true among immature one-and-one-half- or two-and-one-half-year-old bucks.

As a means of intimidation, one of the bucks is likely to rub a sapling while the other two watch. Another buck is then likely to respond by saying, in effect, "oh yeah, well watch this!" whereupon he demonstrates his prowess by rubbing another tree. The third buck then predictably responds by putting on his own show. This rubbing activity can go on for an hour or more, and when the animals finally depart, it looks as though not a single tree has been left untouched.

Although the appearance of a rub concentration can be quite impressive, even awesome, it probably will not prove to be a good hunting location when the season opens. By then the bachelor groups will have long since disseminated, abandoned their late-summer/early-fall travel patterns, and adopted their own individual breeding territories elsewhere.

Getting It All Together

One of the best times to study whitetail rubbing behavior is early spring, before lush vegetation has had a chance to emerge and hide last year's deer sign. The exposed cambiums of rubbed trees will not have weathered yet, and trails will be easily discernible. Moreover, like the game "connect the dots," an astute hunter can often spot consecutive rubs leading off into the distance, and by drawing imaginary lines between them, he can determine that particular buck's precise travel pattern.

The value of this scouting exercise has many facets, just one of which is the possibility of finding shed antlers. That way, you know for sure that the buck who made the rubs survived the hunting season and approximately what his new rack will look like next year.

Additionally, keep in mind that mature bucks frequently rub the same trees from one year to the next. If you closely examine a fresh rub, you'll probably detect weathered scarring that has healed over from the previous season. Be absolutely sure to note the locations of these particular trees, because if the buck that created them survived this hunting season, he's almost sure to rub them again next year.

By following a rub line and its associated trail, a hunter can also ascertain the bedding area the buck is using. This is vitally important, as the hunter will not want to situate his stand too close to the bedding area.

Aside from the rubs of alpha bucks serving as olfactory signposts and thereby having an influence upon the estrus cycles of local does, their secondary and equally important function is to serve as visual signposts among local bucks. In effect, an antler rub is an extension of a given animal in that deer's absence, and it serves to communicate information to other bucks which may filter through that region at a later time.

Advanced hunters can use this insight in a very novel way, if they'll keep in mind that no matter where they're hunting, there's a likelihood that at least several bucks are sharing the same area and are even using the same trails.

When a buck comes ambling down a trail littered with rubs, an observant hunter should instantly know whether the deer is just a so-so deer or the dominant buck in the immediate region. If it's a subordinate deer, the visual stimuli of the large diameter rubs along the trail will cause him to outwardly display his inferiority. The most common submissive body posture exhibited by a low-ranking deer is a slinking gait that reminds me of a dog that has just been swatted on the rump

with a newspaper for wetting the floor. The tail is held tightly against the hindquarters, the back is somewhat sunken, and the head is held low.

If a buck exhibits this behavior, you can take him or not, depending upon what fulfills your expectations for concluding a successful hunt. But realize that the deer is using body language that reveals, in no uncertain terms, that he is intimidated by the rubs in the area; and this means the trail in question is also being used by a much larger animal.

A dominant buck, however, is sure to reveal an entirely different personality. He'll proudly hold his head high and may actually have a somewhat prancing appearance to his gait, almost like a high-stepping quarterhorse. But the sure tipoff is that he will periodically lift his tail to half-mast and extend it straight back for long moments at a time. If you observe this behavior, you might as well go ahead and take the deer at the first opportunity, because, in that particular region, he's at the top of the social hierarchy. The only other alternative, if he is not what you're hoping to take, is to pull your stand and devote your remaining hunting time elsewhere.

In any event, the long and short of it is to find the early rubs. They're the best way to hedge your bet that you'll collect the biggest buck in the region you're hunting.

When hunting a rub-line, observe the behavior of any bucks that come along. This is a nice buck, but he's exhibiting inferior body posture, which tells the hunter it was another bigger buck that made this rub.

Opening Day

PETER FIDUCCIA

For most of us, thoughts of opening day hold most of our expectations and dreams of bagging a buck. We have all read and heard that up to 80 percent of our chances to kill a buck take place on opening day, with our next best chance on opening weekend.

With that in mind I thought it would be sensible to include some of my best opening-day hunting tips. These tips are common-sense based and easy to apply. They are meant to give novice hunters some strategies to get the best edge to bag their first buck. They also include some tips that are geared more to the seasoned deer hunting veteran.

I hope they make a difference in your success for your next opening day hunt—good hunting!

During the first few days of deer season (bow or firearm), pack your lunch and stay on your stand all day from sunrise to dark. This is also a good bet for opening weekends as well. Deer will react to the sudden increased hunting pressure and will move continually throughout their habitat, circling hunters and may eventually come into sight of your stand.

I have always felt that scouting too early can be more harmful than not scouting at all. In places not subjected to intense hunting pressure, scout for sign as close to opening day as is reasonable. By scouting too early, the sign you find may no longer be relevant when the season opens and, more importantly, you can spook, or at least give warning to mature bucks in the area that the hunt is about to start!

I have longed believed that having several stands in place for opening day and the rest of the deer season is crucial to success. Savvy hunters understand that consistent success depends on how they pay attention to wind direction. With

An opening-day eight-point buck and a matriarchal doe taken on our farm in 2006.

It pays to remain in your stand on opening day because you never know when a buck like this will show up under your stand.

too, and even the lousiest weather will not keep them out of the woodlands, so deer will remain on the move. It's later in the season, when hunters are tired, that bad weather keeps them home, but it shouldn't, as deer like to move even in the foulest of weather conditions.

If you're sitting on stand and another hunter bumbles noisily through your area, don't become discouraged and abandon your stand. He'll undoubtedly keep on moving, and any deer that are in and around the area will circle and give him a wide berth, never realizing that another hunter (you) is there, waiting motionless.

Whether you're hunting with a bow or firearm, opening day is not the time to take the first legal animal that comes along. There's plenty of time left in the season, so enjoy the hunt, be relatively picky and take the opportunity to look over several animals. It's during the waning days of the season that most hunters begin lowering their standards.

Deer quickly abandon their normal routines on opening day of the firearms season, especially if there's intense hunting pressure. Because of this, you're likely to have much success grunting in a buck, using rattling antlers or hunting in open feeding areas. So, take a stand on elevated terrain that overlooks a heavily covered funnel or travel corridor. Keep an eye out for bucks using these routes as they elude hunters who have infiltrated their domain.

When opening day of bowhunting season arrives, bucks are likely to be hanging tight with does that are just about to enter estrus. In this type of situation, your chances of calling a buck to your location are between slim and none. Try using a fawn bleat to call in does instead, any bucks tending them will follow.

many stands to choose from, you get the edge by being able to select the one that offers the best wind direction before heading out to the woods.

As I have said for over 40 years, deer, especially mature bucks, move about in strong wind and rain more than most hunters believe. If you get up on opening morning (or any day during the hunting season), to strong wind and hard rain, don't go back to bed. Instead, dress for the weather and go to your stand. Other hunters have waited for opening day

Little-Known Deer Facts

PETER FIDUCCIA

The old adage that you never stop learning applies to this chapter. While you may already know some of the tips I share here –there may be some that are new to you.

This is a chapter some of you may choose to skip over or browse through. That would be a mistake. I have always felt that consistently successful deer hunters are those who understand their quarry to the ninth degree. Many of the tips in this chapter are geared to providing you that type of information.

You will find some of these tips strategic in orientation, others are biologic in nature, and fact related and others are about the deer's anatomy. All are important for you to have at your finger tips to help you take your deer hunting to the next level.

Knowing your quarry inside and out is the key to consistent hunting success. Credit: Ted Rose

According to researchers a mature whitetail buck makes an average of 195 rubs on saplings each fall.

In the study of whitetail stomach contents, it was determined that the animals regularly feed on more than 600 different varieties of plants.

The hollow hairs comprising a deer's winter coat are equal in their insulating qualities to the most sophisticated wool or other high-tech fibers developed by man.

The reason you see fewer bucks during the spring and summer months is because bucks restrict their movements during this time of year in order to avoid injuring their growing antlers. As they grow, antlers remain soft, tender, and pliable and are very easily damaged.

Scientists tell us that whitetails defecate an average of 13 times every 24 hours. That means even when you locate a lot of scat, it may not indicate that there are a lot of deer leaving the sign. The best way to determine if you have a large herd of deer on your land is to make actual survey counts of deer scat, which is too much trouble for most hunters. I like to see large scat in piles. At the very least, these indicate mature deer–bucks and does.

There are more than 30 known subspecies of whitetails in North and Central America, all of which are believed to have evolved from the "prototype" Virginia whitetail (*Odocoileus virginianus*) species.

Research has proven that deer will defecate up to thirteen times every hour. Glad you're not a deer now, aren't you!

Many hunters confuse the species and think that *Odocoileus virginianus'* range is widespread especially through the Northeast and New England. This is not so. *Odocoileus virginianus virginianus'* range includes Virginia, West Virginia, Kentucky, Tennessee, North Carolina, South Carolina, Georgia, Alabama, and Mississippi. This is a moderately big deer with fairly heavy antlers.

The northern whitetail known as *O.v. borealis*, is the largest subspecies of deer and has the darkest coat. It also has the widest range throughout Maryland, Delaware, New Jersey, New York, Pennsylvania, Ohio, Indiana, Illinois, Minnesota, Wisconsin, Michigan, Connecticut, Rhode Island, Massachusetts, New Hampshire, Vermont, Maine, and in the Canadian provinces of Quebec, Ontario, Nova Scotia, New Brunswick, and a part of Manitoba.

The Dakota whitetail, *O.v. dacotensis*, is another very large deer almost as big in body weight as borealis. Interestingly, this deer has more high-ranking trophy heads in the book than the borealis species. The Dakota whitetail's range encompasses North Dakota, South Dakota, Kansas, Wyoming, Montana, parts of Nebraska and the Canadian provinces of Manitoba, Saskatchewan, and Alberta. Unlike borealis, which is known as a woodland deer, dacotensis calls the timbered coulees, gullies, draws, fields, breaks, and river and stream bottoms of the prairies home.

The Northwest whitetail, *O.v. ochrourus*, is also a large deer. It's range covers parts of Idaho, Montana, Washington, Oregon, California, Nevada, Utah, and the Canadian provinces of British Columbia and Alberta.

This buck's rack probably made short work of a lot of the soft bark on the conifer trees he rubbed. Credit: Ted Rose

The Columbia whitetail, *O.v. leucurus,* has been declining in numbers for years. They are only found along the Columbia River near Cathlamet, Washington.

The Coues (pronounced "cows") is also know as the Arizona whitetail (*O.v. couesi*) and is a small deer. This deer is found in the arid areas of southeastern California, southern Arizona, southwestern New Mexico, and in Mexico.

Other whitetail sub-species include the Texas whitetail, *O.v. texanus*; the Carmen Mountains whitetail *O.v. carminis*; the Avery Island whitetail, *O.v. mcilhennyi*; the Kansas whitetail, *O.v. macrourus*;

the Bull's Island whitetail, *O.v. taurinsulae*; the Hunting Island whitetail, *O.v. venatorius*; the Hilton Head Island whitetail, *O.v. hiltonensis*; and the Blackbeard Island whitetail, *O.v. nigribarbis.* All of the last four subspecies have small antlers. The Florida whitetail, *O.v. seminolus*, is a good size deer that has a fair antler size as well. However, the Florida coastal whitetail *O.v. osceola* is not as large bodied and has slightly smaller antlers. The smallest of all the deer found in North America is the diminutive Florida Key whitetail, *O.v. clavium.*

I can't give you a reason why, but most researchers say that studies have shown deer respond most frequently to the sounds of grunt calls and/or antler rattling when they must travel uphill or at least remain on level ground. They seldom respond if it'll require downhill travel. I tend to agree to a degree. I have had bucks come down hill to my calling and rattling but not as much as going uphill or on level ground.

Ninety percent of all antler rubs are made on aromatic or resinous tree species, such as cedar, pine, spruce, shining sumac, cherry, and dogwood. It is believed this happens because the oily cambiums of these trees will hold the buck's forehead gland scent for longer periods of time, even during rain or snow.

Research by Georgia deer biologist Larry Marchington has documented that during a given year, a buck will make from 69 to 538 antler rubs on trees, with a mature buck averaging 300! (That's a pretty amazing statistic, I know I have never seen that many rubs on my farm!)

Deer possess a supranuclei ganglion, or an internal clock, in their brains. This allows them to fall into restful sleep just as humans can. But unlike us, deer can spring into total alertness in only a third of a second (Sounds like me when I'm napping and I hear the music of one of the old *Star Trek* shows on television).

The size of a scrape is a pretty reliable marker of the size and age of the buck that created it. Mature bucks paw scrapes that are minimally 18 inches in diameter, and some up to six feet.

One of the most argued facts about deer is that deer are not limited to seeing only black and white vision. Recent research has confirmed that deer can see a wide range of colors, including ultraviolet light, which is invisible to humans!

Chasing does is a lot of fun, but by the end of the rut, an average mature buck will have lost as much as 25 percent of his body weight (Hmm, honey–where are you?)!

Radio-tracking studies have documented that the largest bucks generally make the largest antler rubs on trees, and they begin engaging in their rubbing behavior a full month before younger bucks. So if you locate a big rub early, the chance is you have probably located a big buck too. To be sure, look at the rub carefully. If it has indents or tiny holes in the tree, they were probably made by the tips of the tines on a buck's antlers. If you look very carefully, you can almost count the number of tines on the buck's rack.

Many hunters are skeptical about how well deer calls work. Remember, biologists using sophisticated audio recording equipment have identified at least 13 distinct vocalizations that whitetails make to communicate with each other.

For generations, our fathers, grandfathers, and other old-timers told us that cold air temperatures triggered the rut. Now we know that shorter day lengths trigger the rut because reduced amounts of sunlight entering the preorbital glands in the corner of the deer's eyes. These cause changes in a deer's endocrine system, spurring the onset of breeding.

I'm often asked (mostly by guys who hunt in Maine), "What was the heaviest buck ever killed?" It was a 511 pound buck, taken by a Minnesota deer hunter in 1976. This was followed up by two deer that weighed 491 pounds and 481 pounds from Wisconsin in 1980.

Laboratory studies of deer suggest their sense of smell is at least ten times more acute than that of a human. Deer are able to separate and analyze seven different odors simultaneously through an organ in the roof of their mouth called the vomeronasal organ.

Can you look at a pile of deer pellets and learn anything from it? You bet you can! The largest individual pellets are most likely from a buck, because mature bucks are larger in anatomical body size that mature does. Research by a biologist in New Jersey documented that a mature buck will leave a pile of 75 pellets or more.

As most seasoned veteran deer hunters know, when running, a doe is far more likely than a buck to "flag" with her tail. It helps the fawns, yearlings, and other deer in her group to follow her in dim light or when she is fleeing through thick cover.

When making rubs, mature bucks a) deposit priming pheromones from their forehead glands, b) drip urine over their tarsal glands and c) deposit more scent from their vomeronasal organ when they lick the rub. These pheromones attract hot does, tell other bucks the particular buck's rutting status and even help to induce late-estrus does into coming into heat. The scents also chemically intimidate younger bucks into submission so they are less inclined to attempt to refresh the rub or try to breed does that are near the rub.

When the weather turns bitterly cold, seek out places where staghorn sumac grows, if possible. When it gets this cold, deer feed heavily upon staghorn sumac. They instinctively know that this plant is higher in fat than any other native food and thus helps generate body heat.

Deer have a so-called odor comfort zone of about 250 yards. Beyond this distance, foreign odors, some noises, and even predators are not likely to alert or alarm them.

A whitetail's tarsal and interdigital glands carry its unique "signature," just as fingerprints do among humans.

As most seasoned trackers know, the width of a deer track—not its length—is the most reliable indicator of the animal's age. As a deer's body weight steadily increases with age, a progressively wider based platform to support its weight is also needed.

Many hunters are unaware that a doe makes good use of a buck rub and scrape. She is able to sniff and chemically analyze all the scents left by the buck that made it, and then evaluate the health, virility, and the exact status of the buck to determine if he would be a worthy sire.

A lone bed measuring 40 to 60 inches in length is most likely that of a big buck. If the bed you find is barely 40 inches and is accompanied by one or two smaller ones, it's undoubtedly that of a doe with offspring.

Studies of deer that are penned have shown that they have an attention span of about three minutes, after which they forget whatever it was that frightened them. This is good to know. If you step on a branch while still-hunting or walking to your stand, stop and remain motionless for at least three minutes before you take another step. That way, you may keep the deer from running out of the county.

Immature bucks commonly check their scrapes by walking right up to them. Don't count on that when it comes to a mature buck. They normally scent-check their scrapes from 50 to 75 yards or more downwind while remaining in thick cover.

Although a whitetail's home range may span several square miles, radio-tracking studies indicate

Use a snort or grunt call when passing heavy cover (standing corn, a patch of laurel, blow-downs, etc.) to coax a buck out of the cover and into the open.

This is the bed of a doe, as it is small and had several smaller beds around it.

I was still-hunting through blowdowns when I stopped to rattle. The rattling sounds, along with some grunt call I made, got this buck to stand up from behind a downed tree.

that mature bucks have a core area of approximately 40 acres where they spend up to 90 percent of their time. Hence the term, core area, which refers to where the buck spends most of his life.

A scrape is always found near a low, overhanging tree branch that has been chewed and broken by the buck that made the scrape. Sometimes, within five feet of the scrape, you will also find a licking stick, which is a very thin sapling about two to three feet high The tip of the sapling will be chewed and frayed. The buck deposits saliva on both the overhanging branch and the licking stick from his vomeronasal organ and his forehead-gland, as well as scent from his preputial and tarsal glands in order to pass along olfactory information telling other deer that this is his breeding area.

Whitetails have a vomeronasal organ in the roof of the mouth, which allows them to "taste" odors detected by the nose. After this chemical analysis is performed, the information is then transmitted to the brain for deciphering. The vomeronasal organ is very important and is used throughout the rut to scent hot does, and to deposit saliva scent on rubs and scrapes.

Still-Hunting

PETER FIDUCCIA

There are four distinct ways to bag a deer and each way has a specific term.

When a hunter waits for a deer at a specific location on the ground or from above in a tree stand, the term used to describe this hunting method is called *posting*. This hunter depends on knowing the travel routes to and from feeding and bedding areas, as well as the prevailing wind directions and a host of other elements. He often

includes calling, rattling, decoying, and patiently sitting and waiting for a deer to walk past his hunting location or tree stand among his list of necessary hunting skills.

Another good tactic involves a hunter picking up a deer's track and following it until he either finds the buck in his bed or jumps him. This is known as *tracking*. This hunter depends on woodsmanship and hunting skills to bag his buck. He must be able to locate and decipher the smallest amount of fresh sign left by his quarry in order to follow the track to success.

Another strategy entails hunters grouping together to move deer out of the cover of safety and into or past the men who have taken up locations at known escape routes. Of course, the term for this type of hunting is called a *deer drive*.

Finally, there is the hunter who slowly and methodically picks his way through the woods and fields, not so much to find fresh sign or to follow a track, but in hopes of getting into cover where he expects deer to be bedded down. This technique is known as *still-hunting*. This hunter has unlimited patience. He may cover only 100 yards in an hour's time—sometimes longer than that depending on the terrain. His success is solely dependent on his ability to move not only carefully, and slowly, but also his ability to pick out his next step prior to putting

Cody Fiduccia with a deer he hung on our game pole for me. I was still-hunting through a thick patch of pines when I bumped the buck from cover.

his foot down so that he will not spook a deer by accidentally snapping a twig.

The still-hunter watches his back trail constantly and carefully scans for deer that might be lying down, waiting for him to pass by. All his hunting instincts and senses are on full alert from the moment he begins to stalk through the woods until he decides the hunt is over. This hunter is referred to as a still-hunter or stalker.

The image of still-hunting a buck puts goose bumps on most hunter's backs. It conjures up rustic feelings of the skilled hunters from yesteryear. Many of these men entered the woods not for sport, but to put food on the table for their families. Today, some hunters want to relive that vision because it is not only an exciting way to hunt, but it is also demanding and challenging.

For the hunter who still-hunts or for those who want to try the tactic, here are some tips I have garnered over the years through a lot of trial and error. The many flagging tails I have seen while still-hunting dramatically outweighs the number of bucks I have killed using this method. But in the end, the few bucks I have taken like this have etched the deepest memories in my mind over the last 15 years.

The old Native American adage about still-hunting still applies today "walk little, watch a lot." Keep this one piece of advice in mind when you still-hunt and you will find hunting success.

Contrary to what most hunters have heard, you don't always have to still-hunt with the wind constantly in your face. With this tactic the wind can also be quartering toward you from the left or right. The key is not to allow your odor to be carried directly ahead of your intended route of movement.

Some feel that midday is not the best time to still-hunt; I don't. Although it is true that most deer are bedded down then, they are not unapproachable. If you still-hunt during the midday hours, you are

Filson wool is our favorite wool to wear. Here Kate is dressed to keep warm in a Filson wool camo hunting jacket.

also inclined to bump into a buck that has risen out of its bed and is feeding, rubbing a tree, making a scrape, or simply looking for a hot doe. Any time you still-hunt you will have a chance to jump a deer.

As I have said over and over again, bad weather makes for good hunting. A rainy day, or a steady drizzle or a gentle snowfall seems to relax deer and make them feel safer than they actually are. This is a terrific time to still-hunt as you are more inclined to catch a deer feeding in an open area than on a blue bird type day. The ground is also much quieter during this type of weather, giving you a greater opportunity to surprise a bedded or feeding deer.

When still-hunting use all available cover. Avoid open, bright places with little cover.

Always carefully plan your next several steps in advance before moving. Look at the available type of terrain and cover that is ahead of you. Select

This deer didn't make an alarm-snort, instead it made an alarm-distress snort and is heading to the next county. Credit: Ted Rose

routes that will muffle your steps such as fallen pine needles, moist leaves, moss, or non-moving rocks.

Never place your heel down first. The toe end of your boot is more sensitive and it will enable you to feel what is underfoot better.

For me, there is no other choice than wearing Filson wool when I'm still-hunting. Wool is the quietest fabric you can wear. All other clothes are far too noisy to wear when still-hunting. A good backup for wool clothing is fleece.

When you're still-hunting and cross fresh tracks, don't hunt directly over them. Immediately adjust your direction and take a route that parallels the tracks to one side. Watch your back trail, as the buck you're following is watching his and may decide to circle around you.

The savvy still-hunter doesn't spend too much time investigating tracks; he knows they only tell you that the deer passed here earlier. Spend your time looking carefully ahead of you in the distance, in the direction of the tracks. This way, you may just get a good look at the buck that made them.

Let's say you spot a buck too far ahead of you for a clean shot. If you have enough cover, try to make a wide semicircle to get ahead of him. Then, pick a spot with good cover. Stop and wait without making any movement. There is a good chance the buck may end up walking right past you.

If a deer sees, hears, or smells you and snorts and runs off, snort back at it. This is a good way to not only stop the deer but also attract it. If it doesn't see or wind you it probably won't travel far or it might even start walking your way! If it does walk off, wait about 15 minutes and then begin to slowly make a wide arc to the left or right. You may get an opportunity to intercept the deer within a few hundred yards.

For still-hunters, the Game Sled helps makes dragging deer quick and easy--even over long distances. CEO of Coventry Log Homes, Jeff Elliott, drags out a hefty 9-point with the Game Sled.

The worst and the noisiest choice of footwear to wear when still-hunting is a heavy pair of leather boots. They will give your presence away to deer every time. I often wear sneakers in the early fall and light leather or rubber boots later in the season, especially when snow and rain make for slippery terrain.

If you happen to jump a buck and he isn't aware of you, don't rush to change your position or to take a shot. Rushing usually ends up with the hunter making a careless mistake, which inevitably alerts the buck to your presence. I know what I'm talking about here; I made this mistake countless times as a young, inexperienced still-hunter.

A seasoned still-hunter isn't always on the move. If you come upon a good spot to watch for deer like a natural bottleneck, deer ravine, or a primary scrape, take a rest. Sit down and quietly watch the area for just about an hour or so before moving on again.

Deer are most active when the barometric pressure is between 29.80 and 30.29, when the wind is from the south or southwest, and there's a relative humidity of less than 70 percent. This is a good time to still-hunt.

Researchers say that deer go to water at three specific times each day: around 7:00 AM, 11:00 AM, and 6:00 PM Why? Because of the deer's body metabolism and cud-chewing periods. If there are water sources in the area you're still-hunting, it pays to check any known water sources during these times, especially during a period where there has been less rain or during a drought.

Rut Hunting

PETER FIDUCCIA

This tip chapter supplements the more detailed chapter in this book on the rut. To be frank, I could dedicate an entire book to all aspects of the rut biology, strategy and science. But until I get around to writing that book, this chapter and the more detailed chapter will give you a lot of straight information on a subject eliminating all the horse crap that is often spread about the rut.

What you read here and in the other chapter will be material you can rely on and not have to question. It is information that has taken me years to accumulate. I have tested it through trial and error and share with you the cream of information that rose to the top.

I'm very confident that between this tip chapter and the full chapter on the rut, you will gain insight to this often misunderstood and misspoken subject. It will hopefully shed some light on the inner workings of rut behavior, biology, and some new tactics you can try on the very next rut.

Using a scent out of season, like estrus-urine before the breeding or the "chase phase" starts, won't attract bucks. They interpret the aroma as unnatural and will only shy away from it. Pay attention to the timing of scent use, and use such scents only when the rut is clearly under way. Use them sparingly and you will also get a more natural response.

This buck is on the trail of a hot doe. By making an enticing estrus doe blat, you would get the buck's attention quickly. Credit: Ted Rose

The preorbital gland senses decreasing daylight stimulating the pineal gland which sends a chemical message to the pituitary glad to increase testosterone and the onset of the rut begins.
Credit: Ted Rose

You have heard me say over and over again that it is hard to judge what size buck made a rub. As a rule, the larger the diameter of the rubbed tree, the larger the buck that made the rub. Big-antlered bucks do rub small saplings, however, and although young bucks don't usually rub large trees—they do on occasion. Look for hook marks in the tree trunk or little indents or holes. These are made by the tips of antler tines. Usually, this is a good way to judge if the buck that rubbed the tree had at least a multi-pointed rack.

Biologists say that the scrape of a mature buck averages 18 to 36 inches in diameter. Find one that is greater than 24 inches and you have a scrape to hunt over.

Biologists don't have a definitive explanation why the quantity and quality of the acorn drop affects the number of rubs bucks make each fall. Basically, when there are fewer acorns, there will be fewer rubs, so finding only a few rubs doesn't necessarily mean that the buck count is down. There may be more bucks in an area with lower acorn drop than the lack of rub sign would lead you to believe!

When you're setting up a stand so you can watch a scrape, don't get too close, or a returning buck is very likely to detect you. Since bucks commonly scent-check their scrapes from 30 to 40 yards downwind, the spot for your tree stand should be 50 to 60 yards downwind of the scrape if you're a bow hunter, and further still if you're a firearm hunter. Then the returning buck should pass right between you and the scrape with his attention focused in the opposite direction.

Don't pay much attention to scrapes and rubs made around field perimeters bordering woodlands. Most of this rutting sign is made and revisited only after dark.

When you're scouting, never touch a scrape, licking branch, or rubbed tree with your bare hands or clothing. Even the tiniest amount of human scent transferred to the sign will alert deer to your presence and cancel the sign's significance.

The rut is triggered when a decreasing amount of daily sunlight passes through the eyes of deer. This reduction of light stimulates the pineal gland, which in turn sends messages to the pituitary gland to increase testosterone levels in bucks and progesterone levels in does.

Bucks are capable of breeding whenever they have hard antlers, which lasts for a five-month time span. But does are capable of breeding only when in estrus–which runs a 26-hour time span. So in reality, it's the does that "go into rut," not the bucks.

When does are in estrus, it's virtually impossible to call in a buck with a grunt call. Use a doe bleat or fawn call to call in does instead. Any responding does that are in heat will have bucks trailing behind them, right to your deer stand.

When you rattle antlers, don't rattle too loudly at first. Just tick the tines to make "click-clicking" sounds that simulate the sparring of immature bucks. If you start off loud and aggressive, you may intimidate and scare away bucks.

If a doe comes by your stand with her tail extended straight back, freeze! She's at the peak of her estrus and is signaling to a following buck that she's ready to breed.

The most intense action during any region's well-defined rutting period occurs when there is a 10 to 20 degree drop in the temperature. Conversely, rutting action slows dramatically when the temperature suddenly rises above the norm. This is not to be confused with the rut-regulating influence of sunlight; it's a separate, year-round phenomenon. Deer are always more active in cool weather, becoming lethargic when the temperature rises above the norm.

Biologists tell us that the types of places where bucks most frequently make scrapes are (in descending order of importance) field edges, ridge crests, terraced hillside benches, narrow bottomland flats adjacent to creeks, and old logging roads.

During the rut, bucks can to travel as far as seven miles per day and as little as 300 yards per day. It all depends upon how many does are available to a buck in a given region.

When you're rattling antlers, simulate the sounds of a genuine buck fight by stomping the ground with your boots and raking the antlers through brush. Since the buck will come in focused on your sounds, make sure you are well camouflaged.

Many experts agree that hunting a scrape area is more likely to result in success if you use a portable, climbing stand that you carry in and out each time you visit. If you use either a fixed-position stand or a ladder stand and leave them in place, a buck visiting the area during your absence is likely to see or smell the stand and avoid it from then on.

If you're hunting a scrape area and spook a mature buck or shoot at one and miss, it's unlikely that he'll give you a second chance in the days or week to come. Relocate your stand to another scrape area at least 300 yards away.

If you see a buck approaching a scrape cautiously, in a timid manner, with his head held low and his tail tucked between his legs, you might want to pass him up. He's exhibiting subordinate behavior that indicates the scrape he's investigating was made by another higher-ranking buck.

Bucks commonly scrape in the same locations year after year. They may even lay down scrapes beneath the exact tree branches and rub the very same saplings as the year before. When scouting, be sure to check the scrape and rub locations you hunted the previous years. You may even find yourself being able to use the same exact tree for a stand as you did last year.

Ignore so-called estrus-response scrapes. These are small and are commonly found in open fields and meadows. They're simply places where an estrus doe has urinated and a buck (in his random travels) has detected the scent and briefly pawed the ground. The buck may never return to that spot again.

If a scrape you're hunting begins to dry out and is slowly becoming covered by windblown leaves and forest duff, it's no longer being visited and freshened by the buck that originally made it. Scout somewhere else for a hot scrape that's being regularly tended.

Severe weather ordinarily causes whitetails to lay up in cover, often for several days, until things blow over. The exception is the peak of the rut. This is the time when most of the does are in full estrus. They are very restless and continually on the move. Bucks, likewise, are traveling and searching for does, regardless of what the weather is doing. So don't stay home just because high winds or driving sleet are ravaging your favorite deep woods. Get out and be in the woods during this time of peak deer activity.

Unless the weather is extremely bad during the rut, bucks and does will continue to move in search of a mates.
Credit: Ted Rose

Tree Stands

PETER FIDUCCIA

One of the most common mistakes about deer hunting is not having confidence in where you placed your stand. I have heard many times from hunters who email me (peter@fiduccia.com) about this one subject, "Please give me some sound advice on where I should place my stand."

In this tip chapter, I share with you my best advice on this subject. Whether you hunt a farm, remote ridge in big woods or on heavily hunted state lands there is something here for you to glean.

Remember while you are reading these tip that while they may seem basic, many hunters despite knowing of them–do not use them to the best of their ability. The truth is paying attention to the dozen tips I mention here will help improve you deer sightings and shooting opportunities dramatically.

If you're hunting a farm, it may be better not to walk in with your portable stand–unless you have

This is one of my favorite deer blinds. It is called a DeerBox, and it comes in all shapes and sizes.

no other choice. Remember, that on every farm or ranch, the farmer or rancher doesn't walk around his land. Farmers constantly drive tractors, trucks, or four-wheelers on their property and deer soon become accustomed to the comings and goings of vehicles. They even get more familiar with the one vehicle that is used most often. So if you have the opportunity to ride a tractor or ATV set up your stand you may wind up arousing less suspicion by the deer than if you walked in.

When you're trail watching, don't position your stand along a straightaway stretch. Instead, place it on the inside of the bend. Deer usually walk the trail looking toward the outside of the bend and therefore, they are less likely to notice you.

When you're hunting a bedding area, position your portable climbing stand so you can hunt the downwind side of the cover. If the wind direction changes on a particular day, go to a different stand location.

For the best concealment from every direction, hang your stand in a multi-trunk tree clump–I like three-trunk trees. You will be spotted much more often from a single-trunk tree standing alone. Single trees just don't hide your presence as well as multi-trunk trees do and when a deer approaches, it usually makes you out.

Early in the season, it is wiser not to go too high in your stand. With leaves on the trees, your vision is obstructed and there is more in your way when trying to get a clear shot. Instead, stay below the heavy leaves and foliage to see and get more action. Plan to set up higher later in the season, after the leaves have dropped.

Once your stand is mounted and secure, try it out for comfort and to see if there are any dead branches, twigs, or loose bark in your way. If so, rub away the loose bark and snap the branches and twigs from the trunk. That way, you will prevent any unexpected noise as well as getting your clothing caught and making noises as you climb or turn your body to get into shooting position. More deer are spooked like this than you can image. Most deer are never seen because they hear your noise and avoid the spot–leaving you thinking you got skunked for the day.

I know it is hard, but try to avoid taking the same route to your stand every day; you'll eventually alert the deer to your presence. With a mature buck it won't take but a few times, at best, for him to get the picture of what is taking place. Try not to hunt from the same stand every day either. I like giving my stands a rest of at least one day, and preferably

This stand gets its best action when the wind is blowing from the southwest. The savvy hunter sets lots of stands to take advantage of different wind directions.

two or three days, between hunts. Of course, this means having other stands set up and ready to go so you can play the shell game when the wind is wrong or so you can avoid over-hunting a certain stand.

Even the most active big-buck stand can be ruined if you hunt it when the wind direction is not completely in your favor. It takes a lot of determination, but if you know the wind is coming from the wrong direction or swirling erratically, don't go to the stand. The best advantage for having multiple stands in place is that you can choose the best location to hunt each day as conditions dictate.

I regularly set out markers to help me not under- or over-estimate distances when I am bowhunting. I place markers at various distances around my stand for quick reference that I have measured off with a digital rangefinder. In the woods, there are plenty of places to hang markers. In a stand at the edge of a field, I use markers that stick in the ground.

Whenever you have a choice, hang your stand on the north side of a tree. You will be less visible to deer because most of the time you'll be in the shade of the trunk.

On our farm, we have at least 24 tree stands in different locations. Now, I don't recommend setting up that many unless you also own at least 300 acres, but if you are hunting a 50–150-acre parcel you should have at least a half dozen stands up so you can work the wind and avoid hunting the same stand twice in a day. That way you will always have a hot stand to hunt from as the season progresses and conditions change. There should be a stand overlooking a prime feeding area, one overlooking an escape trail, swamp, a thick patch of pines, a hot primary scrape or rub, as well as one in a funnel, near a water hole, and one near a stormy-weather bedding area.

I look for new tree-stand locations in March or April, because vegetation has not yet grown up to hide last year's sign. I also look during turkey season.

Calling All Deer

PETER FIDUCCIA

My most successful tactic over the last 45 years is using deer calls to attract deer, hold others from leaving, and stop running deer or even to intentionally spook deer from heavy cover. No matter what circumstance comes up in deer hunting–using a deer call can benefit you.

These are tips that can complement all the other information I have provided on deer calling over the years. Some of the tips I have mentioned before in my calling DVD *Tactics for Talking to Deer* or in other books or on my television show. I mention them again here to demonstrate their importance. You can take what you read in this chapter to the deer hunting bank–used as recommended you will be dressing out your buck or doe this fall!

As I have mentioned many times, never call to a deer when it is walking toward you and especially when it is looking straight in your direction. The odds of the deer seeing you are much greater if you do. It may also see you move the call to your lips and just that movement alone may be enough of a warning for the deer to leave the area. Always give deer an angle before calling to them or at least wait until the deer looks another way. If you excite their sense of curiosity and keep him guessing where the call is coming from, a buck or doe will eventually get close enough for a shot.

As many of you have heard me preach in my seminars and on our television show, blowing a grunt call like you're the biggest, "baddest" buck in the woods will only work against you. A loud, aggressive grunt only serves to intimidate most bucks–even mature bucks–and will scare them away almost every time. If you keep your grunt tone low so you sound like a "beatable" buck, you'll draw greater response from bucks that think they can whip you.

If you see a distant deer respond to your call and begin coming your way, stop calling! Let the deer's curiosity work for you. By continuing to call to the deer, you'll only increase the buck's chances of pinpointing your exact location. Also, most deer do not vocalize repeatedly. This does not sound natural to them.

This buck is making a lip curl (flehmening). He would respond immediately to a doe estrus blat.
Credit: Ted Rose

An adult estrus doe blat is the perfect call to use at the peak of the rut. When a doe is in heat, she seeks out a buck. Often, the doe periodically stops and makes several soft blats, then looks around and listens for a soft grunt response from a buck. The cadence of this particular sound by the doe sounds almost like a standard grunt call; the difference is that it isn't continuous but includes three-second pauses between each one-second blat.

If you blow your call at a distant deer, he will react almost one hundred percent of the time. He may not always turn and immediately come your way, but you'll see some recognition of the call. He may flag his tail twice, raise his head slightly, either slow down or speed up its gait, look in your direction, or simply cup an ear toward you. If none

These are the tools of a deer caller. They include a grunt, snort, two adult blats, and a fawn bleat.

of these body language signals takes place, the buck most likely did not hear your call. It is worth trying to call to this deer once more, slightly louder.

More and more hunters, especially bowhunters, are using the alarm-distress fawn bleat to call in does. Why call does? Because a doe's maternal instinct causes her to respond to what she perceives is a fawn in trouble. And if you call her in, any buck that's with her or even near enough to hear the fawn bleating may just follow the doe to your stand as well!

When you rattle with a partner—antler rattling is doubly effective. Place the shooter in a tree stand, ground blind, or in heavy cover, about 35 yards from the rattling hunter. If a deer responds, he'll usually walk right by the shooter to find the two "other bucks" that are sparring or fighting—many times offering the shooter an exciting shot.

Learning not to grunt too loudly or aggressively will enhance your success post-haste. You can take that to the deer hunting bank!

Deer don't continuously vocalize among themselves, so don't overdo your calling. The exception to this rule is during the rut, when both bucks and does use a variety of vocalizations far more frequently. During this time of the season, you can risk calling more often—say every 20 or 30 minutes throughout the course of the day.

Calling when you actually do not see a deer can be effective, but calling to a deer you can see works best as you can watch to see if the deer is interested or not.

When you're using any type of deer call, don't always expect a deer to immediately respond and head your way. Quite often, a deer will stare for a long period of time, trying to see the other deer before venturing closer. This is where my natural deer tail decoy works its magic. Full size decoys also work well to entice deer to come in as well.

When you rattle, pay close attention to your immediate right, left, and behind you. A majority of bucks I have called in didn't come straight to me from the direction I expected. Instead, they often circled and tried to come in downwind of me. Keep that in mind when you are using pro-active tactics like calling, rattling, and decoying.

I wish I had a dollar for every time I could not control the need to cough or sneeze while on stand. When it happens, I try to muffle my mouth against my jacket sleeve. Then, I immediately try to cover my sound and stimulate some other type of deer vocalization that will match the time of throat-clearing noise and then a grunt, or blat, or some other deer vocalization won't be alarmed as he would've been if you'd just coughed. When I sneeze—I quickly make a soft, social snort to cover the noise made by the sneeze.

In addition to my deer calls, I carry a small predator call that imitates a screaming rabbit. Many deer respond to predator calls based purely upon curiosity.

It is important to use your eyes and ears when calling. Here, the editor of this book uses a grunt in a cedar swamp.

Using your ears and eyes are critical to successful calling. It is said that 80 percent of the animals called in by hunters come in without being seen. Whitetails have an uncanny way of slipping in close without making a sound or exposing themselves in the open. Continually scrutinize the cover in all directions around you for the slightest glimpse of a wary buck putting the sneak on you. I have often heard a buck make very soft guttural grunts before I ever saw him. Other times, I heard and saw a sapling being rubbed or brush being attacked by a buck that responded to my call, but kept himself well hidden in cover. When this happens, sometimes a soft doe blat draws the wary buck closer to you.

Generally, antlered game does not want to spill blood when they fight. On rare occasions, a serious injury or death may happen, most fights are nothing more than shoving and sparring matches.

During the pre-rut, savvy callers combine what I term the "Big Four." Use a grunt call, mixed with an estrus doe-blat, rattling antlers, and a decoy. Note: During the firearm season I only do this on my farm in an area where no other hunters are present. For safety's sake, either do this on your own land or only during the bowhunting season. For goodness sake—don't do it on the opening day of firearm season anywhere!

Throughout the year, does are far more vocal and social than bucks. Because of this, many deer you call in will be does. Young 1½ year old bucks also fall into this category.

If you call in a buck and he hangs up just out of shooting range and won't come any closer, wait a few minutes before doing anything more. Allow him to turn and walk away until he's almost out of sight. Then, make a soft grunt quickly followed by a slightly louder estrus blat. Many times I have had a buck stop in his tracks, spin around, and come trotting in with his guard down. It creates the entire illusion for the buck.

Take this to the deer hunting bank: There is no truth to the legend that large rattling antlers will call in the biggest bucks. Again, big bucks are frightened of their own shadows most of the time and when they are spurred on to be brave during the rut, they still avoid encounters with big or bigger bucks. Use an average set of antlers and you will have greater response. Yes, it's true that bleached or dried-out antlers don't yield the same authentic sounds as fresh ones—I guarantee that. And yes, I have used synthetic antlers for over 20 years when I rattle. You can find them at www.woodsnwater.tv .

If hunting pressure is usually intense in your region, you'll have your best success calling deer during the off-hours and midweek, when fewer hunters are in the woods. Hunt the heaviest cover you can find during this time.

Most buck fights are nothing more than sparring sessions. Only where there is a one-to-one buck-to-doe ratio do bucks get into more serious fights. So don't smash your antlers together hard especially during the early fall or you'll scare off even the big bucks. Many times this type of over-aggressive rattling will scare off a hot doe during the rut and then you might as well move your location. By just lightly tickling the antlers you will attract more bucks. The time to clash your antlers a little louder is later during the big chase, when bucks are fighting more aggressively, but still not getting into all-out fights.

When calling or rattling, remember if you call in a small buck, you may want to let him pass. Or, at least wait a few minutes to see if he is being followed by a larger buck—which often happens. Don't expect the bigger buck to just walk in. When you spot the young deer, take a moment to scan the cover for the bigger buck.

When you're rattling, this is the time to create the entire illusion. Add more realism by meshing and grinding the antlers together. If you're on the ground, kick dirt and rustle leaves with your boots and don't be afraid to break dry branches to simulate the various sounds that bucks make when fighting. If you're rattling from a tree stand, rake the tree's bark and break smaller branches. Don't get over aggressive but make sure to include all of the above. I know I have said in earlier books to be very aggressive when rattling. Well, we all continue to learn the more we hunt. After rattling for 40 years, I can now say being less aggressive pays more dividends than being overly aggressive.

Don't expect deer to respond to your calling every day—it just won't happen. That's the reality of calling, rattling, and decoying. Sometimes deer will come to you one day, and they won't respond the next day. Don't be frustrated and give up calling. Instead stick with it—it will be worth your while.

I often carry my deer calls during the spring and summer while I work on my farm. It gives me an opportunity to practice on any deer that I happen to come across. Practicing during the off-season is crucial to becoming a confident caller during the hunting season.

Hunting Farmlands

Several years ago, my cousin Leo Somma and I purchased over 300 acres of land in Otsego County, New York. Leo's 110 acres has about seven tillable acres and my property has 35 agricultural acres. Between both our farms we have not only learned how to become pretty good farmers, but we have also learned how to improve the soil, pH, and the mineral content of the soil.

We have gained invaluable experience on how to successfully grow many different types of crops that attract, hold, and help the overall health of the deer and other wildlife.

We regularly grow different types of vegetables, melons, clover, grains, legumes, brassicas, buckwheat, sugar beets, turnips, and millet. We also plant and grow specialty crops like white acorn trees, wild fruit trees, soybeans, sunflowers, a wide variety of shrubs, and even inedible cover crops.

By growing these crops (through trial and error), we have come a long way to understand what deer eat, when they eat it, what they prefer to eat and how they use the fields and other areas on our farms in their daily routines.

The day we bought our land we decided we would improve our soil minerals, create sanctuaries, and manage the crops, woods, water sources, and the game as the first step to begin our quest to start a genuine quality deer management program.

We have also learned that deer not only respond very well to having fields or food plots to feed in, but they also develop a predictable pattern regarding travel routes, feeding times and places, and other behavior that helps our hunting to be more successful.

Following are some suggestions for anyone who hunts on lands that include agricultural fields, small food plots, or other types of plants, shrubs, trees, or vegetation that deer eat.

Biologists claim that the preferred domestic foods of deer are soybeans, corn, cabbage, sugar beets, carrots, navy beans, turnips, apples, pears, peaches, and legume grasses such as alfalfa and clover. You can take that to the deer hunting bank. On our farm, alfalfa is the number one favored crop followed closely by soybeans, corn, and carrots. Next are apples and pears. I'll bet they are also favored in this order on most farms you hunt.

We have noticed over the years that deer normally enter crop fields at the inside or outside corners, not along one of the side edges. When you're looking for a stand location, spend most of your time scouting for entrance and exit trails at these corner spots.

Hunters don't often pay enough attention to harvested cornfields or other croplands when they are covered by snow. I promise you, deer can smell the food beneath the snow. I've seen them paw down through a foot of the fresh snow to get at the broken corn cobs, grasses or other food.

As a rule of thumb, it is easier to get deer hunting permission on a farm where crops are grown than on a tract of land not used for agriculture. Too many deer can destroy certain crops (like soybeans) making most farmers welcome hunters in hopes of keeping their deer population in balance.

I discovered that deer love all types of melons—which are like ice cream to deer (so are turnips). They stomp the melons apart with their hooves, and then eat the sweet inner fruit. A field littered with broken melon parts is a deer hunting hot spot you should never overlook. Pumpkin fields also produce the same attraction to deer.

When fields of low-growing crops (grains, grasses, and large plantings of garden vegetables) are close to dense cover, woods, or stands of evergreen pines, deer feed on them most often during daylight. Other fields that place deer out in the open (especially mature bucks), aren't worth hunting after the hunting pressure gets going. Does and young bucks may eat there during the last 30 minutes of light, but mature bucks will not venture into the open fields until well after dark.

I have seen deer on my farm walk right through my cornfields, without stopping to even nibble on the corn, to reach a small five-acre soybean field. Soybeans are so highly sought-after by deer that they eat the entire plant; first the beans, then the leaves, then the stems. That is why if you are going to plant soybeans plant at least five acres. Despite being warned by my cousin Ralph to "double or triple" the number of acres I was planting, I didn't. The deer never gave my soybeans the chance to grow. They ate them to the ground. Ralph regularly hunts huge soybean fields in Colts Neck, New Jersey, and knows well how fast deer will eat up a small field planted in soybeans. After the beans have been

This is a field of corn on my farm. I often spot deer leaving the woods and feeding during the midday on my corn.

I plant corn and sorghum for food, cover, and as a natural fence along my property's borders and roads. I leave the crops standing through deer season. As the hunting pressure increases deer quickly use them to bed and escape from hunters on nearby properties.

harvested, they'll revisit the field to paw the ground and get at the roots. If you have a choice of various types of cropland to hunt, always pick the soybean field—even over alfalfa when the area around you has other alfalfa fields but no soybeans fields available!

I have also discovered that when there's no heavy bedding cover adjacent to a cornfield, and sometimes even when there is, deer regularly bed in the standing corn—right through the firearm season! If hunting the perimeter edges doesn't produce, put on very small pushes. One hunter should slowly walk through the standing corn zigzagging back and forth. If there are deer bedded there, they will slowly move ahead of the hunter and when they get to the edge of the corn they will trot out into the surrounding woods or other cover surrounding the corn field! I also use standing corn to make an

alarm-distress snort. If deer are there, they will move from the corn offering you a shot.

It didn't take me long to find out deer don't like to dig for their food. As soon as we cut a crop or harvest it, they'll eagerly head to the fields to eat the broken pieces of these vegetables that the harvester or other farm equipment leaves behind and are turned up to the top of the soil.

The number one question I get when I give food plot seminars is, "What should I plant on my land?" My answer is from what I have learned through six years of farming experience, "Always try to plant what your neighbors are not planting!" By planting crops your neighboring hunting clubs or numerous farms don't plant, you will offer the deer something new and interesting to eat that they can't find anywhere else! If everyone is growing clover, there

To draw as many deer as you can from your land and your neighbors' properties, plant crops that are not planted by your surrounding neighbors or farmers.

is no reason that deer have to come to your land to eat clover. But if you offer chicory or sugar beets or anything else other than what is growing around you, deer will make a beeline to your place first. That means they will be there during shooting hours!

If you don't have your own land to grow crops, always try to gain hunting permission on a farm where something different is grown than on other farms in the area. Deer are varietal feeders, meaning that their body metabolisms don't function properly on just one type of food. Therefore, if most of the farms are planted in corn and hay, the lone farm that has leafy vegetables will act as a magnet to the local deer population. If most of the farmers in the area raise apples and other fruits, the lone farm with grain (i.e. wheat or oats) will be high on the deer hit list.

When hunting any cropland, stay on stand as long as possible each day. A good way to do this is to hunt one stand from dawn till around 9:00 AM. Then if you want, go back to camp and eat a quick breakfast (not bacon or other smelly foods). Then head back out to another stand—not the one you were in—and hunt there from 11:30 AM to 2:30 PM Then, move to a third stand to hunt until legal light is over. This strategy doesn't take long before it produces more deer sightings for the average hunter. Deer living in farm areas are more accustomed to having close encounters with vehicles, farm equipment, and farm workers, so they're not nearly as nocturnal as in non-farm country where they will dart to the thickets to bed soon after sunup.

Many farmers know that whitetails focus their attention on soybean and cornfield spillage and remaining orchard fruits during bitter-cold weather. As I have often mentioned, deer instinctively know these particular food types yield the highest conversion rate (conversion is the metabolic transformation of food into energy, body warmth,

and accumulated fat store). Therefore, when the temperature suddenly drops below 27 degrees, head to corn or soybean fields to hunt.

In my first book, I wrote that during the rut, find the does and you'll find the bucks. Nothing has changed about that plan over the years. When hunting on farms, you'll locate the does in the fields of whatever crop happens to be in its prime. The bucks will be skulking close by in any available cover.

The very worst thing you can do during the firearm season is to hunt directly over a crop field. Instead, put your stand at least 100 yards from where you think the deer will be feeding. During bow season, put it on the entrance trail at least 50 yards back into the adjacent woodland cover. Does and small bucks may enter a cropland well before dusk, but mature bucks commonly stay back within the protection of cover until full dark.

After you have permission to hunt on a farm that's raising crops, ask the landowner where he sees deer feeding, where they come out of surrounding woodlands, and how they travel back and forth across the property. He sees the activity day in and day out and knows best where the deer feed most every day. Following this advice can turn your scouting time into hunting time instead!

If you have a stand that overlooks a crop like alfalfa or soybean, don't go to your stand in the pre-dawn darkness, by walking across the open field. It is more than likely you will spook deer that are feeding in the field and you will send them scurrying off to find cover. Instead, walk the edges or circle around to approach your stand by coming through adjacent woodland cover. During the evening post, reverse that practice. Don't walk through the woodlands to reach a stand that overlooks a field, because you'll probably spook deer from their beds or who are moving slowly toward the fields. Instead, take the shortest route across the open field to get to the stand unnoticed and unheard.

Although grass legumes such as alfalfa and clover are deer magnets, their attraction is strongest in the early fall when they're still lush and green. Later in the fall and into early winter, after several hard frosts, the grasses go into dormancy, become dry and aren't as palatable or nutritious. This time of year, deer seek out crops like turnips and sugar beets as these plants become much sweeter after they have frozen. Turnips have 17 to 24 percent crude protein and their roots have 12 to 15 percent protein. Turnips are another "ice cream" plant for deer especially after heavy frosts when other crops are less attractive to deer.

We set up a lot of our food plots in areas where our stands are at least 40 to 50 yards in the woods so the deer don't associate the food plots with danger. During bow season we will hunt the edges of our fields more, however.

During periods of drought, the hot spot for deer hunting is in a field planted in legumes. The prime time to be on stand is early morning when deer eat the wet grass and lick the dew from it (as an added benefit). Soon after the sun burns off the dew, the deer will boogie for nearby shaded woodland cover.

We never let a planting season go by without putting in turnips for the deer. After a heavy frost turnips are to deer as iron is to magnets.

Deer Drives

PETER FIDUCCIA

I'm not big on driving deer especially in heavily hunted areas or in places where driving small acreage only sends deer to the neighbors. I'm also never too impressed by killing a deer that was driven to me. It seems to take something out of the hunt for me. But let me be clear that by no means am I being critical of anyone else who enjoys the strategy. I feel to each-his-own when it comes to how you like to hunt deer.

The way I drive deer isn't really a drive at all. It is more like a strategic low-key push. Small drives always seem to work better than large ones do—for me anyway. The real fact is that hunters seldom really drive, push or move deer in directions the deer really don't want to go!

Remember that all deer drives do include elements of strategies that to the best of our hunting skills try to get deer to move in a direction that makes it more vulnerable to moving past another hunter lying in ambush.

Any type of push or drive requires a lot of pre-planning not only to get the deer moving but also to get both the pusher and stander coordinated. All drives must include the utmost concern to safety. They must include a drive master whose is in charge of the push and whose instructions are followed in unwavering detail and are viewed as the final word by all other participants of the deer drive.

When you're a poster on a deer drive and you want to stop a running deer that is moving by your stand, make a loud alarm blat. The buck or doe will skid to a halt giving you a better opportunity for a safe and accurate shot.

The tips in this chapter are only suggestions and should be adjusted to the type of drives or pushes you do. They are in no way meant to suggest that driving deer is inherently dangerous or any more unsafe than any other type of hunting. But with that said, they do require your utmost concern to safety and overall participant numbers. One final suggestion—it is wise not to include first time hunters on deer drives for the obvious reason that they lack experience in this type of hunting.

If you employ deer drives as one of your tactics remember this: Always appoint a drive master to be in charge of your drive group. His word is the last word on anything related to how the drive is to take place. No one overrides his instructions or decisions.

The drive master should have the best knowledge of the terrain and the habits and whereabouts of the deer on the land including where deer bed. The drive master should also know where they usually move when pushed.

I don't recommend pushing deer with a large group of hunters, because it is less effective than driving with smaller groups. Larger drives also take more time and effort to organize for maximum success. Smaller groups of three to six hunters are easier to organize and move around.

Driving large tracts is usually a waste of time as it takes a lot of time and gives deer too many opportunities to take advantage of all the escape routes. The savvy driver understands that it is to

In order to get the best results from his pushers and standers, the savvy deer drive captain uses a wind detector before making the plans for his drive.

everyone's advantage to drive a 50-acre piece versus a 100-acre tract. Smaller plots offer better results.

Over the years, I have noticed that when driving thick cover, if there's a big buck in the cover and he has other deer with him, most often, he's either the first one to break out, or he is going to hold tight and won't come out at all.

On my farm, we began planting over 100 six- to eight-foot pine trees in a five-acre pasture in order to provide future cover and a place for deer to seek refuge during heavy snow or extreme cold temperatures. Immature pine plantations, with individual trees no more than eight feet high and packed tightly together, can hold a surprising amount of bedded deer. Evergreen patches become prime places for two- or three-man drives in just a few short years. The thick groups of branches close to the ground limit visibility to only feet and give deer a feeling of great security. When I consult with landowners about deer management or what types of food plots to plant, I always strongly recommend that they including planting a patch of pines as part of their quality deer management program.

When you're planning a drive and considering the wind direction, it's advantageous to allow the deer to get a nose full of human odor from the drivers. The best situation of all is driving in a crosswind, as the deer won't be able to directly catch the scent of either the standers or the drivers.

An old tactic to get a wily buck out of a thick patch of cover is to drive it slowly the first time. If you're sure he is in the cover, but your first drive didn't push him out try the drive again. This time, however, make sure you drive the cover from a different direction.

To prevent deer from circling back past the drivers, consider using what some call a fishhook drive. The drivers move through the thick cover in the usual manner. About half way through the drive, two drivers reverse their line of travel and slowly hunt back in the direction they came from. Often they'll get up-close shots at deer that are focusing their attention on the drivers moving away in the distance.

Try a drop-drive to ambush any bucks that try to sneak through the driveline. A drop-drive has the drivers moving through the cover in the usual way, trying to push deer to other standers positioned ahead. But soon after the drive begins, a couple of stand hunters stop and take stands behind the drivers at the spot where the driveline initially enters the cover. These hunters often get action about halfway through the drive.

Remember that mature bucks act a lot like rabbits. They take advantage of the smallest amount of cover. So don't overlook even the smallest pieces of isolated cover. After hunting pressure has been on for several days, a brushy culvert in the middle of a farm field, or thick patch of undergrowth only one acre in size may hold a your trophy buck.

One of the most effective drives is a two-hunter drive. One enters the cover and begins to slowly still-hunt. The other hunter waits at least 15 minutes and, from a higher or lower position, takes the same general route as his partner who, by now, is 500 or more yards ahead of him. Deer that detect the lead hunter will often make either a circle to get behind him or escape to his left or right and offer a shot to the trailing hunter.

Ah, how often have I preached that windy days are excellent to post, still hunt and especially drive. Deer drives often have the most success on windy days, even with gusts exceeding 15 miles per hour. Bedded deer usually don't hear the approach of drivers or posters going to their stands. The sounds and effects of the wind and swirling air currents carry human odors in random directions often confusing the senses of driven deer, causing them to travel slowly and cautiously, presenting easier shots.

If you drive a piece of cover one day and don't push a deer out, that doesn't mean you shouldn't give that patch of cover a second chance the next day. Deer may have moved into the area during the night.

The designated drive master should always make it clear to a stander that once he has arrived at his assigned location, it is crucial that the stander not move from his stand even if he thinks he spots a better vantage point only 50 yards away. Always trust the drive master's knowledge of the terrain and how deer move through it.

The one drive situation that's more successful than most other drives is made through a long, cover-choked ravine that, at some particular spot, bottlenecks down into a narrow passage or funnel that escaping deer naturally get pinched through to make their escape.

Any savvy driver knows that it is not wise to walk by large brush piles or blown-downs. Remember what I said above, mature bucks act like rabbits. When making your way through cover like this, make sure to kick the brush and snap twigs on blow-downs. Often deer hide right in the middle, waiting for you to pass and then try to escape unnoticed. Shaking things up is likely to put a good buck on his feet.

If you're a stander and see deer running toward you, but they're moving fast, make a loud adult alarm blat call. Guaranteed that the buck that's about to run by you will briefly slam on his brakes and skid to a halt to try to determine where the danger is, giving you precious seconds to get him in your sights.

It is in blowdowns like this that you are likely to jump a buck. The deer are well-camouflaged and can observe their surroundings without being detected by hunters.

Bitter Cold Weather

PETER FIDUCCIA

Many years ago I hunted for whitetails in Lamar, Colorado. The area was choked with deer– some of which were monster bucks. I came away from that hunt with two thoughts. The first was that I was sure over the next ten years Lamar would produce a buck that would challenge my good friend Milo Hansen's world record. Second, I swore I would never again hunt in bitter cold conditions without "dressing to kill" and without having an arsenal of cold-weather hunting tactics to use to help me bag my buck.

Since then, I have developed a much better routine for staying warm and some key tactics for bagging deer in extremely cold weather. Here are some tips that will put a big buck in your sights in really cold conditions and also keep you warm, too!

While hot coffee or tea will help keep you warm on stand, a thermos of beef or chicken broth will keep your body temperature higher and keep you more comfortable every time. The broth offers nutritional value and will kick-start your internal body temperature to generate body heat. Coffee and tea won't be as effective.

If you have staghorn sumac on the land you hunt, plan to be there when the temperatures fall.

Hunting deer in extremely cold weather requires wearing the right clothes, and keeping your head and feet warm. When you stay warm you will remain on stand longer and possibly get the opportunity to shoot a buck like this. Credit: Ted Rose

This plant has a higher fat content than any other native forage. Deer instinctively (there's that word again) know that this plant generates high levels of body heat. Deer seek the plant out quickly, particularly when the temperatures fall into the single digits. Staghorn sumac is easily identified by its bright red seed clusters and long branches. It stands two to six feet tall and grows in thick groves.

When the temperature begins to drop like a rock it is time to plan to hunt near where deer seek food. Deer need extra energy in bitter-cold weather and will search for high-energy foods. This includes corn, acorns, winter wheat, and turnips. Find and hunt near these foods or the trails leading to them and it won't be long before you'll be sitting by the camp's fireplace recounting the hunt!

Have you ever noticed while driving along a highway after a snow fall that one side of the road is

Here is a full leaf of staghorn sumac. Its fruit is a tall red hairy structure, present from June through September. Credit: Brandeis University

bare of snow and the other isn't? Well that's because south-facing slopes may be as much as 15 degrees warmer than north-facing hillsides. When you're afield keep this in mind. South-facing slopes are where you will see the most deer activity and you'll be warmer hunting there too!

When the temperature gets frigid, some gun oils and lubricants may slow your firearm's action down considerably. During the colder part of the season, use a solvent to remove the present oil and lube, then lightly lube them with a high-viscosity oil.

On the coldest of days, I carry two heat seats to my stand; one thin one and one thicker one. I place the thinner Thermaseat inside the back of my jacket around my kidneys. I use the thicker seat to stand on. With my kidneys and feet warm, the rest of my body stays comfortably warm too.

When the weather gets just too cold to bear, go to a backup ground blind that you can use instead of suffering in your tree stand, especially during snow, ice, or sleet-filled days. On our farm, we have over a dozen shooting houses to retreat to when the weather turns sour. The ground blinds also enable us to hunt in heavy rain as well.

Biologists say that some of the deer's favorite foods in winter include white cedar, red maple, mountain maple, aspen, and sumac. Find out if you have any of these trees on your land and hunt them just before and after storms.

On cold days it is wise not to bring your firearms, optics or other equipment into a warm house, cabin, or tent. Condensation, fogging, and other problems are sure to happen if you do. Leave your gear on the deck, in your vehicle, or on a free-standing gun rack.

Ever have trouble starting your vehicle (or ATV) at deer camp after a cold night? Ever have it parked the wrong way when you need a jump at deer camp? Well here's an idea that will help you. When you park your vehicle after the day's hunt, make sure it is facing in the direction you want to leave the next morning. You may also want to keep the transmission in first gear and the transfer case engaged. This will enable the engine to kick over easily in the morning.

As mid-winter approaches the circadian rhythm, or daily activity cycle, of deer shifts. During this time they don't move a lot between dawn and dusk. Instead, they move about during the midday, from 11:00 AM to 3:00 PM If you ever heard one of my seminars, the best tip I share is to hunt these so called off-hours. Most times it is way too cold to stay on stand all day. So, sleeping in until 10:00 AM is a welcome break. Head to your stand around 10:30 AM and you'll get there during the peak deer activity period.

In heavy rain or snow, I place a piece of tape over the muzzle of my rifle to prevent snow and sleet from going down the barrel. This is really handy in case I trip or fall while walking through the woods. You can shoot through the tape without worrying about any loss of accuracy.

In driving winds, look for deer to bed on lee hillsides or in the middle of thick cover.

When the weather has been cold and a warming trend is predicted, you can bet you will see an increase in deer movement. Keep in mind a warming may be only a few degrees above what the current temperatures have been over the last few days. For instance, if it has been in the mid-teens and the temperature jumps only five degrees higher, that's a warming trend for the deer and they will be on the move.

When the weather turns really cold on our farm, we look for deer in the swamps. Usually, swamps are located in lower elevations than the surrounding land and are protected from cold blasts of northerly winds that are blown off ridges or across

We keep our firearms outdoors during the hunt. It is not only safer than bringing them into the house, but it also keeps the scopes from fogging up.

open fields. Lowlands, swamps, and boggy areas can be as much as 10 degrees warmer than higher ground only a few hundred yards away.

When harvested crop fields are covered in snow, don't think the deer will not feed in them. I have seen deer paw through several inches of snow (as long as it hasn't frozen on top) to get to old corn or other vegetable or legume spillage left in the field after it was harvested. Deer can easily smell the food under the snow.

When you're still-hunting or staging drives, concentrate on thick groves of cedars. When the trees are packed tightly, cedars are a preferred bedding cover for whitetails. They're also a favorite cold-weather food and deer don't have to spend a lot of energy traveling long distances from bedding sites to feeding areas.

In frigid weather, deer will move with the sun during the day. You'll find them bedded on east-facing slopes in the morning, south-facing slopes during the midday, and west-facing slopes in late afternoon. You won't find them on north-facing slopes.

A dry, cold day does not stop deer from moving as much as a damp cold day will. If the relative humidity is higher than normal on a given day, don't expect much deer movement.

There are many brands of portable heaters on the market that burn odorless gas (I use Mr. Heater). They can be used for waterfowl hunting and deer hunting. They work to warm your whole body when used in a ground blind or you can put them between your feet when you're in a tree stand to keep your feet warm during severe cold weather.

When a storm is approaching, the barometer begins to drop rapidly. Deer will quickly head to thick cover to bed. A rising barometer signals the storm is over which causes the deer to leave their beds and head to feeding areas.

An old but true adage is that if you want to stay warm, wear a warm hat, because the head and neck region is where most body heat escapes. Keep you ears and head covered and you can last at least two more hours on stand on a cold day.

This is the railing of one of our stands that overlooks a group of thick pines. We use the stand every time there is a heavy snow storm or bitter cold wind. We can count on the deer moving in and out of the pines in front.

Anatomy of the Pre-Rut

JOHN TROUT, JR.

It's late summer, the time of year when whitetail bucks commonly hang together, sometimes grooming each other and removing insects. They share the same bedding areas, trails and food sources. They have no quarrels to speak of. Their antlers are covered in velvet, necks remain thin and the breeding is months away. Amazingly, within days it will all change. While many deer hunters are occupied with outside projects and not yet thinking about the deer woods, the velvet on antlers will come off, testicles will swell and testosterone will rise. The pre-rut period has begun!

A buck's antlers start growing the moment he sheds them in winter or early spring, although they won't be visible for several weeks. The antlers will grow hour by hour, reaching maximum size by the middle of summer, when bucks' testosterone is at its lowest level. That's not to say a buck won't breed if opportunity allows.

I have been fortunate to study several pen-raised whitetails over the years. One old doe named Julie gave birth to fawns each summer from the time she was two-years-old until she turned eight. She has had no more fawns since after her eighth birthday, even though she remains quite healthy and her teeth still get the job done on the high-protein diet she is fed. Despite not impregnating, though, she comes into estrus in late November or early December each year and continues to breed.

Sis (don't ask how he got that name), a seven-year-old buck in the same pen, always breeds her, and breeds her and breeds her. In fact, Julie and Sis breed monthly up until April.

Sis typically loses his antlers in February. Thus, even though his testosterone is at its lowest, he won't pass up a golden opportunity. I should add, he breeds other does and all of them give birth to fawns each year, so clearly Julie's lack of fawns is not due to any problem with Sis. For all this Sis is grateful, even though he's worn out and down to skin-and-bones when the breeding finally ends.

By midsummer the antlers harden and a buck's testosterone level begins to rise.

A captive doe named Julie is shown here with the last two fawns she had at age eight. Now eleven years old, she still breeds from November through March, although she never becomes impregnated.

By the way, at the time of this writing, Julie is eleven-years-old and still breeding at least five months out of the year like she always has, with twenty-four to twenty-eight days between her breeding episodes. Research has shown that some does have bred six times without impregnating. Wouldn't you like to have one like that running around in your hunting area?

When you stop and think about it, it's good news that the old doe doesn't impregnate when bred in spring—one of nature's marvels. It makes certain that fawns will be born when they have the best chance of surviving. Consider that a doe will carry a fawn more than two hundred days. Cold weather and scarcity of food would make it difficult on both the fawn and doe if she gave birth in November.

It is the long daylight hours of summer that cause a buck's hormones to increase and testicles to grow—the first progressive stage of the pre-rut period. This is when sperm first appear in his semen and blood stops circulating in the velvet covering of his antlers.

Some hunters have gotten the idea that velvet comes off the antlers because of rubbing, but the skin is actually ready to come off soon after the bone hardens. Once the blood no longer flows through, the velvet decays, shreds and begins to separate from the antlers. Portions might hang by threads, often prompting a buck to scrape his antlers against a bush, tree, or the ground in an attempt to rid the nuisance. Bucks make it a point not to leave even one small piece of the velvet. When the velvet is first removed, the antlers might have a reddish color, which is actually a blood stain. Some claim the entire velvet-shedding process can take up to thirty-six hours, although I have never seen it last more than twenty-four. In every case, I have observed a buck one day, only to see his velvet gone the next.

The removal of the velvet, and the thrashing of antlers against objects to remove it, seem to spark the buck's desire to rub trees, an act of frustration and, actually, another sexual stage of the pre-rut. Bucks love to get real nasty, breaking and destroying anything within their power. Locating and hunting these early-autumn rubs are often beneficial, as you'll read later in this prerut section. Keep in mind, once a buck starts rubbing in the pre-rut season, he may rub several trees daily.

It's also true that some bucks, particularly young ones, will begin sparring within days of removing the velvet. Sparring builds up neck muscles for future battles and establishes who's king-of-the-hill. Some young bucks probably spar for entertainment.

The pre-rut phase begins the moment bucks begin shedding their velvet. The velvet is usually removed within twenty-four hours.

Regardless of why bucks spar, it is the reason that rattling often lures them in during the pre-rut period.

I've spent hours photographing wild turkeys and have recorded numerous pecking order fights among the toms when breeding occurs, but pecking order events among whitetails are different. The only ones I've seen had nothing to do with the rut. In areas where numerous mature bucks exist, a hierarchy is usually established before the breeding begins, usually during the early portion of the pre-rut. This can change in late pre-rut, or during primary rut. When one buck overlaps another's territory, knock-down, drag-out fights can occur. During pre-rut, most mature bucks will not challenge each other, unless there's a breeding doe around.

Note the distinction between fights and spars. Sparring is quite friendly and more of a practice amongst young bucks than mature ones. When they spar, bucks poke antlers without much force and shove at each other with little energy. When bucks actually fight, body size is just as much a factor as antler size, and the energy behind the pushing, antlers against antlers, often decides the winner.

Some buck fights never get started during the pre-rut period only because one buck simply intimidated another by slicking back his ears against his neck. His hair rises like he just stuck his hoof in an electrical socket, and the aggressive gestures often scare away an opponent.

Sparring begins almost the moment velvet is removed and intensifies as autumn progresses. It is one of the first noticeable gestures behaviors of the pre-rut phase. even though mature bucks do very little sparring, if any sparring.

Bachelor groups are common in both late summer and even early autumn after the velvet has shed. Does usually avoid bucks, but it doesn't really matter since the bucks don't really want to hang out with the does. What's crucial for hunters to know is that mature bucks in pre-rut seem to have their own areas away from other bucks. They tend to form their own groups or, more often, they hang out alone. It's uncommon to see a three- or four-year-old buck hanging out with two or three others just past their first birthday. The bachelor groups typically fall apart before or within days of the velvet shedding.

Scraping in the pre-rut period is common. Bucks often begin scraping the ground shortly after removing the velvet, although some deer have been noted scraping one month before the velvet came off. Pre-rut scrapes typically show up along fringes, but bucks seldom visit them regularly. Scrapes that include "licking branches" and applications of glandular substances are usually the most important. These usually start showing up about one week before the breeding begins, and I've found that the more bucks there are in a given area, the more pre-rut scraping occurs.

However, I have never enjoyed success hunting scrapes during pre-rut. Hunting scrapes is tough business anytime, but I believe early-season scrapes only cost you precious time. In other words, you will have the best chance of killing a mature buck during the pre-rut season if you concentrate on other tactics. (The primary rut is a different story, which you'll read about later.)

The difference of what happens in each of these rut phases is astronomical. Although we commonly see doe-chasing occur during the primary rut, it's far more typical of the pre-rut. A young buck will consistently "bird-dog," coming up behind a doe and rapidlyapproaching for a short distance of about

In late summer and even early autumn, mature bucks often hang together. This routine subsides shortly after the velvet is removed.

thirty yards, stomping his feet hard against the ground, with his head low and his neck extended as far as it can go. Mature bucks seldom chase does in pre-rut, knowing the time is not right. They wait, and will even tolerate the younger bucks making total fools of themselves.

We know that decreasing sunlight affects the estrus cycle of the does just as it affects the testosterone rise in bucks. The difference, during pre-rut at least, is that does give no outward signals of the coming rut— at least none that researchers and hunters can see. Bucks rub antlers, make scrapes and get aggressive. Does don't pay any attention to scrapes, nor do anything aggressively with their heads and glands, and they don't care about other does of the same age group nearby. Make no mistake, though, the pre-rut phase is working on them, and the bucks know it, probably through the scent of the does' gland secretions and urine.

So how long does the pre-rut last? Of the three phases—pre-rut, primary rut and post-rut—the prerut and post-rut periods offer the longest hunting opportunities. The primary rut is shorter—governed by the does' major but brief breeding cycle— and typically lasts for about two weeks, including a peak-day. Thus, consider that one week before and one week after that peak day is the primary rut period. Every moment that follows the bucks' loss of velvet, up to one week before the primary rut, can be considered the pre-rut period. This could be just a few weeks or perhaps several.

Most bucks in a given area will shed their velvet during a two-week period, but not all bucks in the area lose their velvet the same day. I remember seeing one buck in the process of losing his on August 13— extremely early for the area I was in—and another buck in the same area with his velvet peeling off

The length of the pre-rut phase is dependant upon when the breeding begins. In some areas, the breeding begins as early as September, although in most regions it will begin some time between November and January.

during the second week of September of the same year. Researchers have noted that older bucks often lose their velvet before yearling bucks, primarily because of higher peaks in testosterone levels.

Consider, too, that breeding starts earlier in some areas than others because decreasing sunlight is not the only factor that controls buck and doe hormones, as once believed. For this reason, some bucks and does breed as early as September, while others breed in November and some breed in January.

There is no question in my mind that weather affects your chances of intercepting a pre-rut buck. During the breeding season, weather might not matter as much, but when the bugs are plentiful and Indian summer persists, it can hurt. I've most certainly had better luck some years than others, simply because of temperatures and an early arrival of the first frost. Nevertheless, don't think for a moment you can't kill a mature buck if it's ninety degrees and mosquitoes are buzzing. Many hunters have done so because they patterned a buck.

I've always said that anyone can kill a buck during the primary rut if they hunt hard. You only have to be a little lucky to end up in the right area at right moment. It takes little scouting to get lucky, and little knowledge of a rutting buck's habits to take advantage of an easy kill. Bucks make mistakes by moving consistently in search of does. Some folks hunt all their lives hoping to shoot a record-book deer, yet some individuals do it on opening day the first time they go hunting, but only because that hunt took place at the peak of the breeding period. That's not to say that any of us can shoot a mature buck every season during rut just by getting lucky, however. Section II of this book includes several chapters dedicated to tactics for killing big bucks during rut. I'm just saying that the primary rut is the easiest time to get the job done.

On the other hand, I believe hunters who have enjoyed successes in pre-rut have accomplished great feats. During pre-rut, bucks are not vulnerable and prone to making "dumb" mistakes. Whitetails have always been creatures of habit, but during pre-rut, they stick even closer to certain rules. They seldom move about four hours after dawn or four hours before dusk like they often do in primary rut. They seldom cover a mile or two overnight and wind up in a strange area, like they consistently do in primary rut. They seldom cross open fields in the middle of the day or bed down just anywhere they happen to be, like they often do in primary rut.

Nevertheless, a good hunter can cause bucks in pre-rut to make mistakes. As I just said, deer are creatures of habit in late summer and early autumn, and this sets the stage for patterning a buck during the pre-rut period. Figure out what he's eating and where he's bedding, get to understand his personality, and he could be yours. That's all easier said than accomplished, but some hunters have taken plenty of big whitetails during the pre-rut period because they patterned a buck accurately.

A limited home range makes it easier to pattern bucks in the pre-rut period, although the distance they roam will vary from area-to-area. Weather, predators, and hunting pressure play a key role. However, most of the time during primary rut a buck says goodbye to his home range and, as you know, many never make it back.

In pre-rut, a mature buck's home range might be only a hundred acres or up to a square mile. The latter is usually not the case in pre-rut. Either way, you can bet that when the breeding begins, a buck won't be spending much time at home.

In early autumn, most deer refuse to leave their home range. For example, a 1970 study indicated that one young buck fitted with a radio collar was chased out of his home range by dogs on several occasions. He always returned within a few hours. After so many chases, he finally set up a temporary home a long way off, only to return close to the home range on a couple of other occasions. The young buck spent the primary rut in an entirely new area.

Does typically have smaller home ranges than bucks. One five-year study in Texas showed that some does shared a home range of about 93 acres, two does

Unlike bucks in the breeding season, that when bucks often move through open areas at any hour of the day, bucks during in the pre-rut seldom make those mistakes.

had larger ranges of 502 acres, while another had a home range of 690 acres. The same study indicated the bucks had an average home range of 1,079 acres. Researchers noted, however, that the deer's home range decreased in spring and summer when bucks were growing antlers and does were with fawns. The does then kept their home ranges to twenty-four acres and, strangely, the bucks settled for thirteen.

Another interesting study occurred on Crab Orchard National Wildlife Refuge in Illinois. It showed that in 1962, only one percent of the deer observed early in the year on the refuge were killed elsewhere later that year, compared to seventeen percent in 1965. The researcher linked the difference to increasing population and human pressure.

As for mature bucks, I'm not so sure they get as far away from their home range as do young bucks. I'm speaking of the primary rut, of course. It's just that I have seen several big bucks in one area during the pre-rut, only to see them again in the primary rut close to where they were the first time. I sincerely believe that mature bucks become home-range conscious, seeming to prefer an area they know best as opposed to one they know nothing about. This is probably the exception to the rule, but I mention it just to let you know that if you don't get a certain buck in the pre-rut phase, you could get lucky and see him again in the same vicinity after the breeding begins.

We could assume that the more an area is left alone, the better the chance that those bucks in the area will remain there, at least through the pre-rut phase. Intense interruptions in a bedding area or some form of harassment along trails and in feeding areas may force a deer away long before the primary rut arrives. With these facts in mind, we should view it as a demonstration of how we can easily cause harm to the areas we hunt.

I know of some archery hunters who claim this is why they do not want to hunt before the primary rut arrives. They know that if their presence becomes known, it's all over but the shouting.

I don't agree. First, I love hunting too much to limit myself to only the primary rut. Although I know how important it is to remain undetected during the prerut, I also realize that it's the prime time to pattern a buck and kill him. I look at it this way: You only need to sharpen your hunting skills to make sure you don't interrupt a buck's habits before killing him. And if you do screw up a big buck during the pre-rut, the game is not necessarily over.

From experience, I can tell you that big bucks won't always leave the country during the prerut just because they know you are hunting them. As mentioned previously, even the young buck

Although the stakes are high during the pre-rut period, the rewards are worth the effort. One goof is all it takes to let a home-range buck know he's being hunted. However, the pre-rut is one of the best times to pattern a mature deer.

was run out of his home range by dogs numerous times before he finally gave it up. Don't think for a moment that a wise old buck will tolerate you sending him running too often, but you might get by with one time. On two separate occasions—different years, different areas—I sent big bucks into never-never land after bumping them out of bedding areas early in the pre-rut period. I spotted each of these bucks again within a couple of weeks after they left, however. Of course, I wouldn't want to make a habit of running a trophy buck out of his home range.

One final thought about bucks leaving and returning to the home range: You never know for sure how many mature bucks you spook, and if any of those came back. You can't help leaving human scent behind and making disturbances each time you pass through a hunting area. I truly believe that you must take many more precautionary measures when hunting the pre-rut phase than when hunting the primary or post-rut. During the primary rut, bucks stay on the move, and your main concern then is not spooking the does. During post-rut, the bucks are worn out, which makes them want to stick around

in their home ranges unless you really scare them consistently. These bucks, sometimes already in a near nocturnal state of mind, will only get worse if you allow them to detect your presence.

The less nocturnal a buck is, the better the chance you can kill him. I'm sure you already know that. The good news is, during pre-rut a buck often moves during daylight hours, and mature bucks are closer to being diurnal during the primary rut than any other time of year. But the pre-rut only ranks second in the diurnal ratings.

Early in the pre-rut period, bucks commonly feed in daylight hours due to the lack of previous hunting pressure and the continuation of summer habits. They need to eat all they can to get ready for the primary rut.

Another good point: During the primary and post-rut periods, you have to be much more selective when choosing ambush locations to remain hidden. It's easy in pre-rut period, when there is plenty of natural camouflage. I also like the groundhunting opportunities during early autumn, a new and exciting challenge at a time of year when you can use foliage to hide.

Whitetail bucks are creatures of habit in early autumn, often utilizing the same bedding areas, food sources and trails.

I have taken several mature bucks, but I'm most proud of those that I've taken during the pre-rut and post-rut periods. I have discovered the best chances of taking a mature buck in pre-rut occur at two times: One is the first week of the hunting season. The other hot period comes a few weeks later. There is a simple explanation for this. Early in the hunting season, the bucks don't know they are being hunted. Thus, they follow the same habits they did before the hunting began. After the first week of the season, a lapse of opportunity typically occurs. Some hunters take bucks during this dead period of the pre-rut, but the best chance follows two to three weeks after that first week, when the pre-rut frenzy begins. The chapters that follow outline many of the tactics used to take bucks that are still weeks away from kicking the rut into high gear.

Hunting debuts in most states and provinces as an early archery season in late summer and early fall. This gives bowhunters a good chance to challenge a buck during the pre-rut period. Firearm seasons usually open several weeks later and closer to or during the primary rut, but that doesn't necessarily mean that there are no other windows of opportunity for a gun hunter. Some states and provinces host special hunts with muzzleloader, rifle, or slugster during the heart of the pre-rut season. There are also youth hunts held in early autumn, sometimes before Jack Frost has visited an area. Special hunts with a firearm are common, and although they might be limited to one, two or three days, you can gain an edge if you have an understanding of a buck's habits and the tactics to fool them during the pre-rut period.

I've always been an avid record keeper, tracking the number of deer spotted throughout the season by ambush locations. Surprisingly, on more occasions than not, the records show that I see more deer, including bucks, during the first week of the pre-rut period. I should mention that I'm speaking of averages per efforts hunted. Averages have always been more meaningful than totals.

Personally, I'm glad to be an avid archer just to have the opportunity to hunt hard during pre-rut. True, some bowhunters wait until the cold days of the primary rut to begin hunting. Yet we die-hards love the challenge of hunting the pre-rut while dreaming about the primary rut. Conditions may be less than favorable when hunting early autumn, but if you pattern the animal with a high degree of accuracy, the potential is there to cash in on a bruiser buck. Of course, you must know his whereabouts.

The Rut's Golden Rules

JOHN TROUT, JR.

For just a moment, think about the number of times I've mentioned that it doesn't take a lot of skill to kill a trophy whitetail during the primary rut. All you need is a little luck. If there's a big one in the area, he could walk by you or some other hunter leaning against a tree two hundred yards away. However, things can still go terribly wrong for folks like you and I who work so hard to shoot a mature buck.

Most serious deer hunters spend countless hours reading about rut-hunting tactics that can be applied during the hunting season. Let's face it,

Some hunters stick to one favorite ambush location where they were successful in the past. Keep an open mind, scout continuously and keep an eye on the does.

in the past decade, there has been no shortage of articles on the subject. Some tell you how to hunt big bucks during all portions of the archery season, and there are stories that suggest proven drills—from luring bucks into range with a call, to hunting food sources, rub lines, scrapes, and trails. You've already read about these topics in this book, and you'll read more about them in the chapters ahead. However, there's much more to the story.

Don't get me wrong. Articles that focus on tactics to fool rutting trophy bucks deserve the full attention of any serious trophy whitetail hunter. I read them with interest and I always keep an open mind. However, in most of these stories, at least six ingredients are commonly overlooked. In fact, regardless of the tactics you use, you must consider the following advanced common-sense topics if you hope to tag a trophy.

1. Pattern The Does

Despite our desire to hunt the same stomping grounds year after year, we must be sure that a trophy buck exists before deciding on a location. For instance, I have "favorite" areas that I know as well as the inside of my hunting closet (my wife disagrees). It's fun to hunt these areas because of past experiences and successes, but they are not necessarily the places to be during the rut. Simply said, a mature whitetail buck must roam this territory if I am to have a chance at intercepting him.

If you pattern the does during the primary rut, you will soon know if a big buck is in the area during the primary rut. However, be realistic and aware that quality private lands and remote public areas are the places where big bucks prefer to roam in search of does.

Getting stuck on an old spot can be detrimental to tagging a big buck. It's true that some favorite spots are almost always good places to be, and there are often good reasons why certain ambush locations consistently produce big bucks. Nonetheless, I would suggest keep one eye and ear open. Returning to a spot where you once took a trophy buck does not mean that lightning will strike twice in the same place.

Since "seeing is believing," many veteran bowhunters spend several hours watching food sources before the season. Take my good friend Tim Hillsmeyer, who has tagged several Pope and Young caliber bucks. Near dusk, Hillsmeyer often drives the roads in agricultural areas to locate big bucks, because the deer are visiting food sources in daylight hours. He also sets up near food sources with his binoculars handy, making certain that his presence is not detected while watching a particular field.

We discussed this tactic in the pre-rut section, but I mention it again to remind you that it's the existence of does that will attract bucks during primary rut. For this reason, you must know where the does will be. My point is, never limit your scouting to the pre-rut only. It's necessary to know exactly where a big buck is feeding and bedding if you want to pattern and kill him during pre-rut, and the same is true during the primary rut. It's necessary to know exactly where the does are feeding and bedding if you want to pattern and kill that same big buck you didn't shoot during the pre-rut.

2. Build Landowner Relations

It pays to have a good relationship with a landowner to tag a mature buck. It's no big secret; most successful trophy hunters pursue bucks on private lands that have little pressure. However, always consider gaining access to remote public ground that borders private land. Topographic maps are essential tools because many public-land bucks that survive year after year take refuge on or near adjoining private lands or hard-to-reach public ground when they feel pressured.

One item that will be helpful is an Atlas and Gazetteer by DeLorme, which provide topo maps of entire states in book format and are available at many sporting goods stores and bookstores. Finally, consider visiting the assessor's office in the county you hunt and purchasing a plat book to learn names of landowners.

3. Avoid Temptation

If you really want to tag a trophy buck, common sense dictates that you must overlook bucks that have not yet reached their full potential. If you want to take only a buck that makes it into the record books, you must be able to judge antlers quickly and effectively in the field—on short notice. Of course, your idea of a trophy may be different from that of another hunter.

If the area you hunt offers numerous tags, it can be more difficult to pass a smaller buck that offers a shot. You could simply take the lesser buck and continue hunting for a wall-hanger. Unfortunately, though, bad news accompanies that practice.

First, consider that shooting any deer may disqualify the area as a potential trophy-producing site. When you shoot a deer in a particular region, you are sure to create a disturbance and leave behind scent—a situation that can become critical if you must track the deer for a long distance.

It is also possible that shooting the smaller buck will cause the does, which would have brought in

If you have more than one tag, you might hold off on shooting a lesser buck until you kill a trophy. Shooting just any buck can quickly spoil a hunting area for days to come.

the wall-hanger, to vacate the area. For this reason alone, many dedicated trophy hunters refuse to harvest a smaller buck just because they carry an "extra" tag. I don't have a problem with shooting does and small bucks when tags are available. I'm just saying that serious trophy hunters know where their priorities lie, and will wait until the time is right before shooting just any deer.

4. Error! Error!

Hillsmeyer claims that the most serious error a trophy hunter can make is scouting too often in the wrong places. He added that once a mature buck know she is being hunted, the hunt might be over.

"Flush a buck out of hiding a time or two, and you can bet he's going somewhere else," said Hillsmeyer. "It's imperative that you do your scouting wisely, and then get in and out of an area without the buck knowing you are there."

I discussed this error in the pre-rut section, but I want to emphasize that a big buck will not appreciate getting bumped, even during the primary rut. If there are lots of does in the area, he might have spent several days there, even if it's unfamiliar territory. If you spook him, he'll probably take his chances looking for does elsewhere. Unlike subordinate bucks, mature bucks seldom "forgive and forget."

Since second shots at big bucks are rare, most trophy hunters never take chances when it comes to wind direction. In fact, hunting where the wind blows toward the area you expect the deer to come from is one way to insure you never see the buck you are waiting for. Thus, if the wind is wrong for your best ambush location, choose another even if it doesn't look as promising. It's better to sit in a bad location and not see any deer than to sit in a good location and spook one.

You should also pay close attention to air currents as you approach an ambush location, since they may differ from the actual wind direction. This can be accomplished easily by using scentless wind testing powder.

5. Hit It Hard

I'm proud of several bucks I've taken that now hang on my living room wall, and I can honestly say that most of them did not come easy. It seems I always have to walk so many miles, hang so many stands, lose so much sleep and see so many other deer before my shooting opportunity comes. It's like having a quota that must be filled, except there still are no guarantees that I will enjoy success even when the quota is met. Many readers have probably had the same experiences.

The one thing I must always do is hunt hard. I make it a point to be out there every chance I get. In other words, "Never put off till tomorrow what you can do today." Sure, you could get lucky and have a wall-hanger walk past you any time, but when the primary rut is in high gear, "Tomorrow may never come." The odds are more in your favor for getting one "tomorrow" if you're out there today.

Hillsmeyer hit the nail on the head. "You can think of a thousand excuses why you shouldn't hunt, but the buck you are after is the one good reason to be there." The best point Hillsmeyer makes about hunting often, though, is that you learn something each time you are there. You might not see the right buck today, but the experience could teach you something that will help you next time.

Logically speaking, we can safely assume that the whitetail's habits change considerably from week to week. They might not, but if they do and you are not aware of it, you'll be a day late when you head for the woods. Food sources change, as does hunting pressure. Each plays an important part in the whitetail's habits, and the hunter who is there at every opportunity may stay one step ahead of the bucks. Actually, change that to "does," the most important word in the rut dictionary when you are trying to kill a big buck.

Tim Hillsmeyer points out that you must hunt hard, even during the primary rut, if you hope to get a chance at a trophy whitetail. He claims that even if you don't get him today, you'll learn something that will help you tomorrow.

Don't think for a moment that hunting from the perch is the only way to kill a trophy buck. The primary rut is one of the best times to choose a ground ambush location and to still-hunt.

6. Choose Versatile Ambush Locations

It does help to stay on the move when it comes to ambush locations. I mentioned this in part I, but it's also valuable during the primary rut. Never limit yourself to hunting only from a tree stand when the breeding is underway.

Bowhunters are the world's worst about getting into a tree-stand rut, and some archers refuse to hunt from a ground site even when they switch to hunting with a firearm. Most assume they have no chance of killing a mature buck from the ground. I used to feel that way many years ago, but that was before I had taken several whitetails from a ground ambush.

Don't get me wrong. I'd rather be in a tree. I feel my best chance of intercepting a trophy buck is when I'm elevated in any portion of the hunting season. But when bucks are going crazy during the rut, why limit yourself to hunting from a tree? The rut is prime time to take a big buck from the ground, which means you can set up quickly in remote locations that have not been touched by others.

Then there's the still-hunting side of killing trophy bucks. Hillsmeyer, who usually hunts from a tree stand, has taken several bucks on the ground. He prefers a stiff wind and a quiet floor for still-hunting during the primary rut, when the foliage is thin, but he hunts on the ground during all phases of the rut. Ground hunting tactics and some of Hillsmeyer's tips are discussed in chapter 15.

You could say that hunting for a trophy buck is like baking a cake. You need to use the right methods and ingredients if you hope to get a top notch finished product. In the case of hunting trophy whitetails during the primary rut, the scrapes, rubs, trails, and food sources of the does are the methods. The six previously mentioned topics are the ingredients. On the other hand, you might just try tempting a buck.

Second Rut Madness

JOHN TROUT, JR.

The final rut of the year is usually called the "second rut" by avid hunters who fight it to the bitter end. Some consider it the best and last opportunity to shoot a mature buck. One thing I'm sure of: Sometimes the second rut is the time to kill a whopper and some tactics are more reliable than others for taking that late-season trophy.

You see, the second rut needs a little explaining, since many folks have the wrong idea about this part of the breeding cycle. There are lots of factors that might contribute more to your chances of taking a big whitetail buck during the post-rut period than the second rut itself. Don't get me wrong. The second rut provides a great opportunity if you fully understand the mechanics of it, have the time to hunt, and then get the right breaks. However, other things happen during the winter that can really boost your odds of taking a trophy buck in late season, such as the whitetail's hunger pains. His need for adequate nutrition must be satisfied.

First, you should know that mature does have little or no bearing on the second rut. Nope! Most of

Only a small percentage of yearling does come into estrus their first year. When they do, it's usually several weeks after the mature does have bred.

them—those one and one-half-years and older—will come into estrus during the first rut, and they will breed and impregnate at that time.

Lots of hunters think the does that didn't get bred during the first rut decide when the second rut will arrive. That is partially correct. Does that don't impregnate during the first rut will come into estrus again about thirty days later. But let's be practical. Do you really think for a moment that a doe is going to walk around in estrus, ready to breed for more than twenty-four hours, and end up getting the cold shoulder from every buck she encounters? You and I both know that there are bucks willing to die for a piece of the action. For this reason, we can safely assume that mature does have little or no bearing on the arrival of the second rut.

It is possible that a mature doe will not impregnate during the first breeding cycle, but this is a rare phenomenon. Earlier in this book, I told you about Julie, the old penned deer that continues to breed each year for a few months, yet never

impregnates. There are other tales, and we can all appreciate having such does in our area during the late season.

However, there's another side to the story worth hearing. While writing this book, Kelsey, a five-year-old captive doe, impregnated in November during the first rut when she came into estrus. On June 2, the healthy doe delivered three fawns. I arrived on the scene late and watched the last two being born. Kelsey responded to the fawns, cleaned them up and fed them faithfully for the next twenty-four hours. Then all Haiti broke loose.

Thirty-six hours after Kelsey gave birth, I saw the old buck in the four-acre pen sniffing her south end. Moments later, he climbed on her back and did what none of us can believe. The buck's growing antlers were in velvet and the temperature was in the high eighties. But that didn't matter to the buck. He continued to breed Kelsey for the next thirty-two hours, which proves that bucks are always willing. Meanwhile, the old doe did

A mature doe will come into estrus about thirty days after the first estrous cycle. However, this is rare since most mature does will breed and impregnate during the first rut.

Who knows when the second rut will arrive. Hunt as often as you can, dress for the weather, and you might be out there at the right time. Credit by Vikki L. Trout

not give her youngsters the time of day. They were desperate to feed, and displayed their emotions by walking around bleating the whole time Kelsey was with the buck. Once the breeding ended, the doe would run away from the buck each time he came near. Thankfully, she got back into the fawn-rearing business before it was too late.

Who knows what happened with this doe. Maybe something went haywire with her hormones. Could it happen in the wild? Probably; anything like this is possible. Perhaps that is why I was inclined to believe one individual who claimed he saw a small, spotted fawn in February.

Enough said about mature does. It is the yearlings—those that have not yet enjoyed their first birthdays—that will decide when and if you enjoy success during the second rut.

I don't know of any research that provides us with an "average" number of young does that come into estrus their first year. Still, although you should understand that very few six-month-old does come into estrus, you can bet that some will. Being around captive deer for many years, I can attest to only about twenty percent of the yearling does breeding their first year. That one in five, however, can be your ticket to tagging a whopper buck.

The problem is knowing when the hot second rut will occur. Most young does come into estrus about four to six weeks after the primary rut. However, they are not limited to that time period. Moreover, they don't all come into estrus at once. Of the young does that will breed their first year, one might come into estrus three weeks after the primary rut, while another does eight weeks after.

Consider December 31st many years ago when my son and I hunted in southern Indiana. That cold evening we both witnessed three bucks—one of them a wall hanger—chasing one young doe. The primary rut had been over for many weeks, but we witnessed a brief flurry of late-season rut activity, thanks to being in the right place when a young doe came into estrus.

Nevertheless, the second rut is not like your annual New Year's celebration party. It can go unnoticed. You could be sitting in a tree waiting for the fireworks to start, not knowing that the best part is still several weeks away, or worse yet, not knowing that the late-season action has already ended. That's a shame, to say the least, but it's a fact. If you are sitting in the wrong spot when the second rut kicks in, you'll miss the action for sure. You could even miss the action if you are in the right spot. You might also give up too quickly if nothing happens; it's easy to become bored during the late season—unless you experience that one great day that keeps you going back for more.

During the late archery season in Illinois two years ago, I had no idea when or if the second rut would occur. But one cold, fair evening, I spotted a yearling doe heading for a small field. Behind her was a buck. Behind that buck was another buck and, well, there were at least two more. Four bucks following one young doe!

I had seen a couple of straggler bucks during the past few days, but both were small. They hadn't been with does, nor had they shown any sign of the second rut. Yet here I was now with four bucks after one doe, and none of them were more than fifty yards from my tree stand.

As the five deer moved into the field, I examined the bucks closely. The first one on the tail of the doe was a mature ten-pointer, which I estimated would score in the high 130s. The next in line was a six-point buck. Another young buck was

behind him, followed by what looked like a two-year-old eight-pointer.

After a few minutes, the young doe made a turn toward me. The biggest buck followed and I raised my bow to prepare for a shooting opportunity, but my hopes only lasted about thirty seconds. When the doe hit the thirty-yard mark, she put on the brakes, threw her head up and scented the air. My scent was blowing right to her and I knew it was over. She promptly ran a short distance into the woods, stopped, and looked back. All the bucks went with her, although that none of them, not even the big buck, had any idea what had bugged the doe. The ten-pointer got after her almost immediately, grunting and finally chasing her over a hill and out of sight. The other bucks followed, hoping the big buck would drop dead of a heart attack so they could get in on the action.

I provided the details of this scenario just to give you an idea of how one little hot doe can attract all kinds of attention. A breeding doe in winter will bring big bucks you never knew existed out of the woodwork and into the hunting arena.

The second rut is never as hot as the first. Unlike the primary rut, it comes without warning and could might even go unnoticed.

During the second rut, a hot young doe will promptly bring a mature buck out of hiding.

It's really hard to say just how much effect the second rut has on bucks. I believe it does fire them up and sometimes spark them to do those things that bucks love to do during the primary rut. New scrapes are sometimes opened, and old scrapes are sometimes hit. However, I don't know of any avid late-season hunters who have depended upon hunting scrapes for success. In fact, I believe that most late-season scrapes are the result of bucks becoming fired up for the brief period that young does are in estrus. I also believe the mature bucks promptly go back to the usual feeding and bedding habits once the does are done. The scrapes are merely temporary scent stations and will do a hunter no good.

I'm often a bit shocked to locate rubs and scrapes during late season, but never totally surprised. Only last season, I found a couple of scrapes that had been reopened along the edge of a small clover field during the first rut, and they stayed active for a couple of weeks. However, after the rutting activity subsided, they remained idle for about four weeks. I discovered they had been pawed furiously during the late season, but this action was brief, to say the least. In fact, had I hunted near and waited on the scrapes to get hit again, it would have taken about nine months—until the primary rut the following year.

The same is probably true for rubs; you probably can't count on them to produce action. There are exceptions, though, such as the rub line I found during the late archery season several years ago, about five weeks after the primary rut.

I seldom locate fresh rubs in the late season, and when I do, I rarely consider setting up an ambush nearby. This time it was different. I had just passed through the area three days earlier and hadn't seen any rubs. So when I discovered about ten to twelve rubs, all within a one hundred-yard stretch connecting to a thicket and probable bedding area, I had to set up a stand.

Nothing showed for two hours on the first morning I hunted the stand. Around 8:00 A.M., though, I spotted movement to the south. I saw gleaming white antlers bobbing up and down with each step the big ten-pointer took. He was walking precisely along the rub line, and I knew that if he stayed on course, he would pass by at twelve yards. He did. My arrow hit a little too far back, but the doomed buck still went down only 150 yards from where I shot him.

I can honestly say that most of my late-season second-rut action has occurred in the afternoons, long before dusk. Don't get me wrong; I've seen bucks at both dawn and dusk during late season if there was a young hot doe in the area. But most second rut activity, such as bucks pursuing young does, takes place early in the afternoons.

The previously mentioned late-season buck has been the only one I've taken along a rub line. Today, I typically don't depend upon rub lines, or scrapes for that matter, for any second-rut success.

Late-season rutting behavior is probably more common among mature bucks (those that do most of the breeding) than we realize. I believe breeding is always on their minds, even when there is no pretty little doe around. I made a disturbance while preparing a ground blind one year in late season, many weeks after the primary rut. I was clearing a couple of shooting lanes when I heard something behind me, turned and spotted a huge buck standing there. Maybe he thought all the breaking of limbs meant there was a battle going on. But he noticed me at the same moment I noticed him, and that buck was gone in a flash.

If you stop and think about the tactics that lead to success during the second rut, they're really not much different than those you use in the primary rut. You hunt for the does! If you find yearlings coming into estrus, you will find bucks. If there are no breeding does, you wait them out and hope that sooner or later one will breed. That's the good news about the second rut. It only takes one hot little rascal to pull all the bucks out of hiding. From one day to the next, your hunting area can change from "poor to superb."

Finding the does is a pretty straightforward task. You just find out where they are feeding. Sometimes, it's helpful to locate a bedding area, but it's usually foods, particularly anything green, that will lead to late-season action.

Deer Calls

PETER FIDUCCIA

One of the chapters that received the most response in my first book *Whitetail Strategies* was "How to Use Deer Calls Effectively." Many of the folks who e-mailed me after reading the book remarked how their deer hunting had improved after they began using deer calls. Some ardent trackers even told me that by adding calling to their arsenal, they were able to see and bag more deer.

Deer calls have always been underrated and underused. I believe this can be attributed to the way many of us were taught to hunt deer by our fathers, uncles, and grandfathers. A lot of hunters from the older generation are ardent believers in not making any noise that might spook a deer in the woods, including sounds that deer naturally make. Trying to convince these old-timers that using deer calls can improve their hunting skills has been frustrating for me. No matter how many times they've been shown the effectiveness of deer calls through my television show, magazines articles, or in my books, these dyed-in-the-wool anticallers remain steadfast in their belief tnat using calls to attract, hold, or intentionally roust deer is foolhardy at best and a bunch of malarkey at worst. But they couldn't be more mistaken.

Using deer calls has consistently improved my ability to see and take bucks. It is by far the most natural strategy a hunter can use, although it isn't a foolproof strategy that works every time out. Still, I've employed deer calls more than any other tactic during my many years of hunting across North America.

In order to be an effective deer caller, you must first learn how to mimic the primary vocalizations deer make. Practicing each cadence of each of the vocalizations long before opening day will give you the confidence necessary to place a call in your mouth and blow without worrying about whether

The whitetail bucks in this part of my trophy room were all bagged using deer calls. Even the moose, caribou, and gobbler were called in. (So far, my young lab hasn't responded.)

the noise will be beneficial or harmful to your chances. When you call correctly, you'll definitely attract more deer. Once you gain this mindset, you'll incorporate deer calls into your hunting strategy season after season with amazing success.

Back in the 1960s, using calls to attract deer was a well-kept secret known only to seasoned, savvy woodsmen who hunted remote wilderness areas of North America, especially in Quebec, Canada. These hunters used rudimentary calls made of rubber bands and balsa wood to regularly attract whitetails, but they rarely talked about them.

It was one of these cagey old hunters who first introduced me to deer calls early in my hunting life. I was sitting on a stand overlooking a swamp in New York's Adirondack Mountains. Every so often I heard a soft lamb-like bleat. I had no idea what the sound was or what was making it. But I did know that every fifteen minutes or so the sound emanated from

a dip about one hundred yards below the ledge I was sitting on.

Since this was only my second year of deer hunting, my patience level wasn't very high. If I didn't see a deer within the first hour or two, I usually got up and skulked around hoping to jump a buck. I still smile when I think about my impatience in those days. It never seemed to fail; as soon as I got up and started walking around, I'd hear a shot ring out close by. I'm sure I unknowingly drove a lot of bucks to a lot of other hunters back then.

In any event, by 7:30 that morning my patience had waned and I was determined to find out what was making that noise. As I stood up, I heard the sound again. This time, however, I heard a similar noise coming from the swamp in the opposite direction. A big doe emerged from the swamp and trotted toward the ledge below me. Never swerving, she went straight to the source of the noise.

I watched as she stopped and then began pacing nervously back and forth. Then the excitement started. Two bucks ran out of the swamp, hot on her trail. I started shaking and was still trying to decide which one to shoot when a gunshot rang out. The bigger of the two bucks dropped in its tracks. I threw my .30-30 to my shoulder and attempted to draw a bead on the second buck as he and the doe weaved and darted through the hardwoods, but there was no chance to pull the trigger. Naturally, I was shocked at what had just taken place.

As I sat there disgusted, a hunter who had been posted well below me stood and approached the downed buck. I grabbed my gear and went down to talk to him. I soon discovered that this old gentleman had been the source of the doe blats I'd heard all morning.

He told me that he'd been using doe blats to attract whitetaih for many years, especially "to pull bucks from heavy cover" like the swamp we were overlooking. He laughed until there were tears in his eyes when I told him I thought I was posted near a sheep farm. "Boy," he said, "there ain't a sheep or a farm between Childwold and Tupper Lake, and they're thirty miles apart!"

The Olt deer call was the first call I learned to use to talk to deer. It has worket successfully for many years.

While he field dressed his eight-point buck, I stood there in amazement as he told me story after story of how successful he had been over the years using a blat call. "Hell, boy, if you wanna kill bucks like this, learn to blow one of these here doe calls," he said, placing an Olt deer call in my hand. "Your friends will think you're crazy for using it, but I betcha it'll work."

I bought an Olt call that afternoon in a tiny general store in Tupper Lake during a heavy snowfall. I blew it on almost every hunting trip that season without success. But I didn't give up. The memory of that morning's hunt and the old gent's stories remained vivid, so I continued to use and practice the doe blat call.

Within a few short years, I became proficient with a blat call and some of the other deer vocalizations. I had enough reaction from deer to know that I was onto a tactic that could provide me with more success than just sitting and waiting for a buck to pass my stand. I promised myself that through trial and error and continuous practice I would gain the experience and confidence needed to become an accomplished deer caller.

Over the next thirty-five years, I did just that. I learned all thirteen primary vocalizations that deer make and the myriad sub-calls, also known as cadences, that go along with each one. I practiced in spring and summer when deer are easy to see along roads and in fields. I made bleats, blats, snorts, and even grunts, and I watched their reactions to each

This veteran hunter told me he regularly used a doe bleat to call in bucks like the eight-pointer shown here.

This buck is vocalizing to the doe with soft, guttural grunts, a common sound throughout the deer woods during the breeding season. Credit: Ted Rose

I've had good results with a variety of deer blat calls over the years. The Deer Stopper from F.I.K., Inc. is one of my favorites. Credit: Kate Fiduccia)

call. I learned that there was a definite difference between a blat and a bleat. I saw deer react in many different ways to a variety of snorts. And I discovered that does even grunt during the off-season.

Learning how vocal deer really are gave me the confidence 1 needed to use calls during the archery and firearm seasons. After all, if deer "talked" to each other as much as I had witnessed during the spring and summer, why wouldn't they continue to communicate during the most important time for does and bucks—the rut.

It became apparent to me that any hunter who resists learning how to use vocalizations to attract deer is only hurting himself. He is missing out on what I've long referred to as one of Mother Nature's natural seductions. Whitetails aren't the only ruminants that respond to calls. All thirty species and subspecies of deer in the Americas vocalize and respond readily to the sounds made by hunters using deer calls.

Calls You Need to Know

While biologists have recognized thirteen primary deer vocalizations, there are four basic sounds a hunter must incorporate into his bag of tricks in order to see and tag more deer. Thankfully, they are the easiest of all the vocalizations to learn and mimic. These sounds include the snort, the blat, the bleat, and the grunt.

Each one of these has a variety of sub-calls (cadences) that mean something other than the primary vocalization. For instance, the blat has five cadences: the alarm blat, the feeding blat, the

These deer calls imitate common variations of the primary snort, blat, bleat, and grunt.

locating blat, the trail blat, and the social blat. As you become more experienced, you can start learning and adding these subvocalizations to the four primary calls to make yourself a more complete deer caller.

I'll go over each primary call and its sub-calls in detail in the chapters ahead. I advise you to learn each thoroughly. Doing so will improve your deer hunting success immediately and exponentially. But first let's look at some general principles related to calling.

Talking to Deer in Spring

Each spring, I practice using bleat calls to attract does. It is important to understand the difference between bleats and blats. A bleat is made by fawns from birth to about eighteen months of age. At that point, the fawn's voice changes much like a

teenager's. The bleat evolves into a deeper-toned call known as a blat. Be cautious about this, as there are times when an adult deer will respond negatively if you're trying to imitate a blat and it comes out sounding like a bleat.

During the spring and summer, why wouldn't they continue to communicate during the most important time for does and bucks—the rut.

It became apparent to me that any hunter who resists learning how to use vocalizations to attract deer is only hurting himself. He is missing out on what I've long referred to as one of Mother Nature's natural seductions. Whitetails aren't the only ruminants that respond to calls. All thirty species and subspecies of deer in the Americas vocalize and respond readily to the sounds made by hunters using deer calls.

Calls You Need to Know

While biologists have recognized thirteen primary deer vocalizations, there are four basic sounds a hunter must incorporate into his bag of tricks in order to see and tag more deer. Thankfully, they are the easiest of all the vocalizations to learn and mimic. These sounds include the snort, the blat, the bleat, and the grunt.

Each one of these has a variety of sub-calls (cadences) that mean something other than the primary vocalization. For instance, the blat has five cadences: the alarm blat, the feeding blat, the locating blat, the trail blat, and the social blat. As you become more experienced, you can start learning and adding these subvocalizations to the four primary calls to make yourself a more complete deer caller.

I'll go over each primary call and its sub-calls in detail in the chapters ahead. I advise you to learn each thoroughly. Doing so will improve your deer hunting success immediately and exponentially. But first let's look at some general principles related to calling.

Talking to Deer in Spring

Each spring, I practice using bleat calls to attract does. It is important to understand the difference between bleats and blats. A bleat is made by fawns from birth to about eighteen months of age. At that point, the fawn's voice changes much like a teenager's. The bleat evolves into a deeper-toned call known as a blat. Be cautious about this, as there are times when an adult deer will respond negatively if you're trying to imitate a blat and it comes out sounding like a bleat.

The spring is a good time to practice because adult does are most vocal after giving birth to fawns. A fawn's neonatal vocalizations are crucial to its survival. The different cadences made by a fawn include a feeding bleat, an alarm bleat, and a locating bleat. There are also more subtle types of bleat calls made by fawns to demonstrate a wide variety of emotions such as pleasure, discontent, and so on. The doe readily reacts to any of the vocalizations a fawn makes. It is nature's way of making the doe a better caretaker of her offspring.

Keep It Low

An experienced caller learns how to call softly. Occasionally, a louder sound may be necessary. On very rare occasions, a more aggressive call may be the key to success. But if there is one thing I can promise you about calling, it's that a hunter who makes loud, aggressive vocalizations to does and/or bucks, even mature bucks, will scare away more deer than he attracts. Many times, a hunter will never hear or see the deer approaching over the noise he's making, or worse yet, won't even get the deer interested enough to respond because his calling has frightened it away.

Deer react negatively to loud, aggressive vocalizations, even when they're as far away as two hundred yards. Loud calls are unnatural in the deer world, so they usually interpret them to mean trouble is afoot. When faced with an alien sound, deer will fade away into the cover like ghosts.

I often refer to the phrase "common sense hunting strategies" to help hunters relate to a specific tactic. I'm sure many hunters have been tempted by merchandising campaigns that promote loud deer calls, mostly grunt calls, as the only ones to buy to ensure success. Nothing could be further from the truth. Take a moment to stop and think about it. Most of us have heard the varied low guttural sounds of a buck grunt. Even at its most aggressive levels, it isn't a sound that can be heard by hunters over long distances. Subtler grunt vocalizations made by a buck are even harder to hear, even at close ranges. A buck making a soft grunt can be difficult to hear at just twenty yards.

Once you know all this, it quickly becomes obvious that a grunt call other hunters can hear over two hundred yards away won't sound natural. I don't think there is a hunter out there who has heard a buck in the woods grunting as loudly as a bull. If they did, we'd all be in our stands listening to a crescendo of loud brp . . . brp . . . brp sounds reverberating through the woods. It just doesn't happen that way.

So keep your calling soft and subtle most of the time and you will have much more success as a deer caller.

Need further proof? Imagine that you're in your stand and you spot an eight-point buck walking through the woods. You decide to make a loud, aggressive grunt. The buck turns his head, looks in your direction, then swings his head back, drops it slightly, flags his tail twice, and continues on his way. You grunt again, thinking that maybe he didn't hear you or that he just isn't interested in responding. Neither of these two assumptions is correct.

Basically, by grunting too loudly, you've sent the buck an emphatic verbal message that you're a mature, aggressive buck issuing a challenge. Initially, he looks to make eye contact, but he instinctively knows this is a serious mistake. By swinging his head away and dropping it slightly, and then flicking his tail and slowly walking away, he avoids

This buck heard a deep, aggressive grunt that caused him to leave the doe and trot off. The signal he received was that a huge buck was ready to kick his rump unless he cleared out fast. Credit: Ted Rose

a confrontation with what he perceives to be a more powerful buck. This is the real reason he won't look back or react to the grunt again. All he wants to do at this point is put as much ground between the two of you as possible.

Unfortunately, most hunters interpret the buck's behavior as an apparent lack of interest or presume that he didn't hear the grunt. The hunter's natural response is to grunt again, and in most cases even louder. Now it's the buck's turn to do some interpreting. He instinctively believes that the more aggressive buck is going to pursue him, so he moves away with more determination than ever.

No matter how long or hard you grunt at a buck in this situation, he won't respond to your call. It's only natural that he'd want to get as far away as he can from what he perceives to be the biggest and baddest buck in the woods. Even if this buck is large and heavily antlered, he'll try to avoid a fight with a buck he thinks is even larger and more aggressive than he is.

If you still have doubts about this, think back to all the times you've seen this exact reaction from a buck you were grunting at in a loud and aggressive manner. Trust me, keep your calls soft and you will be more successful.

Don't Over-Call

The next most common reason for a lack of success in calling deer is over-calling. Any turkey hunter can tell you that a gobbler not only hears the seductive calls a hunter is making from up to two hundred yards away, but he also is able to immediately determine exactly where the call is coming from at closer ranges. A savvy, call-shy gobbler then quietly slips in to check out the sounds he is hearing. If the turkey hunter continues to call as the gobbler approaches, he never even realizes that the bird "made" him and is just as quietly sneaking off. The same holds true for a wary buck.

So keep the volume of your calls low, but also make them infrequently enough to not give yourself away. It's always better to build a buck's curiosity with infrequent calls and then let him get frustrated enough to give himself away as he searches for the sounds you made. Use common sense to limit the number of calls you make, whether imitating a competing buck or an estrus doe.

One critical mistake the hunter often makes is to call when a buck has already responded to an earlier call and is walking toward him. Once you see or hear the deer responding, stop calling. Again, let the deer's curiosity work for you instead of against you.

Practice

The most important advice I can give you about calling is to practice each call long before the season. Practice not only makes you a better caller, it also enhances your confidence level tremendously. In Whitetail Strategies, I wrote, "Concentration + Positive Thinking X Confidence = Consistent Success." And it bears repeating here, because being confident in your ability to imitate different deer sounds and knowing when to use an alarm snort as opposed to a social snort will put antlers on your wall and venison in your freezer.

When you think you've practiced your calling techniques enough, practice, practice, and practice some more.

This buck "made" the hunter who was calling to him and took off at top speed. Over-calling often gives the hunter away. Credit: Ted Rose

The Snort and Its Variations

PETER FIDUCCIA

The snort is the most often misunderstood primary vocalization. It's often thought of as a sound a deer makes when it's alarmed or running away, so hunters don't use this call very much. That is a real shame, because the primary snort and its four sub-sounds, or cadences, may be the most effective deer vocalization a hunter can make. However, as with any of the vocalizations, a hunter must know when he should blow a particular

Credit: Ted Rose

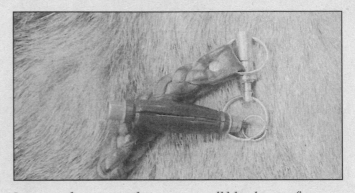

I never go hunting without a snort call like this one from Lohman. (It can be hard to find in stores, but is available on my web site at www.deerdoctor.com.)

sub-call or the inevitable result will be a deer streaking away with its tail flying high behind it.

As soon as you decipher what each snort call actually means —or, for that matter, what every cadence of each primary vocalization means—you'll discover how potent this call can be. A snort can be used to stop, relax, attract, and even spook or roust deer from heavy cover. The latter is my favorite way to use the snort sound.

As early as 1988, I decided that the different vocalizations of the snort needed to be given specific names in order for hunters to better differentiate between each call. I labeled the primary snort's four cadences as the alarm snort, the social snort, the alarm-distress snort, and the aggressive snort. Each sound has a distinct meaning to deer.

When the proper snort is used at the right time and under the right set of circumstances, a hunter can trick a buck or doe into thinking he is just another deer. Use the wrong cadence at the wrong time and place, though, and the deer you're calling to will turn itself inside out as it tries to get away.

The Alarm-Distress Snort

The alarm-distress is by far my favorite snort cadence. Why? Because its sound forces the deer to react out of instinct. Nothing is better when it comes to hunting a wise old buck. Locate thick cover, like a cedar patch or a swamp, and then post hunters along the networks of trails that are known deer escape routes. Don't let the hunters penetrate too deeply into the center of the cover. After all the standers are posted, wait a good half hour for things to settle down. Then walk into the middle of the thickest part of the cover without worrying about being too quiet. When you've reached the spot where you want to be, take out interdigital scent and lay down several drops. Now stomp your foot several times while blowing the alarm-distress cadence of the primary snort.

The call sounds like this: *Whew . . . whew . . . whew . . . whew, whew, whew, whew.* Make the first three snorts loud and hesitate about a second between each one. Then make the next four snorts quickly, without any hesitation.

It's important to always create as natural a display as possible when calling, or when rattling or decoying. Try to duplicate what deer would do when they're vocalizing, responding to antler rat-tling, or coming in to check out a decoy.

Make an all-out effort to create all the sounds, smells, and motions (shaking brush or saplings) that deer make when they're calling. All of this helps put a deer at ease when it responds to you. The deer naturally thinks it is hearing, smelling, and sometimes seeing another deer, so it responds more enthusiastically and with less caution.

The alarm-distress is also useful when you're hunting alone, which is when I've had the most success

with this cadence of the snort. I use it to roust deer from cattails, ledges, brush piles, small woodlots, laurels, and standing corn. In addition, I've done very well with this call when walking through blowdowns.

Several years ago I was hunting in a place I call the "Honey Hole," a deep bowl surrounded by mountains. It takes a lot of effort and time to reach, which keeps most hunters away. As the hunting season progresses, I find more and more mature bucks using the Honey Hole to escape the pressure in the surrounding valleys and mountains where most hunters post.

I've taken several nicely racked bucks at this location over the years. It's the perfect terrain from which to call or rattle. There is a big swamp in the middle, which is rimmed with large blowdowns along its edge. I have often seen bucks rise from behind deadfalls in the middle of the day to feed or move away from the area.

On this particular morning I reached the Honey Hole after a two-hour hike, just as large snowflakes began to fall. I took up a po-sition on a side hill and soon spotted a doe that walked behind a large blowdown and disappeared. I studied the area with my binoculars and finally found the doe's face as she lay comfortably under the downed tree, looking back over

The snort is one of the most misunderstood of all the deer calls. Learn when and where it should be used and you will see and take more deer.

her shoulder. My gut told me that she was looking at a buck, so I kept watching the area intently.

About twenty minutes later I saw what I thought was one side of a set of antlers. I wasn't sure if my strained eyes were playing tricks on me or if there really was a buck bedded with the doe. I had two options. I could try to outwait them, hoping they'd eventually rise and move. Or I could take a more proactive approach by trying to make something happen without the deer exploding out of the cover and running off before I could get a shot.

I decided the best strategy would be to blow an alarm-distress call. I put out several drops of interdigital gland scent, and from behind a large oak I stomped my foot several times and blew the alarm-distress: *Whew . . . whew . . . whew . . . whew, whew, whew, whew.*

Within seconds, the doe stood up and began to intently scan the area to find out what caused the other "deer" to blow an alarm-distress cadence. While she was swinging her head from side to side, the buck stood up. I could see instantly that he was a keeper. Not wanting to take any chances by waiting around, the buck scaled the big blowdown, sniffed the air,

The alarm-distress call has provided me many shot opportunities at bucks and does bedded in the safety of blowdowns. Their instinctive response to this call gave their locations away.

and was about to take off in another direction when the report from my Ruger .44 Mag echoed off the surrounding mountains. (I always use my lightweight Ruger in areas that require long walks up and down mountains and through thick cover, especially when a quick second shot may be necessary.)

Without the alarm-distress call, I seriously doubt I'd have ever gotten a chance at this buck. The snow was already falling hard, and trying to wait him out would have probably been the wrong tactic. By using a cadence I knew would pull the deer from cover, I created a shot opportunity I otherwise wouldn't have had.

I've used this call to roust bucks out of small patches of cover on farms, in swales, and even in heavy thorn brush. Most hunters walk by this type of cover, thinking the undergrowth is either too small to harbor a buck or too impenetrable to check out.

A small buck I shot in the early 1970s offers a classic example. I was hunting on a farm we called "Weissmans." As I walked across an open field, I passed a thick patch of overgrown brush I had probably walked by a hundred times before. As I looked at it this time I thought to myself, I wonder how many times I've walked past a deer bedded in there.

I flung a heavy branch into the thicket. Nothing happened. So I took my snort call out and blew the alarm-distress. I was still learning the nuances of calling back then, which meant that I wasn't using interdigital scent and I wasn't stomping my foot to create the full illusion. I just blew the alarm-distress a few times.

I hadn't even finished the second sequence when a small buck broke from the cover and started running across the field. I dropped him just before he reached the bordering woodlot. Even though I suspected the call might work, it was still early enough in my trial-and-error days that I was totally shocked to see it actually do the job it was supposed to do. The young

Leo Somma paused to blow an alarm-distress call while walking through some thick blowdowns. This buck stood up long enough for him to get a clear shot.

Here Leo is drawing a bead on a buck he rousted from a patch of standing corn with an alarm-distress snort.

buck reacted predictably and immediately to what it perceived to be a serious problem.

Again, I never would have had the opportunity to shoot this buck if I hadn't used the alarm-distress to force him out.

Remember, this call works so well because all deer learned from the time they were old enough to run that this particular cadence of the snort requires an instant flee response. It is ingrained in their heads as a natural behavior.

Blowing the alarm-distress snort has created numerous shot opportunities for me through the years. Without it, many a buck would have remained safely hidden within sanctuaries of thick cover.

The Alarm Snort

The alarm cadence of the primary snort is the most recognized vocalization deer make. I can even tell you when and where hunters probably encounter a deer making this snort. Often, a hunter jumps a deer while walking along a logging road or making his way through the woods to his stand. Because the deer doesn't see or wind the hunter first, it reacts only to the noise the hunter is making. If it had

winded or sighted the hunter, it would have quietly snuck off or blown the alarm-distress call as it made a hasty retreat.

But this deer is confused, so it blows the alarm call. It doesn't really know what spooked it, and it often remains standing or slowly walks a short distance and blows the call again. This call is a specific noise. Every hunter has heard this snort often. And the deer that makes this call can be easily called back if you know exactly what to do.

When you encounter a deer unexpectedly, the deer may respond by blowing a single snort, and then running several yards before stopping and blowing a second single snort: *whew . . . whew*. It's alarmed, but it hasn't been able to pinpoint why. It knows instinctively that it's safer not to run any farther until it can determine exactly what made it nervous.

This is the point at which you either make or break your opportunity to call the deer back. I've learned through trial and error to stop in my tracks as soon as the deer sounds the alarm. I immediately blow a single snort back at the deer.

Be careful here, though. If the sound you heard appears to be fifty yards or closer, one single snort is all you can risk without being discovered by the deer. If you estimate the range at over fifty yards you can make two single snorts: a snort, a brief second or two of silence, and then another single snort: *whew ... ...whew.*

The deer is trying to locate and isolate the danger. By blowing back at the deer with the alarm cadence of the primary snort call, you stimulate its curiosity. Often, after hearing what it per-ceives to be just a call from another deer, it decides to slowly make its way back toward the location where it first perceived the danger.

As long as the deer remains at a distance and continues to blow one or two snorts, you can keep blowing a single snort. Con-tinue to do this unless the deer begins to walk toward you. The in-stant the deer moves in your direction, stop calling. Even if the deer continues to snort at this point, you must remain silent to let its curiosity build. This is your best chance at pulling the deer within shooting distance.

Years ago, my wife shot her first buck while still-hunting toward her tree stand. She spotted a deer, but as she tried to position herself for a shot she stepped on a branch. The deer heard the snap and blew an alarm snort. True to form, it ran off several yards and then blew a second snort. Kate blew back at the deer and the buck answered.

Each time the deer answered, it blew two snorts but didn't move. And each time Kate blew back two snorts. The buck, curious to see what had frightened it, finally came closer with each series of alarm snorts. After several minutes of exchanging snorts, the spike buck made its last move, stepping out from behind the cedars where Kate dispatched him with one clean shot. She would never have had the chance to shoot that buck if she hadn't known how to call back an alarmed deer.

I also use the alarm snort to help roust deer from cover when I'm still-hunting with my bow. I intentionally walk through heavy cover with the wind in my face. Every few steps I snap a twig or kick some leaves, hoping the noise will alarm a buck. Once I make contact with a buck and he makes the alarm snort, I know I have a better than average chance of calling him back.

I often refer to the alarm snort as mv "too late" call. Too late for the buck, that is. As the buck and I exchange calls, he usually approaches without knowing I'm hidden in heavy brush or pines, and he continues to walk by me in search of the other "deer." I've shot a few nice bucks at distances less than ten yards while using the alarm snort. Again, the trick is to stop calling when the buck closes to

I shot this buck in western New York while still-hunting through a recently logged woodlot. He was bedded behind a tangle of brush but rose to the sounds of my calling.

within fifty yards or less. This heightens the curiosity of the buck, drawing it all the way in for the shot.

While all variations of the snort work well, you'll find that the alarm snort is the easiest call to master. Keep in mind, however, that a critical aspect when using a snort call is to not blow an alarm snort to a deer who is vocalizing an alarm-distress snort. You must recognize the different cadences of each call to use them effectively.

The Social Snort

The social snort is usually made by a nervous deer warily feeding at the edge of a field or in a woodlot. I'm sure you've seen and heard a deer make this call.

The animal puts its head down to feed while focusing its ears in a particular direction. It then lifts its head quickly, looking in the direction its ears were pointing. Reluctantly, the deer lowers its head to begin feeding again, only to repeat the process. This nervous behavior goes on for several minutes before the deer decides to blow a single non-aggressive snort. By blowing the snort, the deer is trying to encourage whatever is making it nervous to reveal itself by approaching it, or at least answering. If it's reacting to another deer nearby, that deer will often answer with a single snort of its own.

This return call immediately relaxes the first deer, which then begins to feed more contentedly, without lifting its head every few seconds. Often the deer feeds in the direction of the deer that answered it—safety in numbers. If it doesn't hear a return social snort after making one, the deer usually stops feeding and retreats from the area.

When I see a deer acting like this, I know I can relax it and sometimes even attract it to me by using the social cadence of the primary snort. But it's important to remember that the social snort only works on deer that are exhibiting the type of behavior described above.

Never make this call unless the deer first makes a single quick snort. When it drops its head back down to feed, make one soft snort to the deer. Try to blow the call in the opposite direction of the deer. If the call is made correctly, the deer typically lifts its head, cups its ears toward you, and then begins to feed again, many times heading in your direction. If the deer lifts its head and becomes even more nervous, you probably blew the call too loudly. Don't try to make another call until the deer starts to feed again.

I used the social snort to attract a good eight-point buck once while bowhunting in Hope, New Jersey. The buck was nervously feeding on acorns in a small woodlot that bordered an agricultural field. Every few seconds he perked up his ears and looked behind him. Then he put his nose into the leaves and resumed the search for more acorns.

Before long, the buck's ears started playing the radar game again. He lifted his head, stared into a thicket, and walked off a short distance in the opposite direction of the bushes. I noticed that he was getting more and more spooked with each passing minute, and that he was moving away from my stand.

I waited until the buck put his head down to feed again, and then I turned away from him and softly blew a single snort. The buck lifted its head, stared in my direction, and then began to feed again. Only this time, he moved purposefully and steadily toward me while feeding.

I knew enough to stop calling at this point, letting the deer dictate my next move. Within two minutes of my first snort, the buck was under my tree stand. I released my arrow as the buck's nose was buried in the leaves looking for acorns. He never suspected a thing.

If I hadn't relaxed the buck with a social snort, I doubt a shot opportunity would have presented itself.

I think the buck would have eventually become too nervous from the original noise, moving out of bow range and maybe even out of the area entirely. This encounter may have come to nothing if I'd lacked the understanding and confidence to make a social snort.

Knowing when, how, why, and where to use this cadence has been crucial to my success.

The Aggressive Snort

The aggressive snort is the fourth cadence of the primary snort. This is sometimes referred to as the grunt-snort-wheeze. But this isn't correct. A buck that is annoyed and trying to establish itself within the social pecking order makes the aggressive snort. This is a loud and overblown call, meant to get the attention of another, offending deer. It's often made so powerfully that the deer expels air and mucus from its nostrils.

Does make this call to fawns, yearlings, and other competing does when food sources are scarce. The call is also associated with an action known as "flailing," which occurs when a deer rises on its hind legs and strikes at the head or body of another deer with its forelegs.

All deer that are lower on the totem pole than the deer making this vocalization pay attention to it instantly. These submissive deer quickly move off several feet from the more aggressive deer.

Mature bucks regularly vocalize to lesser bucks with this type of snort. They use it to let them know they are about to convert their antagonism from a simple call to a greater physical confrontation. It is most often used by bucks during the three phases of the rut. A younger satellite buck typically hangs close to an estrus doe with a mature buck in the hopes of getting into the action. Many times, when all other body language fails to dissuade the youngster, the mature buck blows an aggressive

An aggressive snort call helped Jay Cassell lure this monster within range.

snort. It's a warning to the smaller buck to back off or deal with the consequences.

Normally, this cadence of the snort scares more bucks than it attracts. But there is a time when it can be used to attract a buck. If you encounter a situation like the one I described above, wait until the mature buck blows the aggressive snort and then make an aggressive snort of your own in his direction. The message you're sending is that you're a competing mature buck of his age-class and rank in the pecking order. The call is telling him you aren't afraid of his warning and, in fact, are daring to challenge him for the doe he is tending.

In all the years I've used this call, I've noted only two types of reaction. Either a buck immediately uses his antlers to prod the doe to retreat to another area, thereby leaving the "challenging buck" in the dust, or depending on his mood, he stiff-legs his way toward the challenger with his ears laid back, nostrils flared, and the hair on his neck standing up. All of this happens while he blows aggressive snorts. It is a visual and vocal demonstration that he is big enough and strong enough to not be intimidated by any other buck in the area.

Using the aggressive snort is always a gamble. You quickly lose the buck or get him to respond. But I think it's better to have a 50-50 chance to get the buck rather than to helplessly watch him walk off.

This is a neat call to master. And while it may not attract a lot of bucks, when it does it'll be an experience you'll always remember.

To do the aggressive snort call correctly, you have to break my cardinal rule about calling softly— just this one time. After hearing the buck or doe make this call, muster up all the lung power you can and blow two hard snorts back-to-back—*Whew, Whew*—and then wait. If the deer moves toward you, don't make another call. If he moves away and continues to blow an aggressive snort while doing so, you can also blow an aggressive snort until the buck responds or moves off entirely.

The wise hunter never assumes that a buck that doesn't initially respond, or one that moves off into heavy cover, has decided not to respond at all. Sometimes, the aggressive snort is nothing more than a bluff, even when the deer is a mature buck. He heads to cover only to cautiously circle the challenging buck in an attempt to catch him by surprise.

When I blow an aggressive snort to a buck and he moves off into the woods, I wait a good hour before giving up on him. Heed my advice: Watch the surrounding cover and listen carefully for a good hour. The buck may be circling with the wind in his nose, looking to sneak up on the interloper. This is a good time to be off the ground!

Bleats and Blats and Their Variations

PETER FIDUCCIA

The four primary vocalizations deer make include the blat and the bleat. All deer younger than eighteen months old—yearlings and fawns—generally make bleats, while all adult deer make blats. There is a significant difference in the sound of each of these calls. Any seasoned turkey hunter will tell you the same thing is true with this species. The sounds of an adult boss gobbler or hen are markedly different from those of a poult or jake.

It's important to note that some manufacturers who make deer calls refer to both the fawn and adult sounds as bleats. And some companies identify the adult sound as an "adult bleat." To keep from getting confused, keep in mind that any package labeled "adult bleat" really just means "blat." If you're looking for a fawn bleat, make sure the package is marked as a fawn or yearling call.

If you have trouble locating the correct blat or bleat call, visit my web site, www.deerdoctor.com, where you can purchase either type. Or you can e-mail me with any questions you have about using these calls at peter@fiduccia.com.

Fawn Bleats

Because fawn bleat calls are most productive from September through the end of October, they're primarily helpful for the early season bowhunter. When made correctly and used at the right time, these calls can be lethal.

Don't confuse bleat and blat calls, which are made by deer of different age-classes. Here, I'm using an adult blat call.

Fawns make several variations of a bleat. They bleat when they're hungry, lost, hurt, in immediate danger, frightened, or simply when they want attention. Each sound is broken down into the following categories: the locating bleat, the alarm-distress bleat, the social bleat, and the feeding bleat.

The Locating Bleat

A fawn that is unexpectedly separated from its group will make a whining bleat over and over again in an attempt to locate the doe or another deer (once the danger has passed). This is one of the easiest fawn bleats to imitate, and it's also one of the more effective calls.

Unlike the way she responds to the alarm-distress sound of a fawn, a doe doesn't respond to the locating bleat with much urgency. Instead, she calmly makes her way toward the area the sound is coming from in an attempt to locate the lost fawn or yearling. The entire family group often follows her, including any young bucks that are still with the group. At other times, mature bucks hear this sound and respond instinctively, knowing that a doe must be close by.

Whenever I see a fawn separated from the group, I immediately make the locating bleat. Sometimes the doe stops in her tracks and slowly makes her way back. Other times, bucks appear out of nowhere in response to the sound.

The Alarm-Distress Bleat

When the doe hears the alarm-distress bleat made by a yearling, or especially a fawn, it only takes her moments to respond. As she urgently makes her way toward the sound, the rest of her group will again instinctively follow in most instances. As I noted above, this group frequently includes a yearling buck or two. A mature buck may occasionally respond since he's likely to locate a doe near the source of the distress call, but he usually does so with caution because the sound means the fawn is in danger.

My newest DVD, *Tactics for "Talking" to Deer*, includes footage of does being called in with the alarm-distress call. The does react immediately,

My new DVD on calling covers all four primary sounds—the grunt, blat, and snort—and their variations. I explain how, when, why, and where to use them most effectively.

racing in to rescue the fawn or yearling they think is in trouble. The response to this call can be so dramatic that it often catches the hunter off-guard.

Once you blow this call, you must be ready for action. No other sound prompts deer, especially does, to respond so quickly. This can be one of the most fun calls to use. There have been times when I haven't been able to draw back my bow or make the shot because I'm laughing so hard at the response of the doe.

The Social Bleat

The social bleat is a sound regularly made by yearlings and fawns as a greeting call. It is a soft sound, barely audible to humans, but deer hear

Several companies make blat and bleat cans, but I think the Primos can calls make the most realistic sounds.

it easily. Youngsters usually make it as one group moves into an area with other deer. It is meant to be a relaxing call or an introductory sound to the other deer. I use it when I see a group of deer passing my stand and I want to stop them to get a shot or to see if there is a buck following them.

The Feeding Bleat

A fawn that wants to be fed, which may still happen as late as September or October, will make a long, whiney bleat over and over again until the doe responds. During September, this neonatal sound still plays heavily on the doe's maternal instincts, and she will usually respond to it. In October, however, she is less inclined to feed the fawn because by this time she wants it to be permanently weaned off her milk. But even then it's hard for her to ignore her maternal duties, and most times she eventually seeks out the source of the sound. I don't use this call at all after October, as it is rarely effective.

The Adult Blat

All adult deer—over 1½ years old —make the loud blat. It is the most common vocalization among all deer in the woods. The blat is used in a variety of cadences to locate, warn, fend off, attract, and generally communicate. Because it's the primary sound used by all deer, it arouses the curiosity of both bucks and does without question. As with the bleat, hunters will benefit from recognizing some of the most common blat variations.

The Social Blat

The social blat is used when deer communicate with one another under non-pressured, casual circumstances. This sound—*Baa-Baaaaaa* . . .

Markus Wilhelm, President of Outdoorsman's Edge Book Club, poses with a hefty ten-point buck I called in from over two hundred yards away using a social blat.

Baa-baaaaaa — should be blown gently. Stretch it out to a whine at the end of the call, and do not blow the call often. Once every thirty to forty-five minutes is enough. If a deer approaches, stop calling. This spurs the deer to intensify its search for the source.

Just like yearlings and fawns use the bleat, adult deer make the social call as they approach other deer. Does also make it when they approach a buck. It is a relaxing sound to deer and will calm the nerves of spooky whitetails. I use it to keep nervous does from leaving my area, especially during the rut.

My long-time adage, "If you want to kill a buck, hunt the does," should be taken to heart. While bucks can be elusive most of the time, they are on the hunt for does during the chase period of the rut and during the rut itself. By keeping does in sight during these periods, you automatically up your chances of seeing and bagging a buck.

It isn't widely known that mule deer, especially bucks, respond readily to adult blats. This buck came in within minutes of my call.

Stopping a monster buck like this, especially when he is chasing a hot doe, shouldn't be left to chance. Whisteling may or may not work, but an alarm blat will always stop him in his tracks for at least a few seconds. Credit: Ted Rose

The Alarm Blat

This is one of the most useful calls you can make to stop deer dead in their tracks. I don't care how fast a deer is running, when it hears an alarm blat it skids to a halt to discover where it came from.

This is one of the few calls that I recommend blowing loudly. If you see a buck making his way past your stand and he's moving too fast to get a bead on, just blow a single loud alarm blat: *Baa-Baaaaaaaaaaaa*. I can almost guarantee you that the deer will slide to a stop in order to determine why another deer is blowing an alarm. It doesn't want to move in a direction that would put it in harm's way, so it stops to get its bearings.

Sometimes a deer will only stop for a few seconds before moving off again. Other times, a deer will remain motionless for several minutes. In either case, the hunter now has time to make a shot on an animal that was running too fast for a clean, accurate kill.

Many hunters have told me they simply whistle at running deer to make them stop. While this tactic does work on occasion, my experience has been that whistling is more likely to send a running deer into warp drive. Trust me, correctly blowing an alarm blat with your mouth or with a call will stop a deer in its tracks every time.

I suggest learning to make this call, and all the adult blats, for that matter, with your mouth. This is easy to do. Simply tuck in your chin and make a deep, lamb-like sound: *Baaaaaaaaaaaaaaaa*. In fact, it's not difficult to mimic each of the adult blats with your mouth. The more you practice, the better you will get. Before you know it, you'll be able to make all variations of the blat with your mouth just as effectively as any manufactured call.

This call is also excellent for hunters who shoot long distances. I used an alarm blat in Wyoming years ago while taping one of my *Woods N' Water* TV segments. There were three mature bucks on a ridgetop about three hundred yards away. They were slowly walking from right to left along the ridgeline. My rifle was wedged in the fork of a tree and I made a loud blat (louder than normal because of the distance). All three bucks immediately stopped and stared down in the direction of the call.

I placed my crosshairs on the middle buck because he was the largest. While the three bucks stood there motionless, I had plenty of time to figure the wind direction and distance. I then took my shot. I heard the bullet smack the deer, and we watched the buck drop like a lead weight between the other two. As the remaining bucks ran off, I blew another alarm blat, again stopping them cold. This was quite a testament to the effectiveness of the call.

I have stopped and taken many deer since then with the alarm blat. Last year, while hunting on my farm in New York, I jumped a small buck that bolted off through the woods. I made an alarm blat with my mouth, and he stopped about sixty yards from where I'd jumped him. I quickly put the scope on him, only to discover he was a seven-point. I passed on the shot because part of our management policy on the farm is to not take any bucks with fewer than eight points or with racks less than eighteen inches wide.

Anyone who wants to improve his shot opportunities by bringing deer to a standstill needs to learn this call.

The Estrus-Doe Blat

One of my favorite calls during any of the three phases of the rut is the estrus-doe blat. I find it extremely effective from mid-December through late January during the late, or post, rut. This is a time when a lot of yearlings and fawns come into their first or second heat. Since most adult does have already been bred, these hot younger does are absolute magnets for bucks.

It isn't unusual to see a single doe being followed by more than one mature buck during this period. Countless times over the years I've seen several bucks on the trail of one hot doe over the course of a few hours. The estrus-doe blat will work magic on any buck following the trail of one of these hot young does.

Another advantage to using the estrus blat occurs when a buck hangs up after you've rattled or grunted to it. Too many hunters get stuck in the mindset that the only call that will attract a big mature buck during the rut is the grunt. If you want to increase your success hunting bucks by at least 50 percent, learn to make an estrus-doe blat.

Find an area that does use frequently. During the rut, an estrus doe walks through the woods emitting these blats to attract bucks that haven't yet picked up her scent.

Blow the call with reasonable volume —but not too loud—to create a drawn-out *Baaaaaaaah . . . Baaaaaaaah*. Repeat this call two or three times and then stop. Wait about fifteen minutes and then make

My neighbour used on estrus-doe bleat to stop this terrific ten-point as it walked past his stand.

another two or three calls. Repeat this sequence for up to an hour. After that, it has been my experience that waiting an additional hour to make the calls again is more beneficial than continuing to blow regularly.

This call brings bucks in from long distances. Sometimes a buck even runs right in. But most times they respond cautiously, even though they come in quickly. Once again, the key to success is to stop calling the moment you see or hear any kind of response. Let the buck's curiosity build enough that he continues to search frantically for what he believes is a hot doe.

This is the one call I can depend on to pull in deer that are hung up in cover, and it's a terrific late-season deer vocalization that has attracted big bucks for me in many different states.

Because deer move about much more during the midday hours late in the season, I strongly recommend hunting the "off hours" between 10:30 AM and 1:30 PM. In fact, if you follow only one recommendation from this book, make it this one. In order to consistently kill mature whitetail bucks, you must believe from the bottom of your heart that big bucks don't go totally nocturnal. Take that to the deer hunting bank. Big bucks become extremely sensitive to your scent and pressure, no matter how slight. It only takes a few days of a hunter scouting or walking its home area before a buck knows that something has changed and that the hunt has begun.

As soon as he figures this out, he adjusts his movement patterns accordingly. He understands instinctively that between the morning hours of 6:00 and 9:30 his home range is being invaded by hunters. He has lived ten months of the year without such pressure, and even the dumbest of bucks is able to react to this kind of unusual activity.

These bucks get the same message from about 2 PM to dark. Common sense tells you what options are left for the buck. If he is interested in feeding or looking for does, nothing short of hunting pressure or human scent stops him from getting up during the midday hours and moving out. He may not move far, but trust me, he will move.

If you truly believe that all mature bucks "go nocturnal," at some point you have to wonder how big bucks still manage to get shot during daylight hours.

When you're hunting the midday, or off, hours try not to stay in one stand all day. You won't be hunting as effectively as possible. Your scent will permeate the area and you will eventually become distracted enough to miss things. If you want to stay in the woods all day, try the following. Hunt one stand from daylight to 9:30 AM, and then move to another stand a few hundred yards away from 10:30 AM to 1:30 PM. Finally, return to your original stand from 2 to 5 PM.

Chances are, you won't need to return to your evening stand. I have taken 60 percent of all my mature bucks between 10:30 AM and 1:30 PM. In fact, on many occasions I've gone out only during the off-hours, especially in extremely cold weather, and still bagged a mature buck.

By the way, because November through January can be cold, particularly in the northern states, protect your blat call from freezing—assuming you're using a commercial call —by placing it inside the breast pocket of your shirt underneath your jacket.

One of the most dramatic examples of the usefulness of an estrus-doe blat call occurred on a hunt I had in Canada. It was a colder than normal morning, even for northern Saskatchewan. A doe broke from the woodlot about 150 yards from my stand and quickly ran fifty yards or so into an open field. She only paused for a moment before darting just as quickly back into the woods. She repeated this routine several more times during the next ten minutes. Each time she entered the field she made several short, loud blats and then dashed back into the woods.

I quickly realized this doe was in peak estrus, and the odds were great that a buck was hovering in the cover of the woods near the edge of the field.

The next time she ran into the field, I made several short estrus blats. Instead of running back to the woods, she nervously trotted along the wood line toward me. Moments later, she was below my stand, trying to locate what she thought was a competing estrus doe. Ignoring her, I focused my concentration on the woods, searching for her would-be suitor.

It didn't take long for me to see parts of a buck as he steadily but cautiously moved through the trees toward the doe. I heard his soft guttural grunts and the sounds of leaves crunching and twigs snapping as he got closer and closer to the stand. He was moving quickly enough that I couldn't risk taking a shot at him.

When he got within fifty yards of my stand, I blew one soft blat. The sound made the doe run a dozen or more feet closer to me, blatting as she came. The buck stood motionless at this point. I raised my rifle and quickly scanned his ten-point rack. Without a doubt, he was a keeper.

I flipped the safety off the Ruger and was about to fire when a slight movement behind the buck caught my attention. At first I thought I was seeing a large heavy branch moving in the background, but then I saw an eye and an ear. I quickly put the crosshairs on the spot and saw a huge-racked buck. Without counting points, I instinctively knew I should shoot him.

This all took place in a matter of seconds, although it felt like several minutes. Before I could settle the crosshairs on a vital area of the buck, the doe reacted to my movement, despite how carefully I was trying to avoid alerting her. With a leap, both bucks disappeared into the woods.

I spent the next hour trying to call the doe back without success. The temperature was minus 30 degrees, and it was way too cold to remain on stand. In fact, my wife, who is also my longtime cameraperson when she isn't in front of the camera hunting or cooking, whispered to me, "Actually, in a way it's a blessing that they ran off. It's so cold the camera isn't operational —it's frozen!"

It took five long, very cold days, but on the last day of the hunt I called in another doe from another location using an estrus blat. She trotted from the woods and ran across an open field and past my stand, looking for the competing doe. Moments later, the huge buck broke from cover and chased after her.

I shot him as he reached the end of the field. Unfortunately, I hit him farther back than I'd intended, and he swerved hard and ran into the woods below me. I thought I'd missed him because he didn't show any reaction to being hit. But I did hear the bullet smack into something, so we checked the video and it was clear that I hit the buck in a vital area, albeit behind where I was aiming.

When I reached the hit site I discovered dark-brown and grayish hair with black tips, a strong indication that I had hit him in the liver or kidney area. I immediately realized that even as excited as I was, I had to give him at least thirty minutes before following his blood trail. The dark-red, almost maroon, blood was another indication that I'd hit the liver or kidney. Hits in this area bleed profusely, so the trail was easy to follow.

I waited the half hour and then took up the trail. After following it for a couple hundred yards, I noticed the buck bedded down in heavy cover. He strained to get to his feet and wobbled as he stood. A second shot to the neck ended the hunt.

The buck turned out to be an atypical sixteen-point with a rack that had mass from burr to antler tip. His green score was 207 1/8, with a net Boone & Crockett score of 195 3/8.

The fact that this buck is now in my trophy room all boiled down to knowing when, where, how, and why to use an estrus-doe blat. Hunters should be aware that an estrus blat can often be more successful in calling in wary bucks and does than a grunt call. This even applies to bucks that hang up when called to with a grunt. I've learned through experience that during the chase period of the primary rut, it's better to call to hot estrus does than it is to try attracting a buck with a grunt call. (See chapter 10 for further details on this aspect of the rut.)

Once you attract a doe, it doesn't matter how big or wary a buck is; she will lead him to your stand as neatly as if he had a ring through his nose.

Rattling North and Rattling South

KATHY ETLING

The rates of rattling success hunters can expect differ from one area to another. Yet there are plenty of places a hunter can go to tempt whitetails with the sounds of mock battle with a reasonable expectation of success. In Texas, ranches that offer hunting have such a variety of price ranges that most hunters can find several to accommodate their budget. Be aware, though, that on some ranches the average deer may sport only average racks at best. On the other hand, visiting a top South Texas ranch, one that can boast of balanced buck-to-doe ratios and balanced age classes of bucks, will set a hunter back some major dinero. Hill country ranches and outfits in the Texas panhandle, while often more reasonably priced, may provide just as much action but far fewer true trophy-caliber deer. It's the rare whitetail hunter who wouldn't be happy with one of the 125- to 150-point Boone and Crockett bucks it's possible to score on at one of these spreads. So little public land exists in Texas that if you want to experience Texas rattling the way it's depicted in so many videos and TV shows, it's going to cost you. It may cost you quite dearly, too, depending on where in Texas you go.

Wonderful rattling opportunities exist in many other areas of the country as well. Eastern Colorado, if you stick it out by garnering an extra preference point each year you are unsuccessful in the draw or simply apply for points, has some truly tremendous whitetail hunting with excellent buck-to-doe ratios in many areas. Although much of eastern Colorado is private, hunters report good rattling success on Division of Wildlife landholdings as well as on the hundreds of thousands of private acres leased to the Division each year.

South Dakota and Wyoming are just two of the states with great whitetail hunting as well as plenty of walk-in areas, public easements, public hunting grounds, and cooperative agreements with private landowners. Many other states have similar arrangements, and these other states, quite possibly, will also provide some great rattling.

Visiting a top South Texas ranch will set a hunter back some major dinero. Credit: R.E. Zaiglin.

Hunters can even book pack-in western hunts to experience the best of rattling, calling, and decoying for whitetails. Credit: Kathy Etling.

One state with which I'm extremely familiar is Montana. I've hunted white-tails there on many occasions. Montana is chock full of public land that's open to hunters. Although a Montana deer license is expensive, and you might not draw one, a do-it-yourself hunt where you can rattle in your own whitetails would be easy, particularly in the state's westernmost reaches. If you'd rather book with an outfitter, there are many excellent hunting outfits in the state. Two of the best—and ones with which I'm familiar—are Flat Iron Outfitters in Thompson Falls and Horizons West Outfitting in Dodson.

I wouldn't hesitate to plan a do-it-yourself whitetail hunt anywhere whitetails can be found. Idaho, Washington, and Oregon all have plenty of public land and aburgeoning population of whitetails. Be sure you check out winterkill rates before applying for licenses, though. If the winterkill was severe during any of the previous three, four, or even five seasons, deer numbers may be scarce, particularly trophy buck numbers.

Call the game department in the state where you would like to hunt. You already know the questions to ask: license fees; license application period; availability of public land; availability of state land and state-managed or leased land maps; buck-to-doe ratios; buck age class structure in the areas you are considering; the best trophy or quality areas; names of campgrounds or nearby motels; the type of weather you can expect at the time you'll be hunting; the approximate dates of the whitetail pre-rut period, the rut's peak, and the post-rut period.

To give you a better idea of what two different rattling hunts would be like in two completely different areas of the country, here is a comparison between a Texas hunt in the state's Hill Country and a hunt in Montana's rugged Cabinet Mountains, on the western slope of the Continental Divide:

Texas Hill Country

Several years ago, I hunted on a Texas Hill Country ranch owned by the Harrison Ranches and managed by Bob Zaiglin. Although this ranch has since been sold, it was there that I experienced, firsthand, the finest whitetail rattling of my life. My husband, Bob, and I hadn't gone to Texas to hunt the Harrison property. But when we discovered the outfitter with whom we'd booked had absconded with all the hunters' deposits—and his secretary—and that he'd hired no guides, we called Bob Zaiglin. Zaiglin kindly opened up this ranch even though it had been shut down for hunting only a few days previously. Zaiglin's guides were supposed to travel to another ranch in South Texas to help him there. Instead, they opened the ranch and its outbuildings again, and rattled, called, and guided for us over the next three days.

A Texas whitetail hunt may be one of the most unforgettable experiences of your life. In some places whitetails are so thick they jump from behind mesquite bushes and bed down next to roads. You

Bob tagged out the first morning of this Texas hunt after his guide rattled in several bucks to their position. Credit: Kathy Etling.

can't drive at night without seeing hordes in your headlight beams. Seeing so many deer boggles your mind as you recall hunts where, after days of futile waiting, you actually wondered if there were any deer left in your area.

Needless to say, with so many deer—and little hunting pressure, at least on well-managed ranches—the buck-to-doe ratio is right where it should be. Plenty of bucks are roaming the hills, ready to spar with willing contenders.

Experiencing rattling at this ranch was being exposed to a little bit of heaven. When I was there,

finding a good buck was no problem. I just waited as deer charged in nearly every time my guide took me out. I was able to pick and choose from among more than ten bucks. Finally, in the misty grey light right after dawn on the third day of our hunt, a buck I knew was far better than any I'd seen before suddenly materialized through the fog. I shot and the buck fell.

Bob had tagged out the first morning when his guide rattled and several bucks raced in to their positions. He wasn't going to shoot, or so he said, but when one fine buck almost leaped on top of him, his reflexes responded and he fired. Bob's buck grossed a little over 125 Boone and Crockett points, while mine scored right at 130.

When we hunted the Hill Country we stayed in a trailer and cooked our own food. The largest deer taken that year went a little over 140 Boone and Crockett points. Although there were plenty of deer, there was little chance of taking a real trophy. Other Hill Country ranches advertise larger bucks, but the chance of taking an animal that exceeds 160 Boone and Crockett points on most Hill Country spreads is probably remote. The more a hunt costs, however, the more likely you will be to take a high-scoring buck. Otherwise, to simply sample the best rattling of your life, book with an operation that advertises its services as such. The rut usually peaks in the Hill Country during the first two weeks of November. We were there the first week in December. Previous groups of hunters had had hard hunting. Rattling wasn't working well, and calling was tough. But our flight arrived with a cold front. The next morning when we went out hunting, that cold front must have inspired the ranch's whitetails to be footloose and fancy-free and to be dead set on racing in to the sounds of rattling horns. On this occasion, Bob Zaiglin told us we were out hunting at the best possible time.

Jerry Shively used M.A.D.'s Power Rattle® and the Grunt-Snort-Wheeze® to call this buck in for Kurt Kraft. Credit: Jerry Shively.

Montana's Western-Slope Conifer Forests

Think of Montana and what most people imagine is an immense state of snow-capped mountain peaks. While Montana is often thought of as a great destination for trophy mule deer, only recently has it come into its own as one of the country's premier hunting spots for taking buster

whitetails. White-tailed deer are so adaptable that they've moved into river bottoms and conifer forests all over the state. Believe me, little compares with a walk through forestland thick with Douglas firs that are so tall they almost block out the sun's rays. In these ancient northwestern rain forests, moss dangles eerily from the ends of tree branches, just as it does in a swamp. Tree limbs sometimes are woven so tightly together overhead you seem to be walking through a living tunnel. The forest's rugged, remote beauty and sweet conifer smell are reason enough to plan a visit. An even better reason, though, is to see the tremendous amount of big whitetail sign almost everywhere you look.

We hunted western Montana several times with the late Terry Kayser's outfit. Kayser, who was killed when he was thrown from his pickup truck while setting out deer stands, was a great whitetail guide. His operation has been taken over by his wife, Cheri DuBeau, who now operates out of Dodson, Montana. Cheri outfits and guides for whitetails and other critters on Montana's eastern plains. She calls her outfit Horizons West Outfitters.

Sparring circles are common place in Montana. So are huge rubs, room-sized scrapes, and heavily used deer trails. Easily accessed public land is plentiful. Local hunters rarely stay out all day, so if you find a good place to hunt, you'll generally have it to yourself. In some areas, mainly those close to the roads, locals simply may park their vehicles, walk through the area, and then

Easily accessed public hunting ground is plentiful in western Montana's conifer forests and so are whitetails. Credit: Kathy Etling.

I took this buck while on a rattling hunt to north western Montana's thick conifer forests. Credit: Bob Etling.

leave. If you can stay put, this extraneous activity doesn't seem to bother deer. I have noticed that Montana whitetails are more predictable—active—early and late in the day than deer I've hunted in other parts of the country.

The late Terry preferred to rattle and call from his location a top a slight knoll overlooking a recent clear-cut. Credit: Kathy Etling.

Both Bob and I took good bucks in the 125 to 135 Boone and Crockett class-while hunting western Montana near Noxon. Bob was being guided by Kayser when a big buck in the 150 to 160 Boone and Crockett class wandered by. From where Bob sat waiting in his tree stand, however, he wasn't able to get a clear shot at the buck. Kayser was rattling for Bob not far from where I was waiting when a dandy whitetail burst into the forest opening in front of me. I am not certain he was responding to the horns, but I wasn't about to give him a chance to race away to where Terry was rattling. I shot him and he dropped.

The next day, one of Kayser's guides rattled in a 160 Boone and Crockett class buck for another hunter. Although we were hunting during the peak of the rut, rattling was not yet producing fast and furious action. Temperatures were extremely frigid. On most days it would warm up to ten degrees below zero.

Kayser relied a great deal on his rattling skills. One of his favorite tactics was to skirt the edge of a recent clear-cut searching for fresh sign. We'd set up nearby, leaving an open area on our downwind side where deer would be able to dash out when lured by the sounds of Kayser's horns. Kayser always made certain that this down wind area was a place deer would naturally be drawn to. Several trails feeding into such an area were necessary for success. After we'd returned home, Kayser mailed us photos of the bucks his hunters had taken. Rattling always seemed to come into its own as soon as we boarded the plane for our return flight.

I wouldn't hesitate to return to Montana. Luckily, Jerry Shively outfits and hunts in an area not far from where we hunted with Kayser. Since Shively has a great reputation, he is the outfitter with whom I will book the next time I plan to hunt Montana's wild conifer forests.

Getting Started Rattling

KATHY ETLING

Does rattling sound like a hunting tactic you'd like to try, yet you're not quite sure then saw off its antlers? Perhaps you have a set of antlers from a deer you took last season then saw off its antlers? Perhaps you have a set of antlers from a deer you took last season or before. Or, perhaps you can prevail upon someone you know for his or her next set of antlers. Should you wait until spring when you can go hunting for a nice, fresh set of matched sheds? And what's wrong with synthetics, anyway? Do they work as well as the real McCoy? Do sheds work as well or sound as realistic as fresh antlers? What about rattling devices? Surely whitetails must suspect that any "rattling" created by store-bought devices is phony, right?

Through the years I've interviewed many whitetail experts for the express purpose of learning what each believed was the most foolproof way of rattling in whitetails. While each expert's methods are amazingly similar to those of the others, and while even their preferred rattling sequences bear more than a passing resemblance to those of the other experts, and while the parameters they look for when they are preparing to set up are not that much different, it's clear that each of our experts has definite opinions about what another hunter should do and use to create the most realistic-sounding mock buck battles possible.

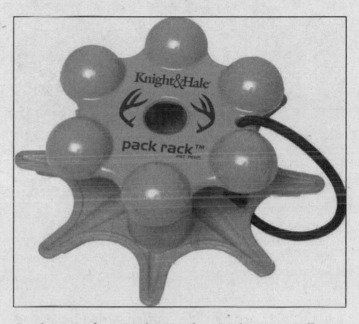

Synthetic Antlers. Credit: Knight & Hale Game Calls.

Synthetic, Real, or Something Else?

I've used both synthetic antlers and real antlers, and I honestly have never been able to tell much difference between the two. I've rattled in deer using both types. If I were asked to put my feelings about the two antler types into words, I suppose I would say that real antlers sound more solid when clashed together. The synthetics I used seemed to be slightly higher-pitched, and they seemed to reverberate a bit more. I can't truthfully say this reverberation is a negative, though. The sound from the synthetic

Although Bob Zaiglin prefers to use fresh sheds to rattle in bucks, he has done quite well with synthetics, too, as evidenced by the buck in this photo. Credit: Bob Zaiglin.

with a scent-free product to preserve that "just-off-the-buck" degree of freshness.

Bob Zaiglin uses a large set of real antlers for his rattling horns. Mickey Hellickson looks for the heaviest, freshest pair of shed antlers he can find. "I've been using some massive horns lately," Hellickson said. "I cut off the brow tines and then shaved the surrounding area smooth to the beam so they're easy to grip. A large set of horns produces the greatest volume. My study revealed that volume is more important than any other factor to rattling success. The higher the volume, the greater the distance over which it will be heard. The greater the distance, the more bucks that will hear it. And if more bucks hear your rattling, more bucks are bound to respond."

Proponents of using real antlers include other successful hunters, too, experts like Peter Fiduccia, Jay Cassell, and Jim Holdenried. "Using smaller antlers won't discourage smaller bucks from investigating," Fiduccia pointed out. "And

antlers might actually have carried farther because of it than the sound from my real rattling horns. Were I to go rattling at this very moment, whether I would grab the synthetics or authentics would be a moot point. In fact, I'm so impressed with a few of the rattling devices I've recently seen that I just might use them instead. But more about them later.

Some hunters swear that nothing sounds like a fresh set of rattling horns. But if you bring antlers inside at the end of each day and rarely expose them to the elements, even a twenty-year-old set will sound identical to a set removed from a buck's head today. To get that so-called "fresh" sound, some hunters soak their sheds in water, no matter how new they may be, for several hours. Others rub their sheds down with petroleum jelly to seal in freshness Still other experts prefer oiling or waxing their sheds

Although he usually prefers synthetics, Jerry Shively used real antlers to lure this fine Montana buck in for Mark Easterling. Credit: Jerry Shively.

According to Peter Fiduccia, not only will smaller antlers rattle in bucks of all sizes, they're easier to pack around. Credit: Fiduccia Enterprises.

Modify real antlers before using them to rattle by cutting off the ends of tines; otherwise you could be seriously injured—or worse—if you fell on them while walking or climbing into a stand. Credit: Kathy Etling.

smaller antlers are far easier to pack around." Cassell agrees. "I want to imitate the sound of smaller bucks fighting," he said. "By doing so, I hope to lure in a larger buck who's hoping to whip both their [smaller bucks'] butts."

Fiduccia noted that synthetic antlers usually don't have to be modified for safety's sake, but that if you don't modify real antlers you could be hurt in an accident while pulling them into your stand, climbing hills, or negotiating bluffs. "Always be cautious when using real antlers in a public hunting area," he warned. Fiduccia modified his set of smaller antlers by trimming off sharp tines and drilling a hole through each base where he threaded a lanyard.

"I use real antlers for the most part," said Jim Holdenried. "I prefer a set of sheds the would score

about 125 Pope and Young points. Smaller rattling horns don't do it for me, particularly not for more intense, 'hard' rattling sequences." Holdenried also removes sharp tines to keep them from cutting or jabbing his hands. "I've used a rattling bag, but I have better luck with real antlers," he concluded.

"I've used real antlers, synthetic antlers, and rattling bags," noted M.R. James. "I like actual antlers, real and synthetic, because of the sounds produced when I tickle the tines together or really grind the beams. Artificial antlers don't sound as true to me, but the deer don't seem to mind or notice. My

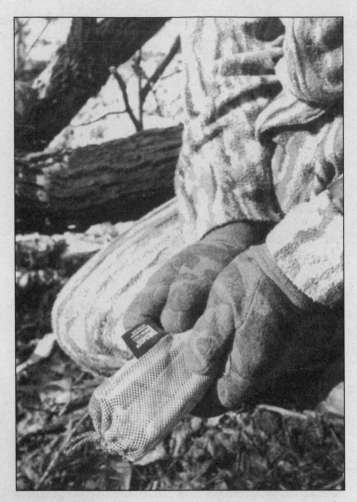

A nylon mesh rattle bag containing ceramic dowels is both easier and safer to carry than antlers and sounds authentic enough to fool rutting bucks. Credit: M.R. James.

favorite set of horns is a pair of sheds I found that score about 135 Pope and Young points."

For ease when packing into a hunting area and climbing into tree stands, James says it's hard to beat a rattle bag. "Rattle bags may have their drawbacks, but they're sure handy to tote," he said. "I prefer rattling bags full of ceramic dowels rather than wooden dowels. Ceramic just seems to work better, especially in wet weather when wood may swell and lose its crisp tones."

"I've heard it all, and the best sounds are produced by real antlers or good quality synthetics,"

said Gary Roberson of Burnham Brothers Game Calls in Menard, Texas.

Other Rattling "Tricks"

Somewhat in the same vein, M.R. James will sometimes tie a rope to his rattling horns, then tie the rope to a bush or tree below his stand. He then lowers the antlers on this "haul" line so that they are resting in the bush or next to the sapling. When he jerks on the line, the antlers thrash about in the brush where they might attract a nearby deer.

One thing all of these hunters have in common is a high degree of originality and an ability to take tricks they've learned about and make them their own. "Some hunters will fasten a string to a sapling, then pull on it from their stand, high above, to create the illusion of a buck rubbing the sapling," Peter Fiduccia said. Fiduccia sometimes fills a third of a plastic zipper lock bag with fish tank gravel. He places the gravel-laden bag inside another plastic bag. He then makes a small hole through each bag,

Mick Hellickson uses the largest set of real antlers he can find to produce the loud rattling that attracts big bucks like this one. Credit: Mickey Hellickson.

Rattling from Ground Blinds

The argument about whether tree stands or ground blinds are better continues to rage among rattling experts. "I prefer ground blinds," said Fiduccia. "Ground blinds work better for breaking up your profile or as something easy to hide behind. I've often made my ground blinds from stacks of cedar trees."

In agricultural areas, many hunters who rely on rattling report excellent success when set up behind a blind made of straw bales. The advantage here is that the blind is fairly stable, even during high winds, and it provides a great screen for hiding hunter movement. Being able to mask movement is vitally important to trophy bowhunters like Judy Kovar of Illinois.

Scouting for Sparring Circles

"What I'm looking for is an open spot that's surrounded by fairly heavy cover," said Jerry Shively. "The places that seem to work the best are those where I've watched bucks fighting over the years. Bucks seem to have very definite locales where they prefer to fight. You can identify one of these spots by the sparring circle evident on the ground. I've hunted this one piece of property for more than twenty years and I know all the bucks' favorite places to fight." As its name suggests, a sparring circle is a large, round area where you can tell animals were trampling the ground beneath their hooves. Grass may be flattened within this circle, or the earth may be mostly bare because bucks have fought there for many years. Brush and undergrowth may be battered and beaten, too. The ground may also reveal paw marks and antler gouges. The more such sign you discover in a particular location, the better your chances will be of rattling in a buck there.

A rattle bag can be rolled against a tree trunk—or your leg—to create the sound of sparring bucks with a minimum amount of movement, as Wilbur Primos demonstrates. Credit: M.R. James.

runs a long string through both, and attaches the bags to his ankle. In this manner he's able to rattle with his foot, with a minimum of movement, while he's waiting in his tree stand. As he rattles, he moves his foot back and forth to drag the bag over the undergrowth and forest litter beneath his stand. "This is just another way of setting the stage so that any buck listening will think a battle is going on," he said. "It provides a realistic sound, right down to the 'hooves' moving back and forth across the forest floor."

"I don't really return to certain rattling locations per se," Bob Zaiglin said. "But I get these vibrations about a spot. I know, everybody laughs, but as I'm walking through the brush I really start feeling like This is an area that I'd be in if I were a buck. Or, man, this looks really deery. Look at all those fresh scrapes. So, I move on to step two of my process: looking for a good place to station both my hunter and myself. I want to be in a spot where I can see in both directions. I really believe I rattle up more deer due to confidence than technique. I'm so confident when I think I've found a good spot that I'm almost positive that's why I've had such fantastic success." Zaiglin has rattled up whitetails everywhere he's hunted, even back home in Pennsylvania. In Texas, he's rattled up several hundred deer that have been taken by his hunters and hundreds more that his hunters have passed up.

One Rattler, Two hunters

Shively's favorite rattling tactic, when guiding hunters, is to position two hunters on stands two or three hundred yards apart. He then splits the distance between them and rattles. "My hunters usually see deer, but I won't," he said. "Since they're elevated they have a better view of the terrain. Since hundreds of yards separate them, one may see one buck while the other sees a different buck. I once had two hunters shoot at two different bucks at the same exact moment. None of us were aware of it until we got together afterward. 'I shot,' said the one. 'No, I shot,' said the other. My head started spinning, but then I found out they'd both scored on really nice whitetails."

Rattling from Tree Stands

If you decide to do your solo rattling from a tree stand, choose a tree with a trunk that is large

A tree with a thick trunk and plentiful foliage will break up your silhouette and prevent the deer from spotting you. Credit: Randy Templeton.

enough to hide you, should the need arise. "It's a good idea to always rattle from the side of the tree where you do not expect the buck to appear," Peter Fiduccia said. "Natural cover to break up your outline is a must. It's particularly helpful beneath your feet so that any deer looking upward will be unable to make out your human silhouette." Deer

A rattle bag can be rolled against a tree trunk—or your leg—to create the sound of sparring bucks with a minimum amount of movement, as Wilbur Primos demonstrates. Credit: M.R. James.

peering upward are a fact of life when rattling or calling emanates from the treetops rather than from down on the ground. You can sometimes mitigate that effect by rattling from the sides of steep hollows where the sound appears to be coming from farther up the hillside, even if you are in a tree stand. The risk in this maneuver is that a deer may come in higher up on the hillside, be on the same level as you, and be able to see you in the tree stand. "Another good ploy is to position yourself where you can whack your rattling horns against a leafy limb," Fiduccia said. "This simulates the sounds of a buck thrashing its rack in a bush or sapling. Don't be afraid to thwack the rattling horns against the tree's trunk, either. Doing so provides an even greater degree of realism."

"I find it hard to get deer to commit to coming in when I'm waiting in a tree stand in an area where deer can see quite well," Don Kisky said. "One of my favorite tricks is to make them think that the rattling is going on just over the hill. Whenever deer can see well, they become extremely cautious. That's why I like rattling from the edge of a bluff or creek where it's difficult for them to circle downwind of me."

Rattling Sequences

"I'll always make a snort-wheeze before I start rattling," Kisky continued. "If I see two bucks in the distance, I'll use the snort-wheeze, too. When I rattle, I really go at it. I think it's impossible to make too much noise when you rattle during the rut. Of course, when you're busy flailing around rattling, it's easy for a buck to spot you. That's one reason I keep my sequences loud, but short. My normal sequence lasts just ten seconds. If you rattle too long, bucks may sneak in and spot you and you'll never even know they were there." Kisky has used rattling to take many of his biggest deer. These include bucks

Don Kisky likes to play with a big buck's mind by making him think that the rattling—the "fight"—they hear is going on just over the hill. Credit: Don and Kandi Kisky.

that were gross-scored at 197, 181, 179, 177, 171, 167, and 161, among others. To say that Kisky knows what he's doing with a set of rattling horns in his hand would be a major understatement.

"I do all my hard rattling from mid- to late October," Jim Holdenried said. "Prime time for me is from the eighteenth to the thirty-first and perhaps during early November, particularly if the action is somewhat dead. Those are the days when you

Don Kisky keeps his rattling sequences loud but short to pull in trophy bucks like this to within bow range. Credit: Don and Kandy Kisky.

might not be ready and suddenly, here they come at a dead run!"

"One thing you have to know about antler-rattling is that it's as much about what you're feeling as anything else," added Bob Zaiglin. "Say a buck is two hundred yards away—or maybe you only think he is. If you have the feeling that you are close to the buck of a lifetime and you want to bring him in, try just tickling the antlers at first. This is a great tactic to use during the cold, early morning hours following a warm spell. Some people like to clash those antlers together as hard as they can, but I can't help but think that this type of noise might inhibit deer from coming in. It's only on the second or third time I grind those antlers together that I begin to get louder and enhance my sequence so that it appears to any buck that may be listening that the ground and the brush are being torn apart by those 'two battling whitetails.' And that's what I want him to think."

"I'll start rattling right before the rut begins, around the first of November," Jerry Shively said. "We'll start with some light rattling and some get-

Kandi Kisky has taken deer as large as some of husband Don's, including this massive 170+ whitetail shot with a muzzleloader. Credit: Don and Kandi Kisky.

acquainted grunts, nothing dominant or too loud. Our deer aren't yet fighting at this time. They aren't acting really aggressive. When you see them sparring, they're still just tickling their horns. I rattle just enough to work on their curiosity."

Shively doesn't get serious about his rattling and grunting until about a week before the rut starts on November 15. "You can make a tremendous amount of noise out there if you're trying to mimic two deer seriously going at it," he said. "There is no way a single hunter can make enough noise to accurately duplicate it."

M.R. James begins his rattling sequences with buck grunts, and then starts raking a tree trunk with his antlers. "I start off slow, as if the 'bucks' are merely sparring," he said. "I'll mesh the antlers for several periods of ten to fifteen seconds with soundless intervals between the sequences. I let the action build in intensity as the 'fight' progresses, with prolonged grinding of the beams and clicking of the tines, but with occasional pauses. I seldom rattle for more than 90 to 120 seconds per sequence. I conclude by 'tickling the tines' one final time, then finishing off with three or four aggressive buck grunts." As a bowhunter, James will seldom move on to a different stand site. Instead, he may rattle from the same stand site six to eight times during a four-hour period to attract any bucks that may be traveling through his hunting area.

"Do I vary my rattling sequences?" asked Brad Harris, rhetorically. "Yes, quite a bit. The way in which I vary my sequences intrigues hunters. I tell them that you have to get in tune with your surroundings. I rattle the way I feel, the way the weather makes me feel. On some days, it just seems like deer should be more responsive, so I'll rattle or call more often. On doldrum days, I'm more laid back, quieter, and I don't rattle as much."

One of Harris's typical rattling sequences will begin with one loud aggressive grunt in every direction. "That should get the buck's head up," Harris said. "He's now listening, so I pause a few seconds, then start rattling as though one buck has just confronted another, and then the battle begins. I rattle five to thirty seconds, just swiping the antlers together, and then I'll pause, listen, and wait, because you never know if a buck is just over the next ridge. I'll rattle, then pause, then rattle perhaps two times more while pausing and listening. I'll rattle, wait, and then maybe grunt. Even after I've quit rattling, I'll probably make a grunt every now and then in case the buck is coming but I'm unable to see him."

If it's windy, Harris will rattle loudly and more often. "You have to adjust to conditions," he said. "If I'm in an area where I'm able to see long distances, then I'll probably rattle less. Cold, clear conditions usually mean rattling will be more productive than on warm or hot days."

Peter Fiduccia explained every detail he puts into his rattling sequences. "First, I find a good spot where I can set up," he said "I'll start by dribbling some buck urine around the area. I then do my best to create the illusion I'm after. This means stomping my feet, stepping hard upon leaves and twigs, adding some aggressive grunts, hitting my horns against tree limbs, and then slamming the antlers against the ground or tree trunks. I'll do this for fifteen seconds, thirty seconds, forty-five seconds, or even an entire minute. I'll then pause to look and listen in all directions. You must stay alert. If you think it might work, shake a nearby sapling or stomp on the ground to entice any nearby whitetails into showing themselves."

Fiduccia then waits between fifteen and twenty minutes before rattling again. "The next time I'll wait thirty minutes," he said. "Some people move to a new area, but I prefer to stay put. Should a buck appear, try always to be positioned in a place where you're able to shake a sapling or grunt or do both. If you are unable to do this, then try to have a rattling buddy along who can. This simple motion or call may be the last nail in that buck's coffin. What you do is provide him with one final motive to rush in and see what's going on."

Fiduccia warns hunters who are new to the rattling game to remain at high alert for any sign of a nearby buck, including the sound of a snort or grunt, the slight movement of legs beneath nearby brush, sunlight glinting off an antler tine, a silhouette where you don't remember seeing one before. "Deer are shifty critters," he said. "Now you see them, now you don't."

The Best Times to Rattle?

Although all of our experts would rattle all day long, their consensus "best time" was early morning, particularly one that was frosty cold and windstill. Bob Zaiglin qualified his choice when he said, "I've rattled all day long, for many years. It doesn't matter where you might be rattling from—if it's not close to a deer you'd like to take, it will be for naught. Sunup is my favorite time to rattle, but you must be woods-wise enough to figure out where the buck you want is hiding, then decide how best to try to rattle him in. If you can get to within five hundred yards of where that is without disturbing him, your rattling and calling techniques will be perhaps 60 percent effective. If you can close that distance to two hundred yards, those techniques may increase in effectiveness to as much as 90 percent."

"I learned one time-management lesson the hard way," added M.R. James. "I owned this one place in the Indiana suburbs that had some great whitetail hunting. One morning I went in early and climbed up into my stand. It was still dark when I began rattling. I heard something, looked down, and saw a buck. It walked right under my stand. The only problem was it was still dark. I could see antlers, but it wasn't legal shooting time yet. I learned the hard way not to rattle too early or too late. It's difficult passing up a nice buck that you rattled in fair and square because you couldn't wait until it was time to shoot."

"Without a doubt, the first ten minutes of light and the last ten minutes are the very best times to rattle," said Don Kisky.

Jerry Shively reports having better rattling luck in the afternoons and evenings. Even so, he admitted, "There are days when I can't do anything wrong—but there are just as many days when I can't do anything right."

From Which Direction Will Bucks Come?

Mickey Hellickson's Texas research study confirmed that bucks are more likely to approach a rattler's position from the downwind side. Surprisingly, as he stated in the previous chapter, mature bucks were no more likely to approach from downwind than younger animals were. A few bucks from all age classes broke precedent to come in from directions other than downwind. "I've rattled bucks in from all directions," said Bob Zaiglin. "They don't always come in from downwind. What will happen, though, is that the buck will usually circumvent the rattler to come in from the downwind side. That's why rattling with a team works so well.

"Say you have a north wind," he said, to illustrate his point. "One person is in a stand in a mesquite tree that's south of where the other person is rattling from the ground. The person in the stand to the south of the rattler will always see far more deer than the one who is rattling."

"I've rarely had bucks come rushing in except in Texas," M.R. James said. "The bucks I rattle in in other places usually approach my position slowly, their ears back, hair standing up on the backs of their necks, walking stiff-legged, and posturing. I've watched plenty of these bucks raking trees or brush with their antlers as they came closer to my stand. I've arrowed several that swaggered in and stopped directly beneath my tree. I really believe deer can pinpoint the exact location of any 'buck fight' they hear. It's a big thrill for me to rattle or grunt a good buck close enough to shoot at with a bow."

To which, I'm sure, the rest of our experts would add a fervent "Amen."

When rattling or calling, stay alert to any buck that might walk in stiff-legged and posturing, just waiting to work over a sapling with its antlers. Credit: Bob Etling.

Rattling: What to Expect

KATHY ETLING

Okay, you're out in the field. You've started rattling. What should you expect to happen, and when?

To begin, remember that deer don't *only* vocalize. Nor do they merely tickle, mesh, or clash their antlers together in the sounds of battle, mock or authentic. Deer will also stomp their hooves to communicate with each other. Whether the stomping emanates from a doe that's trying to warn her youngsters or a buck reluctant to continue on the path it is taking, foot-stomping provides not only an aural warning via other deer's ears, but also a visual warning during periods of high winds. In the latter case, nearby deer may be able to see an agitated animal better than they can hear it.

Foot-stomping imparts a chemical message as well. A deer's hooves emit a pheromone—a chemical message—from the *interdigital gland*, a scent gland between the two parts of the deer's cloven hoof. A white-tail stomping on a trail, for example, is providing an olfactory warning to any deer that may follow that something wasn't quite right here. Whether it was the scent of a human hunter carried from afar or something along the trail that seemed out of place and, therefore, potentially dangerous, the interdigital gland does its work subtly and swiftly. Many hunters sweeten mock scrapes and mock rubs with commercial interdigital gland scent or with hooves frozen and preserved from previous seasons. Should a deer you decline to shoot discover your rattling setup and start stomping its foot because it suspects a human is nearby, your best recourse is to relocate. Any other deer that comes by will immediately be alert to the presence of danger. Move, but do so carefully. Don't stand up, believing that you haven't rattled in a buck, and then be startled to see a white tail bobbing off into the distance.

If an agitated buck races in looking for another buck, his pawing and stomping of the ground will not leave a negative olfactory warning for other deer. Although his hoof-stomping provides an auditory signal, if an olfactory threat or agonistic signal is

Jay Cassell with a buck he rattled out of some heavy mesquite brush on a ranch near San Antonio, Texas. Credit: Jay Cassell.

Create the total illusion when rattling from the ground by using your antlers to rake trees, leaves, and brush and to thump the ground like a buck's hooves. Credit: M.R. James

communicated as well, biologists, at least as far as I know, are unaware of it. Should a buck race in and stomp prior to a "fight" that never materializes—and you miss your chance to take him—no olfactory warning will be given unless the buck realizes that a human is there. If it fails to do so, you might even be able to rattle him in again. Should he run off unaware that a human was nearby, there's no reason for you to leave.

Moving your rattling location may work wonders, especially if there's a lot of great hunting ground and few other hunters, as in much of Texas and the West. Such a strategy may prove less lucrative in the East, Midwest, and South, where hunter densities are much higher. In states as scattered as Michigan, Missouri, Pennsylvania, and Georgia, staying in one place—even all day—is preferable unless you are hunting a large tract of

Avoid moving your rattling setup too frequently, because thick undergrowth can work to a whitetail's advantage and you might not see a deer approaching. Credit: Don and Kandi Kisky

private land with few other hunters. One reason to avoid moving your rattling setup too often is that thick undergrowth can work to a whitetail's advantage by camouflaging its presence until the last possible moment. If you move and reveal your position, you're aiding the whitetail's cause. Stay put. Let *him* make the mistakes.

For every buck that bursts onto the scene in response to your rattling sequences, probably four or five others choose to take a wait-and-see attitude and remain hidden. These deer may be subdominants, their native caution holding them back to see what will transpire next. Or perhaps a dominant buck is biding his time, waiting for the best moment to charge into view. It's always possible that no buck has heard your rattling, but a buck is heading your way as you prepare to give up for the day. Should you leave the stand and risk spooking a possibly responsive buck? Granted, there are no guarantees that this theoretical "buck" will ever make its appearance. But it might also be the buck you bag.

A Rattler's Most Important Quality

Should you decide to give calling, rattling, and decoying a go, you must also work on the one quality that will help you succeed more than any other when using these techniques: patience. The more you rattle from any given stand, the more likely a buck will eventually investigate. Perhaps his curiosity finally maxes out. Perhaps he just traveled into hearing range. Perhaps he's finally bred the doe he was following, and he's looking for another. When he hears the sound of antlers clashing, he might think the "fight" is being waged over another hot doe and come storming in. Or maybe you've finally agitated him beyond all reckoning and he stampedes in to find out what in tarnation is going on. In any event, patience is a crucial part of the art of deceiving whitetails.

Where to Rattle?

If conditions are right, whitetail bucks—unlike turkey gobblers—will come in to almost any location. Bucks responding to rattling will race up hills and down, may storm across creeks, and will

In most states, rattling from one place all day is preferable to moving, as archer Holly Fuller demonstrates. Credit: Holly Fuller.

Successful rattlers like Iowa's Don Kisky agree that the one quality that will most help you succeed is patience. Credit: Don and Kandi Kisky.

even race across bare fields, so great is their desire to view or participate in the "fight" now underway.

"I've experienced some of my best November rattling in eastern Colorado, along the Arkansas River," M.R. James said. "At this one ranch you could see deer at such a great distance you could actually watch as bucks ran across pastures or hopped fences to reach the rattling. That was some of the most exciting rattling I've ever experienced."

Don't be reluctant to set up anywhere you feel there's a halfway decent chance of rattling in a buck. Just be sure there is a good place for you to hide until you or your hunting partner is able to make the shot.

Early in the season, rattle in areas where you have seen bucks moving about in their bachelor groups. Look for core areas where early rubs have been made on small, insignificant saplings and where platter-sized scrapes roughly mark the animal's semi-territorial boundaries.

Bob Zaiglin team-rattles by setting up in a thicket that will disguise his movement well upwind of where his hunter is positioned in a tree stand. Credit: Bob Zaiglin.

As the primary rut approaches, remember that bucks will be traveling. They may return to core areas regularly, but they are more likely to check in only occasionally. No matter what size a buck's normal home range may be, once the rut commences, all home range bets are off. While some bucks may remain true to their annual home range, others may look for estrous does elsewhere. Some radio-collared bucks have been tracked thirty miles away from their annual home ranges, although this is the exception, not the rule. Don't waste your time targeting a particular buck that may no longer be in the area. Instead, set up close to an area frequented by one or more doe family groups. Whenever does are in estrus, bucks won't be far away.

Stay Alert

Once when M.R. James was hunting in Illinois he set up his stand in a point of woods where three trails converged. "I climbed into my stand and began rattling," he said. "Now, I could see for a long way in every direction. I mustn't have been looking in the right place, because all of a sudden I saw something move out of the corner of my eye. This buck must have run all the way across the corn field in front of me without me seeing it. When I did, the buck was only fifty yards away. He walked in, licking his nose, and I shot him."

Can You Rattle Too Much?

Too much of a good thing can sometimes work against you. That may be as true of rattling as it is of partaking of too many boilermakers on a Saturday night. Don Kisky believes too much rattling during past hunting seasons has worked against him more recently. "I've rattled so much in the past that I honestly think the five- and six-year-old bucks on

M.R. James's whitetail hunting tools: rattling antlers, a rattle bag, and deer calls. He won't leave home without 'em. Credit M.R. James.

our farm have become conditioned to the sound. Older bucks don't respond as readily as they once did. Yet I can hunt a farm where deer aren't used to the sound and rattle one right in. I've rattled in most of my larger bucks, but now, when they get to within seventy or eighty yards, I'll rely on grunting to bring them the rest of the way in. Three of my five largest whitetails have been grunted or rattled in."

Advanced Antler-Rattling

MICKEY HELLICKSON

Wham! I hit the shed antlers together as hard as I could and then quickly pulled them apart. Again, I slammed the antlers together with all of my force. This time I kept the antlers entwined and twisted the tines and beams against each other for several seconds. I repeated this several times. Two minutes into the rattling sequence I noticed movement and a flash of gray out in front of me.

The deer stopped out of sight behind a thick clump of mesquite trees. I continued to rattle, but tried to shield all of my movements from the deer. After several anxious moments, the deer stepped into view. His rack was huge. The main beams were over twenty inches apart and carried eleven typical points. The tines were also very tall and symmetrical. The only flaw, if there was one, was his lack of mass.

The buck had been sighted and photographed earlier, during the fall deer survey, by ranch owner Stuart Stedman. Based on these photographs and my sighting, we estimated the buck's gross Boone and Crockett Club score to be in the 160s. The only reason this buck was still alive was because of his age—he was only 4½ years old!

The buck, #180, was one of 130 bucks that we had captured and equipped with radio-transmitting collars since my research started in 1992. We captured this buck in October of that same year. At that time, Dr. Charles DeYoung of Texas A&M University-Kingsville had estimated the buck's age at 2½ years. DeYoung, who has aged literally thousands of live deer, aged every buck we captured each fall based on the amount of lower jaw tooth wear. In 1992, this buck's rack tallied up a gross Boone and Crockett score of 89, with seven points and no brow tines.

It was now mid-November. I was collecting data for an ongoing study on buck responses to antler-rattling. Dr. Larry Marchinton, from the University of Georgia, DeYoung, and I had been studying this aspect of breeding whitetail behavior

Wearing a camo headnet or face mask and gloves when you rattle will help hide your moving parts from sharp-eyed—and suspicious—bucks. Credit: M.R. James.

Mickey Hellickson's first antler-rattling study proved that the post-rut and the pre-rut periods were the best times to rattle in mature, trophy-caliber bucks. Credit: Mickey Hellickson.

for three years. This project would satisfy part of my doctoral requirements at the University of Georgia.

The first part of this study was conducted at the Rob and Bessie Welder Wildlife Refuge, north of Sinton, Texas. Our primary goal was to determine which type of rattling sequence attracted the highest number of bucks. The results of this three-year study were reported in an issue of The *Journal of the Texas Trophy Hunters*.

Recap of Earlier Results

To refresh your memory from Chapter 13, we tested four rattling sequences on whitetails. These sequences varied by length as well as rattling volume. We rattled a total of 171 times during the three periods of the whitetail breeding season. Our rattling attracted a total of 111 bucks. We found that loud rattling attracted nearly three times as many bucks as quiet rattling, and that the length of the rattling sequence was not important. We discovered that the post-rut and pre-rut periods were the best times to rattle in mature, trophy-caliber bucks. The rut's peak was tops if the objective was to rattle in

large numbers of bucks. Rattling sessions that took place between 7:30 and 10:30 am attracted more bucks than sessions conducted either at midday or in the afternoon. Cloudy days with little wind and mild temperatures represented the most productive weather conditions for rattling.

A Second Antler-Rattling Study

The goal of this, the second part of our antler-rattling study, would be to rattle to specific radio-collared bucks, and then measure each animal's responses. Each of the 130 collared bucks was outfitted with a transmitter attached to a neck collar that produced a unique radio signal. We tracked each buck using telemetry for an entire year. We located each buck's position a minimum of one or two times each day.

To track the bucks, we used a radio receiver connected to a large antenna. We dialed the frequency of the buck we wished to locate into the receiver and then drove the ranch roads, stopping every quarter mile to search for the animal. At each stop, the antenna would be swung 360 degrees in an

Hellickson's study also revealed that cloudy days with little wind and mild temperatures were the most productive when rattling for whitetails. Credit: Mickey Hellickson.

attempt to detect the buck's signal. Once we picked up the correct signal, we determined the direction from which the signal was strongest. A compass was used to plot a bearing in that direction. We then stopped two more times at locations farther down the road, where we repeated the process. When we had three bearings to use for triangulation, we drew each on a map. The intersection of these three lines represented the buck's approximate location.

Forty-three of the 130 bucks that we had captured and radio-collared had been equipped with special activity-sensing transmitters. These transmitters told us whether each buck was bedded or active whenever we located him, even though we were usually not able to see him. Each buck's collar produced a radio signal at a rate of one pulse per second if the buck was not moving and the collar around its neck was stationary. Whenever the buck moved, the collar would also move, which would increase the radio signal to two or more pulses per second. Therefore, whenever we located one of these bucks, we could tell if he was not moving and bedded, or active, simply by the radio pulse rate.

One day I used radiotelemetry to map Buck #180's position. On this particular occasion I drove

downwind of the buck and parked the truck. I eased in toward him quietly until I believed I'd closed the gap between us to no more than two to three hundred yards. At that point, I turned on the receiver and zeroed it in on the buck. In this manner I was able to detect his responses as I rattled to him by the pulse rate of his signal. I started the rattling sequence related at the beginning of this article.

Buck #180's radio signal became active almost immediately. As I continued to rattle, the pulse rate quickened even more, while the signal became louder. Based on this information, I knew not only that the buck was active, but that he was moving toward me. One minute into the sequence the signal had become so loud that I knew the buck would appear at any moment!

The buck stepped into the opening and almost immediately turned and disappeared back into the brush. I gathered up the telemetry equipment and returned to the truck. After I'd reached the truck, I waited thirty minutes and relocated the buck with three new bearings. I was thus able to determine how far and in what direction he had traveled after responding to my rattling.

Through the use of this cutting-edge technology, we were able to measure the individual responses of many whitetail bucks both during and after we rattled to them. We could tell whether or not each buck responded to our rattling, even if the animal did not move close enough for us to see him. Finally, rattling response rates were determined based on the gross Boone and Crockett scores of each buck as well as its age, which had been determined by patterns of tooth wear.

The Results

The results of the second part of our study were extremely interesting. With research assistants Fred

Steubing and Justin McCoy aiding us, each autumn from 1994 to 1996 we located the same eighteen bucks. We'd previously collared them with the activity-sensing radio transmitters described above. During this phase of the study we located each buck, walked quietly to within two or three hundred yards of him, then created a long, loud rattling sequence. In all, we rattled 33 times near these 18 bucks. Five of the bucks were located and rattled to during the pre-rut period, 14 during the rut's peak, and 14 others during the post-rut.

During 24 of the 33 sessions (73 percent), bucks responded by becoming active and moving closer to the source of the rattling. In other words, *nearly three out every four bucks responded to rattling if they were upwind and within hearing range.* I doubt whether most hunters could have predicted that bucks would respond at such an incredible rate. Before I conducted this study, I personally believed that fewer than 25 percent of the bucks within hearing range would respond to our rattling.

During our 33 rattling sessions, the horn rattler succeeded only 11 times in spotting the collared buck that was the object of our rattling. Rattling during this second study was performed by one person situated at ground level. We realize that not having a second observer nearby in a 30-foot-tall tower significantly reduced the number of bucks sighted. And yet the 33 percent sighting rate during the second part of the study compared favorably with results from our first Welder Refuge study. During that study, the person rattling from the ground spotted only 48 of the 111 bucks (43 percent) seen by the observer in the tower.

This illustrates how critical it is for a hunter to be waiting in an elevated position.

Rattling with a partner is probably the most efficient way to consistently see and take whitetail bucks. While the shooter climbs into a tripod or some other type of elevated stand, another person should rattle from the ground. Stand sites should be selected upwind of open areas to even further increase the number of bucks seen, since the majority of bucks respond from downwind.

Fewer bucks responded to rattling during the pre-rut than during the rut's peak and post-rut periods. During the pre-rut, 2 of 5 (40 percent) rattling sessions culminated in the buck becoming active and moving closer to the rattling. During the rut's peak, 11 of 14 (79 percent) bucks became active and moved closer, while 11 of 14 bucks (79 percent) became active and moved closer during the post-rut period. The rut's peak response rate was slightly lower than what had been observed during the study's initial Welder Refuge phase, while the response rate during the post-rut period was higher.

Buck response rates were highest during morning rattling sessions. Midday and afternoon sessions elicited identical response rates that were

During thirty-three research study sessions. the horn rattler spotted the buck targeted by the rattling only eleven times. Hence the need for a rattling team.
Credit: Mickey Hellickson.

When this old Montana buck responded to rattling during the rut period, M.R. James arrowed him at fifteen yards. Credit: M.R. James.

slightly lower than those registered after morning sessions. Eight radio-collared bucks responded to 9 morning rattling sessions (89 percent response rate). Six bucks responded to the 9 midday sessions (67 percent), while 10 bucks responded to 15 afternoon sessions (67 percent response rate). Midday buck response rates during this second phase of the study were higher than those attained during the study's first phase at Welder Refuge.

During nine sessions, bucks either did not respond at all or they became active but moved away from the person rattling. The average age of bucks that responded to our rattling was 5.8 years, while the average for bucks that did not respond was 7.4 years. This seems to indicate that older bucks may be less susceptible to antler-rattling.

Thirty minutes after responding to the rattling, a buck would move an average of almost a third of a mile. Two bucks traveled nearly three quarters of a mile. Two other bucks moved very

little. We were able to relocate them in their original positions. After responding to our rattling, most of the bucks (73 percent) moved to an area upwind of where they had been originally, even though we had rattled from a downwind location. In other words, a buck typically first moved downwind toward the rattling. After responding in this manner, each buck then usually moved back upwind beyond the place where we'd originally located him. Buck movements away from our rattling site were highest during the post-rut and lowest during the pre-rut periods.

We rattled more than once to 11 bucks to determine if bucks learned to avoid rattling. In every case but four, bucks responded during either the second, third, or fourth rattling session in the same way that they had responded during the first. The four exceptions failed to respond during the initial rattling session, but responded during the second. We rattled to Buck #1940, a 6.5-yearoldduring the

M.R. James rattled in this rutting buck less than 150 yards from his Montana home. Credit: M.R. James.

study's first year, four times. Each time he responded by becoming active and moving closer. Our results seem to indicate that bucks will continue to respond in a positive manner to rattling, even if they have already responded to a previous rattling session.

When the data were analyzed based upon each buck's known gross Boone and Crockett score, the results were surprising. Most hunters probably believe that trophy bucks are less likely than other bucks to respond to rattling. In this study, we found that the opposite was true. The bucks were separated into two groups. One group, which we called the "cull" group, included every buck with antlers that scored less than 130 Boone and Crockett points. All bucks with gross antler scores that exceeded 130 Boone and Crockett points were placed in the "trophy" group. Sixty-seven percent of the trophy bucks responded to our rattling compared to only 50 percent of the cull bucks. In addition, bucks in the cull group moved, on average, nearly two and one-half times farther between pre- and post-rattling locations than did those bucks in the trophy group.

Our Results Should Improve Hunting Success

Our hope is that hunters will use our research results to increase their chances of success during upcoming seasons. Antler rattling is perhaps the most exciting deer hunting technique there is. Little compares to the sight of a mature buck with an immense rack rushing into view in response to rattling—that much we know.

We thank the many individuals who assisted with our antler rattling and data collection. Rob, Fred, Bronson, Brent, Don, Justin, Scott, George, and William happily volunteered their time to work on this project. We also owe a debt of gratitude to the Rob and Bessie Welder Wildlife Foundation and its staff, the Neva and Wesley West Foundation and ranch owner Stuart Stedman, the University of Georgia, Texas A&M University-Kingsville, and the Caesar Kleberg Wildlife Research Institute for financial support of this research. See results on the following page.

Table 1. Radio-collared buck response rates to antler-rattling by time of day and period of the breeding season (number in parentheses is number of bucks that responded divided by the number of bucks that were tested).

Period Of Breeding Season	Number Of Bucks Tested	Time Of Day			
		0730–1030	1030–1330	1330–1630	TOTAL
Pre-rut	5	No Sessions Performed	50% (1/2)	33% (1/3)	40% (2/5)
Rut peak	14	100% (5/5)	67% (2/3)	67% (4/6)	79% (11/14)
Post-rut	14	75% (3/4)	75% (3/4)	83% (5/6)	79% (11/14)
Total	33	89% (8/9)	67% (6/9)	67% (1OT5)	73% (24/33)

Table 2. Age and type of response (Y = yes, buck did respond; N = no, buck did not respond) of eleven radio-collared bucks that were rattled to on more than one occasion.

Buck Identification Number	Age	Rattling Session			
		1	2	3	4
180	4.5	Y	Y		
602	4.5	N	Y		
1540	4.5	N	Y	Y	
1721	4.5	Y	Y		
1300	5.5	Y	Y		
1462	5.5	N	Y		
924	6.5	Y	Y		
1940	6.5	Y	Y	Y	Y
1326	7.5	Y	Y		
980	9.5	N	N		
1561	9.5	N	Y		

The Moon Is Unique and Influential

JEFF MURRAY

Since the dawning of civilization, the Moon has fired man's imagination and challenged his intellect, spawning the extremes of superstition and analytical thought. The annals of Sumerian priests, who charted the Moon's progress in the sky more than 4,000 years ago from their towering ziggurats, represent both extremes. Cuneiform tablets indicate that Mesopotamian sky gazers kept such accurate lunar calendars that they could predict lunar eclipses... yet they worshipped the Moon by rendering premonitions from its ever-changing faces.

In stark contrast, the Scriptures mention the Moon 61 times, proclaiming a beneficial relationship between it and mankind. For example, Deuteronomy 33:17 speaks of "precious things" brought forth by the Moon; Psalm 104:19 and Jeremiah 31:35 reveal a loving God appointing the Moon for seasons and as a guiding light at nighttime; Psalm 121:6 encourages man not to be afraid of the sun by day nor the Moon by night.

Even today the Moon's mesmerizing countenance has a hold on humanity. For example, people in Moslem countries still measure the year by the Moon's cycles, similar to American Indian culture. And in spite of this present age of hybridization and genetic engineering, savvy gardeners religiously consult planting tables updated annually in the *Old Farmer's Almanac*. At the other end of the spectrum are moviegoers who treat themselves to Hollywood's latest version of Bram Stoker's classic, *Dracula*. Perhaps in between are the millions of discriminating anglers who plan fishing trips around favorable Moon periods.

So, like it or not, we're hopelessly hooked on our most dominant companion in the night sky. Moon madness is no less a part of our culture than baseball, bubble gum and blue jeans. But are we

flirting with folklore or fact when we seek the Moon's advice on earthly matters? It depends. In some cases, ignorant superstition overshadows common sense, as evidenced by ancient Romans worshipping their Moon goddess, Diana (interestingly, the goddess of the hunt as well as guardian of wild beasts). But just as often, ageless empirical wisdom can be traced to the complex but predictable lunar cycle. Although the final issue may never be resolved in the minds of incurable skeptics, a startling record of scientific inquiries awaits open-minded truth-seekers. If that includes you, and it obviously does, read on.

Lunacy—From Pearls to Man

We begin our exploration with pearls of lunar wisdom. Oysters are wellknown to be wired to the Moon as much as any poet, lover or farmer, but is it because of tides, or unseen forces creating the tides? Dr. Frank Brown decided to find out. The pioneering biologist relocated a study group of oysters from a Connecticut seashore to a laboratory near Chicago. After placing the oysters in trays, enough salt water was added to cover their shells. Light and temperature were held constant. During the first two weeks, each oyster continued to open its shell, feeding according to the tides at its former seashore home site. But by the end of the second week, every oyster had changed its "cycle" to feed as the Moon peaked at its highest point over their new location.

Research from California and Texas proves that the lunar cycle can help predict bollworm outbreaks. Dr. Clyde Sartor, an agri-science consultant, helps clients fend off cotton pest infestations—before they get out of hand—with the findings of colleague Dr. Stan Nemec. His dissertation "Influence of Lunar Phases On Generation and Population Cycles of the Bollworm" explains that New Moon periods are bad news for cotton, tobacco, cabbage and beet growers:

egg deposition begins to pick up about three days following a Full Moon, peaking around the New Moon.

As an example, bollworms typically don't threaten San Joaquin Valley cotton fields until late July. But during one research year, Dr. Louis Falcon, an insect pathologist at the Berkeley campus, noticed egg populations escalating shortly after the Full Moon of July 26 and peaking near the New Moons of August 7 and again September 9.

We must include birds in our discussion. Recent investigations at Cornell University show that homing pigeons determine direction by observing the position of the sun and Moon in relation to the birds' internal calendars and clocks. How do the pigeons find their way in cloudy weather? It was discovered using electromagnets that they couldn't navigate unless the sun was out. This sensitivity to magnetic fields probably comes from magnetic iron oxide that has been discovered in the tissues of the heads of the birds. Which shouldn't come as a surprise, given the Moon's influence on ocean tides.

The lesser whitethroated warbler is another example of a bird-brained organism functioning just fine in its environment, thanks to benevolent solar/lunar forces. This migrating songbird summers in Germany and winters near the headwaters of the Nile River, in Africa. Amazingly, its internal navigation system allows the vacationing warbler to find its parents thousands of miles away across unfamiliar land and sea—the parent birds take off for Africa ahead of their young brood, leaving the offspring to fend for themselves on a totally unguided trip! Human behavior doesn't seem to be exempt from lunar influences. Consider studies conducted by psychologists Arnold Leiber and Carolyn Sherin, who researched 4,000 homicides occurring between 1956 and 1970 in Miami and Cleveland. Leiber wrote," The results were astounding. . . . murders become more frequent with the increase in the Moon's gravitational force." Interestingly, homicides peaked during Full Moons and again after a New Moon. Leiber theorized that hormonal activity in the brain is affected by solar and lunar gravitational forces——just as ocean tides are caused by the Moon, people are subject to biological tides that can be set on edge by the Moon. "These tides do not cause strange behavior," Leiber conceded. "They only make it more likely to happen."

Skeptics like astronomer Nicholas Sanduleak and psychologist Alex Pokorny disagreed with Leiber, stating that insufficient data led to generalities that, in turn, lead to self-fulfilling prophecies. A leading contemporary psychologist told me (confidentially) that the "Moon debate is on a par with Friday the 13th." However, police reports—generally more copious during certain lunar phases—seem to contradict this point of view. Toss in the records from hospital emergency rooms and observations from establishments that serve alcoholic beverages, and you have to wonder. As the manager of a popular restaurant in a large Southern city recently remarked, "You can just about tell what the Moon phase is by the activity in the cocktail lounge. A full house is bedlam during a Full Moon."

The latest research on "earth tides" is equally compelling. We've long known that the ebb and flow of ocean tides is caused by the Moon. I got a graphic illustration of the Moon's power when I hunted moose along the Alaska coast near Cordova recently. Each morning I had to time my route according to low tides, and I had to return on time to avoid being stranded by a rising Pacific Ocean. Just as Earth's oceans are like clay in the "hands of the Moon," so is our planet's landscape. Thanks to satellite-assisted photography, we now know that the Earth's crust shifts a foot or more when the Moon's electromagnetic force peaks during key lunar

periods. Perhaps this force, rather than the Moon's gravitational influence, is a better explanation for human behavior during Full and New Moons. (We're comprised of 80 percent water, after all, in which iron atoms are abundant).

As for fish, the late John Alden Knight founded a fraternity of loyal "Moon anglers" with his Solunar Tables, which are presently published bi-monthly within the pages of the nation's largest-circulation outdoor publication, *Field & Stream*. Not to be outdone, *Outdoor Life* occasionally prints Maori fishing charts; Bassmasters has recently added Rick Taylor's Astro-Tracker; *Game & Fish* publications showcase Dan Barnett's tables; *North American Hunter* recently signed on with Vektor Game Activity Tables... and so it goes.

Mounting evidence suggests that anglers might want to check into lunar tables if they haven't already done so. My friend Kurt Beckstrom, senior editor with *North American Fisherman,* where my fishing column appears in each issue, discovered that approximately 70 percent of all world-record fish were caught at times "when the Moon was exerting a significant influence." Ralph Manns, a respected investigative writer/angler, was recently commissioned by the *In-Fisherman* group, an esteemed team of research-oriented anglers for which I served as field editor, to find out once and for all if the Moon's influence is fact or fiction. After an exhaustive literature search, Manns concluded that there is indeed a lunar/fish connection, provided environmental factors do not intervene.

So we know the Moon influences the physical Earth and some of its inhabitants. Does this include deer? If so, how does it impact deer hunting? Do you have an open mind? If so, you're about to discover that the "lunar connection" is the latest breakthrough in deer and big-game hunting. Join the many astute hunters who have learned to use the Moon to hunt smarter in spite of what naysayers claim. But the intellectual foundation of unbelievers is eroding like a California mud bank. As you're about to discover, even the academic world is catching up with empirical observation.

A Lunar Deer Cycle?

Research biologists have long studied the "lunar effect." Until recently, however, conclusive evidence on a significant deer/Moon relationship failed to materialize. A major constraint was the lack of deer sightings for a statistically valid study. Before the advent of high-tech computerized radio tracking, the job was cost-prohibitive in terms of both dollars and man-hours. For example retired University of Georgia professor R. Larry Marchinton was forced to shift his focus from Moon-related study because isolating the Moon's influence was a time-consuming, tedious chore.

Another obstacle, I believe, is that investigators focused on the wrong variable—the phases of the Moon. No wonder Al Hofacker, then-editor of *Deer & Deer Hunting* magazine, drew a blank when he tried correlating the four Moon phases with a 1981 survey in which 7,148 deer were sighted during 13,517 hunter-hours on stand.

But eventually pieces of the lunar puzzle began falling into place. The first major clue involved a study of 25 radio-collared trophy bucks monitored from 1985 through 1987 in South Texas. Headed by Texas Tech University biologist Steve Demarais and whitetail management consultant Bob Zaiglin, the study yielded results that broke new ground in many respects. But you have to dig beneath the surface to mine Moon gold.

The pair's extensive background enabled them to interpret and express their data in hunter-friendly terms, first published in the September 1991 issue of *Buckmasters*. "Radio-tracking the bucks was actually a sidelight of our main duty of deer management on the Harrison holdings [107,000-acre Piloncillo Ranch," Zaiglin told me. "Still, we managed to cull a lot of data that can help hunters [better understand the] Moon."

Of the many insights gleaned from tracking reclusive, mysterious trophy whitetails, one particularly stands out. It was expressed in Zaiglin's revelation involving big-buck activity at dawn and dusk:"[It] most closely approached the typical [low light] pattern when there was a Quarter to three Quarter Moon. Interestingly, the Moonless and Full Moon phases seemed to "break this pattern down." In other words, something about Quarter-Moon phases increase buck movements during the traditional hunting hours around sunrise and sunset. And that something was notably absent during Full and New Moon when the researchers recorded few bucks up and about apart from limited midday activity and sporadic middle-of-the-night excursions.

The key variable couldn't be light (or darkness). It wasn't changing atmospheric conditions, either. The only viable alternative remaining was Moon position: Quarter-Moons peak in the sky during low-light periods of sunrise and again at sunset. Coincidentally, bucks use the reduced light as cover and are more comfortable with their surroundings at that "Moon time."

A landmark study all but confirms the Moon position theory. One of the most comprehensive telemetry studies ever conducted (assisted by computerized activity collars and continuous monitoring receivers) was completed under the direction of Dr. James C. Kroll, with the School of Forestry at Stephen Austin State University at Nacogdoches, Texas. The respected whitetail

Note the funny gizmo around this buck's neck; it enabled researchers to put the first pieces of the lunar puzzle together.

researcher recorded thousands of movements from two dozen mature buck and hundreds of does in Louisiana. His findings substantiated the fact that deers are "cued to the position of the Moon." When Dr. Kroll decides to release the full details, they're sure to be illuminating.

When I recently asked Dr. Kroll if the Moon's influence is due to gravitational or electromagnetic forces or some sort of internal clock triggering deer, he replied, "Yes, there's a built-in mechanism, as with many other animals, that allows [deer] to cue on the position of the Moon. We definitely see an increase in deer activity when the Moon is directly overhead and occasionally at other times. We're trying to find

out why, and I'm forced to rethink earlier biases. The Moon is a significant factor [in hunting], almost as much as the weather."

Dr. Kroll's observation on Moon position may be hot news in whitetail academia, but it's old hat to a number of sage hunters, guides and outfitters I've talked to over the years. Take Bill Lankinen, an Ontario logger who is a very successful big-game hunter. Lankinen times his efforts to coincide with a specific lunar period. "It just won't work that well at other times," he says. "The Moon's the key." Keep in mind that Bill has killed more than 30 bucks and 65 moose with this system.

Another tracking expert, Minnesota's Noble Carlson, uses the Moon to predict how close deer will be to bedding areas during a given outing. Carlson is the best deep-woods hunter I've ever met, having killed more than 100 bucks, all but a handful by tracking.

Larry Weishuhn is a former state biologist in Texas and a popular lecturer and consultant who is unusually successful with whitetails mainly because he hunts with the Moon in mind. In 1994, Weishuhn killed eight bucks that scored between 130 and 170 Boone & Crockett points.

Ontario woodsman Bill Lanikenen uses a morning Moon to track trophy whitetails in the "bush." It works on Boone and Crockett bucks!

Minnesota Moon hunter Noble Carlson needs a skidder to haul this monster buck out of the back woods.

Another believer is Hayward Simmons, who manages the Cedar Knoll Club near Allendale, South Carolina. Simmons has hunted this area since the 1960s and farmed it since 1977. An observant hunter, Simmons noticed deer enter ing fields at certain periods on some days, but not showing up until after dark on others. He began comparing deer sightings with various Moon charts and, sure enough, a correlation unfolded. "One thing led to another," he said. "I kept notes on when deer were harvested in the community, and plotted Moon schedules on the calendar. Then I came up with a glaring statistic: 70 percent of antlered deer were harvested during a two-week lunar period; 37 percent were taken the week before the Full Moon, 33 percent the week following it. Moreover, two-thirds of the bucks were killed in the afternoons." No wonder Simmons hunts religiously by the Moon.

Many Western outfitters keep a close watch on the Moon when guiding clients. Stan Graf of Desert Outfitters specializes in Coues deer in Arizona, and he correlates "Moon times" with Moon phases. So does Colorado elk outfitter Bill Jackson. The list of Moon hunters grows each season. What you're about to learn is no longer a guarded secret: Hunting by the Moon, not in spite of it, pays!

As the Moon Turns

A basic understanding of the Moon is necessary to help translate its mysterious pull into practical hunting terms. The Moon actually functions with the Earth as a double planet, rather than a distant satellite; an accurate physical representation of the pair would be a basketball next to a tennis ball (the Earth's diameter is about 8,000 miles, the Moon's 2,160 miles). This size comparison is unique in our solar system—the rest of the planets' moons are

The Moon's elliptical orbit complicates matters.

proportionally smaller, and therefore exert minimal influence on the mother planets. Factor in the Moon's relatively close proximity—a mere 30 Earth diameters away—and it's no wonder we feel its effects on this planet.

That the Moon is perplexing and often paradoxical is an understatement. The Moon:

- Actually travels from west to east in its orbit around the Earth, yet appears to travel from east to west in the night sky.
- Goes through phases that require mental gymnastics to keep straight; for example, a New Moon isn't visible, and a Quarter-Moon is actually half-full.
- Completes one rotation on its axis in the same time it takes to orbit the Earth (known as synchronous rotation). This is why it keeps the same "face" toward the Earth at all times.

LUNATION

New Moon is 0 days old

Quarter Moon is
7.4 days old

Full Moon is 14.8 days old

Last Quarter Moon
Is 22.1 days old

29.5 days later

Beginning of
lunar month
(invisible to
Earth)
0

New
Moon

Quarter
Moon   7.4

Full
Moon   14.0

Last
Quarter
Moon   22.1

New
Moon   29.5
Completion of
lunar month

Understanding the faces of the Moon It takes 29.5 days for the Moon to complete a synodic month (lunation), going from New Moon. A numbering system was introduced on January 17, 1923, and it serves as a handy reference for predicting the "age" of a given lunation: A New Moon is 0 days old; Quarter Moon, 7.4 days old; Full Moon 14.8 days; Last Quarter, 22.1 days; and so on.

- Completes one revolution (around the Earth) in 29 days, 12 hours, 44 minutes and 2.8 seconds, but actually returns to its original position opposite the Earth in 27.3 days.

- Maintains an elliptical (oval-shaped) orbit that varies in distance to the Earth from 225,742 miles to 251,968 miles (238,856 is average).

- Creates tidal friction on the Earth that slows our planet's axial rotation .002 second, thereby lengthening the day that much every century.

- Has a day that differs from a 24-hour Earth day, instead averaging 24 hours, 50 minutes.

- Rises and sets at different times each day—every 24 hours, while the Earth has turned on its axis, the Moon has moved about 12 degrees eastward in its orbit, causing it to rise an average of 51 minutes later each day.

On top of all this, the Moon's height above the horizon varies from season to season. For example, in early spring, the First-Quarter Moon is highest, Last-Quarter is lowest; New and Full Moons are about equal. This changes substantially in the fall: In September, Last-Quarter is highest, First Quarter is lowest, and a New and Full Moon coincide with the sun's midday high-point. In December, the Full Moon is highest, New Moon is lowest and the two Quarters are in-between. So when we use terms like "directly overhead or underfoot," we really mean "as high [or low] as the Moon gets above [and below] the Earth."

Consider the Full Moon/New Moon controversy in light of the above. Whereas some hunters swear by the New Moon and swear at the Full Moon, others do the opposite. Because we live in an age when doctors don't make house calls, we should keep up with the times and seek the truth about these particular phases.

As you can see, an explicit description of the Moon's motion is quite an astronomical feat. No wonder the Moon's complicated personality has helped keep its secrets under lock for so long. But a well-designed "Moon guide" can easily change that.

Zoned Out

JEFF MURRAY

When Native Americans kept track of seasons, many Moons ago, they didn't need computer-generated astrological tables. Time was as endless as game was abundant. Today's hunters, on the other hand, must budget their time as conscientiously as their money. To avoid the painfully familiar "you should have been here last week" syndrome, contemporary hunters need to know the Moon's daily positions in the sky (ideally expressed in hours and minutes, rather than astronomical coordinates). Keeping up with the times is the cornerstone of planning a successful hunt.

Moon Times—The Right Time

More than any other lunar event, the Moon peaking in its daily orbit fore-tells deer movement patterns. As Dr. Kroll pointed out in the October 1994 issue of *Outdoor Life*, "Hunting factors are really in your favor when the Moon is straight overhead."

What about Moon phases? Well, it's time to phase them out. Whereas they serve as a general guide for tracing the Moon's ever-changing arc in the sky, hunters really need a handy reference tool to track the Moon accurately. The chief advantage of a "Moon guide" is for trip planning. I and many of my acquaintances have successfully mapped out hunts months, even years, in advance by taking advantage of favorable lunar periods and avoiding more difficult ones.

The first thing to keep in mind is that not all lunar charts are created equal. Some are cumbersome to read (I lost the directions for a particular model and couldn't remember how to interpret the information). Others add spurious information that may or may not affect fish but doesn't apply to deer and big game. (I'm not interested, for example, in the Moon's right or left-angle position to the Earth, nor am I concerned about after-dark Moon times when I can't hunt.) Still other char are too general for orchestrating daily game plans for whitetails: Instead of listing exactly when the

Smart hunters know that moon phases affect deer behavior.

Superior Transit
(Moon overhead)

Your position
on the Earth

Inferior Transit
(Moon underfoot)

When the Moon peaks at its superior transit most directly overhead, it exerts its maximum influence upon the Earth's inhabitants; a similar effect occurs about 12 hours and 25 minutes later, when the Moon swings underfoot to its inferior transit. These positions are typically expressed in astronomical coordinates that can be converted into times of the day.

Moon peaks for the central meridian of a given time zone, a ½ to three-hour period is typically listed.

Until the advent of the Deer Hunters' Moon Guide™ finding a hunting table with specific Moon times was next to impossible. The Moon Guide™ predict to the minute when the Moon peaks over heard or underfoot for the middle of the Central Standard Time Zone. This means the times are accurate for the middle of all other time zones as well. (Incidentally, hunters located new time zone boundaries will want to fine-tune the Guide. Check local hunting regulations listing sunrise and sunset times. Or simply add or minute for each 12 miles traveled west and sub tract one minute for each 12 miles traveled eas ward of your Time Zone's central meridian. For example, if the Moon peaks over your deer stand at 8 a.m., it wouldn't peak over your buddy stand, located 50 miles to the west, until 8:04.)

Ruminate on This

At this point you may be wondering why ungulates (deer, elk, sheep, moon and so on) feed according to two specific Moon times and not random throughout the day. A clue lies with a distinguishing characteristic of this clar of animals—their unique stomachs. Grazing prey are designed to feed in has to reduce exposure to danger, then retreat to the safety of cover to "bed and chew their cud." Understanding the ungulate's digestive system helps explain why two major daily lunar influences come into play.

Deer, once considered browsers of fibrous stems and branches, are also gracing ruminants (like cattle). A four-part (rumen, reticulum, omasum, abomasure stomach allows them to digest and metabolize foods that other animals cannot Food—from forbs to fruit, from legumes to tree limbs—is consumed very rapidly (practically swallowed whole) before it is stored in the rumen, the stomac largest chamber. Eventually the nutriments are regurgitated, remasticated and reswallowed. In fact, microbial breakdown is actually promoted by food movie back and forth from the rumen to the reticulum in this rather strange mannor

Deer can eat so much at one feeding that a full rumen and reticulum my account for as much as 10 percent of the animal's live weight (the rumen along can easily hold 10 quarts of food). The fining of the rumen consists of papills tiny string-like projections one-half-inch long that number about 1,600 to the square inch. The reticulum holds less than a quart and looks like a honeycon Hard-core digestion actually begins in the omasum, which has 48 "lobes" of do. ferent sizes and shapes that act as strainers. The abomasum is completely the opposite—smooth and slippery. An adult deer also has about 65 feet of intestines, and it takes 24 to 36 hours for food to pass through the animal.

This cud stuff is quite a process. Renowned wildlife photographer Len Rue III has studied cud-chewing extensively (as he has just about every other aspect of whitetail behavior). "I have found that they masticate each piece of cud with about 40 chews," he says. "This takes, on average, 45 seconds. This masticated cud is then reswallowed and a new one is regurgitated. It requires from six to eight seconds for the cud to go down and the next cud to replace it in the mouth. You can see the cud from quite a distance—each is about the size of a lemon."

Interrupting this natural process can spell danger. A satiated deer deprived the opportunity of chewing its cud risks severe sickness or even death. Enterprising Ukrainian deer hunters in Saskatchewan and Manitoba have discovered a clever strategy for capitalizing on this biological fact of life. After locating a good buck feeding in a wheat or oat field, the hunter allows the animal to fill its stomach at least 20 minutes to a half-hour. Then the chase is on. Once on track, the hunter doesn't stop for a moment, not even for a quick cup of coffee. As often as not, by the end of the day he gets his buck. During the chase he hopes to find a clue to the deer's whereabouts—regurgitated digestive matter. When he finds it, he knows the buck is on its last legs, likely bedded in a nearby pocket in hopes its pursuer will pass by unawares. With skill and patience the hunter can literally walk up to the bedded buck.

Studies substantiate this strange phenomenon. Unlike carnivores and omnivores, deer feed rhythmically, chewing their cud during alternating periods of rest. While researching the heart rates of whitetails, Cornell University's Dr. Aaron Moen discovered that deer spend about 70 percent of their time bedded during the day. This can be interpreted that deer hole up more for digestive purposes than for rebuilding from muscle fatigue.

Bob Zaiglin has observed deer on a near-daily basis for more than 20 years, and he sees strong feeding movements every 12 or so hours, with a notable exception. "The only kink to this is artificial feeding in the Hill Country of Texas," he says. "Regardless of the Moon phase or Moon position, deer literally leap out of the brush at the sound of the [feeding] truck. Bucks are more reticent, but once they become hooked on the vocalization associated with feeding, they seem to plan their day around it. It's

This bedded buck is chewing its cud- in this case, regurgitating, remasticating and reswallowing acorns that fell from nearby oaks. Research indicates that deer spend 70 percent of their time bedded down.

uncanny. This suggests that deer can be conditioned to feed out of synch with their natural link to the Moon."

Suburban deer represent a similar example. Human activity—vehicular traffic, joggers, dog-walkers, sight-seers—predictably peaks during early morning and late-afternoon hours. Deer respond with suppressed activity at these times.

Another factor that can alter a deer's predictable lunar feeding cycle is a strong weather front. As the animals sense the impending loss of feeding opportunities, they chow down. Also, intense hunting pressure can shift feeding periods toward evening hours. Nevertheless, deer feed in remarkable conformity to the Moon's superior and inferior transits about 70 percent of the time. Hundreds of hunters, after comparing deer sightings to respective Moon times, wrote me confessing their conversion from skepticism to fanaticism: Hunting by the Moon may be heresy in their deer camp, but it's not lunacy.

Deer belch to eliminate gasses such as methane and carbon dioxide byproducts of microbial fermentation in their abomasum and small intestine.

Moon Spots™—The Right Place

The Deer Hunters' Moon Guide™ is more than a Moon table; it's a legally protected system that takes Moon hunting to the next level. Instead of merely listing when deer and other big-game animals are likely to be moving to feed, the Guide indicates where to set up at those times. Savvy Moon-hunters have learned to rotate hunting locations to jibe with ever-changing Moon times. I've coined a little saying that sums up the significance of this breakthrough: Being at the wrong place at the right time isn't much better than being at the wrong place at the wrong time.

Now the key to getting the most out of Moon times is first realizing that deer spend 90 percent of their time in three distinct areas: feeding and bedding areas and "transition belts" connecting the two. In some situations, a general area may meet a buck's feeding and bedding needs. Traditional deer yards in severe weather come to mind; so does the brush country of South Texas and the travel a considerable distance between the feeding and bedding zones, thus travel a considerable distance between the feeding and bedding zones, thus setting up a third zone: transition belts.

What about so-called breeding territories? This is an unfortunate misnomer. Rutting areas are usually concentrated near primary bedding areas and therefore don't qualify as a distinctly unique area. A buck doesn't say, "Hey, Debbie Doe, let's mosey over to that scrape line on Estrous Ridge where we can, you know, have some privacy." To the contrary, bucks breed does wherever does happen to be when they're receptive. And don't forget, dominant bucks often lead does away from areas of normal deer traffic to isolate them from rival bucks. The misunderstood concept of "breeding territories" has led to many a failed game plan. No matter how you slice it, there are only three basic zones deer frequent on a predictable basis, and this forms the foundation of hunting by the Moon.

So let's take a closer look at this trio of "Moon spots." The Man in the Moon sees to it that each area has its glory period during a typical lunation, and if we know ahead of time when it will occur, we'll know precisely where to set up as well as the best method to tackle the situation.

It's not the right time if it's the wrong place,
And it's not the right place if it's the wrong time.
Time will tell if it's the Time and Spot,
It'll all fall in place... if it's not for nought.

The Deer Hunters' Moon Guide™ lists exact Moon times for the middle of the Central Standard Time Zone. This puts all hunters in North America in the ball park, regardless of their location. The weatherproof seven-inch dial is easy to operate. Spin the outer wheel to a chosen date to find when deer and big game feel the urge to feed; this, in turn, calls up a key hunting location for that Moon time.

A detailed illustration on the flip side of the Moon Guide™ shows how to rotate hunting locations, or Moon Spots™, according to each day's best Moon time(s).

M.R. James, founder and former editor of *Bowhunter*, with a dandy Montana buck arrowed in November, 1994. M.R. "had his doubts" but "gradually became a believer" after testing out the Deer Hunters' Moon Guide™ system.

Scouting with the Man in the Moon

JEFF MURRAY

"The lazy man does not roast what he took in hunting,
But diligence is man's precious possession."
Proverbs 12:27

A nanosecond is one-billionth of a second—about the time it takes me to recognize the importance of scouting. Don't take my word for it, though. Listen to "Iron Mike" Weaver who, at this writing, has 35 trophy whitetails entered in the Pope and Young record books. That's right, 35 and still counting! Weaver owns his own automobile repair shop and schedules work around deer hunting, especially scouting. Though this Virginia bowhunter knows as much as anyone on how to get within spitting distance of cagey whitetails, he's pretty old-fashioned when it comes to scouting.

"It's tempting to cut corners and spend extra time hunting instead of observing," he says "But it's a monumental mistake to hunt big bucks prematurely. You have to figure them out first or they'll figure you out first."

When you're tempted to give up prematurely or cut that seemingly insignificant corner, remember one of Weaver's hunts that involved two weeks of watching and absolutely no "shooting." The following year, however, he managed to arrow four record-book bucks from the same spot. There's just no such thing as failure when it comes to

scouting. Call it something tried that didn't work out the way you planned, but don't label your lack of success failure. As my Dad used to say, "Better to try and fail than not to try at all. In due time you, too, shall reap the rewards."

Scouting can be critical to hunting success.

Pre-hunting

I define scouting simply as patterning deer before they pattern me. Consider it pre-hunting, similar to the methods professional anglers use to "pre-fish" a body of water before a big tournament—as quickly as possible they must assemble clues that unlock the fishery. Likewise, you must find out what makes a particular animal tick. Your biggest obstacle is figuring him out before he's onto you—once a buck gets wind of your presence, the party's pretty much over. In spite of what some "experts" say, you never want to get into a game of cat 'n' mouse with a mature buck—you're better off hunting traveled routes than socalled escape routes.

To be sure, there's a difference between scouting hard and scouting smart. Prudent paperwork can save miles of legwork.

To get to first base, I suggest a handy "overlay map." As a former land-use planner, I've worked with every conceivable visual aid—from orthographic maps to three-dimensional aerial photos (viewed with a stereoscope). None, however, has enabled me to map out deer country as efficiently as the overlay procedure I'm about to disclose.

To cut to the chase, sandwich together a topographic map and an aerial photograph (make sure they're the same scale). Start with the time-honored topographic map. Its contours connecting areas of equal elevation show "relief" in surprising detail. A piece of flat paper depicting a real-world scene requires you to visualize somewhat, so keep in mind the following:

- The scale of the map is at the bottom. The 7.5-minute quadrangle (1:24,000 scale) is the most handy (an inch equals .38 mile).

- A square mile is known as a "section" and equals 640 acres.

- Black squares are generally occupied buildings; open squares are outbuildings such as barns, garages and sheds; new buildings are usually red or purple.

- Green is vegetative cover (from bushes to trees); white is open (from bogs to cultivated fields).

- The unique blue marsh symbol indicates bogs that could range from open teaberry to thick reeds to willows, tag alders and second-growth brush.

- The contour lines on the above scale indicate a rise or fall of 10 feet. Now start looking for these details:

"With 35 Pope and Young bucks (and still counting) Mike Weaver knows the scouting game as well as anyone."

- In relatively flat habitat, zero in on brushy creek beds. (If there's a contour line on each side, the bed is fairly deep and could attract transition-time movement.)
- Ribbon cover connecting larger tracts of timber is equally enticing to deer, and elbows in the contours (or cover) constrict deer at the joint of the "L."
- In hilly terrain, learn to identify points, fingers, saddles and benches.

Try to find a local commercial source so you can browse at your own clip without shelling out $3 to $4 every time you need to examine an adjacent quadrangle (look up "Printing" or "Maps" in the Yellow Pages). Otherwise you'll have to start with a phone call to the U.S. Geological Survey (1-800-USA-MAPS). Hopefully your nearby map source also stocks aerial photos. If not, visit the closest planning agency or government field office—state natural resources department or Forest Service and Fish and Wildlife Service branch.

By the way, "soil maps" produced by the USDA Soil Conservation Service (SCS) are an excellent resource for trophy deer hunters (other factors remaining equal). If you've ever wondered why a certain drainage system or belt of land seems to produce better racks than another one just a few miles away, it's probably the soils.

For example, biologists know that sandy soils lack nutrients like calcium and phosphorous necessary for optimum antler development. More important, a fertile soil will produce vegetation with a higher percentage of protein—the key ingredient to growing larger racks. Because soil types are listed on the SCS maps, at a glance you get a good indication of the area's nutritional potential. These maps are a lot more helpful than Pope and Young and Boone and Crockett record books, which, at best, give county-by-county statistics. Factor in glaciers and floods, that distribute nutrients in a haphazard manner across North America, and you're looking at a huge time-saver.

A classic example of the significance of soils is the black belt phenomenon in the Southeast. This east/west swath of highly nutritious soils accounts for some dandy bucks in Alabama, where on lands outside of the "antler zone," hunters are lucky to raise bucks with racks much wider than 14 or 16 inches. Naturally, a conscientious program of "doe management" must also be applied in regions like this where deer tend to propagate themselves beyond the carrying capacity of the land.

Trophy hunters should also seek out areas with expanding deer herds, ideally where populations are about one-half the carrying capacity of the land. The notion of innumerable wide-racked bucks in a bumper-to-bumper deer herd is a pipe dream. Also know that antler growth levels off visibly at the 2 ½ to 3½ -year mark if the buck-to-doe ratio isn't balanced (and there isn't more than enough nutrition to go around). So look for areas with low hunter pressure where bucks can reach the golden antler-producing age of four or more years.

Now for a slick trick. Have the topo and aerial photo enlarged at a quality print shop so that a particular area covers one square mile on an 8½x 11-inch piece of paper (again, maintaining the same scale). Now you can overlap the two against a bright light (light table, living room window, windshield of your car) and read vegetative cover and elevation at a single glance. Of course, you can always switch back and forth if you want to analyze a particular detail, but with them together, you get quite a story on one versatile working map.

Which leads to another point. You can locate likely daytime bedding areas by finding dark spots on the aerial photo and slopes on the contour map.

Tom Indrebo studies a saddle, located in Wisconsin's Buffalo County, on his homemade map. By enlarging section 36, subtle details leap off the page.

If these spots are within with a mile or two of prime food sources, you're almost home free.

The significance of daytime bedding areas cannot be understated. They're the hub of a buck's daily routine. Every evening he leaves; every morning he returns. What a clue! Incidentally, be sure to identify primary areas for prevailing winds as well as secondary sites for variable winds. And don't forget about hunting pressure. Invariably, out-of-the-way pockets become more productive than easy-access bedding areas as the season wears on.

The next step is to locate topographical barriers that might constrict or encourage deer to travel along key routes, or corridors. During the day, deer avoid certain danger zones—particularly open areas void of cover—but they also avoid tight spots that make

travel difficult. As you piece together travel patterns, don't overlook the fact that human traffic tends to steer deer around certain areas, too.

Like the seams of a football team's zone coverage, bucks like to run "pass routes" around and between the "cornerbacks of human activity." So consider roads and trails when mapping out deer country. Let's face it. Hunters are basically lazy. No more than one out of 100 two-legged predators ventures farther than a half-mile from the nearest two-track.

As you study the areas deer skirt—such as fields, clearings, beaver ponds, rivers, lakes, swamps and bluffs—and those they dive into—such as roadless areas and difficult access points—several "buck corridors" will eventually emerge. Now all you need to know is whether a good buck or two made it through the hunting season in one of the areas you've selected. Then you can hunt with confidence...

Old Antlers Shed New Light

The woods smelled different—kind of sweet, kind of musty—when a sudden breeze swelled out of the southwest. I just had to stop and drink it in, as did my daughter, Janell, who often accompanies me on my early spring vigils. Yep, we were hunting for shed antlers and soaking up every moment.

"Found one, Dad," Janell shouted gleefully.

"One what?" I teased.

"A rack," she said, somewhat annoyed at me playing dumb. She knew she was as good as I was at this game, probably better. What did I think she'd found, a dead skunk?

"That ain't no rack, it's an antler," I said, seizing the opportunity to spoonfeed some whitetail lore to my favorite young lady. "Find the other half, and we'll have an honest-to-goodness rack." With that, Janell scurried for a heap of compacted, dried leaves

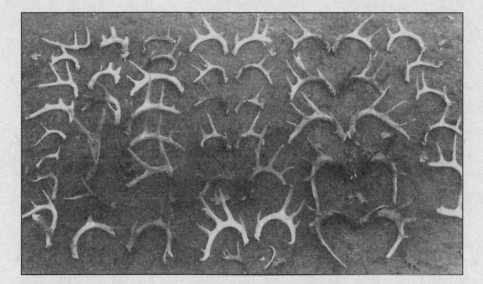

Antlers cast a bewitching spell on many hunters, including me! The sheds from an old buck hanging out in the same general area really boost my confidence.

and kicked at it. Then she scooted over to another pile and kicked again. And so went our day. We built a few memories while I managed to piece together another missing part of the whitetail puzzle. I knew that if I could find the drops of a good buck, more than likely he'd be fair game the next fall.

An added bonus of this pastime is that it fills a vacant niche in my calendar—after late-season bowhunting and before spring turkey and bear seasons. It can do the same for you.

As with many endeavors, timing is everything. Although it's impossible to predict when bucks will drop their headgear, a few generalities hold true. For one, the farther north you go, the sooner racks seem to hit the ground. For another, the better the local food supply, the longer bucks tend to hang onto their racks. (The "disposable" head adornment of the Cervidae family is unique among the animal kingdom in that the rack only grows during the vegetative season. Consequently, droughts can severely hamper antler development.)

But there are so many local variations that you must remain flexible and keep current with conditions. A case in point involves a deer yard I visited several years ago. I photographed the thicket where the whitetails had instinctively gathered in

hopes of documenting the harsh elements' toll on the herd. I was amazed at the diversity among the bucks: Some were in full-rack splendor; others sported only one side of their rack; still others were as bald as eagles. My notes reflect that the last rack was shed a full eight weeks after the first one; a particularly impressive 12-pointer hung onto his headgear until late March.

The casual whitetail student interprets this as meaning that the best time to get in the woods for sheds is when it's convenient. Fanatics see it differently: If competition in a given area is keen, better get out often, possibly revisiting potential hotspots if you want to score on a matched set. Some guys get so "antlerized" that they hit the woods in waves, organizing a telephone network. Indeed, a buddy system can save wear and tear on the nerves and keep your vehicle's mileage down.

Snow depth can be a factor. In the upper Midwest, where I do most of my shed hunting, a crust of refrozen snow camouflages antler tines well. And busting through knee to thigh-high drifts makes shed hunting more like work than play. Ideally, try to time shed-hunting forays for when the snow is almost, but not quite, gone. Then a bleached, bonewhite tine protruding out of the earth is easy to spot—even for a teenaged girl. Don't wait too much longer or rodents, especially squirrels, will be out in full force, gnawing away at the calcium-rich drops.

Interestingly, research shows that deer south of the snow belt begin antler development about the same time as their northern counterparts—mid-March to April. As a result, antler shedding is surprisingly uniform across the whitetail's range, largely due to increasing daylight and prolactin secretions. However, if you live a considerable distance from the area you intend to scout, a quick phone call to a natural resources field office can help fine-tune your timing.

The where-to aspect of shed hunting is an inexact science. As a friend remarked, shed hunting is like picking mushrooms. "They're where you find 'em," he said. "No rhyme or reason to their whereabouts." I'd say he's at least half-correct. An open field could cough up state-record sheds as easily as a river bottom. And a thicket in a residential area is just as likely to produce as a cattail slough bordering a farm several miles away. Still, there are good spots and there are better spots.

If you are just into sheds and not necessarily using them to target a huntable buck, some of

I photographed this buck in a deer yard shortly after he dropped half of his rack. I returned a month later and collected the other half.

the best spots in the country right now are in suburbia Deer are creatures of the fringe. Housing developments spreading outward like spokes of a wheel don't curb nearby deer populations that much. To the contrary, when you factor in local laws that typically prohibit the discharge of firearms, deer numbers escalate.

The game of suburban shed hunting is relatively straightforward. Many residents love to watch deer, so they set up feeders to encourage whitetail visitation. In the process, predictable patterns emerge. All you have to do is locate several such feeders and backtrack from them to a thicket or two that deer use to avoid daytime human activity. It could be a cattail slough, grassy drainage ditch or tangled woodlot. The best time to locate these areas is in early winter, when deer trails are most pronounced.

Keep in mind that these areas are under private ownership, so you need to know boundary lines and get permission for access. A plat book or a trip to the city (or township) assessor's office will help identify landowners. Or you could just knock on a few doors."Which reminds me: The sport of shed-hunting provides an excellent opportunity to convey the hunting heritage message to non-hunters who outnumber hunters in the 'burbs 10:1. You never know where these contacts might lead...

In the big woods during years of below-average snowfalls (actually the rule rather than the exception the last decade or so), look for sheds in lowland areas and not necessarily in traditional yarding areas. Certainly don't rule out feeding areas, either. Thick cover is readily available in the big woods, and deer often bed within yards, not miles, of food sources such as fields, cut-overs and slashings associated with active logging operations.

In agricultural areas and semi-arid regions, river bottoms get the nod because vegetation is concentrated mainly along creeks and drainages. So-called ribbon cover is the easiest whitetail habitat to shed-hunt in. Again, you know where deer are likely to spend most of their time in such spots so you can pretty much rule out low-percentage areas.

Transition habitat, with its characteristic mixture of croplands and woodlots, can be tricky. Not only do deer spend a considerable amount of time in Conservation Reserve Program (CRP) plots, but they traverse open fields after sundown. If it's "that time," they could drop an antler or two just about anywhere along the way. You might want to glass plowed fields before heading into the thick stuff.

Sheds are valuable (perhaps too valuable in this age of commercialism). Who doesn't relish the thought of running their fingers along the thick main beams, counting the burrs of the brow tines, inspecting the pedicels? Like fingerprints and snowflakes, the Creator made each antler truly unique. So what are you going to do when you accumulate a mess of "dust-collectors," as my wife calls them? Don't store them away in the rafters of your garage. Instead, consider a mount like the one my friend Mike Kohler had made up for his young son, Ross. The youngster's crowning pickup, a matched pair grossing about 160 Boone and Crockett points, graces the family's fireplace mantle. The attractive plaque gives the date Ross found the set, and each side can be removed—for toying with, of course—by unlatching a metal clasp. I agree with Kohler that sheds ought to be preserved the way they were found—no putty, no burnt umber and certainly not mounted on another deer's cape.

If you've discovered the spoils of decoying deer, save a not-so-matched set for a buck decoy. Try several pairs, experimenting to find which ones attract/spook deer in your area (here's betting you won't want to go too small or too big).

Sheds serve another useful purpose: for rattling up bucks during the hunting season. Again, you'll have to experiment because some sheds crack loudly whereas others "tinkle" with a muffled, hollow ring.

Just because sheds have been cast by their maker doesn't mean their useful life is over. For some lucky relics, it's just the beginning.

The Bachelor Party

The month of August reminds me of a singles' bar—it has the appearance, but rarely the results, of a rewarding relationship. Indeed, when bucks group together in so-called bachelor groups, they tease hunters by feeding in broad daylight in open alfalfa fields (up north) and bean and milo fields (further south). Although this is an excellent time to observe big bucks from a distance—perhaps confirming what shed antler scouting has revealed—it isn't a reliable indicator of where those deer will be come hunting season.

"The bucks will disperse with a few ending up in some fairly distant places," Dr. Kroll says. "The dominant individuals habitually stake out preferred core areas, sometimes a considerable distance from summer loafing and feeding areas."

Translation? By all means get out the spotting scope and put your number on the widest, heaviest-racked buck in the area. But don't count on him showing up in the same field with his buddies... unless you find his bedroom rubs nearby.

Don't Forget the Moon

As you snoop for whitetail clues, keep track of Moon times when you're afield, especially as the hunting season approaches. This tip alone could save the season. For example, suppose you're driving a backcountry road and notice a set of tracks along

Late summer and early fall bucks gang together in bachelor groups; however, where you find them now won't be where they'll be during the heat of the hunting season.

the shoulder. Are they heading from open fields toward a patch of woods... or the opposite way? Recall that the lunar cycle (complete phase) repeats itself every 29.5 days. If you find deer traveling along a particular route during, say, a midmorning Moon time, chances are the deer will show up along that same route when the Moon waxes into its next lunation.

Stop and think about this! Should you fail to connect this week, you might have a chance to redeem yourself. Get in the habit of tracking deer activity in accordance with the lunar calendar.

Signs of the Tines

With general bedding, feeding and connecting corridors identified on your map, it's time to step into the woods. Over the years a ritual of scouting during late winter has evolved for me. Trampled trails and leftover sign are oh-so-obvious and, with the deer season behind me and next year's hunt months away, I won't have to worry about bumping deer out of their daily routine. If you've got the

time and inclination, take advantage of this unique window of opportunity.

What to look for? In a word: rubs. And old ones are just as telling as new ones because a buck will retrace his general comings and goings in successive years. In fact, the best tip-off is a rub line a buck has worked several years in a row.

Bucks keep an eye on the moon, and so should you.

I caught this buck in the act of rubbing a mountain maple during the first week of September. Notice that early fall rubs do not resemble larger signpost markers associated with the ruts.

Find a series of trees with two or more rub scars—distinctive oval-shaped "scabs" formed on the bark—and you're probably looking at the handiwork of an older buck (at least three, maybe 4 ½ years old or more). No wonder my mind does cartwheels when I discover a tree or three with multiple scabs! These rubs are easy to distinguish. For some strange reason, bucks tend to rework a tree or bush from a slightly different angle each year. Rather than polishing the exact same spot, the buck attacks the tree just above the scar, just below it, or off to the side. And this fall the buck could return, if you don't rub him the wrong way.

Rub-scouting in late summer demands a change of plans. Now you should be concerned with an entirely different kind of rub (and it's not the impressive leg-size rubs many hunters go ga-ga over). You want to be rubbed in the direction of reality, not imagination, so let's first rehearse some basic facts about rubs.

Not all rubs are of equal significance to hunters. Whether or not rubs carved out by dominant breeding bucks are territorial markers (reportedly establishing home ranges to "warn" juvenile bucks and potential rivals) is largely academic. From a practical standpoint, rubs can help us locate the bedding areas of mature animals and give insights into possible weak links to their seemingly invincible armor.

The small-rub/small-buck, big-rub/big-buck axiom holds some water, but has been oversimplified. Researchers Larry Marchinton and Karl Miller, after examining 529 rubs in five study areas, found no substantial difference in rub sizes in areas with varying deer age structures; rubs in yearling-dominated habitats were about the same size as those where two out of three bucks were older than a year and a half. Other research suggests that although a big buck may make seemingly small rubs, young bucks are rarely responsible for those impressive scars showing up on eight to 12-inch trees. Also, bigger bucks make more rubs "because they have more to advertise," says retired Michigan biologist John Ozoga.

Whatever you do, don't discount all small rubs. In fact, some of them can tell you more than the imposing, so-called signpost markers I used to drool over. In September, about the only rubs you will find are those made by mature bucks. This really simplifies the rub interpretation game, doesn't it? Again, you have to know what to look for.

"[A buck's first rubs] look more like thrashings than the deliberate [scraping] of tree bark associated with rubs later in the fall signaling the onset of the rutting season," Marchinton says. "If you find a lot of early-season rubs, there's a good chance the age structure of the deer herd could be an older one."

This is why I shift into overdrive as I cruise new territory for early season rubs. Not only is their relative abundance a good reflection of an area's

This buck is attacking a tree that he worked over the previous fall. A series of trees with multipleyear rubs is an invaluable clue.

big-buck potential, but it indicates where bucks are probably bedding, because a majority of early rubs are made near the inner sanctum of the bucks' daytime lairs. Studious bowhunters should scout hard in late summer and early fall, before the archery season opens, if they want to intercept the rub-maker when the time is right. (Keep in mind that deer haven't been hunted for several months and are more apt to tolerate minor disturbances before leaves fall and small-game and bird hunters invade the woods.)

Punctuate your field map with every fresh rub you find in September. Again, the ultimate goal is zeroing in on a buck's preferred daytime bedding area. Better get ready for some serious grunt work, though. You won't find these rubs along field edges or in open country like the late-season signpost markers. Instead, head for the thickest foliage you can find. (Remember those dark patches on the aerial photos?) And come prepared for a lot of crawling on all fours—the best way to see under the canopy of leaves and through lush undergrowth. Search for these rubs with the diligence of a pirate digging for buried treasure.

Incidentally, if you strike out, you get a second chance to locate a boss buck with another distinctive type of rub. As the breeding season draws near, signpost rubs proliferate. The latest theory on these large, unmistakable markers is that they are a part of a complex communication system within the sexes as well as between them. When a buck rubs his antlers and forehead on a tree (and licks it repeatedly), he deposits "priming pheromones" that likely serve as a biostimulant to induce ovulation in does. This is one of Nature's remarkable processes. Studies involving pen-raised deer in Michigan and wild deer on the Mt. Holly Plantation in South Carolina show that the absence or presence of these rubs can impact the timing of the rut. Of course, photoperiodism (the diminishing ratio of daylight to dark) triggers hormonal releases in does and determines the general breeding season. But in habitats where breeding bucks are abundant, local does may go into heat as much as two weeks early. (The reverse is also true; a lack of bucks can delay does entering estrus.)

Myles-A-Head

Meet Myles Keller. This easygoing Minnesota bowhunter has more than two dozen Pope and Young whitetails in the record books—more than any other bowhunter. I make this distinction, in spite of the "trophy mentality" that seems to have spread through hunting camps across the country like an electrical storm. (All big game harvested under fair chase principles are prized, especially those taken with a bow.) But because so many "professionals" have emerged of late—often advocating conflicting advice—I feel the public needs some sort of barometer to measure a spokesperson's credibility.

Myles Keller with the smallest of four record-book bucks he arrowed in 1993.

Take fishing. Outdoor writers used to be the primary source of angling knowledge because they had the platform of books and magazines to advance their theories. That information hierarchy changed dramatically when sanctioned fishing tournaments spawned a new generation of credible tournament pros. Though there aren't any "tournament hunters," we do have record books. Those maintained by the Pope and Young Club can be particularly helpful for recognizing prominent members of the hunting fraternity. (Assuming that game-law violators such as Don Lewis and, more recently, Noel Feather don't confuse the issue.)

I'm not the Wizard of Oz empowered to bestow titles, but after interviewing thousands of dedicated hunters and professional biologists, guides and outfitters, I have reached a simple conclusion: Only Myles Keller is a whitetail expert. A few come close; more than a few are impostors; and most are wannabes. When penned the first magazine article on Myles back in 1985 (appearing in *Outdoor Life*, entitled "World's Greatest Bowhunter?"), I suspected he might be in a class by himself. Now I know he is.

To say Myles is miles ahead of contemporary bowhunters is to say Einstein was good at math. So when Myles speaks, I try my best to comprehend the meaning of his message. It isn't always easy. Myles' thoughts on whitetails aren't always mainstream, and he doesn't always tell his audience what they want to hear. "A lot of times a guy will ask me a series of probing questions," he once told me. "I can see him shaking his head as he walks away, thinking, 'That guy doesn't know any more than me.' Too bad he's looking for a secret formula instead of examining his hunting system for weak links."

For the record, Myles makes his living field-testing and promoting bowhunting-related products; contracts with Indian Archery (Xi bows), Scent Shield and Advantage camouflage (a division of Realtree) keep him hopping.

Scout-hunting

Once the season opens, you should continue to scout while you hunt instead of depending on previously scouted deer sign. Scout-hunting is the

Claude Pollington keeps tabs on the rut-without tipping bucks off-by checking the status of boundary scrapes.

only zeroimpact tactic acceptable for effective trophy hunting. No one has translated this principle into a practical hunting strategy better than Myles.

"It's critical that a buck thinks his Back 40 sanctuary is safe," Myles says. "This means staying out unless I know exactly when and where I can kill him back in there." In other words, the typical strategy of snooping around for rubs and hot scrapes, then hanging a stand downwind and hoping for something good to happen is usually futile for mature animals.

Sounds like a Catch-22: To find rut sign signaling the breeding season you've got to prowl the backwoods, but in so doing you risk bumping the buck out of his bedding area. Well, it is. My association with Myles over the years has caused me to re-evaluate my entire system of hunting whitetails. In the old days, I wouldn't have thought twice about keeping a low profile and playing the wind, figuring if I jumped a buck he wouldn't wind me and should continue his routine. Not any more.

"Bowhunters expecting a legitimate shot at an impressive Pope and Young buck have to realize what they're up against," Myles says. "This animal's different from an alpha doe or a 2 ½-year-old buck. There are no shortcuts... only extra miles.

This always brings us back to no-impact pre-season scouting: The only way to deal with major-league rut sign is before the hunting season. In short, while nimrods set up on top of rubs or so-called scrape lines, one of two scenarios typically unfolds. The first is failing to map out a buck's core area, resulting in the hunter locating where the animal sojourns infrequently. The second is digging deeper to get a better picture... and spooking the buck.

"Hunting big-time rutting sign is very tempting but most often self-defining," Myles says. "You're much better off hunting where you can catch the beer entering or leaving." There's no better place to start than a food source, especaily when the Moon signals deer to chow down before the sun sets. Of course scout-hunting will pay off when Moon times force hunters to lay back for food sources. I'm just glad we've got the Moon to show the way.

This buck is heading for the next food source, and so should you.

Blood Trails and Tracking

JOHN TROUT, JR.

The best trackers are those who are patient. Following the trail of a wounded deer effectively requires you to do so slowly, cautiously, and quietly. You must consider many factors before starting to blood trail. This chapter will focus on tracking techniques, beginning with the precise location of where the deer was shot. Following a blood trail can be simple, or it can be difficult. Sometimes we make it more difficult than it is, while other times it is much more difficult than we expected. The location of the wound, the type of terrain, and how soon you begin tracking will all play essential roles in trailing the deer.

Tracking a wounded deer is an art that some have mastered through experience. Others jump right in and do a fine job the first time out. Good trackers do much more than follow drops of blood on the ground, however. A skilled tracker knows to look for blood smears, tissue, and hair. He knows if a wounded deer has bedded, is walking or running, and he can often follow a trail when blood does not even exist. Most important, he does not assume anything.

Before going on, let me say that there is one fact that stands out above the rest. A large amount of external blood does not necessarily mean that a deer is going down. Many of us have experienced these types of blood trails, but they do not always lead to a downed deer. I have seen some superficial muscle wounds bleed extensively for long distances. On the other hand, I have seen wounded deer go down within 100 yards, without leaving one drop of blood on the ground.

First Blood

There are many reasons why you might find blood at the location the deer stood when you took

How long should you wait before tracking a wounded deer? Each hunter should make his decision based on the wound.

the shot. There are also many reasons why you might not find blood until you have gone a considerable distance from where the deer was standing. Moreover, there are also reasons why a deer may not bleed at all. The location of the wound, angle of the shot, diameter of the entry and departure hole, penetration of the projectile or arrow, and height of the entry and departure hole will decide how quickly a deer bleeds externally.

Extremely low wounds sometimes result in blood getting to the ground immediately, whereas high wounds will seldom result in blood getting to the ground until the deer has run a fair distance. Such was the case when southern Indiana bowhunter Ed Rinehart shot a small buck only a few yards from the base of his tree. The arrow entered high and just behind the shoulder, but did not exit. We spent more than an hour looking for blood of this lung-shot deer, but could not find anything. We finally found the buck piled up 125 yards from where Ed shot it. This deer did not leave one drop of external blood.

My dad once shot a buck from a tree stand, hitting it low in the stomach. Blood was splattered everywhere at the precise location where the deer stood. However, the blood slacked off to pin drops only fifty yards from that spot. After tracking the buck another twenty-five yards, the blood stopped. We later recovered the deer and discovered that the arrow had entered the deer in the bottom of its paunch, and exited in the middle of its underbelly.

I used these examples to give you an idea of why you do or do not find blood quickly. As mentioned previously, every wound will vary. Despite these variations, I will always look for blood at the location where the deer stood when shot. If I don't find blood, I will do my best to locate hair and scuffed marks. Then I will widen the search and attempt to find the first blood. In the

following chapters, you will read about each type of wound imaginable, and how soon you can expect to find blood. Most tracking endeavors cannot begin until you find the first blood. After finding the first blood, you can examine its color and know when to begin tracking.

Colors of Blood

Blood is not just red. It can be bright or dark. It can be darker than dark, or crimson instead of bright. Each wound gives off a certain color of blood, and that color should guide you when deciding how soon you should track the deer.

For instance, dark blood is the result of an abdomen wound. Muscle wounds result in bright blood, similar to lung-shot deer. However, a lung-shot deer may produce blood that appears almost pink. Heart, some artery, and kidney wounds usually result in bright to crimson blood.

If the hunter does not pay special attention to the color of blood, he may not know how long to wait before he begins to track the animal. The bowhunter, if he or she retrieves the arrow, can often determine the color of blood by looking at the shaft. If the shaft cannot be located, the bowhunter must do the same as the firearm hunter and locate the first few drops to make a determination. However, always consider the angle of the deer and the path of the projectile or arrow shaft. It is possible for a deer to leave both bright and dark blood. For instance, if your arrow or bullet enters the deer near its hip and exits through the paunch, it is possible you could find bright and dark blood. In this case the bright blood is usually more prevalent, but the fact remains that both colors could exist. If a hunter shoots a deer quartering toward him, his broadhead or projectile may enter the animal just behind the shoulder and exit in front of the hip. He will also find bright and dark blood. The bright blood would be from the wound to one lung, and the dark blood would be the result of the wound to the stomach and/or intestines.

Complete arrow or projectile penetration may determine how quickly you find blood. In case you're wondering, two holes are always better than one. First, consider that the path of the arrow or projectile is longer than it would be if it did not exit. The more it penetrates, the better the chance it will hit a vital organ, or artery. Additionally, an exit hole increases the chance of external blood getting to the ground, and the possibility that you will find blood sooner than you would have if only an entry hole existed.

Examining Arrows

Bowhunters can often obtain facts from a spent arrow, facts that can aid them in tracking. First, let's look at penetration.

Some trackers believe that good things come from an arrow that remains in the deer. For instance, it could keep the entry and/or departure hole from clotting. There is probably some truth to this theory, since coagulation can occur. I would much rather see a pass-through, though, simply because I will probably locate the arrow, and there will be a better chance the broadhead has hit vitals.

If tallow is present on an arrow, it indicates certain wounds. These wounds will be discussed in later chapters. However, many wounds where tallow is found do not result in easy-to-follow blood trails, or dead deer. Exceptions do exist, however. You may determine a pass-through by the straightness of the arrow shaft, and the blood you find between the nock and the broadhead. Bent or broken arrows, even when found at the location the deer stood when shot, sometimes indicate the arrow did not pass through. When the arrow hits, the deer often lunges.

If the arrow hits a tree or heavy brush, it may break off or bend. You can usually determine penetration by how far the blood comes up the shaft, and by the location of the bend or break. If the arrow is bent or broken on the front half (nock end), you probably did not penetrate totally.

On the other hand, if the bend or brake is on the business end, the arrow has probably penetrated totally. You may also find blood on just one side of the arrow. This may indicate a graze, but not always. Debris and foliage, particularly when wet, can clean an arrow on one side, or all sides. An arrow that is found after you track a deer for a given distance also tells a story. For instance, an arrow that has penetrated totally will usually come out broadhead first, and fall to the ground from the exit hole. This is true whether you shot the deer from a tree stand or the ground. It will not work its way out through the entry hole if it has penetrated totally.

Sometimes, if a deer carries the arrow, it will bump into debris or trees, causing it to break apart and flip away from the blood trail. I can't tell you how many times I have tracked and found a deer, yet failed to see the arrow along the blood trail. Backtracking will usually turn up the arrow, however.

Waiting Before Tracking

How long should you wait before tracking a wounded deer? Will waiting increase your chances of finding the animal, or will the delay hinder you? These questions are always sources of debate among hunters. Some hunters say you should push every deer, while others say it's best to go after some deer right away. A few believe you should delay tracking any wounded deer immediately. I will give you my opinions, and in doing so, explain how I have come to these conclusions. Although research has played a part in my opinions, my primary beliefs have come from in-the-field experiences.

When I started deer hunting in the 1960s, hunters always thought it best to sit back and wait twenty or thirty minutes before picking up the trail of a wounded deer. It was believed that the deer would bed down, stiffen, and eventually die if left alone, or be stiff enough so that it couldn't get out of its bed. If you jumped the deer, and it obviously had not stiffened enough to lay there and give you another shot, you should have waited longer before you started tracking.

Today, we know that a wound does not cause a deer to stiffen and die. It is the severity of the wound that will cause the animal to succumb, coupled with the length of time you wait before tracking it.

Rigor mortis is the stiffening of muscles after death. After a deer dies, it will begin stiffening. Various muscles will stiffen first, after a given length of time, although variables may affect the results.

John D. Gill of the Maine Department of Inland Fisheries, and David C. O'Meara, of Maine's Department of Animal Pathology, conducted a survey in the 1960s to estimate the time of death in white-tailed deer. For several days, they observed the carcasses of eighty-five deer shot by hunters. The two gathered data on body temperature, eye appearance, pupil diameter, and muscle stiffness. Their article and findings appeared in the Journal Of Wildlife Management, Volume 29, No. 3, July 1965.

To check rigor mortis, Gill and O'Meara gently flexed various joints by grasping the outer edge of the jaw, the upper end of the neck, the forelimb above and below either the wrist (corpus) or the elbow (humerus), the hind leg above and below either the ankle (tarus), or the knee (femur). The team made certain they did not reduce or break rigor, and the degree of stiffness present was recorded as "None", "one-quarter inch", "one-half inch", "three-quarter inch", or "complete".

Hours since Death

Rigor Mortis		1	2	3	4	5	6
Jaw	None	0					
	Partial	6	6				
	Stiff	1	18	28	24	14	18
Neck	None	4	14	6	1		
	Partial	2	16	28	14	20	
	Stiff	1	4	10	13	17	
Wrist (Carpus)	None	7	23	15	8	2	2
	Partial	5	24	37	33	26	
	Stiff		1	5	4	15	
Elbow (humerus)	None	7	10				
	Partial	12	20	12	10	5	
	Stiff	3	20	38	29	49	

Hours since Death

Rigor Mortis		1	2	3	4	5	6
Ankle (Tarsus)	None	4	3	1			
	Partial	1	12	14	11	8	3
	Stiff		2	12	16	16	18
Knee (femur)	None	4	2				
	Partial	1	12	5	3	1	2
	Stiff		3	20	21	18	20

Rigor Mortis Table: Numbers of observations of rigor mortis in deer. (Journal of Wildlife Management July 1965, John D. Gill and David O'Meara).

It was observed that muscles gradually stiffened soon after death, but would later relax because of internal chemical changes. Temperatures and other factors contributed to the rate of change in various parts of the body. Although more stiffening occurred in this sequence - jaw, knee, elbow, ankle, neck, and wrist, exceptions were mostly due to these four reasons:

1. Wounds may prevent, weaken, or delay rigor near tissue damage.
2. Rough handling may reduce or eliminate stiffening.
3. Differences due to air temperature (possibly masked by other variables).
4. Freezing confused with rigor mortis.

It was noted that jaws stiffened within two hours. Gill and O'Meara claimed the lower jaw clamped tightly with the lips concealing the teeth, although the tongue protruded. As the jaw relaxed, the front teeth became visible and the outer end of the jaw would flex about inch.

Stiffness, of course, may help you determine how long a deer has been dead, but it is not a factor before death. However, there is another consideration when wondering how long to wait before tracking a wounded deer.

We know that a running whitetail has about three times the heart rate per minute of a bedded deer. Thus, it is safe to assume that a moving deer will bleed more than a bedded deer, whether the bleeding is internal or external. Does this mean that a wounded deer should be tracked right away?

I say no, even though these facts have led some to believe that we should push all wounded deer, regardless of the location of the wound. Some hunters claim that a moving deer will bleed out and die sooner than one that is bedded. Personally, I believe we should throw this theory out the door along with the stiffening hypothesi.

I will agree that heart rate and bleeding increases with movement. However, keep in mind that a moving deer is getting farther away with each step. I've had times when it took me an hour to follow a deer for 100 yards or less, simply because blood did not get to the ground when the deer was walking. And that's the bottom line: A wound that allows blood to get to the ground, particularly muscle wounds, could call for immediate tracking. On the other hand, a gut-shot deer that may leave very few drops of blood, or no blood at all on the ground for a long distance, should never be tracked immediately. Consider that stomach and intestinal matter may clog a hole in a deer, preventing blood from getting to the ground. A large broadhead or projectile may make a big hole, but that doesn't necessarily mean that an entry or departure hole will remain open and allow blood to reach the ground. I also know that a gut-shot deer will not succumb quickly, and will usually bed down if not pushed.

When tracking a deer, it is primarily a blood trail that will lead you to the animal. Obviously, the tracking becomes more difficult if no blood is present. Now consider the distance a deer may travel. In the case of stomach and intestinal wounds, many deer lay up a short distance from where they were shot. These wounds are fatal, and deer with such wounds will die within a given number of hours depending upon precise location of the wound - organ and artery damage. However, if you push the animal to increase the heart rate and induce bleeding, you still may get no more blood on the ground than you would have if you left the deer alone. Meanwhile, the deer gets farther away, and the chances of recovering it grow slimmer. Consider slowly pushing a deer for five minutes, and how far it could travel. If you allow the gut-shot deer to stay bedded, it will still bleed internally - perhaps slower than it would have if moving, but nonetheless the end result is still death. The best advice I can give is to consider distance. The further you must track a deer, the less chance you have of a recovery.

Fortunately, many hunters do wait to track stomach and intestinal-shot deer. But some insist upon waiting to track any deer, including those with muscle wounds, where increased bleeding could lead

the animal to succumb when it otherwise may not have. Thus, you should evaluate every wound when deciding how long to wait. For instance, why wait to track a double lung-shot deer that will probably go down in seconds, a short distance away? Then again, waiting a few minutes and sizing up the situation won't hurt anything since the animal will obviously not be going anywhere. Waiting too long to track a deer with a muscle wound, though, could be damaging when coagulation begins.

I have provided a table that you can use as a guide. I have stuck to this waiting schedule, as have other veteran deer hunters I know. The results have been spectacular and have led to the recovery of more than a few deer. Of course, you must know the location of the wound, and be aware of how it will affect tracking. Other factors, such as too many hunters in the area, terrain, weather, and darkness may also affect the length of time you should wait to track a deer. In the following chapters, I have supplied anecdotes, and information about specific types of wounds that tell why it is best to wait or delay tracking.

Lack of patience should never tempt you to begin tracking a deer immediately. When I shoot a deer, I'm as eager as the next guy to get after it and see my trophy up close. However, you must be patient and wait if necessary. I would that many hunters who pursue an animal right away do so because they just couldn't stand the agony of waiting. Just as harmful would be waiting, but not waiting long enough. For instance, if you should wait for four hours and you wait for only one hour to track a stomach-shot deer, you will probably push the deer farther away, just as you would have done if you had started tracking at once.

Throughout this book, I suggest that some wounds call for immediate tracking. After viewing

Location of Wound	Time to Wait Before Tracking
Artery (major)	20 minutes
Heart	20 minutes
Hip (muscle only)	20 minutes
Intestines	8 – 12 hours
Kidneys	20 minutes
Leg	20 minutes
Liver	2 to 3 hours
Lungs	20 minutes
Neck (muscle only)	20 minutes
Shoulder (muscle only)	20 minutes
Spine or Neck Vertebrate	0
Stomach	4 – 6 hours

Time to Wait Table: The author's schedule for waiting to track a wounded deer, by wound location. Variables may exist that will prompt or delay time to wait.

the table, you might wonder why these wounds suggest you wait twenty minutes. Actually, staying put for a few minutes after shooting an animal will help you gain composure, and recall a few events that may help to put you on the blood trail. You may not pick up the trail until twenty minutes after the shot, but you are still in immediate pursuit and will probably prevent coagulation.

When you do pursue a deer right away, you must move slowly and quietly from one drop of blood to another. Avoid getting ahead of yourself if you lose the blood trail, and keep a constant look ahead for a bedded or moving deer.

Reading Tracks

Just finding tracks when you trail a deer is helpful, but being able to read those tracks will provide valuable tracking insight. Tracks show you if a deer is running or walking. Tracks may indicate other factors, including the sex of the deer, size, and sometimes the type of wound the animal encountered.

Various types of wounds will cause a deer to run differently than it might have otherwise. For instance, a heart-shot deer often runs much more erratically than a lung-shot deer does. The running tracks of a deer with a stomach wound are totally different from one with a hip wound. Joseph Bruner, a German tracker, studied eight different sets of tracks of wounded deer. In 1909, Bruner provided an illustration of the track patterns in a book titled Tracks And Tracking (see table). In recent years, I have attempted to determine the accuracy of the track patterns and wounds depicted in the table. In many cases, the tracks I followed did not stay visible long enough, the deer stayed in woods and thickets and did not produce tracks, or the animal dropped dead before I could evaluate the tracks. Although I have yet to compare precisely the tracks recorded by Bruner and deer I have trailed, I have seen similarities - primarily the track patterns as a result of wounds to the foreleg and hind leg.

The back hooves of a deer are slightly smaller than the front hooves. It is difficult to provide measurements, since the size of the track is dependent upon the subspecies of the deer, age, and size. However, most adult whitetail tracks will be two and one-half to three inches in length when the animal walks. When running, the length and width of the tracks are slightly larger.

When you follow the tracks of a wounded deer, they often lead into other tracks, leaving you confused. This can happen in snow, even when it appears for a moment that you could follow the animal to the end of the continent. When the tracks you follow merge with other tracks, it is best to bend over, get close to the ground, and proceed cautiously.

One thing you can bet on is that most wounded deer do not attempt to travel with others unless the wound is minor, such as a scrape under the brisket, or a nick on the leg. I've also noticed that severely wounded young deer do not attempt to get back with the doe, nor does a severely wounded doe try to find her fawn.

Whenever I shoot a deer that is with others, it may run away with them, but will not stay with them long. After a short sprint, the wounded animal usually separates from the others. Thus, if you can't find blood near the location where you hit a deer, follow all the tracks but pay special attention to a track that suddenly separates from the others, or a track pattern that differs from the others.

When tracking a deer, it also helps to know if a deer is running or walking. For example, if walking tracks suddenly change to running tracks, it could be the deer detected your presence. Alternatively, the deer may have been bedded and detected your approach. Whenever a walking deer suddenly runs, I evaluate the situation carefully. I may stay on the trail, or I may sit down and wait.

There are two ways to tell if a deer is walking - by tracks and by blood. First, we'll discuss tracks.

A running deer brings its back feet ahead of the front feet. The tracks will appear as a set of four tracks, with the tracks of the back feet parallel with each other, and in front of the tracks made by the front feet. Each set of four tracks will be spaced two and one-half to three feet apart. When a deer walks, you will find two straight lines of tracks about fourteen to twenty inches apart.

That's understandable, if you consider the body width of a deer. The toes of the tracks will also be turned outward slightly. The straight-line appearance of the tracks can differ, as well as the outward angle of the toes when certain conditions exist. For instance, when a doe's udder is filled with milk, the tracks made by the back hooves may be farther apart than the tracks made by the front hooves, and the tracks of the back hooves may curve more outward than the front ones. It is also believed that track patterns of does in estrous, and bucks in rut change slightly. A certain wound may also have an affect on how the tracks appear.

For many years, veteran hunters and trackers have argued about determining the sex of the deer by its tracks. The debate will continue, as some tracks may allow you to determine the sex of the deer, while others will leave you scratching your head.

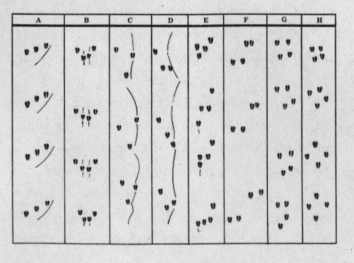

Wounded Deer Walking Patterns: (A) Trail of a deer shot through brisket with leg broken low in shoulder. (B) Trail of a deer shot high through the shoulders. (C) Trail of a deer with a broken foreleg - the lower the leg is broken, the more pronounced the drag mark. (D) Trail of a deer wit a broken hind leg - the lower the leg is broken. the more pronounced the drag mark. (E) Trail of a deer shot through the ham. (F) This trail usually means that the animal was shot through the intestines, liver or lungs. (G) Same as F but did not penetrate to the lungs. (H) The cross jump results from a bullet through the intestines or liver with the animal standing broadside to the hunter. (Joseph Bruner, Tracks And Tracking).

A running deer brings its back feet ahead of the front feet. Instead of evenly spaced tracks, you will find set of four tracks each.

A walking deer's tracks will be in two straight lines, those made by the left, and those made by the right hooves.

The size of the track may help, but only when it comes from a big buck, and you are familiar with the size of the tracks of an average adult deer in your area. If you have seen hundreds of tracks in the area made by deer weighing 125 to 150 pounds, and then come across the tracks of a 200-pound deer, you will probably see a noticeable difference, and believe they are that of a buck. However, I have seen one and one-half-year-old, 150-pound bucks with tracks as large as two-and-onehalf-year-old, 200-pound bucks. In addition, tracks may appear larger and deeper in snow and soft soil than they would on a dry, dirt surface. And since a running deer's track appears larger than a walking deer's track, it wouldn't be wise to estimate the sex or size of the deer if it is running.

You will often find drag marks in snow when you follow the tracks of a buck, providing the snow is a certain depth. A buck seems to walk more clumsily than a doe, and it's a fact that does raise their hooves slightly higher than a buck's, probably because their pelvic structure differs from bucks. In deep snow, all deer leave drag marks. In fact, when examining the tracks of deer in captivity, I've found that the only way to see drag marks of bucks is when the snow is one to three inches deep.

In heavy leaves, you may also determine drag marks. However, that is very difficult to do since the depth of leaves and terrain can vary every few yards. The best chance of seeing a buck's drag marks in leaves is when the terrain is level, most of the leaves have fallen and are dry, and there has not been heavy deer traffic through that specific area.

A deer's hooves are designed to provide traction, but not on slick surfaces. On ice, a deer walks very carefully, and appears to know that its hooves could slide out from under him. If the animal goes down, it may not be able to get back up.

Blood Trailing

Tracking a wounded deer, particularly one that does not leave an easy-to-follow blood trail, requires

Bucks will leave drag marks behind their tracks when they walk in snow. However, if the snow gets deep, all deer will leave drag marks.

skill. Most hunters, who have mastered the art of tracking, did so because of experience. However, help is advantageous, regardless of your abilities.

I always find myself much more nervous when tracking my own deer. Secondly, it really helps to have more eyes looking for blood and a downed deer. My son and I have shared many tracking experiences in the past two decades, and I am always glad to have his help. He is a patient tracker, as are many of my friends who are proficient trackers. In recent years my wife, Vikki, has also assisted me with trailing, and while she usually stands patiently on the last drop of blood, she often finds more blood in that location while I'm out ahead somewhere.

Just how many should be involved when the tracking begins? I prefer a party of two or three. Four hunters are pushing it. I have often assisted when the tracking party consisted of four, five, or more. I find things too noisy and careless, which can lead to a trampled blood trail or a spooked deer. When three people track the deer, one can stay on the last blood while four eyes continue looking for the next drop.

Although some blood trails are easy to see and can be followed rapidly, most difficult trailing episodes go from drop to drop. When you find one drop, look closely for another without moving too far ahead. If you can't find another drop within sight of the last, mark the spot before getting too far away. Never get in a hurry and start looking for a downed deer too quickly. Some hunters would rather look for a deer than a drop of blood. Their eyes never focus on the ground and surrounding debris for sign. This leads to careless tracking, and may spoil a recovery opportunity.

Walk to the sides of a blood trail as you follow it. If you walk over the blood, you'll kick up any drops that you've already found. While this may be okay if you find the deer a short distance ahead, it certainly won't do you any good if you have to return to the blood drops later on. For instance, what if the deer you're following suddenly begins backtracking? Surprisingly, some deer do turn around and go back in the same direction they just came from. If you walk a couple of feet to the sides of the blood trail, and mark it consistently, you should have no problem returning to the original trail if the deer turns around and walks back from where it came.

As mentioned previously, it helps to tie white tissue paper or trail-marking ribbon a few feet above the ground each time you find blood. Don't lay your marker on the ground, or tie it a foot or two above the ground, since it would be hard to see from a short distance away.

It may not be necessary to mark the trail if you are finding large amounts of blood, but it is necessary whenever you find blood droplets several feet apart. The markers allow you to return to the last blood, and they allow you to see the directional travel of the deer you are trailing. Many times, after losing a blood trail, I have looked back through the woods to see 100 yards or more of markers. I can then notice if the deer is veering right or left, and can concentrate on looking for blood in another direction. When the tracking ends, return to your location and remove the markers. Tissue paper will decompose eventually, but this may take several weeks. Seeing tissue paper strung through woods is not a pretty sight, and it won't do much for your hunting area.

Speaking of hunting areas, be aware that a major tracking episode will probably hurt your hunting area for several days. Consistently, I have seen areas dry up immediately following a trailing endeavor. However, when you consider the disturbance and the human scent left in the area, it's no wonder the hunting becomes stale. I always hope for a good rain to wash out human scent as soon as the tracking ends.

I've said this before: Despite what you may have heard, the volume of blood you find on the ground has little to do with your chances of recovering a deer. I have heard hunters (myself included) say, "This deer is about to go down." These opinions are often based on a heavy blood trail. However, many scrape and muscle wounds cause excessive bleeding that do not always result in a downed deer. These wounds produce blood trails that would make you believe an artery was severed, but after a couple of hundred yards or less, they begin to tell a different story. On the other hand, many stomach and intestinal-shot deer leave little or no blood, but will result in a downed deer. For this reason, it is best not to speculate when it comes to the amount of external blood, since it could affect your persistence to continue tracking if the going gets tough.

Large cuts across the bottom of the deer may result in excessive bleeding when the broadhead or projectile does not penetrate into the body cavity. They simply make a long incision. You might determine this type of wound at the location the deer stood when you shot. A large section of hair, sometimes up to several inches, will be found on the ground after grazing an animal.

When the blood trail becomes difficult to follow, get down on your knees, or bend down to look for blood. You'll be surprised how much more blood you can find when your eyes are only a foot above the ground, particularly when nickel-size droplets suddenly turn into drops the size of pinheads. Getting on all fours is probably better than bending, but it can also damage an existing blood trail.

Many blood trails intensify as you follow them, while others begin to weaken. Several factors will determine the amount of blood that gets to the ground as the deer moves farther away. For example, you may follow the trail of a running deer that received a muscle wound. Each time the deer's heart pumps hard, blood is expelled through an entry and/or exit hole. If this deer begins walking, the blood trail may weaken.

A low hit can also cause more blood to get to the ground early in the tracking than it will later. A high hit works the opposite, since the blood you find on the ground may intensify after the deer travels a short distance. Then, consider a low hit, and blood in the body cavity. As the deer travels, internal bleeding may occur. This blood soon reaches the hole in the deer

The amount of blood that gets to the ground often depends upon the location of the wound. Don't be mislead if you find very little blood. Many deer that do not bleed much externally may still be mortally wounded.

and finds its way to the ground. Thus, the blood trail begins intensifying as the deer moves farther along the trail. Later, I discuss specific wounds and what kind of blood trails will occur as a result of these wounds.

You may find two trails of blood instead of one when complete penetration occurs. The possibility of two blood trails depends upon the location of wound, and the height of your entry and exit holes. However, if a single blood trail suddenly turns into two, make certain the deer is not backtrailing.

Previously, I told how you can tell if a deer is running or walking by its tracks. You can also determine if a deer is standing, walking, or running by examining blood droplets. When a deer walks slowly, you will find a line of droplets. Each droplet is round and completely encircled by thin splatter marks. The shape of the droplets is the same as those made by a standing deer, except they are not in a line. Instead, you may find several droplets in one location, perhaps covering a one- or two-foot area. When a deer stands, you might find a pool of blood

Get close to the ground if the blood trail becomes difficult to follow, but make certain you stay to the sides of the trail and don't walk over blood.

as each drop merges with another. The amount of blood you find on the ground depends upon the wound, and how long the deer stood there.

When a deer runs, the blood droplets are oblong. You may find splatter marks on the wide end of the oval droplet, but not on the opposite end. The wider portion of the droplet, which has the splatter marks, also indicates the direction the deer is traveling.

When you find blood in the deer's tracks, it usually indicates a leg, shoulder, neck, or ham wound. The blood ends up in the track after running down a leg, but this usually doesn't occur until the animal has traveled for a distance. It is also possible you may find blood on the ground between the left and right hooves, or about the center of the deer. This often occurs when you track a neck-shot deer, or if your departure hole came out on the bottom side of the deer.

Always examine the blood carefully to make certain it is indeed blood. There's nothing worse than losing a blood trail, then to have someone holler, "Blood," and then discover it isn't blood at all. The woods floor is full of red, maroon, and purple colors. I've seen some maple leaves that had red blotches on them that look exactly like blood. Many types of berries splatter on the ground and appear as blood. When you are uncertain, use your saliva to wet the spot you suspect is blood. If it doesn't wipe off, you know it isn't blood. Another thought is to use hydrogen peroxide or a commercial blood tester.

When blood dries, it becomes darker and is harder to see. The more blood there is in one location, the longer it will stay wet. However, if you follow a dry blood trail and it suddenly turns wet, you probably got close to the deer and sent it moving.

When a blood trail expires, I will begin looking for blood smears on rocks, trees, tall weeds, and other debris. If I don't find smears, I resort to

When you find two blood trails instead of one, it probably means the deer is bleeding out of both sides. However, always make certain the deer hasn't walked back the same trail it came through earlier.

A deer that walks will leave blood droplets that are round with splatter marks surrounding the drops.

following trails and looking for tracks. If tracks are not visible, I look for another means of trailing the deer. For instance, when a deer runs in leaves, it leaves an obvious trail. The leaves are kicked out and piled up near the locations where the deer's hooves come off the ground. Even if the deer walks in leaves, careful tracking may allow you to follow the trail. When the hooves of a walking deer come down, they curl the leaves under each hoof.

Finally, don't take things for granted when tracking a wounded deer. This can get you into trouble. I try to look at each trailing experience as a unique one. I often know what to expect, but avoid making guesses. I stay on a blood trail as long as possible, and then resort to tracking the animal the best I can when blood is not getting to the ground. When I can't track the deer any longer by blood or tracks, and all other efforts to locate them have been to no avail, I begin the recovery attempt. For this reason, it's important for you to read the chapter, "Last-Ditch Efforts."

The String Tracker

The bowhunter who chooses to use a string tracker may find it beneficial when it comes to recovering a deer. However, you should be aware of a few disadvantages.

A friend of mine, Woody Williams, used a string tracker in Ontario while hunting black bear. After shooting a bear, he nervously watched the string unwind until it stopped. He believed the bear was down.

Shortly after dark, Woody and I got on the trail of the wounded bear. We found blood here and there,

When a deer runs, it leaves a different blood trail. Notice the oval shape of these blood droplets, and that splatter marks are only at one end of the droplet.

Many leaves and berries can resemble blood. If you have any doubt if what you found is blood, test it with hydrogen peroxide or a commercial blood tester.

but easily followed the line that had unraveled from the string tracker. About 150 yards later, we reached the end of the line (I mean that literally). It had caught in debris and broken. We never recovered the bear.

String tracking line is tough, but it can break. Archers should also be aware that arrow flight and accuracy can change when using a string tracker. The farther you shoot, the more drop you will have. When I used a string tracker for the first time several years ago, I found it necessary to adjust my sight when shooting at twenty yards. My arrows dropped

about four inches. At thirty yards, the drop increased dramatically. If you plan to use a string tracker, plan to practice often.

Wind can also cause problems when using a string tracker. The loop of line that dangles loosely from the canister to the business end of the arrow may catch on accessories or limbs, causing the string to unravel.

On the positive side, a string tracker can give you several hundred yards of easy tracking if you make a bad hit. If the line gets to the end of the spool, simply tie on line from an extra spool. This can add another few hundred yards of easy tracking. A string tracker may also help you track a deer if it rains. Finally, a string tracker makes it easy to locate your arrow when you miss, or if it totally penetrates. If the arrow does go all the way through the deer, however, you may find two trails of line when you follow it.

Tracking with Dogs

No hunter will dispute a dog's ability to follow a trail. We also know that a dog will do a better job than we can of tracking a wounded deer. After all, they can follow a trail by scent, while we must use our eyes.

However, the idea of using dogs does not appeal to every hunter. Instead, they believe that it is the hunter's responsibility to do everything humanly possible to recover the animal, without the aid of a dog.

This is a touchy subject, so I might as well jump in and give my opinion. I don't have a problem with using dogs in some tracking situations, but a thin line exists. Where dogs are legal, I often wonder if it can lead to careless shooting on a hunter's part. If they have access to a quality dog, would they take risky shots? Stress is another factor. Is it possible that an unleashed dog would cause undue stress when it trails a deer that has received only a minor wound? I believe so. If I started deer hunting in a state that allowed dogs to trail deer, I might see it from a different perspective. But I have another opinion. If a deer is doomed and will surely die, such as a gut-shot deer, and all tracking efforts by the hunter have failed, it would seem better to use a dog than to not find the animal at all.

At the time of this writing, trailing dogs are legal in fifteen states. In one of these states, however, dogs must be on a leash. There is also an organization dedicated to helping others recover deer with the aid of dogs, but not until the hunter has made a thorough recovery attempt.

I must tip my hat to Deer Search, Inc. (D.S.I.), a New York group of volunteers that uses leashed dogs to track and find wounded deer. There are sixty members in the western chapter, where Mike Coppola is a trustee, and past president. According to Coppola, his chapter received about 550 requests to track wounded deer in 1999. He reported that the chapter assisted in about 200 of the requests. Each request is evaluated when the call comes in. Coppola said that a large percentage of the wounds are shoulder hits. However, D.S.I makes every effort to help hunters recover liver and gut-shot deer. Even the organization's brochure states, "D.S.I. is NOT a hunter's crutch, it is an agency of Last Resort. After you have tried everything else you know to do and still circumstances prevent you from recovering your wounded deer (or bear), call Deer Search, Inc. For more information, contact Deer Search, Inc., P.O. Box 853, Pleasant Valley, NY 12569, or call 716/648-4355.

States that Allow the Use of Trailing Dogs

Alabama	New York
Arkansas	North Carolina
California	South Carolina
Florida	South Dakota
Georgia	Texas
Louisiana	Virginia
Mississippi	Wisconsin*
Nebraska	

* Dogs must be on a leash.

Tracking Accessories

Deer hunters pack along all kinds of gadgets, from grunt calls and scents to wind-checking devices. Why not prepare a tracking kit? Surprisingly, you can include about everything you could possibly need in a fanny pack or small daypack. If you are hunting close to home or a vehicle, you can leave the pack stored away until duty calls.

The most important items are probably markers to place above blood droplets, a proper light for tracking in the dark, and hydrogen peroxide, or a commercial blood testing chemical. However, there is an array of other items listed in the Tracking Kit table that you may find useful. Some of the items you may have with you, but nonetheless the kit makes certain they will be there when tracking a deer. I would also suggest you pack along this book if space allows. This will make it possible for you to recognize the type of wound you are dealing with by blood color and hair. Additionally, you will have quick access to tracking tips.

I consistently pack a tracking kit, hoping that some of the items won't be used. As they say, though, "It's better to have it and not need it than need it and not have it."

Tracking Kit Essentials

Compass	String Tracker
Field Dressing Gloves	Toilet Paper
Hydrogen Peroxide	Topographic Map
Knife	Tracking Book
Light/Lantern	Trail Marking Ribbon
Radio	

Store these items in a fanny pack or daypack, and keep them close by.

To make certain you have everything when tracking becomes necessary, consider packing a tracking kit in a daypack or fanny pack.

Credit: Ted Rose

Taking time to evaluate all the signs and then planning a course of action is often crucial to locating a wounded deer.

Field Dressing Your Deer

STEPHEN D. CARPENTERI

You've made a good shot and found your deer. Good job! For safety's sake, approach your downed deer from behind and above its shoulders. Move in slowly with your gun still loaded (but with the safety on).

Watch the animal for signs of life. If its eyes are open and there are no signs of breathing or other movement, the animal is likely dead. Touch the deer's rump with your foot and wait for a reaction. If nothing happens, this phase of the hunt is over.

If the deer appears to be breathing or moving, is blinking its eyes or attempts to rise, you must shoot the animal again immediately. Administer a shot at the base of the skull, just behind the ear. Head shots are unnecessarily damaging and unsightly, and body shots will simply ruin meat. Some taxidermists do not like the behind-the-ear shot because it can create a large hole in the hide, but recovery of the deer is

most important. Hides can be repaired or substitute hides may be used for a mount — you can't mount a deer that gets up and runs away from you!

Fortunately, 99 percent of heart-lung shot deer will be dead when you catch up to them. The only deer I've had to shoot a second time were bucks I'd hit in the neck, head or lower chest — and thankfully few of those!

Congratulations! You've accomplished something only 10 percent of this year's hunters will achieve, and you have a right to be proud. Enjoy this moment, let the adrenalin flow, take some pictures and pause to admire and appreciate your trophy. The first thing I do after confirming a kill is affix my license tag to the ear or antler as required by state regulation. Next, I'll take a few minutes to admire my hard-won trophy, pausing just a moment to appreciate the beautiful animal that has been the object of off-season dreaming and many hours of travel, preparation, anxiety and effort. Any deer is a hard-earned trophy and worthy of a moment of introspective reflection. For most hunters, success in the deer woods is a long time coming. Savor the moment every chance you get!

NOW, LET'S GET TO WORK!

Gutting Your Deer

Tasty, palatable venison depends on what you do once your deer is down, and there is no time to

waste. Your bullet did some internal damage to the animal, and death begins a process of deterioration that must be managed.

The first thing to do is gut the animal. Gutting a deer is not as complicated or "gross" as most people tend to think. The goal is simply to remove all the internal organs from end to end. This removes most of the blood from the animal, shot-damaged tissue and debris that may have leaked into the body cavity from damaged organs, the stomach or intestines.

The process can be confusing to a first-timer who may not even know where to begin, but, on a bet some years ago, I completely gutted a large Maine buck in 56 seconds — it's not a particularly difficult procedure if you know what you are doing.

The gutting process is as varied as the number of hunters who perform the task, and I have seen it done many ways. It's not important how you do it. It's simply important to empty the animal of its viscera in order to halt the bacterial process and help cool the remaining meat.

Here's one way to do it:

1. **With the deer laying on its side, lift the tail and "core" the anus just as you would an apple**. Pull the anus upward and insert your knife

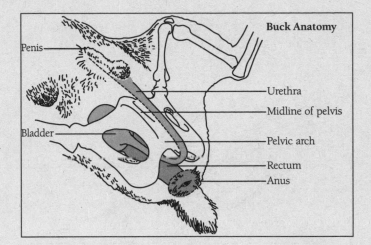

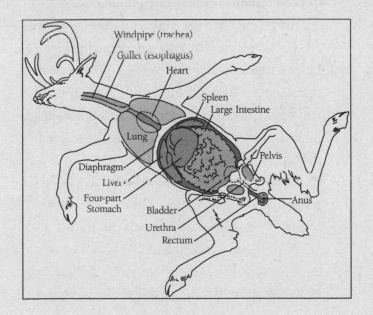

blade to the hilt about an inch away from the opening. Now, cut around the anus, gently pulling the anus away from the body as you go. This separates the end of the digestive tract from the body, making it easier to remove the entrails later.

2. **Lay the animal on its back with the shoulders slightly higher than the hindquarters.** You may need to move the animal to another location to accomplish this. In most areas the ground is uneven so there's rarely a lack of elevated ground that can be used. You may prop the animal on a rock, log or even your backpack, just as long as the shoulders are above the hips. Straddle the carcass facing the animal's head and run your free hand down the breast bone until you can feel the beginning of the soft abdominal wall. This is usually the area where the black-haired breast and white belly fur join. Press down firmly with one hand and insert the knife blade to the hilt horizontally through the skin and muscle below. Aim the knife point toward the deer's head, not straight down into the body cavity. Doing so will puncture the stomach or intestines, creating interesting sights, smells and sounds most hunters prefer to avoid! Cut forward as far as your knife will go (just an inch or two) creating a hole in the hide through the skin and abdominal muscles. This is the start of your belly cut.

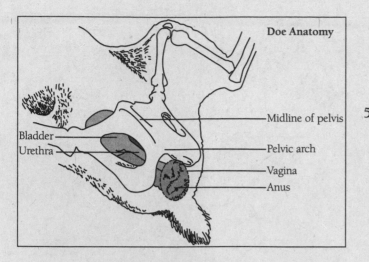

Doe Anatomy

Bladder
Urethra

Midline of pelvis

Pelvic arch

Vagina

Anus

3. **Turn and straddle the carcass with your feet placed on either side of the deer's shoulders, steadying the carcass.** Place two fingers of your free hand into the initial cut. Pull up sharply, and you will create a small space between the belly muscle and the stomach. Carefully insert the tip of your knife blade into the hole between your fingers, blade up. Moving the knife and your fingers as one unit, slice carefully straight ahead down the center of the belly to a point midway between the rear legs. Your cut should end just beyond the testicles (if it's a buck) or the udder. Work slowly because it's important to keep the abdominal wall away from the stomach and intestines. These organs may protrude slightly as you progress with opening the stomach cavity, but that is normal. Just be sure to keep the knife point and blade away from them!

4. **Straddle the deer again, this time facing the head.** Reach forward inside the carcass along the left and right ribs until you can feel a smooth, red membrane just in front of the stomach. This is the diaphragm, which separates the heart and lungs from the lower digestive system. Move the stomach away from the diaphragm with your free hand and cut along the diaphragm, separating the red membrane from the rib cage.

In heartshot deer, this invariably releases a gush of thick, hot blood, a graphic illustration of why it is not necessary to "bleed" a shot deer by cutting its throat.

5. **Remove your coat or jacket, roll up your sleeves and put on your rubber gloves if you have them.** With your free hand, reach as far up into the chest-neck cavity as you can until you locate the esophagus, a taught, rubbery, hose-like organ. Then, pull your hand out and grip the tip of your knife and work both hands back into the opening. Guide the knife blade to the farthest point of the esophagus you can reach and hold the knife there while your free hand reaches down and grips the esophagus a safe distance away. Maintaining a tight grip, slice through the esophagus and pull the organ back toward yourself. Use the knife to snip away any tendons or muscles that are attached to the ribs or spine. Back away from the deer as you pull making the necessary cuts as you go. In short order the heart, lungs, liver, stomach and intestines will be outside the carcass.

6. **Reach into the rear of the exposed abdominal cavity and pull the pre-cut anal section out of the animal.** You may need to make a few additional cuts here as well. That baseball-sized, creamy white bag you now see is the bladder. Do not puncture the bladder! Find the neck of the bladder with your free hand, pinch it tightly and cut it off above the pinch. Step well away from the carcass and carefully toss the severed bladder well away from you.

7. **At this point the internal organs have been removed.** You may cut away the reproductive organs if you wish, or wait until the animal is skinned. Reach inside the belly cavity and find the two long, thin, smooth muscles that lay along the spine. These are the tenderloins, the

most tender cuts on any animal. Slice either end of each piece and carefully pull the muscle away from the spine. Wash the blood off of the tenderloins and refrigerate as soon as possible.

8. **Move the deer away from the gut pile** and turn the carcass belly-side down with the legs propped open so any blood or material left inside the animal may drain freely. Take a break and let the carcass drain. Pay attention in gathering your equipment and gear. This is where knives, compasses, ammunition and other items end up being lost or misplaced!

It was once traditional to remove the heart and liver to be eaten as a ceremonial dinner in camp the night of a kill, but most states now caution hunters against eating organ meat due to chemical contamination. Check local regulations for cautionary statements regarding game organ consumption advisories.

Transporting Deer Out of the Woods

With your deer down, gutted and draining, the next order of business is getting the carcass out of the woods. The goal is to do so without damaging the hide or meat due to excessive dragging or pounding against rocks, logs and other obstacles. If you are hunting alone far from roads or trails there is not much you can do except start dragging, especially in areas where quartering deer prior to tagging is not legal.

Are You Ready For This?

The first thing you must do is admit to yourself that you may not be strong or healthy enough for the task, which involves dragging 100 to 200 pounds of dead weight over rough ground for long periods of time. Hunters who are too old, in poor condition or unaware of their vascular problems die or suffer major heart attacks while dragging deer out of the woods. Be honest about your own physical condition and do not attempt to drag a deer if you have shortness of breath, dizzy spells or chest pains, even occasionally. There are other ways to deal with transporting dead deer, and killing yourself in the process is the least desirable method!

I once shot a buck on a state-designated "primitive area" where no vehicles were allowed. My trophy was over two miles from the nearest gate with elevations varying from 1,100 to 1,400 feet. I was in what I consider the best shape of my life at the time, participating in 10k races several times each year, often running 40 or more miles per week to keep in shape. Most hunters do not walk or run 40 miles per year, and in fact are probably not in very good shape for any kind of physically challenging venture.

In any case, after state foresters refused to allow me (at age 45) to enter the area by vehicle, and with no one else around to help, I elected to drag the deer out on my own. On the way in I had deposited full water bottles about every 200 yards, figuring I'd stop for a break and a drink as I reached each way point. I simply attached a rope to the buck's antlers, turned around and started dragging. Eight hours later I had my deer at the first exit gate where I could drive up and load the buck into my truck. I was exhausted, cut, scratched and bloody but I was alive and the job was done!

Would I do it again? Probably, if there were no other way. Would I recommend it? Definitely not! Hunters I know who have accompanied me to that spot on subsequent trips have told me they would not even want to walk back in there again, let alone go that far while dragging a deer and carrying a pack and rifle!

Dragging Deer by Hand

There was a time when a hunter and his partners would simply grab a deer by its antlers and, through sheer strength of will, drag the animal to the nearest road. Of course, hunting close to roads was always in the game plan, and many hunters refuse to shoot a deer if it were so far back in they'd have trouble getting it out. Hunters today still remark about how they won't hunt certain areas because of the difficulty of dragging a deer back to camp.

The worst way to drag a deer is by hand, using nothing but the antlers or, in the case of a doe, the legs or ears. The bare-handed method is too much work, too inefficient and too rough on the hide and meat. *Avoid hand-dragging if you can!*

The next best technique is to tie a rope around the deer's neck or antlers (with or without the front feet tied in). A deer will "drag" relatively smoothly this way, even smoother if you cut a 12-inch stick and use it for a drag handle. If other people are available, use a longer stick (stout enough for the job) with one or more draggers on each side. The added manpower will make the job much easier.

Adaptations include using shoulder or body harnesses (a shirt or jacket slung diagonally across the chest with lengths of rope tied to the deer), tying the rope around your waist or looping the rope around your forearm.

All of these methods work well on snow, wet leaves or grass. It's still work and will still take some time and effort, but it is easier than dragging a deer through open woods, swamps, brush or clear-cut areas. If possible, avoid dragging your deer down creek bottoms, wet or dry. The terrain in such places is wet, slippery, rocky and uneven, often with entangling brush and vegetation. It's true that creek bottoms are at the lowest elevation, but the tradeoff is that you'll be dragging your trophy through some of the worst terrain you can imagine!

The nostalgic, deer-on-a-pole approach, in which the deer's legs are tied to a single pole with one hunter on either end, should be illegal! I have tried this technique several times and it seems that no matter what you do the deer swings and sways with the rhythm of the carriers, pounding the pole down into your shoulders and nearly dislocating your hips in the process. It's not easy to find carriers of the same height, speed and build, and so the deer rocks and rolls like a pendulum all the way back to camp. The technique looks great in pictures, but the last time I tried it was over 20 years ago and I still get back spasms just thinking about it!

Slides and Wheeled Aids

Much progress has been made on the inventive side of deer transportation. Plastic sleds, sheaths and the like are designed to surround the carcass in slippery nylon, plastic or rubber, thereby reducing the amount of drag encountered in rough woods. These products work to an extent, but I have found that there is a loss of control as well because they are often too slick — the deer shoots ahead like a bullet or wobbles from side to side as it slides too quickly over every obstacle it encounters. Going uphill, they are fine, but downhill drags can be an adventure.

The best non-motorized way to transport deer over dry ground (you can't beat a canoe if there's a stream or lake nearby!) is with a wheeled cart or wagon. One-wheeled carts work well enough when two hunters can work together, but you will run into balance problems if you try to single wheel a deer out of the woods on your own. There are many two-wheeled carts on the market that are excellent for transporting deer on even terrain, roads or trails. I usually try to drag my deer to the nearest logging road or trail, and then use my two wheeled cart for the remainder of the trip.

The secret to transporting a deer with wheeled vehicles (including bicycles) is to tie the deer securely to the cart (including head and feet) so that there is no wobbling or shifting during transport. No matter how you bring your deer out, be sure to tie it down securely and travel so that the antlers and legs are tucked out of the way and don't catch on every sapling, branch and vine along the way.

Motorized Vehicles

The easiest way to transport deer is by vehicle. Simply strap the animal to the deck of the vehicle or load it into the back of the truck and head for home. This is definitely the way to go if the area you're hunting is open to motorized vehicles. Many state forests, wildlife management areas and state parks do not allow such vehicles, but in many cases you can drag your deer to the nearest unrestricted road and then transport it by vehicle to camp or your car or truck.

Use Caution with Potential Mounts!

No matter how you decide to transport your deer, use extra caution if you intend to have the animal mounted. Do not tie ropes or cords around the deer's head, neck or shoulder region. Damage done to deer hair cannot be repaired by a taxidermist, and if the damage is severe it may require the use of a substitute cape, adding to the cost of the mount.

Also, do not drag the deer. Most taxidermists recommend that you carry it out of the woods to avoid damaging the hide or hair, which of course means a more complicated, time-consuming job. I have participated in a few "deer carries," and it is not easy. The finished product is certainly worth the effort, but plan on having at least four helpers and double the amount of time it would normally take to drag a deer to a road or trail.

To transport a deer meant for mounting, bring a 10x12 tarp and two 12-foot poles. Wrap the poles into the 12-foot length of the tarp to create a stretcher. Tie the wrapped sides tight so they don't unravel enroute. Place the deer on the tarp and, with two carriers per side, head for the road! It would help to have a fifth person walking ahead with an axe or brush cutter to trim away saplings and branches, creating a trail that can accommodate four carriers, a deer and a stretcher. It sounds like a tough job, and it is, but it's worth the effort if you want an exceptional mounting job.

Retrace Your Steps

Many hunters I've known who shot a deer and dragged it out, alone or with friends, end up leaving some item of personal gear at the gutting site. Knowing this, I've retraced their steps and have recovered cellphones, knives, gloves, hats, backpacks, and Thermos bottles. It's always worth returning to the scene, with or without a firearm, just to look for and recover lost equipment.

For example, one year I left a stainless steel pocket saw in the woods. I had used the saw to cut a drag pole. I forgot about the saw till I was halfway home and had to wait a full year before I was able to go back and look for it. I knew exactly where I'd left it and found it there the following November, dusty and dirty but none the worse for wear.

Go back to the site of each kill and look for lost gear — good advice for you and for me!

Preparing to Butcher Your Deer

JOHN WEISS

In getting ready for butchering, the hunter will need to assemble a selection of tools that will enable him to reduce big pieces of venison quickly and efficiently into many smaller ones ready for the freezer. In accomplishing this, first-hand, trial-and-error experience plays a role in determining what works best for you. And those special routines, methods, and equipment preferences you eventually come to rely upon year in and year-out are sure to differ somewhat from those of another hunter who is equally proficient in handling his deer.

Then there is an entirely different class of hunters—the professionals—whom we should all watch and talk to whenever the opportunity arises.

One such "professor emeritus" of the chopping-block table who long ago took me under his wing is Minnesota hunter Charlie Hause. Aside from being a fanatical deer hunter, he's a professional meatcutter by trade. In addition to annually cutting up hundreds of carcasses from beef steers and hogs, and the deer he harvests himself, he moonlights during the hunting season by doing custom-butchering for local sportsmen.

I don't know how many deer Charlie has cut up over the years, but there was a particular day that stands out in his memory, a day when he was so swamped with orders he just couldn't handle everything himself. So he bought a couple of cases of premium beer, which is always a good persuader, and then called three fellow meatcutters to help him out

of a jam. Beginning at three o'clock in the afternoon, the foursome set to the task and continued working through the late night hours until four o'clock in the morning. During that time Charlie and his pals completely butchered a total of forty deer. Not only that, they also made 1,200 pounds of burger and sausage from all the lesser cuts and trimmings, swapped stories of hunts past and, yes, even managed to polish off both cases of beer.

It must have been a wild and woolly night, but everything was completed to perfection and many hours later hundreds of wrapped, labeled, and frozen packages of venison were waiting for their respective owners to pick up. I remember Charlie saying that

When conditions are right and everyone in camp is filling his tag, a meat-cutting marathon may be in your future. To make the job easy, first spend some time assembling your tools and preparing your work area.

about the time he finished cleaning up his home butchershop from this marathon meatcutting session, he had just enough time to shower and gulp down several cups of black coffee before having to open his meat market downtown. A pro's pro, indeed!

Getting Your Work Area Ready

Even though professional butchers have personal preferences when it comes to certain brands of cutting tools and supplies, their common bond is that, before setting to the task at hand, they invest a lot of time readying their work sites.

This is critical to success, speed, and happiness because you don't want to be so physically uncomfortable that the butchering operation becomes a miserable ordeal. Nor do you want it to take twelve hours to complete a six hour task, and perhaps even do a sloppy job at that. And with several venison quarters lying before you, now is certainly not the time to launch a search for your knives, try to locate your whetstone, or find you have to go to town to buy freezer wrapping paper and other supplies; this is nothing more than poor planning, and it often dooms what should be a proficient butchering effort right from the get-go.

First decide upon the best place to do your butchering. Since everyone's living circumstances are different, I'll simply describe the best and worst places and the reader can adjust this insight to his own situation.

The best location is a clean, well-lit, spacious garage that is cool enough for meat handling but warm enough that you can work in shirtsleeves.

The least favorable location is your kitchen, and with good reason. The kitchens of most homes are high-traffic areas where meals must be prepared several times a day and hunting dogs must be fed and kids are always looking for snacks or wanting

a drink. Also, most kitchens are too warm for long meat-cutting sessions, and available table or counter-top workspace isn't really large enough for major butchering operations.

What you need is ample time and space to complete your meat-cutting without hassles and interruptions. You need a large work surface and plenty of elbow room, particularly if someone else will be working alongside you. And you need the peace of mind, not the constant worry and concern, that some errant speck of blood or scrap of meat that falls to the floor is not going to draw the wrath of other family members.

A large table is fine as your work surface. This is most commonly a picnic table brought inside, but it can be a simple four-by-eight sheet of plywood resting upon sawhorses. Just make sure it's as clean as possible and situated in such a manner that you will be cutting at comfortable waist level.

To ensure cleanliness, cover your work surface with protective paper. Lay it down in several long, overlapping sheets with the shiny, plastic-coated side up; secure the edges in place around the perimeter of the table with masking tape.

The purpose of this tabletop covering is to have a neat, clean place to set various cuts of meat before and after working on them. However, you won't want to do actual cutting on this surface because your knife blade would quickly reduce the paper to shreds.

For cutting work, you need some type of cutting board. This can be a standard kitchen model, if it's extra-large in size, that's made of strips of laminated hardwood and intended for food-preparation work.

Better still is a professional meat-cutting board made of pressed styrene and thermoplastic resin that is both sanitary and impervious to knife cuts. In either case, the ideal size is something about twenty-four inches wide by thirty-six inches long by one-inch thick.

A large, flat cutting surface, such as a chopping block table is essential to meat cutting. Wooden cutting surfaces are porous, however, and require regular cleaning. A one to four-inch thick block of hard plastic is easier to clean than wood and requires less maintenance.

Avoid the commonly seen use of a square of plywood. The soft wood will become scarred with deep knife cuts that attract bacteria, and the wood laminations are glued with chemical adhesives that may be toxic.

Instead of a cutting board that's placed upon the larger work surface, the hunter might want to consider a stand-alone chopping-block table. They're worthwhile investments on the part of serious sportsmen who take several deer every year because, in addition to accommodating venison, they have numerous other fish and game-dressing uses throughout the year.

Just be sure to carefully follow the manufacturer's instructions before and after each use of the table, because even the hardest wood must periodically be cleaned and maintained. The chopping-block table I'm presently using is made of hard-rock maple impregnated with a special food-safe polyurethane coating that requires no maintenance whatever, other than occasionally wiping it down with a rag dampened in very hot water. Most, however, require periodic scraping

with a stiff-bristle wire brush and then a soaking application with disinfectant followed by a treatment with a bactericidal mineral oil.

Cutting Tools That Get the Job Done

"A meat-cutter is no better than the knives he uses," Jim Borg, a professional butcher from Nashville, Tennessee, remarked as we began working on two deer. With that, he opened his special briefcase, a hallmark that distinguishes such tradesmen, and gave me a peek at a gleaming array of knives of every conceivable design, all assigned to their own protective slots in plastic foam.

Borg's opening comment was right on target because, like a master mechanic given only one size and type of wrench, a hunter who has only one poorly chosen knife can expect to do little more than an amateurish, hacked-up job on his deer.

Since every skilled meat-cutter eventually acquires preferences in his chosen assortment of cutting tools, it's impossible here to recommend a specific selection of knives as better than any other. Yet, we can talk in generalities.

First, some type of conventional butcher's knife with a blade at least ten inches in length is needed to reduce large chunks of meat to smaller ones in one fell swoop; otherwise, with a shorter blade, several smaller cuts will have to be made instead of a single slice, and those cuts will seldom meet, leaving a ragged, irregular appearance.

A boning knife also is imperative. As the reader will soon discover, I'm a strong proponent of boning-out meat whenever possible, for two important reasons. Bone-cutting with a saw is eliminated, so marrow "dust" cannot sprinkle the meat; many butchers believe marrow, in addition to deer fat, is what's often responsible for the overly strong,

An assemblage of knives is important, each intended for a specific task. The author recommends (from top to bottom) a cleaver, a long- and short-bladed butcher's knife, and a boning knife. Also needed is an all-purpose utility knife, not shown because your choice of hunting/field-dressing knife is adequate.

pungent, gamey flavor that many people object to. Second, you save on freezer space if you don't have to store forty pounds of bones (which you cannot eat, anyway) along with your venison.

Most boning knives have a long, slender blade that culminates in an upswept tip. They are also quite thin, which gives the blade flexibility to allow a cutter to guide the blade around irregular bone curvatures. And guess what? One way a sportsman can make at least one of his knives perform double-duty is to use his long-bladed fish-fillet knife as his venison boning knife; it's a near-perfect substitute.

An all-purpose or utility knife, or even a paring knife, will also come in handy for final trimming operations and other close work calling for a meticulous touch. And from time to time you might also find use for a heavy meat cleaver, especially when working on ribs and steaks prepared bone-in.

Some type of meat saw is also sure to be periodically needed in the processing of venison. As already mentioned, I'm a proponent of minimal bone cutting, but since some cutting is inevitable, a quality saw is a delight to work with. Such a saw is chiefly used to cut off the lower legs and separate the head from the carcass by cutting through the neckbone. Then, during actual butchering operations, you may desire to cut sections from the rib cage for broiling, and certain types of roasts, such as front-shoulder blade roasts. There's even one preliminary butchering technique to be described later that involves first halving the carcass by cutting down the centerline of the backbone. There are many models of meat saws to choose from, depending upon your needs and how much you can afford to spend. The smallest I'm aware of is the Wyoming Saw, available through hunting mail-order catalogs and designed primarily for field use or in camp.

The largest and most expensive saw is an electric, table-mounted bandsaw of the type found in professional butchershops. Although they do extremely high-quality work in short time, their prices generally limit their use to those who do custom-butchering of deer for others, and hunting clubs where many members can share both the saw and its cost.

In between these two extremes are moderately priced, professional meat saws that resemble giant hacksaws but are specifically intended for cutting meat and bone.

Do yourself a favor and don't cheap-out by attempting to use a conventional hacksaw from your garage workshop. Hacksaws, generally used for metal cutting, typically have twenty to twenty-six teeth per inch; since the teeth are so small and close together they quickly clog with bone and meat residue, which renders them inoperative until they're scrubbed down with a stiff-bristle brush. You don't need this continual hassle. Buy a professional meat saw, which has only ten to twelve teeth per inch. It will be a pleasure to

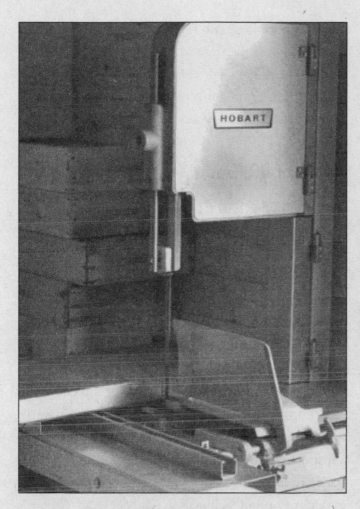

A traditional butcher's meat saw is a smart investment for any serious hunter. Though not cheap, such a saw will last a lifetime.

A professional meat saw can make short work of many deer, but they are pricey, which usually limits them to hunting clubs where many members can share the cost.

use, will last the rest of your life (you'll probably never even have to replace the blade), and the only maintenance you'll have to give it is to wash it with hot, soapy water at the end of each day's use.

Some means of keeping your knives scalpel-sharp through the duration of your meatcutting also is imperative. A quality whetstone such as an Arkansas or Ouachita is a good choice, and so are the ceramic rods and diamond-dust-impregnated steel rods now available to hunters.

It would be impossible to describe a universal knife-sharpening procedure here, because so many variables are involved, including the type of steel the blade is made of, the shape of the blade, whether

the blade is flat- or hollow-ground, and whether the bevel of the cutting edge is straight or chiseled. Good advice is to follow the sharpening instructions in the booklet that came with each specific knife; you did save them, didn't you?

Once a knife is sharp, most expert meatcutters make periodic use of a sharpening steel. A steel looks like a large rat-tail file in that a long, tapered, rough-surfaced rod is inserted into a wooden or hard-plastic handle.

The purpose of a steel is not to actually sharpen a knife in the conventional sense, by removing metal and forming an edge, as with a stone. Rather, in the midst of cutting chores, a steel allows the user to quickly but temporarily restore the blade's sharpness by removing the wavy edge all knives take after use;

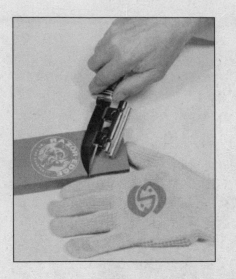

Some means of keeping your knives sharp is essential. Since blade designs widely differ, study the instructions that came with your specific brand for the manufacturer's recommendations.

A butcher's steel is both inexpensive and a fast and easy way to keep knives sharp between sessions at the sharpening stone.

with the microscopic edge of teeth periodically once again made straight and "true," the worker can delay actual stone-sharpening for lengthy periods of time.

At first, using a steel may seem somewhat awkward, but with some practice it will quickly be just like second nature. Basically, the knife is held in one hand, tip pointing up, and the steel is held in the other, tip pointing up. The knife is then gently sandpapered against the steel in rapid up

and down fashion, with each pass seeing the knife alternate across the front of the steel and then the back, to work both sides of the blade. If you find any difficulty performing this maneuver, ask a butcher at a meat market to give you a firsthand demonstration.

Tricks of the Trade

Among the little tips and techniques you can pick up by watching other experts is one that Charlie Hause passed onto me many years ago, and that is making sure that the meat is very, very cold. The shoulders, haunches, and other primal cuts should be almost but not quite frozen. The reason for this is that when it is warm, any kind of meat is loose, floppy, soft, and uncontrollable, and in this condition it's virtually impossible to make neat, precision cuts.

Furthermore, a large quantity of relatively warm meat from any kind of animal, domestic or wild, has a distinct odor. It is not at all an unpleasant aroma, but after six or eight hours of continually breathing it in you may begin feeling a bit nauseous.

Very cold meat, on the other hand, has almost no odor whatsoever. And since it is so firm, you can handle it with ease, propping it up just so to make certain cuts, turning it this way or that to perform all manner of surgical operations cleanly and neatly without the meat sagging, separating, and seemingly having a mind of its own.

Another characteristic of very cold meat is that it is not sticky, which is something no one can really appreciate until he's had the experience of working with warm meat, particularly small pieces being trimmed for burger. Like flypaper, the stuff sticks to your hands, your work surface, your knife blade, and everything else it touches, which generates so much frustration that you want to shoot the deer a second time.

So make a point of ensuring that your venison is quite cold, even if it means putting a large primal cut on a tray and briefly slipping it into your freezer to firm-up while you take a coffee break.

Another thing Charlie Hause emphasizes is the importance of working with clean meat. It is inevitable when working with deer that countless, tiny hairs from the hide will adhere to the venison. These are all sources of contamination if not removed, but picking them away one by one can test even the most patient.

That's why Charlie thoroughly cleans all surfaces of the meat before the first knife cut is made. He does this by using a small piece of terrycloth towel soaked in very warm water and then thoroughly wrung out. Amazingly, several swipes in one direction and then another removes every stray hair easily and quickly. Although this step is also done just before hanging the carcass and letting it age, it's necessary to do it a second time when each primal cut is removed from the carcass and set upon the meatcutting table to be worked upon.

Still another tip—this one from Jim Borg—has to do with testing the tenderness of various meat cuts. Merely pinch a small piece of each major meat cut between the fingernails of your thumb and forefinger. Meat that is not so tender will offer resistance at first and then, upon exertion of more fingertip pressure, will begin to slightly dimple or compress itself. Conversely, tender meat will readily be cut by your fingernails and begins to signal that it's about to "mush" if still more pressure is exerted.

There are several advantages in knowing how tender various parts of the anatomy of that particular deer are likely to be. First, you know how the meat should be cut. Should it be sliced into steaks to be broiled, made into roasts to be baked, or cut into cubes for stew meat? In producing roasts and such, you know whether you should go to the extra trouble to lard or bard particular ones (both of these techniques are discussed later). You even know whether certain cuts should be tenderized more just before cooking by applying a commercial meat-tenderizing salt or soaking them in some type of marinade.

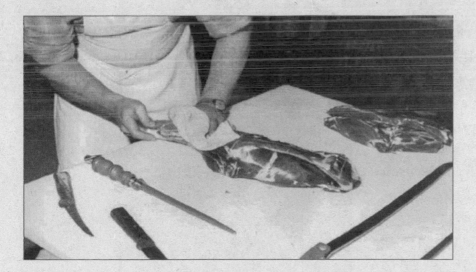

Just before butchering, a neat trick for quickly removing the countless little hairs that cling to deer meat is to wipe the venison down with a damp, hot towel.

Butchering the Front Legs

JOHN WEISS

Butchering a deer is easy if you look at it from this standpoint: the basic thing you'll be doing is using a modest assortment of tools to reduce big pieces of meat into little pieces. It's not exactly rocket science. The somewhat difficult hurdle many hunters must confront is psychological, in that they feel overwhelmed by the enormous size of that deer carcass hanging in the garage and simply don't know where to begin. Several weeks ago, before the deer season opened, they bagged two rabbits and in a matter of minutes after arriving home had them in the frying pan. But now, the antlered beast hanging before them is intimidating.

It needn't be that way, because butchering is not unlike changing a flat tire in that once you've learned which steps have to be performed and then acquire some practice, you can do a professional job almost blindfolded.

My recommendation has always been to approach the hanging carcass piecemeal. In other words, remove one piece of meat that is relatively easy to handle, such as a front leg, take it to the cutting table and, following the step-by-step instructions I'll give in a moment, thoroughly reduce that leg to wrapped cuts of meat ready for the freezer.

Then go back to the carcass and get the other front leg and proceed as before, momentarily forgetting about all the rest. Since you've just finished a front leg and learned something in the process about its unique anatomical features, the second front leg should be a snap. Then butcher a hind leg, as described in the next chapter, and so on. By following this suggested routine, the carcass will steadily become smaller and smaller

while, conversely, your confidence level will grow and greatly reduce that seemingly formidable challenge you initially faced.

Keep in mind a key thought expressed in the last chapter. You need not follow any specific butchering sequence, such as the front legs before hind legs, or whatever. Feel entirely free to tackle any of the meat-cutting procedures in this book in any order you like.

Moreover, don't worry about making mistakes! Sure, you'll occasionally goof, but will life as we know it on this planet come to a screeching halt?

Don't allow that huge hanging deer carcass to intimidate you. Divide and conquer by simply tackling the job piecemeal. Let's begin with a front leg.

Of course not. And besides, you're going to need to accumulate a hefty pile of scraps and trimmings to produce all the burger and sausage your family is looking forward to.

Some Words about Fat

Before we begin cutting meat it's important to briefly discuss the trimming away of fat we'll be encountering in various places of the deer's anatomy as we go along.

Previous books and magazine articles dealing with the handling of venison have preached the dire necessity of trimming away every speck of fat you find, claiming it is so distasteful that if left intact no one will enjoy eating your venison. This information is not entirely accurate.

Actually, deer possess three types of fat, and according to studies at Utah State University, not all of them are sources of disagreeable or so-called gamey flavor. There is cod fat, which is found only on the brisket (lower front chest region). There is tallow fat, which is found mainly on the back, covering the rump, and to a lesser extent around the perimeter of the neck and on the rearmost areas of the front shoulders. And there is marbling fat, which is found

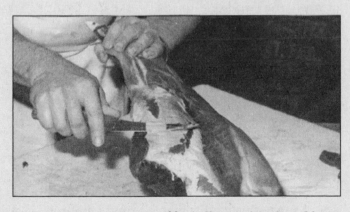

Deer possess several types of fat (tallow, cod, and marbling), but only the tallow, found on the surface, should be removed. A boning or fish-fillet knife makes the job easy.

throughout the body but concentrated in muscle tissue and between series of opposing muscle groups.

Cod fat and tallow fat are both designed to help keep the animal warm in cold weather, so nature has located them on the exterior surfaces of the anatomy just beneath the hide. Cod fat and tallow fat have flavors not terribly disagreeable but indeed noticeable and upon occasion a bit strong, particularly in mature animals (those which are three and one-half years of age or older). Good advice is to try and remove as much cod fat and tallow fat as possible. But there's no need to freak out and be so meticulous about this that you end up spending twice the amount of time it should ordinarily take to butcher a deer.

Marbling fat, on the other hand, is deep fat woven interstitially through and between the muscle fibers. It looks like thin, elongated, white streaks, and as much of this fat as possible should be allowed to remain! Not only is marbling fat virtually tasteless, but the research at Utah State proved its presence significantly increases the tenderness of cooked venison compared to other cuts of meat that had much of their marbling removed. As a result, since deer are very active animals possessing very lean meat compared to sedentary animals such as beef steers, it is important to not remove what little marbling the critters possess.

Consequently, when you first lay each large chunk of venison on the cutting table, no matter what part of the anatomy it came from, turn the meat this way and that and, as you do so, carefully trim away as much surface fat as you can see on all sides of the meat. However, after this is accomplished and as you begin to reduce the meat to various freezer-ready cuts, leave intact the remaining fat found deeper inside.

Let's Cut Meat

Removing a front leg/shoulder assembly from the carcass is easy because there is no ball-and-socket attachment as there is with the hind legs. Instead, the wide, flat shoulder bone, which is essentially the size and shape of a ping-pong paddle and is known as the scapula, is free-floating and independent of any other bone connection with the body. It's attached to the body only by several thin muscle segments covered by thin skin and is easily cut with a knife.

At the meatpole, all that's necessary is to grab the leg in the knee region and pull it away from the carcass a bit while simultaneously using a long bladed butcher knife to cut the connective muscle tissue on the backside of the scapula adjoining the rib cage. Keep the blade flat and tight against the rib cage as you to continue to lift and pull away the shoulder and cut it free. In this manner, you should be able to remove the entire front leg and shoulder assembly in less than one minute.

With the front leg and shoulder now lying on your cutting table, wipe it down with a warm, damp cloth to remove any stray hairs or other debris.

Then, with a thin-bladed knife (a fish fillet knife is fine), begin carefully trimming the meat of unwanted tallow and the very thin, protective, skinlike glazing crust the meat acquired during aging; in many places this procedure will expose pure meat.

There are three meatcutting methods for the front leg and shoulder region, depending upon how you intend to use the meat later on. None of

this meat is sinfully tender, so the first and easiest method is to merely cut all of it from the bone, then reduce it into chunks to be used in stews, soups, casseroles, or in the grinding of burger and sausage.

Blade and Arm Roasts

The second method, a bit more time-consuming but not at all difficult, involves laying the leg and shoulder assembly before you with the inside of the leg down and the lower part of the leg facing to the right, in order

The lowermost leg part, just below the knee, is sinewy and goes into the burger pile to be ground later. Now cut the remaining shoulder in half, approximately through the middle so two roasts of equal weight are created.

to produce two bone-in roasts as shown in the accompanying diagram. The first cut removes the lower leg just above the knee; since this lower leg is thoroughly laced with sinew and ligaments, the only value it has, after a good deal of judicious trimming, is fodder for the meat grinder. In creating the two bone-in roasts, the one nearest the lower leg is called an arm roast and the second cut of meat, located beyond this and higher up, is called a blade roast.

When engaging in these two operations, make them neat and professional looking by trying to avoid cutting the meat itself with your saw. Cut down as far as possible through the meat with your knife, using the saw only when you come to bone.

I suggest using this method, in the producing of two shoulder roasts, only if you have an adult buck or doe. Younger deer have front leg-shoulder regions

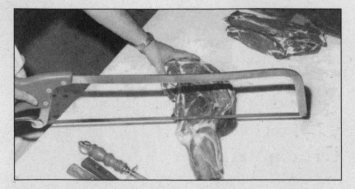

For those who prefer blade and arm roasts (rather than rolled shoulder roasts), simply reduce the front leg to three pieces.

that simply do not possess enough meat to produce arm or shoulder roasts of any significant size that would provide a meal for more than one person.

Rolled Shoulder Roasts

The third meatcutting method, still a bit more time-consuming, involves boning out the meat to produce sumptuous, rolled shoulder roasts. Since the meat from both the arm and blade regions of both legs is combined into one roast, there is, in this case, enough meat even on a smaller, younger animal to produce a single roast that's adequate in size to feed a family of four; if it's a larger, adult animal, the completed roast will be so sizeable it can actually be sliced in half to yield two four-person meals.

To produce a rolled shoulder roast, begin by laying the meat with the inside of the leg down and the lower leg pointing away from you. You'll immediately see a distinct white line vertically separating the right one third of the shoulder from the left two-thirds. This is actually the top edge of a bony

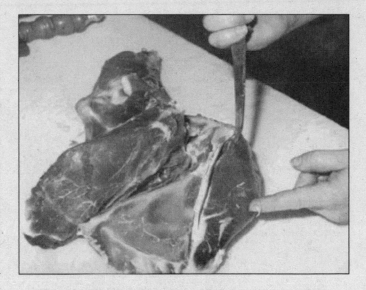

Next run your knife blade down the opposite side of the vertical bone ridge and around to that opposite side.

ridge standing upright on one side of the ping pong-paddle-shaped scapula. Butchers commonly refer to the oblong meat on the right side of the bony ridge as scotch roll meat, and that to the left as the clod meat.

Run your knife blade close to the left side of the vertical bone ridge and down through the clod meat until the knife edge stops on the flat scapula, then turn the blade flat and continue slicing toward the left until you almost reach the edge of that side of the shoulder.

Now cut down on the right side of the vertical bone ridge through the scotch roll meat until the knife blade stops on that side of the scapula, and continue slicing all the way to the right (a distance of about two inches).

Use just the tip of your knife blade in carrying out these two steps. As you approach the far left and far right edges, be careful not to cut the two pieces of meat free from the bone just yet, because you want to next turn the works over and continue separating the meat from the entirely flat surface of the scapula on the back side.

The end product is one large, flat slab of shoulder meat with a smaller, almost detached

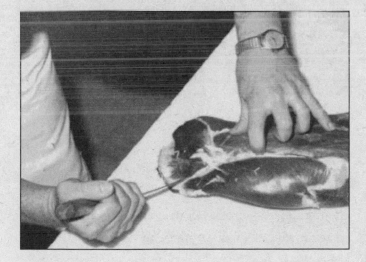

To produce a rolled shoulder roast, the meat needs to be boned-out. Find the vertical-standing bone ridge in the middle of the shoulder and run your knife blade down one side, across the adjacent boney flat and around the edge, being careful not to cut all the way through the meat.

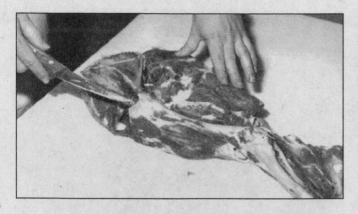

Now turn the shoulder over and separate the remainder of the meat from the wide, flat scapula bone.

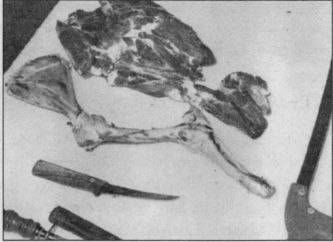

When finished, you should have one large slab of boneless meat. Here, the remaining shoulder bone is shown for an anatomical reference.

segment constituting the lower leg meat which, again, should be cut free and tossed into the burger bowl.

It is now necessary to set aside this large slab of meat and remove the opposite foreleg and shoulder from the carcass in order to obtain a comparable slab of shoulder meat from that side of the deer.

Now take the two identical slabs of shoulder meat and, insides facing each other, lay one on top of the other. Form them somewhat with your hands to create a nice-looking, football-shaped roast.

Tying the roast is the next step, and a few tricks of the trade will make it quite easy. Use cotton string (never nylon) and the so-called surgeon's knot. This is basically a common square knot, but with one exception. Instead of two double-overhand ties, you first make a triple-overhand tie followed by a conventional double-overhand tie. When snugged up against the meat, the triple-overhand will grab it tightly and hold it in place, and won't come loose when you release a bit of tension on the string to make the double-overhand tie to complete the knot.

Another tip is to make your first two string ties at opposite ends of the roast. This will serve to hold the two slabs of shoulder meat firmly together into the shape you've formed; you can then make subsequent string ties moving progressively toward

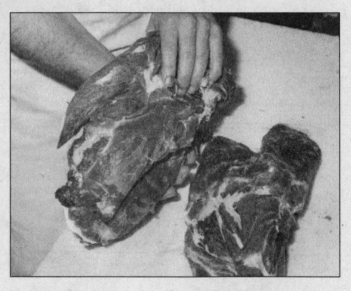

Momentarily set your slab of boned shoulder meat aside, remove the second front leg from the deer carcass, and bone it out in the same manner. This produces two large slabs of shoulder meat that can be placed on top of each other.

the middle of the roast. Conversely, if you were to instead make the first string tie in the middle of the roast, it would tend to compress the two meat slabs in such a way as to force them out to the opposite sides, which would result in a long, slender, tube-like roast instead of a more desirable thick, plump one.

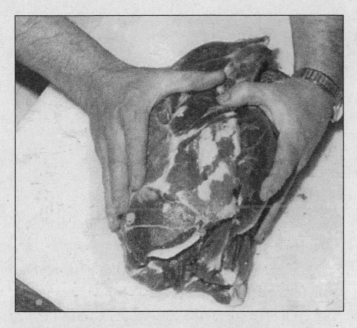

Use your hands to form a single large shoulder roast from the two slabs of boneless meat, then tie the works together with cotton string.

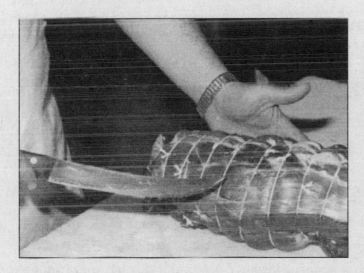

The finished rolled shoulder roast weighs about ten pounds and can easily be reduced to two or three smaller roasts by simply slicing down between the string ties. End pieces and other small "mistakes" can be trimmed away to go into the burger pile.

When all of your string ties are completed (about ten should be sufficient), trim the ends of the roast so it looks neat and toss these end-scraps into the burger pile. Then trim the ends of the string ties to about one half inch in length.

You now have a professional-looking rolled shoulder roast of venison. If you have a large family (six to eight), this roast can be wrapped for the freezer, as is, in one piece for a future meal. For a smaller family, you can slice it in half right down the middle, between two of the string ties, to give two medium-sized roasts.

Final Words

Never make a very small shoulder roast or try to reduce a large one to a smaller one that would be less than two pounds in weight. This is a common mistake made by hunters when there are only two or three people in the family. The result is a roast that sees the marbling quickly melt and cook away, causing the meat from that point on until it reaches doneness to become dried out and tough. You need a somewhat large or medium-sized roast whose bulk will help the meat retain its internal basting moisture, and therefore tenderness, through the duration of the cooking.

With a small family, this obviously means there may be a good quantity of meat left over when the meal is done. But this does not mean the venison will be wasted, because the remains can be cubed and added to soups and stews. You can also slice it thin and create delicious hot or cold sandwiches.

The last step in butchering the shoulder and leg meat is to go back over the bones with a small knife to remove any additional meat remnants, salvaging these tender tidbits found closest to the bone but missed by your knife, on behalf of the meat grinder.

See how easy it is to become an expert meatcutter? In fact, it's worth mentioning that my friend Charlie Hause, who wielded the knife while I operated the camera, produced the shoulder roast shown here in less time than it took you to read this particular chapter.

Butchering the Hind Legs

JOHN WEISS

At the beginning of the previous chapter I mentioned that there is no particular sequence in which butchering various parts of a deer must be undertaken. I then started off describing how to butcher the front legs, and with good reason. Anatomically, they're the easiest, and so this gives the hunter a feel for his work–gets him started–and makes him feel comfortable with the job at hand, all of which reduces his head-scratching time and thus adds to his level of proficiency.

Removing the rear legs from the carcass is slightly more difficult because the haunches are attached to the pelvic girdle by means of a ball and socket. Moreover, the pelvis itself presents many irregularly shaped contours that must be blindly followed with the knife blade to separate muscle from bone.

So I still hold by the statement that you can butcher-out the various deer parts in any sequence you wish. But someone who is a beginner to all of this is well-advised to begin with the easier front legs; once he has several deerbutchering sessions under his belt, he may choose to vary his routine.

In starting work on the back legs, many hunters prefer to use their saw to cut the spine, horizontally, in the region of the small of the back, just before the hams, whereupon both rear legs, still joined by the pelvis, are allowed to fall free. Then they carry the awkward, two-legged hunk to the butcher table and saw down vertically between the two, through the Aitch bone, to separate the legs.

But know in advance you're making far more work for yourself than necessary, because once you have each hind leg on the cutting table, you still have to bone it out and remove the meat from that half-side of the pelvis. Why not simply eliminate the aforementioned effort and, right from the start, cut the leg from its attachment, leaving the pelvis attached to the skeleton.

Start at the root of the tail and begin cutting down through the meat on the left side of the spine to initiate removal of the left leg. Always use just the tip of your boning knife and try to keep the flat blade as close to bone as possible to minimize lost meat; technically, no meat is ever "lost," because when small goofs are committed, as they inevitably are by all of us, the quality of the growing burger pile is enhanced with the tender addition of rump-meat scraps. In any event, you may wish to occasionally use your hands to pull the leg away from the body to somewhat enlarge your work area and better see what you're doing.

As you continue to cut down and around the ham, allow your knife blade to gently travel over the irregular surfaces of the pelvic girdle; when you hit bone, adjust the angle of the blade edge just a bit inward or outward to allow the knife to continue onward through adjacent meat. In time you'll come to the ball and socket assembly, but there is no need to do any bone cutting here. The ball sits loosely in the socket, attached only by a small piece of cartilage. If you slip just the tip of your knife blade down into and between the ball and socket, you can easily cut the cartilage and the leg will begin to fall almost entirely free at this point, requiring just a bit more meatcutting in the vicinity of the Aitch bone.

Back at the Cutting Table, Again

With the left leg now separated from the carcass and on the work table, once again spend a few minutes getting the meat ready for cutting as you did with each of the front legs. Trim away the large portions of surface tallow, most of which will be high on the leg where it was previously attached to the spinal/pelvic region. Then trim off the thin, protective "rind" or darkcolored casing, which the surface of the venison acquired during aging. After this, go over the entire leg with a damp rag to remove any stray hairs or other debris.

If you wish, you can now use your knife and saw to cut away the lower leg just above the knee. The standard procedure is to first use a knife to cut down through the meat around the diameter of the leg, then use the saw to cut the bone. As with the front legs, the lower sections of the rear legs are laced with sinew and therefore have no use other than feeding your meat grinder.

Cutting the Steaks and Roasts

Now let's get down to the nitty-gritty. The rear leg is composed of three adjoining muscles. Due to their odd shapes the tissue fibers run in somewhat different directions, but there is a thin membrane that covers and unites the three into a whole.

Consequently, there are two ways to butcher the rear leg, depending upon the types of meat

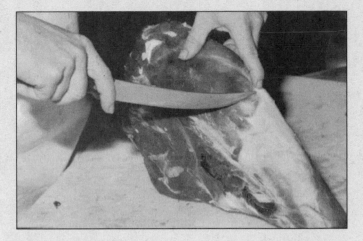

With a back leg separated from the carcass and now on the cutting table, most hunters prefer to first remove the sirloin tip section. After propping the leg up, find the tip of the white knuckle bone as your starting point.

cuts you'd like to obtain. You can remove the thin membrane covering the entire haunch and separate the three exposed muscles to produce three roasts (two rump roasts and a sirloin tip roast); or, you can remove only that part of the membrane covering the sirloin tip in order to remove it (which you can then use as a roast or slice vertically into sirloin tip steaks), but leave the membrane intact on the remaining two muscles and slice them into round steaks.

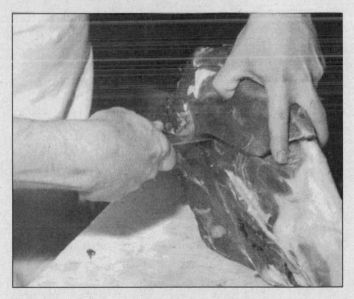

Just forward of the knuckle tip, slice down through the meat until the knife stops against the leg bone. Then turn the blade and, keeping it flat against the leg bone, continue cutting in that direction to remove the entire sirloin tip.

The sirloin tip should come free and entirely intact.

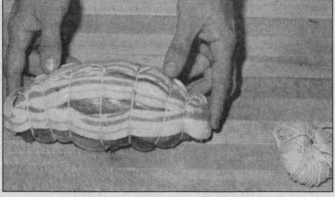

The entire sirloin tip can also be tied with cotton string to produce a three-pound sirloin tip roast. This one has been first layered with bacon to baste the roast as it cooks.

There is no right or wrong way here, simply a matter of preference as to meat cuts. First remove the sirloin tip by propping up the entire leg on its edge with the lower leg bone facing away from you. You'll easily see the tip of the hard white-knuckle bone and this is your starting point. Cut down through the meat just above the knuckle at a slight angle as shown in the accompanying photo.

After going only a short distance, your knife blade will come to an abrupt halt against the leg bone. Now turn the blade flat and bring the knife cut toward you, keeping the blade continually against the bone until the sirloin tip is cut entirely free.

You now have an oblong chunk of solid, of two things with this footballoneless meat called the sirloin tip. Easy, huh? You can do either of two things with this football-shaped piece of meat. You can leave it whole, to be cooked as a sirloin tip roast. If this is the case, it's a good idea to tie the roast incrementally along its length, every inch or so, with cotton string as described for roasts from the front shoulder. Since this is very tender meat, it will tend to fall apart during cooking if it's not tied.

You can also vertically slice the meat into about five sirloin tip steaks, each one-inch thick, which are fine for broiling over coals or can be made into Swiss steaks. Since the meat is football shaped, and hence thicker in the middle, you'll end up with steaks of uniform thickness, but those toward either end will

be a bit smaller in size than those in the middle. This works out perfectly for dinner guests, who might prefer steaks a bit smaller (or larger) than the others.

Incidentally, the very ends of the sirloin tip have several membrane layers within them, so we usually cut these one-inch pieces free at each end and toss them into the burger pile.

The next step is the same, regardless of whether you want to use the remainder of the rump for roasts or round steaks. Lay the remaining leg portion with the inside down and the partially exposed leg bone facing you; this is the bone that became exposed when the sirloin tip was removed.

Now remove this entire bone without damaging the meat wrapped around it. Begin by using just

The sirloin tip can now be sliced vertically into about five sirloin tip steaks; the end pieces go into the burger pile.

Now go back to the remainder of the hind leg and, using as a guide the exposed bone where the sirloin tip was removed, entirely encircle the bone with your knife to remove the remainder of the rump meat intact.

the tip of your boning knife to slowly go all the way around its perimeter, gently pulling away the meat as you proceed, and eventually you'll reach the other side. Now make two vertical slices, one to the far left and the other to the far right, to complete the separation of the meat from its attachment at the lower-leg and upper-pelvic regions, and the meat will fall free in one large, boneless slab.

The meat, now without the bone through the middle that previously held everything together, can now be returned to its former shape by molding it with your hands so it looks almost exactly at it did a minute ago. Here is where working with very cold meat pays off in easy handling, compared to meat that is warm, floppy, and difficult to control.

What to do with this large chunk of rump meat? Very popular with many hunters is to simply use a long-bladed butcher knife to slice it vertically into about five one-inch-thick round steaks.

Another way of producing these round steaks is by merely skipping the boning-out procedure just described and, instead, slicing the steaks with the butcher knife down through the meat until the bone is reached, and then cutting the bone with a

The entire slab of rump meat, with the bone removed, can be molded by hand back into its former shape, then sliced vertically to produce about six round steaks. Instead of boning out the meat, some hunters prefer to use a meat saw; the same size round steaks are produced but with a small, round bone in the middle of each.

saw. In this manner, you'll create round steaks that will be the same size and shape, and each will have a disk-like piece of round leg bone in the center. As mentioned previously, I prefer boneless cuts of venison, but the choice is yours.

If you'd like roasts instead of round steaks, that is also a splendid decision because, coming from the rump, they'll be as tender as any cut the deer has to offer. Rolled rump roasts are produced in the same way as rolled shoulder roasts.

Use your hands to shape and form the meat back together so it looks the same as before the leg bone was removed. Now use cotton string to tie the roast in ten or twelve places, beginning at opposite ends and working gradually toward the middle. Once it's secured with string, you can leave the roast whole for a sumptuous repast that will serve eight, or you can slice it in half to produce two meals that each serve four.

Despite his most valiant efforts, any hunter is likely to end up with numerous, smallish chunks of rump meat. The excuse I use is that my knife blade sometimes has a mind of its own. These pieces of meat will predictably be so irregularly shaped and of varied sizes that one will be tempted to reserve them for the meat grinder. That's fine, because it will result in the most delicious burger and sausage imaginable.

On the other hand, keep in mind that burger and sausage are traditionally made from cuts of tougher meat that must be chopped by a grinder's blades, but what you now have is an accumulation of very tender rump meat. Our choice is to wrap and freeze these miscellaneous pieces in one-pound packages. Later, when defrosted, they can be further reduced to one-inch chunks or half-inch thick strips that can be used in stroganoff, stir-fry, and similar recipes that call for tender meat.

The last step is to go over the rear leg bone one more time and clean it thoroughly of the smallest scraps of remaining meat for the burger pile.

Now it's time to move on to the other rear leg and, since you've gained a good deal of practice, the work should go quickly. You can butcher it exactly the same way if you like, or you may decide to do it just a little differently to add variety to your future meals. For example, if you left the sirloin tip intact as a roast, you may wish to use the other one, sliced vertically, for sirloin tip steaks. Similarly, if you previously sliced the rump meat into round steaks, you may wish to use the rump meat of the right leg for rolled rump roasts. To each his own pleasure!

Larding and Barding

Before proceeding to other butchering procedures, let's take a few moments to discuss two techniques for tenderizing venison that you may wish to incorporate into meatcutting operations dealing with either the front shoulder roasts or the rump roasts produced from the rear legs.

In earlier chapters we discussed being a selective hunter and what to look for in body conformation that signals tender venison. Sometimes, however, after his deer is down, the hunter may have reason to suspect that the venison is not likely to be as tender as he'd hoped for. This may tempt him to shove the entire deer through the tiny spout of his meat grinder–but wait!

There are two after-the-fact techniques, known as larding and barding, that can be instituted during the butchering of the front and rear legs, that will transform even a grizzled old buck's venison into such tender fare you'll feel compelled to bow your head in reverence as you dine. To understand the benefits of these two techniques, let's once again briefly visit a comparison between domestic livestock and wild game.

In finishing the butchering of a rear leg, there will be several large chunks of rump meat left over. The largest can be assembled into rolled rump roasts and tied with cotton string. The smallest are prime rump meat. We don't use them for burger, but cut them into chunks for later use in stews, stir fries, and meat casseroles.

If you goof and some of the round steaks are not of uniform thickness, a bit of quick work with a meat mallet solves everything.

Beef steers, for example, spend lives of leisure lazing around pastures and feedlots awaiting their destiny and seldom utilizing their muscles to the fullest extent of their physical capability. And, all the while, they dine complacently upon assorted high-fat and high-carbohydrate foods,which in turn make them quite fatty in their musculature. Additionally, about a month before they are to be slaughtered, they are subjected to a "finishing" process in which they are force-fed milk, and grain such as corn, to even further increase the fat content of their musculature.

The result of this modern animal husbandry is that domestic livestock meat contains a very high level of marbling throughout its flesh. This marbling fat is found in striations between and through the tissue fibers of the meat, and during cooking it melts and subsequently helps to break down (and greatly tenderize) the tissue's cellular structure.

Exactly the opposite sequence of events occurs during the lives of deer. Although they may occasionally lunch at some farmer's cornfield, a majority of the year sees deer dining upon whatever native foods they can find, and often they do not find all that much, particularly during winter. Further, deer spend much of their time on the run, and this continual exercise, as with a human athlete, hardens them off in the building of tough musculature. You just don't see fat, flabby deer and, of course, they do not undergo a finishing process prior to opening day; indeed, when they are taken by hunters they may be in a state of stress and lactic acid build-up.

Consequently, unlike domestic livestock, venison does not possess a high level of marbling. Instead, it is a dry, very lean meat with very little in the way of tissue fat to internally lubricate the meat as it cooks.

There are several ways to remedy this state of affairs. First, as emphasized previously, trim away as much tallow fat as time and convenience allow, but leave whatever marbling fat you find woven between the muscle and tissue fibers. It is easily identified because unlike tallow fat, which is formed in thick layers on the outside surfaces of the meat, marbling appears as long, thin streaks and flecks within the interior of the meat. Second, consider barding the meat. This involves adding fat to the venison. .

One method,when you have a large slab of shoulder or rump meat you are preparing to assemble into a roast, is to first lay several slices of bacon in the folds of the meat before forming it into a roast with your hands and tying it with cotton string. This will do a good job of tenderizing the meat, and will also impart a very subtle, yet pleasing, bacon flavor. Instead of using bacon, you can also use thinly cut strips of beef suet or salt pork, each of which will impart their own flavors as well.

Another barding method is to drape the exterior of the roast with bacon strips just before tying it securely with string. As the roast cooks, the bacon will slowly melt and drip-baste the venison.

When rolled roasts are created from either the front or rear legs, and they're from a deer you suspect may not be so tender, use the technique called barding, in which bacon or salt pork is layered between the folds of meat before it is tied. It will melt during cooking and lubricate the meat to tenderness.

There are two slight disadvantages to barding, one of which is that the hunter does not obtain a pure, unadulterated venison flavor but one of venison slightly accentuated with beef or pork characteristics.

The other drawback is that any kind of beef or pork fat does not keep very long in your freezer, which means that venison roasts that have exterior bacon drapes or interior insertions of bacon, beef suet, or salt pork must be used within several months.

If you desire to conserve your cache of deer meat and make it last as long as possible, you won't want to use barding as a meat-tenderizing technique. So go ahead and produced your rolled, tied roasts as described earlier, and place them in the freezer

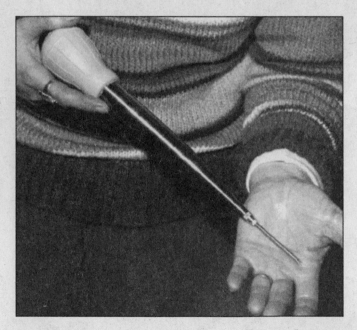

Another technique for tenderizing roasts from the front and rear legs is larding, using a larding needle. The utensil is filled with melted butter, bacon fat, or cooking oil and injected into the roast in random locations.

where they'll remain in good condition for up to two years (believe it or not) if you follow the steps described in the chapter devoted to freezing venison.

Then, each time you remove a roast from the freezer, and just before cooking, use another technique called larding, which accomplishes the very same tenderizing as barding but without the drawback of limited storage time in the freezer. Larding means injecting fat and similar lubricants into the meat by means of an inexpensive larding needle.

As before, you can use bacon, suet, or salt pork,which will impart subtle flavors of their own, but first rendering them down; that is, very slowly cooking them in a pan to reduce them to liquid fat. If you'd prefer to retain the exclusive flavor of the venison, with nothing to detract from it, use a relatively tasteless larding fluid such as melted butter, cooking oil, or a combination of the two mixed together.

A larding needle looks somewhat like a siphon, in that a rubber squeeze bulb is fitted to one end of a stainless-steel tube, with a long, hollow needle at the other. Simply squeeze the bulb to expel its air, insert the needle into the larding liquid, release the pressure on the bulb, and it will suck in as much larding fluid as the bulb will hold. Then insert the needle in random locations in the meat, briefly squeeze the bulb, and the larding fluid will saturate the inside of the roast.

If you're in camp or some other location, and a larding needle is not available, use a long, narrow knife blade to pierce numerous holes into the roast and then use the tip of the blade to insert slivers of bacon or salt pork.

Butchering Loins and Ribs

JOHN WEISS

You can refer to them as loins, tenderloins, steaks, backstraps, or other common names, but by any description they are the tenderest cuts of venison a deer possesses. They are located along both sides of the backbone. If they're on the underneath sides of the spine within the chest cavity, they're most correctly, in the case of deer, referred to as tenderloins; their counterparts on a beef steer are called filet mignons.

If they're located on the top, exterior sides of the spine, just beneath the hide, they're most correctly, in the case of deer referred to as backstraps; their counterparts on a beef steer are simply referred to as different types of steaks such as porterhouse steaks, which have the filet mignon present, or T-bone steaks, in which the filet mignon has been cut away.

There are several ways to remove these delectable cuts of venison, depending upon whether you like pure, boneless steak meat or whether you prefer bone-in steaks.

If you'll recall, in an earlier chapter I suggested the tenderloins be removed, and how to do it, shortly after the field-dressed animal arrives at camp or home. The tenderloins are so tender that they require no aging whatever; and besides, they are relatively small in size, and after even a brief exposure to air they quickly develop a hard, glazed surface that must be trimmed away, at the sacrifice of a good deal of prime meat.

The backstraps, on the exterior of the skeletal system, lie adjacent to the backbone, running from just behind the front shoulder back to where the front of the rear legs begin. They're situated in a type of triangular-shaped pocket created by the offset vertebrae of the backbone.

Removing the backstraps intact, in long strips, is accomplished by using a fillet knife or boning

When a hunter takes a beautiful buck like this, he's first captivated by the antlers. Then his attention turns to the deer's most tender cut, the backstrap steaks. Credit: Northern Wildlife Ventures

The backstraps lie on either side of the spine and are easily filleted right out of their triangularshaped pockets. This hunter is working on the tenderloin steaks, also found along both sides of the spine but inside the chest cavity.

Each backstrap weighs about eight pounds; it is pure, boneless meat that is easily and quickly butchered.

knife with a flexible tip that will easily bend to conform to the curvature of the bones. Insert the tip of your blade just behind the front shoulder and, with the blade flat against the backbone, carefully guide it all the way along the length of the spine to just above the pelvic girdle where you made your first incision in the removal of the back leg on that side. It will feel at times as if the blade is traveling over a rippled surface (these are the vertebrae), so proceed slowly and work the blade slightly in and out as you go along in order to retain as much meat as possible.

Now, back at that point where you began the shoulder cut, make another cut, this time perpendicular, about four inches in length. Then it is quite simple to cut and lift, cut and lift, gently filleting the backstrap right out of its spinal pocket until its entire length is removed. Then do exactly the same on the opposite side of the spinal column to remove its strip of back-strap meat.

At the butchering table you'll notice a thin, silvery-colored membranelike sheath covering the exterior of the backstrap. You can trim this away with your knife, if you wish, by starting at one end and

alternately lifting the membrane while running the flat of the blade between it and the meat. However, this operation is merely for the sake of appearance; it is not necessary because the membrane, also called silverskin, will cook out as very tender.

Next, you'll want to slice the lengthy backstrap horizontally into numerous steaks. On a very large deer, which in turn will have large backstraps, you can simply begin slicing the steaks any thickness you prefer (I recommend from one to two inches thick).

However, when a deer is only average size, this technique results in the sliced steaks being rather small, and so I use the butterfly method of cutting them. In this procedure, you begin slicing a steak of the desired thickness but do not cut all the way down through the meat. Now, make a second cut another inch or so away, and this time do slice all the way through. What you'll have, then, is a pair of steaks side by side, connected to each other by a type of hinge that, when the steaks are opened and laid out flat, produces a steak double the usual size.

Most hunters prefer to slice their backstraps into one-inch-thick steaks. If desired, however, you can butterfly them as shown to produce larger portions.

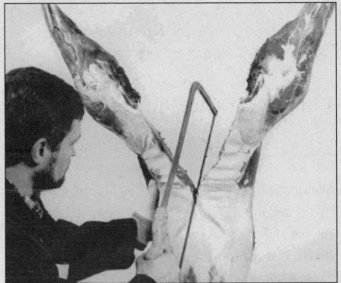

Instead of boneless backstrap steaks, some hunters prefer bone-in steaks, commonly called chops. After the front legs are removed, saw the carcass in half lengthwise down through the middle of the spine. After the rear legs are cut free, the so-called saddle is then sawed horizontally into steaks.

As you approach either end of the long backstrap it will become progressively smaller in size, so begin making your cuts just a bit thicker. Then use a wooden mallet to gently pound them out flat. This will spread out their surface areas somewhat, so that all the steaks from the backstrap are of uniform size, rather than some small and some large.

You can also leave the eight-inch-long end cuts intact and freeze them whole. We like to place these on a grill and slice them very thin at the table, as in chateaubriand, or to make steak sandwiches.

The other meatcutting method for the backstraps, which produces bone-in steaks (some hunters call them chops), requires considerably more work, but the procedure is easily described.

Begin by sawing the deer lengthwise into two halves, down the centerline of the backbone. This is done before butchering-out the hind legs, as the two rear legs left intact can allow the carcass to remain hanging from the gambrel; once the deer is in halves, each hind leg can then be removed and dealt with as described in the previous chapter, leaving the remainder of the backbone halves and their attached backstraps. Next, each side is simply laid upon the cutting table and steaks are vertically sawed to whatever thickness you prefer. Then the rib ends, which contain very little meat, are removed.

If you harbor doubts as to which method you might like best, here's a good suggestion: try both. Halve the deer down the centerline and saw steaks bone-in, and then on the opposite side of the backbone fillet-out the boneless backstrap intact.

As mentioned in a previous chapter, the tenderloins found against either side of the backbone

A third option is to cut the entire backstrap into only four lengthy sections of about two pounds a piece, to be grilled whole or baked.

but inside the chest cavity are generally left in whole condition when removed, to be cooked intact in a variety of ways, such as grilling.

Final Meat-Cutting Tasks

All that should now remain on your deer carcass is the neck meat, ribs, and brisket meat. The neck meat has many uses. Remove it from the carcass by boning it out. The easiest method is to begin at the back of the neck with a horizontal cut just below the ears, and another one just above the shoulder. Then make a lengthwise cut down the centerline on one side of the neckbone or the other. Make it a deep cut as this will produce a large flap of neck meat and simultaneously expose the neck bone, allowing you to easily continue working around its perimeter.

With the slab of neck meat on your cutting table, remove as much surface tallow as possible, but retain the more deeply imbedded marbling fat. This large slab of meat can now be rolled into a large roast and tied with string, then halved or even cut into thirds for very slow cooking over low heat (as in a crockpot) for six or eight hours. Or, you can cube the neck meat for use in stews. Or, you can reserve the entire quantity of neck meat for burger and sausage.

Only the forward two-thirds of the rib-plate, closest to the neck and measuring about a foot long and half again as wide, is worth cutting out and saving; farther back, there's so little meat on the bones it's hardly worth working for.

Many hunters don't care for venison ribs, saying the meat contains so much tallow that it's like chewing a mouthful of paste. The trick to eliminating this problem is to pre-cook the ribs. That is, place them on a slotted broiler pan and slip them under the broiler at just a medium-heat setting for about forty-five minutes. This will cause the tallow to melt and drain away into the bottom of the broiler-pan assembly. From that point on, you can proceed with any rib recipe you like, such as basting them with barbecue sauce on a charcoal grill, slow-cooking them in a crockpot, or slow-cooking them in a baking pan in the oven ... all with tender, delectable results.

Other hunters take still another approach to using their ribs. Using a knife, they cut the rib meat free from between the bones comprising the rib cage and add it to their accumulated pile of burger and sausage trimmings but slightly reducing the quantity of beef fat or pork those recipes call for, as described in the next two chapters.

The meat on the brisket has many uses, such as going into burger or sausage; when removing it in a slab with the flat of your knife against the lower-front chest region, be sure to trim away as much surface tallow and cod fat as possible.

As with the neck meat, that of the brisket meat is especially well-suited to being cut into inch-thick chunks and used as the main ingredient in stews. Both the neck and brisket meat are flavorful but also quite tough, which is actually to their advantage. You want stew meat to hold together well during long hours of slow simmering but eventually become tender. Brisket and neck meat do this very well. Conversely, trying to make stew from already tender cuts of venison such as rump meat is often futile. By the time it has slowly cooked for several hours over low heat, the meat no longer is firm and something you can sink your teeth into, but mushy and fallen apart.

About this time, all that should remain of your deer carcass is a skeleton that has been picked clean, without even an ounce remaining that isn't at least suitable for burger and sausage.

Undoubtedly, however, as you've been carrying out your butchering you'll have accumulated a hefty quantity of skin remnants, junk meats, and other trimmings that are too fatty or too sinewy to be used for human consumption. Instead of throwing them away, they make splendid dog food.

In fact, whenever we first begin butchering a deer we always place a five-gallon pot on the stove, half filled with water and turned on low heat. We toss any undesirable meat scraps into the pot as we go along. This "stew" slowly simmers for many hours, to the point that even the gristle becomes tender.

We usually end up with as much as forty pounds of nutritious, high-protein food our dogs absolutely love. After the food has cooked, allow it to cool, then ladle it into half-quart plastic containers (the type in which cottage cheese is sold). Every few days, defrost one container, heat it up a bit, and then mix it with your dog's usual dry kibbles. He'll attack the meal as if there's no tomorrow, especially if it's bitter cold outside.

Not only do you save a lot of money making this dog food, but you gain the satisfaction of knowing you utilized the entire deer, throwing away nothing but bones.

Part 2

Firearms Hunting

Introduction

JAY CASSELL

If you like to hunt with a rifle, shotgun, or muzzleloader, then this section is specifically for you. The chapters on bolt-action rifles, by Wayne van Zwoll, are my favorites, because I like to hunt with an Ultralight Arms 30-06, and I enjoy reading about other bolt actions. I've got a few Brownings too, for that matter, but I'd sure like to try some (or many) of the rifles Wayne is reviewing.

Some of my own material is in here, as well. I like to still-hunt, so some of my favorite tactics are included in this section. Some of my favorite calling and rattling techniques are also included, as are some tips about using a climbing treestand or building and hunting out of your own. And don't miss the chapter by master Maine hunter, Hal Blood. This man knows how to hunt the deep woods, and is more than happy to share his knowledge with you – as are Dave Henderson on shotgun hunting, and John Weiss on blackpowder (and rifles and slug guns, for that matter).

Ultimately, you hunt with a firearm, you're successful if you know how to use it, and know how to shoot it straight, for a well-placed bullet is going to take down your deer, no matter what caliber you are using.

Big Names in Bolt Guns

WAYNE VAN ZWOLL

The stillness of a snowy woods holds promise for whitetail hunters. But my plans to slip quietly through this Washington thicket had been dashed by a hard frost. It had struck before the snow, and the leaves crackled underfoot. Alice was not so frustrated. She had grown up in northern Wisconsin, where stumpsitting was a local tradition.

"Let's stop for a snack," she whispered.

Grudgingly, I complied, shedding my pack to dig out her chocolate. I was wolfing raisins when she tugged at my arm. "There!" she hissed.

I turned. A buck was slipping through the oaks behind us. Slowly, I eased the Remington to my shoulder. Too many branches! I whistled softly. The deer stopped, and in the 6X Lyman, I found a small alley. At the blast of my .280 Improved, the buck vanished. Again the snowy woods were still.

Deer live and die silently.

Paul Mauser's Popular Door Latch

Mauser is to rifles as Mercedes is to automobiles—in Germany. Worldwide, Mauser may have a bigger following. The huge factory in Oberndorf that supplied German troops with rifles in two World Wars, and exported military arms to countless other republics, covers more acres than the market warrants these days. And though it remains one of the most popular high-power magazine

rifles across generations of hunters in Africa, it has given way to the competition Stateside. Ironically, the competition is co-opting the design that made Mauser rifles famous a century ago.

While the Mauser label has been applied to a variety of firearms (some with the Mauser banner stamped in the receiver, others simply because they are bolt rifles), most shooters associate the name with the Model 1898. This was not the first Mauser rifle; in fact, it came about when Paul Mauser was 50 years old. Like John Browning, Peter Paul Mauser was a gifted designer who could think mechanisms onto paper and fashion parts that did just what he wanted them to do. His products, like those of Browning, showed an attention to detail that ensured reliable function. His work married inventiveness with artistry, a mastery of mechanics with a drive to achieve what had not been attempted before.

Oddly enough, many riflemen think of Mauser only as a machinist who developed a breech bolt that worked like a door latch. Almost anybody could have done that, and some probably did it before Peter Paul Mauser. In fact, one of his first experimental rifles derived from the turn-bolt action of the Dreyse needle gun, German's primary shoulder arm in the Franco-Prussian War. That work brought no contracts from the Wuerttemberg, Prussian or Austrian War Ministries. But it intrigued Samuel Norris, an American traveling in Europe as an agent for E. Remington & Sons. Norris offered Paul and older brother Wilhelm financial incentive to convert the French Chassepot needle gun to a metallic-cartridge rifle. In 1867, they moved to Liege, Belgium, to begin work. When Norris failed to interest the French government in a new rifle, he bailed out of the agreement. Paul and Wilhelm returned to Oberndorf, where Paul had been born 29 years earlier. There they opened shop. Wilhelm's business savvy complemented Paul's mechanical talent.

As the brothers struggled to establish a firearms business, the Royal Prussian Military Shooting School was testing a Mauser rifle Norris had furnished earlier. It so impressed ordnance people that they asked the Mausers to make specific improvements. The young men followed up and resubmitted the rifle, a single-shot breech-loader firing an 11mm black-powder cartridge. Early in 1872, the Mauser Model 1871 became the official Prussian shoulder arm.

Elated, Paul and Wilhelm were quickly informed that the Prussian army would pay them only 15 percent of what they'd been led to expect for design rights. Also, the rifles were to be built in government arsenals, not by the Mausers. The brothers still needed work. They wound up with a contract to produce 3,000 sights for the Model 1871. A Bavarian order for 100,000 sights eventually led them to build a Mauser factory in Oberndorf. Not long thereafter, the Wuerttemberg War Ministry awarded Paul and Wilhelm a contract to build 100,000 rifles. To do this, they immediately formed a partnership with the Wuerttemberg Vereinsbank of Stuttgart to buy the Wuerttemberg Royal Armory.

On February 5, 1874, it became Mauser Bros. and Co. The sprawling Armory, which had begun life as an Augustinian Cloister, shipped the last of the

Model 71s in 1878, six months ahead of schedule. Production of sights and an order of 26,000 rifles for China then kept the brothers busy. Paul invented a single-shot pistol and a revolver, but neither of these succeeded at market. Wilhelm died very early, in 1882, and Mauser became a stock company. Controlling shares were bought by Ludwig Loewe & Co. of Berlin.

In 1889, In Liege, Belgium, Fabrique Nationale d'Armes de Guerre (FN) came about to produce Mauser rifles for the Belgian government. The FN project resulted from development of the Model 1889, Paul's first successful smokeless powder rifle. The 1889 incorporated elements that established Mauser as the dominant gun designer on the Continent. During the next six years, he overhauled the rifle to make it even better. One of the most important changes, a staggered-column, fixedbox magazine, came along in 1893. By 1895 Paul had developed an action that would be perfected as the famous Model 1898. Shortly after its acceptance by the German Army on April 5, 1898, the Mauser 98 became the most popular military arm to that point in history. Exported to many countries, it would be built in many more. France, Great Britain, Russia, and the U.S. designed and produced their own battle rifles; but none surpassed the Mauser 98 in function or reliability.

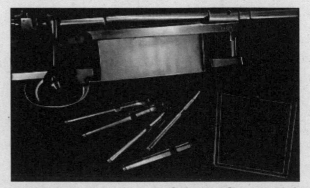

Each Mauser magazine was fashioned for a particular cartridge, here the 10.75x73, or .404 Jeffery.

Among the 98's chief attributes was its stout extractor, a beefy length of spring-steel fastened to the righthand side of the bolt by a forward C-shaped collar with lips on the ends that grabbed a slot on the extractor's belly when you slid the extractor rearward into place. When the bolt pushed a cartridge forward in the magazine, it popped free of the rails, up against the bolt face, and into the massive extractor claw that shadowed the upper right-hand quadrant of the face. The bottom of the bolt face was milled flush with its center to permit smooth travel for the cartridge head into the extractor.

The claw shepherded the cartridge from magazine to chamber, engendering the term, "controlled round feed." It was an asset in the heat of battle because it prevented short-stroking and a jam— or worse, detonation of the primer of a chambered round by the bullet tip of another cartridge rammed forward from the magazine. With Mauser's extractor, if a soldier "double-clutched," chambering a cartridge but not firing it and then withdrawing the bolt to load a second, the first cartridge was pulled out on the bolt's rearward stroke because the claw already had the rim in its grip. One round would have to be ejected before another could be chambered.

In Africa, professional hunters came to favor the Mauser for the same reason. If multiple shots were needed to stop a dangerous animal, the 98's action was forgiving of imperfect bolt manipulation. And in the event of a misfire, the shooter could leave prognostications for later. He knew that as long as there were rounds to strip from the magazine, the rifle would keep firing. While controlled-round feed is less important to deer hunters taking deliberate shots or one quick poke at a bounding whitetail, the feature has legions of advocates. Winchester dropped the expensive Mauser-style extractor from

its Model 70 in an ill-advised cost-cutting rampage in 1964, and riflemen howled. The Mauser claw was later reinstated and remains an emblem of quality— not only on the 70 but also on other rifles. Several makers have adopted it; few magazine rifles for dangerous game are made without it.

But the extractor itself is not the only component of controlled round feed. Bracketing the ejector groove on a 98 bolt face are two cartridge support lugs. The lower of these is angled to guide the rim of the cartridge case as the magazine spring pushes it up. Because a staggered cartridge stack is not constricted at the top into a single column that pops the uppermost round into the middle of the action, this lower lug is important. It must herd cartridges from both sides of the magazine toward the center of bolt travel and, as the bolt slides forward, coax the case rim into the extractor claw. Once there, the case head is held tight against the claw by both lugs. The angle, bearing surface and thickness of the lower lug affect how readily the case will step across the bolt face, yield to the extractor, and stay centered as the bolt slides into battery.

D'Arcy Echols, an accomplished contemporary riflesmith who openly marvels at Paul Mauser's engineering, says that the cartridge should spring the extractor claw about .004 for a tight fit. "Trouble is, there's that much variation among various brands of the same cartridge. Weatherby cases manufactured by Norma have extractor grooves that average .010 deeper than the grooves in Weatherby cases turned out by Remington and Winchester." Result: A Mauser-style extractor that properly fits the Weatherby case will be too tight for others, and may prevent the case head from climbing all the way up the bolt face until chamber contact with the case body forces it. An extractor fitted to the Remington or Winchester rim will not hold a Norma cartridge

Mausers have been chambered for almost every conceivable deer cartridge. This buck fell to a .280.

because there's no tension on the claw. In neither instance do you get controlled-round feed—no matter what shape the extractor!

Incidentally, Mauser purposefully did not design his extractor to jump over the rim of a round loaded directly into the chamber by hand. But there's roughly .030 extra clearance broached in the right lug raceway of the receiver ring, should single loading become necessary. You just pinch the extractor spring toward the bolt body as you seat the bolt. The extractor claw, which subtends about 20 percent of the rim's arc, makes the jump. To prevent sticky cases from slipping from the extractor's grasp, Mauser undercut the extractor tongue and its groove in the bolt body so that an extra tug during extraction puts the claw deep into the extractor groove.

After World War II, the Mauser firm was renamed, "Werke" (works) replacing "Waffenfabrik" (arms factory), and Mauser's business shifted toward the sporting trade. The U.S. agent, A.F. Stoeger, Inc., of New York, assigned numbers to the various Mauser actions. By the end of the Depression, there

were 20 configurations in four lengths: magnum, standard, intermediate, and short. The short, or "Kurz" version, featured a small receiver ring and was factory-barreled for only three cartridges: the 6.5x50, 8x51, and .250 Savage. Magnum and Kurz actions were made strictly for sporting use. Mauser did not adopt the Stoeger numbers, 1 through 20; however, collectors still use these designations.

While surplus military Mausers have been sold at ridiculously low prices, commercial versions came dear, even before the second World War. In 1939, a new Model 70 Winchester cost $61.25, while a Mauser sporting rifle listed at $110 to $250. Square-bridge actions cost more. For an additional $200 you could have a left-hand Mauser!

Though few shooters these days pay it much attention, Paul Mauser's magazines may top the 98 extractor as his star achievement. He figured out that a staggered column would enable him to fit the most cartridges in the belly of a rifle action. But how to shape the box? Each cartridge needed support– from the box on one side, from the next cartridge or the follower underneath, and on the other side. He decided the stacking angle should be 30 degrees, so viewed from the end, the primers of three cartridges touching each other would form the points of an equilateral triangle. D'Arcy Echols explains that the magazines were made for specific cartridges.

This elegant Mauser was crafted by the late Maurice Ottmar, a custom maker from Coulee City, Washington.

"Mauser didn't fashion one box for many hulls, like the gun companies do today to save money. When you think about what makes Mausers so reliable, you conclude that it's mainly the cartridge-specific magazine. And you have to admire the guy who came up with the formula."

The numbers are easy to crunch once you know the formula: Multiply the cosine of 30 degrees (.866) by the case head (or belt) diameter, then add head diameter to that product. For example, a .300 H&H Magnum case is .532 across the belt. So .866 x .532 = .460 + .532 = .992. Theoretically, that's the correct rear box width for any cartridge deriving from the .300 case. But cartridges are not straight. They taper. To provide adequate support, a magazine must taper too. At the point of shoulder contact or, on a case without a neck, just behind the crimp, you use the same formula to get front box width at that point.

A .458 Lott, for instance, has a front measure of .480; .866 x .480 = .415 + .480 = .895, proper inside width of the box at the case mouth. A box designed for one cartridge will work for others only if they share front and rear diameters and have the same span between them. Overall cartridge length should be close to the same as well. So if you subscribe to Mauser's reasoning, magazine interchangeability is limited. A 7.65 rifle rebarreled to .270 needs a longer magazine, of course—but also one slightly wider up front. A 7.65 box is .801 wide at the shoulder of a .270 round. A properly engineered .270 magazine is .822 wide at that point. With a .270 in a 7.65 box, the triangles between cartridge centerlines get steep up front, and the rounds tend to cross-stack. The bullet emerges from the box craning its neck. A jam may result.

Paul Mauser knew that not all cartridges have straight sides and that some rimless cases might contact the box between base and shoulder. So he relieved the box sides from just ahead of the

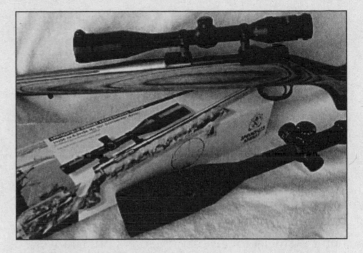

This modern Mauser from Legacy wears a Boyd's stock and a Springfield scope.

cartridge base to just behind the shoulder. He paid equal attention to magazine followers, tapering each to fit the box and shaping the top surface "just so." The width of the follower's lower shelf is matched to the case, with a 61-degree step between the upper and lower shelf. To make the next-to-last cartridge feed, the top shelf is high enough to support that round without lifting it off the last cartridge in the stack. The follower slopes like a ramp to accommodate cartridge taper and keep the rounds level in the box.

Paul engineered considerable side clearance into his followers. Says protégé D'Arcy Echols, "It's common to see floorplates machined to hold the Mauser magazine spring tightly. At first I made a couple that way myself—I figured Mauser's machinists were just sloppy in cutting spring slots .180 too wide at the rear of the floorplate. Was I ever wrong! Those springs are supposed to wiggle back and forth on the plate as cartridges are stripped off the top. If you don't let the spring shuffle, it twists; and the follower tips or gets cocked sideways."

D'Arcy Echols makes his followers .060 narrower than their boxes so they can shimmy a bit. A follower allowed too much play, however, will bang into the front of the box during recoil. While length is perhaps the least critical follower dimension, a short follower will dive in front, and a long one may bind.

Paul Mauser obviously didn't engineer his Model 1898 bolt rifle on a weekend. His ingenuity and insight as well as the time required on this project become evident to any hunter who investigates closely the rifle's design. Cartridge feeding is just one function of any magazine rifle, but it is crucial to reliability. Mauser's brilliant work in this area was largely responsible for the ready acceptance of the 98 by so many armies—and for the enduring popularity of Mausers among hunters and the makers of fine custom rifles.

When I was young, I ogled double-page spreads of Browning's High Power Rifles in catalogs that set the standard of their day for seductive photos. The High Power was assembled by Browning, but unlike the current A-Bolt, of Browning design and manufacture, it featured more than one action type. For long rounds, the mechanism was commercial Mauser. It was impeccably finished and married to impeccably polished barrels. The bluing was deep and lustrous, a perfect match for the hand-checkered, figured walnut in the stock—which also had a mirror gloss. Alas, the High Power is no more.

The latest rendition of the 98 for hunters is an action imported by Global Trading, an Italian firm that came along in 1995. The mechanism now appears in the lineup of Legacy Sports International, which also offers Howa bolt rifles, Puma lever rifles and Silma and Escort shotguns. Legacy's Mauser shows its military heritage. Two massive locking lugs, plus a safety lug, are pure 98. So are the full-length extractor, sturdy fixed ejector, and gas-deflecting shroud. Refinements include a three-position Model 70-style safety and hardened single-stage trigger

Charles Daly manufactures this Mark X' style Mauser, synthetic stocked to hold down the cost.

adjustable for weight of pull, sear engagement, and overtravel. The bolt handle has an M70 look but is not to my eye as attractive. A square-shouldered bridge and front ring are reminiscent of double-square-bridge actions owned mostly by people who drive Jaguars. Both top flats are drilled and tapped and machined with dovetails for your choice of scope mounts. Steel rings specifically for this rifle come in two heights.

The Legacy's is a heavy action: 3.17 pounds of 32CRM04 steel. Like the bolt, the receiver is investment-cast. Its 8.66 inches includes an extra-long receiver ring for additional barrel support. It has a M70-style gas vent. The 3.11-inch ejection port promises plenty of clearance for long magnum cartridges. An Oberndorf-style latch in the front of the trigger guard secures a hinged floorplate. Magazines hold three magnum cartridges or five standard rounds. You can order deep-well, fiveround magazines for magnums. While it's not cataloged at this writing, I'm told Legacy will offer an alloy trigger guard with a detachable steel box magazine. Many hunters apparently think detachable boxes offer a handy alternative to loading from the top and releasing loose cartridges or running them through

A British Columbia guide carries this Mauser in .30-06. There's no more durable, reliable bolt action!

the chamber. My jaundiced opinion: box magazines are an abomination, no more appealing on a classy rifle than snooze stickers on your Jaguar. But then, you didn't ask me.

A professional-grade polish graced the steel of Legacy Mausers I've examined. High-gloss blue and Teflon finishes are optional. So is a "Big Five" action for dangerous-game cartridges. A forged, super-size 98 with all the refinements of the standard action, it is 9.37 inches long with a 3.60-inch ejection port. So it can accommodate truly husky rounds like the .505 Gibbs. The traditional straight bolt handle is a nice touch, as is the drop-box magazine and lower tang extension. Unlike the standard version, which Legacy offers in the white, finished or in a completed rifle chambered to .300 Winchester Magnum, the Big Five comes only as an in-the-white action. It weighs 3.77 pounds.

Next time you have a few moments at a used-gun rack, pick up a Mauser. Commercial beauty or battle-worn service rifle, it deserves a look. Beneath the scars, you'll see genius. Cycle that action and consider the components—their shape, dimensions, and, the fact that for more than a century, Mauser

rifles have been the most dependable repeaters around. In the trenches and now in the field, there's never been a more reliable mechanism. Our Springfield and the Winchester 70 borrowed heavily from the Mauser 98. Browning used it in raw form until it became too costly to market. Now Legacy keeps the name and distinctive profile of commercial Mausers alive.

Everyman's Deer Rifle: The Remington 700

Cloud shadows raced across ahead of the wind over black sage and red Wyoming earth. I bellied to the crest and peeked. The buck was alone. Slowly I slid the rifle ahead of my face and snicked off the safety. In the 4x Lyman Challenger, he looked awfully small. I held a foot into the wind and high and fired. The pronghorn streaked away as I rolled over to cycle the Remington 722. In the scope once again, he slowed and stopped. Smaller now. I held farther into the wind, decided I'd shot high and kept the wire on his back. At the report, he sprinted off, but this time I heard the "thwuck" of a 90-grain .244 bullet in the slats. The buck wobbled a bit, staggered, and fell.

Remington rifles, like Chevrolet automobiles, date to the beginnings of their industry here in the

Remingtons Model 700 made big news in 1963. This first-year-production .30-06 carries a Weaver K4 scope, very popular then.

U.S. And because they're both of common cloth, you'll find lots of Remingtons in the window racks of Chevy pickups. Where I hunt big game, the Model 700 bolt gun is more popular than even the Winchester Model 70, which predated it by 25 years and has long been hailed as "the rifleman's rifle." Among custom 'smiths, the 700's is the action of choice for hunting rigs when accuracy is a chief concern.

For more than 40 years at this writing, the 700 has been the flagship of a long line of Remington rifles beginning in 1816, when Eliphalet Remington II fashioned a rifle in his father's forge in upstate New York. A gunmaking dynasty emerged. By the late 1840s, E. Remington & Sons was supplying government arsenals and had acquired the services of ace designers William Jenks and Fordyce Beals. Manufacturing contracts for the Jenks breech-loading Navy carbine, initiated in 1841, eventually went to Remington—and with them, high-precision gunmaking tools. War with Mexico kept government agents shopping for rifles, while Eli Whitney pioneered the use of mass-produced interchangeable parts. In 1846, Lite Remington adapted Whitney's ideas and tooling to make Model 1841 military rifles. During our Civil War, the North's mass production of weapons was decisive. By 1865, this machinery had also helped Remington become the biggest armsmaker in the country.

Before that war, Remington designer Joseph Rider had worked with Beals and William Elliot on percussion revolvers. His split-breech carbine, patented late in 1863, contributed much more to the firm. It was refined to become the Rolling Block, a huge success for Remington. Military and commercial orders came from all over the world. But when Winchester's Model 1873 lever gun appeared, Remington shifted its focus to repeaters. John Keene, a New Jersey inventor, had what Remington wanted,

in a bolt-action magazine rifle bored to .45-70. But this tube-fed rifle was costly to build, and when the Army rejected it in 1881 trials, the rifle's prospects tumbled. Remington made relatively few of this, its first bolt gun, before falling into receivership in 1886.

The company's financial woes during this era were only partly due to the Keene's flagging sales. Remington had diversified beyond reason, and despite the success of its sewing machines, suffered losses to high overhead and poor investments. Heavy reliance on military contracts left tooling idle in peacetime. Hartley and Graham, a New York firm that also owned giant Union Metallic Cartridge Company, bought E. Remington & Sons. The first military contract after its acquisition was for the bolt-action Remington-Lee Model 1885 Navy Box Magazine Rifle, invented by James Lee. The first sporting version, a Model 1899, didn't reach market until Winchester's controlling interest in Remington (1888 to 1896) ended. Possibly the New Haven company had sought to nix any repeater that would threaten its lever-actions. Remington-Lee sporters were offered in 7x57, 7.35 Belgium Mauser, .236 Remington, .30-30 Winchester, and .30-40 Krag.

Twelve years after these rifles were dropped, in 1909, Remington announced a new bolt-action for hunters. The 30S derived from the 1917 Enfield, which Remington had produced on government contract during the Great War. Heavy and expensive, the 30S sold poorly. In 1926, it was replaced by the Model 30 Express, offered not only in .30-06 but in .25, .30, .32, and .35 Remington—all developed for pump guns. The 30 Express cocked on opening, had a shorter (22-inch) barrel than its predecessor and a lighter trigger pull. A slim stock helped reduce overall weight to seven-and-a-quarter pounds. Priced at $45.75, the 30 Express became reasonably popular; deluxe and carbine versions followed. In

1931, the 7x57 made the list of chamberings; five years later, the .257 Remington-Roberts. Beginning in 1933, service rifles with 1917 and 30S receivers were produced for Latin America. The last 30 Express came off the line in 1940.

The Model 720 High Power Rifle, developed by Oliver Loomis and A.H. Lowe to replace the 30 Express, had a short life. Its 1941 debut, in .30-06, .270, and .257 Roberts, amounted to only 4,000 units before Remington's production shifted to military hardware. In fact, the Navy acquired many of the first 720s. Those not issued during the second World War were presented, beginning in 1964, as marksmanship trophies by the Navy and Marines.

Clean-looking, with a functional grace, Remington 700s support the cartridge with three rings of steel

Remington manufactured many thousands of 1903 and (beginning in 1942) 1903A3 Springfields in a wartime effort that all but cancelled manufacture of sporting guns at the Ilion, New York, plant. Just before adoption of the M1C Garand Sniper rifle, Remington delivered 28,365 Model 1903A4s—the first mass-produced run of sniper rifles in the U.S.

Instead of resuming manufacture of the 720 bolt-action rifle at war's end, Remington adopted a new design by engineers Merle "Mike" Walker and Homer Young. One goal was to reduce costs. Walker, a bench-rest competitor, insisted on an accurate rifle. The Model 721 and short-action 722 were announced early in 1948, with receivers cut from cylindrical tubing. A clip-ring extractor, washer-type recoil lug, self-contained trigger assembly, and stamped bottom metal helped pare costs. But there was no compromise in function.

The stiff receiver helped accuracy. A bolt head shroud added support to the case and security in the event of case rupture. The 721 in .270 and .30-06 originally sold for $79.95. The 722 in .257 Roberts and .300 Savage cost $5 less. All had 24-inch barrels. In 1949, the .300 H&H was added to the 721 list. At eight-and-a-half pounds (with 26-inch barrel) it weighed considerably more than the standard 721 (seven and a quarter) and 722 (seven) and retailed for $89.95. In 1960, the .280 Remington was offered in the 721; a year later, the .264 Winchester Magnum. The 722 would be barreled in .222 Remington (1950), .244 Remington and .308 Winchester (1956), .222 Remington Magnum (1958) and .243 Winchester (1959). High-grade AC and B versions of both rifles were replaced in 1955 with the ADL and BDL designations familiar to Model 700 owners.

The only flaw in the 721/722 design was with appearance. The rifles had stampings where hunters were used to machined parts. Plain, uncheckered stocks shouted "economy!"–though they performed on par with costlier models. A better-looking option from two Remington designers, Wayne Leek and Charlie Campbell, was the Model 725, introduced in 1958. It featured 721/722 receivers but with hinged floorplate, checkered walnut, hooded front, and adjustable open rear sights. A 22-inch barrel came standard on initial offerings in .270, .280, and .30-06, also in .244 (1959) and .243 (1960). A 24-inch tube bored to .222 came along in 1959. During 1961 and 1962, a Kodiak Model 725 was produced in Remington's Custom Shop. Chambered in .375 and .458 Magnum, it wore a 26-inch barrel with built-in muzzle brake. Just 52 of these nine-pound rifles left the factory. They listed for $310, about the same price as Winchester's M70 African.

Three years before the 725 appeared, Remington had introduced the 40X. Designed to

Gunsmiths find M700 actions easy to customize. This one has been lightened by fluting

replace the costly Model 37 .22 target rifle, the 40X was of single-shot design but included features from the 721/722. The centerfire version arrived in 1959, barreled to .308. In 1960, Remington added the .222, .222 Magnum, .30-06, and .300 H&H Magnum. Free Rifle variations followed, with two-ounce and half-ounce triggers.

In 1962, Remington fielded its most successful bolt-action rifle to date, one that immediately drew accolades from hunters. The Model 700 borrowed heavily from the 721/722. In fact, the basic mechanism is the same. Remington hung much of its early advertising on the 700's strength, "three rings of steel" (the bolt shroud, chamber wall, and receiver ring) supporting the cartridge head. But the trimmer tang, swept bolt with checkered knob, cast (not stamped) bottom metal, and more appealing stock pulled shooters to the cash registers in droves. A big assist came from Remington's brand-new 7mm Magnum cartridge, which offered the reach of a .300 H&H Magnum with less recoil. It was one of two magnum rounds listed for the M700's initial run. The other: Winchester's similar but less ably promoted .264. Both these rifles came with 24-inch barrels, as did the .222 and .222 Magnum. A 20-inch barrel was standard for the .243, .270, .280, .308, and .30-06 (all at $114.95). Two action lengths accommodated

this wide range of cartridges, which has since expanded to include almost every modern cartridge made in the U.S. for bolt-action rifles. Indeed, the list of discontinued M700 chamberings is longer than the list of current offerings in many rifles!

Initially cataloged in ADL (blind magazine) and BDL (hinged floorplate) versions, the 700 got its first face-lift in 1969, when Remington jeweled the unblued portion of the bolt and installed a longer rear bolt shroud. A restyled stock featured a buttplate of black plastic instead of anodized alloy. Checkering—pressed into early stocks—got its first overhaul in '69. Now M700 wood stocks have attractive, functional machine-cut checkering. Over the years, changes in manufacturing methods have shown up in the finished product (compare trigger guards now with those of the early 1960s), and the quality of walnut has slipped a bit because figured wood is now hard to come by. Many refinements and economies have been imposed on 700s. Still, a standard version is much the same now as it was before Viet Nam made the six o'clock news.

Myriad variations in the Model 700 have appeared over the last four decades. The most notable:

1965—M700C, a special-order high-grade rifle with fancy wood.

1967—Varmint Special, with 24-inch barrel in .222, .223, .22-250, .243, 6mm.

1973—Left-hand stock and bolt, in .270, .30-06, and 7mm Remington Magnum.

1978—Classic, with satin-finished straight-comb stock, hinged floorplate, in .22-250, .243, 6mm, .270, .30-06, 7mm Magnum. Starting in 1981, limitededition Classics came in one chambering per year. The 6mm was dropped in 1983; all other original chamberings in 1986.

1982—Safety alteration that locks the bolt down when the safety is "on" to prevent opening of the bolt during carry. This change would later be blamed (not justly) for accidental discharges when hunters unloaded their rifles. Remington would respond by reverting to the original safeties.

1984–Sportsman 78 rifle, a Spartan version of the M700, with uncheckered wood and metal and a blind magazine, in .270, .30-06 (the .243 and .308 were added in 1985, the .223 just a year later). The Sportsman 78 was dropped in 1989.

1986–Mountain Rifle, a six-and-three-quarter-pound, walnut-stocked rifle with slim 22-inch barrel tapered to .560. Initially chambered in .270, .280, and .30-06, it came out in short-action form two years later: .243, .308, and 7mm-08. The .257 Roberts was added in 1991, the .25-06 in 1992.

1987–Kit Guns, finished barreled actions with rough-shaped, inletted wood for do-it-yourselfers. Available in .243, .270, .308, .30-06, and 7mm Magnum, Kit Guns were discontinued in 1989.

1987–Rynite stocks (RS) and fiberglass stocks (FS). They survived just two years, to be replaced by synthetic stocks of lighter materials.

1987–Left-hand stock and bolt in short-action rifles chambered for the .243 and .308.

1988–Laminated stock on the ADL/LS, first in .30-06. A year later: .243, .270, 7mm Magnum.

1992–Stainless Synthetic (SS) version of the BDL, with a 426 stainless barrel, receiver, and bolt, black synthetic stock and blind magazine. It came in .25-06, .270, .280, and .30-06, four magnum chamberings: 7mm, .300 Win., .338, and .375.

1993–European 700 with oil-finished stock in .243, .270, 7-08, .280, .30-06, 7mm Magnum.

1994–Varmint Synthetic Stainless Fluted (VS SF) with aluminum bedding block per the earlier VS model (1992) but with six grooves on a heavy 26-inch barrel and a new spherical, concave crown. Chamberings: .223, .22-250, .220 Swift, .308.

1994–Sendero Special with graphite composite stock, bedding block, heavy blued barrel (initially 24 inches, then 26). This nine-pound rifle started out in .25-06, .270, 7mm, and .300 Win. Magnums.

1994–African Plains Rifle, with laminated straight-comb stock and 26-inch "magnum contour" barrel. It was assembled in Remington's Custom Shop in five magnum calibers: 7mm, .300 Win., .300 Wby., .338, .375.

1994–Alaska Wilderness Rifle, with Kevlar-reinforced stock. Receiver, bolt, and 24-inch barrel were of stainless steel. This six-and-three-quarter-pound Custom Shop rifle was initially offered in five magnum chamberings: 7mm, .300 Win., .300 Wby., .338, and .375. The 7mm STW was added in 1998.

1995–DM or Detachable Magazine versions of the BDL and Mountain rifle. 1996–Sendero SF, or stainless fluted, in .25-06, 7mm, and .300 Win. Magnums (later 7mm STW and .300 Wby. Magnum).

1996–MLS black-powder rifles on the 700 action, with a breech plug and nipple at the rear of the 45- or 50-caliber bore. A cylindrical striker replaced the firing pin. The rifle had a synthetic stock and stainless or chrome-moly barrel, iron sights.

1998–VS SF-P, with two ports on the muzzle to reduce jump and deliver an uninterrupted sight picture during recoil of this rifle in .22-250, .220 Swift, .308.

1998–Youth model with synthetic stock, 13-inch pull, in .243, .308.

Remington has since added significantly to the line, including a five-and-ahalf- pound 700 with titanium receiver, and—now discontinued—a 700 Etronx that fired specially-primed cartridges with an electronic impulse provided by a battery in the stock. New cartridge listings include the Remington Ultra Mag series: 7mm, .300, .338, and .375, and the 7mm and .300 Remington Short Ultra Mags.

Remington has built M700s for both military and police forces, beginning in 1966. Paul Gogol, a Remington design engineer and Custom Shop foreman, came up with a sniper rifle based on a 40X action. It won a contract from the Marine Corps. Substituting the Model 700 mechanism, Remington built 995 of these M-40 Sniper rifles for the Corps over the next six years. Many wore Redfield 3-9x scopes; many saw service in Viet Nam. All were chambered for the 7.62 NATO (.308 Winchester). In 1986, the U.S. Army approved for its troops a Model 700 SWS (Sniper Weapon System), with long-action receiver, synthetic Kevlar-reinforced stock, and free-floating 24-inch stainless barrel. These rifles (2,510 for U.S. forces and another 1,000 for Egypt) were shipped with a bipod and a range-finding Leupold M3A 10x scope.

More recently, Remington has supplied domestic law-enforcement agencies with a heavy-barreled Model 700 Police Rifle in .223. An alternative version, in .308, features a detachable box magazine. The sight: Leupold's Vari-X III 3.5-10x. A Harris bipod comes standard; so too a Michael's shooting sling and Pelican case.

Remington has fielded other bolt rifles since the Model 700's debut. The 788 was an inexpensive but serviceable rear-locking gun that remained in the line from 1967 to 1983. The 600 and 660 carbines, with dog-leg bolts that were more distinctive than marketable, had a shorter run—from '64 to '71. They've become sought-after in the used-gun market because now short, lightweight, accurate guns are chic. And because the profile that put everyone off in the '60s has retro appeal.

Remington's handsome Model Seven, introduced in 1983, has been a resounding success and now comes in many guises, including one dressed like the old 600 Magnum. The 710, radically different in its mechanism from traditional bolt rifles, delivers durability and good hunting accuracy

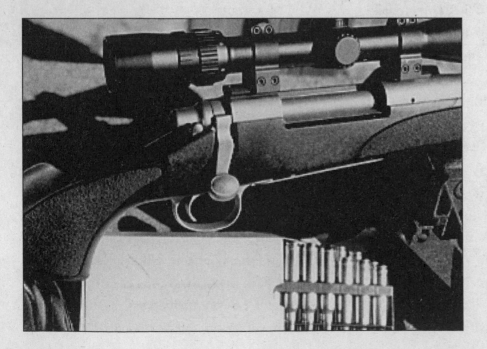

The most recent Remington 700s wear synthetic stocks with grip panels. Stainless steel is popular.

at a Wal-Mart price. But no rifle ever boxed up at Ilion comes close to matching the Model 700 in sales. Current Remington catalogs list 20 variations, including four Custom Shop entries (but not black-powder guns). Take your pick of 29 chamberings, from .17 Remington to .416 Remington Magnum.

Not long ago, still-hunting in a Montana thicket, I spied the nose of a mule deer buck through a slender alley in the lodgepoles. The rifle came up as if it had been part of me for 40 years. Well, that was almost true. The Model 78, rebarreled now to .280 Improved, handled just like countless other Remington bolt guns that have snugged to my cheek and nudged my shoulder on crisp autumn mornings. It homed in on the target like a .244 did long ago, when a pronghorn buck stood briefly behind a dancing crosswire.

You can kill big game with just about any rifle. But tradition counts for a lot among hunters. And you get a fistful of tradition whenever you pick up a Remington 700.

Bill Ruger: An Eye for What Works

William Batterman Ruger, founder and Chairman Emeritus of Sturm, Ruger & Company, died at his home July 6, 2002, at age 86. He was a rarity, a 20th-century pioneer.

Born June 21, 1916, in Brooklyn, New York, Bill Ruger found his passion for guns when his father, attorney Adolph Ruger, gave him a rifle. Bill was just 12 but had often accompanied his father on duck shoots to eastern Long Island. One day afield, he met a man with a .30-06. The blast of that rifle was intoxicating, and soon he and a pal, Bill Lett, had anteed up $9.75 for a surplus .30-40 Krag. Later, Ruger practiced riflery on a high school shooting team—then designed a light machine gun and built a prototype!

At prep school in Salisbury, Connecticut, Bill had to keep his guns off campus. He spent weekends and holidays in Brooklyn machine shops, learning how to fabricate things from metal. Later, as a student at the University of North Carolina, Chapel Hill, he converted an empty room into a machine shop. There he built an auto-loading rifle from a Savage Model 99 lever-action. In 1938, he came up with an idea for what eventually became a machine gun. He finished the technical drawings on his in-laws' dining room table. Army Ordnance officers liked the result, and Ruger was ready to charge ahead full-time as a gun designer.

Bill Ruger wedded Mary Thompson in 1939. Shortly thereafter, he approached Army Ordnance with plans for another machine gun. The Army turned him down. With money running short, Bill accepted a job at Springfield Armory. The $130 monthly check held him there for a year. Eventually, though, claustrophobia set in. The Rugers moved to North Carolina, where Bill renewed his efforts to develop a better machine gun. His work brought no orders from Winchester, Remington or Smith & Wesson—but several job tenders followed. Ruger accepted a position with Auto Ordnance, which made Thompson submachine guns. The firm thought Ruger's prototypes had promise, but the end of World War II killed government interest in new ordnance.

Bill Ruger stayed with Auto Ordnance for three happy years, earning $100 a week at the design table. There he met Doug Hammond, who broached the idea of building guns from sheet metal to trim production costs. Ruger concluded that modern factory machinery could hold acceptable tolerances, that parts could be made to fit easily and interchangeably, yet closely enough for a solid feel, positive functioning and acceptable accuracy. Short years later, the first Ruger auto-loading pistol would prove him right.

William Batterman Ruger's first dive into the waters of free enterprise had him gasping for air in no time. The product–carpenters' tools–cost too much to make. Lesson: No matter how good the item, it must also be a bargain. Hard on the heels of World War II, the Ruger Corporation expired quicker than had Italy.

But in 1948, Bill Ruger got a boost. Alex Sturm, a graduate of the Yale Art School, had no interest in carpenters' tools. He did have $50,000 to invest, however. And he collected guns. Ever the opportunist, Bill was all too willing to take the small grubstake offered him for the manufacture of the .22 pistol he'd designed to be manufactured from sheet steel. This gun must have generated some snickers from the cognoscenti, but at $37.50, it was substantially less expensive than its competition. Bill Ruger had managed to make his gun look good and shoot reliably, too. A 1949 review by NRA's technical staff (including Major Julian Hatcher, Ruger's mentor) helped promote the pistol. An avalanche of orders followed.

The quick rooting of Bill Ruger's new gun company was marred by the death of Alex Sturm. He was not yet 30. To commemorate his partner, Bill had the Ruger "red eagle" emblem (in fact, the likeness of a griffin) changed to black, although red emblems remained in some company literature.

Bill was not just a shooter; he studied guns. Their history and function, changes in metallurgy and marketing–all were interesting. Ruger had started collecting in his teens. Those first Luger and Colt pistols, Sharps and Springfield rifles whetted an appetite that remained. But knowing what came before did not satisfy Bill Ruger.

In 1952, he discarded plans for a tip-up revolver in favor of a solid-frame .22 patterned after Colt's famous Single Action Army revolver. Announced in 1953, this gun gathered a huge following. Like Ruger's auto-loader, it was affordable; but instead of sheet steel, it featured an investment-cast frame–a solid casting held to fine tolerances, and smooth finish by what is commonly called the "lost wax" process. This technique uses wax templates as cores for parts molds. Each part (the frame, in this case) is cast in a mold formed around a template, which

A more comely deer rifle than the Ruger Number One A is hard to find. This a 7x57.

has been melted out. The mold's interior is thus wax-smooth. Final machining is either elim inated or reduced, cutting production time, and expense.

The Ruger Single Six sustained a few early modifications, one of the most brilliant being the addition of an auxiliary cylinder in .22 Winchester Magnum Rimfire. More than 250,000 of these guns have been sold.

Bill Ruger was always quick to build on success, and in 1955 he brought to market a centerfire version of the Single Six. The Blackhawk revolver, initially chambered in .357 Magnum, would eventually be offered in .41 and .44 Magnum, .30 Carbine and .45 Long Colt. In 1959, the .44 Magnum Super Blackhawk appeared, with an unfluted cylinder and a square-backed trigger guard. These guns appealed to deer hunters keen to try a handgun on whitetails. That year, a trim single-action .22 revolver called the Bearcat also made headlines. It had a brass frame, fixed sights, and lightweight four-inch barrel. Eventually it was discontinued, along with the single-shot Hawkeye, which looked like a single-action revolver. The Hawkeye was chambered in .256 Winchester, a marginal round for big game and not as popular with varminters as Remington's .221 Fireball in the XP-100 pistol. Ruger later announced the Fireball as a Hawkeye chambering, but no guns were produced for that round.

In 1961, Ruger started building rifles, first with a .44 Magnum Carbine designed for the deer woods. The five-and-three-quarter-pound gas-operated auto-loader with an 18 1/2-inch barrel and factory-fitted peep sight certainly made sense for close-cover whitetail hunting, but in 1986 the company dropped it. As I recall, the first retail sticker on this delightful little gun was only $108.

But the Carbine's design didn't die. In 1964, Ruger announced a look-alike, the 10/22 rimfire

Long shots come often on the Texas gulf plains. Here a shooter steadies his Ruger Number One.

rifle, with a clever 10-round rotary magazine that fit flush in the action well of the stock. This gun has now become one of the most popular .22 rifles ever. A cottage industry in custom accessories and services has grown up around the 10/22.

By 1968 Bill Ruger had become well known for his innovative thinking. All of his guns were truly fresh designs, with internal features that made each model better than its competition. In some cases there was no competition, because Bill Ruger wasn't afraid to try something nobody else would—like build a single-shot hunting rifle. The last centerfire of this type had been designed by John Browning when Teddy Roosevelt was in his twenties! The Ruger Number One, introduced in 1968 at a list price of $265, got a lukewarm reception.

Fashioned after the British Farquharson action, but trimmer, it had strength, good looks, a crisp trigger, and an ingenious quarter-rib that accepted Ruger's scope rings—no other mount base needed! But it lacked a bolt handle and a magazine, defining features of contemporary hunting rifles.

The Number One has since gained a loyal if limited following among hunters serious enough to make their first shot count. Available in six styles, in

This left handed shooter likes the straight, plain comb of his Ruger 77—and the tang safety!

chamberings from .218 Bee to .458 Winchester, it has even generated competition, the true mark of success.

While some combinations of stock style and chambering have been discontinued, the Number One retains its most pleasing and useful forms. The "B" with 26-inch medium-weight barrel (no sights) and a forend of clean, conservative line offers the widest choice of cartridges. This eight-pound rifle remains a good choice for deer hunters who want to shoot long with powerful cartridges. The "S" version is similar but wears open sights and a barrel-band front swivel stud in front of an abbreviated "Alex Henry" forend. That forend style carries over to the "A," whose trimmer 22-inch barrel (also with sights and stud) makes it easier to carry and quicker to the shoulder. The most recent Number One of interest to deer hunters is the "International," a full-stocked

rifle with sights on a 20-inch barrel. Varmint and Tropical (heavy-caliber) versions complete the line.

Bill Ruger introduced another single-shot rifle several years later. The Number Three carbine offered a more utilitarian look, with an action reminiscent of the Winchester 1885 High Wall. A straight grip and the curved steel butt and barrel band of the .44 Magnum Carbine complemented an uncheckered stock. There was no quarter-rib on the 22-inch barrel. Open sights included a leaf rear and a bead front. Chambered initially in .22 Hornet, .30-40 Krag, and .45-70, the six-pound Number Three was later offered in .223, plus .357 and .44 Magnum. A full-stock version appeared briefly. The rifle was retired in 1987, 15 years after its introduction.

Ruger brought out its bolt-action Model 77 in 1969, just a year after announcing the Number One. If a single-shot seemed a lonely venture, this bolt gun faced even greater risk in a field dominated by Winchester's Model 70 and Remington's 700. Sending a new rifle into the ring with these heavyweights, Bill Ruger showed not only confidence in his product, but a willingness to gamble and a fine sense of timing.

The 77's investment-cast receiver kept costs down. Its conservative-style stock appeared at the height of a revolution against garish angular stock designs. Its great range of chamberings and sensible barrel choices gave it wide appeal. Integral Ruger bases and machined-steel rings provided with each rifle made scope-mounting a snap. A Mauser claw extractor helped both reliability and appearance–though it did not provide controlled-round feeding. In short order, Ruger's 77 muscled aside the giants for a slice of market share. An understudy rifle, the 77/22 rimfire, followed in 1983.

Ruger changed the Model 77 in 1989, replacing the sliding tang safety with a three-position side-swing tab. It also introduced controlled-round

Ruger 77s come in myriad configurations. This deer hunter likes his rifle short and light

feeding and a fixed ejector. The trigger guard was reconfigured, and new versions with stainless steel and synthetic stocks began to appear. The 77 Mark II eventually fathered All-Weather, International, Magnum, Compact, and Ultra Light rifles in a variety of chamberings and with barrels of 16 1/2 to 26 inches in length. The Compact weighs just five-and-three-quarter pounds; the Ultra Light, six. You can get the standard 77 Mark II with open sights or a "clean" barrel. Receivers are forged with the integral base that accommodates Ruger scope rings. Recently, Ruger added to the 77 line with the 77/44, a bolt-action rendition of the original autoloading Deerstalker. It weighs six pounds, with an 18 1/2-inch barrel, and feeds from a rotary magazine. Announced in 1997, it followed, by a year, a lever-action .44, the Model 96. It too features the spool that made the Deerstalker the talk of deer camps in the early 1960s.

Consistent with his pioneering bent, Bill Ruger followed up his original Model 77 with a cap-and-ball revolver. That was in 1983. Next came a 15-shot double-action autoloading pistol and an over-under shotgun with no visible action pins. His Mini-14

carbine in .223 and 7.62x39 has become a popular selfloader, not only on the farm and ranch, but in police cars. The firm's doubleaction revolvers, which come in various frame sizes, have also been selected by law enforcement officers. And the DA .44 Magnum Redhawk is among the bestselling hunting handguns. The subsequent Super Redhawk, with extended frame and integral scope mounts, is even better. Since then (1987), Sturm-Ruger has expanded its line of firearms mainly by cataloging multiple variations of proven models..

"There's really only one gun company in America," Bill Ruger told me once during my visit to his New Hampshire facility years ago. He said it as if he were recommending chowder over sandwiches at a local cafe. No swagger: you want the straight scoop, don't you? Making guns, like making

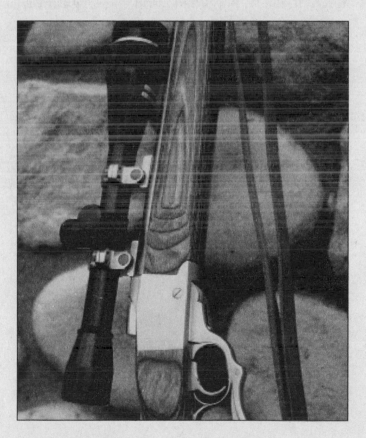

This Ruger Number One is equipped with a powerful Leupold AO scope designed for long shooting.

chowder, is something anybody can try, but it's easier to go broke making guns. Bill Ruger was not broke. During 53 years designing guns, he had helped invent and patent dozens of sporting rifles, pistols and shotguns.

Debt-free and with assets of over $100 million, Sturm, Ruger & Company remained for years in Southport, Connecticut, where Bill Ruger's first manufacturing enterprise struggled in 1946 and where the first guns were built. Now the corporate offices are in Prescott, Arizona. The Newport, New Hampshire, factory, currently the biggest Ruger plant, evolved from an investment casting operation called Pine Tree Casting. Most pistol frames and rifle receivers originate here, as do all but the longest revolver barrels, which come from the outside source that supplies Ruger rifle barrels. Shotgun barrels are forged in-house. Ruger button-rifles its long barrels, but short pistol barrels are broached.

The company operates its own wood shop next to the Pine Tree Casting plant, where it fashions rifle and shotgun stocks from American walnut. European walnut is standard on some guns. Ruger lists synthetic stocks for most models. These are supplied by outside vendors, as are revolver grips. Assembly is done in-house. Afterward, the guns are proofed on a range that also serves the company's armorer program, offered to police agencies. Four million bullets fly down Ruger's test tunnels each year!

When not involved in firearms design, Bill Ruger collected antique firearms, early Western American art and automobiles. His garages held more than 30 antique and modern vehicles, including Bentleys, Rolls-Royces, Bugattis, Stutzes, and a lovely 1913 Mercer Raceabout. In 1970, Ruger commissioned the design and construction of a sports tourer he dubbed the Ruger Special. It was based on a 1929 Bentley four-and-a-half-liter model.

Bill Ruger's philanthropy supported several charities and the Buffalo Bill Historical Center in Cody, Wyoming, where he served as a Trustee for 15 years. His son, William B. Ruger, runs the firearms business now (son James Thompson "Tom" Ruger and wife Mary Thompson Ruger died before Bill). The company has, to date, produced well over 20 million firearms for hunting, target shooting, self-defense, and tactical use. Deer hunters know it best for the practical, affordable rifles that began rolling off Ruger lines in the 1960s. Rifles that look and feel good enough to compete with the biggest names in deer guns.

More Bolt Rifles of Consequence

WAYNE VAN ZWOLL

We gulped lukewarm oatmeal by flashlight, cinched our packs tight and marched silently up over a rocky plateau. The black rim of the basin cut clearly into the night sky. Dawn was yet two hours off. On top, wind cut through the sweat and we huddled in the lee of a spruce while the eastern sky turned to steel, then rose. Then we split, Vern easing downslope into this untrafficked basin, while I still-hunted slowly enough to break even with him at the first rockslide.

Just beyond, with the sun now a strong promise, we began the still-hunt we'd shared for years. A rifleshot from ridgeline, I picked my way slowly, throttling my step. Vern, probing thickets of whitebark pine, would be on the deer first.

But he didn't see the pair of bucks that ghosted out in front of him. They stopped on talus to look back. In the 2 1/2x All American, they looked very far.

Sitting, with the sling taut, I nudged the quivering dot up on the big deer's scapula and crushed the trigger. The Model 70 jumped, and its crack echoed from the basin's headwall as the buck collapsed. Vern got busy with his .30-06 then, and the other deer died.

My .270 has been with me for decades now, in places like this basin that I want to show it again. It was my idea of a rifleman's rifle before Winchester came up with that name.

Sako, Scandinavia's Brightest Star

It's not "Sayko." Nor is it "Sacko." It's "Socko." At least, if you want to sound like you know what you're talking about when in Finland. It was there that Suojeluskuntain yliesikunnan asepaja was established the first day of April, 1919. Sako may be a big firm by local standards, but the factory is small compared to the competition's plants in the U.S. This is a rural area, where in the dark of cold mornings I jog a few easy miles along deserted streets. No skyscrapers in Riihimaki—though the Finns make good use of space and heating dollars with multi-story apartments. They're not high-rise, the tallest structure in town, it appears, is still a church steeple. Birches swing lazily with the wind in pools of yellow light cast by the street lamps. As the sky behind them turns from black to steel, old men and women sift onto the sidewalks. They are bundled in sweaters and greatcoats but obviously used to the weather and just as clearly bound for distant places. Some carry ski poles and walk with the long, pendulous stride of people who spend much of each year coursing snow.

It had been the same in Helsinki, the capital and as metropolitan a city as you'll find here. In the pre-dawn chill of its docks, I passed many people walking to work. Some slowed as the boats backed to the main thoroughfares, their owners setting out smoked fish. An elderly woman sat under a canvas awning, a cup of coffee between her hands. Raw, cold wind raked the awning and teased the woman's black shawl. I jogged toward a park. With a population of just over half a million, Helsinki would hardly qualify for big-city status in the U.S. Roughly 10 percent of the Finnish people live here, hard against the Gulf of Finland. Facing the dock, across the boardwalk, brick street and rails, loom federal buildings built—well, not that long ago. Finland didn't become an independent republic until 1919, two years after breaking with Russia.

Explored by Swedish missionaries as early as 1155, Finland remained a Swedish protectorate until 1809, when it was surrendered to Russia. The Czar proclaimed it a Grand Duchy. Many Swedes remained in-country, and Swedish is still taught in some schools. Of the roughly 91,000 foreigners now in Finland, many are Swedes. Oddly enough, the Finnish language (of the Finno-Ugric linguistic family) is closer to Hungarian than to Swedish. Sami, the tongue of Lapland, is also an official language. Lapland comprises the northern part of Finland and extends well above the Arctic Circle, where the sun doesn't set for 73 days each summer—and doesn't rise for 51 days each winter.

Nearly 80 percent of Finland is forested; forest products account for about 30 percent of exports. But as I was to find out shortly, there are lots of openings in the rolling woodlands—small farms that bring to mind the upper Midwest where so many Scandinavians have settled in the U.S. It's perfect whitetail habitat, but I didn't know that Finns shoot 17,500 of these animals annually. Where'd the deer come from? The U.S.! In 1934, six whitetails were imported from Minnesota. They escaped from an enclosure in 1938. A decade later, six more fawns arrived from the States; four survived and were released. By 1960, Finland had

nearly 1,000 deer—enough for a hunting season. Their subsequent increase is due partly to the lack of predators. Wolves, which raided farms in the closing years of the 19th century and took dozens of children, were trapped and shot aggressively. They remain only in the wildest areas. You'll see foxes here, but no big cats. Bears are an occasional hazard to fawns. Feral dogs don't get much sympathy from Finnish hunt clubs that manage the game—though they use dogs to drive moose and often to move or trail deer on hunts.

Sako rifles evolved to serve an active hunting industry. Compared to that in the U.S., it is highly regulated, but no less tradition-bound. I was told that all big game is managed by 300 state-sanctioned hunting associations that currently comprise 2,370 clubs and 140,000 members. The country is divided into 15 game conservation districts administered by a Central Association of Hunters. You needn't be a club member or landowner to hunt, though membership has advantages. About 300,000 riflemen take to the woods each fall, more per capita than in any other European country. Moose (or, traditionally in Finland, elk) are by far the most important economically. Moose hunters spend the most, and moose meat sold at market adds to the coffers. Of 10 million kilograms of game (roughly 22 million pounds) sold in the year 2000, a whopping 84 percent came from moose. Some places in Finland, moose trails snake through the woods like deer highways in our high-density whitetail coverts.

Given the local importance of big game, it might seem strange that the first rifle from Finland's best-known firearms manufacturer was built for small-game hunting. In fact, it was named after a fox.

By the end of the second world war, Sako had developed its "Vixen," a nowlegendary bolt rifle scaled for small centerfire cartridges like the

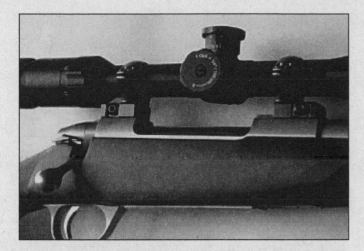

Sako's reputation for clean lines and fine workmanship shows in this Zeiss-scoped .300 Weatherby.

.22 Hornet and .218 Bee, which had appeared in the 1930s. It was subsequently offered in .222 (circa 1950) and the .222 Magnum and .223 (developed beginning in the late 1950s). Stoeger brought the Vixen Sporter to the States in 1946. A heavybarrel version and a fullstocked carbine with 20-inch barrel came along the next year. Production of these rifles followed a tough time in Finnish history. During the winter of 1939-1940, the Soviet Union attacked Finland. Brutal fighting ensued, in what has come to be known as the Winter War. As Europe fell to the Nazis, Finland renewed its struggle against the Russian Bear in the Continuation War, which cost the smaller country some territory. But when the smoke cleared in 1944, Finland was still independent.

In 1955, Finland joined the United Nations, a year later the Nordic Council. By this time, Sako had committed to expanding its rifle line, and two years later announced the L-57 Forester. This action, built on the Mauser design but with refinements, was sized to accommodate the then-new .308 Winchester and its derivative, the .243. L-57s were also chambered in .22-250. Like the Vixen, the Forester came in Sporter, Carbine, and Heavy Barrel configurations. They became available to U.S. shooters in 1958.

Three years later, Sako came up with another, longer action. It looked like the Forester, but the L-61 Finnbear chambered the popular .30-06. You could also specify .25-06 or .270, the .264 Winchester or 7mm Remington Magnum, the .300 or .338 Winchester Magnum, even the .375 H&H. Catalogs listed no Heavy Barrel option, but did include a full-stocked carbine (20-inch barrel), as well as a standard version with 24-inch tube.

In 1961, Sako also came up with the Finnwolf, a hammerless lever-action rifle with a one-piece stock. Available in .243 and .308 with a four-shot detachable magazine, it looked a little like Winchester's 88 and lasted for about a decade. You'll search hard to find one now. A Model 73 followed the Finnwolf. Identical save for its flush three-round magazine and lack of a cheekpiece, this rifle sold only until 1975.

By this time Sako was eight years into new ownership and had designed a new rifle to replace the Vixen, Forester, and Finnbear. The Model 74 maintained separate action lengths for three main classes of cartridges. Produced from 1974 until 1978, it was succeeded by the A1 series (the A11 and A111 were the medium- and long-action models). In the mid-1980s, Sako replaced it with the Hunter, again in three action lengths. A left-hand version appeared in 1987. By the time the company's current TRG rifle came along in 1993, only Sako collectors could tell you all the minor differences that distinguished the various series of rifles that had evolved from the lovely Vixen. Along the way, Sako built a Model 78 rimfire, a classy box-fed bolt-action sporter cataloged from 1977 to 1987. You could also buy this model in .22 Hornet.

Early Sakos were characterized by hand-checkered walnut stocks that, from the late 1950s, wore a glossy finish. It seems to me a few early stocks came from Finnish birch, common on other, less expensive rifles. Metal finish was uniformly excellent, the resulting blue gleaming but not glittery. Wood-to-metal fit as well showed great care. Never inexpensive, Sako rifles earned a reputation for fine accuracy and caught the fancy of riflemen who wanted something a cut above ordinary Remington and Winchester rifles. Crisp, adjustable triggers, and buttery bolt operation helped sell the Sakos. Dovetail receiver rails that required the purchase of costly Sako rings worked fine but may not have added market share. The extractor, an external claw much smaller than the 98 Mauser's, apparently matched its reliability if not its strength.

In 1997, Sako's current flagship, the Model 75, appeared in four action lengths, to accommodate a broad spectrum of cartridges from the .17 Remington to the .416 Remington. Its three locking lugs are a departure from the early sporters, offering a 70-degree bolt lift. The right-side two-position safety has the traditional look, so, too, the steel bottom metal, and the barrels are

A flush-fit detachable magazine gives Sako rifles a clean profile; and unloading is a snap.

still hammer-forged–though by a new, more fully automated process. Sako's catalog points out that there's .02 inch-clearance between the barrel and forend channel. Perhaps the most striking feature of the 75 is its bolt shroud. It incorporates a lock you can manipulate with a supplied key to render the rifle inoperable. I don't like this, but then, neither do I like heavy triggers, crossbolt safeties on lever guns or any other device that diminishes the utility of a rifle in the name of safety. Rifles difficult to cycle quickly or shoot accurately are like dull axes.

Enough said on that.

The Sako 75 comes in several versions: The Hunter, Hunter Stainless, and Deluxe feature walnut stocks and 22-, 24-, and 26-inch barrels. The Finnlight, with 20- or 22-inch fluted barrel, and the Synthetic Stainless are both stainless, synthetic-stocked models. There's a walnut-stocked Battue, with quarter-rib and 19-inch barrel. And Varmint and Varmint Stainless configurations with 24- and 26-inch barrels. The 75 comes in 18 chamberings, including the .17 Remington and .22 and 6mm PPC. You can order it in .340 Weatherby and .338 Lapua, and if your tastes run Continental, in 6.5x55, 7x64, and 9.3x62.

Smooth cycling makes Sako the choice of this Scout-rifle shooter, here reload at a speed-shooting event at Arizona's Gunsite Academy.

Sako's other centerfire is the TRG. Most renditions are for target and tactical shooters, but there's a TRG-S in .338 Lapua or .30-378 Weatherby. The three-lug action differs from the 75's and includes a detachable box magazine, straight stack. Like the 75, the TRGs feature integral top rails on the receiver. These dovetail cuts, angled 3.7 degrees, secure Sako's Optilock mounts under the force of recoil. There's a center cut in the rear bridge, a stop that accepts a pin in the mount base. The Optilock base clamps to the receiver with a right-hand clamp. Scope rings feature rotating polymer inserts to guarantee perfect ring alignment with the scope's axis. Available in three heights and two diameters (one inch and 30mm), the rings are also supplied with quick-detach bases and thumb levers.

Though Sako's line of shooting irons is limited by U.S. standards, the company is more diversified than it appears. The Sako Finnfire, cataloged in Hunter, Varmint, and Sporter versions, is Finland's premier .22 rimfire, stocked in walnut. In 1983, Sako conspired with another Finnish firm, Tikka, in a

Finland's premier riflemaker. Sako at the Riihimaki facility also produces Tikka rifles.

joint effort to produce the Model 555 rifle, seldom talked about now. At that time, Tikka was older than Sako, having manufactured gun parts for 80 years. During the second World War, it had built sewing machines and sub-machine guns. By 1970, it had abandoned its own brand of sewing machines to concentrate on the Tikka Models 55 and 65 rifles and 17 shotgun. The 77 shotgun followed.

During the 1980s, Sako acquired Tikka, along with the shotgun manufacturer, Valmet, established in 1925. Valmet had auto-loading mechanisms in its past, but the strength of the union came from its over/under smoothbores. By 1989, all Tikka production at its Tikkakoski Works had been moved to Sako's Riihimaki plant. Tikka's Whitetail rifle was well built but poorly publicized in the U.S. Its successor, the T3 has received much more attention here. It is built in the Sako plant, using components of the same quality as are used in Sako rifles. Tikka barrels come from the same bin and must meet identical specs. Yet the T3's list price is much lower.

Since I was old enough to keep my fingers off their finely polished steel, I've held and coveted quite a few Sakos. I've shot a few but owned only one. It's a little embarrassing to admit that, because these rifles are commonly acknowledged as the best bolt rifles east of Cape Cod. But while they've been imported steadily through Stoeger, they've not been as common in the U.S. as our own domestic rifles. Some Sakos, in fact, have stayed pretty much within commuting distance of the Riihimaki plant. Take those in 9.3x66, a proprietary cartridge I saw for the first time on a visit to Sako's plant. It's a powerful number, on the order of the .338 Winchester Magnum, a 9.3-bore

I shot this Austrian roebuck with a Sako short-action rifle in .308 Winchester.

cartridge a tad longer than the 9.3x64 but with a .30-06-size case rim. It won't come Stateside.

"We're marketing Sako rifles more aggressively to U.S. hunters now," said Paavo Tammisto, who handles press relations for Sako. "Since Beretta bought the company in 2000, we've benefited from their selling style and muscle. But the rifles will continue to be made the same way, right here in Riihimaki, to our highest standards."

Roy Weatherby: Magnum Man

During the late 1940s and 1950s, post-war prosperity plowed returning GIs back into civilian life. Many popped up again soon as entrepreneurs, new industries fertilizing their ambitions. California called some away from more pedestrian places. Whatever you had to sell, there was a market in the Golden State. Roy Weatherby no doubt considered that when he began selling rifles and ammunition. But he went a step further. He packaged an image, and his ability to peddle that image to people with disgusting amounts of money brought success to a fledgling company. It would become, in time, the sequined gun company, one that courted favor with Hollywood and flourished in a period that redefined American culture and big game hunting.

Roy Weatherby belonged in the California that produced Tinseltown. The quintessential promoter, he placed himself in photos with actors like Roy Rogers, worldtraveled hunters like Elgin Gates, even foreign dignitaries like the Shah of Iran. He shared the lens with Elmer Keith and Jack O'Connor, with Jimmy Doolittle, Joe Foss, and Robert L. Scott. He parlayed his associations into business because he believed what he preached: Weatherby rifles can bring you extraordinary hunting success. He reminded customers that owning a Weatherby is

joining elite company. The subliminal message: Weatherby helps you become more than you are.

Roy certainly became more than his boyhood promised. Born in 1910 to a sharecropper in central Kansas, Roy knew poverty. He and his nine brothers and sisters moved a lot. There was no automobile, no electrical service or indoor plumbing at the George Weatherby house. Roy recalled walking behind an old plow-horse, watching a neighbor pull five bottoms three times as fast with a Fordson tractor.

In 1923, George opened a one-pump filling station in Salinas. Then there was the move to Florida, "nine of us in a four-passenger Dodge, camping in a tent along the way." George laid bricks while Roy hauled mortar. Growing up, Roy would clerk in a music store, sell washing machines, and drive a bread truck. He later enrolled at the University of Wichita, where he met Camilla Jackson. They married in 1936, and Roy got work at Southwestern Bell Telephone. Not long thereafter the couple headed west, winding up in San Diego. Employed by a local utility, then the Automobile Club of Southern California, Roy was soon making very good money: $200 a month.

Since his boyhood days trapping possums, Roy had indulged an interest in the outdoors. He liked to hunt, and he liked to experiment with guns. Working in his home shop with rudimentary equipment, he reshaped the .300 Holland and Holland case to increase its capacity. He reduced body taper and gave it a "double-radius" shoulder. The full-length version became the .300 Weatherby, but his first magnums were necked to .257, .277, and .284 and shortened for .30-06-length magazines. In 1946, he pledged "everything I owned" to get a $5,000 business loan from the Bank of America. It was a start. But for the first couple of decades, Roy Weatherby's custom-rifle enterprise teetered. With bankruptcy a constant threat, Roy pushed ahead. One day, behind the counter at his small retail store, he watched Gary Cooper walk in the door. It was a pivotal moment. Soon Roy was meeting other Hollywood stars. He wrote an article, "Overgunned and Undergunned" for a magazine; Sheldon Coleman saw it and became a customer.

By 1949, Roy's hard work had produced a larger shop and store, but he needed more capital to put the company on the next rung. Business partner Bill Wittman agreed to incorporation, and in May the two men offered $70,000 in stock. One of the company officers was Herb Klein, a wealthy Texas oilman who owned a .270 Weatherby Magnum rifle. Herb bought $10,000 of that stock. He would later become a key source of business acumen and additional capital. (The early growth of Weatherby's company is chronicled in a book, *Weatherby: The Man. The gun. The Legend,* by Grits and Tom Gresham, Cane River Publishing.) The company would remain true to Roy's vision. Now, under the leadership of Roy's only son, Ed, it has also shown itself nimble, adapting to market changes and bringing a stream of new products to shooters.

Roy built his first rifles on Mauser actions. In 1957, he and company engineer Fred Jennie came up with an action of their own: the Mark V. They engaged Germany's J.P. Sauer & Sohn to produce it. Since then, this mechanism with its low-lift, interrupted-tread, lug-diameter bolt has remained essentially as Roy and Fred fashioned it. In 1971, rifle manufacture moved to Japan, then came Stateside in the 1990s. Now all Weatherby rifles are built in the U.S.

During the 1990s, a six-lug Mark V appeared. This scaled-down action weighs 26 ounces—10 ounces or 28 percent less than the Mark V Magnum. Teamed with slim, fluted barrels, this receiver better fitted .30-06-size cartridges and enabled Weatherby to build rifles as light as five-and-three-quarter pounds. It became the nucleus of several hunting models, and heavy-barreled varminters for traditional short-action rounds. In developing the Ultra Light rifle, Weatherby did not chop the barrel to pare ounces. That ploy would have reduced bullet velocity and impaired rifle balance. Barrels for Weatherby Magnum rounds have remained at 26 inches,

Beginning in the 1940s, Roy Weatherby promoted his rifles and cartridges by stressing their reach.

Weatherby's Mark V (left) and the Remington 700 both accommodate long cartridges.

but those for standard cartridges and the 7mm Remington and .300 Winchester Magnum measure 24. A deer hunter who doesn't want the power of a full-length .300 Weatherby Magnum cartridge certainly won't want to carry the heavy original rifle up a mountain or prowl the woods with something so cumbersome. The six-lug Mark V with a lightweight barrel makes more sense.

One of my all-time favorite rifles is the .338-06 Ultra Lightweight. It weighs an even six pounds with 24-inch barrel, a few ounces more than its Ultra Lightweight siblings. That's because the Kreiger barrel is of slightly greater diameter to leave enough metal at the base of the flutes around a .33 bore. To me, this rifle seems ideally balanced. The efficiency and versatility of the .338-06 has appealed to me since I first read of its forebear: the .333 OKH, developed in the early 1940s for Jeffery bullets. My friend Larry Barnett at Superior Ammunition in Sturgis, South Dakota, provided the first .338-06 A-Square ammo fired in this Weatherby, with 210-grain Nosler Partition and 225-grain Swift A-Frame bullets. Norma, which manufactured cartridge cases for Weatherby beginning in 1953, now loads .338-06 ammo with the rest of Weatherby's line.

Larry's Noslers clock 2,765 fps. That's only 65 fps shy of chart values for these bullets in the .338 Winchester Magnum as factory loaded! With nearly 3,600 footpounds of thrust at the muzzle, the .338-06 Superior loads hit harder than any 180-grain bullet from the .300 Winchester Magnum! A 200-yard zero puts the Partitions eight inches low at 300, 24 inches low at 400. Deer hunters who might also hunt elk and moose with the same rifle owe themselves a few shots with a Weatherby in .338-06. The 225-grain Swift bullets leave the muzzle of my .338-06 at 2,685 fps. For tough game, this bullet excels.

Like other Weatherbys, the Ultra Light wears a high-backed comb that reduces cheek slap. Even

with heavy loads, it is not unpleasant. The Weatherby one-and-ahalf-inch guarantee means less to me than a rifle's "pointability" and its field accuracy from hunting positions. Still, barrels that deliver tight groups inspire confidence. Button-rifled Criterion barrels from John Krieger's shop are cryogenically treated in-house. That is, barrel temperature is lowered to -300 degrees F to relieve stresses bound in the steel by manufacturing operations. At the Brainerd MN Acrometal plant that assembles Weatherby's rifles, I once examined targets from then-new Super VarmintMaster rifles. The hand-lapped barrels kept some clusters to less than .six inch.

Not long ago as this is written, Weatherby introduced a Special Varmint Rifle. The plain-vanilla seven-and-a-quarter-pound rifle wore a 22-inch barrel in .223 and .22-250. Initially priced at $999, it cost considerably less than the Super VarmintMaster. The SVM was followed by the Super PredatorMaster, a six-and-aquarter-pound rifle for the "walking" varmint hunter. PredatorMasters sold better than expected in .243, 7mm-08, and .308. Weatherby's Marketing VP, Brad Ruddell, decided that the buyers weren't all shooting 'chucks and coyotes. "Hunters thought it was an ideal deer gun."

Weatherby quickly developed a lightweight big-game rifle patterned on the PredatorMaster. A

Super-accurate Weatherby rifles are now so designated. Deer hunters who shoot long take note!

year later, it announced the Super Big GameMaster. Built on both the six- and nine-lug actions, this rifle weighs five-and-three-quarter to sixand-three-quarter pounds. Barrels are stainless and hand-lapped, with six flutes and an 11-degree crown. The adjustable trigger is factory-set at four pounds, with .012 to .015 sear engagement. Like its predecessor, the SBGM wears a "laid" stock of Aramid, graphite and fiberglass. Its aluminum bedding block ensures precise recoil lug seating and stiffens the magazine mortise. Magazine capacity for the SBGM: five in .240 Wby., .25-06, .270 Win., .280, .30-06, .338-06. Capacity is three for magnums: .257 Wby., .270 Wby., 7mm Wby., 7mm Rem., .300 Win., and .300 Wby. In many ways, the SBGM is the modern version of Weatherby's original Mark V rifle, stocked in figured Claro walnut and listing, in 1964, for $285. The SBGM retails for $1,561 (standard calibers) and $1,623 (magnums).

The Weatherby Vanguard, a mid-priced rifle on the Howa action, is also chambered for short magnums.

Weatherby's Custom Shop has become more flexible, offering not only "California style" stocks, but also more conservative handles. Despite the steep pitch of the Mark V tang, Weatherby gunmakers have managed to make the grip long and attractive. They also build guns for dangerous game, chambered for the likes of the .458 Lott, as well as for Weatherby's own hard-hitting .378, .416, and .460.

The Vanguard, once the "entry level" Weatherby, reappeared in the line late in 2003. Built on the Japanese Howa action, it is an affordable alternative to the Mark V. A Butler Creek injection-molded stock helps keep retail of the least expensive rendition at $476 ($595 for the stainless version). The Vanguard is offered in 11chamberings, from .223 to .338 Winchester Magnum. The Howa action has been used for a number of U.S.-produced sporting rifles. It's a bit heavy (though not in comparison with the magnum Mark V!). The trigger is a good one. I've used this stout, smooth-cycling mechanism on both deer and elk hunts.

Weatherby has been in the shotgun business for years. Best-known are its boxlock over/unders. The Athena and Orion come in 12, 20, and 28 gauges. A modified Greener crossbolt with automatic ejectors and single selective trigger complement back-bored barrels with long forcing cones and interchangeable chokes. A Prince-of-Wales grip and trim lines bring these guns quickly on target.

Weatherby rifles are popular among deer hunters in the West, where flat-shot bullets rule.

Deer hunters in slug country have more truck with the Weatherby SAS, a revamped SKB. Its self-compensating gas system lets you interchange target and hunting loads. Field guns with walnut stocks, and specialty guns wearing camo, are a step up from the $649 SAS with black synthetic stock. At seven-and-a-quarter pounds, these auto-loaders are not lightweights, but they seem nimble in the hand, and they point where I look. The weight and gas system soak up recoil from heavy loads—a real blessing on the SAS slug gun. Its 22-inch rifled barrel wears a cantilever scope mount. While earlier SAS shotguns came from Japan, the new models come from Italy and include shims that let you change stock dimensions that most affect fit: cast and drop.

Winchester and the Rifleman's Rifle

By 1890, gun design in the United States had eclipsed the development of cartridges. Black powder was essentially the same mixture the Chinese had used in the 14th century. Developments in Europe, however, would soon make it obsolete. Following the work of the Swiss chemist Schoenbein and the Italian Sobero, who discovered nitrocellulose and nitroglycerin, Vielle, a Frenchman, found in 1885 that dissolving nitrocellulose in ether produced a stable colloid that could be dried and used as propellant. The compound became single-base smokeless powder. Alfred Nobel and Frederick Able later added nitroglycerine to get double-base smokeless.

Winchester didn't catalog smokeless ammunition until 1893, when it advertised shotshells with new "nitro" propellant. Within a year, the company was offering 17 smokeless centerfire cartridges. Ammunition fueled much of Winchester's growth in the early days of the automobile. By 1914, the company was loading 175 smokeless cartridges. Though it marketed to hand-loaders, Winchester called the hand-loading of smokeless cartridges "impractical."

Between the advent of smokeless powder and the start of World War I, Winchester developed some of its most famous guns: the Model 1890 .22 rimfire pump rifle and Model 1897 pump shotgun, its models 1892 and 1894 lever-action rifles. The Model 1903 auto-loading .22 was the first successful self-loader produced in quantity in the United States. The Model 12 pump shotgun became one of the most popular smoothbores ever.

Winchester pioneered the use of nickel steel barrels in the Model 94, perhaps the most popular whitetail rifle in the past century. The 92, chambered for shorter, less potent rounds like the .44-40, was advertised it as "the rifle that helped Peary reach the North Pole."

The 20th century brought new men to Winchester. Thomas Bennett's split with John Browning was a blow, but in Thomas Crossly Johnson the company found another gifted gun designer. Johnson specialized in auto-loading mechanisms, developing the recoil-operated Winchester Self-Loading Rifles, Models 03, 05, 07, and 10. Johnson engineered Winchester's first auto-loading shotgun, a recoil operated, hammerless, five-shot repeater designated the Model 11. He had to work around the Browning patents—which he had helped write!

During the first World War, Winchester supplied more than 50,000 Browning Automatic Rifles, plus thousands of short-barreled Model 97 shotguns for trench fighting. Each shell had six 34-caliber pellets. They proved so devastating that the German government protested, warning that any American carrying a shotgun when captured would be shot. Other contracts called for 44 million

.303 British cartridges and 400,000 Enfield rifles for the British government, plus nine million .44 WCF rounds for the British Home Guard's Winchester 92 rifles and 50 million .22 Long Rifle cartridges, also for England. Winchester's plant had doubled in size, to three-and-one-quarter-million square feet. During hostilities, 17,519 people worked there. But long term military contracts didn't cover steeply-rising labor costs. At war's end, with demand on a slide, these oversights crippled Winchester.

In 1920, Thomas Bennett and other patriarchs reorganized the firm. The Winchester Repeating Arms Company made guns and ammunition, while its sister firm, the Winchester Company, manufactured cutlery, gas refrigerators, skates, flashlights, fishing gear, hand tools, washing machines, baseball bats, skis, batteries, paints, and household brushes. This diversification failed to reduce debt; ironically, the gun division prospered.

For some time after armistice, Winchester gun designers had almost no budget. Still, they came up with two fine rifles: the Model 52 bolt-action rimfire in 1919 and the Model 54 centerfire in 1924. The 54 was Winchester's first successful bolt-action centerfire rifle, though the company had tried to enter that field for 30 years. The .45-70 Hotchkiss was discontinued in 1900; the Lee Straight Pull, lasted from 1897 to 1903. Engineers working on the Model 54 borrowed the 1903 Springfield's coned breech. The ejector was of Newton design. The Mauserstyle bolt cocked on opening and wore a beefy extractor and safety. The stock was patterned after the popular Sedgely sporters of that period. A nickel-steel barrel on a cyanide-hardened receiver bottled pressures from the new .270 WCF cartridge, whose 130-grain bullet at 3,000 fps awed hunters used to .30-30s. The 54 cost more than a surplus military rifle, but much less than a Sedgley or Griffin & Howe sporter. Though it never earned the accolades given the earlier Model 94 or the Model 70, Winchester's M54 appeared at a pivotal time. The Springfield had introduced shooters to the potential of bolt rifles and powerful cartridges. The 54 was delightfully nimble, and the .270 shot flatter than anything most deer hunters had ever seen.

When the Depression hit, Winchester was too weak to stand. In February 1929, the old organization was dissolved and The Winchester Repeating Arms Company of Delaware took its place. The company went bankrupt January 22, 1931, the

This three-position side-swing safety is a Model 70 hallmark. Several makers have adopted it. This rifle is a Kimber.

A stainless synthetic, this rifle in 7mm WSM is unmistakably a Model 70.

year the Model 21 shotgun would come to market. In December, Winchester was acquired by the Western Cartridge Company. Western assumed the Winchester Company for $3 million cash and $4.8 million (par value) of Western stock. The company entered the Depression under Franklin Olin's son, John, who had a keen interest in firearms. In the next decade, 23 new Winchester guns would appear.

The decision to replace the Model 54 with another rifle was prompted largely by a desire for a better centerfire target rifle. Since its introduction in 1919, the Model 52 rimfire had steadily built an unassailable record on small-bore ranges, and Winchester wanted centerfire laurels to match. Western had kept the 54 alive, allowing T. C. Johnson

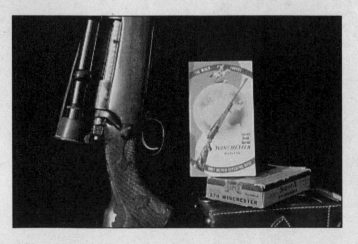

This early Model 70 is one of the most ornate ever produced by the Winchester Custom Stop.

and his staff to refine the rifle they had engineered. Ten configurations came about, with 10 chamberings. Prices (in 1936) ranged from $59.75 for the basic Model 54 to $111.00 for a Sniper's Match.

The Model 54's main weakness was its trigger. Fashioned after military triggers of the day, it also served as a bolt stop. Competitive shooters grumbled. Hunters content to fight a mushy trigger balked at the high-swing safety, which precluded low scope mounting. Bill Weaver's affordable Model 330 scope had shown shooters what optical sights could do, and rifles that wouldn't accommodate them had a dim future.

The Model 54 was cataloged and available through 1941, but production became a trickle during the last five years. Beginning December 29, 1934, Winchester started work on a stronger, better-looking rifle—the Model 70. It came to market slowly. The 54 was still viable, and changes were given close scrutiny. Also, lots of men were still eating in soup kitchens; there was no screaming demand for a new hunting rifle. On January 20, 1936, the first M70 receivers got serial numbers. On the official release date (January 1, 1937), 2,238 rifles were awaiting shipment.

The 70's barrel and receiver looked a lot like the Model 54's. But the trigger was much better, a separate sear allowing for adjustment in take-up, weight, and overtravel. The bolt stop was also separate. To eliminate misfires—too common with the 54's speed lock—striker travel on the Model 70 was increased 1/16 inch. The first Model 70 safety was a tab on top of the bolt shroud. It swung horizontally; four years later it would be redesigned as a side-swing tab, a middle detent blocking the striker while permitting bolt manipulation. Like the Model 54, the Model 70 had three guard screws, but instead of a stamped, fixed magazine cover and guard, the 70 wore a hinged floorplate secured by a spring-loaded plunger in the separate trigger guard. A low bolt handle acted as a safety lug. The square bolt shoulder precluded low scope mounting and was later eliminated.

Model 70 barrels (with the same contours and threads as Model 54 barrels) were drop-forged, straightened by hand with a 15-pound hammer, then turned true on a lathe. They were deep-hole drilled, then straightened again. Next, each bore was reamed to proper diameter and hook-rifled by a cutter slicing progressively deeper on several passes, one groove at a time. Rifling took roughly 11 minutes per barrel. After lapping, barrels were threaded and slotted for rear sights and front sight hoods. Forged, hand-stippled ramps appeared on the first 70s; later ramps were soldered on and machine-matted. Just before chambering, each barrel was inspected, then stamped underneath with caliber designation, and the last two digits of the year of manufacture. The last of four chambering reamers left the chamber undersize for headspacing. The barrel then was roll-marked, given a caliber stamping, polished, and blued. Barrel material had evolved by several stages in 1936. In 1925, stainless steel had appeared; in 1932, chrome-molybdenum.

Model 70 receivers were machined from solid bar stock, each beginning as a seven-and-a-half-pound chrome-moly billet. After 75 machinings, a finished receiver weighed 19.3 ounces. It was 8.77 inches long, 1.357 inches through the receiver ring. Spot-hardening the extraction cam behind the bridge preceded a full heat treatment. Next, each was immersed in a 1,200-degree salt bath for 24 hours. Hardness after cooling: 47C. The test left a dimple in the tang. Most small parts were drop-forged, then machined. The extractor was fashioned from 1095 spring steel.

The Model 70's stock was more substantial than the 54's, though similar in appearance to the late Model 54 version. Standard stocks were roughed by bandsaw from 2x36-inch American black walnut. After center-punching, they went eight at a time to the duplicator for contouring. Final inletting was done by hand. After buttplate fitting, the stock was drum-sanded, then hand-sanded. Minor flaws were repaired with stick shellac, glue or a matching wood match. The first stocks got a clear nitrocellulose lacquer finish over an alcohol-based stain. Because these lacquers contained carnauba wax, they produced a soft, oil-like finish. After the war, when carnauba wax became scarce, harder lacquers appeared. Hand checkering with carbide-tipped cutters followed.

Headspacing came first in assembly, then the matching of bolt parts, trigger, and sear honing and a function check. The Winchester Proof (WP) stamp signified firing of one "blue pill" cartridge (70,000 psi). After its serial number was etched on the bolt, each rifle was zeroed at 50 yards. List price in 1937: $61.25. Early Model 70s were offered in .22 Hornet, .220 Swift, .250-3000 Savage, .257 Roberts, .270 WCF, 7mm Mauser, and .30-06—plus .300 and .375 H&H Magnums. Between 1941 and 1963 nine more chamberings were added; however, the .300 Savage was never cataloged. The rest of the stable of Model

A deer hunter shoulders his Featherweight, a Model 70 variation that first appeared in 1952.

70 cartridges (all from Winchester) appeared in the 1950s and early 1960s: the .243, .264 Magnum, .308, .300 Magnum, .338 Magnum, .358, and .458 Magnum. Eventually, "pre-64" Model 70s would come in 29 basic styles and 48 sub-configurations—not including special orders. Deer hunters kept sales of standardweight .30-06 and .270 rifles at the top of the charts. The first rifles retailed for $61.25.

So successful it earned the title of "the rifleman's rifle," Winchester's Model 70 became less and less profitable as labor costs escalated. In 1960, company accountants urged reducing production costs. Two years later, engineers had identified 50 changes; these were implemented in 1963. The most visible drew public outrage. The stock wore crude, pressed checkering and a barrel that "floated" in its channel between gaps wide enough to swallow Tootsie Rolls. The recessed bolt face had a tiny hook extractor instead of the beefy Mauser claw. Machined-steel bottom metal was supplanted by aluminum, solid-action pins by roll-pins, and the bolt stop's coil spring by music-wire. A red-painted cocking indicator stuck out like a tongue from under the bolt shroud, arrogance on insult. The overall effect was depressing. Prices of pre-64 Model 70s shot through the ceiling; new rifles languished on dealer racks.

Winchester improved the "new Model 70" with an antibind device for the bolt in 1966, a classier stock in 1972, a Featherweight rifle that looked and handled much better in 1980. A short-action Model 70 arrived in 1984. Three years later, Winchester reintroduced the Mauser claw extractor on custom-shop 70s, and three years after that, a "Classic" version with controlled-round feed entered the catalog line. Current Model 70s, while lacking the handwork of the originals, are accurate, attractive, and thoroughly dependable.

Winchester's accountants still ponder profits, but they've apparently learned that no matter how

much money you save in manufacture, you don't make any if rifles don't sell. New Haven's 1964 changes gave Remington, with its new Model 700 rifle and 7mm Magnum cartridge, a big break.

In 1936, the M1 Garand rifle became the main infantry weapon for U.S. armed forces. The first Winchester-built Garands were delivered a year before Pearl Harbor. In 1940, Winchester also developed a lightweight carbine. In preliminary work, company designer David "Carbine" Williams used a new short-stroke piston to operate the

I shot this Washington whitetail with an early Winchester 70 in .270.

action, later scaled down to accept the .30 Carbine cartridge.

The second World War fueled huge production jumps at Winchester-Western. Total wartime output: 1.45 million guns and more than 15 billion rounds of ammunition. After the war, John Olin's ammunition firm concentrated on the development of sporting ammunition. Ball powders came in 1946, Baby Magnum shotshells in 1954, the .22 Winchester Magnum Rimfire round in 1959, a compression-formed shotshell in 1964.

In August 1954, Olin was swallowed by the huge Mattheson Chemical Corporation. Ten years later, Winchester guns were redesigned to take advantage of cheaper materials and manufacturing processes. Sound on paper, the change triggered a colossal revolt in the marketplace. Pre-64 Winchesters suddenly commanded premiums on the used gun market. The company scrambled to correct its blunder. In relatively short order it was offering guns with the traditional features shooters wanted, but without the hand finishing that had become prohibitively expensive. When Olin-Mattheson sold the Winchester Sporting Arms business in July 1981, the new company, U.S. Repeating Arms, continued improving its products, contracting some shotguns from Japan.

In 1984, USRAC filed for Chapter 11 bankruptcy. In 1987, five investors bought the company. Among them was Fabrique Nationale (FN), a Belgian firm that also owned Browning. FN is itself owned by Societe Generale, which controls 70 percent of Belgium's GNP. Early in 1991, a French conglomerate bought FN and, with it, USRAC. These days, you'll likely hear "Use-rack" in talk about guns of New Haven lineage. They're still Winchesters to shooters who value history.

Still-Hunt at a Variable Pace

HAL BLOOD

Becoming a successful still-hunter is a very rewarding accomplishment. Still-hunting for deer in the big woods dates back to a time when Native Americans quietly moved through the forest in buckskin clothing trying to get within bow range of the animals so they could kill them and feed their families. Their whole existence depended on their hunting ability. Today, even with modern firearms, it's still the challenge of man against beast that lures us to the woods each season. Still-hunting requires a combination of stealth, patience, and knowledge of the whitetail's habits and habitat. Still-hunting pits man against deer in the game of hide-and-seek.

When you still-hunt for a big buck, you have to become a part of his environment. To be successful, you have to think like a buck so you can put yourself where he is. A still-hunter must be able to adapt to ever changing forest conditions. If you hunt the big woods, whether in the Adirondacks or New Brunswick, you must realize that these areas have low deer densities, so you may have to travel a long distance to find one.

Hunting the Sign

When I still-hunt, I always hunt the sign—that is, I set my pace according to the deer sign I find as I move along. If I see very few tracks or droppings, I move through the area fairly quickly. Once I start seeing sign, whether it's droppings, a scrape, or a rub, I'll slow down and start to analyze what I'm seeing. Of course, I'm always looking for buck sign. The way scrapes and rubs are laid out in an area tells me a lot. Signpost rubs determine my still-hunting

Mike Featherstone with his wide-beamed nine-point buck taken on a remote hunt with Cedar Ridge Outfitters. Mike's success was directly related to knowing when to pick up the pace and when to slow down while following the buck's tracks.

route. I hunt slowly around these areas, hoping to catch a buck making his rounds.

Hunting the Signpost Route

When hunting at one of my remote camps one year, I routinely hunted one of these signpost routes. The first signpost rub was about half a mile from camp at the base of a hardwood ridge about a hundred yards from a stream.

It was the best place to cross the stream, so we usually passed that rub going to and from camp every day. In two weeks of hunting we saw three bucks within fifty yards of the rub. Two were big; one we shot, and the other got away. The third was a four-pointer we let go for another year. When you hunt where the sign is, your odds increase tremendously.

Hunting the Ridges and Mountains

When hunting in country that has ridges or mountains, spend most of your still-hunting time high up. There are two reasons for this. First, bucks bed high the majority of the time in this type of terrain. Second, when you still-hunt high up, you have the advantage of being able to see better by looking down from above. Bucks feel more secure when bedded high and do not expect danger from above. Often they lie on bluffs overlooking their back tracks. If the wind is at their backs, they can detect danger from behind.

Usually, a buck will bed in the green growth on top of a ridge or where the green growth meets the hardwoods. The only way to approach a buck bedded like this is to sneak through the green growth and peer over the bluffs and knolls, hoping to catch him bedded or get close enough for a running shot should you jump him.

Lessons for the Hunter and the Hunted

One year, the first week of the season was especially warm. I was guiding Sue Morse that week, and we hadn't seen as many deer as usual. The last day of the hunt, we were still-hunting around a mountain where the green growth meets the hardwood. It was another warm, sunny day with leaves crunching underfoot—the kind of day that makes it easy for a hunter to get discouraged. We hadn't see any deer that morning, so we stopped for a sandwich at about eleven o'clock and then decided to continue around the mountain for the afternoon hunt. We eased along as quietly as possible, using the green growth for cover and looking out into a hardwood chopping.

We had covered only about a hundred yards when I looked across a ravine and spotted a buck bedded on a ledge under some fir trees, staring in our direction. He was a beautiful eight-pointer with heavy beams and tall points. He was about eighty yards away, and he looked like a statue lying there. Sue brought her gun up and fired. To my amazement, he never moved. She levered another shell and fired again. This time he jumped up and bounded off. We walked over to check for sign of a hit. I found where the bullets had kicked up dirt underneath where he had been, and I knew he wasn't hit.

Sue was using an old octagon-barrel Winchester .30-30 her grandfather had given her, and we discovered that the flip-up peep sight wouldn't lock. It had tipped forward, causing the rifle to shoot low. That was an expensive lesson in checking equipment, and I think that was the day Sue retired her nostalgic old weapon.

That old buck felt secure bedded where he could look down the ravine. He had fir trees behind him for cover so he wouldn't be seen by anything approaching from that direction. If something did approach from behind, all he had to do was make one jump into the ravine and disappear.

Checking out a scrape with an overhanging limb.
Credit: Susan C. Morse

I'm sure he must have heard us walking in the leaves, but I'm convinced he thought we were other deer. When we got to his bed and looked back, we found that the sun must have been in his eyes so he couldn't see us behind the screen of green growth. The hunter and hunted all became a little wiser that day.

Hunting Flat or Densely Forested Country

If you're hunting in country that is low, flat, and swampy or is heavily forested with evergreens, use different still-hunting tactics. In these areas, deer tend to travel more on runs because the woods are usually quite thick. Some of these areas are where deer spend the winter, and they'll have well-worn trails. If this is the case, the best way to still-hunt is to walk these trails. They'll follow the easiest route and are quiet to walk in, since the ground has been packed down from years of use. Move slowly and spend a lot of time looking around. Rely on your eyes—chances are, when you see a deer it will be close. You never know when you might meet a big buck coming down the trail toward you. When I guide hunters that want to still-hunt, I send them into this type of area with the confidence that they'll be able to see deer on their own.

One That Got Away

One year at remote camp, we had planned on hunting a new area the first week of the season. Before the season my other guide, Fred, and I had made some ground blinds in and around a thick tangle of spruce surrounding a huge cedar bog. When we headed down to hunt this area for the first time, all the hunters agreed to take a stand except one.

Larry said he couldn't sit still for five minutes and wanted to still-hunt. I sent him into the cedar bog with instructions to stay on the deer trails and move slowly. Later that morning I heard a single shot ring out of the bog. I knew it had to be Larry, but there were no signal shots. That evening, after everyone had gathered back at camp, Larry told us his story. He had been walking a trail that led him into a thick patch of cedars. He pushed his way through the thicket, and when he broke out on the other side, standing there in the trail facing him was a monster buck thirty yards away. Larry said he had never seen antlers that big before.

Just as he put up his rifle to shoot, the buck whirled and hightailed it back where he had come from. Larry had time for one quick shot, but he never touched a hair on that buck.

Following the Trails

The first year I guided a remote deer hunt, I booked hunters for the last two weeks of the season. We arrived in camp with the first group on Sunday afternoon of the third week.

Everyone had high expectations, because they were the first hunters in this area, and six inches of soft snow covered the ground. Of the five hunters, only one wanted to take a stand; the rest wanted to still-hunt or track. They all agreed to post up for a while the first morning to give us guides some time to figure things out.

Rob's 150-class ten-pointer. Rob shot this buck while still-hunting along a well-worn deer trail.

Guide Fred found a beaten-down trail through the spruces in an area around a small pond. He went back and told Rob to still-hunt in the trail. Rob followed the trail to where it crossed a logging road and then up a hardwood ridge.

As he worked his way up the ridge, a doe came running down the trail and veered off. When he looked back up the trail, he saw a four-pointer coming along the doe's track. He tried to get off a shot but never had a good chance. He was kicking himself about it when he heard a snap and looked up to see a monster buck bringing up the rear. He was trying a running shot when the buck suddenly stopped and gave Rob a broad side. Rob made the shot good and had himself a nice ten-point buck.

That night at camp, we compared notes about the deer sign we had found. George, the oldest hunter in camp, said he had found an area he liked and would hunt there again the next day. He described trails crisscrossing through an area of spruce knolls. Late the next afternoon, as all the hunters were drifting back to camp, we heard two shots several hundred yards away. We waited for signal shots, but there were none. One of the hunters decided to go up the trail and check it out anyway. Five minutes later, we heard signal shots. We all headed up the trail to see what had happened.

When we got to him, George had a ten-pointer lying there that looked like the brother of Rob's buck. He said he was still-hunting the trail out of the thicket, and when he looked ahead of him up the ridge, he could see a deer standing in the trail. He didn't know whether it was a buck or a doe, so he waited. When the deer turned to run, George saw antlers and fired. The buck didn't made it thirty yards before piling up. When we asked George why he hadn't signaled, he said he had carried only three shells, so after he had fired two at the buck, he didn't have two to signal with!

Walking the Trails—Silently

Walking trails is a great way to still-hunt. If you're a new hunter, you'll find it easy to stay where the deer are traveling, and you'll be able to walk more quietly if you stay on the trails. When you walk trails in thick cover, you shouldn't have to go too far to get near deer because you'll be in the areas they like to use for cover. Be alert at all times when you hunt these areas. It doesn't take long for a buck to disappear when the visibility is fifty yards or less. This type of hunting requires that you pay more attention to the wind as you travel. Stop, look, and listen often, because you are on the buck's turf, trying to fit into his world.

The "still" in still-hunting has two meanings: to move slowly and to be quiet. Sometimes, though, conditions in the woods are not conducive to moving about silently. It would be nice if every day you hunted there was a carpet of fresh snow— or at least damp leaves—on the ground, but that won't always happen. In reality, you'll hunt a good part of the time in dry, frozen leaves that crunch underfoot. It's important to be able to use whatever conditions you have to your best advantage and realize that there are pluses and minuses to all kinds of conditions.

Hunters who choose not to track when there's snow on the ground always have the option to still-hunt. I often still-hunt as I look for a particular track to follow.

To me, it's much more rewarding than if I were just riding the roads looking for a track. It's

not unusual for me to change from tracking to still-hunting in the course of a single day. Still-hunting in the snow is exciting, because your chances of seeing deer increase. You can tell whether you're around deer by the number of tracks, and the deer stand out like beacons on the backdrop of snow. One thing to remember, of course, is that you also stand out on the snow. For this reason, it's important to use the available cover to your advantage. Skirt around the edges of hardwood openings instead of walking right through the middle of them. If you have to cross an opening, stop often and look as far as you can in the distance. Deer can detect distant movement on the snow. Your eyes are your most valuable asset when still-hunting in quiet snow. In this game of hide-and-seek, the winner will be the first one to spot the other.

If you're the loser, the only sounds you may hear are brush cracking and deer snorting. If you're the winner, you may peek around a bush and see a buck lying or standing there with no idea he's in any danger.

If you still-hunt on a run like this, your chances of seeing a buck increase greatly.
Credit: Susan C. Morse

George (left) took this wide-racked ten-pointer while still-hunting on a deer trail.

Be Quiet—Or Else

Craig and I were still-hunting back to camp. We'd been tracking a buck all day and decided to leave him when he turned west and camp was to the east. We were about three miles from camp, and it was going to be dark in an hour, so we were moving right along. When we came to a spruce ridge with a steep ravine on the other side, I told Craig to wait while I looked for a place to get down the other side.

As I eased out along the edge of the bluff, I noticed where a good buck had milled around during the night. The track lead down into the ravine, so as I neared the edge, I kept looking down. I spotted the buck lying on a little knoll in the ravine about seventy-five yards away. He was facing toward me looking up his back track, but he didn't see me. He had an exceptionally wide rack, and I knew we wanted him. Craig was just out of sight from me, so I gave a light whistle. He started toward me but made no effort to be quiet. When he snapped a couple of sticks, the buck stood up and looked our way.

As Craig came out of the firs, I tried to motion for him to stop. He didn't notice me, and after he took a few more steps, the buck turned and sailed away toward the other side of the mountain. That was a tough lesson for Craig. He learned about the need to be as quiet as possible at all times, because the buck of a lifetime could be just around the corner.

Successful Still-Hunting

Another time, I was still-hunting along a ridge in some choppings during the last week of November when the rut was in full swing. There were tracks of bucks chasing does everywhere. I figured I'd be better off sneaking around trying to catch a buck that was chasing instead of trying to unravel the spider web of tracks. I worked my way along a shelf for a while, then dropped down into a ravine where I found tracks that were only hours old. As I followed a skid trail through some thick firs, two does jumped into the trail and stopped about seventy-five yards away. I could see only one of them, and she began to feed on raspberry stems. I noticed that she kept looking up the ridge where I couldn't see so I figured there just might be a buck up there getting her attention.

The buck I call Pretty Boy. I shot this eight-point 203-pound buck after a doe tipped me off to his location while I watched her feed.

I waited for a few minutes and tried grunting. I waited another fifteen minutes and still couldn't see anything. however, the doe kept looking in the same direction, so I eased ahead, looking where she was looking. All at once, I saw a rack coming up out of the brush as the buck bolted downhill toward the doe. All I could see were flicks of brown, so I couldn't get a shot. Then it dawned on me that the buck was going to cross the skid trail I was standing in!

I swung my rifle as he moved, and when he jumped into the skid trail, I let fly with two shots before he disappeared over the ridge. I ran to the bottom just in time to see him make his last jump before piling up. He was a nice two-hundred-pound eight-pointer.

When there's snow on the ground, tracking isn't the only way to hunt. A patient still-hunter who takes the time to read the sign can be very successful.

Tricks for Still-Hunting in Crusted Snow

Days that warm to above freezing or rain followed by cold nights often cause a crust to form on early-season snow. This is probably the most discouraging condition to still-hunt in. Every step you take sends a signal to every creature in the woods that danger may be approaching. Combine that with the fact that you stand out on the snow, and the odds are definitely against you. Don't throw in the towel, though, because you can capitalize on this condition. Remember, deer also will make a lot of noise when they walk in the crust. The key is to hear them first. To do this, you'll have to spend more time standing and listening than walking around. Deer don't like to travel much in the crust, so when you locate fresh tracks, a deer may be close by. You won't get too close to one if he's bedded, but if you hunt with a partner and one of you spooks a deer, the other has a chance of hearing it and getting into a position to shoot.

When you're traveling through the woods trying to locate deer, don't try to sneak in crusty snow. To the deer you'll sound like a predator, and they'll be gone before you see them. Instead, move along at a steady pace, stopping every fifty yards or so depending on the terrain. Look around, but mostly listen. It's surprising how far away you can hear footsteps. This is the way deer travel, and they just might think you're another deer approaching. By keeping in good cover, I have walked surprisingly close to deer before they sensed something was amiss.

I've also spotted a deer in the distance that I knew was not going to move my way. When this happened, I ran at an angle not directly toward it until I was close enough to tell whether it was a buck. To a deer, this sounds more like another deer than a hunter. By combining any of these tricks with a call, you'll increase your chances of making them work.

Don't hang around camp when the snow is crusty and all the other hunters are discouraged. Get out and enjoy the woods and the hunt. Every day is a new learning experience. Don't be afraid to try something new. I always say, if you try something enough, something will work. But if you try nothing, nothing will work.

Still-Hunting with No Snow

I do most of my still-hunting when there is no snow for tracking. With plenty of practice, you can get good at it and be successful. If there's no snow, the best you can hope for is rain-soaked leaves—you'll be able to slip along as quietly as a mouse in a cotton factory. This is when you'll really have to use your eyes. The deer blend in perfectly with their surroundings, and they are silent like ghosts. The only sound you might hear is the thump of their hooves hitting the ground when you spook them. These are the kinds of days when you can get close to deer before being detected. On such days my favorite places to hunt are ones with lots of bluffs and knolls where I can sneak up and peek over the top. I can't tell you how many deer I've seen over the years hunting like this.

Sometimes, wet leaves freeze and become crunchy. But they may be that way only for the morning, because as the day warms, they thaw and become quiet once more. With enough sun, though, they may dry out completely, and then you might as well be walking in cornflakes. If this happens, use the same tactics as you would in crusty snow. Another silent technique is to walk on downed logs or step on rocks when you get the chance. This will help you to cover ground with as little noise as possible.

I hunt an area with three- or four-year-old choppings. Skid trails crisscross the whole mountain. Some of them cut through the green growth almost to the top. It's a perfect place to still-hunt in noisy conditions. I can start from the road in the morning and hunt all day without having to leave a skid trail. Some of these trails that go through the thicker areas have developed into deer trails, making the hunting even better.

The first hunter I took into this area was Sue Morse. It was the first week of the season and we had bare ground, mostly with dry leaves, the whole time. We still-hunted the skid trails all week and saw seventeen deer, four of them good-racked bucks. As luck would have it, though, I couldn't get Sue in position for a shot at any of them. I've been hunting in that area ever since, and it's a rare day when I don't see deer.

Train Yourself to Recognize Sounds

When you're still-hunting, you have to train yourself to hear the sounds around you as you walk. If the leaves are crunchy, most people tend to hear their own footsteps, but you can train your mind to block out the close sounds and concentrate on the distant ones. To be successful, you have to hear and identify these sounds. Some sounds, such as a deer snorting, may seem obvious, but a raven can make a similar sound. Stop and listen to make sure it's a deer. Other sounds are subtle, and you may question whether you even heard them. A deer getting to its feet makes a distinct thumping sound. Once you hear it, you won't forget it. Pay attention to this sound, as a deer may be just standing there waiting to identify you. I've been caught discounting

that thumping sound all too often. I'll hear it while I'm walking and pause to listen. Then when I'm listening, I'll talk myself into thinking that I'm hearing things. Then when I take the next step, all I hear is hooves pounding and brush cracking! It all goes back to being patient.

A squirrel rustling or running in the leaves sounds nothing like a deer, but if you hunt where there are turkeys, you know that they can sound like a deer. Moose walking can also sound like a deer, except that moose tend to snap more sticks. If I spook a deer by snapping a stick, I'll often give a moose call. Most big woods bucks are used to living around moose and know the sounds they make. Once you've heard enough deer walking or running in the woods, though, you won't mistake their sound for many other sounds. The one sound that is like no other in the woods is that of a big buck on a mission. It won't be the tiptoeing sound of a doe. A big-woods buck walks with a steady, deliberate, foot-dragging pace, pausing every so often to survey his surroundings. Like the thumping sound of a deer getting to its feet, you'll never forget this sound either.

Choosing the Right Route

Another important element to becoming a good still-hunter is being able to choose the right route as you go. You not only have to be able to read the sign and decide where to go, but you also must learn to pick your way through the woods to get there. I've seen many hunters walk into thickets or blowdowns only to have to back out of them and go around. When I started guiding deer hunters, I had the hunter walk in front of me while I pointed out the way to go. But I found that it was too much of a distraction to keep pointing out the way to them, as invariably they would walk toward the worst mess in the woods. Now, I have them follow me. It's important to scan ahead and pick a route. By doing this, you can concentrate on looking for deer instead of stumbling over things.

Don't Be Afraid to Cover Ground

To still-hunt in the big woods, you have to be willing to cover some ground. You may find deer close to a road, but you'll probably find other hunters, too. There is nothing like getting back into the most remote country you can find and going one-on-one with a buck on his home turf. When hunting like this, you never know what kind of buck you might run into. I often walk back in a mile or more and spend the day still-hunting where most hunters don't go. I know that there are areas across the North and West and probably the South where bucks grow up never having contact with human beings. This doesn't mean they are any less wary than bucks that do. On the contrary, I think big bucks have a natural wariness of anything strange to them. That's why they've been able to grow up to be the majestic creatures they are.

Still-hunting is an art. To master it, you must be willing to take the time to hone the skills necessary for success. You'll have to leave the ways of the civilized world behind and learn to blend in with nature. You'll have to go wherever your instincts tell you to go without worrying about getting lost. Still-hunting for big-woods bucks is demanding, yet rewarding. Once you master it, hunting any other game animal will become less of a challenge.

These are the ten best bucks I have taken in the last fourteen years. Eight of these deer dressed out at more than two hundred pounds each. I spent an average of three days hunting per buck.

Timing is everything in life, especially when related to deer hunting. Catching up with big bucks requires skill and a little timing. Knowing when the rut is in full swing will help you set your sights on a trophy like this one. This 208-pound buck was shot by Steve Coleman on Thanksgiving Day.

Be a Deer Whisperer

JAY CASSELL

Take a look at almost any deer hunter and chances are he has a grunt call hanging around his neck. Do these devices really work, or are hunters wasting their time snorting and grunting as they make their way through the woods?

Vocalizations

Deer make three basic calls—the snort, the bleat and the grunt. We've all heard deer snort.

When combined with calls, rattling can draw bucks in from long distances.
(Credit: Summit Treestands)

You're tiptoeing through the woods, trying to get close to some heavy brush, and all of a sudden you hear a loud wheezing sound; a second later you see a white flag go bounding off through the trees. That sound is the snort, which deer make when alarmed and to alert each other to danger. For the hunter, making a snort on a deer call is of little practical use.

On the other hand, the bleat, made mostly by fawns and does, can be used to advantage. A hunter calling in an area that does frequent can usually bring a doe by making a pleading, crying bleat. "You have to put feeling into it," says Jim Strelec of Knight & Hale Game Calls. "A lot of hunters just blow into the call and produce a dull, boring bleat. That's not going to attract any deer's attention. For a bleat to work, you have to make it sounds as if a fawn is really in distress. Cry through that call and you'll see the difference. Does will practically come running."

And following the does, one hopes, will be a buck.

Grunt Work

A deep, guttural vocalization made through a tube call imitates the sound bucks make when they're either with a hot doe or actively looking for one. I've seen and heard bucks grunt throughout all stages of the rut. Unfortunately, although I've used the call during that period, I've had limited success. I have come to the conclusion that with all those

Grunt calls can stop a rutting buck in his tracks. Just don't overdo it!
(Credit: Summit Treestands)

This is true especially at the beginning of the season, when the woods are full of grunting hunters, so in the past few years I've remained quiet at this time, during the gun season in particular.

In the early bow season, or in the latter half of the gun season, I use the grunt call fairly often. And while I've spooked deer with the call—they either figured out that I was a human grunter, or else thought I was a larger buck that they didn't want to mess with—I have also called a few bucks in. It really seems to depend upon the individual buck. If a buck is hot after a doe and hears a grunt, he's more likely to investigate than if he were just going about his daily routines. Sometimes rattling antlers in conjunction with grunt calling has worked, too.

Is Calling Worth It?

Yes. There will be times when you spook deer with grunt calls or bleats. And there will be times when deer pay you absolutely no attention. But there will also be times when the call will either draw a buck into range or make him stop in his tracks, giving you an opportunity for a shot.

In short, calling is not a panacea but merely another tool in a deer hunter's arsenal. Don't expect too much from calls, and use them at the appropriate times.

hunters in the woods blowing on grunt calls, many deer now associate the sound with the presence of a human being and have therefore learned to avoid it.

The Still-Hunting Advantage

JAY CASSELL

The buck never knew I was there. I had been pussyfooting down an old logging trail, pausing every five yards or so, stopping every 20. I was standing next to a large hemlock, my body partially obscured by branches, watching the road in front of me, when I saw movement off to the right. A deer was moving down a trail that intersected the logging road 40 yards ahead.

Head down, nose to the ground, the buck was obviously following the scent of a doe. Caution was the last thing on his mind. When he reached the logging road, he skidded to a stop, turned and looked right at me. Too late. I took him with one shot.

Still-hunting. It's a highly effective way of hunting deer, especially if you do it at the right time, in the right place, the right way

When

Much depends upon the weather. On still days, with crunchy leaves or icy snow covering the ground, still-hunting is out of the question. No matter how quiet you try to be, you'll still make too much noise and spook any deer way before you can get within gun range. Better to remain in a tree stand on still days, and still-hunt on windy days, when gusts conceal your leaf crunching, or on damp or rainy days, when ground cover is wet and won't make noise when stepped on. Deer also tend to bed down on rainy and especially windy days, so your best chance of getting a shot at a buck under such conditions is to go find one, on foot, quietly.

Where

No matter what the weather, I like to still-hunt when I'm in new territory. While I prefer a tree stand when the situation is right, I don't have a clue where to put up a stand when I'm in unfamiliar country. Still-hunting lets me learn the property, plus it gives me a better chance at a deer than just putting up a stand in any old tree.

In damp or windy conditions, when deer are probably bedded down, I head to the thickest cover I can find. Rhododendron stands, hemlock groves, cedar swamps, thickets, steep ledges; anyplace a buck is likely to bed down is where I'll go. When hunting such spots, wear camo if the law allows, and move slower than slow. Deer pick these spots not only because they're sheltered, but also because they can watch for approaching danger.

When hunting tough-to-reach cover, pay special attention to the wind. Even if you're wearing a cover scent that's consistent with the area's vegetation, moving into an area with the wind at your back dictates that you stop and figure an alternative route. The brush may be ridiculously thick, or the ledges perilously steep, but common sense says you should try to circle around and approach from downwind. Being lazy and just barging ahead anyway will only ensure that you won't see deer.

How

This may sound like a cliché, but it's true: If you think you're going too fast, you are. Serious still-hunting means going painfully slow, so slow that it's almost boring. But you're doing this for a number of reasons. With each step you take, you have a different perspective of the woods. A bedded buck can come into view with just one or two steps. Take five or six, and that buck will detect your movement and be history before you even know he's there.

You're also moving slowly because you want to be quiet. Take each step carefully. Watch where you're putting your feet. If you suspect there might be a stick under the wet leaves you're about to step on, put your foot down slowly. Gradually increase the pressure, putting your weight first on your heel, then on the rest of your foot. As you go, if you can put your foot on a rock that won't tip, on moss,

When still hunting, always be ready to shoot, as the element of surprise is on your side.

on snow—anything that you're certain won't make noise—do it. If you're in an area where you know your footsteps will be silent, then don't watch your feet. Instead, watch the woods in front of you and around you. I'm not talking woods that are 25 yards in front of you, either; rather, 100 yards or more. That's where you're likely to see a buck, not close up. Train yourself to look as far as you can see, and you'll start spotting deer you wouldn't have seen otherwise.

As you move through a given patch of woods, be aware of where the large, silhouette-breaking trees are located. Pause by them. The last thing you want to do is pause out in the open, because that's exactly when a buck is going to come walking into view and see you. Pause by trees, as I did on that logging road, boulders, blow-downs, anything to break up your silhouette. And do it no matter where you are; even if you think you're in an area where you know a buck won't be, still-hunt carefully, and pause by large objects.

Be Ready

Three years ago I was hunting in New York's Catskill Mountains. I was way down the mountain, hunting virtually inaccessible ledges. With a lot of hunting pressure up top, I figured deer would be down low, away from the crowds. It was nearing the end of the season, there was snow on the ground, it was late afternoon. The snow was somewhat, crunchy, so I was moving extra carefully, placing my feet on rocks whenever feasible.

Dropping down to another ledge, I stopped next to a boulder. Generally when I stop, I don't move for at least five minutes, usually 10. Just as I was about to end my break and move another 25 yards or so, I heard something crunching off to my right. Sure enough, a doe and yearling appeared, moving along my ledge. To my surprise, they came to within 10 yards of me, then stopped and started to paw the ground, looking for food. They didn't see me at all. And while I was tempted to quietly say Boo, I stayed silent and motionless. I wanted to see what would happen.

What happened was that I heard more crunching off to my right. Now antlers came up over the lip of the ledge. It was a 7-pointer, just 30 yards away. He looked at the does and then froze, his widening eyes riveted on me. He had me, but he didn't move; obviously the presence of the does so close to me had him confused. What would he do? I figured I'd better do something, because he'd probably bolt any second. Ever so slowly, I started to raise my rifle. If I could get it just halfway up to my shoulder, I could take a snapshot and maybe get him.

Naturally, it didn't work that way. The retractable scope cap snapped on the zipper of the camo jacket. Both the doe and yearling heard it and looked right at me; then all hell broke loose. Throwing the gun to my shoulder, I looked through the scope and immediately saw brown. But it wasn't the buck! It was the yearling, running to my left, blocking my view of the buck. And within seconds it was over, as all three deer disappeared over the edge of the ledge. I took no shot at the buck, as the only shot I had, at the last split second, was a running kidney shot. Too risky, in the situation.

Lesson learned? Whenever I stop somewhere now, I never, ever, hold my gun low on my body, no matter how tired I am. Port arms is always my rule now. And so is that time-honored piece of advice: Always be ready, because you never know.

Climb Higher, Hunt Better

JAY CASSELL

This past season, I used climbing tree stands more than I have in all of the past 10. One reason is that I got permission to hunt some new property, near my home, just before the opening of deer season. I didn't have time to scout the area at all, so I just took my climber into the woods each day and set up in areas that looked promising.

Using a climber helped me learn the new property in a hurry. That's one reason for using a climber. Another is when you aren't seeing anything out of your permanent stand, and want to watch a different spot.

The following routines help me get into the woods, up a tree and settled, fast.

Climbers let you learn new property and set up in areas where deer aren't pressured. Credit: Summit Treestands

Quiet and Quick

The biggest drawback of climbers is that they make noise. You clank into the woods, pull this bulky thing off your back, attach it to a tree by turning bolts and nuts, then scrape your way up to a vantage point. Yes, climbers do make noise, but you

can reduce it. I always strap an extra bungee cord or two around my stand, which keeps the two pieces together and prevents them from banging as I walk. For setting up at the base of a tree, replace wingnuts with large, accessory-type knobs; they are quieter and easily tuned with gloves on. If you drop them in the leaves, you won't lose them. When you go up the tree, go as quietly and rapidly as you can, but do it while keeping an eye out for deer. If you're silent in your approach and setup, you'll be surprised at how many deer may be nearby.

The Right Tree

When I hike through the woods with a climber on my back, I search for trees that overlook frequently used deer trails. I also look for a tree that's at least 10 yards off my chosen trail; set up too close to a trail and deer will peg you in a hurry. Search for a straight tree, one whose diameter is right for the size of your climber (mine is about 14 inches). Rule out trees that are crooked, that lean, or that have an abundance of broken branches you'll have to deal with. The final variable is to find a tree near others that can break up your silhouette.

If you find a tree you like, hunt it that day. If you plan to hunt out of the tree again, though, consider that you want to get to it as quickly and quietly as possible the next time. Find the best trail leading to the tree, one that you can move along quietly, with concealed movements.

A good sling will help you make steady shots from a stand. Credit: Summit Treestands

Camo cloth helps conceal this hunter's movements. Credit: Summit Treestands

Set your stand in a tree large enough to break up your silhouette. Credit: Summit Treestands

A shooting rest is the mark of a quality treestand. Credit: Summit Treestands

Have a Routine

Devise a routine and stick with it no matter where or when you hunt; if you know where everything always is, you have fewer chances for making mistakes. My routine is this: Before I start into the woods, I strap my safety belt around my waist. The part of the belt that goes around the tree is in my left pocket, ready to be pulled out as soon as I get onto the tree. A rope for hauling up my rifle is attached to the top part of my stand. Safety Tip – *Always* make sure your rifle is not loaded when pulling in up with your haul rope, or letting it down at the end of the day.

When I get to my tree, I take the climber off my back, undo the bungee cords (these go into my pants pocket), undo the nuts, and attach the blades of the climber around the tree. I next tie my rifle to the haul rope, then climb into the stand, put my feet in the straps, attach my safety belt, and start to climb. A handsaw is in the right outside pocket of my daypack, if I need to saw off any tree limbs. Gloves and handwarmers are in the left.

When I reach my desired height—normally 15 to 20 feet depending on the tree and the terrain—I tighten my safety belt. Once I'm secure, I attach a bungee cord between both parts of my climber, which ensures that the bottom platform won't fall away, should I take my weight off it. My second bungee goes around the top blade.

Next, I take a screw-in step and insert it into the tree. I hang my daypack on the step, then turn around, pull up my rifle. Once secure, I chamber a cartridge, then settle down.

Coming Down

To descend, do your climbing routine in reverse. Take your time, because something might be headed your way, and don't step on your rifle when you get out of your stand.

Take a Stand

JAY CASSELL

If you intend to build your own permanent tree stand, first make sure that it's okay in your hunting area. In my case, the land is owned privately, and the owner gave me the go-ahead. If you hunt on state land, you'll have to go with a portable, as it's illegal to build there.

However, if you are in a situation where you can build a permanent stand, the next thing to do is scout the area thoroughly. Once you've found the spot, planning begins. In my case, I found a sturdy, forked beech tree that overlooked the exact area I wanted to watch. Next, I made a sketch of my proposed stand, and then gathered the necessary materials. With the help of two friends (one of whom had an ATV for transport), we set to it.

First we cut down a third, nearby beech, about the same diameter as the forked tree. We topped it so that its total height was about 20 feet, then carried it over to the forked beech and pushed it upright so that it leaned against it. With a flat rock for a support under our makeshift corner post, we chain-sawed some of the 2 × 4s in half. These we nailed into the corner post and then into both living trees, as supports, to form a triangle with the trees.

Moving up the trees, we constructed another level of support, then started on the floor. Here, again, we nailed two halves of a 2 × 4 onto the corner post and real trees, to form another triangle. We then cut the 1 × 6s into three-foot and two-foot sections, which we nailed on top of the 2 × 4s for

A room with a view. A well-constructed permanent stand will last for years if properly maintained.

floorboards. A railing went on next, about three feet above the floor; then, three feet about that, we put on the roof, using the same method we used for the floor. Some shingles on the roof, some trimming of excess woodland overhangs, and the basic structure was complete. There was even enough wood left over to fashion a seat, with two short lengths of 2 × 4s nailed between the back two trees, and a few pieces of 1 × 6s nailed on top! Spikes were nailed into the side of one of the live trees to serve as the ladder. Next year, I may even add plywood or camouflage-netting sides to block the wind and further conceal myself.

A few thoughts here. We found it necessary to cut down the third tree, as I didn't want to change the location of my stand and there was no third tree close enough to incorporate into the stand. If you can find three (or four) trees growing close together, or one sturdy tree that splits into three trees as it goes up—"triangle trees," I call them—by all means use them. Live trees will be sturdier, and last longer, than dead ones or a combination of live and dead ones. A large double tree, for that matter, can also become an excellent tree stand.

On the subject of picking a tree, make certain that your tree is in good shape before you start building on it. The last thing you want to do is build a tree stand in a set of trees that may rot out in a few years.

When building a stand, do it in spring or summer. Deer know the forest, and anything out of the ordinary is going to be suspect to them. If you build your stand well before hunting season, they'll get used to seeing it there, and won't view it as potentially dangerous. Building it during summer will also give the wood some time to weather, so it won't stand out once the leaves have fallen.

If you somehow find yourself in a situation where you must build a tree stand just before or during hunting season, it might make sense to use natural wood, as the deer may not notice it as readily. I generally prefer 2 × 4s from the lumberyard, however, as they last longer, and are easier to work

Sturdy rungs ensure safety. Check them often.

with. Natural wood is wet, too, which means it's more apt to split.

Once your stand is completed, go sit in it for a while. Like the view? If not, it might pay to carry a limb pruner or handsaw into the woods and clear shooting lanes and any limbs that obscure your vision.

Finally, clean up the ground around your stand. Let the woods revert to its natural state; the less human odor and evidence of human presence, the better. Never urinate near your stand, before or during deer season, as you'll simply be advertising your presence to the deer. For that matter, you should use scent on your boots, to further mask your presence.

Driving Deer

JAY CASSELL

Deer season is on its last legs. If you haven't gotten a buck yet, you have to get serious if you want to put venison in the freezer. Tactics that worked earlier in the year won't cut it now. The rut is pretty much over, so rattling, calling or watching scrapes and rubs aren't the answers. And still-hunting heavy cover, which always gives you a chance, isn't as effective, since deer in most parts of the country are going to hear you crunching across frozen ground before you even see them.

No, if you want to get a buck, then it's time to drive. And to do that, you need planning and proper execution.

Last Chance

Where I hunt, most hunters have hung it up by the last weekend of the season. Some have already gotten a whitetail, others have simply moved on to new activities. In camp, there are often only three or four of us left, but somebody in our group usually fills his tag at the end of the season. The reason for this is that we concentrate our drives where we know deer are located.

With two to four hunters in a drive, we key in on two prime late-season areas: steep ledges, especially those on south-facing (warmer) slopes; and smaller (one- to three-acre) hemlock groves or cedar swamps.

The Ledge Game

When we hunt mountainside ledges, we position two standers downwind of likely deer hangouts, in spots on the slope where they can survey as far downhill or uphill as possible. The uphill stander is placed where deer will be unable to move above him, such as at the base of a rock face or an extremely steep ledge. At the agreed-upon starting time, the drivers begin walking across the ledges, with the wind at their backs, about 75 yards apart. Everyone wears hunter orange, and no one even thinks about shooting in the direction of other people. We move slowly, making minimal noise (too much commotion will spook deer into terrified flight, making any shots difficult; it's better to have deer simply get up and walk away). If any deer are kicked up, they usually move straight away from the drivers, giving the standers easy shots across the ledges; or the deer head downhill, giving the downhill stander a chance.

This type of drive also works well on ridgetops and longish saddles.

Groves and Swamps

When deer are holed up in hemlock groves or cedar swamps, we drive only small patches that we can effectively cover. It makes no sense to drive large hemlock groves, where deer can sneak around the drivers or simply stay hidden. We position two or three standers at the downwind perimeter of a small hemlock stand, usually where it opens up into hardwoods. Then one driver, preferably two, will enter the woods at the specified time; if there are two drivers, they move parallel to each other, never losing visual contact. Deer kicked up from the thick stuff will move either straight away from the drivers, toward the standers or out the sides in an attempt to double back. Either way, someone usually gets a shot.

Woodlots, marshes and small fields can also be effectively hunted with this type of drive.

I Was Almost Shot on a Drive a Few Years Ago

It was a stupid mistake, but most accidents are. I was one of three standers surrounding the perimeter of some hemlocks interspersed with blowdowns and thick brush. We were set out as a triangle, with me on the right corner. The drivers walked right by me. They didn't see me; I didn't see or hear them. Suddenly, there was a shot from just uphill of me; then a bullet came whizzing across the forest floor, kicking up leaves not 10 inches from my feet.

At the end of the drive, one of the drivers said he had taken a shot at a running deer but missed. When I told him that he almost shot me, he was horrified. This is a guy who has been hunting for 40 years, and it was the first time he had ever jeopardized anyone on a hunt. After that, we made a few drive rules that we follow to the letter, every year:

- Everyone—driver and stander—always wears hunter orange.
- Before the drive, we make explicit plans. Everyone knows exactly where the other people will be; and the drivers in particular always keep each other in view.
- No one shoots in the direction of anyone else. The only shots that can be taken will be at deer that have broken out the side of the driven area, or have gotten into an uphill or downhill position where a backstop—ledge, knoll, boulder—will stop any errant bullets. If you are unsure of your target, or of what's behind it, do not even think about shooting.

And a final reminder: Hunters who have already filled their tags always act as drivers since they cannot, by law, carry firearms.

Why Use a Shotgun?

DAVE HENDERSON

Shotgunning for Deer

Hunting deer with a shotgun is a lot like going to bat in a baseball game with a broomstick. Both implements may be used somewhat effectively, but neither represents the most efficient nor preferred method. As suburbia continues its relentless expansion into deer habitat and humans and whitetails compete increasingly for elbowroom, more and more municipalities are mandating shotguns for big game hunting rather than permitting the use of long-range modern rifles. This is not to say that

The New York State record typical buck — once the world record — was taken in 1939 with a punkin ball slug fired from a shotgun.

shotguns are not effective for deer hunting. In fact, the largest-grossing typical whitetail buck recorded in the history of the Boone & Crockett Club's scoring system was taken by an Illinois shotgun hunter in 1993. The two largest bucks taken in the history of my native New York, a 198-plus typical and a 267-plus nontypical, were both killed during the 1930s with old "punkin ball" slugs.

Today about 4.1 million of the nation's 10 million whitetail hunters go afield armed with shotguns, and the number is growing every year. More than 20 states mandate the use of shotguns for deer for at least some of their hunters. Eight states limit all of their hunters to shotguns or muzzleloaders for deer. Delaware, Massachusetts, New Jersey and Rhode Island allow buckshot or slugs while Illinois, Indiana, Iowa and Ohio limit everyone to slugs. Connecticut used to prohibit rifles but now allows them for hunting on holdings larger than 10 acres, with written permission from the landowner. Eight other states limit at least 40 percent of their hunters to slugs and/or buckshot. Pennsylvania, historic home of the American rifle, now restricts more than 100,000 of its hunters to slug guns and muzzleloaders by mandating special regulations areas around Philadelphia and Pittsburgh. New York has nearly 400,000 slug shooters. Even such frontier outposts as Helena, Montana, and Edmonton, Alberta, have shotgun-only hunting areas in their outer suburbs.

At last count only about 3 percent of today's shotgun deer hunters must or opt to use buckshot; the rest use slugs of one form or another. Given a fast-growing market, development of slug loads and slug-shooting shotguns has advanced more in the last 20 years than any other aspect of the firearms industry. Today's high-velocity, high-tech sabot slugs and rifled barrel slug guns have turned shotgun deer hunting from a "wait-'til-you-see-the-whites-of-their-eyes" proposition into an event where the hunter can no longer be faulted for preheating the oven when a rack appears a couple of hundred yards away. Regardless, being of sound mind and body, if I'm given a choice, I'll use a rifle for hunting deer rather than a shotgun. I thus found it surprising

Richard Paulli displays the mount of the Boone & Crockett 267-plus buck that he took with a shotgun in Illinois in 1983. It is still one of the largest scoring whitetail bucks taken with a slug.

when, in my native New York, there was staunch opposition to a legislative proposal to allow rifles in the largely agricultural western portion of the state, which has been restricted to slug guns ever since deer hunting was regulated in the late 1930s.

There is obviously a core of deer hunters who are satisfied with shotguns for deer, but the majority of us who do hunt with a shotgun probably do so becau   the matter. Most of us   loads and guns, and g   ology in this area, there   hich one is right for yo

The author cautiously approaches a fallen buck taken with a slug gun. Most shotgun hunters select slugs as their ammunition of choice.

Slugs or Buckshot?

First of all, if you have a choice between buckshot and slugs, there is no choice. Slugs are absolutely the most effective load you can put into a shotgun. Granted, buckshot is a devastating close-range load. In fact, the Germans complained to the Hague and Geneva Conventions regarding the shotgun's horrific effect in trench warfare during World War I. That's the reason shotguns were

Shotguns are effective tactical weapons for the military and law enforcement personnel.

outlawed under the Law of Armed Conflict, Article 23, by the Hague Convention, a decree that the United States chose not to observe. American armed forces used a variety of pump shotguns in the Pacific Theater du... ...Korea. While the ...le was readily ide... ...ce, the lion's bellow of ... ...double aught buc... ...ost feared sound in t... ...le environs of Vietnam. Ithaca, Mossberg, Winchester and Remington all built tactical scatterguns for U.S. troops.

Buddy and fellow writer J. Wayne Fears says he favored the companionship of a Winchester 97 while serving in the jungles of Southeast Asia with U.S. Special Forces. Wayne said of the 97 that it was one gun you always knew whether it was ready or not, by the hammer position. Any slug, full-bore or sabot, 20-, 16-, 10- or 12-gauge, has a much, much more extensive effective range than buckshot in the same gauge and, although the margin for error is slightly less, is every bit as deadly in close quarters. But given the choice, the vast majority of American shotgunners will go with slugs every time.

Types of Slugs

Despite all of the hype about saboted ammunition that you read in magazines and see on television, the conventional full-bore slug still represents more than 60 percent of the retail sales to slug hunters. Does saboted ammunition have a longer effective range? Definitely. Is it more accurate when fired from a rifled bore than full-bore slugs are from a smoothbore? Absolutely. Does everyone need that extra wallop and extended range? Nope. Longstanding (and somewhat outdated) surveys have shown that 97 percent of all deer killed with

Modern sabot slugs shoot very flat and perform very well on deer-sized game.

Buckshot is a very effective deer hunting load when used at limited ranges.

shotguns are taken at ranges of less than 100 yards. An impressive 94 percent are actually taken inside of 75 yards. Foster-type full-bore slugs, such as those loaded by Winchester, Federal and Remington and the various non-saboted Brenneke-style designs, are very effective at that range.

If you shoot a smoothbore shotgun and take typical shots within these parameters, you are not at a disadvantage with full-bore slugs. Saboted ammunition, at least before the new high-velocity stuff hit the market, offered little advantage over full-bore slugs at traditional deer hunting ranges (40-80 yards). The high-tech ammunition didn't really show its stuff until it had a chance to stretch out and run at longer distances. At that point the high-tech ammunition's superior aerodynamics and ballistic coefficient and the stabilizing effect of the spin generated by the rifling helped the projectile maintain its velocity, trajectory and energy over a greater distance than did the bulky full-bore slug.

Foster-type rifled slugs and the 2¾-inch Brenneke smoothbore slugs look essentially the same as they did when they were introduced — (*Foster's in 1933 and the Original Brenneke in 1935*) — but have undergone some subtle improvements over the years. For instance, Winchester redesigned its Double-X load in 1982 by swelling the diameter to fill all bores and by making it more consistently concentric. Federal Cartridge followed with a redesign in 1985 and again in the early 1990s while Remington finally swelled the diameter and made some changes to its venerable Slugger in 1993.

An extraordinary array of shotgun slugs are available to modern deer hunters.

Barrels Make a Difference

What about chokes for slug shooting? Odds are that your smoothbore will shoot a slug more accurately with a relatively open choke. The industry, in fact, used to suggest improved cylinder for slug shooting. But shotgun bores vary in dimension, bore to bore, even in the same brand and model. A slug that has been squeezed tightly throughout its journey down the barrel will react differently when it hits the choke — regardless of the constriction of that choke — than one that fits loosely and tipped slightly as it traversed the same distance. I've seen some modified choke shotguns that were real tack drivers and the post-war Belgian Browning Auto-5 that I inherited from Dad shot Brennekes like they were designed for each other — despite its fixed full-choke barrel.

Will shooting high-tech sabot loads through your smoothbore increase your effective range? Maybe, but certainly not to the point that would justify paying 7 or 8 times as much as you would for full-bore slugs. In fact, you will find that saboted ammunition is less effective in a smoothbore than conventional slugs since, if the slug is not spinning, the sabot sleeves will have difficulty separating from the slug and will actually destabilize the projectile. Sabot slugs are designed for rifled barrels; the soft

ORIGINAL BRENNEKE   FOSTER

Today's Original Brenneke slug and the Foster-style rifled slug (loaded by Winchester, Remington and Federal) are visually identical to their original 1930s prototypes.

material of the sabot sleeves grips the rifling and imparts spin to the projectile, which it needs to maintain stability. Full-bore slugs rely on a nose-heavy design for stability during a relatively short flight.

If you shoot a smoothbore but would like to take advantage of the high-tech loads, your best bet is to add a rifled choke tube. All major shotgun manufacturers offer rifled tubes and they are improving all the time. You can also look into aftermarket tubes from Hastings, Colonial, Cation and others — The length of the choke tube is a factor in how well it stabilizes slugs. After all, asking 2 to 3 inches of spiraled grooves to impart a rotation of up to 37,000 rpm on a projectile that has already reached terminal velocity is asking a lot. Regardless, I've seen some rifled tubes that shot far more accurately, particularly inside of 100 yards, than the laws of physics should allow.

The fact remains, however, if you want to take advantage of the latest innovations and vast ballistic superiority of today's high-tech slugs, you'll need a rifled slug barrel. Be advised that a rifled barrel dedicates the gun to slug shooting only, it will not

effectively pattern shot. It will, however, stabilize any slugs — sabot or full-bore Foster or Brenneke-style — and extend their effective range. In fact, full-bore slugs actually skid a bit in the rifling and leave copious amounts of lead fouling in the grooves in a very short period of time, but they will shoot well in a rifled bore. The best slug gun models will have fixed rifled barrels, which means they can't be used for anything but slug shooting, unlike models with interchangeable barrels. As with rifled choke tubes, all major shotgun manufacturers offer at least one model with a rifled barrel and most offer optional rifled barrels that can replace your conventional barrel for the deer season.

Rifle-sights or optics are a necessity for a slug gun. Slug shooting is a specialty use of a shotgun — you must aim the gun rather than just point it.

Knowing what loads are designed for what type of shotgun barrels makes a difference in the deer woods.

More than 60 percent of whitetail deer hunters choose smoothbore shotguns and use full-bore (non-sabot) slugs.

With a stiff barrel, good trigger and solidly mounted scope your rifled barrel slug gun should be able to consistently put three conventionalvelocity saboted slugs through the same hole at 50 yards from a solid rest. Accuracy at 100 yards will vary with the wind conditions, trigger pull, load and the shooter's ability. To sum it up, what you need from a slug gun depends entirely on how you are going to use it. There's nothing wrong with smoothbore shotguns and full-bore slugs for the relatively short ranges encountered in most deer woods. If you're looking for longrange performance in your slug gun, however, that option is available in rifled-barrel shotguns and high-tech saboted ammunition.

Shotguns for Deer

DAVE HENDERSON

State-of-the-Art Slug Guns

For three-quarters of the 20th century small game shotguns became deer guns by simply changing the load. The market just wasn't big enough to warrant much innovation and manufacturers made few design concessions for slug or buckshot shooters. Ithaca Gun was the first shotgun company to cater to slug shooters, introducing its 12-gauge Deerslayer in 1959. The Deerslayer was a John Browning Model 37 bottom-ejection pump design that Ithaca pulled off the scrap heap when Remington discontinued its predecessor, the Model 17, in 1936.

A spokesman at the Remington Museum assured me that Big Green had willingly given up the design when the original Browning patent had run out to avoid any charges that Remington held a monopoly in the shotgun market. Ithaca Gun historian Walter Snyder, however, says that Ithaca Gun actually built a few Model 37s while Remington was still producing Model 17s and stored them until the patent expired. The original Deerslayer featured iron rifle sights on a straight-tube barrel (no forcing cones or chokes) with a tight .704-inch internal diameter barrel (conventional 12-gauge barrels are .729) that firmly squeezed all of the slugs available on the market that time.

"Tolerances were really strict," said former Ithaca Gun service manager Les Hovencamp. "I guess if a barrel came off the reamer at .705 or .706

it was scrapped." Most any slug on the market filled this bore, thus retaining the essential square-to-bore orientation before exiting the barrel. The result was vastly improved accuracy, even though the bore diameter was eventually bored out to .719 in the early 1980s to lessen pressures, as slugs got bigger.

Shotguns designed and manufactured specifically for slug shooting are a relatively new concept.

The accuracy of today's slug guns, firing modern loads, is better than ever before.

All major manufacturers eventually followed by offering optional "buck barrels"— shorter, open-cylinder versions of existing designs fitted with rifle sights.

The length of a slug barrel is of very little importance. You'll find that while the powder burns in the first 16 to 17 inches of the bore, there will be a slight increase in velocity up to about 25 inches. Anything longer than that actually begins to work as a brake on the ejecta, slowing it down. Most production guns come with 22- to 25-inch barrels while a few hand-built guns have 20-inch barrels.

Birth of Rifled Barrels

Rifled shotgun barrels have been used by trapshooters and produced by European designers for the better part of a century, but until BRI's Bob Sowash achieved a certified MOA group (*five shots measuring 1 inch center to center at 100 yards*) with his slug and a custom-rifled barrel in the early 1970s, the spiral spout was largely unheard of on these shores. In fact, until the 1980s federal law prohibited rifled barrels over .50-caliber for civilian use. They were deemed "destructive devices." The grandfather of rifled shotgun barrels is probably Olie Olson, head gunsmith for E.R. Shaw Barrels of Bridgeville, Pennsylvania, until his retirement in 2001.

A transplanted Californian living in the shotgun-only environs of Allegheny County, Pennsylvania, Olson was frustrated by the relative inaccuracy of conventional slug guns. He toyed with rifling shotgun bores with various twist rates in the late 1970s. When Shaw obtained permission from the feds to build spiral tubes for civilian shotguns in 1982, the door was opened for slug shooting to enter the 20th century. Shaw started producing rifled barrels that could be retrofitted to certain solid-receiver, fixed frame shotguns like High Standard Flite Kings. Today

Randy Fritz's Tar-Hunt Rifles uses Shaw barrels on its custom bolt-action and pump slug guns and once toyed with the idea of importing today's version of the High Standard receivers from the Philippines.

Rock Barrels in Oregon and Pennsylvania Arms of Duryea, Pennsylvania, ventured into the fray early but the only company that would have a lasting presence was the Hastings Company of Clay Center, Kansas. Originally conceived as a barrel-maker for interchangeable choke systems, Hastings owners Phil Frigon and Bob Rott began importing rifled Paradox barrels from France in 1985 and quickly became the prime after-market source of rifled shotgun barrels. Hastings encountered very little competition in the aftermarket rifled barrel market until Ithaca Gun tested the waters in 2003. The venerable upstate New York gunmaker was famous for its "Roto-Forged" smoothbore barrels

The advent of rifled barrels sparked a revolution in slug shooting.

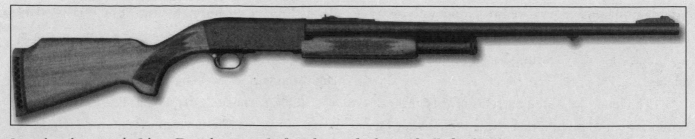

Introduced in 1959 the Ithaca Deerslayer was the first shotgun built specifically for slug shooting.

until its plant moved in 1989 and the forge proved too expensive to rebuild at the new facility. The company was outsourcing barrels for its own M37 pumps from 1989 to 2002 when it purchased a computerized barrel lathe and, for a brief time, marketed aftermarket barrels for other brands of shotguns. The lathe, however, was lost to a creditor when Ithaca closed its doors in New York in 2005.

There are conflicting schools of thought on rifling twist rates. An inar-guable fact is that the faster twist rates (*one turn in 24 or 25 inches*) accentuate expansion of slugs. Hastings' Bob Rott and gun builder Mark Bansner say that they saw no difference in accuracy of sabot slugs between 1-28 and 1-36 barrels. Randy Fritz and Shaw's Olie Olson, however, claimed that the sabots preferred 1-28 and Foster slugs preferred 1-36 with 1-34, a good compromise for both. Fritz, who has been in on the development of Lightfields since their inception, actually builds his custom guns with a special twist rate — I think it's 1-34 — to shoot Lightfield Hybreds. I have noticed that the soft Foster slugs, when spun too much (1-28 for example) seem to want to "flow" or fly apart due to centrifugal force. I have also noticed that guns with 1-28 twists (1-24 in 20-gauge) do seem to handle high-velocity slugs better than those with 1-36 twist rates.

First Production Rifled Barrels

Ithaca and Mossberg were the first companies to offer production guns with rifled barrels in 1987 — Ithaca with its Model 37 Deerslayer II and Mossberg introducing the Model 500 Trophy Slugster. Heckler and Koch started importing Benelli autoloaders and affixing them with Shaw rifled barrels. Thompson Center's custom shop and tiny New England Firearms (H&R) started marketing single-shot rifled-barrel guns in the very late 1980s. Today all major shotgun manufacturers — Remington, Mossberg, U.S. Repeating Arms, Browning, Ithaca, H&R, Marlin, Savage, Beretta, Benelli, Franchi and Traditions — offer at least one model with a rifled barrel. Although smoothbore shotguns and conventional slugs still make up nearly 65 percent of the retail market, rifled barrels and sabot slugs are the most advanced and accurate and represent the fastest-growing segment of the industry.

Slug Gun Shortcomings

The effectiveness of a slug gun is limited by chamber pressure (*shotguns operate at less than 12,000 pounds per square inch, rifles up to 60,000*) and, due to looser construction, vibration. Vibration is not nearly as much of a factor with buckshot guns simply

twist rates (*at 1,400 fps*)	
1-25 inches .... 37,440 rpm	1-34 inches .... 27,528 rpm
1-28 inches .... 33,428 rpm	1-35 inches .... 26,742 rpm
1-32 inches .... 29,250 rpm	1-36 inches .... 26,999 rpm

The author took this 8-point buck with a Remington 11-87 autoloader. The autoloader, however, is the heaviest and inherently the least accurate of any slug gun design.

Despite all the advances in slug guns and loads, the shotgun hunter will never achieve the range and effectiveness enjoyed by rifle hunters.

because the whole idea there is to spray a pattern of pellets as opposed to centering a single projectile. Slug guns definitely need to be more precise. That's why the bolt-action and break-action singleshot are the most accurate actions. The barrel is fixed (*screwed*) to the receiver and the entire function of the gun is in a straight line with nothing hanging off it, which means less barrel-shaking, accuracy robbing vibration. That's also why today's slug barrels are typically short. A long barrel used to be an advantage since older powders needed more space to burn and efficiency was compromised by gas leaking past under-sized wads. But the high-tech powders used to propel today's gas-sealing wads

is burned in the first 16-17 inches of barrel length, so any barrel of at least 18 inches should be adequate in that respect.

Slugs, like shotshells, thus gain nothing ballistically from a longer bar-rel. In fact, unlike shotshells, slugs have characteristics that may actually make the shorter barrels more accurate. Slugs are so slow that the gun recoils nearly 5/8 inch before the slug can get out the muzzle. Because of this phenomenon a longer barrel is actually detrimental to accuracy because the longer the

slug stays in the tube the more it is affected by the barrel movement caused by recoil and vibration. Autoloaders are inherently the least accurate action because there is so much movement when the trigger is pulled. At ignition the gun starts recoiling, the bolt slides back to eject the empty hull and a fresh load is levered out of the magazine and up to where it can be slammed into the chamber by the returning bolt.

Pumps, with the fore end slide and magazine dangling from the barrel, which is loosely fitted to the receiver, also experience a great deal of vibration at ignition. Ithaca's Deerslayer II line, featuring a free-floating (*not attached to the magazine*) barrel that is fixed permanently to the receiver, is the only exception among pump guns. Although the single shot is the simplest design, it usually is a very inexpensive model shotgun with a less-than-bank-vault-solid lockup, heavy trigger and cheap barrel — factors that negate the action's accuracy potential. Exceptions are the Mossberg SSi-One, the Thompson Center single shot that was phased out of its custom shop in the late 1990s and the H&R and New England Firearms (*identical except for wood and finish*) 980 and 925 (*20-gauge*) series. These guns used extremely heavy bull-barrels to tame harmonics

A good barrel and a relatively light, crisp trigger are the hallmarks of a good slug gun.

The bolt-action shotgun is the state of the art in slug guns.

and offset the effects of the heavy triggers. Mine were both hand-fitted at the factory to maximize the tightness of the lock-up and the triggers were tightened. The result is two simple but extremely accurate test guns that I've toted to deer stands on many occasions.

State-of-the-Art Slug Guns

Bolt Actions

The state of the art in slug guns is the bolt action. Once the least expensive, simplest shotgun action, the addition of the rifled barrel and a few other amenities (*like fiber-optic sights, rifle-style synthetic stocks and scope mounts*) has turned the bolt from a beginner's gun into the most inherently accurate slug gun available. If you're old enough to have seen Vietnam "live" through binoculars or on the evening news or to have voted for McGovern, chances are you're familiar with the concept of bolt-action shotguns for beginners.

Who among we gray-templed outdoors types doesn't remember a sibling or crony who started deer hunting with a slug-loaded, inexpen-sive bolt action or single shot? Seems like there was always somebody with a Polychoked Mossberg 195, Marlin 55 or Sears 140 bolt gun. Or, by the same token, an Ithaca 66 Super Single — or even a crusty old uncle

SteadyGrip

From the "What-Will-They-Think-of-Next?" Department comes Benelli's SteadyGrip system. The company's Super Black Eagle and M1 Field autoloaders offer optional stock system that consists of a soft-rubber coated pistol-style grip that drops away from the stock just behind the trigger guard at a 60-degree rear angle. The concept actually dates back more than a decade. In the late 1980s—before the formation of Benelli USA, when the Italian line came from Urbino to the United States through Heckler ft Koch — the company's tactical shotguns were offered with a similar-looking "tactical" grip. But no one has ever put one on a sporter until now. Having extensive experience with M-16/AR-15s, which feature a grip and stock configuration virtually identical to the SteadyGrip, I was well aware of the advantage the system afforded off-hand shooting, but I'd also tried some aftermarket tactical grips on other shotguns in the past and found that their abrupt drop actually accentuated recoil when the gun was fired from a seated position.

It was thus with admitted skepticism that I first approached the SteadyGrip. But after a couple of range sessions and a week-long turkey hunt with the Super Black Eagle on the Nail Ranch in west-central Texas, I came away impressed. The rearward angle and soft rubber grip actually made the inertia system (recoil-operated) Benelli autos comfortable to shoot from a seated position — even when the Super Black Eagle was loaded to the tips with 3.5-inch, 2-ounce Federal Grand Slam turkey loads. The SteadyGrip-fitted guns weigh exactly the same and have the same stock dimensions (in terms of length of pull, drop at the comb and drop at the heel) as their conventionally stocked versions and are priced only moderately more. (*M1 SteadyGrip is $90 more than its conventionally stocked version; the Super Black Eagle just $80 more.*)

When shooting off-hand on the range, the SteadyGrip provided the familiar suppressed recoil and, well, steadiness I remembered from my Service Rifle competition days with the AR-15. In fact, the session engendered a mental note to pick up an optional rifled slug barrel (both the Super Black Eagle and M1 Field have them). Afterall, the SteadyGrip models of guns are drilled and tapped for scope mounting. The SteadyGrip system definitely makes the guns "dedicated use" ordnance. But while the SteadyGrip concept doesn't lend itself to comfortable wing shooting, it'll make a great companion in the turkey woods or deer blind.

who put slugs in his "Long Tom" Marlin goose gun or one of the old break-action single-digit model H&Rs. Back then singles and bolts were "starters" reserved for kids, or they were multipurpose ordnance used by folks who weren't as serious about deer guns as they were in simply having something in the truck or the barn that could be of use in all seasons. The bolts and singles of those days were at the lower end of the shotgun spectrum. But you've also got to remember that shotguns and slugs per se weren't accurate back then, either. But, as I say, that was then — this is now. Today's bolt-action slug guns are definitely not reinventions of the wheel. Comparisons between them and yesterday's simple actions are about as valid as racing the *Spirit of St. Louis* against a Stealth bomber.

A rack of bolt actions *(left to right)* Savage 210, Tar-Hunt RSG-12, Marlin 512P and Mossberg 695.

The Savage 210 bolt gun was replaced in the line with the clip-fed, Accu-Triggered 212 in 2011.

"Years ago the bolt action was simply an inexpensive shotgun with little more than reliability to justify its existence," said Mossberg CEO Alan 'Tver" Mossberg, whose company was one of the prime providers of entry-level bolt shotguns decades ago. "The growing popularity of the pump and autoloading shotguns nearly retired the bolt action. Oddly enough, when bolt action interest was waning, many states were changing their deer seasons to "shotgun only," slug ammunition was improving tenfold. Suddenly the bolt-action was reborn and repositioned." But Mossberg's 695 was discontinued at the end of the twentieth century, leaving the Savage 210 alone in the genre. In the twenty-first century, however, used Browning A-Bolts were routinely selling for four figures and the company brought them back in 2011, just after Savage introduced the Savage 220F (20 gauge) in 2010 and the revamped 12-gauge 212 in 2011.

Marlin's 512 was the first-ever bolt-action rifled barrel gun, starting off in 1994. The story goes that veteran *Outdoor Life* shooting editor Jim Carmichel suggested to Marlin that a rifled barrel on its bolt-action Model 55 Goose Gun would be a big seller and thus it was born. The 512, which featured unique side-saddle scope mounts, a 1-28 twist rate in its 22-inch barrel and later a synthetic stock and fiber-optic sights, was discontinued due to slumping sales in 2001. The Browning A-Bolt slug gun, essentially that com-pany's bolt-action rifle design chambered for 12-gauge, was probably the best-built production slug gun ever made, but it enjoyed a short life span, being discontinued in 1998 after just three years of production. The gun cost more than twice the price of the Mossberg and Marlin bolts and consumers just weren't willing to pay the difference. If you can find one today in good shape, grab it. The problem is that most people who have them know what they have and aren't going to part with them.

The Savage 210 Master Shot is similarly a rifle design (Savage's inexpensive but accurate 110 series) chambered in 12-gauge. Like the Browning, the Savage 210 uses a rifle-style bolt with front locking lugs and a 60-degree throw. The Mossberg and Marlin are shotgun bolts that lock up when the bolt handle is dropped into a recess cut into the stock. The Savage uses a synthetic stock that is virtually identical to the one on its bull-barreled varmint and tactical rifles, the exception being an integral box magazine that protrudes from the bottom of the receiver like a molded goiter. The Savage has a 24-inch rifled (1-35) twist receiver is drilled and tapped to accept scope mounts. Unquestionably, the ultimate in slug guns today is the custom-built Tar-Hunt RSG (Rifled Slug Gun) bolt-action series made by gun builder Randy Fritz of Bloomsburg, Pennsylvania. The RSG-12 Professional and its 20-gauge counterpart, the RSG-20 Mountaineer, are basically Remington 700 rifle clones chambered for shotgun loads. Fitted with Shaw barrels, Jewell triggers, McMillan composite stocks, Pachymar Decelerator recoil pad and the custom-made action, the guns retail for thousands. Fritz also fits custom barrels and does trigger work on Remington 870 pumps, calling that model the DSG (Designated Slug Gun) series.

Single Shots

Single-shot, break-open slug guns such as the H&R 980 and 925 Ultra Slugster (bull-bar-reled 12- and 20-gauge models) and Mossberg's 12-gauge SSi-One are similarly accurate but tend to be heavier and lack the quick follow-up of the bolt actions. Because the scope rail is mounted directly on the chamber, these guns also tend to be rougher on scopes. New England Firearms, the Marlin-owned sister company to H&R, makes the 980 in a less expensive version and both companies market (NEF Tracker and H&R Topper) light, compact single-shot versions with rifled bores. The very inexpensive Pardner series is a smoothbore version.

The H&R 980's barrel is heavy enough to offset the effects of a heavy trigger-pull

The single-shot H&R Topper is available with a rifled barrel.

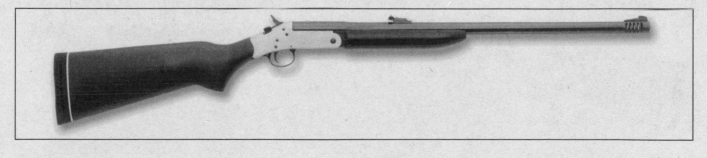

New York hunter Roger Scales took this 13-point doe with an Ithaca Deerslayer using a Brenneke slug in 1994. It was one of the largest-racked does ever recorded.

Pumps

Pumps are the most popular slug guns, probably due to retail price point as well as their light weight, durability and simplicity. The compact, lightweight aspect of the pump makes it the darling of the stalker as well as the stand-hunter. Follow-up shots are easier with a pump than with any action other than an autoloader, but heavier recoil is the price one pays for light, compact design. There are nearly 10 million Remington 12-, 16-

and 20-gauge 870s wandering around the country while the 12-gauge Mossberg 500 and 835 Ultri-Mag are among the sales leaders every year. Ithaca's M37 pump comes in several 12-, 16- and 20-gauge configurations for deer hunters, including the 11-pound 12-gauge bull-barreled Deerslayer HI, which is available only by special order through the compa-ny.Ithaca Gun failed again in 2005 but resurfaced in Ohio under new ownership that changed the face of the company. The newest Ithaca Gun offers the old Deerslayer II but the newer Deerslayer HI is a trimmed down version of the New York model, with a lighter bull barrel and new twist rate (now l-in-28) that, coupled with the free-floating concept, leads outstanding accuracy.

The Browning BPS, Winchester SpeedPump, Benelli Nova, NEF Pardner and a couple of pumps from other companies offer rifled barreled versions.

Autoloaders

The autoloader is popular due to its tendency toward lessened recoil and quick follow-ups. The trade-off is that they are generally much heavier and far more expensive than other actions. They are also more complicated and often less reliable and somewhat less accurate due to the excessive vibration caused by the cycling action. The Remington 1100 is the lightest and oldest autoloading model on the market and is available in both 12- and 20-gauge slug versions. It's a long

The Benelli inertial recoil operating system used in the 12-gauge Stoeger Model 2000 slug gun permits the use of a wide range of 23A- and 3-inch loads.

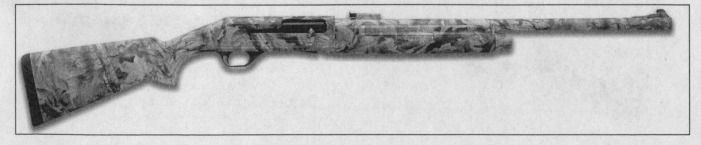

Double-barreled shotguns are notorious for shooting in two different directions and thus are not suitable for slug shooting. Occasionally a buckshot hunter will use a double for short-range shooting.

Is Remington planning a proprietary smallbore slug gun built on the Model 710 rifle frame?

time favorite with slug hunters, as is its successor, the 11-87 and the newer Versa, Browning's Gold, Silver and Maxus, Winchester's Super X2 and Super X3, Benelli's Super Black Eagle and Ml and Beretta's 12-gauge ES100 (formerly the Pintail), Weatherby's SAS and Traditions' Spanish-built XL-2000 autoloaders are all popular with slug hunters in both rifled barrels and smoothbores. Mossberg's 9200 fits that bill until it was discontinued in 2000, as was Winchester's 1400 a few years earlier.

Doubles

Double-barreled shotguns, be they side-by-sides or over-unders, are notoriously inaccurate for slug shooting, since both bores often have their own point-of-aim. For that reason, no doubles are currently made with rifled barrels.

What's Next?

In the late 1990s, with bolt-action shotguns well established as the state of the art, Remington director of firearms product development Jay Bunting told me that there would never be a slug gun built on the Model 700 rifle action. Bunting noted the whole industry learned a lesson through Browning, which built an excellent bolt-action gun based on its A-Bolt rifle action but with a $700 price tag it simply could not compete with the Mossberg, Marlin and Savage guns that were pouring out of mass merchandisers for less than half that price.

But when Remington brought out its 710 rifle in 2000, a bolt-action designed for Mart sales at $350 including a Bushnell scope, many of us thought the door was open for Remington to enter the bolt-action slug gun market with a competitively priced unit. "No, you won't see a 12-gauge 710," Bunting stated emphatically when questioned on the matter. "But how about a smaller gauge? How about one even smaller than 20 — a bolt gun designed around a very flat-shooting proprietary slug? Stay tuned." Intriguing.

43 Tips for Rifle Hunters

JOHN WEISS

*A*ccuracy at any range is critical to the rifle hunter. *Choosing the right calibers, firearm actions, bullet designs, and scopes all come into play.*

1. The ever-unpredictable human element is the most important component in any rifle-shooting equation. Virtually any brand or caliber of rifle taken right from the box, secured in a ballistic laboratory's vise, and fed with standard factory loads will be more accurate than 99 percent of all the hunters afield. When a live deer is in your sights, and you must estimate the distance instantly and then shoot offhand through cover with poor lighting conditions and pumping adrenaline, pinpoint shooting accuracy can quickly go down the drain. So don't believe the hype that buying a new gun in a different caliber will instantly turn you into an expert marksman. There's a lot more to it than that.

2. Most rifle authorities will tell you that the four calibers best suited to whitetail hunting are the .243 Winchester, .270 Winchester, .30-06 Springfield, and .308 Winchester. Many other calibers can get the job done just as well, but the above four are far and away the most popular— accounting for more than 80 percent of all centerfire rifle sales.

3. When shooting the calibers recommended in tip 2, 100-grain bullets are considered best for the .243; for the .270, I use 130- or 140-grain bullets; and for the .30-06 and .308, I recommend 150- or 165-grain bullets.

4. Most proficient hunters rely on jacketed bullets—also known as controlled expanding bullets—in which most of the lead, except for the tip, is covered with a tough alloyed metal, or where the tip has a thin coat of metal but is notched or has a tiny hollowpoint to facilitate rapid expansion. In either case, the jacket gives the bullet good accuracy, performance, and penetration, allowing the bullet to hold together on impact but then quickly begin peeling back from the tip and flattening as it opens a large path. Two examples of such bullets are the Winchester Pointed Soft-Point and the Remington Core-Lokt.

The most popular calibers for whitetail hunting are the .243 Winchester, .270 Winchester, .30-06 Springfield, and .308 Winchester

5. When you're hunting, don't use full-jacketed bullets. They invariably pass entirely through a deer, leaving only a small hole and sometimes not inflicting enough collateral shock or tissue damage to prove fatal. Full-jacketed bullets are designed to hold together on impact and penetrate deeply through tough muscle and thick bones before beginning to expand. They're intended for game animals much larger than deer, such as elk, moose, brown bears, and large African species.

6. For a variety of reasons, different regions of the country have become associated with different rifle actions. Throughout the northern border states and into the East and Northeast, for example, the most popular actions seem to be the lever-action and the autoloader. In the plains, western, and southwestern states, many hunters carry either a bolt-action or lever-action. And in the Midwest, South, and Southeast, you'll see mostly autoloaders, with someone in the crowd occasionally carrying a pump gun. There are pockets where the rules don't hold, of course, but in any case, there is no advantage to being a conformist. Regional firearm choices are almost

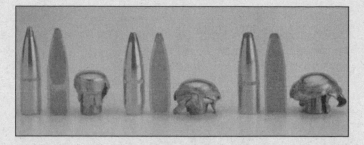

Ideally, a whitetail bullet should offer a combination of good penetration and good expansion without breaking apart.

always dictated by tradition, not technical applications.

7. The bolt-action is the most accurate of all the actions, which is why it is unanimously chosen by match shooters and varminters, who typically require precision accuracy at long ranges. It's also the most rugged, the most trouble-free, and the easiest to break down for cleaning, even in the field.

Lever-action rifles and open iron sights dominated hunting for decades but are quickly fading from the scene. Lever-action mechanisms are not as strong as the popular bolt-action. And iron sights limit your shooting distance to 100 yards.

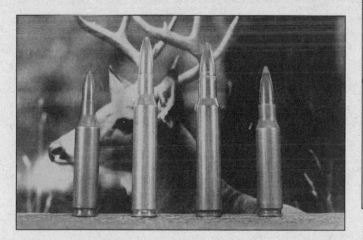

Firearm experts recommend that whitetail hunters use jacketed bullets in which most of the lead, except for the tip, is covered with a tough alloyed metal.

A perfect, one-inch, three-shot group on the range is what every rifle hunter should strive for before heading afield.

8. If you're in the market for a bolt-action, get one with a twenty-two- or twenty-four-inch barrel. These two lengths account for 95 percent of all bolt-action sales. Some brands may offer slightly longer barrels, but they don't afford noticeably better accuracy at deer hunting's customary shooting distances, and they can be unwieldy in thick cover.

9. A bolt-action rifle intended for whitetail hunting should weigh no more than seven or eight pounds. If you add the scope with its base and rings, the rifle suddenly weighs nine pounds. Then, there's the weight of the sling and fully loaded magazine to consider. Remember, additional ounces here and there can feel like pounds when you're climbing steep terrain. If the total weight of your shooting equipment can be kept close to ten pounds, you've done a good job.

10. The pump gun (slide-action) is not as accurate as the bolt-action, but many hunters find it faster to use. This is because they can quickly chamber additional rounds by simply working the slide in a straight-back/ straight-forward manner, as opposed to working a bolt in a 90-degree right-angle eject direction and then working it again in a 90-degree cartridge- feed direction. If you decide on a pump gun, go with the popular twenty-two-inch barrel length. Stripped down, such rifles weigh seven pounds or so, which means that a fully outfitted firearm will tip the scales at nine or ten pounds.

11. The lever-action is especially popular with those who prefer to stillhunt or drive deer, as opposed to stand-hunting. Being continually on the move, such hunters need a rifle that still feels light at the end of the day. Barrel lengths average eighteen to twenty inches. When stripped down, most lever-actions weigh 5½ to 6½ pounds. The lever-action design allows fast use but, as in the case of the pump gun, it isn't as strong or accurate as the bolt-action.

12. The autoloader (or semi-automatic) isn't impressively accurate. It isn't overly rugged, either. Feeding and extraction malfunctions or jams are common when the firearm is not immaculately clean, whenever the weather is unusually cold, and sometimes when you're working with handloads. Barrels average eighteen to twenty-two inches in length. Stripped-down autoloaders weigh in the vicinity of 7½ pounds. The autoloader's deficiencies are compensated for by the fact that its action is by far the fastest. All you need do is repeatedly squeeze the trigger, and the rifle's action will rapidly do the rest.

13. Iron and aperture-type peep sights are waning in popularity, except perhaps among a small contingent of hunters who exclusively stage drives or hunt deer in very thick cover where short shots are the rule. On the plus side, iron sights and aperture-type peep sights are extremely rugged, almost entirely failsafe, and relatively inexpensive.

14. Because they don't magnify anything, iron sights and aperture-type peep sights generally

restrict you to shooting distances of less than 100 yards, which means you'll never be able to take advantage of the long-range capabilities of the four calibers described earlier. The Weaver Scope Company once had a ballistic lab compare a rifle's performance first with a scope and then with open sights. In both tests, exactly the same slugs were used. The scoped rifle offered a 35 percent increase in accuracy at 100 yards, an 85 percent increase at 200 yards, and a whopping 400 percent increase in accuracy at 250 yards!

15. Many hunters err by using scopes of greater magnification than the shooting situation warrants. With any scope, the higher the power, the more restricted the field of view at closer ranges. Many times, this prevents you from quickly finding your target and centering the reticle on it. This is especially the case when a deer is on the move in cover. Likewise, because the higher magnifications tend to reflect the slightest of normal body tremors (such as excited breathing), holding steady on a faraway target is sometimes futile.

16. For decades, standard-field, fixed-power scopes such as the venerable 4X outsold all others. These are still adequate, but today's deer hunters much prefer the various types of wide-angle, variable-magnification scopes.

17. The most popular wide-angle, variable-magnification scope is the 2.5 x 8X. Its versatility is its hallmark. When you're stillhunting, waiting on stand in heavy cover, or participating in drives—all of which are likely to present shots as close as twenty-five yards—the scope remains on its lowest magnification setting. Yet if you change location to watch a cover edge at a somewhat longer distance—say, 100 yards—a midrange setting can be instantly selected. If you move yet again to watch even more distant terrain (out to 250 yards or so), just bring the highest magnification setting into use.

18. In addition to enlarging the target image, scopes allow you to take greater care in picking your shots in heavy cover. In other words, you're better able to find small openings and tight shooting alleys through tangled branches and vines, which is seldom possible when using open iron sights at distances beyond fifty yards. This reduces the risk that a tiny, unnoticed branch will deflect the rifle bullet, perhaps wounding the animal or missing it altogether.

19. Many optics companies offer light-gathering scopes in their line-ups. This means that a target's resolution, or degree of brightness, is far greater through the scope than what the human eye can ordinarily discern. By utilizing an oversized bell (the scope's front, objective lens), the scope channels a greater quantity of available light back through the ocular lens, or eyepiece. The advantage of this feature is that you can see your target more clearly during the hours of dawn and dusk, in the shade of deep cover, and during inclement weather. This serves as not only a hunting aid but also a safety feature that helps ensure positive target identification.

20. Optics companies offer many types of reticles for deer hunting. Most hunters favor some type of crosshair configuration rather than a post or dot reticle, which can obscure too much of the target at longer ranges. Crosshair reticles are available in fine, medium-fine, and coarse thicknesses. For deer hunting, avoid the fine crosshair variety, which can be difficult to use in thick cover or low-light situations.

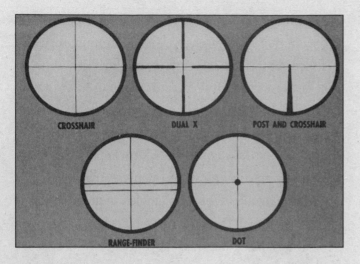

Of the numerous scope reticles available, the crosshair and Dual-X are the best for most shooting applications.

Scope rings with hex-head screws are far more secure and pleasing to the eye than those with slot-type screws.

21. In the category of crosshair reticles, the most popular are the so-called 4-Plex, Dual-X, or DuPlex designs, in which the thick outer wires of the crosshairs taper down either gradually or abruptly to medium-fine at the center. This design quickly draws the eye to the target and permits easy centering of the crosshairs without obscuring the aiming point.

22. Rangefinder scopes are generally of interest only to those hunters who hunt in regions where shots at deer typically are at long range and across open ground. By using a scale seen through the glass and a calibrated dial on the side of the scope, you can first judge the distance to the deer and then manually adjust the crosshairs, so that aiming calculations can be more precise. In this manner, you won't need to guess at how much holdover to use when a deer is in the distance.

23. In mounting a scope, base, and rings, *tight* is the key word. It's also a good practice to check the mounting screws periodically throughout the hunting season. Laboratory tests have shown that if any of the three telescopic sight components can be wiggled just 1/100 inch, it will translate into a shot that's off as much as 100 inches at 100 yards.

24. Most companies are doing away with scope-mounting bases and rings that are held in place with slot-type screw heads. As you begin to tighten such screws, the screwdriver is prone to slip and either strip the screwhead slot or scratch the finish. In their place, most manufacturers are opting for scope-mounting screws with recessed hex heads that can be tightened only with an Allen wrench. Not only are these more pleasing to the eye, but they can be tightened securely with no damage to the screw, scope, mounting parts, or the firearm itself.

25. Scope hardware is often shipped from the factory with a fine coating of lubricant to prevent rust. For the tightest possible scope mounting, it's essential to remove this slippery film. Simply go over all the parts with a toothbrush and small dish of solvent, then dry with a soft rag.

26. When you're mounting the scope base and rings, treat each threaded screw with a droplet of Gun-Tite adhesive, available at any store that sells firearms. This adhesive helps hold the screws in place despite constant recoil and barrel vibrations.

27. Sighting-in a deer rifle is easier if it's first bore-sighted with an optical collimator. Any gunsmith can do this in five minutes at a minimal charge, but if you own a number of firearms, you may

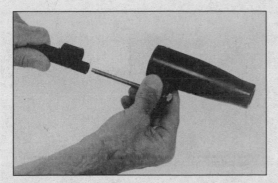

Use an optical collimator to bore-sight the firearm prior to going to the target range to sight-in a deer rifle.

A shooting bench and sandbags are essential for optimum accuracy.

wish to buy your own. A bore-sighter fits into the firearm's muzzle; the scope's crosswires are then adjusted to match those in the collimator. This allows you to immediately get bullets on paper rather than having to take many guess shots. Once the collimator has been removed, you can fine-tune your rifle's accuracy.

28. On the range, there's another important step to take before your first fine-tuning shot. Virtually all scopes have a rear, ocular lens that can be adjusted to accommodate any hunter's particular visual deficiencies. Yet some hunters, strangely, never use this eyepiece feature. Do it. It's as easy as focusing binoculars, and it will give you a much sharper image of your aim point. Once the eyepiece focusing ring is tightened, it stays that way permanently—until your vision changes or someone borrows your gun and changes the settings.

29. After the ocular lens has been adjusted to your personal vision, check for proper eye relief—distance from the scope eye to the ocular or rear of the scope. A scope that's mounted too far forward in its rings doesn't allow a complete sight picture. Loosen the scope rings a bit, and slide the scope to the rear until you get a clear and complete sight picture. A scope that's too far to the rear, on the other hand, may clout you in

the eyebrow region when the rifle recoils. For most hunters, proper eye relief is somewhere between 2½ and four inches.

30. Fine-tuning a rifle's accuracy should always be done on a shooting bench with the firearm cradled in sandbags. Never try to sight-in a rifle or any other firearm by holding it offhand—you simply won't get the stability necessary for consistent, accurate shooting. This is due to normal body tremor, breathing fluctuations, and every hunter's inability to hold a firearm perfectly steady without any means of artificial support. The result is erratic shot placement.

31. If you need to check your rifle's accuracy in a camp with no shooting bench or sandbags, the hood of a vehicle is a good alternative. Support the firearm in a cradle of rolled-up blankets or towels, cut two V-slots in opposite ends of a cardboard box, or rest the rifle on a backpack or even a hunting coat.

32. On the target range, a firearm's accuracy is fine-tuned by turning the windage and elevation knobs on the scope. Each time you make a scope adjustment, fire a three-shot group. Then rest the rifle for at least five minutes to allow the barrel to cool down. As the barrel becomes hotter and hotter (sometimes too hot to touch), accuracy deteriorates noticeably. Besides, when leveling your sights on a deer, your first (and

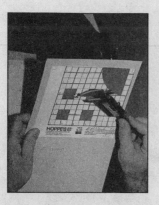

Shot at the upper left-hand square, this first group is low and to the right. Ideally, it should be three inches above the square and moved left by one inch.

hopefully only) shot will be from a cold barrel, so you want the utmost in cold-barrel accuracy.

33. Most whitetail hunters sight-in their rifles so that, on the target range, the bullets print dead-on (center of bull's-eye) at twenty-five yards. This should put the slugs approximately three inches high of the point of aim at 100 yards, and approximately dead-on again at 200 yards. Of course, bullet weight and the caliber of the firearm may skew these figures slightly. Why this particular sighting-in formula? Because a deer's twelve-inch squared lung region is the ideal aiming point. With this formula, you can hold dead-on at any range from point blank to 250 yards and still be sure you'll connect with the chest cavity.

34. To make the rifle shoot higher or lower, the scope's elevation knob is adjusted, and adjustments to the right or left are made by turning the windage knob. Most such knobs have arrows on them, indicating the direction to turn the dials if you want the point of impact to be raised, lowered, or sent to the right or left. Both knobs are also graduated in click stops, with each click representing an angle of .25 minute (at 100 yards, one minute of angle is one inch).

35. If slugs are consistently printing one inch high at 100 yards (which is two inches below the desired point of impact), turn your elevation knob up by eight clicks.

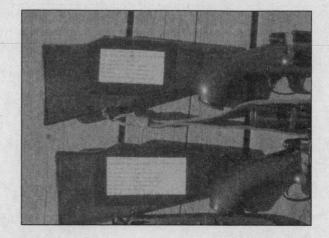

Taking a backup rifle on every hunt is good insurance. If it's of a different caliber, tape reminder cards on the stocks as to their sighting-in specs.

36. If slugs are consistently printing four inches to the left of point of aim, turn your windage knob sixteen clicks to the right.

37. What's considered good accuracy for a conventional (noncustomized) deer rifle? As a rule, at 100 yards two-inch groups are considered acceptable, 1½-inch groups are very good, and one-inch groups bestow bragging rights upon the shooter.

38. Get into the habit of regularly cleaning your scope's lenses. Otherwise, a gradual buildup of dust and grime will reduce the sharpness of the image you see through the optics. Avoid using the common spit-and-handkerchief method because dust or grit embedded in the cloth's fibers may scratch the lenses. Instead, use the same lens-cleaning fluid and tissue that photographers use on their expensive camera lenses.

39. When hunting in inclement weather, many hunters use scope covers. These are rubber or plastic affairs that quickly fit over the front and rear ends of the scope to keep the lenses free from rain and snow, and to prevent the glass from fogging. They can be quickly removed when you want to take a shot.

Use lens covers that flip up instantly if you're expecting rain or snow.

Bipods, such as this Harris model, are excellent for hunting while prone, sitting, or kneeling. The legs extend out to three feet in length. When the legs are collapsed, they fold up against the forearm for easy carrying.

40. Every deer rifle should be outfitted with a sling, which lets you shoulder the firearm while you navigate steep or slippery terrain. Those with extra-wide straps are the most popular because they stay on your shoulder and don't cut into your skin when you're hunting in warm weather and wearing light clothing.

41. Most rifle triggers come from the factory preset at anywhere from four to six pounds, which is difficult enough to squeeze (for safety reasons) and affects accuracy. A much smoother and crisper trigger pull is around two to three pounds. The creep, or distance the trigger must travel before the sear is released to discharge the round, should likewise be removed. If you can't do this work yourself, have your gunsmith make the adjustments.

42. Never climb up or down from a tree stand with a rifle slung over your shoulder and a cartridge in the chamber. Always use a haul rope to raise and lower the firearm, and always tie the rope to the *rear* sling swivel, so the rifle's muzzle is pointing downward.

43. When you're preparing to take a shot, use a rest whenever possible to stabilize the firearm and increase accuracy. If you're shooting from a prone position, you can do this by cradling the firearm in the crook of a western hat or in a piece of clothing. You can also attach a bipod to the rifle's forearm. In a sitting position, lay the rifle's forearm on your upturned palm placed on a raised knee. If you're kneeling, use two cross sticks (several companies make excellent ones). If you're standing, lean against a tree trunk. However, when you take any kind of rest, make sure that the rifle's forearm is always resting on something that provides a cushioning effect. Never lay the forearm on a rigid, hard surface such as a boulder, which will cause shots to fly higher than your point of aim. This occurs because the hard surface exerts slight upward pressure on the stock forearm, which in turn exerts slight upward pressure on the free-floating barrel.

36 Tips for Slug-Shotgun Hunters

JOHN WEISS

How to get the most from the new high-tech shotguns.

1. The past ten years have seen tremendous strides in deer-shotgun technology. It's a good thing, too, because some state wildlife agencies are predicting that only shotguns will be legal for deer hunting east of the Mississippi by the year 2020. With more and more people moving to the countryside, short-range shotguns are simply safer than long-range centerfire rifles in many situations. When fired at a thirty-degree angle of elevation, some centerfire rifle bullets may travel as much as several miles, whereas the maximum range of most 12-gauge shotgun slugs is only about 2,400 feet.

2. Just because slug shotguns are short-range firearms, don't mistakenly assume that their accuracy leaves anything to be desired. Ballistic tests have shown that a finely tuned modern shotgun equipped with a scope is more accurate than many venerable deer rifles of a generation ago, including the .30—30 Winchester, .35 Remington, .32 Winchester Special, and .44 Magnum.

3. The only reasonable bore to use for deer shotgunning is the 12-gauge. All others fall far behind in terms of deer-slug performance. A one-ounce Foster-type slug leaves the barrel of a 12-gauge with a velocity of only 1,600 feet per second but possesses a walloping 2,485 foot-pounds of energy. Thus it packs the same amount of knockdown power as a 150-grain, .30-06 bullet at fifty yards. Other slugs, such as the 12-gauge exception is a single-shot 20 gauge "youth gun" three-inch magnum

The two best types of deer shotguns are pump guns and autoloaders. Use only 12 gauge. The one exception is a single-shot 20 guage "youth gun" when one member of the group is a youngster being inroduced to his or her first deer hunt.

There are a wide variety of 12-gauge deer slugs on the market. The author has found superior down-range performance with sabot-type slugs encased in plastic sleeves that fall away when the slug exits the muzzle.

Brenneke Golden at a hefty 600 grains, have a muzzle energy of 2,913 foot-pounds of energy, giving them the same smack as a 150-grain, .30—06 bullet at 100 yards!

4. Ballistics tests have revealed that in most 12-gauge deer shotguns, three-inch magnum loads are less accurate than standard 2¾-inch loads. And the additional recoil is torture. Until the Federal Bureau of Ballistic Standards raises the allowable chamber pressure in shotguns beyond the current 12,500 feet per square inch—to accommodate the extra extenders in the longer shells and the greater amount of powder being burned—stick with standard 2¾-inch loads.

5. For hunters, the least-desirable deer shotgun action is the break-open single-shot. This doesn't mean that those currently on the market are of poor quality. Its simply that the procedure of cocking the hammer takes practice if you're to avoid making an audible click that may spook deer. Also, because there's little or no receiver length on which to mount a scope, you must be satisfied with open rifle-type sights. Plus, of course, you've got only one shot. However, most brands on the market are nevertheless fine starter guns for youngsters or first-time older hunters. This is because their single-shot capability and uncomplicated loading and unloading make them very safe and easy to master for those who don't have much firearm experience.

6. Deer hunters should also avoid double-barrel shotguns such as over-and-unders and side-by-sides. Because of the canted way in which the barrels are married to the receiver, slugs fired from doubles cross over during their trajectories. In other words, with a side-by-side, a slug fired from the left barrel will, on a target, print to the right of a slug fired from the right barrel, and vice versa. Similarly, with an over-and-under, a slug from the bottom barrel will print higher than a slug from the top barrel, and vice versa. You can add to this confusion the fact that the two barrels of over-and-unders and side-by-sides are nearly always of different chokes, which also results in erratic slug flight. Finally, scopes and aperture-type peep sights cannot be mounted on these firearms, and any semblance of accuracy using only a front bead sight is reduced to pure guesswork. For deer hunting, avoid these shotguns entirely.

7. Bolt-action shotguns, such as the famous Tar-Hunt and Browning A-Bolt, are currently the state of the art in whitetail slug hunting. They're every bit as high in quality as branded centerfire rifles. The downside is that they usually carry price tags as much as three times higher than autoloading and pump shotguns.

8. Autoloading and pump shotguns offer a five-round capacity but, increasingly, states are passing laws requiring the use of a plug in the magazine tube that reduces the capacity to three rounds. If you don't have a plug or one didn't come with your new firearm, it's not necessary

For the highest down-range accuracy performance, always sight in from a bench rest.

to order one from the manufacturer. Simply cut a piece of ¾-inch-diameter dowel rod to a length of five inches and insert it into the tube.

9. One disadvantage of autoloading shotguns is that feeding and ejection problems can occur, especially in cold or inclement weather. Also, if you wish to mount a scope on an autoloader, expect to run into difficulties. Because most autoloader receivers are made of aluminum, when the thin metal on the top of the receiver is drilled and tapped, screws cannot be embedded deeply enough or subsequently tightened enough to securely hold a scope mount.

10. Some shooters try to solve the shotgun scope-mounting dilemma by buying a slug barrel that has a scope dovetail mount welded right where it fits into the receiver. But this usually

The receivers of many shotguns are made of thin aluminum that cannot be drilled and tapped for secure scope mounting. One alternative is an aftermarket slug barrel with a cantilever scope shelf that extends back over the receiver.

works out poorly because the scope ends up being mounted so far forward that its eye relief is substantially increased, which prevents you from gaining a full sight picture. It's better to purchase the type of aftermarket slug barrel that has a cantilever scope mount. The cantilever is welded to the rear of the barrel just like a dovetail scope mount, but it incorporates a shelflike device that extends still farther to the rear. The scope is mounted onto this shelf, allowing for an acceptable eye-relief distance. Another option is to buy a scope mount that attaches to the side of the receiver. The gunsmith will still have to drill into soft aluminum, but it's thicker on the side of the receiver than on top.

11. Pump shotguns are far and away the most popular with whitetail hunters. They're ruggedly built and virtually fail-safe in operation. Moreover, their receivers are usually made of

The most popular slug gun is the 12-gauge pump. This is Ithaca's Deerslayer with a Hastings aftermarket rifled barrel and a 2 x 8X Bausch & Lomb scope.

Left to right: the Winchester Foster-style, BRI-500, Remington Foster-style, and Brenneke shotgun slugs.

case-hardened steel, allowing you to drill and tap a strong scope mount.

12. With smoothbore shotguns, a deer slug will pass through all types of muzzle choke constrictions without damage to the firearm. But you sacrifice a great deal of accuracy if you use an improved-cylinder, modified, or full choke. It's better to use a cylinder choke (which has the least constriction). Better still, if available, is an optional, interchangeable slug barrel with a straight bore (no choke at all).

13. When you obtain an interchangeable slug barrel to replace your shot-pellet barrel, it will come equipped with rifle-type sights. These usually consist of a front elevated blade on a ramp and some kind of adjustable, notched rear sight. But most hunters who invest in a slug barrel want maximum performance, and this means mounting a scope on the receiver.

14. When you're using a smoothbore shotgun, use only Foster-style slugs, which have a weighty nose section and a hollow base and fly much the same as a badminton shuttlecock. Contrary to what some hunters believe, the helical fins on Foster-style slugs do not impart any degree

of spin that might increase accuracy—they simply allow the slug to squeeze through any size of choke constriction in the shotgun barrel. It's the weighty nose section that stabilizes the slug in flight and keeps it in line with the aiming point.

15. The most popular Foster type slugs are made by Winchester, Federal, and Remington, and range in weight from 435 to 547 grains. Buckshot loads are not recommended because of their garden-hose spraying effect. And, besides, only four states allow the use of buckshot.

16. A variation on the Foster-style slug has a fiber wad attached to its base in the belief that this will enhance stability in flight. The jury is still out on this speculation. The most common examples are made by Brenneke and Activ, and they range in weight from 492 to 600 grains.

17. When you're using a high-tech deer shotgun with a factory-installed rifled barrel, or when you're removing a smoothbore barrel from a shotgun and slipping on an aftermarket rifled barrel for deer hunting, always use a sabot (pronounced SAY-boh) slug. This is a slug

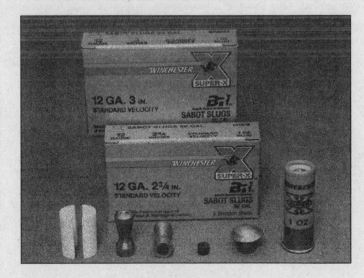

Use only sabot slugs for optimum performance in deer shotguns fitted with rifled barrels.

Keep in mind slug shotguns for deer hunting are short-range firearms. A shot farther than 100 yards is a long poke.

encased in a two-part plastic sleeve. When fired, internal gas pressure causes the plastic-sleeve assembly to expand and grip the barrel's inner lands and grooves. This phenomenon causes the slug to exit the muzzle with near-perfect gyroscopic stability. It also imparts spin to the slug, and—as with a centerfire rifle bullet—a spinning shotgun slug is far more accurate than one that doesn't spin. After traveling about twenty yards from the muzzle, the lightweight, two-part sabot meets air resistance and falls away while the slug continues on.

18. The most popular sabot slugs are made by Winchester, Federal, Remington, and Lightfield, and they range in weight from 423 to 485 grains.

19. Because various sabot slugs come in different weights, it's best to experiment with several brands to determine which fares best in a particular shotgun. If you eventually decide to switch to a different brand of slug with a different weight from your current brand, you should sight in your gun to see if any slight adjustments are necessary. The same holds true when you're switching between any of the Foster-type or Foster-Attached-Wad slugs.

20. There's a consensus among deer shotgunners that the ideal weight for a high-tech slug gun (be it a bolt-action, autoloader, or pump) is between seven and eight pounds. Add a scope mount, scope, and sling, then fill the magazine with slugs, and the firearm approaches ten pounds ... the same weight as the ideal deer rifle. When you're considering different brands of guns, keep in mind the recommended barrel length of twenty to twenty-four inches.

21. Which brand, style, and weight of shotgun slug is best for deer? Because virtually all of them are of high quality, this is a tough decision.

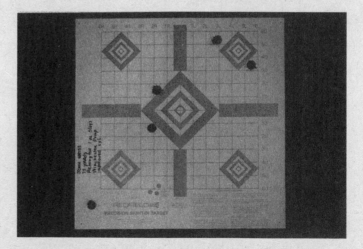

Every shotgun has a personality all its own, so it pays to range-test several different types of slugs to determine which performs best in your firearm. This group was not acceptable.

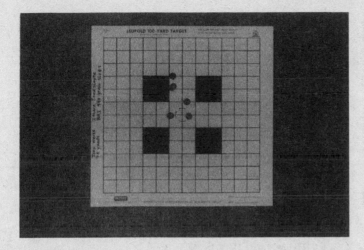

This first group at seventy-five yards, with sabot slugs, is acceptable, but testing other slugs and a bit of fine-tuning could improve it.

It sounds unscientific, but each shotgun has its own personality and will, therefore, shoot certain types of slugs better than others. I watched one hunter sighting in with Remington-Foster slugs, and at 100 yards the best he could achieve was five-inch groups. When he switched to nearly identical Winchester-Foster slugs, though, his groups tightened up to nearly half that. Another hunter's experience was that neither Remington-Foster nor Winchester-Foster slugs yielded acceptable performance in his slug gun, but he was amazed with the accuracy of Federal-Foster slugs and Brennekes. Buy a small quantity of all brands, head for the range, and allow your shotgun to decide what it likes.

22. What's the best downrange performance you can expect from a smooth-barrel deer shotgun with Foster-style slugs and aperture-type or peep sights? Generally, you'll be doing well if you shoot four-inch groups at seventy-five yards, and your shooting distance should be restricted to 100 yards.

23. What's the best downrange performance you can expect from a smooth-barrel deer shotgun with Foster-type slugs and a scope? Generally, you'll do well to shoot three-inch groups at 100 yards, restricting your shooting distance to no more than 125 yards.

24. What's the best downrange performance you can expect from a rifled barrel shotgun with sabot slugs and a scope? Generally, you'll do well to shoot 1½-inch groups at 100 yards, with the shooting distance restricted to 150 yards.

25. The information about scopes and scope-mounting procedures in Chapter 14, "43 Tips for Rifle Hunters," applies almost entirely to slug shotguns as well. There is one exception, however. A wide-angle scope with variable magnification is still suggested for slug shotguns, but the magnification need not be as high, simply because the maximum recommended shooting distance is only 150 yards. This means that a scope of 1.5 x 3X or 2.5 x 5X is fine. Also, in accordance with rifle-scope recommendations, a Dual-X crosshair reticle is favored by most hunters. This is the type in which the thick outer extremities of the crosshairs taper either gradually or abruptly to medium-fine at the center.

26. Sighting in a slug shotgun using rifle-type sights or an aperture-type peep sight is most commonly done by adjusting the rear sight up or down and sideways. The rule of thumb is to always move the rear sight in the direction you want the slug to go. In other words, if slugs are printing to the left of the bull's-eye, move the rear sight to the left. If slugs are printing lower than you'd like, lower the rear sight. However, because there are so many open-sight variations on the market, consult the manufacturer's instructions for more specific information.

Because slug shotguns are relatively short-range guns, the perfect set-up is commonly a food plot adjacent to heavy cover.

you can adjust your holdover if a 150-yard shot presents itself.

29. Slug-shotgun accuracy can be improved significantly by stiffening and lightening the trigger pull. Most shotgun trigger assemblies come from the factory set at either five or six pounds. These heavyset triggers are designed to be "slapped," not squeezed as with a rifle trigger, so have your gunsmith adjust your slug-gun trigger to a three-pound pull with little or no travel.

27. In addition to adjustable rear sights, some aftermarket barrels also have adjustable front blade sights mounted in dovetails. This allows them to be moved right or left by lightly tapping on them with a hammer and small centerpunch tool.

28. Sighting in a deer shotgun with a scope differs from sighting in a scoped centerfire rifle in two significant ways. First, the distance capability of even a high-tech shotgun is far less than that of a centerfire rifle, so no allowance need be made for shooting possibilities beyond 200 yards. Also, rifle bullets fly on a different trajectory from shotgun slugs. Slugs have a relatively flat trajectory out to about 100 yards before dropping rapidly. Consequently, most deer shotgunners sight-in their scopes so slugs are dead-on (center of bull's-eye) a twenty-five yards. This also puts them nearly dead-on at the 100-yard target. If you're using a high-tech shotgun with a rifled barrel and sabot slugs, however, you'll have to fire several groups at the maximum recommended 150 yards to determine how much drop occurs in that additional fifty yards. Then you need only make a mental note of the amount of drop so that

Because slug shotguns are most commonly required by law where high human populations and hunter density afield prevail, keep in mind there will be many hunting groups that exclusively stage drives. So you can't beat a stand location that serves as a known travel corridor.

30. If your particular slug gun's trigger cannot be adjusted to a lower-pound pull and its creep cannot be removed, consider buying an aftermarket, fully adjustable, rifle-type trigger assembly. It can be installed in minutes.

31. The weakest part of any shotgun is the linkup where the barrel is attached to the receiver. In some cases, the barrel screws into the receiver; in other cases, it twists in and locks with several lugs. In either case, it's often a sloppy, imprecise fit. This matters little when you're shooting at pheasant or rabbit, but it can cause problems when you're trying to achieve deer-slug accuracy. Ask your gunsmith if he can remedy this problem with your specific firearm by using epoxy or some other method. If he can, be forewarned that the change will probably be permanent. You'll now have a full-time deer shotgun . . . but one that is far more accurate than before.

32. It's especially important to thoroughly clean a slug shotgun at the end of the season. Foster-type slugs are made of very soft lead, which will foul a smooth barrel as quickly as lead shot will. Saboted slugs are equally damaging, but in their case it's the plastic sabot sleeves that leave residue on the lands and grooves of rifled barrels. In either case, use a quality barrel solvent and a stiff-bristle brass cleaning brush to do the job.

33. In regions where slug shotguns are mandated, you can be sure there's a relatively large human population. This means more hunting pressure, so it's probably futile to set up a stand or blind overlooking a feeding area such as a field, hay meadow, or low-growing cropland. Pressured deer simply won't venture into such open places, except after dark. Your best bet is to scout the heaviest cover you can find, especially funnels and travel corridors that deer will use to evade hunters.

34. Because pressured deer circle and dodge hunters all day, dusk and dawn aren't the only productive times to see animals. Shotgun deer hunters accept the fact that they're just as likely to see a buck sneaking through their area at noon as at first light. It consequently pays to remain on stand all day.

35. Slug-shotgun hunting is scheduled for later in the year in most states, with the early deer seasons given over to bow- and blackpowder hunters. When you scout for food sources then, keep in mind that foods that are abundant in the early fall may be depleted by the time early winter arrives. Zero in on mast-bearing trees such as oaks and beeches—if the mast crop was normal, there should still be plenty of acorns and beechnuts on the ground when the slug-shotgun season opens. Many farmers will also still have standing corn in their fields late in the year, and this is a magnet for deer. So are abandoned orchards. These food sources should be next to the heavy cover, however, or deer will avoid them during the day.

36. As a rule, tree stands used by slug shotgunners should be placed somewhat higher than stands used earlier in the season with other forms of shooting equipment. The reason is that the leaf drop is complete before most states' slug-shotgunning seasons begin, leaving hunters who are aloft far more exposed. Low stands are acceptable if you can find trees with many gnarled, spreading branches to break up your outline, or if you can place yours in a conifer (which retains its leaves year-round).

50 Blackpowder Hunting Tips

JOHN WEISS

*H*ere's a quick review of things to remember that will ensure trouble-free muzzleloading.

1. When you take your flintlock or percussion-cap rifle out of offseason storage, run several dry patches down the barrel to remove the oily coating that you put there to prevent rust. Otherwise, the oil may deactivate the first powder charge you load and prevent ignition. Use a pipe cleaner to remove oil from the nipple.

2. Place a short strip of tape over the bore to prevent rain or snow from entering the barrel and causing rust or possibly deactivating the powder charge. You can shoot right through the tape with no loss of velocity or accuracy.

3. At the end of a hunting day afield, it's not necessary to discharge your muzzleloader. All states consider the firearm legally unloaded if you simply remove the cap from a percussion rifle or the powder charge from a flintlock's pan.

There are numerous styles of percussion cap and flintlock rifles on the market. Devoted "powder burners" typically own several.

At the beginning of a new hunting season, run dry patches through the barrel to remove last season's protective lube.

4. If you use Pyrodex pellets, don't touch them with your fingers—oil or moisture on your skin may lessen the potency of the charge. Included with each box of pellets is a short pipe cleaner designed to slide through each pellet's centerhole for hands-free loading.

5. Always load Pyrodex pellets into the barrel with their blackened ends facing down. This blackening is an accelerant smearing of black powder that, when seated against the percussion cap, ensures full ignition of the Pyrodex.

6. Before you load a percussion-cap rifle, place a clean patch on a ramrod, push it down the barrel, and fire three caps. Then, extract the ramrod and patch. You should see a black star pattern on the patch and a burned hole in the center, indicating that any residual oil or cleaning solvent has been blown out of the nipple, nipple port, and breech, and that they're clean and dry.

7. As you consider your first purchase of a blackpowder gun for deer hunting, remember that a rifle in .50 caliber is generally considered best for most situations.

Most hunters carry spare accessories in a small tacklebox in their truck or camp.

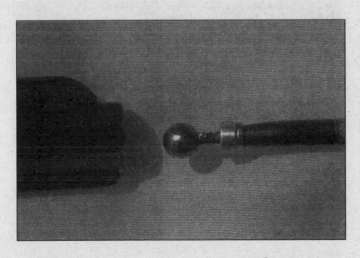

For whitetail hunting, experts agree that a rifle in .50 caliber is best.

To ensure maximum accuracy, clean a muzzleloader's barrel after every shot when you sight in on the target range.

8. For deer hunting, two Pyrodex pellets (equivalent to 100 grains of black powder) are recommended.

9. If you're using black powder, experiment on the target range with loads ranging from 100 to 125 grains to determine which specific charge yields the best accuracy with your chosen bullet.

10. Among deer hunters, the most popular .50-caliber bullets for use in the new high-tech in-line and Outer-Line rifles are 250- or 300-grain copper solid hollowpoints or copper solid bullets with lead noses.

11. Every blackpowder hunter carries a possibles bag full of assorted supplies and tools. However, one item that should never go into this bag is your nipple capper. Keep it close at hand on a neck lanyard, so that you can instantly recap your rifle if a dud cap fails to ignite.

12. When you're hunting, it's not necessary to clean a blackpowder rifle barrel after every shot unless time and convenience allow for it. *Do* clean the barrel after every shot when you're sighting in on the rifle range, however, to ensure optimum shot-to-shot accuracy.

13. Immediately after you pour a charge of black powder down the barrel of a percussion-cap gun or flintlock, always firmly slap the barrel several times with the palm of your hand. This ensures that all the powder has settled into the breech before you load the bullet.

14. If either a percussion cap or the powder in a flintlocks frizzen ignites but the powder charge in the barrel fails to burn, consider it a misfire and act as though the rifle could fire at any second. Keep the rifle pointed in a safe direction for at least one full minute before you recap the nipple or recharge the pan and attempt to fire again.

15. When you're sighting in a flintlock or sidelock percussion rifle on the rifle range, make sure there are no bystanders to your immediate right. Flames, sparks, and bits of percussion cap metal or flint chips may spray in that direction.

16. Speed-loaders, each containing a premeasured powder charge and bullet, allow for quick reloading afield. Three or four of them in your possibles bag should be enough for a day of hunting.

In inclement weather, put a piece of masking tape over the muzzle to keep out rainwater. You can shoot right through the tape.

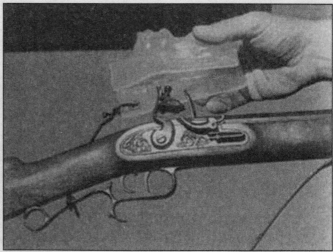

A molded-plastic hood will protect the hammer-pan-frizzen area from rain and snow.

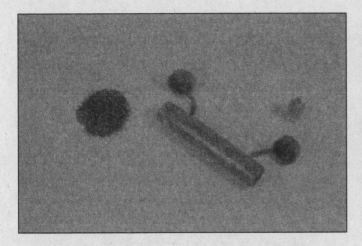

Speed-loader tubes, each containing a powder charge and ammo round, can save a day's hunt afield if the first shot is a miss.

Wide-angle scopes are most popular.

17. Heed the old adage about "keeping your powder dry" by loading your rifle at home or in camp, not outside in inclement weather. A rifle pre-loaded in this manner is safe to handle and legal to transport in a vehicle so long as there is no percussion cap on the nipple or powder in the pan.

18. If you suspect that your powder charge has become deactivated due to moisture or oil in the barrel, unscrew the nipple and trickle a few grains of powder into the nipple port. Then replace the nipple, install a fresh cap, and fire the rifle in a safe direction. The added flash from the additional grains of dry powder is often enough to cause ignition. If not, your only alternative is to unscrew the breech plug and use a ramrod to force the powder and bullet down the length of the barrel and out the bore.

19. When you're ramming a bullet or ball down the barrel, it's critical to seat it firmly against the powder charge. If it's not seated, it's a barrel obstruction and can result in an exploding barrel.

20. The priming powder you use for a flintlock's pan should be exceedingly fine four-F powder,

not the coarser double-F variety poured down the barrel.

21. When you're readying a flintlock to fire, pour enough powder into the pan, so that it comes up to a level meeting the touch hole but not covering it. The powder is so light that some of it can fall out of the pan even when the frizzen is closed. When you're hunting, get into the habit of frequently checking it and adding more powder as necessary.

22. In the most inclement weather, protection should be given to the blackpowder rifle's locking area. For a percussion-cap rifle, place a three-inch square of plastic wrap around the drum and capped nipple, and hold it in place with a twist-tie. You need only cock the hammer and fire without having to remove the plastic.

23. To protect a flintlock in bad weather, buy a molded-plastic hood that covers the entire hammer-pan-frizzen assembly. This protector must be removed before shooting.

24. The most weatherproof, surefire blackpowder ignition system currently on the market is the Markesbery 400 SRP found on Markesbery Outer-Line rifles. The standard nipple is

replaced with a two-piece stainless-steel housing. A small rifle primer is placed in the bottom half of the housing; the top half, containing a free-floating firing pin, is then screwed on. The procedure takes only a few seconds, the ignition system is 100 percent waterproof, and the small rifle primer puts ten times as much fire into the breech as even the hottest percussion cap.

25. Although patched-ball loads will kill deer at ranges of up to seventy-five yards, most hunters like to take advantage of the their muzzleloader's fullest capabilities by using maxi-balls, full-bore conical bullets, jacketed handgun bullets, or saboted bullets. In addition to extending your shooting distance by fifty yards or more, they're easier and faster to load.

26. Each time you discharge a percussion-cap gun, check the hammer's recessed head for deformed remnants of the cap. If left in place, they can dull the hammer's impact on a fresh cap as you take a second shot.

27. In bitter-cold weather, don't bring your blackpowder rifle inside a warm dwelling—condensation may form on interior and exterior metal parts. Simply remove the percussion cap or powder in the pan, and stow the rifle in your car trunk, your truck gun rack, or a shed or outbuilding protected from rain and snow.

28. In states where it's legal, most owners of high-tech in-line and Outer-Line muzzleloaders prefer to outfit them with scopes. Because blackpowder rifles are relatively short-range firearms, the most popular scope is a

Tony Knight, inventor of the famous MK-85 and other Knight rifles, displays one of his newer blackpowder models.

A perfect broadside shot. If you hit him, remember exactly where he was standing, so you can trail him if he runs off.

wide-angle model with a variable magnification of 2 x 7X.

29. Few blackpowder hunters completely strip down their rifles and use hot soapy water to clean them. A superior and much faster cleaning job can be achieved by removing the nipple and breech plug and allowing them to soak in a solvent bath such as Black Off. Meanwhile, run solvent-soaked patches through the bore. When everything is sparkling clean—usually within only ten minutes—reassemble the components, apply a light coat of protective lubricant, and you're finished!

30. An often overlooked tool that should be in every possibles bag is a patch puller or worm. This is a hooklike snare that screws into the end of the ramrod to retrieve a cleaning patch that has separated from the cleaning jag.

31. Another indispensable accessory is a nipple pick, used to clean fired-cap residue from the nipple hole before a second, fresh cap is installed. A simple safety pin attached to your jacket works just as well for this.

32. If you want to add a scope to your blackpowder rifle, use a quick-detach scope mount and rings. Blackpowder rifles require cleaning far more frequently than centerfire rifles, and a quick-detach mount is not only faster to remove and reinstall but also allows the scope to retain its zero without your having to sight-in the firearm after each cleaning.

33. If you're in the market for a new blackpowder rifle and plan to shoot saboted all-copper bullets or jacketed handgun rounds, pick a model that offers a fast rate of barrel-rifling twist for the best performance. For these bullets, a barrel with a twist of one turn in twenty-six inches or one in thirty-four inches is recommended. If you plan to shoot patched round balls or bore-sized conical bullets such as maxi-balls or Buffalo Bullets, a barrel with a twist of one turn in forty-eight inches or one in sixty-six inches performs best.

34. Patched balls and all-lead conical bullets that pass entirely through a deer create small entrance and exit holes. As a result, there may be no immediate blood trail. If you hit a deer but can't find the animal or its blood trail, begin walking in increasingly wider back-and-forth arcs from the location where you last saw it. Do this carefully, and chances are you'll discover either the blood or the dead animal itself.

"Many of the high-tech blackpowder rifles now on the market, when mounted with a scope, have an effective shooting distance of up to 150 yards."—Russ Markesbery, inventor of the Markesbery line of rifles.

35. When you're shopping for a new blackpowder rifle, keep in mind that a twenty-four-inch barrel yields the best overall performance with the widest range of bullet types and powder charges. This is because ballistic tests have shown that a barrel shorter than twenty-four inches does not allow all of the powder to be burned before the projectile leaves the muzzle. A barrel longer than twenty-four inches, on the other hand, reduces a projectile's muzzle velocity and foot-pounds of energy.

36. Never pour a powder charge from a can, flask, or powder horn down a barrel. If a smoldering ember is present from your last shot, it could ignite not only the new charge being poured but also the powder in the larger container. It's better, and safer, to use a small measuring device that holds only the amount of powder to be loaded.

37. Black powder is extremely corrosive, so make sure you clean your firearm thoroughly after each use. A blackpowder rifle put into storage at the end of the hunting season without being cleaned will have a rusted and pitted barrel by the time next year's hunting season opens.

38. If you use a flintlock, check the metal surface of the frizzen frequently. If it begins to develop a bit of scale rust, there will be a reduction in the amount of sparking that occurs when the hammer strikes the flint across the frizzen. A light touch-up with a piece of steel wool (kept in your possibles bag) quickly remedies the problem.

39. When you load a round ball, always center a well-lubed patch on the bore, and then position the ball with the sprue "up." (The sprue is the small flat place on the ball created when molten lead is poured during the manufacturing process.)

40. Blackpowder rifles with iron sights are easy to sight in. The front blade is fixed, so you only have to adjust the rear dovetail up or down, right or left. Fire a three-shot group at a twenty-five-yard target. If the group is right of the bull's-eye, move the rear sight to the right; if you're shooting left, move the rear sight to the left. If the group is low, elevate the rear sight; if it's high, lower the rear sight. Then, fine-tune your group at 100 yards.

41. When you're using a ramrod, never grab it more than eight inches above the muzzle. Doing so will cause severe side stress on the rod, possibly causing it to break and injure your hand.

42. To determine proper load depth, insert the ramrod when the rifle is fully loaded, and then use an indelible-ink pen to mark the ramrod at the point where it protrudes from the barrel. This mark now serves as a reference point each time you load. If the mark is above the muzzle, you know the projectile has not been seated deeply enough, causing a dangerous barrel obstruction if fired! Ram the load deeper until it's tight against the powder and the ramrod mark is flush with the bore.

43. When you remove the rifle's percussion cap or the powder from a flintlock's pan at the end of the day, a wise safety measure is to tie a tag on the trigger guard. This informs anyone around that even though the rifle is legally "unloaded," there's still powder and a bullet in the barrel.

44. If you want to cast your own round balls or maxi-balls, use only pure lead. Lead alloys, as used in the manufacture of wheel weights or Linotype from a print shop, contain large amounts of antimony; using this results in very hard projectiles that are difficult to properly load and seat against a powder charge.

45. Pyrodex is *not* recommended for use in flintlock rifles because it isn't as flammable as black powder. This can substantially increase hang time (a dangerous situation) if frizzen sparks occasionally are not hot or intense enough.

46. Hammer blow back occurs when the hammer is driven back to the half-cock position an instant after the rifle is fired. It's a dangerous occurrence, the result of very high pressure caused by excessive barrel fouling or the use of too much powder. Clean the barrel immediately. Then, before you attempt to fire the rifle again, consult your owner's manual to make sure you're loading the recommended powder charge.

47. When you're sighting in a rifle with a patched ball, recover a few of the fired patches to learn if they're doing their job—they'll be on the

ground about ten yards in front of the muzzle. A lubed patch that's performing well will be blackened in the center, where it was exposed to the burning powder. A patch that is not only blackened but also burned through either is made of thin, inferior material or wasn't lubed thoroughly.

48. If it's ever necessary to pull a round from a muzzleloader, always deactivate the powder first. The easiest way is to remove the priming powder from a flintlock pan or the nipple from a percussion-cap rifle. Then squirt cleaning solvent into the breech plug, or remove the barrel from the stock and soak the breech area in a bucket of hot water for half an hour.

49. When loading a patched ball, some hunters try to economize by simply spitting on the patch rather than using lube. The trouble is that a spit patch can dry out in hot weather or freeze in cold weather; both conditions result in poor shooting performance. Lube is cheap. Use it.

50. Many replica blackpowder rifles, such as the Thompson-Center Hawken, have double-set triggers. If you first pull the rear trigger, you "set" the front trigger, so that only slight finger pressure is needed to fire the round. To eliminate this two-step firing method, some hunters simply yank the front trigger, but this can destroy the sight picture and cause a miss. Use the set trigger as it was intended.

End-of-season cleaning of a blackpowder firearm is easy. Simply disassemble the breech parts and soak for an hour in gun solvent. Next, run through the barrel dry patches, then oil the barrel as you would any rifle.

Part 3

Bowhunting

Introduction

JAY CASSELL

Some tactics for hunting from a treestand, from a ground blind, in the early season, with some excellent advice from Richard Combs on using cover, attractor, natural and synthetic scents. There are also some really helpful chapters on hunting other members of the deer family (other than whitetails, by far the most popular and widely hunted deer). Elk, moose, caribou, mule deer and blacktail are all covered. If you ever get the chance to hunt any of these, do it! Aside from getting to see territory completely different from what you normally hunt, each of these deer family members has very different habits – they'll test your skills as a bowhunter. And if you are able to bring down a heavy critter like a moose or elk, well, you have really accomplished something. Not to mention filling your freezer with some of the best venison on the planet.

Pursuit of the Perfect Arrow

TODD A. KUHN

My first "bow," hand-fashioned from a heavy willow branch, was as crooked as a dog's leg. It was strung with cotton cord spooled on a wooden spindle that had been bought from a dusty mercantile in upstate New York. The cord was destined for my grandmothers clothes line.

My grandfather, an outdoorsman, squirreled away the remnant twine on a hand-hewed header in a tool shed he'd built in the early 1920s. Its roof pitched and yawed, having grown temperamental, afflicted from decades of heavy snows and legume growth that enshrined the ancient structure. Teetering on its floor joists, its once firm stance had succumbed to the roots of a neighboring balsam fir.

To a four-year-old, that shed held a unique fascination for a vivid imagination and a spirit for adventure. Rusty tin-lidded jars of milky glass held untold treasures: snelled hooks, brass buttons, curtain rings, and a pocketknife that was bequeathed to me when I turned old enough to handle it with respect and care.

On the front step of this shed, my grandfather spun dramatic tales of his adolescence and fascination with the bow. Once he finished, I'd run off with that stick and twine in hand, searching for rabid grizzlies and other foe worthy of attention from my finely-crafted weapon.

My first real bow was a Fred Bear. I remember it vividly. I stood tall in the backyard of our house

Author on an early morning South Dakota turkey hunt.

in central Florida, my lemonwood Ranger a thing of beauty in the eyes of a youthful beholder. It had its share of nicks and scratches—all badges of courage etched by mighty warriors from distant lands who too stood tall behind this bow. Mighty men of stern resolve who'd fought hand-to-hand against overwhelming odds. They'd been bloodied in battles, but had emerged victorious. The spoils of victory were theirs.

My knobby knees rattled as I strained to bend those limbs and stretch the frayed string. I longed to be a warrior, too. Years later, my mom told me the bow's patina wasn't earned in battle but from bouncing from one garage sale to the next. Nonetheless, for one scrawny kid, the seed was sown and the dream was born.

Fast Forward

Those who haven't been exposed to archery often ask me why I shoot. For me, (and hundreds of thousands of other archery fanatics), the answer is relatively simple: I love it. For us, the bow and arrow are somehow addictive, casting a spell of intrigue and romance over those who shoulder it.

I consider myself an atypical archer, shooting around sixty arrows a day on weekdays, close to double that on weekends. For anyone who drops by my house, it's immediately obvious that I'm an addict. For starters, there's a hundred-yard range in my backyard. Well-worn bag targets hang on pressure treated 4x4s, arranged incrementally and staggered at twenty, forty, sixty, eighty, a hundred yards. The ragged target faces are testament of the hundreds, if not thousands, of arrows they've been pounded with over time.

Now that I live north of the Mason-Dixon line, there are occasions when the weather turns persnickety. When it does, I move indoors to my twenty-yard range in my basement. While my wife isn't overly thrilled with the idea of arrows zinging around in the basement, I've yet to hit anything down there of real or sentimental value.

Archery has since morphed into a lifetime pursuit of perfection—perfection in the sense of

Archery is a sport of solitude, not one given to crowds.

the human machine (that of muscle, tendon, and bone) mastering the mechanical machine (the bow's components).

As I mentioned, I have a hundred-yard range. A bag target hanging 100-yards away is a daunting sight. For most visitors, it holds such intrigue. Those uninitiated to the archery game immediately assume they've stumbled on a neighborhood gun range. Once I explain the function of my range, visitors are stupefied. The first question out of everyone's mouth is "How far is it to that target down there," there being the farthest target. And so begins my sermon on the virtues of archery.

You see, archery is an odd sport—one of solitude. Not unlike that of the long distance runner. It's a sport of seclusion and relative recluse for those who choose to participate. There are no referees, no umpires, or line judges. There's no clock to run out other than when daylight recedes into night on a day's hunt. There's no overtime—no mulligan, handicaps, or cheering crowds. For team members, the uniform is a favorite brand of camouflage.

Cause for Intrigue: 100-yard backyard range.

Archery is a sport requiring discipline of the hand, head, and heart. You see, to excel you must train the hand through much repetition and discipline the head through mental calisthenics. And to *really* excel, you must possess a heart whose desire is to achieve.

In engineering terms, a compound bow is a simple machine. It's so simple, you'll be hard pressed to name more than five or so components that actually move. In contrast, an automobile has more than 20,000 moving parts. But how could this mechanical contrivance, one of such rudimentary intent—that of casting arrows downrange—possess such a degree of intrigue for countless generations of archery enthusiasts?

When the compound was first introduced, it was much maligned by traditionalists. It was, after all, like shooting a gun, right? Well, not so much. The modern compound, with its array of accessories, is at best only as accurate as the human machine throttling it.

A bowhunter's team uniform is his favorite camo brand.

While the act of drawing the bow isn't too difficult, it is extremely challenging to do it with a complete concert of an amalgam of muscles. When working in perfect concert, the mind and body achieves flawless form and the perfect shot. While most believe that is defined as a "pie-plate sized group at twenty yards," that is far from "perfection attained."

Achieving the perfect arrow with a compound is rare. No matter how good you get (or think you are), you can still improve. No archer can consistently hit the mark. In fact, it is for that reason we keep coming back to the sport. It's what draws newbies and challenges the most ardent of archers to continue improving. It is, in its purest form, a lifetime pursuit of the perfect arrow.

Making a Case for Compounds and Bowhunting

Bowhunting has experienced unparalleled growth as a sport. A sport of meager beginnings, the first "compound" was kludged together by Holless Wilbur Allen in the mid-1960s. Allen's contraption was a longbow with the limb tips cut off. He then lashed crude pulleys to the limbs and configured a makeshift string and cable system. Crude at best, the first "compound" cobbled together would be the predecessor of all that is "compound" today.

Today's modern compound is an astounding feat of mechanical engineering and materials science. From its meager beginnings in a tinkerer's crowded Missouri garage, the compound has morphed into a stealthy, powerful machine capable of clustering arrows into tight target groups at exaggerated distances.

Weird Science

With the whirlwind of advances that we witness each year, it seems these machines are only

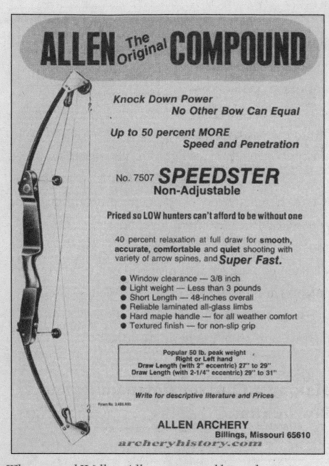

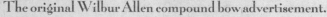

The original Wilbur Allen compound bow advertisement.

physically limited by the imagination of those who use them. Advances in materials science continue, offering compound designers more options. Solid fiberglass limbs have been replaced by limbs reinforced and lightened with space-age carbon fibers. Carbon nanotube technology will be available in compound limbs within the next year or so, offering even more stout and resilient materials from which to design and build archery components.

New copolymers blend resins with long-strand carbon fibers, and other proprietary fillers are incorporated into designs with improved performance. This slurry is molded into parts and assemblies that rival machined aircraft quality aluminum for structural integrity and are physically lighter.

Scientific advancements in coatings have contributed to the rapid advancements in compounds. Progress in fluoropolymers, aluminum surfacing science, and elastomeric coatings have led to reduced friction on bow component surfaces, as well as resistance to wear. All of these have led to more mechanically efficient bows.

Cam systems are modeled using complex computer aided design (CAD) programs that plot their efficiencies and match them perfectly to the compound's limbs, riser, string, and cable systems. These programs can actually simulate drawing and firing the compound; enabling design engineers to predict where structural inefficiencies may manifest prior to cutting the first prototyping part. These efficiencies make a more rugged bow with higher mechanical efficiencies, tighter tolerances, and top-end performance while lowering the overall mass weight.

Technology Rules

As compounds have evolved, so has the sport of bowhunting. Modern compounds are capable of harvesting animals at dizzying distances. Consequently, the evolution of accessories and hunting tactics has accelerated to keep pace with the quantum leaps in bow performance.

Early bowhunters carried compounds into the field that were capable "of astounding performance" (as one was advertised) comparable to lobbing arrows at 180 feet-per-second with a whopping 30-some foot pounds of kinetic energy. These modern-day compound predecessors limited the bowhunter to shoot distances of 20 yards or less. In stark comparison, today's compounds are capable of shooting arrows more than 360 feet-per-second and carry over 100 foot pounds of kinetic energy. Today, a bowhunter's effective range is limited only by his or her physical ability, not by his or her equipment.

Beyond the bow itself, modern archery equipment has evolved, keeping pace with the advances in compound technologies. As we will see in later chapters, sights, arrows, arrow rests, stabilizers, quivers, and other ancillary equipment have made the bow more efficient while increasing the enjoyment of shooting.

Even with a bow's impressive performance, it's still a primitive weapon. So why bowhunt? Well, the answer is quite rudimentary. For me, bowhunting presents challenges unparalleled by other forms of hunting, and the up-close-and-personal style of bowhunting adds to the challenge. Having to slip within a short physical distance from the animal for a shot also adds to the excitement. Narrowing this

Bowhunter glassing field from the confines of a ground blind fashioned from native prunings.

distance also requires the hunter to be more skilled, both in woodsmanship and in the skill required to make an ethical kill shot. Neither of these are easy nor are they learned anywhere other than in the woods or afield.

Contrast this with hunting using high-powered rifles. Please understand first and foremost that I hold no prejudice or malice toward rifle hunters. I have hunted with a rifle and loved every minute of it. However, I prefer bowhunting. That being said, rifle hunting removes some (not all) of the woodsmanship factors— those skills requiring the hunter to negotiate close to his or her target animal.

Spot-and-Stalk, Treestands, and Ground Blinds.

The need to get close presents significant challenges, depending on your method of hunting— spot-and-stalking, tree standing, or ground blinding. Getting close using a tree stand or ground blind

A bowhunter glasses from his elevated perch.

requires hours of scouting and surveillance. Each observation is used to paint a tactical picture of what a particular deer is doing.

Once this is decided, the bowhunter can formulate a hunting strategy. But it doesn't end once you're committed to a specific tree or ground blind position—the game has typically just begun. Rarely does a new tree stand or ground blind position pay off with an animal. As you hunt and observe the movement of the animals, the strategy changes and so the hunter must evolve and adapt.

The same rigors apply to spot-and-stalking. However, for me, spot-and-stalking is the most challenging (and rewarding) bowhunting technique. It demands incredible bowmanship, that of being capable of executing the most difficult of nontraditional shots. Nontraditional as in kneeling, seated, crouched, angled, leaning, and so on.

Adding to the difficulty is the need to be physically capable of closing the distance between the animal and yourself. This may include literally hours of crawling, slipping, jogging, and anything in between. All require the bowhunter to be in top physical shape.

The challenge is not all physical, however. You must also consider the mental chess match you enter into with the animal and the environment. Every move made to negotiate closer to the animal is predicated on past experiences, those that educate the bowhunter on what can be done tactically and those that cannot be done tactically but are still successful. In most cases, sadly, the animal and the environment win the chess match. Whether the animal sees you or the wind changes, tipping the animal of your approach— you lose. That's what makes it challenging.

An Economy of Scale

One of the last reasons folks are flocking to bow-hunting (both compounds and crossbows) is there simply isn't enough contiguous ground on which to rifle hunt. Larger tracts of farmlands have been split, segmented, and subdivided throughout the past few decades. The family farms of yesteryear simply don't appear with the frequency they once did. Challenging economic times have led to family farms being sold off in small plots.

So a depressed economy has led to an economy of space for hunters. These plots, sometimes as small as a few acres and once a large aggregate of property, were hunted with high-powered rifles. Now, they no longer offer a safe opportunity to gun hunt. However, in contrast, these small tracts offer ample bowhunting space. In fact, my largest deer to date was taken on a postage stamp-sized tract of land in a neighborhood that was adjacent to a farm. These small tracts often times offer protected sanctuary for mammoth whitetails.

An Abridged History of Archery

Early historical facts surrounding the bow and its development are sketchy at best. As a weapon, it dates back a few millenniums As such, much of what is surmised about early archers has been discovered

Spot-and-stalking requires an archer be able to execute shots from a number of positions.

Large expansive tracts of land are shrinking at an accelerated pace.

through archeological digs. To date, the oldest archery relics were unearthed in Africa. Arrowheads discovered in the area date back to approximately 25000 BC.

More than 5,000 miles south of Africa, scientists discovered a burial tomb in Italy containing a skeleton with a fragmented flint arrowhead lodged in the pelvis. Through carbon dating, scientists estimate that the flint dates back to 11000 BC. Ancient Egyptian drawings dating from 7500 to 5000 BC depict humans using early bows for hunting food and for warfare.

Scientists estimate that around 2800 BC, the first composite bow (built from two separate materials glued together) was made of wood, tipped with animal horn, and lashed together with animal sinew and some type of ancient glue. The bowstring was made of sheep intestines, which launched very light arrows.

In battles, early Egyptian armies utilized archers on chariots to outflank the enemy on the battlefield. The chariots and skilled archers proved too much for opposing foot soldiers and their handheld weaponry. Literature found in ancient China dated between 1500 and 1027 BC included the first description of crossbows built and used in China.

Somewhere around 250 BC, the Parthian civilization (now modern Iran and Afghanistan) mounted expert archers on horseback. These archers developed an odd but highly effective battle technique. The archers would pretend to flee the battlefied, and the enemy would give chase. Once their opponents were in bow range, they would turn around on their horses and launch arrows back at the advancing army. Historians venture that this is where the term "parting shot" came from.

Qin Shihuang, the first emperor of China, was buried with six-thousand life-sized terracotta figures, some of which modeled carrying primitive crossbows. In Rome, a fellow named Sebastian was the commander of the Praetorian Guards for the Roman Emperor. He was shot to death with arrows when his deep Christian faith was discovered in 228 AD. Oddly enough, after being shot repeatedly and assumed dead, he was found alive and nursed back to health by family friends.

Once he was again healthy, Sebastian announced his Christian faith on the steps of the Emperor's palace. The guards were ordered to beat him to death with their clubs. After he was pummeled to death, his body was recovered by friends (probably the same ones that found him the first time) and was secretly buried in the catacombs under Rome. Sebastian became known as the Patron Saint of Archers.

Infamous Mongol warrior Genghis Khan was documented as utilizing composite bows of seventy pounds of draw weight and thumb ring releases to unleash the bowstring in 1208 AD. These bows were far superior to those used by other armies. These same Mongol soldiers would wrap silk cloth under their clothing as an arrow shield. When struck by an enemy's arrow, the silk fabric wrapped around the enemy's arrowhead, impeding penetration.

In 1307 AD, the legendary William Tell refused to bow (in a display of indentured servitude) to the imperial power and was thus ordered to shoot an apple off his son's head. Legend has it that Tell had another arrow hidden just in case he injured or killed his son. If he had, he was going to kill the government official who had ordered him to shoot at his son. Naturally, as the story goes, he successfully shot the apple off his sons head, sparing the official's life, too.

In 1346 AD, the French army included crossbowequipped soldiers. Their crossbows were powerful because they were drawn via hand crank. During the Battle of Crécy, Edward III of England led his army into battle against the French. The French were defeated handily when rain moistened their bowstrings the night before the battle, causing them to stretch. The waterlogged strings misfired and broke during the battle. The French, knowing the rain would compromise their strings, had placed them under their helmets during the rainstorm. The dry strings proved deadly.

Both crossbows and compound bows were considered the most effective battle weapons throughout what is modern day now modern day Europe and Asia until the early 1500s when the musket was invented. The year 1588 AD marked the last time bows were used in warfare when 10,000 soldiers from the English fleet, armed with muskets, defeated the Spanish Armada which was armed with bows. In the latter half of the 1600s, contests of archery skill became vogue in England.

In 1545, *Toxophilus,* a book about longbow archery by Roger Ascham, was published in London. Dedicated to King Henry VIII, it was the first book on archery written in English. According to legend, Ascham was a keen archer and scholar, lecturing at St John's College, Cambridge. The premise of the book was his defense of archery as a sport fitting of the educated.

The beginning of modern archery arguably dates back to 1879 when inventor Ephraim Morton of Plymouth, Massachusetts, was granted a United States patent for his wood handled bow equipped with steel rod limbs.

Archery gained international exposure as a sport when it was included in the Olympic Games in 1904, 1908, and 1920. It was discontinued for a while, and then reinstated during the 1972 Olympics. Meanwhile, in 1934, the first bowhunting season opened in Wisconsin, and in 1937, the first modern sights were used in target archery competitions.

The patent Ephraim Morton of Plymouth received for a bow equipped with steel rod limbs marked the beginning of modern archery.

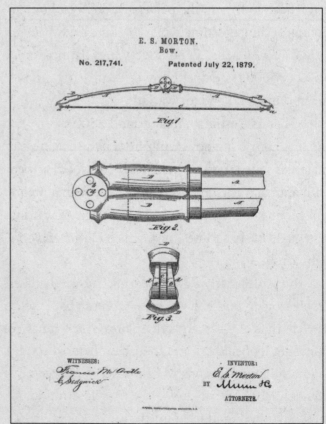

In 1939, James Easton began tinkering with manufacturing arrows out of aluminum instead of the traditional wood. By 1941, Larry Hughes won the American National Championship using Easton's aluminum arrows. Easton, of course, went on to found Easton Technical Products, which continues to be a leader in the archery industry. Easton produced its first trademarked aluminum arrows, the 24 SRT-X, in 1946.

In 1942, Earl Hoyt, Jr. founded Hoyt Archery, Co. In the decades to follow, Hoyt's company would go on to become one of the largest and most successful archery companies in the world. In 1951, Max Hamilton introduced the first plastic fletching, the Plastifletch, which marked the start of today's arrow vane industry.

Meanwhile, Fred Bear of Bear Archery introduced the first recurve bow in 1953. Previous

Earl Hoyt, founder of the company that bears his name.

bows were longbows, that is, bows with straight limbs. Bear's recurve had oddly shaped limbs that were purported to improve accuracy and increase speed.

By 1956, Earl Hoyt developed the first pistol grip bow handle, and Easton introduced his new XX75 aluminum arrow shaft in 1958. In 1966, Easton continued innovating arrows, extruding their X7 aluminum shaft. However, the largest advancement in modern archery is attributed to a Missourian.

Holless Wilbur Allen was born on July 12, 1909. Allen was a tinkerer and avid archer. Legend has it that Allen had grown tired of the drawbacks of traditional bows and longed for something faster and a bit easier to shoot.

So one day in his garage, Allen decided to cut the limb tips off his recurve and added two pulleys to decrease the amount of effort it took to draw the bow. With that, he had unknowingly launched the modern archery industry. His new prototype performed considerably better than his recurve, though it was very, very crude.

On June 23, 1966, Allen applied for a patent titled 'Archery Bow with Draw-Force Multiplying Attachments." In December of 1969, the US Patent and Trademark Office issued Allen his patent

James Easton, inventor of the aluminum arrow.

Archery icon Fred Bear in his shop.

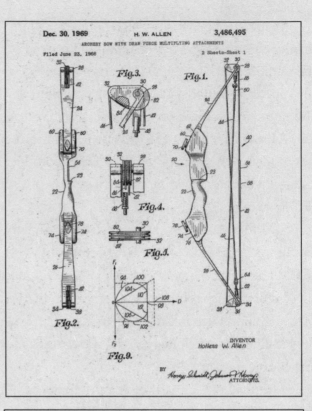

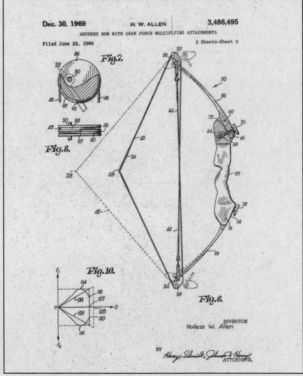

Holless Allen's original compound patent USPTO Patent 3,486,495 Archery Bow with Draw Force Multiplying Attachments

(patent number 3,486,495). Allen joined forces with Tom Jennings, a revered traditional bowyer, to begin manufacturing of the first compound bows. Tragically, Allen was killed in a two-car collision on June 28, 1979.

In 1970, the compound bow and release aid made their national debut at the United States National Archery Competition. In 1971, Andy Simo, founder of New Archery Products (NAP), invented the first flipper-style rest, increasing archery accuracy ten-fold over shooting off a padded bow shelf. Simo's NAP would grow into one of the largest archery accessory companies, offering a wide variety of over-the-top engineered shooting components. That same year, archery legend Pete Shepley founded Precision Shooting Equipment (PSE) in Illinois. Shepley, an engineer by education, worked for Magnavox as a product engineer. Shepley's love for shooting led him to tinker with different designs. The company he founded continues to lead the archery industry in innovative engineering today.

In 1974, archery legend Freddie Troncoso invented the first dual prong arrow rest, elevating archery accuracy even further over Simo's flipper-style rest. The year 1982 marked the first time compounds with actual lobe-shaped cams were introduced (previous compounds featured round wheels). The following year, Easton introduced the first carbon arrow shaft. From here on out, the timeline of improvements begin to blur as innovations are developed seemingly overnight and more archers and hunters become archery inventors and manufacturers. We will review these improvements and the history of these accessories and bows in detail in subsequent chapters.

The Arch of Innovation

Archery companies are pressured to one-up their products each year. Throughout the late 1960s and early 1970s, improvements in compound design were happening on an almost daily basis. The compound design was in its adolescence,

Precision Shooting Equipment's founder Pete Shepley, today and circa 1969.

Andy Simo, founder of New Archery Products.

and improvements came quickly and easily. These quantum leaps in technological advances continued through the eighties and nineties. The new millennium saw technological advances slow as the fundamental design of the compound had matured.

As is the case with any industry, the bowhunting industry evolved in cycles and eventually matured. The improvements that followed became incrementally smaller. For instance, solar power was harnessed and collected in the late 1 760s. Swiss scientist Horace de Saussure was credited with building the world's first solar collector in 1 767. Yet some 245 years later, our government still pitches "new" solar power green initiatives as though this idea is something new.

As a student of the game of archery, I watch each year for new and innovative improvements, yet they have appeared less frequently in the past twenty years. Admittedly, small tweaks in design are made by manufacturers and then advertised as earth-shattering new designs. In reality, these are simple twists on current designs polished with marketing hype.

For example, about ten years ago, one bow company espoused at length about their new and innovative cam system. Ads screamed of this breakthrough technology; cutting-edge science, engineering, and manufacturing melded together to form the ultimate power propulsion system for compounds. Well, truth be told, the design had been patented some twenty years earlier and never really marketed with zeal. So much for the latest and greatest innovation!

When asked where I see the industry going in the next decade, I hesitate to provide a definitive answer. This is because, barring any new discoveries in materials science, the industry and their compounds have squeezed almost every pound of power out of the compound machine.

In Chapter Two, I discuss what it will take, in purely theoretical terms, to break the mystical 400-feet-per-second barrier with a compound. I think that once you read this, you'll understand the limitations that bow designers are faced with and what it will take to break the next great barrier of compound design.

Despite its limitations, the archery game continues to intrigue many. I'm hoping you'll

find something to your liking in this book—something that will enlighten or stir your interest in bowhunting.

Up Close and Personal

Humidity drapes on you like a warm, wet bed sheet. You struggle against gravity and impending sunrise, inching your climber ever higher. Your lungs offer their objection, burning as you quietly gasp to draw your next breath of this air you wear.

Once you've reached hunting height, you settle into the pre-dawn darkness—one so dark you need a flashlight to find your pocket. Your heart pounds uncontrollably and your temples throb with each rustle of leaves and snap of a twig. The anticipation of what the first fingers of sunlight will reveal on the forest floor some thirty feet below is deafening.

The acrid smell of repellent fills your nose and stings your eyes as it shoulders itself against the airborne horde that clouds around your head and hands. The early light stretches through nature's mossy hardwood window shades, and you stare cross-eyed as a salty bead of sweat trickles down the bridge of your nose.

Resolute to remain motionless, you battle the urge to brush it aside. Finally, it drips onto the standing platform with a gentle, yet discernible "tink." Welcome to the archery opener and early season bowhunting!

This precious time is what the fraternal brotherhood of bowhunters yearns for. To the uninitiated, this ritual is remotely odd and seemingly painful. To those of the order, those with unwavering resolve, it's what defines our being. Adrenaline is our drug of choice. We are, proudly and passionately, after all, bowhunters. I invite you to join the ranks. Here's why.

Learn to Be a Better Hunter

I'm not going to beat around the bush or sugarcoat this for any number of reasons; bowhunters are the best hunters in the woods. Don't get mad at me; it is what it is. Consider the following.

Close your eyes and picture the first days of the war in Iraq. Remote images of sorties dropping smart bombs filled our living rooms and dens. We cheered as bombs dropped several miles away found their way to the intended targets.

Gun hunting, to me, is much the same. There you sit in a shooting house, covering a 100-acre agricultural field with a high-powered rifle. In stark contrast, a bowhunter has an effective range on a good day in the south of about forty yards. With this diminutive affective range, a bowhunter must get into a deer's comfort zone, into their living room if you will, to deliver a lethal arrow.

Scent Control

Being a good bowhunter means being a master woodsman. As such, many individual facets must be considered and contemplated. Scent control is exponentially more important to a bowhunter than someone hunting with a gun. Make a mistake here with the wind and it's over. Much has been written on the subject, so we won't be laver the point.

Author and his Texas Axis deer.

Stand Management and Etiquette

Stand management is another consideration that's critical. Several factors require forethought including shooting lanes, animal travel direction, sunrise and sunset, predominant wind direction, hunting height, stand orientation, and more.

Stand etiquette is also of paramount importance. There are two distinct entities here: 1) management of yourself and 2) equipment management. Managing "yourself" refers to the ability to cloak yourself from an animal's eyes and ears. This is not an easy skill to learn. Curbing or minimizing movement takes practice.

Equipment management takes time to perfect as well. This affects your ability to setup your hunting platform (stand) in the most ergonomically and efficient manner. You must know how to place your essentials about the stand to make you as comfortable negotiating them as you are driving your automobile.

Early Season Pattern ability

A distinct advantage early season bowhunters have is that deer are very predictable now. While many hunters center their season's hopes, dreams, and much-coveted vacation time around the rut,

Author with his Wyoming antelope.

rutting bucks wander willy-nilly in search of breed-able does. This search may take them miles from their core area. Conversely, during early season, whitetails fall into a predictable pattern, one that puts grounding one in your favor.

Early season deer are driven by the need to feed and rehydrate themselves. When the temperature rises, a deer's metabolism goes into overdrive. As whitetail binge on readily available nutrition, their need for water increases. This need for water makes them susceptible. Locate their water and food source and you'll find success.

Go Where No One Has Gone Before

As urban sprawl continues to cast its shadow across the landscape, whitetails are being pinched out of their natural habitat. No matter if you agree with urban expanse, more whitetails are forced to live within the confines of this urbanscape.

Hardwoods, swamps, and other intimate places of refuge are diminishing. Whitetails are squeezed like frosting through a batter bag into backyards, small woodlots, and neighborhoods. The family farm and its corn fields and CRP succumb to suburbia, concrete, condos, and corporate America.

Author with an Illinois buck shot with a muzzleloader, although he prefers archery equipment.

Author with a rare white deer—not an albino, but a completely white whitetail deer.

Significantly more opportunities to hunt pristine areas where no other hunters have been before now exist. Moreover, we're able to hunt very small tracks of lands where guns are considered off-limits. Along these same lines, the owners of these small tracts are much more likely to allow bowhunting than that of high-powered rifle hunting. In many cases, the animals are unpressured and relatively tolerant of humans and their presence.

It's Just Fun!

Admittedly, shooting a gun has its distinct appeal. The smell of gunpowder and seeing a quarter-size group at 100 yards is satisfying. However, the thrill of attaining a shaft-to-shaft arrow group at thirty yards eclipses high-powered, magnification-assisted groupings.

Archery and bowhunting can be addictive. It's a sport that can be done year-round in most cases and is one the entire family can enjoy together. There's an archery setup for any age, gender and skill level. It's also relatively inexpensive to get into. Complete combination (i.e., bow, sight, arrow rest, arrows, and quiver) kits retail for as little as $199.

How to Build a Premier Tree Stand for Bowhunting

PETER FIDUCCIA AND LEO SOMMA

TOOLS

Chain saw, hand pruning saw, pole saw	Torpedo level
Hand saw, circular saw, or jigsaw	T-square
Drill and drill bits	Socket wrench or open-end wrench set
Screw gun and bits	Miter box
Air-powered gun with 16d nails	Staple gun and ½" staples

This stand was designed to be large and sturdy, which also makes it heavy. The platform is large and strong enough to accommodate two adults quite comfortably. The archer's premier stand allows you to invite either a beginning hunter or a non-hunting companion (a child, wife, spouse, or friend) with you to experience the excitement of your hunt, or anyone you'd like to accompany as they take their deer as well. In any case, the archer's premiere tree stand provides enough platform space for two to sit safely and comfortably during the hunt.

This stand incorporates a ⅜" threaded rod that is about 3 to 4 feet long that fits around at least two tree trunks and is then secured tightly with ⅜" nuts and washers. The stand must be attached to healthy, tall trees with a main trunk of sizeable diameter (at least 18 inches). We like to attach this stand to a group of oaks. It should be set in a group of trees (at least three or four) or one very large

tree with a few good sized trunks growing from it. Although the rear platform measures 48" in width, the tree stand can be mounted to wider trees since the rear platform measures 72" wide.

This tree stand is one of our favorite designs because it is also intended to give you more height than many tree stands. The height of the platform is approximately 15 feet, when using 16-foot side rungs. Since 2x4s are not readily available in longer lengths, making the platform any higher is not possible unless you want to extend the side rungs by bolting two pieces together. However, we do not recommend that since doing this lessens the overall strength of the stand and makes it very cumbersome and heavy to move.

Although it is most definitely intended to be mounted in one spot as a longtime stand, with some time and effort it can be removed and relocated, if absolutely necessary, by removing the mounting bolts and rods used to secure it to the tree. Unlike smaller and lighter designs, however, this stand will require up to two or three strong people to move it to another location.

We try locating a fairly large group of trees so the base can be mounted to two separate limbs. This also requires you to find only a spot with one solid, good-sized tree trunk for setup.

For this stand and any other stand we build, we strongly recommend that it be constructed from pressure-treated ACQ wood, including all rails, steps, braces, and supports. If built from pressure-treated wood, this stand will withstand the weight of two adults and remain strong and durable over the years, as long as you also check it at least twice a year to make sure none of the components needs to be secured or replaced.

Dimensions: 14' high; 48" wide; 48" long; ladder steps 25" wide

Directions:

Materials: Hot-dipped galvanized nails, 16d, 10d; 1 ½", 2 ½", and 3" wood deck screws; 20d nails and/or hooks; 20' nylon rope; ⅜" x 6" carriage bolts, nuts, and washers; two 4-foot lengths of ⅜" threaded rod, washers, and nuts. Two wooden

CUTTING LIST				
Key	Part	Dimensions	Pcs.	Material
A	Ladder tree steps	1 ½" x 3 ½" x 25"	12	Pressure-treated ACQ
B	Ladder side rails	1 ½" x 3 ½" x 16'	2	Pressure-treated ACQ
C	Rear platform support	1 ½" x 5 ½" x 72"	1	Pressure-treated ACQ
D	Front platform support	1 ½" x 5 ½" x 36"	1	Pressure-treated ACQ
E	Side platform supports	1 ½" x 5 ½" x 46"	2	Pressure-treated ACQ
F	Platform decking	¾" x 48" x 48"	1	Pressure-treated ACQ-plywood
G	Ladder/Platform supports	1 ½" x 3 ½" x 62"	2	Pressure-treated ACQ
H	Ladder tree supports	1 ½" x 3 ½" x 65"	2	Pressure-treated ACQ
I	Safety railing supports	1 ½" x 3 ½" x 42"	4	Pressure-treated ACQ
J	Side railings	1 ½" x 3 ½" x 49"	2	Pressure-treated ACQ
K	Front railing	1 ½" x 3 ½" x 40"	1	Pressure-treated ACQ
L	Seat support	1 ½" x 3 ½" x 48"	1	Pressure-treated ACQ
M	Seat platform	¾" x 16" x 48"	1	Exterior plywood
N	Seat brace	1 ½" x 3 ½" x 16"	1	Pressure-treated ACQ
O	Optional deck supports	1 ½" x 5 ½" x 45"	2	Pressure-treated ACQ

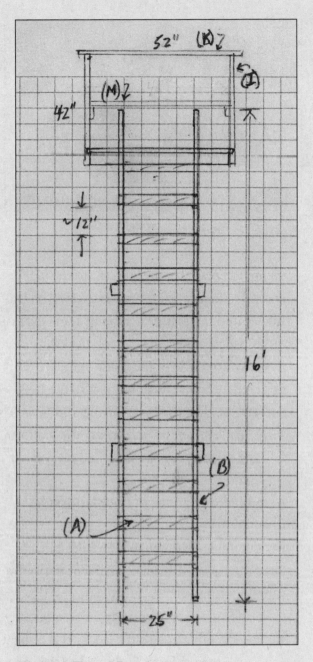

Figure 1 - Front View

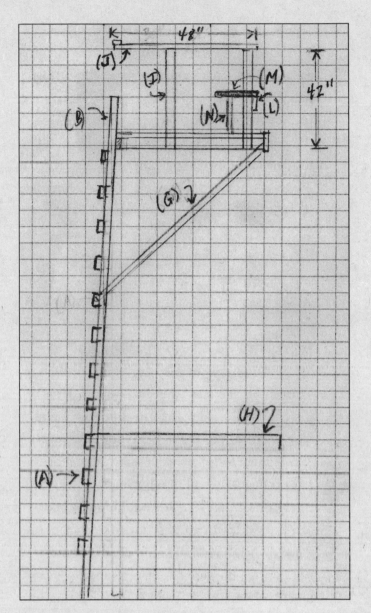

Figure 2 - Side View

wedges (1 ½" x 2" x ¼"). Camouflage burlap, three pieces 48" x 48".

Note: Measurements reflect the actual thickness of dimension lumber.

Construct the ladder. (See Figures 1 and 2)

1. Cut the ladder steps (A) to size as shown in the cutting list, using a hand saw or circular saw.

2. Lay out the two ladder rails (B) on edge on a flat surface. Measure the distance between each step, and mark the edges of each side rail. The actual spread of the steps can be made to vary, depending on your size and comfort level. You will find that the older you get, the closer together you'll want to the ladder steps. For this particular design, using steps that are 3 ½" wide, the spread between steps was made at approximately 12-13", for a total of 12 steps.

3. Secure each step to the side rails by nailing one 16d nail in the center of the step to the rail on each side. If you have access to an air powered nail gun, I highly recommend its use. It will save you lots of time and energy as you are nailing the stand pieces together and to the trees.

4. Provide additional support to the steps by using 3" wood screws. Screw two screws on each side of each step and repeat for both side rails.

Construct the platform. (See Figure 3).

1. Cut the remaining pieces (C), (D), (E), (F), and (G) to size using a hand saw or circular saw as shown in the cutting list.

2. Lay out the two side platform supports (E) on edge on a flat surface approximately 48" apart. Place the rear platform support (C) at the ends of the side platform supports. Make sure that the ends overlap the side supports by approximately 16" on each side. Secure together by nailing a 16d nail into the ends of the side platform support. Provide additional support by screwing at least two 3" screws into each end.

3. Place the front platform support (D) at the front end of the side platform supports. Secure together by nailing a 1d nail from the front into the ends of the side platform support. Provide additional support by screwing at least two 3" screws into each end. (Author's note: The ends of the side platform supports can be cut at a slight angle to make for a closer fit against the rear and front platform supports.)

4. Lay the platform decking (F) on top of the finished platform support with the rear flush with the outside edge of the rear platform support. Mark the underside of the platform to match the support frame. Using a circular saw, jigsaw, or hand saw, cut out the finished shape of the platform. Place it back on the frame and

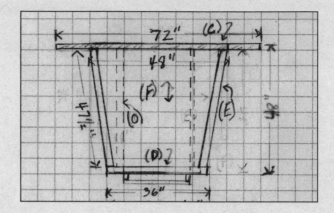

Figure 3 - Top View

secure the platform decking (F) to the side and rear platform supports using 1 ½" nails or screws into the platform support frame edges.

5. As an added option, install two deck supports in the bottom side of the platform. Place them centered 24" apart. Secure them to the front and rear platform supports using 16d nails. Use 1 1/2" nails or screws and secure the platform into the two supports.

Assemble the ladder to the platform. (See Figures 2 and 3).

1. Lay out the platform on end on a flat surface. Place the assembled ladder on the front platform support, so that the ladder extends past the top of the platform by approximately 14". Temporarily support the other end so the ladder is at a slight angle with the platform. Position it so that it sits evenly between the front platform supports.

2. Drill two ⅜" holes through the ladder side rail through the front platform support about 2 ½" apart. Repeat for the other side.

3. Secure the ladder to the platform with two ⅜" x 6" carriage bolts, nuts, and washers on each side. Slip a small wooden wedge (1 1/2" x 2" x 1/4") on each side where the bottom of the front platform support meets the ladder side rails. Tighten the nuts using a socket or open-end wrench.

4. Make sure that the ladder is at a slight angle to the platform.

5. Cut the ends of the platform angle supports (G) at 45-degree angles using a hand saw.

6. Place one of the supports against the inside of the rear bottom of the platform and the other end so it just overlaps the ladder side rail. Secure it in place by using at least three 2 ½" wood screws at each location. Repeat for the other support.

Mount the tree stand, safety railing, and seat.
(See Figures 2 and 3)

1. Pick out the location and trees you want to use for your tree stand. For this stand, we like to look for a grouping of trees with at least two solid main trunks side-by-side, which provides a sturdy footing for mounting the platform.

2. You will need at least three people to erect this stand and secure it against the tree. Have two people pick up the platform from both sides, with the bottom of the ladder on the ground. Start walking it up off the ground. The third person, on the opposite side of the trees, can pull up on a piece of rope tied to the rear platform support.

3. A fourth person could brace their feet on the bottom of the ladder to prevent it from slipping while grabbing and pulling up toward the tree by grabbing the steps. If a fourth person is not available, make sure that the bottom of the ladder is wedged up against the bottom of the tree base.

4. Now that the platform back edge is against the trees, level off the platform by moving the ladder out away from the tree trunk. Have one person lean against the front of the ladder, putting pressure on the platform against the tree trunk. If a rope was used to pull up from the backside of the trees, tie it around another tree to hold the platform in place temporarily.

5. Have one person carefully and slowly climb the ladder with a couple of 3" wood screws and a screw gun. Screw into the back of the rear platform support into the trees. For additional strength and support, use a four-foot length of ⅜" threaded rod on each end. Predrill two sets of ⅜" pilot holes on both sides of the rear platform support. The holes should be spaced at least 14" apart so they align slightly wider than both sides of the tree trunk. These holes will be used for the ⅜" threaded rods.

6. Bend the threaded rod into shape around the backside of the tree, placing both ends into the predrilled holes in the rear platform support. Place washers and nuts and tighten up the nuts until the platform is secured tightly to the trees. Repeat for the other side with another length of threaded rod.

7. Secure two of the safety railing supports (I) on one side of the side platform supports. Place the first one on the tree end and the second one at the front edge of the platform. Secure to the side platform supports using three 3" wood screws in each end. Repeat this for the other side.

8. Place one of the side railing (J) pieces on the top ends of the side railing supports (I). Secure in place by screwing two 3" wood screws into each end. Repeat this for the other side.

9. Place the front railing (K) on the front ends of the two side rails (J). Secure in place at both ends by screwing two 3" screws into the side rails.

10. There are a variety of seats that can be used for this type of tree stand. We have found that a bench seat mounted across the backside against the two trees works best and affords you the most versatility. Secure the seat support (L) against the trees at 17" from the base of the platform. This piece can also be mounted between the rear side railing supports (I).

This is how we used the threaded ⅜" rods to attach the tree stand to the tree. We repeated the process with the tree stand and the other tree next to this one.

11. Place the seat platform (M) on top of the seat support (L). Secure it in place by screwing five 3" screws into the seat support.

12. Place the seat brace (N) in the middle of the seat platform in the front. Secure it to the seat by screwing two screws into the seat brace end. Secure the other end of the seat brace into the platform decking by toenailing 2" screws.

Apply Finishing Touches

1. For additional support, secure the ladder tree support (H) approximately 50" from the base of the tree stand. One end should be screwed into the side of the ladder side rail, and the other end into the tree using at least three 3" wood screws at each location. Repeat for the other side.

2. Using several different colors of exterior spray paint (brown, black, and green), paint the tree stand steps, platform, and railing so the tree stands blends in with the trees.

3. Use hooks or 20d nails, placing several of them at heights above the platform to hang your bow, gun, and other hunting equipment.

4. Measure and cut a piece of nylon cord and secure it to the top of the platform to be used to pull up your bow or gun safely from the ground. Never climb a tree stand while holding a bow or gun.

5. For additional concealment when in the tree, wrap the platform area with camouflage burlap. Simply staple it to the top side and front railing with a staple gun.

6. Using a chain saw, hand pruning saw, or pole saw, trim out any overhanging branches or limbs from around the tree stand location.

Quick and Easy Tree Stand

PETER FIDUCCIA AND LEO SOMMA

Well, it doesn't get much easier than this tree stand design. True to its name, this one is quick and easy to set up. It requires a minimal amount of wood for the small platform and seat, and does not require any wood for the steps, since access to the platform is made through the use of screw-in steps or removable pegs. We have also shown how to build and mount a ladder with steps, for those of you who might feel more comfortable climbing a ladder rather than screw-in steps or pegs. It is so easy that Peter was able to build this one by himself (okay, not actually by himself—he needed the assistance from his amazing son Cody, and the director Katie).

We do not recommend this one for novice hunters, because the platform is small and offers very little protection in the fall. The seat is small, but large enough to be comfortable and a comfortable seat is what I would recommend that you have for this stand.

It can literally be built in less than two hours. Simply find a few tree spread apart by 3–4 feet and you are in business. We have built several of these on the farm, and tend to use them as scouter stands, erecting one of these in an area that we want to scout. If the area proves to be a good one, we tend to follow up by building one of our more solid designs.

When you find two trees spaced apart just like these two - it's easy to build your own simple tree stand. Here we are finishing the floor.

We have provided three options for the steps. Simply use the screw-in steps, removable step bolts, or—if you are looking for more comfort and ease in climbing—construct and install the ladder as described.

The removable step bolts are a great choice when constructing a platform in an area where others may be able to hunt, and you don't want to make it too easy for someone else to climb into the stand. Step bolts are also good to use if you have several different platforms, where you don't want to provide permanent steps. Simply carry the step bolts in your fanny pack, use them to climb into the stand, and remove them as you descend the stand at the end of your hunt.

These step bolts are available from E-Z KUT Hunting Products (www.woodyhunting.com).

They are easily installed using Woody's Convertible Hand and Cordless Drill bit. The step bolts, hand drill, and bit come in a convenient case. We also strongly recommend the use of the E-Z UP Climbing System when drilling the holes, installing/removing the step bolts as you climb or descend the stand. This climbing belt can be worn either right- or left-handed. It is adjustable to fit anyone in your camp, whether they are thin or on the heavy side. It is by far the most comfortable, safest, and most adjustable climbing belt we have ever used. In fact, we keep several extra climbing belts at our camp for our guests. For insurance reasons and to assure the utmost in safety for our guests, we require them to use a climbing belt when climbing any of our stands. All hunters at our camp understand and follow our safety rules. E-Z UP Climbing System belts are highly recommended when setting up or removing portable platform tree stands, as well as when hunting.

Last but not least, this climbing belt makes a great deer drag belt. Simply fasten the belt around your waist, extend the rope to the desired length, and tie the end around the head of your deer or the end of your Game Sled. Now you can walk and drag your trophy to your vehicle or camp.

CUTTING LIST				
Key	Part	Dimensions	Pcs.	Material
A	Platform supports	1 ½" x 5 ½" x 58"	2	Pressure-treated ACQ
B	Platform	1 ½" x 3 ½" x 18"	8-10	Pressure-treated ACQ
C	Seat brace	1 ½" x 3 ½" x 16"	1	Pressure-treated ACQ
D	Seat platform	¾" x 15" x 15"	1	Exterior plywood
E	Seat support	1 ½" x 3 ½" x 17"	1	Pressure-treated ACQ
F	Ladder Tree Steps	1 ½" x 3 ½" x 26"	13	Pressure-treated ACQ
G	Ladder side rails	1 ½" x 3 ½" x 16'	2	Pressure-treated ACQ
H	Safety railing	1 ½" x 3 ½" x 58"	1	Pressure-treated ACQ

Once the stand is erected, prune the trees and branches. Besides the use of an extendable pole pruning saw, we recommend the use of the E-Z KUT Hunting Products heavy-duty ratchet pruner.

Dimensions: 15' high, 18" wide, 36" long

Materials: Hot-dipped galvanized nails, 16d, 1 ½", 2 ½"; wood deck screws, 3"; 20d nails and/or hooks; 20' nylon rope; 10–14 screw-in steps; 10–14 step bolts, available from E-Z KUT Hunting Products (www.woodyhunting.com).

Note: Measurements reflect the actual thickness of dimension lumber.

Directions:

Cut all pieces to the desired lengths as shown in the cutting list, or to the proper lengths depending on your chosen tree.

Install screw-in steps, step bolts, or wooden ladder.

1. Install screw-in steps. This is the easiest approach. If you prefer to use a ladder, skip this step and proceed to Step 3, below.

    A. Depending on the desired height of the platform, screw the tree steps one at a time into the tree trunk. Space them approximately 12–14" apart or whatever makes it comfortable for you to climb.

    B. When installing the screw-in steps, make sure that you use a safety belt.

    C. To make screw-in steps a bit easier to install, I suggest that you use a cordless drill and predrill ¼" holes, approximately 1" deep.

2. Install step bolts. This approach is great when you want easy access to your stand and to deter others from using it. You install the pegs as you climb the stand, and remove them as you

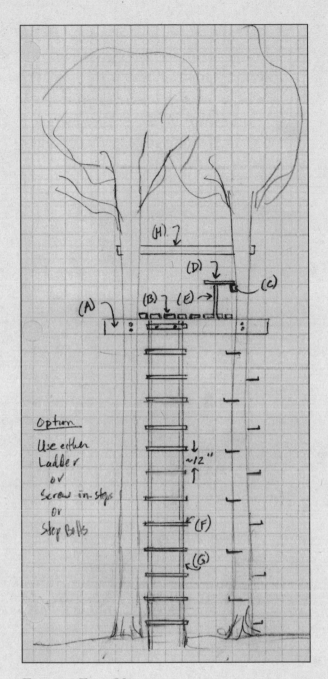

Figure 1 - Front View

descend at the end of your hunt. The steps can be installed using a hand drill with a bit or a cordless power drill with bit.

    A. Using the hand drill, place the heel of your left hand against the tree and grasp the hand drill by its collar with your thumb underneath and your first and middle fingers on the top of the collar. Angle the drill bit down slightly—this will prevent the step bolts from falling out.

B. Exert just enough inward pressure to start the drill; the drill bit is self-feeding and requires no inward pressure while drilling

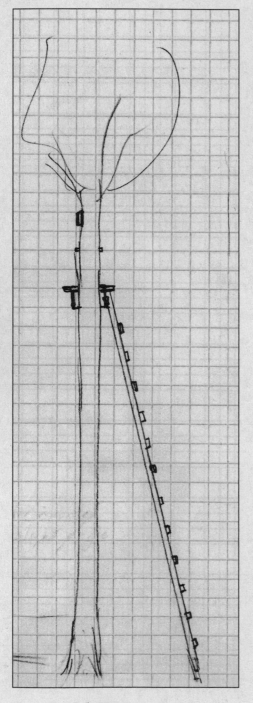

Figure 2 - Side View

the hole. Don't try to change the bit's cutting angle; the selffeeding tip is very hard and may break off. If you're not happy with the angle or placement, remove the bit and start over at a different location.

C. When the bit reaches the proper depth, it will stop drilling. At that point, you will feel the last wood chip break; continue turning the drill a few more times, then grasp the drill by the handle with the bit between your first and middle fingers and pull the bit straight out; there is no need to turn the drill backwards. Pulling the bit out will pull out the wood chips. As you climb the tree, just leave the hand drill and bit in the last highest hole to free up both hands so you can raise up your safety belt, then step up to a higher Bolt Step.

3. Slide in your Woody Step Bolts. Using the Convertible Cordless Drill Bit (these instructions are provided with kit):

A. Place the drill bit in the chuck of your cordless drill. Angle the bit downward slightly and exert slight inward pressure to start the bit cutting. Then just support the drill so the bit doesn't bind; the bit is self-feeding and will pull itself into the tree that you are drilling.

B. When the bits stops cutting just run the drill for a few seconds then pull the drill bit out of the tree. Flick out the chips from the bit flutes before starting another hole. (Authors note: As you ascend the tree it is imperative that you use a safety climbing belt. We highly recommend the use of the E-Z UP Climbing Belt available from www.ezkutpruners.com.)

C. As you are ascending up the tree just leave the drill and the bit in the last highest hole to free up both hands so you can raise up your safety belt and step up higher on the step bolts.

    D. Slide in your Woody Bolt Steps as you go up.

Construct the ladder (optional).

1. Cut the ladder steps (F) to size as shown in the cutting list, using a hand saw or circular saw.
2. Lay out the two ladder rails (G) on edge on a flat surface. Measure the distance between the steps and mark the edges of each side rail. The actual spread of the steps can vary, depending on your size and comfort level. You will find that the older you get, the closer you will want the steps to be. For this particular design, using steps that are 3 ½" wide, the spread between each step was made at approximately 12" for a total of 12 steps.
3. Install the last step at the top on the back side of the side rails.
4. Secure each step to the side rails by nailing one 16d nail in the center of the step to the rail on each side. If you have access to an air-powered nail gun I highly recommend its use. It will save you lots of time and energy as you are nailing the pieces together and to the trees.
5. Provide additional support to the steps by using 3" wood screws. Screw two screws on each side of each step and repeat for both side rails.

Construct the platform and install the ladder.
(Author's note: As you construct the platform, it is imperative that you use a safety climbing belt. We highly recommend the use of the E-Z UP Climbing Belt.)

1. Measure the distance between the outsides of the two trees at the location of the platform. For our tree stand, this distance was 48". Therefore the length of the platform supports (A) should be made 4-5" longer on each end, or in our case 58".
2. Position yourself up the tree, either on the tree steps or using an extension ladder. Get help from your partner to hold the platform in position as you mount it to the trees. When using the ladder, make sure that it is safely tied to the tree at the top step. Using two 16d nails, secure it to the tree. Use at least two 3" wood screws for additional support into the tree. For additional support, use one ⅜" x 5" lag bolt in each end and tighten using a ratchet or hand wrench. Repeat this for the other end into the other tree trunk. Using a torpedo level, make sure that the platform support is level.
3. If you have access to an air-powered nail gun, I highly recommend its use. It will save you lots of time and energy as you are nailing the pieces to the trees.
4. Repeat this same procedure making sure that both sides of the platform supports are at the same height. Place a board across the mounted support and use a torpedo level to align both sides.
5. Secure the platform (B) pieces one at a time by screwing two 3" wood screws into the platform supports at each side. They should overhand each side by 1-2".
6. Repeat Step 4 for each platform piece, spacing them apart by 1". For our tree stand, the inside distance between the two trees was 34", therefore we used eight pieces spaced approximately one 1" apart.
7. If a ladder was constructed, mount it to the stand. It can be mounted on either side of the platform. Secure it to the platform by using several 3" screws through the top back step into the base of the platform.

Complete seat and safety railing

1. Place the seat brace (C) against the side of the tree where you want the seat, approximately 17" from the bottom of the platform. Secure it to the tree by using three 3" screws into the tree.

2. Position the seat platform (D) on top of the seat brace (G) and secure it by drilling four 1 ½" decking screws into the brace.

3. Place the seat support (E) in the middle of the front of the seat. Screw the seat bottom to the seat support by screwing two 2 ½" screws in the top end of the seat support. Secure the bottom of the seat support to the bottom platform by using a 2 ½" wood screw, and toenail it into the platform. Note: Another option is to assemble the seat on the ground, hoist it up with a rope, and then install in to the tree and the platform as described above.

4. Place the safety railing (H) in place against the tree stumps approximately 40" from the base of the platform. Secure in place by using three screws into the tree on each side.

Apply Finishing Touches

1. Using several different colors of exterior spray paint (brown, black, and green), paint the platform and seat so the tree stand blends in with the trees.

2. Place hooks or 20d nails at heights above the platform to hang your bow, gun, and other hunting equipment.

3. Measure and cut a piece of nylon cord and secure it to the top of the platform to be used to pull up your bow or gun safely.

4. Using a chain saw, hand pruning saw, or pole saw, trim out any overhanging branches or limbs from around the tree stand location. (Author's note: When hand pruning we highly recommend the use of an E-Z KUT Hunting Products heavy-duty ratchet pruner.)

Early Season Tactics

BOB MCNALLY

"Deer have home field advantage. So to be consistently successful, you must have a game plan for early season."

Understand from the outset that there is no ultimate game plan for an opening day, or weekend, deer bowhunt, says Chris Kirby, head man at Quaker Boy Game Calls in New York. What works for Chris in the western part of his state in October may not work for you on the Upper Peninsula of Michigan; or for others hunting public land in Maryland; or for those on large private ranches in Texas. But that, ironically says Chris, is the basis for the best deer early-season "game plan"—being flexible.

"Like the football coach who has done his homework scouting the opposing team, planning his plays and positioning his players, a deer bowhunter can do much the same things," says Chris. "But a good, winning football coach also adapts to conditions. If the original game plan isn't working, a smart coach shifts gears, tries other options, probes the defense of the opposition, and capitalizes on those weaknesses. This is why, at half-time, good coaches suddenly can turn a game around from an apparent loss to a decided victory.

"Same is true with an opening weekend deer bowhunt. If the first half of your hunt is a bust, re-group, re-plan, and try alternate hunting sites and/or tactics."

Chris says high-traffic deer travel corridors, like creek draws, can really shine for opening-week bowhunts.

Chris says important factors on where and how a sportsman bowhunts for opening-day whitetails include: hunting pressure in the area, private or public land tapped, weather, wind, wet or dry conditions, herd density, and how close to the rut the hunt is timed.

Naturally, scouting and preparation are keys to any early-season deer bowhunt. Chris begins his preparation for opening day in spring, as early as April in New York, in setting up food plots and places bucks will feel secure through spring and summer. By opening day of bow season, Chris knows where 2½- to 3½-year-old bucks will be available to him.

"I love that first week of bow season. So many adult bucks are not spooky because humans haven't been in the woods all year," he declares. "They are easy to pattern and very susceptible to hunting and calling—even though they are a long way from coming into rut.

"Bucks will be feeding on the highest quality food available, and they'll be living close to it. I spend a lot of time hunting downwind around fields because I can see whitetails in the open areas, and if a good buck is working through, I have good success calling him within bow range. A little soft grunting or using a doe bleat will dupe a lot of two- and three-year-old bucks during that first week or two of bowhunting because they don't have a clue hunters are around. They don't come running to calling like they may later during the rut, but they're curious, and unwary, and that makes them very vulnerable to bowhunting."

As an example of how susceptible adult bucks can be, Chris relates the story of a 137-inch nine-pointer he arrowed one opening week of bow season in western New York. He was hunting with his wife, Michelle, and he put her in stands near the edges of cornfields with ripe apple trees nearby. The place was loaded with deer, and several good bucks. No other bowhunters were in the area, and Chris was careful to see that he and Michelle didn't alarm the animals.

They only hunted afternoons, for fear of spooking deer as they approached stands in pre-dawn dark. During a week of bowhunting, Michelle missed the nine-pointer twice, but the buck never knew he was being hunted—until he wandered by Chris' stand.

"Yeah. I shot my wife's buck," Chris admits, smiling. "But, hey, she had two chances, and I knew we needed to get the buck that first week or we'd likely never have a chance at getting him at all. Once other hunters got in the woods, that buck likely would have gone nocturnal, or been shot by someone else."

Chris says it's smart to be on hunt property long before the season opens, looking for tracks, trails, old rubs, and scrapes. Find choice food sources. Walk perimeters of fields. Learn where deer are feeding and bedding, walking, and getting water. You can't spend too much time afield, he insists.

Chris Kirby says it's smart to be on hunt property long before the season opens, looking for tracks, trails, old rubs and scrapes. Credit: Quaker Boy Game Calls

Late summer and early fall, deer usually are easy to pattern, especially when they haven't been harassed by hunters, says Chris. Most whitetails are feeding in crop fields, around oaks and "soft mast," clear-cuts and thick browse areas early and late in the day. In dry conditions, deer bed around thick draws with water, and they'll visit water holes for drinking. When you're driving a vehicle and glassing with binoculars, such places can quickly pinpoint spots harboring deer, which then must be walked and carefully scrutinized before stands are set. Talk to farmers and friends in rural areas to learn where they're seeing deer, and when, and be sure to ask about bucks.

It's surprising how many large bucks are downed every opening day in places where someone had regularly spotted the deer and reported it to a bowhunter, says Chris, who has a nationwide network of "field staff" bowhunters who also work for Quaker Boy, and keep him informed of such things.

"Timely good buck location information isn't always available, so when it drops in your lap, be sure to take advantage of it," says Chris. "Check out the place where such a buck has been spotted during the 'off' season, because the best chance to collect him is during the opening weeks, before he realizes hunters are on the prowl.

"You might begin a day bowhunting such a known buck at the site where he'd been regularly seen, which frequently is a field corner or field ditch bottleneck. Then, knowing plenty of hunters are afoot, you might move at mid-day to a funnel or neck-down area leading to the closest   thicket or potential bedding area.

"Be sure to have several different hunting locations pinpointed, and stands set, at least a week before opening day. If you have only one area to

Choose a stand that overlooks a number of different trails in a travel corridor where pre-season scouting has shown plenty of deer activity. Credit: Quaker Boy Game Calls

bowhunt, have several different stands hanging in various places, affording good chances to see and tag deer according to wind direction and the 'temperament' of the animals—spooky, calm, in pre-rut, etc.

"I 'grade' the spots I can bowhunt opening weekend, and I only tap the very best locations when conditions are absolutely perfect. Frequently, I hunt the "least good" spots first, particularly 'peripheral' areas if hunting conditions are less than ideal. It can be wise to save the best interior or 'core' spots for when weather and wind conditions are perfect, especially on large tracts of private land."

However, Chris insists that if you have only a few days to hunt, or if you only have the opening day or two to be in the woods, or if you hunt public ground, by all means, hunt the best spots you know. But be certain your approaches to stands are wise, the wind completely favorable. Chris would rather not hunt the hottest of hot spots if the wind is wrong, when he might stumble in to it and alert bucks he's in their neighborhood. You just might be able to squeeze in another day of hunting later or, perhaps, offer the spot to your best friend or brother when conditions improve, says Chris.

"Keep in mind that opening weekend is a great 'first-strike' opportunity to tag bucks lulled into believing the woods are safe—their sole domain," explains Chris, who is nationally known as a game-calling expert. "An open bean field may never have a daytime mature buck in it after the first week of the season. But opening morning, there could be a 'Booner' standing on the field edge feeding, completely oblivious to the danger soon to be around him."

Chris says high-traffic deer travel corridors, like creek draws and overgrown field fence lines, really can shine opening week, when animals are pushed by hunters on the move. That's particularly true in states where there are a lot of archers, like New York, Michigan, Wisconsin, and Pennsylvania. Choose a stand that overlooks a number of different trails in a travel corridor where pre-season scouting has shown plenty of deer activity. Use quality optics, and stay constantly alert.

Sometimes the best places for opening day bowhunting are on border edges of private land, says Chris. One of the best opening day bow stands he ever had was on a large farm that abutted a public hunting area. The state hunting spot was crawling with archers opening morning. But deer that had been living in the WMA quickly vacated the place, heading to cover in surrounding private land holdings.

Chris hunted the place twice, and both times collected nice bucks by mid-morning. He'd found a fence line separating the WMA from the farm, and there were two overgrown creeks that bisected the fence. Deer traveled the cover of the creeks, crossing the fence to the comparative safety of the private farm. A pair of large trees within easy bow range of both creeks made the spot a choice archery stand.

Often on large tracts of private land, where there's low hunting pressure, deer pushed into core areas from adjacent property go right back into their normal routines. Set stands on oak ridges overlooking trails and draws, check field corners and edges, and be sure to have stands set near food sources.

A good game plan for opening-week bowhunting is to get on stand early near a property "peripheral" area or a "funnel" close to a deer-bedding zone, Chris advises, and to stay on stand as late as possible. Bring a daypack with plenty of food and water, making sure you have the right clothing and accessories to make your stay comfortable.

If you've got to get down and move around, walk at mid-day and do a little slow scouting into the wind. Use binoculars often, says Chris, and get back on stand by early afternoon—perhaps a different spot overlooking a feeding area where you've seen deer.

The next day should be a repeat performance, hopefully on different stands, so as not to "over-hunt" a spot, and to help learn what deer are doing at various places on your hunt property.

"Finally," says Chris, "be positive about hunting opening week. Believe you're going to tag a book buck. Sure it can be hot, and bugs can be awful. But it's one of the best times to be in the woods, because big bucks don't yet understand they're being hunted.

"Stay alert. Start hunting early, quit hunting late. Scout, glass, and don't give up. Not ever. It'll pay off—big time!"

Ground-Blind Bucks

BOB MCNALLY

"Tree stands are great, but sometimes you 'gotta get down' to get deer."

Years ago, before the enlightened age of tree stands, whitetail bowhunters routinely took game from terra firma. In fact, some of the biggest bucks arrowed by such legendary bowhunters as Fred Bear and Howard Hill, were taken from the ground. Those days, however, are mostly gone for modern whitetail bowmen. Today, it's likely 95 percent of all deer taken by archers are ambushed from the treetops.

Contemporary bowhunters are so habitually tree-stand oriented, that even when a great hunting spot is found, an archer will not even try to take a deer from the place unless there's a tree to accommodate a stand nearby.

That's a major mistake, though, says legendary longtime Michigan bowhunter Claude Pollington. Plenty of prime spots for bushwhacking a buck have no trees suitable for setting stands. Furthermore, in some locales bucks are so accustomed to bowhunters working from treetops, they are less likely to spot a well-made, well-camouflaged ground blind or "pit."

Effective ground blinds can be simple makeshift "hides" constructed from down timber, stumps and treetops. Great blinds also can be made from other materials, including old, heavy-duty Army blankets. You build a wooden frame, nail

Complete head-to-toe camouflage clothing is even more important for low-level bowhunters than it is for tree-stand archers.

olive-drab blankets to it, then cut several one-foot square "shooting ports" out of the fabric at a level equal to a stool sitting position inside the blind. Finally, pile brush and tree limbs around the outside of the blind to make it blend with natural surroundings at the spot you've chosen for your ambush. Pine straw, and the boughs of fir, cedar and pine are especially good for ground-blind camouflage because they are very aromatic, which helps mask human scent.

Claude is expert in building semi-permanent ground blinds from weathered scrap lumber, because it blends well with wooded terrain. In Michigan, where for years it was illegal to hunt deer from tree stands during the firearms season, such wooden ground blinds, affectionately called "coops," are very popular with sportsmen. Positioned on hillsides, field edges, near deer crossings, fire breaks and power lines, well-made coops, are extremely comfortable and provide both overhead cover and warmth against biting Midwest wind, snow and sleet. A good coop has a couple of shooting holes or "slots," but is otherwise solid, so hunter movement is mostly concealed from game.

Most coops on private land are semi-permanent, and in Michigan, hunters are so accustomed and confident hunting from them that during archery season, they use the same ground-level shooting houses—often with remarkable success. Claude has taken countless big bucks from coops with a bow.

"Bowhunters should concentrate building ground blinds in areas where deer are comfortable and at ease with their surroundings," says Claude, who is widely known in his deer-rich state as the "Whitetail Wizard." "Often, the biggest bucks live in the very thickest, heaviest cover. Frequently those places are alder bottoms, marshes, and swamps that have few large trees for stands. This type cover provides protection for deer, and not many hunters—including bowmen—venture into them because there are no places to 'hang' a stand. But building a coop shooting house from weathered lumber well ahead of season in such places can be the ticket to a bowhunter's biggest buck."

Claude notes that when building a coop, it should be wide enough and high enough to allow for plenty of bowhunter movement. Moving around quietly in the closed-in space with an arrow nocked on a bow is not easy, especially when a good buck is nearby. If there's a coop roof, be sure there's ample height for top bow-limb clearance.

A good bowhunting coop has three or four shooting ports, and it's important to make the holes big enough, roughly twelve inches by eight inches. The rectangular holes should give the hunter enough of an opening to properly aim his bow and loose his arrow.

One vital consideration, Claude emphasizes, is that a ground blind must blend in with adjacent terrain features. A good example of this, and of how being adaptable is key to ground-blind deer-hunting success, is this story about Colorado hunting guide Judd Cooney.

Judd was bowhunting with a pal for Alberta's giant bucks, and they located two Boone & Crockett animals that seemed impossible to ambush. The deer emerged every afternoon from a small strip of woods

Small "shooting holes" are best for ground blinds.

and walked into a cut hay field to feed. Prevailing wind was such that no approach could be made to the spot to hunt in the woods. A standard ground blind would have stood out like an oak in the Sahara because of the close-cropped hay field.

But a farmer had rolled the cut hay into huge bales, and that gave Judd the idea of making a ground blind the same size, shape, and color as the bales. He constructed a round frame with chicken wire and wove hay into the frame so it looked exactly like a real bale—except it was hollow inside, with plenty of space for Judd's bowhunting buddy.

They positioned the fake bale near the woods strip and gave the bucks several days to get used to it. The first afternoon Judd's pal occupied the hollow bale blind, he arrowed one of the massive bucks; its rack easily scored big enough to make the Boone & Crockett books.

A pit blind is another exceptional way to disappear from a deer's watchful eyes, and it's become one of Claude's favorite whitetail hunting sites. A pit can be beneficial because it helps contain hunter scent. The rigorous labor required to dig a human-size hole in rocky or frozen ground may temper your passion for whitetail bowhunting, or at least this method. Still, at times nothing is better than a pit to bushwhack a buck.

While the best pits are deep and roomy, even ones that are just knee-high help conceal a hunter from wary bucks. Such a shallow hole allows a bowman to at least sit down on the pit rim, which can be quite comfortable, particularly if a camouflage cushion is used as a seat. Comfort is something ground-blind hunters never should overlook when long hours of still, silent waiting are on tap, says Claude, since the slightest movement can be spotted instantly by a wary whitetail.

"Be sure to ring the top of a pit opening with brush, tree limbs or corn stalks to conceal your head when peering out of a foxhole," advises Claude. "But make sure such cover is far enough away from you in a pit to allow quiet bow movement. Opening a few 'holes' or ports in natural cover is the ideal way of concealing bowhunter movement during shooting. This is much better than having to come up-and-over brush or tree limbs, or leaving wide 'lanes' in cover through which to shoot. A hole with a top, bottom, and sides of brush and limbs offers the most concealment to an archer while still allowing an arrow to travel accurately to its mark."

If a ground blind is made of natural materials, be sure it matches surrounding features. Claude once hunted with a guy who couldn't figure why he hadn't seen any deer from his ground blind while everyone else in the hunting group was not only seeing deer but getting shots at game. Finally, Claude

Your face, hands, and shiny bow-and-arrow parts are details deer don't overlook, so you shouldn't either.

accompanied him to his hunting spot and quickly saw the problem. It was late fall and all the leaves had dropped from trees. So the prominent cover was bare branches and lifeless looking sticks. The guy had made his blind near two well-used deer trails, but he'd used dark green fir and cedar boughs—as out of place on the barren Michigan oak ridge as a hound at a cat show.

Complete head-to-toe camouflage clothing is even more important for low-level bowhunters than it is for tree-stand archers. Faces, hands, and shiny bow-and-arrow parts are details deer don't overlook, so you shouldn't either. And gloves and masks not only offer concealment, but also protect hunters from mosquitoes and other insects, allowing them to sit longer, with less movement—and eliminating any need for odorous bug repellents that deer can detect from long range.

There are dozens of great camo patterns on the market; just match the hues to your hunting area. If you're in dark, leafy cover, wear dark, leafy camo. If your blind is pine and cedar, mimic it with your camo clothing. Same for cactus and sage, bare branches, autumn leaves, even snow. Blend in with the blind and "break" your human silhouette.

Even with perfect camo, move a bow for a shot only when an animal is looking away, has its head down to feed, or is in cover, its view of you blocked. Should a deer look directly at you, freeze. Some bowhunters never look directly into the eyes of a deer that's looking at them. When they're being "eyeballed" by a nearby deer, they shut their eyes, believing the animal can see the unnatural glassy reflection of their human eyes.

Sometimes a "Mexican stand-off" with whitetails can last many long minutes, and holding a bow at the "ready" position can be very tiring. Resting a bow's lower limb wheel on the ground

can save the day while you wait for a good shooting opportunity. Be sure to clear the inside of a blind of noisy leaves and twigs; resting a lower bow limb wheel quietly on a soft ground cloth or carpet remnant also makes sense.

"Do not sit flat on the ground in a blind," insists Claude. "Sitting on a stump, log, or big rock is better, because it's easier to raise and draw a bow with very little movement. When sitting flat on the ground, an archer must rise to his knees to raise a bow high enough to shoot. This much movement not only is quickly spotted by deer, but the more movement, the more likely the chance for noise. Sitting on a plastic bucket turned upside-down is good, as this affords plenty of lower bow-limb clearance when a shot is made. A dove stool is a perfect ground-blind seat, and I like camouflage lightweight folding aluminum-cloth ones that have a carrying strap. Folding camp stools also work well. They're easily packed to a hunting location, are silent to use, and plenty comfortable. Some even have large pockets for packing snacks, water, and bowhunting accessories."

Bowmen should be conscious of sounds their clothing makes inside blinds. Soft cotton and wool are great for close-quarters ground-blind hunting, while scratchy nylon and some Cordura products, rubbed against brush or limbs, are not so "quiet." Even the slightest sound at ground level alerts mature whitetails.

"The best-made, most camouflaged blind—one even thoroughly doused with deer cover scent—must be positioned correctly in relation to the wind for even a meticulously scent-free bowhunter to be consistently successful," Claude states. "A buck that's three, four or five years old has had plenty of experience with humans, and he's not about to make a mistake regarding wind

"The best-made, most camouflaged blind—even one thoroughly doused with deer cover scent—must be positioned correctly in relation to the wind for even a meticulously scent-free bowhunter to be consistently successful," states Claude.

direction. The wind is a whitetail's greatest ally, and he knows it. So when you're building a ground blind near a trail, creek crossing, scrape or rub line, take careful note of the wind.

"As a general rule, the best place to build a ground blind is crosswind, and slightly downwind, of the place you expect to see deer. If you build a blind directly downwind, a deer will nail you with his nose as he moves toward the place you plan to make your shot. The better position is crosswind from the direction you anticipate deer moving into the area. Even then, be clean, wear full camo, use cover scents, and don't move a muscle until time to shoot."

As always, in an area where wind direction is variable, it's often smart to build more than one blind, then hunt the best spot according to wind direction. Over the last few years, some excellent commercially made portable ground blinds have been developed. They are lightweight, extremely portable, and set up in seconds, which allows a bowman to place a blind wherever it's advantageous on a particular day. Such blinds also save hunters the time and effort of gathering brush, limbs, logs, etc.

One type of commercial blind that works well is simply a length of camo material, with a few stakes that hold it up just high enough to conceal a bowhunter sitting on a stool. It's rather short, with no roof; the camo material, about 16-feet long, attaches to five small poles which can be easily pushed into the ground. This blind can be set up in less than two minutes, rolls tightly into a shoulder-pack, and is extremely lightweight—and that portability is why it's used by many turkey hunters. Also, it's available in five camo patterns and a realistic leaf-type cloth that, from 10 feet, looks like the real thing.

Portable blinds resembling mini-tents have become well entrenched with deer bowhunters. Most have roofs or tops of some kind, four to six sides, and the best models set up and break down fast, and fold easily into compact carrying cases. Many such blinds have no floor, but the good ones are comfortably large and have zip-out windows for easy shooting. You remove the blind from its carrying case, give it a good shake, and in seconds you have a camo tent-blind within bow range of a trail, scrape or other hunting spot, preferably nestled into natural foliage. Just unzip a window or two for shooting on the side game is expected.

It's tempting to sit in such a blind near open windows, watching for game and believing arrow clearance is optimum. But Claude advises sitting on a dove stool or bucket well back from open windows, in the shadows so that bow movement is less visible to deer, and there's less chance of any blind interference when you're drawing a bow or loosing an arrow.

Ground blinds may never replace tree stands for bowhunting whitetail deer. But there are times and places where an archer who stays on terra firma will have a better chance at tagging a buster buck than the one who spends his time searching for suitable trees to "hang in."

"Let deer sign tell you where to set your ambush, not the availability of tree stand sites," says Claude.

ELK

JUDD COONEY

Majestic or magnificent would have to be the words that aptly characterize a bull elk, with his head thrown back, colossal, rapier-tined, ivory-tipped, mahogany-brown antlers caging his heaving chest and flanks. His high-pitched bugling whistles and deep, growling grunts echo and reverberate across the valleys and float up the steep mountain slopes. Add a landscape of frost-sparkled meadows corralled by shimmering gold-leaved aspens, intense green spruce, and pine against a backdrop of snow-capped mountain peaks, and an azure sky flawed only by puffs of clouds, and it's understandable why thoughts of bowhunting the wily wapiti run rampant in almost every bowhunter's aspirations.

If I really and seriously had to choose a single critter (*heaven forbid*) that is the ultimate bowhunting challenge year after year, and one that I never tire of bowhunting, it would be the bull elk. Elk are large, tough, intelligent beasties with survival instincts unrivaled by any other hoofed big-game animal. A mature bull can sport a set of antlers liable to give even an experienced bowhunter the adrenaline rush of a lifetime and the shakes and shimmies of a Greek belly dancer. Best of all, elk meat is about as delectable a table fare as there is, and there's lots of it.

Elk were originally foothill animals that roamed most of northern and western North America, but due to their size, herd instincts,

availability, and edibility, the vast herds were quickly decimated by market hunting and the survivors were forced into the most remote reaches of mountains to escape annihilation. Today, through wise and often lucky game management, the wily wapiti have expanded their range and numbers and have been reintroduced to many former haunts where they were previously eradicated.

Elk are broken down into three distinct subspecies groups, the largest and most extensive being the Yellowstone elk, which was reclassified in the mid-2000s as the American elk as far as the Pope and Young and Boone and Crockett record books are concerned. The Roosevelt or Olympic elk resides in the rain forests of Washington, Oregon, and southern British Columbia, Canada. The Tule elk, whose range is limited to the confines of California, is found in such limited numbers, with equally restricted hunting access, that it is not listed as a separate category in the Pope and Young record books, although Boone and Crockett does have a separate Tule elk category.

The American elk range extends from British Columbia, Idaho, and Nevada eastward through the Rocky Mountains and into the prairie states of North and South Dakota and Nebraska. American elk have been transplanted back into their native haunts as far east as Pennsylvania and southward to Oklahoma. Poaching and lack of the huge tracts of land needed have been the major drawbacks to some of these

Elk country is immense. Your toughest challenge will be conquering the steep and heavily forested land where these majestic animals live.

transplanted herds expanding fully and re-establishing themselves. For the most part, these transplants are holding their own, and in some cases the increasing numbers allow for limited hunting seasons.

American elk are by far the most numerous and widespread members of the wily wapiti family and the most sought after by the bowhunting fraternity. One would think that with hunters, from the earliest native Americans to the current compound-wielding bowhunters, pursuing them, the trophy quality and size of these majestic mountain dwellers would have declined somewhat. Nothing could be farther from the truth. Under modern game management and the wily wapiti's propensity for self preservation and reproduction, American elk are more numerous than ever, and the trophy quality of bulls in many areas has never been better.

I've often heard hunters claiming to have killed a 1000-pound bull elk, but a bull that size is a rarity.

One fall on a private ranch in the south San Juan mountains of Colorado, I guided Billy Ellis to a huge 6x6 bull that about did us in packing it out. When we got the four skinned quarters to the processor, minus the legs, head, hide, and antlers, the quarters weighed a whopping 449 pounds.

It's usually figured that the four quarters without hide, head, and legs will weight approximately 50 percent of the live weight. That would put this bull's weight at 898 pounds, which stood as the heaviest four quarters weighed at that processing plant for many years and may still be the record.

Most mature bulls weigh 600 to 800 pounds live, with large mature cows in the 500–700 pound class. You don't really appreciate an elk's size until you get one down three miles from the truck on a hot September morning and wonder how the heck you're going to haul it out before it spoils or gets fly blown. Unfortunately, many elk hunters are not prepared for this chore and end up losing some of the best eating on hooves.

An elk's sense of smell will rival or exceed that of any big-game animal, including a mature whitetail buck. I've had a herd of elk wind me from half a mile away and not even hesitate in getting the heck out of Dodge. Their eyesight is superb, as is their hearing. Elk have the brain capacity and honed survival instincts to instantly add all the input from their superlative senses into an escape and evasion plan that often leaves bowhunters wondering "wha' happen?" Throw in the elk's tremendous strength, stamina, and penchant for covering miles of rugged terrain with ease, and you have a game animal worthy of the best of your bowhunting efforts.

Elk are herd animals, especially during the fall breeding period or rut. Like other antlered big game, the bulls of summer remain alone or in small bachelor herds while their velvet-covered antlers grow to fighting size. An elk's antler growth is one of nature's most phenomenal occurrences. The bulls don't shed their antlers until February or March, and their awesome headgear is fully grown by August. The only other cells that divide and grow as fast as elk antler cells are cancer cells, and much cancer research has evolved from the study of fast-growing elk antler cells. Asian people have long praised the soft velvet-covered elk antler as a cure-all for many things and as a powerful aphrodisiac.

In August, as the bulls' testosterone levels rise and their antlers harden, they move into pre-rut mode by rubbing the velvet from their antlers, fighting trees and brush, and sparring with each other to build up neck and shoulder muscles. The larger bulls move in and start hanging out with small groups of cows and calves and asserting their dominance over any bull that approaches their harem. Their cow-attracting and competitor-intimidating bugling and grunting activity increases and peaks somewhere between September 15 and October 1 in most elk areas of the West.

It's a no-brainer that calling in a belligerent, bellowing bull elk and arrowing it at point-blank range is the epitome of the elk-bowhunting experience. However, elk are out and about 24 hours a day, 365 days a year, and the peak of the rut isn't the only time to bowhunt them. In fact, it may be the toughest time to kill an elk.

Early-Season Elk-Ambushing Tactics

Archery season in most of the elk states generally opens before the bulls are fully into rut mode, filling the countryside with their high-pitched challenges and announcing their whereabouts to anything with ears. Hunting silent elk is a whole different ball game from bowhunting bugling bulls. The weather during the early part of the archery elk

Elk will retreat to the deep timber shortly after day break. You may find them in small clearings in basins where the hunting pressure is light or non-existent.

season is generally on the warm-to-hot side, and this can be the key to getting your arrow and a bull in the same place at the same time.

Over the years, my clients and I have had a much higher success rate per elk encounter when hunting from ambush than using any other method. During the early season, elk wallows, waterholes or springs, natural mineral licks, and travel routes are deadly places to set an ambush. Elk are not quite as habitual in their daily movements as some of the other species of big game, but they do have favorite haunts that they use regularly enough to make patiently hunting them a worthwhile endeavor.

Pit blinds have long been one of my favorite methods of ambushing elk. Whether they're in an oak brush thicket where there aren't any trees big enough for a tree stand or in an open meadow at the edge of a wide-open pond, pit blinds are the most deadly elk tactic in the book.

Several years ago, I was bowhunting with outfitter Dick Ray in New Mexico in the early season, when it was hot and dry. I'd passed up several small bulls and called in a nice 5x5 for one of Dick's hunters but still hadn't found the one I wanted. I had several days left to bowhunt when Dick told me that some ranch hands building fence on a high bench covered with dense oak brush motts had seen a 6x6 bull watering two afternoons in a row at a tank dam in the middle of a wide-open pasture. According to them, the bull came from one direction one late afternoon and the opposite direction the following afternoon.

The next afternoon, one of Dick's guides and I drove to the area and found the waterhole pounded by elk tracks. There wasn't a speck of cover within 100 yards of the small pond. We finished the three-hour chore of digging a spacious pit blind into the face of the dam and camouflaging it with oak brush and were settled in its shaded interior by 5:00 p.m. At 5:30, I arrowed a huge 6x6 that walked out of the oak brush 200 yards across the meadow and came straight to the waterhole without giving our blind a second glance. I'll trade three hours of digging for a bull like that any day.

Pit blinds can be used almost anywhere you can get a hole in the ground. Elk are accustomed to danger approaching or appearing above ground level, and they tend to overlook things below eye level. A few years ago, my secretary, Dawn Walker, bowhunted a pit blind we'd dug 25 yards from a spring in an open valley within a mile of my house. She wasn't going to be fussy and intended to take the first legal elk within bow range. The first afternoon she sat in the blind, a half dozen elk charged off the oak brush slopes to water just before dark. There were several cows and a nice 4x4 bull drinking 20 yards from her, and she couldn't shoot because there was a spike bull (protected in Colorado) standing *five feet* away, right in the shooting lane, and another just a bit farther out. They shuffled around in front of her, almost kicking dirt into the pit, completely unaware of her presence. The others finished watering and wandered into the meadow to feed and then moved in to water. The next afternoon, she arrowed a hefty yearling and had to call on reinforcements to help her get it out.

A pit blind is about as simple and easy an ambush site as you can get. When possible, I dig them to the same dimensions as covered in the antelope chapter and usually cover them over entirely with sagebrush, tumble weeds, oak brush, or pine boughs, so the bowhunter is sitting in the dark. An elk's sense of smell is acute, so choosing a pit blind location downwind is very important. However, I've found that scent control is much easier hunting out of a pit blind. Unless there is a stiff breeze, human scent tends to hang in the cooler confines of the pit. The surrounding covering, sprayed liberally with scent eliminator or scent killer or doused with a potent elk scent, helps dilute or cover the dreaded human odor. On several occasions, my clients and I have had elk munch on the leaves and branches covering a pit blind. Talk about a heart-thumping encounter.

The other end of the elk-ambushing spectrum is the use of tree stands. I've had clients take a number of elk from tree stands over wallows, springs, mineral licks, and well-traveled trails over the years, and they can be one of the most efficient and effective methods of bowhunting elk. Elk won't hesitate to look up, so movement, or the lack thereof, is a crucial factor.

A lightweight, portable tree stand is an essential item if you're planning an elk bowhunt. Leave the climbers at home, because most western tree types have too many limbs to make them usable, and even though they can be used on quaking aspen, care should be taken to keep your safety belt in constant use because the spongy, soft bark of an aspen can peel out from under the stand and give you a rough ride to the ground.

Background is extremely important when putting up a tree stand for elk. Elk are well-tuned to the dangers associated with the human shape, and getting skylined is a sure way to end your elk bowhunt on a sour note. I've had elk taken from tree stands in cedars and junipers that were only eight feet off the ground because the almost solid background and dense shadows made the bowhunter invisible to the elk. Height isn't nearly as important as good background cover and concealment.

There have been a lot of pros and cons written about how effective it is to bowhunt elk wallows, and there is no pat answer that covers all conditions. I've taken elk bowhunting well-used wallows and spent many fruitless hours sitting over a seemingly "hot" wallow without seeing hide nor hair of a wily wapiti.

Elk are liable to use a wallow at any time of day or night, and there doesn't seem to be a peak time to hunt at one. I've found that during hot and dry weather, bowhunting wallows late morning and early afternoon seems to pay off about as much as any other time. Locating and hunting over a well-used fresh wallow during mid-day is a good way to spend time between your early morning spot-and-stalk or bugling hunt and your late afternoon hunt.

Spot-and-Stalk Elk Bowhunting

Spot-and-stalk bowhunting is the second most productive method of putting an elk on the ground with a bow and arrow and can be a real test of your bowhunting skill and perseverance.

Elk are big animals and live in big country, and this combination is what gives spot-and-stalk

If you hunt public land, let other hunters move the elk around during the mid-day hours. Keep posted during your lunch break where you can glass an area where elk may show.

hunters nightmares. I've heard it said that 90 percent of the elk live in 10 percent of the country, and while that may not be true under all circumstances, it's a pretty fair summation of the situation. Most first-time elk hunters can't comprehend the vastness of elk country and the ease with which these long-legged ungulates roam their home habitat.

Many whitetail bowhunters try the same tactics on elk and come up short because they don't cover enough ground. My spot-and-stalk philosophy is to get into the area I intend hunting in the pre-dawn darkness and try to cover as much ground as I can until I locate elk, either by sound, fresh tracks and droppings, or smell.

Since I am very careful to take advantage of the slightest mountain breeze and hunt with the wind in my favor as much as humanly possible, I can often smell the sweet, licorice-like smell of elk before I see them. I've had clients follow me around for days without realizing that I'm constantly checking the wind with my trusty powder bottle filled with talcum powder. Sometimes all it takes is a small shift in direction to keep the wind in your favor, and it's senseless to try stalking or still-hunting elk if they have the slightest chance of smelling you.

Many times I've glassed elk that spooked at a hunter's scent while the hunter was a half-mile or more away. Doesn't take much human scent to pollute the pure mountain air to the point of spooking a hunter-shy elk. The problem is seriously compounded if you're bowhunting when the elk are herded up and the number of eyes, ears, and noses is multiplied. Keep this fact in mind on your elk hunts: *When the sun goes up, so does the wind, and when the sun sinks, the late afternoon breeze flows downhill.*

I'm always amazed when a client shows up for an elk hunt and doesn't have a good pair of binoculars. Many bowhunters feel binoculars are for use in wide-open country and from a stand, but I make constant use of them when spot and stalk or still-hunting through the woods. I glass every nook and cranny that might harbor a hidden elk, looking for anything that could possibly be the ear, nose, rump patch, or antler tip of a hidden elk.

Even binoculars are not infallible when it comes to dealing with elk. One fall, I was poking along through a dense patch of thick downfall timber when I spotted a light patch of color against the dark background. I froze in mid-stride and glassed the patch for a full 30 minutes, trying to tell whether it was an elk or a patch of sunlight against the rotted end of a stump. A dozen times I decided it had to be the side of a bull elk and two dozen times I decided it was the end of a stump. After half an hour, my eyes burned like someone had poured salt in them as I tried vainly to find ears, antlers, or anything that resembled part of an elk. Finally my patience gave out and I convinced myself that no self-respecting elk would lay there that long without some hint of movement. Even then I wasn't convinced and decided to backtrack and approach from a different angle. Hah! The wily elk was more patient than I

was, because the instant I took a step backward, a 5x5 bull crashed out of its bed and vanished.

Don't waste your money on a small cheapie set of pocket binoculars, because they'll just cause you grief and maybe cost you a trophy elk. Binoculars are a once-in-a-lifetime purchase, so get a second job, save your money, and buy the best set of binoculars you can afford. For elk hunting, I prefer a set of quality medium-sized 7x42 or 8x32s. These glasses are powerful enough for long-distance glassing but gather plenty of light for early-morning and late-afternoon glassing, and they are especially useful in dark-timber situations. Don't just buy them and carry them in your fanny pack or daypack. Get used to using them regularly. They can make a big difference in the success or failure of your spot-and-stalk elk hunt.

High-country, above timberline, spot-and-stalk bowhunting is the epitome of the elk-hunting challenge. There's no way an elk hunt in such country can be anything but successful, even if you never kill an elk.

Fortunately or unfortunately, there are no figures on just how many spot-and-stalk elk hunts are blown by impatience. Judging from my own experiences, I'd say the figure is above the 90 percent level. It seems no matter how long you wait, it's not long enough. If you err, do so on the side of patience.

Spotting elk in the high country can be easy or difficult, depending on how smart you work your spotting. Trying to pick out elk in the early morning or late afternoon grayness of a shadowed mountainside is exceedingly difficult when you're trying to glass *into* the sun. Glassing elk when the early-morning or late afternoon sun is at your back, with its gilding rays of warm light lighting up the scenery and the elk's light-tan hide, is a piece of cake. There are places where I only glass when the morning sun lights up the countryside and any elk around glow like neon signs, and there are places where I only glass in the early evening for the same reason.

There are places where I have to change locations a few hundred yards as the sun moves up or down to see into pockets, valleys, clearings, and hidey holes with the light working for me. Make the shadows and light work for you, rather than inhibiting your ability to pick out the shape or form of an elk long before it has a chance to pick you out. The key to success in spot-and-stalk bowhunting any critter is to pinpoint your quarry *before* it spots you.

Another key to long-distance, high-country spot-and-stalk elk bowhunting is having and making use of a good spotting scope. I have two favorites. The first is my Nikon 15x-45x, 72 mm ED Field Scope with an accessory 60x eyepiece for ultra-long-distance spotting, when conditions are optimum and I need the additional power to judge a trophy or pick a foolproof stalking route. This scope is on the heavy side but is superbly sharp and clear at the higher magnification, and I generally use it with a sturdy tripod or window mount on my truck window.

The second is a lightweight, waterproof, rubber-armored Nikon 16x-48x XL Spotter II. This little scope is also very sharp and clear and easily transported in a fanny pack or daypack into the roughest, back country elk terrain. A small, sturdy tripod increases the scope's effectiveness, but I generally use it supported by my hat or pack over a log or rock with equally good results.

Elk Calling 101

"How the heck can anyone miss an animal the size of a bull elk at 30 yards or less?" my client questioned as we sat down to one of my wife's sumptuous suppers the night before his elk bowhunt started.

"Kind of hard to explain," I replied to the point, "until you've been there."

The second day of his bowhunt, we were slipping our way through the dense oak brush on a side slope in the dark when we heard a bull bugle on the slope above and in front of us.

There was a series of small clearings or meadows interspersed with large and small oak brush motts on the slope, and the bull sounded like he was within a couple hundred yards. I put my client in front of a small clump of oak brush where his green camo would blend with the background and slid down at the base of a Ponderosa a few yards behind him. The breeze was drifting down the slope, so we'd have the wind on the bull unless he circled below us, a definite possibility.

One of the best elk calls is a cow call. Keep the calling light and be ready for action if a bull is within calling range.

The bull bugled every ten minutes or so, and as soon as there was good shooting light, I waited for a bugle, then immediately answered with some seductive (I thought) cow calls. The bull fired back instantly and I could see by my client's body language that he was fully alert and ready for action.

The bull's next bugle left little doubt he was headed our way. Five minutes later, his tan form came drifting silently through the brush 50 yards in front of us. The cautious bull drifted down hill and stopped just out of bow range, where he locked up and bugled several times, trying to get a rise out of the cow he'd heard, and gave us a good look at his tall, massive 6x6 rack.

Much to the consternation of my compadre, I never made a sound. I'd been frequently checking the breeze with my powder bottle as the bull approached and figured, if I called, he'd likely sidehill below us, just out of range, and pick up our scent. After ten tense minutes, the bull finally lost interest and moseyed back the way he'd come. The minute he was out of sight, I slithered to my client and motioned for him to hustle forward 50 yards to another clump of oak brush, where we quickly set up in the same relative positions.

Once again I cow called excitedly, getting an immediate response from the bull less than 100 yards up the slope. I quickly cut loose with a challenging high-pitched spike-bull squeal followed by several more beseeching cow mews. The bull came crashing through the bushes, stopped behind a clump of brush 40 yards in front of my client and proceeded to thrash the brush grunting and bugling his sex-crazed fury.

I was keeping one eye on my client kneeling ten feet from me and could see his arrow bouncing on the rest as the bull circled around the brush and headed our way. When he stepped into a small opening 30 yards below us, I chirped sharply and brought him to a halt where my thoroughly shook-up bowhunter put an arrow right over his shoulders. The bull vanished as quickly as he came, and we could hear him crashing brush and rattling rocks for 200 yards up the hill.

"That's exactly how people miss elk at point-blank range," I chortled to my chagrined, red-faced client. "Now you've been there."

Every elk bowhunter dreams of bugling a bull within bow range, and I'll be the first to admit this is as good as bowhunting gets. However, calling elk isn't the same as it was when I killed my first elk in the early '60s. Today's elk hunter is far more knowledgeable, with a better understanding of elk habits and idiosyncrasies, and calling techniques and tactics, than ever before. With the proliferation of magazine articles, videos, television programs, and live seminars, the plethora of elk bowhunting and calling information available is phenomenal.

Unfortunately, the elk have learned about as rapidly as their nemeses, and those that didn't learn have been removed from the gene pool.

I bugled in my first bull with a coiled piece of gas pipe that sounded horrible compared to modern calls, but the elk were so uninitiated, they responded readily. Today I call less than ever and rarely bugle, but my percent of response is as good or better than ever.

When I enter the woods, elk hunting during the rut, I try to remain totally undetected by the elk until I am in the best-possible position to seduce or infuriate a bull within bow range. I've observed many bowhunters tooting and chirping their way through the woods like the pied piper of the Rockies, and even if they get a bull to respond to their calling, they don't know it.

During the early part of the bow season in most elk states, the elk are just tuning up for the rut and only bugling perfunctorily. They'll respond to good calling at this time, but guardedly and silently. When I feel I'm close to elk in the early season, I set up and use cow and calf mews and chirps for at least an hour or more without moving.

Later in the season, when the herd bulls have gathered their harems, the rules of engagement change. There are lots of eyes, ears, and noses to defeat getting within range of herd bull, and calling him away from his harem is a tough proposition. I've found the best way to do this is to get as close to the herd without spooking them before making a sound. Start calling too soon and the bull will round up his girls and move them away. By the time the dominant bulls have their harems together, they're ready to forgo the fighting for some *loving,* and if given half a chance will drive their cows away from aggressive bugling.

When I'm hunting a herd bull covered up by cows, I try to sneak as close as possible, making sure the wind is in my favor. When I get close (depending on my whims and the conditions), I'll usually cow call softly in hopes of suckering the bull away from his herd. Squealing like a competing spike at this time might just spook him into flight with his harem or bring him on the run.

Several years ago, I slipped to within 75 yards of a herd with a good bull and managed to get between the bull and most of his harem as they crossed an overgrown logging road. I was kneeling behind some serviceberry bushes with the bull just over the ridge above me. When I cut loose with a spike-bull squeal, that dang bull charged down the hill and sideswiped the bush I was behind with his awesome antlers. Try staying in place when that happens. By the time I got my heart off the roof of my mouth and my arrow back on the string, the whole herd had vanished.

As I mentioned, my first elk call was a coiled gas pipe. I went from there to a modified Herters metal-reed deer call that I had to blow so hard to get the breaking bugle, the insides of my cheeks often

Using a two-man approach to calling in a bull elk will allow a hunter to concentrate on the bull and his own movement, while the other partner does the calling. Close encounters like this are not uncommon!

ended up bleeding at the end of a day of elk calling. A diaphragm turkey call and 36-inch piece of 1 ¼-inch PVC pipe as a grunt tube put the variety into elk calling. With this combo, I could bugle, squeal, chirp, and mew to vary my calling to suit the situation. Today I use the Primos palate plate and Quaker Boy diaphragm calls along with Woods Wise and Quaker Boy Hyper cow calls, with a Primos grunt tube for most of my calling. There are hundreds of superb elk calls of every type to choose from, and all will work some of the time; none that I know will work all of the time.

Each and every rutting-elk encounter requires its own strategy and tactics, and while you can learn *how* to call and bugle elk from the profusion of available information, learning *when* to call elk is the key to putting that bull at point-blank range, where you can't possibly miss. And that comes from experience.

Decoying Elk

Elk bulls today are much more cautious and circumspect when they respond to calling, and over the past 10 years, I've had few that came on the run looking for trouble. Most will come in slow and easy looking for the cow or bull that is making the racket. When they don't see the sound source, they tend to get spooky and, at best, circle downwind to scent-check the area. At worst, they just get the heck out of Dodge.

I've hunted with decoys of various sorts all my life, and for years I felt an elk decoy would work wonders in allaying an approaching elk's suspicions and bring him the final yardage needed for a good bow shot. However, I didn't relish the thought of carrying a full-body taxidermy mount or archery target through the woods at 9,000 feet to accomplish this purpose.

When I met and discussed this with Dave Berkeley, owner of Feather Flex decoys, it didn't take long to come up with prototype lightweight foam elk decoys that could be rolled and transported easily. The silhouette decoy we came up with was full-sized, without a head for ease of design and portability. The decoy fastened between two trees with lightweight bungee cords, and the elk looked as if its head was hidden by the tree trunk or brush.

This new decoy worked extremely well and brought a number of elk within bow range for me and my clients, but it still lacked the prime ingredient: extreme portability. I've had several manufacturers approach me for advice on elk decoys, and the one thing I stress is that the decoy has to fit in a daypack or fanny pack. This is a tough requirement, but if you can't take it with you when you leave the truck in the morning and pack it all day every day, chances are you aren't going to have it with you when you really need it.

Jerry McPherson, owner and designer of Montana Decoys, solved that problem with photo-realistic cow elk decoys that collapse in a hoop and are small and light enough to be carried all day, every day, of your elk bowhunt. And they really do work.

On one of my first attempts to decoy a bull, I left my prototype decoy hanging between two immature spruce bushes along the edge of a meadow while my hunting partner and I went pursuing a bull that had come in behind us. When we returned several hours later, another bull had come along and evidently made a pass at my silhouette decoy, tangling his antlers in the cords and the flip-floppy decoy. According to the profusion of skid marks in the meadow, the bull threw a fit for 50 yards trying to get the clinging decoy out of his antlers.

Adding a decoy to your calling set-up and appealing to both the bull's hearing and sight might just tip the balance in your favor when you're dealing

Using a decoy will help tip the odds in your favor. Place the decoy where it can be spotted from a distance as the bull comes in to your calls.

with a curious but cautious or wary bull. As an added attraction, I use elk scent around the decoy to appeal to or confuse the elk's sense of smell.

I make sure my decoy is set where an approaching elk can spot it from some distance, as I've found that a decoy suddenly popping into view will spook an elk or arouse its suspicions. When they can see the decoy for some distance and at the same time they hear elk sounds, it arouses their curiosity and they are much more liable to come closer. When decoying and calling elk, I try to position myself where it is difficult or impossible for an approaching elk to sneak around behind me, and the path of least resistance puts him in good shooting position.

I try to place me or my client off to one side and between the incoming elk and the decoy, but not in direct line of sight between the elk and decoy. I've had elk so engrossed with the decoy, I was able to draw and let down several times within 20 yards without them paying any heed to my slight movement. Decoys

can be a deadly and effective addition to your elk bowhunting arsenal, but only if you carry it with you each and every time you go elk hunting.

Shot Placement and Equipment

Elk are *tough*! I've bowhunted many species of big-game animals, and in my experience, none are tougher nor more survival-driven than elk. Where a hard-hit whitetail buck will travel 200 yards, a bull elk with the same hit can go half a mile. The heart-lung kill zone on bull elk is roughly twice the size of that on whitetail deer, 20 inches to 24 inches. This means that a 40-yard shot on a bull elk is equivalent to a 20-yard shot on a whitetail, *if* you spend the time practicing at the longer distances.

I've had many eastern and Midwestern clients who stated they wouldn't take a shot over 20 yards. I can appreciate their discretion, but they are cheating themselves and decreasing their chances of success. In the wide-open spaces the wary wapiti call home, shot distances may be extended considerably, and you need

The kill zone on a bull elk is about twice the size as that of a whitetail. Practice shooting at 30 to 40 yards with a kill zone target area of about 20 to 24 inches.

to practice, practice, practice at the longer distances to increase your chances of scoring on a bull.

You might surprise yourself at how well you can shoot at 60 yards with a lot of practice, and conscientious practice at these distances will make a 35-yard shot seem close. Also, practice from a variety of shooting positions. Shoot from your knees, sitting, twisted sideways, and to the off side. Elk have a way of coming from the most unpredictable angles, and practicing these shots will prepare you for such an eventuality.

I've had clients take elk with longbows, recurves, and compounds, and the type of bow makes little difference. One bowhunter made a clean one-shot kill on a 5x5 bull with a 42-pound bow. The bow that you shoot the best is the one you want to use for elk hunting. While there's a lot of latitude in bow type and weight for bowhunting elk, the one equipment factor where there is absolutely no leeway is broadhead dependability and sharpness.

I prefer and have taken many elk with "*cut-on-contact*" broadheads, such as the Zwickey, Bear Razorhead, Phantom, and Steel Force. My clients and I have also made clean kills on a number of elk with Andy Simo's trocar-pointed Thunderhead. I *do not* like or recommend mechanical broadheads of any kind. Why base the success or failure of your elk bowhunt on a head that may or may not work, when there are many solid and proven heads that leave no doubt?

Bowhunting elk is the supreme western big-game challenge, so make sure you're prepared for the encounter.

Mule Deer and Blacktail

JUDD COONEY

Taking a trophy mule deer with a bow and arrow just may be today's toughest bowhunting challenge. Throughout much of the west, the mule-deer population is in a drastic decline, and finding a trophy buck that will make the Pope and Young record book is getting tougher with each passing year.

What this boils down to for the bowhunter looking for the best opportunity to arrow a decent mule deer buck is more critical re search and care in choosing areas that have a recent history for producing record-class mule deer bucks. It used to be that a bowhunter could head west and hunt almost anywhere in the mountains of Colorado, Utah, Wyoming, or Montana and have a decent chance at seeing lots of mule deer and getting a chance or two at a good buck. Those days are long gone.

A look at the statistical summary of the last Pope and Young biennial recording period and last record book can provide a wealth of information, not only about where the best bucks were taken, but also the most successful method of hunting them. As a point of comparison, there are roughly eight times the number of whitetails entered into the record book as mule deer. This means putting a mule deer in the book is eight times more difficult than taking a Pope and Young whitetail. These figures should give you an idea of the task you've chosen if you decide you want a mule deer buck for your trophy room wall.

Colorado is still the top trophy-producing state for mule deer (both typical and non-typical), followed by Utah. Wyoming, Oregon, and Idaho also produce many typical and non-typical mule deer, and Kansas is number three in the production of non-typical mule deer.

I can swear by this statistic. Several years ago, I was bowhunting whitetails with my good friends Drew, Mary, and Bob McCartney in north-central Kansas, and I rattled in a 180-plus, non-typical muley buck. The curious buck came right up to my whitetail decoy and stood broadside at 20 yards, while I cussed Kansas law, that prohibits non-residents from taking mule deer on a non-resident archery deer license.

Today you might have a better chance of arrowing a monster muley off the back porch of an urbanite, living on the edge of one of the small towns in the foothills along the front range of the Rockies, than in one of the remote, hidden, high valleys on the western slope. The mule deer have moved close to human habitation and actually invaded many of the small mountain communities to escape from constant pressure by the escalating mountain lion, coyote, and bear populations.

I used to make an annual trip to Estes Park, Colorado, in late November and early December to photograph the huge bucks that migrated to the lower reaches of Rocky Mountain National

Park and then into the city limits, as winter and coyotes pushed them down from their high-country homeland. It wasn't uncommon to find 20 to 30 bucks, from a hefty 170 points to monsters well over 200 points, in the area, along with plenty of does and fawns.

During the fall of 2003, I swung through Estes on my way back from Iowa (for Thanksgiving at home) in hopes of photographing some bucks. Ha! In two days of driving around, I found a dozen mule deer (total) and only two small bucks. According to the local conservation officer, Chronic Wasting Disease (CWD) had wiped out most of the deer in the area, and the few that were left by this insidious disease were further hammered by the coyotes and big cats.

Many of the historically famous mule-deer areas are no longer good bets for bowhunters, and some areas that haven't been noted for producing big mule deer are gaining ground. Many of the prairie states and provinces are producing big bucks, simply because they are out of cougar country and the bucks get a chance to grow to trophy proportions, especially on private ranches and areas where there is still predator control of some sort.

Don't overlook eastern Colorado, New Mexico, Wyoming, Montana, and the Dakotas in your search for a prime mule deer bowhunting location. Alberta is also high on the list of trophy mule deer producers, and there are some areas of the province that offer excellent, non-resident bowhunting opportunities. Start planning well ahead of time, so you can thoroughly research your mule deer bowhunt. It will be time well spent.

Mule deer are open-country, migratory critters that live in and roam much larger expanses of habitat than whitetails, with a far less defined home range. The muleys' yen to roam makes them more unpredictable than whitetails and more difficult to pattern and ambush. However, the broken, more open country they call home makes them an ideal subject for spot-and-stalk bowhunting. Roughly 60 percent of the mule deer bucks entered into the Pope and Young record book were taken by the spot-and-stalk method.

Spot-and-Stalk Muley Hunting

The key to successful spot-and-stalk bowhunting is just what the words imply. First you have to spot the buck and then you stalk him. Sounds simple, but considering some of the large-scale and inhospitable country the big muley bucks call home, bowhunting them by this method can involve lots of time and plenty of patience, not to mention a good share of luck. For my money, spot-and-stalk mule deer bowhunting in the high country, above timberline, is the quintessential bowhunting experience.

If you bowhunt properly using this method, you're going to be spending most of your time spotting, judging, planning, and plotting rather

Wherever you hunt muleys, you'll need excellent binoculars. Your bare eyes won't pick out mule deer (or parts of mule deer) in the draws, gullies, canyons, and other hidey holes they favor.

than stalking. The most important part of your bowhunting equipment will be your optics. Good binoculars and a quality spotting scope will make the job of spotting a trophy mule deer much easier and more comfortable. I've often stayed in one location, glassing for a big buck in good mule deer country, for eight to ten hours at a time. A cheap pair of binoculars with poor-quality lenses will have your eyes feeling like they've been sandpapered and salted after a concentrated couple of hours of glassing slopes and ridges, trying to pick out the well-camouflaged form of a stalkable mule deer buck. Buying a pair of quality binoculars is a lifetime investment, and if you choose carefully, it may just be the most useful and valuable single item of equipment in your bowhunting arsenal.

Any quality binoculars in 7x, 8x, or 10x will work for glassing mule deer. For the longer distances usually involved, I prefer 10x binoculars like my Nikon Superior E glasses. These sharp, center-focus binoculars are tough, lightweight, and medium-sized, and they gather light unbelievably well, all prerequisites for mule deer spotting.

A lightweight, good-quality, variable-power spotting scope is essential for critical long-range spotting, pinpointing deer locations, judging trophy quality, and choosing a stalking route to your quarry. I found that 15-45x is the best all-round power. The lower setting isn't too powerful for general scanning and spotting; yet the higher setting is strong enough for critical long-distance trophy judging and picking out details in terrain features. I have a 60x eyepiece for my 60mm spotting scope, but this is only usable under perfect conditions with a rock solid rest or tripod.

The next most important element of your spot-and-stalk mule-deer hunt is *patience*! It's difficult for any bowhunter in spectacularly open muley habitat to master sitting in one location and have his eyes

do the walking and work. Most bowhunters want to move out and comb the countryside in an attempt to locate any bucks in the area. Not good. The essential element to the success of your mule-deer bowhunt is whether you can spot a trophy buck before it spots you. Guess that's why they call it spot-and-stalk bowhunting.

You'll be a lot less likely to give yourself away to a sharp-eyed muley by sitting quietly and comfortably in the shade of a tree, under a rock ledge, or even in the cab of your pickup, and let your eyes cover the countryside. This is much more efficient than traipsing over hill and dale, rattling rocks, filling the air with your pungent scent, and, in general, letting everything with fur and feathers know there's an intruder in the area.

Locating mule deer is best accomplished during the early morning hours, when the deer are most active and time is on your side. Nothing is more frustrating than spotting a good buck in the late afternoon and not having enough time to get within stalking distance before dark. Of course, this will give you an excellent starting point the following morning and certainly narrow down your search area, so early evening spotting is definitely worthwhile.

Mule deer spend much of their time in the open. They will often bed on an open hillside, at the base of a small tree, under a ledge, or in the shade of a bush, where they have a panoramic view of their surroundings. There are many times when a crafty old buck's bedding or loafing location makes for an impossible stalking situation. Be *patient*. A very high percentage of blown stalks are due to one fundamental faux pas: *impatience*.

When glassing for mule deer, it's important to make use of every little trick you can muster. Always try to glass with the sun at your back, lighting up the area you're glassing. The mule deer's gray coloration was designed to blend with his habitat, and it's unbelievable how well this camouflage works against the broken pattern of shadow, rocks, and brush. The golden rays of early-morning and late afternoon sunlight will reduce the effectiveness of this camouflage and make a muley's hide stand out like a diamond against a lump of coal. Plan your glassing to take advantage of this fact.

Don't sit there in blissful ignorance and figure you're always going to spot a full-bodied, magnificent, heavy-antlered buck perfectly outlined against a grassy background in plain sight! It happens, but you're better off looking for a shape that seems out of place, like an antler sticking up over a bush, a partial rear end patch on the backside of a thicket, or the flick of an ear or tail against a shadowy background. Spot the little things that don't quite fit their surroundings, and then take the time to put together the rest of the pieces and parts with the aid of you binoculars or spotting scope, and you'll locate a lot more mule deer.

The tough part, when patience becomes even more important, is *after* you spot a good buck that has your mouth watering and puts a tremor in your bow hand. This is the time that most spot-and-stalk hunts are blown. The uncontrollable urge to proceed with the stalk often overrides the common sense of taking the time to properly plan it from the first to last step. *Big* mule deer bucks didn't grow to trophy size by being stupid and making mistakes. A mature buck has super eyesight, a keen sense of smell, and phenomenal hearing, combined with the survival instincts to get him out of danger in the most expeditious manner possible. Don't overlook the slightest detail when planning your stalk.

This is the aspect of your mule-deer bowhunt when a good spotting scope can pay for itself in short order. You can use your spotting scope to choose every inch of your stalking route. Study the smallest detail of the terrain features between you and your adversary without ever leaving your observation post and taking a chance on spooking the deer.

If you spot a buck or bucks feeding in the early morning, unless they are close and in an ideal location for a relatively quick stalk with everything in your favor, it might be better strategy to wait until they bed down for a mid-morning siesta. There are, of course, times in a spot-and-stalk hunting situation where you may have a chance at success by pushing the envelope a bit and getting the stalk on without wasting time. On several occasions, I've located mule deer feeding along a slope or flat, and headed for brush or timber that would make an ideal ambush point . . . if I could get there ahead of them. In this situation, go for it, but don't forget the deer's senses of smell, hearing, and eyesight in your stalk and don't rush it.

Big buck mule deer live in rough, rocky, isolated, and lonely places. Don't forget to glass shady spots where they like to feed, bed, and hide.

Once the deer get bedded down and stay put for 15 minutes or so, make sure you know where each and every deer is located. If it's a long stalk over difficult terrain, don't hesitate to draw a rough diagram of the situation and make use of it during your stalk. The countryside and objects look a lot different through binoculars or a spotting scope due to limited depth of field and the compression factor of optics. Make sure you pinpoint the deer's location with a landmark you can identify without question when you get close to where you last saw your quarry. There have been a number of times when failure to fully pinpoint a buck's exact location has let the buck win the encounter. There have been an equal number of times when the untrustworthy deer moved while we were in the process of the perfect stalk, and the buck wasn't where it was expected to be. Stalking mule deer is never cut-and-dried; so don't get overconfident, impatient, or careless at this stage of your hunt. It will cost you dearly!

Spot-and-stalk bowhunting can often be better used by two bowhunters working together. Four eyes are always better than two, and once a deer is located, having one set of eyes glued to the deer while the other bowhunter makes the stalk increases the odds of success considerably. Take the time to work out a set of clear and concise signals to communicate from both ends of the stalk, without miscommunication. Leave the slightest opening in this regard, and you can bet Murphy will pop out of the brush and throw the screws to your best-laid plans . . . big time.

Backpack Mule Deer

One of the major reasons for backpack bowhunting mule deer is that it allows you to get into prime mule-deer country that is almost inaccessible by any other method of hunting. One of my favorite mountain bowhunting axioms always has been, "When you get into country where there are no people, you'll find game!" Backpacking for trophy mule deer may just be your best option for that out-west, high-country hunting venture. There's little doubt that a spot-and-stalk bowhunt for a gigantic mountain muley is the epitome of bowhunting challenges, and a backpack high-country hunt has to be the supreme mule-deer bowhunting experience.

Despite what some bowhunters think, a trophy mule deer buck can be as crafty and spooky as a whitetail. Letting such a buck see or smell you in his home area is just inviting him to disappear without a trace. By carefully backpacking into the area, keeping the mountain breezes in your favor, staying on the back side of the ridges in the heavy timber, and setting up a dry camp with a minimum of noise or disturbance, you won't broadcast the fact that you're around to anything bigger than the local pikas and rockchucks.

One of the major drawing cards to a backpack, high-country bowhunt is cost! You can't go much cheaper than loading the family car with your hunting equipment—backpack, sleeping bag, 8x10 foot piece of plastic, minimum amount of food, an aluminum pot with sterno stove—and driving to the nearest high-country mule deer habitat. Backpack bowhunting can get you into many areas that are not readily accessible by any other method. You can do it on your own or with a bowhunting buddy, rather than having to hire the services of a professional outfitter or guide, thereby saving money, adding challenge, and having the resulting element of self-satisfaction to your hunt.

The first step in setting up a backpack bowhunt is to pick an area where there is a huntable population of mule deer in country that's suitable for

Plan your spot-and-stalk route well in advance. Keep the wind in your face and wait for the right shot. Always keep an eye out for other deer—deer you originally didn't see that would blow your stalk.

backpacking. Get hunting info from various western states, listing seasons and dates, to begin the process. Most western state Game and Fish Departments also provide harvest data or kill figures on the different game management units within the state. With this info and a general state map, you can begin to narrow down your choices.

Look for units that have low density of hunters and a good success ratio in areas with lots of wild and wooly country. There are many areas in the western mountains where you can park the family station wagon (or minivan) along the highway on a high mountain pass, at a mountaintop microwave tower, campground, U.S.F.S. trailhead leading to a wilderness area, or on the end of a logging road at the base of a mountain, and go backpacking. No need for a 4x4 pickup, four-wheeler, or horses and trailer to get you close to some of the best big-buck country available.

Another option that's a bit more expensive, but far cheaper than an outfitted mule-deer bowhunt, is a drop-camp high-country bowhunt. This is a great way to get into good mule deer country if you do your homework and choose the area you want to be packed into yourself. Leaving the choice of a drop camp up to a horse-packing outfit that doesn't do any scouting, and is more interested in the ease of getting into and out of the back country than its potential for trophy bucks, may not be in your best interest. There are outfitters who have set drop camps in excellent deer country and will pack you in and out for a reasonable price. By far the best plan is to thoroughly research a hunting area and then have a packer cart you and your equipment to *your* chosen location.

Still-Hunting Mule Deer

An additional method for bowhunting mule deer bucks is by still-hunting, with approximately 15 percent of the Pope and Young entries taken using this method. This totals up to 75 percent of the bucks being taken by spot-and-stalk and still-hunting methods.

In my experience, it's really tough to differentiate between the two methods. When you're still-hunting through a pocket of timber, keeping your eyes open for a buck, you're basically spotting on the move. When you locate a buck, your still-hunt turns to a stalk even if it's only for a few yards. When you spot a buck from a distance and ease carefully into bow range, are you stalking him or still-hunting him? Who cares . . . as long as you end up with him on the ground?

Still-hunting through a piece of likely mule-deer habitat takes the same patience and locating skills as spot-and-stalk hunting, only this time you don't know for sure exactly where you quarry is located. Remember, you're more likely to see only a portion of a deer rather than the whole animal. Key your thinking to this aspect. Many neophyte muley bowhunters don't even consider binoculars for this type of hunting, but I can tell you from experience that good light-gathering glasses are even *more* important for this type of hunting.

Still-hunting is hunting "up close and personal," in close quarters where a single step can make the difference between success and disaster. Binoculars will tell in short order if a light patch is a deer's rear end or just a sunlit patch of grass, if that slight movement was the tip of an antler showing from behind a tree or bush or the movement of a pine squirrel. Carry binoculars with you all the time and force yourself to use them constantly. Once you find out their value in close quarter still-hunting, you'll never be without them for any of your bowhunting ventures.

Remember the three main detriments to your getting within bow range of a trophy mule deer buck in still-hunting are wind, noise, and movement. *Always* still-hunt through an area with the wind or breeze in your favor. The best way to accomplish this is to use a squeeze bottle filled with talcum powder and let the prevailing breeze dictate exactly how you still-hunt through the area. Try to move as slowly and cautiously as possible, stopping often to survey and glass the terrain you're working into.

Tree-stand hunting for mule deer is not a new phenomenon, but it's one that is rapidly gaining popularity, simply because of its proven effectiveness. Only eight percent of the record-book entries for mule deer were taken from tree stands, while a whopping 78 percent of whitetails are taken using this method. Tree stands for mule deer can be deadly when properly placed.

There have been numerous occasions when I have been still-hunting or spot-and-stalk hunting and have seen a good buck in an ideal location where a tree stand would work, or come upon a mineral lick or heavily used trail from a feeding area that is an obvious location for a tree stand.

A well-placed tree stand with good background cover and good tree-stand hunting techniques is a highly effective mule-deer tactic. Ideal tree-stand locations are overlooking waterholes, travel ways leading to feeding areas or croplands, in saddles and cuts where deer travel from one range or drainage to another, and other locations where a muley's travels are narrowed down to a specific ambush point.

With the mule deer's propensity for open country with sparse tree cover, there are often ideal ambush sites in saddles or along creek beds or meandering streams, on trails leading to a bedding area in the middle of the wide-open spaces, and a million other excellent locations with little cover available and *no* trees. Don't give up!

Get yourself a shovel, pickaxe, and good brush cutter and put in a pit blind or ground blind. This is probably the most overlooked method for bowhunting a trophy mule deer and yet it can be one of the most adaptable and effective methods employed. I have used pit blinds in situations where it would seem impossible to get within bow range of a cautious, open-country, mule deer buck and had them walk within a few yards of the blind within hours of its construction.

Calling Mule Deer

Two percent (or less) of the mule deer entered into the record books were taken by some method of calling. Mule deer are not territorial like their whitetail cousins, nor are they as aggressive during the rut. The mule deer buck's mild manner makes it tough to get one fired up with rattling antlers or grunt challenges to suck them close enough for a bow shot. I've rattled in a few bucks, but they responded out of curiosity more than anger. Several eventually worked their way close enough for a good shot, but the percentage of responses certainly didn't make this one of my favorite methods of bowhunting muley bucks.

I've had much better results using a coarse-toned predator call to imitate the distress bleats of a deer. This is a viable method for bringing in a buck or doe early in the season, when the fawns are still with the does. I've had several good bucks respond when I was calling coyotes early in the fall and again during the winter.

Again, during the late season, I feel it's more of a curiosity response rather than one of aggression or anger, although my late-season calling has brought in some real trophy bucks. I always carry a predator call with me when bowhunting and wouldn't hesitate to try to coax up a trophy buck if he was in sight, with no alternative way of getting close enough for a shot. Calling may not work often enough to use it as your main method of bowhunting trophy mule deer, but it does work and might give you a chance at a trophy buck when nothing else seems feasible.

In states with late-season mule deer hunting, driving is another viable method of putting a trophy buck within bow range. This method can be well used where the mule deer tend to congregate in their wintering areas—along river bottoms, shelter belts, or along wooded slopes or valleys. A mule deer's natural tendency is to move uphill or to more open ground, so take this habit into consideration when choosing your ambush points.

It doesn't take a whole crowd of pushers to move muleys out of cover. In fact, one or two bowhunters moving slowly through a patch of prime, late-season mule-deer cover, with the wind at their backs, will be far more effective than a larger group. Wise old bucks have a propensity for sneaking up side draws, small gullies, or other inconspicuous escape routes, so keep your eyes open for such locations when setting up your late-season drives.

Columbian Blacktails

Columbian blacktail deer are found in California, Oregon, Washington, and lower British Columbia, with Oregon and California producing a major portion of the record-book bucks. California's archery deer season opens in mid-August, when the bucks are still in velvet; consequently, almost all the record-book Columbian blacktails in velvet are taken in California.

The majority of the Columbian blacktails (like their magnum-eared cousins) are taken by spot-and-stalk bowhunting, with the second most effective method being tree-stand hunting.

Most of the foregoing techniques used for mule deer are equally applicable to Columbian blacktails. However, when I bowhunted them again in Oregon, I found that they responded to calling and rattling far more readily than mule deer.

On one occasion, I was bowhunting a densely wooded ridge overlooking a wide valley where the visibility was severely limited by the dense jungle-like vegetation. At mid-morning, I set up along an overgrown logging road and commenced rattling and grunt calling, as if I were whitetail hunting. Within minutes, a heavy, dark-antlered blacktail stuck his head out of a fern thicket 30 yards from me, trying to locate the source of the sound. What I wouldn't have given for a decoy.

That buck appeared and disappeared in the verdant vegetation in front of me for the next 20 minutes while I tried to coax him into the open for a shot. I'd see patches of hide, antlers, or rump, and occasionally a head, but never enough for a good shot. After half an hour of inactivity, I figured the buck was gone and started rattling again. An even larger buck appeared in a small opening at 40 yards, but before I got my wits working and came to full draw, he melted into the background like his compadre. I bleated and grunted softly and got several momentary glimpses of him twice more before he, too, was engulfed by the green labyrinth.

A tree stand would have put me in position to see down into the dense jungle ferns, vines, and moss-shrouded trees and given me a good shot at either record-book buck. I did manage to call in a couple of forky bucks, but after an encounter with the two boomers, I just couldn't bring myself to take the shot.

Sitka Blacktails

Sitka blacktails are found in the northern section of British Columbia and the coastal regions of Alaska. Kodiak Island is definitely the place to go for a record-class Sitka blacktail buck. When I worked for the Alaska Department of Fish and Game in the early '60s, there weren't any blacktails on Afognak Island and darn few on Kodiak Island. Their population exploded shortly thereafter, and not too long ago, the limit was seven deer per hunter. The lush vegetation and abundant food supply make for a high population of fat, healthy deer, but the lack of minerals doesn't do much for antler growth. Consequently, a bowhunter needs to look over a lot of deer to find a Pope and Young qualifier.

Bowhunters weren't the only ones to benefit from the population explosion of the Sitka blacktails. The humongous predatory brown bears were quick to take advantage of the burgeoning red-meat supply and actually learned that gunfire usually meant a fresh gut pile or carcass. This unusual response added a whole new dimension to hunting blacktails for gun hunters, as the voracious bruins started showing up unexpectedly at the site of a fresh deer kill. These close-quarter encounters in the jungle-like thickets of alder and devil's club resulted in a number of fatalities, both human and bear.

Fortunately, a bow doesn't make much noise when it goes off, but I've talked with a number of bowhunters who have lost deer to brown bears. On one occasion, a bowhunter arrowed a deer a bit far back and watched it move slowly into an alder thicket, where it bedded down. The bowhunter backed off and positioned himself on a hillside several hundred yards above the downed deer, waiting. He spotted a brown bear in the valley half a mile above the deer's hidey hole, but didn't think anything about it.

An hour later, he spotted the bear moving purposefully down the valley with his nose in the air and realized he was wind-scenting the wounded deer and headed right for the thicket. A few minutes later, the frustrated bowhunter watched the huge bear carry his record-book blacktail over the hill and out of sight. He was frustrated but darned glad that he hadn't been in the thicket gutting or quartering his deer when the bear showed up to claim the kill.

Almost all Sitka blacktails are taken by spot-and-stalk bowhunting using the same techniques, tactics, and equipment as mule-deer bowhunters. The coastal areas of Alaska are noted for their atrocious weather, so waterproof rain gear is essential for comfort, as is a pair of quality, ankle-fit hip boots that you'll more than likely be wearing day after day.

According to Ed Russell, a bowhunting compadre residing in Anchorage, Sitka blacktails respond readily to bleats and squalls in imitation of a doe or fawn in distress. Ed was one of the first to seriously bowhunt blacktails on Kodiak and has taken a number of bucks by calling them. His favorite call is simply a blade of grass stretched between his thumbs. A variable-tone deer call would work just as well and be easier to master. However, unless you're bowhunting an area with good distant visibility, hunting with a partner who has a brown-bear license and a *big* rifle, or are crazy, calling Sitka blacktails in brown bear country may not be the best bet for putting a trophy blacktail buck on your den wall.

Summing It Up

In my opinion, the future of mule deer in the west is not good, with everything from predators to human encroachment working against them. However, there are still many good mule-deer areas with enough boomer bucks roaming around to fulfill your wildest bowhunting dreams. Don't procrastinate, start planning that mule deer bowhunt *now*. When planning for blacktails, do your homework, research over the Internet, and plan well in advance.

Moose

JUDD COONEY

Moose are the largest member of the deer family and sport the largest antlers of any animal in the world. Not only is bowhunting moose an exciting challenge, but the meat is superb and those antlers make an awesome trophy.

There are four subspecies of moose recognized in North America. The largest is the Alaskan-Yukon moose. An adult bull carrying antlers in the fall, just before rut, can be eight feet tall at the top of the shoulder and 11 feet from nose to tail with a hefty weight of 1500 pounds. As the name implies, this gigantic deer is found throughout Alaska and the Yukon Territory.

The second-largest subspecies is the Canada moose, a term applied to both the western and eastern animals. The western Canada moose ranges from Ontario to British Columbia, while the eastern Canada moose ranges from Ontario to Newfoundland and down into Maine. These two subspecies overlap in northwestern Ontario, a prime area for moose hunting. An adult Canada bull moose carrying antlers in the fall, prior to the rut, can be seven feet at the shoulder and 10 feet nose to tail and weigh in at 1250 pounds, very much in the heavyweight class.

The fourth subspecies, the Shiras or Wyoming moose, found from Colorado and Utah northward through Wyoming and Montana, is the pigmy of the group, but still big! An adult Shiras bull sporting antlers during the fall can stand six feet at the shoulders, be nine feet in length, and tip the scales at 1000 pounds. All moose are BIG!

Moose have considerable attributes that make them a tough adversary to bowhunt under any conditions. Their long-legged, ungainly appearance, with a huge shnozz, dangling fuzzy bell, and humongous rack, may foster the impression of a dull-witted and lethargic critter. Not so. Moose may not exhibit the sneakily alert look of a whitetail buck or the majestic demeanor of a bull elk, but the moose's survival equipment will rival those of any big-game animal.

A moose's first lines of defense are its extraordinary sense of smell and hearing. That stupendous shnozzola can discern the slightest tinge of human scent in the air at phenomenal distances and smell edible greenery under several feet of water.

A bull's hearing is keen enough to pick up the soft, low frequency moans of a cow a mile or more away and the soft snap of a twig at 100 yards. This I know from personal experience. A moose's ears work independently of each other, so it can be checking both the front and back door at the same time. When moose tune in on a sound they want to investigate, they zero both ears and can pinpoint the slightest sound with uncanny accuracy.

Experienced moose bowhunters can also vouch for the acuity of the moose's eyesight. Their daytime vision is equivalent to a human's, but in the dim, early morning, late afternoon, or dark timber light, their vision is far superior to a human's. Their eyesight is highly tuned to picking up the slightest movement, and like their ears, the eyes work independently of each other. A moose's height gives him an elevated perspective that is often underestimated by bowhunters.

According to the Pope and Young record book, calling is the most successful method of getting within bow range of a bull moose, and decoying (where possible) can make calling even more effective. To effectively call and decoy moose, one needs to be aware of the major difference in rutting tendencies between the Alaska-Yukon moose and their Canadian and US cousins.

Because of the vast expanses of tundra and more open alder- and willow-covered country, the Alaskan moose is not nearly as vocal as the Canada moose. Biologists tell us that this may account for the larger antler growth of the Alaska-Yukon moose. Moose living on the tundra make more use of their antlers in communication than do woodland moose.

The Alaska-Yukon bulls stake out the mating areas, tend to be more territorial in defending these areas, and gather harems of cows through calling, perfuming themselves regularly in rut pits and wallows, and making showy antler displays. The bulls hold their cows in brushy creek bottoms, along lakeshores or timbered ridges and side hills, where they can keep an eye on them and run off any interloper bulls that try to horn in on the action. Alaskan-Yukon bulls don't spend as much time or energy roaming their territory looking for cows as do the Canada bulls. They spend their time keeping the competition at bay, their harems intact, and their girls well serviced.

A caller trying to lure an Alaskan bull into bow range should use aggressive tactics and bull sounds to incite a jealous bull. Several Alaskan moose guides I know mix a few cow calls with their bull grunts in hopes of stoking a rutting bull into enough of a jealous rage to leave his harem and come looking for a fight.

One Alaskan outfitter uses a small set of lightweight, fake moose antlers to decoy harem bulls to him by flashing and rattling the antlers in the brush to imitate another bull in the herd bull's territory. According to him, when this method works, the action is fast and furious and certainly not for the faint hearted.

An Alaska bull's huge antlers play an important part in letting other bulls know they are in the country and just how big they are. I've glassed several bulls at a distance challenging each other by simply swaying their heads back and forth to show their opponent the size and width of their antlers. Quite often, this antler display is enough to determine the outcome of the confrontation without any physical contact. In the low Alaskan and Yukon vegetation, a large bull's antlers flashing in the sun can be seen for several miles by both hunters and other moose. This visual signaling alone probably plays a greater role in attracting both bulls and cows than hunters realize.

Several studies have been conducted that strongly indicated decoying with a large set of fake antlers worked with bulls that carried equally large or larger antlers, but would spook bulls with smaller antlers. I would love to bowhunt Alaskan bulls with a lightweight, pop-up cow decoy of some form and a small pair of antlers. There's no doubt such a combination could put a trophy bull right in the hunter's lap.

Carry a small squeeze bottle filled with talcum powder when spotting and stalking moose. Their very sensitive nose will pick up your scent in an instant, so keeping yourself downwind of your quarry is of utmost importance.

Canada and Shiras Rut

The Canada and Shiras moose rut is very different from the Alaskan-Yukon moose rut. The main rut usually starts sometime near mid-September, give or take a week depending on the location. It is the cow that controls when mating will take place. Just before coming into estrus, solitary cows stake out breeding areas approximately one-and-a-half to two square miles, and start to advertise their presence by calling for bulls and frequently urinating to leave their scent for the roaming bulls to find. Cows will defend these areas against other cows and try to drive off any cows encroaching on their mating areas. Cows generally prefer territory around ponds, beaver dams, lakeshores, meadows, or logged areas during the breeding season. Naturally, these are prime locations to set up for calling bulls.

The Canada and Shiras bulls, on the other hand, have home ranges that may cover as much as 16 to 18 square miles, with the ranges of various bulls broadly overlapping each other. During the rut, they travel these ranges in search of cows to

breed. Rutting bulls are not constant travelers, they often stop in a particular area for long periods of time listening for cows that might be calling. Once the bull hones in on a vocal cow, they travel together until she comes into estrus. When the cow allows copulation to take place, they may breed several times during a 24- to 48-hour period, then the bull leaves to find a new cow. Cow moose that do not get bred in this main rut period will come into estrus again 25-28 days later and start calling and trying to attract a bull all over again. Some Canada and Shiras cows have been known to breed as late as November.

Calling and Decoying Canada Moose

Alex Gouthro is a Canadian moose outfitter and guide, with 30 years of experience guiding hunters and bowhunting moose himself, and he is probably one of Canada's most knowledgeable and proficient moose callers. Alex believes the use of a moose decoy, combined with good calling, is the deadliest combination possible for a bowhunter.

Pulling a Canada bull within 70 yards by calling is okay for a rifle hunter, but it doesn't cut it for a bowhunter. After several years of trial and error, Alex finally got a decoy designed that works well for his type of calling and hunting. Alex's silhouette cow moose decoy is life-size, cut from four-inch thick Styrofoam, and divided into three parts for portability. The realistic body, long-nosed head, and prominent ears present a profile that looks like a cow moose from a distance, particularly during the early morning and late afternoon hours.

As with any decoy, Alex believes that movement is the key to effectiveness. To accomplish this, his moose decoy mounts on a lightweight pipe stake through the center, with 30-yard pull cords attached to the head and tail of the decoy. Pulling on the cords swings the decoy back and forth on the pivot stake and allows Alex to fully control the position of the decoy from his calling location. He can swing the decoy to keep it broadside and more visible to an incoming moose or simply move it back and forth to give the impression of life-like action.

Another Canadian moose guide uses a painted foam taxidermy head form of a cow moose. He carries the moose head strapped to his chest with a shoulder harness. This decoy is equally effective when properly used, and has produced many close encounters for the outfitter and his clients. Several have put the outfitter into hasty retreat mode with an overly amorous Canada bull.

Moose Calling

In addition to the decoy, moose calling tools consist of a birch bark calling horn and a dried scapula or shoulder blade bone. Moose megaphones can be the traditional birch bark, plastic, fiberglass, or rolled linoleum. They should be 14 to 16 inches long, with a mouthpiece one and a half inches in diameter, and the bell end five to six inches in diameter. The moose horn simply amplifies the caller's voice and imparts a moosey timbre to the noise. There are also several excellent commercial moose calls on the market that use a reed or diaphragm to produce cow and bull sounds rather than the human voice. The horn can even be used to simulate a cow moose urinating by pouring water from it onto the ground or into a lake, stream, or pond.

A moose or domestic cow scapula is used to imitate the sound of a bull raking his antlers in the brush or knocking against a tree. A scapula isn't as traditional as a set of real moose antlers, but it's a heck of a lot lighter, less cumbersome, and still has a "ring of bone" sound, almost as good as the real thing. In lieu of a scapula, a canoe paddle also works well for imitating the antler action of a rutting bull, and some may find it even easier to use.

Moose calling falls into two categories: passive and aggressive. Passive calling consists of making cow calls to let the bull know there's a cow in the area. Wary, older, trophy size bulls often approach the caller cautiously and generally downwind to let their nose verify the presence of the cow or danger. Bulls may respond from a distance by grunting an answer and continue grunting as they approach the caller's location. These are the easy ones. More cautious, mature bulls are liable to come in as silently as a morning fog and suddenly appear right in the caller's lap. Amazing how such a huge animal, with such an awesome set of headgear, can move like smoke

As with other big game, the call of a cow in heat will quickly bring in a love-sick bull moose. One of the oldest and most reliable calls is a birch bark megaphone.

through the dense timber and brush, but bull moose seem to manage it with ease.

A responding bull may announce his presence by smacking his antlers with single knocks against a tree or by loudly thrashing them in the brush. The single knocks generally indicate a cautious bull that wants the cow to come to him. Use passive calling tactics with this bull.

The bull thrashing trees and brush with his antlers is aggressive and claiming the cow's territory for himself. If passive tactics don't work, use the scapula, pretending to be a small bull raking his antlers in the brush or limbs. I've also had several bulls come to my calling, grunting every step of the way, leaving little doubt as to their whereabouts.

The sheer size and intimidating nature of a rutting bull moose can often turn an avid hunter into a gibbering wreck and leave a guide wondering if he shouldn't take up guiding bird watchers.

Several years ago, Alex called up a nice, 50-inch bull that came in for one of his clients. The bull was creating a major ruckus, raking bushes and trees and grunting loudly. He was deadly serious about intimidating any other bulls in the area.

Alex hand signaled his client to move closer to him and coaxed him into squatting behind a clump of three-foot-high bushes. Alex then proceeded to call the bull past the shooter, broadside at 16 to 18 yards. Five times! The bull would stalk up to the decoy, stop, and eye the fickle female, waiting for her to make some move. Alex was so close, he didn't dare twitch the control cords. Getting no response, the bull would move off until Alex cow called and moved the decoy to entice it back.

As the bull stalked past, the petrified shooter would peek over the bushes and then hunker back down. The bull eventually got tired of going in circles with no visible encouragement from the cow,

and wandered off to look for a more cooperative date. When a very exasperated outfitter inquired as to why the hunter hadn't taken a shot, the flustered client blurted, "The bushes were in the way."

Alex pointed out that the bushes were not all that tall and it would have been easy to shoot over them. "Well you didn't tell me that," the thoroughly distraught, badly whupped bowhunter retorted.

When a reluctant bull hangs up back in the woods or approaches following a cow, switch to more aggressive calling tactics. Use soft bull grunts and the scapula to imitate another amorous bull competing for the favors of the cow. These tactics simulate a smaller, younger bull that won't intimidate the target bull and are especially effective later in the season, after most of the cows have been bred and the bulls are hunting hard for the next encounter. Patience and perseverance are probably more important in moose calling and decoying than any other type of hunting.

The Perfect Moose-Calling Sequence

Move quietly into position on a good crossing, travel-way, or along a lakeshore at least an hour before legal shooting time. Carefully set up your decoy, if you are using one, set out scented rags or canisters or light up your smoke scent sticks, and place them downwind of your blind or tree stand.

After everything is set, walk slowly and noisily around in the brush, slightly downwind of your stand, and splash loudly in any nearby water to simulate the sounds of a feeding or active cow, just in case there is a bull within hearing. After the racket making, get into your blind or tree stand and wait for things to settle down, listening for any bull sounds.

If nothing develops after 15 minutes or so, make a couple of soft communication grunts, using your cupped hands rather than the megaphone. Continue the cow-in-heat calls every 20 minutes, gradually increasing the length and volume of your calling for one or two hours. If there's no action and you're set up near water, quietly leave your ambush, fill your calling horn with water, and loudly pour several containers full into the water, to simulate a cow urinating. The urination procedure can be repeated every hour or so. If nothing develops by mid-morning and you feel the need for a break, move quietly out of the area, leaving your scent equipment in place. If using a decoy, lay it on the ground and cover with brush.

When you return for the afternoon bowhunt, do so with caution, as occasionally a bull will move into the area during the mid-day lull, looking for the source of earlier moose sounds, and he may still be there. The late afternoon session is much the same as the morning hunt, and if you don't do any good, don't get discouraged. Whether you plan on bowhunting the location again or not, vacate the area as quietly and unobtrusively as possible. Even a bull moose spooked by accident may become more difficult to hunt because of it.

A bull moose, for all his size and bulk, can move almost soundlessly through the thickest timber and brush. Add the disturbance of even a slight breeze, and a distant grunt or antler cracking against the brush or a tree may be muted or obliterated by rustling vegetation. I try to cut down on the chances of an unheard encounter by using a pair of Walker's game ears to amplify the sounds around me. The

Float hunting waterways for moose is an enjoyable hunting strategy that will also allow you to take in some stunning scenery. Just make sure the bull is not in the middle of a bog or stream when you release your arrow.

ability to hear the slightest out-of-place, stealthy step or subtle antler scrape may make the difference between success and being snookered.

Partner calling, where the second hunter does the bull imitating while the first does the cow calling, can add even more realism to the ambush, because the simulated cow and bull sounds are coming from two different places. This double teaming will often coax even the wariest of bulls to sidle in close enough for one or the other to get a good bow shot.

Bulls accompanied by a cow can present a whole new challenge to calling moose. If a bull is following a cow, chances are good she has not been bred, and aggressive calling may get the bull riled up enough to come relatively close for a shot. If the cow has been bred, the bull will be in front of her leading the way and ready to find another receptive cow. In this situation, passive calling with seductive cow-in-heat groans, and even the calls of an agitated cow begging for attention, may pull the bull into shooting position.

As with elk calling, when a responding bull is arrowed and starts to leave, a flurry of excited hyper-cow calling may stop the bull and hold him in the area until he drops.

Most of the same tactics used for calling and decoying Canada moose are equally effective for the Shiras moose in the lower 48. The Shiras subspecies cows also establish their own territories and the bulls cover a lot of ground in their quest to locate a breedable cow. Pre-season scouting to locate the cows' home ranges or core areas and travel ways, or corridors within their area, can provide ideal locations for calling during the season. Unfortunately, no manufacturer makes a moose decoy that is realistic looking and easily transported in the mountainous terrain the Shiras moose roam, so decoying these moose is generally not a viable option.

Spot-and-Stalk Moose Hunting

Spot-and-stalk bowhunting is almost on par with calling for producing record-book moose for bow-and-arrow toting hunters.

Spotting moose is a heck of a lot easier than stalking moose. I've flown over thousands of square miles of prime moose habitat in Alaska and Canada and seen hundreds of humongous trophy bulls from the air. Unfortunately, you couldn't get to a high percentage of them from anywhere, and most of them will live and die without ever having encountered a single hunter.

The first axiom for a successful spot-and-stalk bowhunt, as mentioned before, is to locate your antlered adversary before it becomes aware of you. An animal the size of a moose, with its massive headgear, is often easy to spot from a distance in the swamps, tundra, timber, or brush country it calls home. Finding the same critter when you're engulfed in the same impenetrable tangle of moose habitat, at the same level, is a whole different ball game.

Good binoculars are essential for locating moose at a distance and a spotting scope can be invaluable for long-range trophy judging and finite route planning of your stalk. Once a shootable moose is located, don't let the excitement and anticipation override your patience and planning. It's easy to do and disastrous to success. Generally, you'll be hunting with a guide or partner on a moose hunt. Take the time to work out a system, whereby one stays put in a well-marked, visible location, while the other stalks the moose. Work out a fully understood set of signals, so the stalker will be able to ascertain the bull's position relative to his own, its activity . . . bedded, feeding, moving, etc., and the unexpected appearance of other moose (bulls or cows).

Impatience blows a major portion of the stalks on big game, so take your time and do it right. If the wind changes direction, the moose relocates, or anything unforeseen happens, don't hesitate to back off, reconnoiter the situation, and start over . . . even if you have to wait another day.

Since visibility is often very limited when stalking moose in heavy cover, wind becomes even more important, and I make constant use of my powder bottle to keep the slightest trickle of breeze working for me. A string or feather on your bow won't register slight updrafts or downdrafts, and these are often erratic enough to carry your scent the wrong direction. Use your powder bottle.

Moose Bowhunting Gear

Moose are my kind of target . . . big! A bull moose is not exceptionally hard to kill with a well-placed, razor-sharp broadhead. However, as big as they are, it just takes them a bit longer than smaller big game to realize they are dead and supposed to fall over. Any type of bow, 50 pound and above, shooting cut-on-contact, razor-sharp broadheads, will make clean kills on the largest moose when the arrow is put into the huge heart-lung zone of a moose.

The large size of the kill zone on a bull moose (30 inches by 30 inches) gives a bowhunter a bit more leeway on range and a 50- to 60-yard shot on

Spotting moose is hard work. The country moose live in is huge, but they move through rough, log-strewn bogs and sloughs with amazing speed and ease.

a moose equates to a 20-yard shot on a whitetail buck . . . if you conscientiously practice and become proficient at these longer distances.

The moose's enlarged dimensions and overall size make range determination a critical factor in moose hunting, and the best tool to take the guesswork and chance out of this important aspect is an accurate rangefinder. Never leave home without it!

Clothing can go a long way toward making or breaking a moose bowhunt, as the weather where these beasties live during the fall can range from miserably hot to miserably cold and wet. The hot weather can be combated by stripping down to the essentials, but for the wet and cold weather, you'd better have effective rain gear and warm, dry, layered undergarments.

All outer garments should be in a camouflage pattern and color that blends with the background, including gloves and facemask or camo paint. Moose country generally isn't plagued with cockleburs, burdock, and some of the more clingy, poky weeds of whitetail country, so my choice is wool outerwear, with thick or thin (depending on temperature) wicking-type underwear. (I hate wool against my tender skin.) Whatever clothing you choose should be soft and quiet as well as warm and water resistant. Scent Lok has come out with items of clothing that are ideal for moose hunting under a variety of conditions, and they help cut down on the amount of human stinkum floating around the moose habitat.

Moose are water creatures, which means your footgear should be waterproof, insulated, and of sufficient height to keep your feet warm and dry. Unless, of course, you have to cross a lake to get to your moose; then a boat would be nice.

When you walk up to a dead bull moose, your first thoughts are going to be, "What have I done and how far is camp and transportation?" You can have all your portable, packable, and foldable meat saws for smaller critters. I want a razor-sharp, full-sized, steel-handled axe at hand for quartering a moose.

Taking a trophy bull moose with a bow and arrow is an awesome accomplishment, and one that every bowhunter should experience. Sinking your teeth into a sizzling, sputtering, fat-dripping, succulent, two-foot-long, campfire-broiled moose rib ain't a bad experience either.

Caribou

JUDD COONEY

"Rise and shine, it's daylight in the swamps," I hollered enthusiastically to my supine and snoring companions as I stuck my head out the tent flap and marveled at the vast expanse of fog-shrouded tundra surrounding our minuscule campsite. Man I was pumped and ready to go bowhunting for caribou. The seemingly endless (butt-numbing) 900-mile drive from Anchorage to caribou camp, below the north slope of the Brooks Range, was quickly forgotten when we started seeing herds of caribou at the foot of Atigun Pass, along the famed Alaska pipeline. The area adjacent to this engineering marvel is the largest "bowhunting-only" zone in the United States. A no-firearms-hunting buffer zone extending two and-a-half miles on each side of the gigantic tube transporting crude oil from the oil fields around Prudhoe Bay; 850 rough and rugged miles south to the seaport of Valdez in Prince William Sound.

It was well after midnight by the time we'd gotten camp set up at Galbraith Lake, eaten a sandwich washed down with a couple of beers to celebrate our arrival and upcoming adventure, and slipped into our sleeping bags for a short snooze. The grueling drive and camp set-up had done little to stem my enthusiasm, and having been in the outfitting business for years, I'd learned to sleep fast, especially when it never really got dark. At 4:00 a.m. it was light enough to shoot and I couldn't control my excitement any longer. Unfortunately, my experienced companions didn't share my enthusiasm, and after some dire threats mumbled my way, I crawled back into my sleeping bag, wondering what kind of bowhunters I'd teamed up with and what big-game critter wasn't up and about at the crack of dawn.

Caribou bowhunting is different. It's kind of a cross between bowhunting pronghorn antelope and whitetail deer, depending on the subspecies and terrain.

There are four subspecies of caribou scattered across the far north, from the northwestern tip of Alaska to the northeastern tip of Newfoundland.

Barren ground caribou are found only in Alaska and are a larger species, in both body and antler size (by a very small margin), over the equally popular Quebec-Labrador caribou found in northern Quebec. The world-record barren ground caribou stands at 448 6/8 inches, while the Quebec-Labrador record is 434 0/8 inches. Central barren ground bulls are much like their Alaska cousins (only a bit smaller), with the world record at 420 6/8 inches. The mountain caribou is right in there with the world record at 413 6/8 inches, while the woodland caribou tops out at 345 2/8 inches.

All caribou look very much alike and you'd have to see the different species side-by-side to spot the slight differences between them. Caribou are the only big-game species where both bulls and cows

Sometimes caribou hunting involves a lot of waiting. But, generally, when you see one, there are many more to follow!

sport antlers. Their antlers look like they were put together by a committee, and accurately scoring a caribou in the field can drive you to drink. You'll find a bull with long points and good spread with small shovels and bez points, while another bull has wide double shovels and bez with short tines and narrow main beams, etc. Before you embark on a caribou bowhunting adventure, study every photo of caribou antlers you can find. The most valuable time I spent in preparation for several caribou hunts was ogling the numerous record-class antlers at several

Pope and Young competitions and trying to figure out why each set scored as they did.

It didn't take me long on my first day of bowhunting barren ground caribou with pros Curt Lynn, Ed Russell, Dave Neel, and John Colway of Anchorage to realize that bowhunting caribou has its own unique set of rules and timetables that differ drastically from normal big-game bowhunting.

This vast luxuriant tundra country is prime habitat for thousands of barren ground caribou, moose, grizzly, ptarmigan, and a host of other

Caribou antlers come in all shapes and sizes. Take a bull caribou that will bring you memories of your thrilling big-game bowhunt.

harassing anything warm blooded that moves, and caribou in particular. The insatiable pests literally drive the caribou crazy, which can work for or against a bowhunter, depending on his luck.

My Alaskan bowhunting buddies were aware of the bug phenomenon and knew the best time to locate caribou was well after the sun was up, when the bugs were really bugging the caribou. It didn't take me long to realize that the eyes, nose, and mouth of a bowhunter are almost as sought after as those of caribou. Venturing about without a liberal application of Deet insect repellent is tantamount to bowhunting grizzlies with rubber blunts. I also learned to breathe through my mouth rather than my nose and use my clenched teeth to strain out most of the bugs.

Barren ground caribou bowhunting is a spot-and-stalk situation that calls for a good set of binoculars, spotting scope, and patience. The Alaska tundra is very deceptive country for the uninitiated. Stalking caribou across the quaking, waterlogged mat of vegetation that overlays ankle-twisting, ball-bearing-like rocks and boulders is a lot tougher than it appears. A quarter-mile caribou stalk is the equivalent of a mile or longer stalk in antelope or mule-deer country, and the erratic nature of bug-crazy caribou adds a whole new dimension to stalking.

critters. The soggy, saturated arctic tundra is also home to Alaska's state bird, the mosquito, and their equally voracious and aggravating cousins, gnats and flies.

Early fall on the spongy, boggy tundra can be a tough place if you're a caribou with wide-open, sensitive nostrils and eyes. These infernal insects make life miserable for caribou by gathering around their heads and crawling into their noses and eyes. The only peace the caribou get is the few hours of twilight, when the coolness puts the insects down. Once the sun rises and warms things up, the bugs swarm out of their roost in clouds, and start

The only way the caribou can get relief from the airborne pests is to find some shadow or shade where it's too cool for the aerial assault artists. Their favorite bug-evasion tactic is to find a shady spot under a bush, behind a rock, or, best of all, in a small pool of permafrost-cooled water. The caribou stick their heads or noses into these bug-free havens and may stay head down, eyes closed, in this vulnerable position for an hour without moving, or they may get a bug up their nose and run back to where they just came from. This erratic bug-induced behavior makes for some interesting and frustrating stalking.

Stalking caribou over the water-logged tundra or tightly packed, ankle-twisting fields of rocks and boulders, can challenge even the most physically fit of bowhunters.

The first day we must have glassed and judged 200 caribou as we drove along the Haul road. We were all chomping at the bit to try our hand at stalking caribou, but we figured we needed to locate and pinpoint as many trophy animals as possible for the days ahead. Late in the afternoon, a bug-bedeviled, record-book caribou came striding out of

the river bottom, crossed the road in front of us, and ran into a small draw several hundred yards above the road. The annoyed caribou jammed his head into the cool shade of a low-growing willow for relief from the cloud of hovering gnats and mosquitoes.

My companions dropped me off a quarter mile down the road and I quickly circled behind the small ridge to approach the caribou from above and downwind, hoping he'd stay put long enough for me to get into position for a shot. When I eased my head around a bush on top of the ridge, the caribou was still head down at 40 yards, oblivious to the world around him.

I came to full draw from a semi-prone position and then slowly raised to my knees for the shot . . . the bull never moved a muscle. I picked a spot, released and watched my fluorescent-fletched and crested xx75 flit through the arctic air and disappear into the caribou rib cage. Zip, zilch . . . no reaction from the bull.

I quickly snapped another arrow onto the string, wondering if the bull was taking me seriously. He was still head down in the bushes and hadn't showed the slightest indication of being hit, although I could plainly see blood around the first arrow's entrance. I concentrated on the first arrow hit and sent a second arrow his way. The second arrow, slicing through the rib cage in almost the same place, made the bull jerk his head out of the bush and take a couple steps before he staggered and went down.

We spent the next week spotting and stalking caribou to our heart's content, and when we ended the hunt, the five of us had arrowed 13 Pope and Young caribou bulls (limit was three caribou per hunter).

Barren ground caribou are one of the few Alaskan big-game critters that can be bowhunted without the services of an outfitter or guide. Many people have the mistaken notion that Alaska is overrun with game and there are critters behind every bush and tree. Alaska is a monstrous chunk of real estate, with vast areas that contain nothing larger than voles and lemmings for much of the year. I have flown thousands of miles over the Alaskan hinterlands without seeing a live beastie, and then popped over a ridge into a valley crawling with furred and feathered game.

Hunting on your own in Alaska is a great adventure, but make sure you do your homework and plan meticulously, or you could be in for the greatest disaster of your bowhunting career. The most prevalent do-it-yourself way to get into Alaska's caribou country is hiring a flying service to drop you off in the bush for your bowhunt. During the early bow season, barren ground caribou are fairly sedentary and not in migratory mode yet.

The key to success in this type of bowhunt is to make sure you get dropped off where there are caribou. Some drop-camp flying services will drop you into a lake or area where it's easy for them to get in and out, regardless of whether there are caribou in the area. Not a good situation. Thoroughly check out several flying services and their references. Make sure they understand you want to survey the area before being put down. If there aren't huntable numbers of caribou in the area they want to drop you, fly the area until you find caribou within bowhunting range of where they can drop you off.

A good flying service will check on you periodically, and if you need to be moved they will do so. Make sure you both have an understanding of what's going down *before* you send a deposit, and get it in writing. Doing your research and homework well in advance of your Alaskan caribou adventure can make the difference between the success or failure of your bowhunt.

Caribou Bowhunting Equipment

Stalking open-country caribou is an exercise in patience and perseverance because the tundra doesn't offer much cover, and your stalks have to be meticulously planned and executed. Good binoculars and a spotting scope are invaluable in locating the animals and choosing the best route of approach. Combining the judicious use of quality optics with smart bowhunting tactics and persistence should make your caribou bowhunt a blast.

The tundra is like a giant sponge, soaking up the frigid melt water from the underlying permafrost. You can depend on being damp or wet much of the time while bowhunting and stalking caribou. When crawling through low-growing willows, the icy water running in around your belt, down through your shorts, and out your pants legs does a lot to keep you alert during your stalk. Tough as it is at times, grit your teeth, and, as the old Indian in the movie *The Outlaw Josey Wales* quipped, "Endeavor to persevere." Don't let the frigid discomfort or clouds of bugs hovering around your head push you into making a mistake or rushing your stalk.

The damp, breezy arctic conditions make wool or fleece clothing invaluable. Undergarments that cut the wind, maintain their warmth when wet, and dry quickly are an essential part of your gear. Camouflage clothing or outer garments that blend with the background are also a necessity for caribou bowhunting success.

Caribou have excellent noses, but the prevalent arctic breeze generally makes stalking with the wind in your favor a simple matter. You have to let your conscience be your guide on shooting distances in most caribou country. The more proficient you become at the longer ranges, the better your chance of scoring when the opportunity presents itself. Since

I shoot instinctively, a range finder doesn't do me much good, but for a sight shooter, a quality laser rangefinder is essential for your far north bowhunt.

Quebec-Labrador Caribou

I've been snake bit when it comes to bowhunting this species. I've had several hunts booked, and something has come along to spoil the trip every time. On one occasion, the outfitter simply disappeared and hasn't been heard from since. Probably a good thing, since his stranded clients were ready to mount his head on their garage wall.

All of the Canadian caribou species require the services of a licensed outfitter, so do-it-yourself Canada caribou bowhunting is not an option. The Quebec-Labrador caribou are generally bowhunted during the fall migration from summer to winter range. Depending on weather conditions, this northern Quebec bowhunt can range from fantastic, with thousands of caribou on the move in your hunting area, to famine, where you'll be lucky to locate a few local cows, calves, and small bulls.

The key element in killing a trophy Quebec-Labrador bull is being able to glass and judge numerous caribou, so you can pick and choose the bull of your dreams. The hunts are run from a main camp near historical caribou migration routes. Each day, hunters are transported to various crossings on rivers or lakes, where they set up to ambush caribou as they move to the crossings.

According to the many bowhunters I've talked with, the action can vary from fast and furious, with caribou streaming past everywhere, to very boring, with only a couple caribou a day. Once again, good optics are essential; you want to glass and judge oncoming caribou as far out as possible so you can concentrate on getting in position for the shot.

This can be a lot easier said than done, as a herd of caribou on the move presents a jumble of antlers that all look like trophies. Singling out a "boomer" bull in a migrating herd is one thing, but getting within bow range without spooking the whole blooming bunch is another. Imagine there are times when track shoes would be more useful than rubber boots. Caribou are like most other herd animals in that where one goes, the rest of the herd is likely to follow, and this characteristic can often be used to good advantage to put a bowhunter within range of a good bull.

Pre-hunt planning is of the utmost importance for Quebec-Labrador caribou bowhunting due to the dependence on the caribou migration. You want to book your hunt when past statistics and records indicate the peak of the migration in the area you choose to bowhunt. Start the process of booking your Quebec-Labrador caribou bowhunt at least two years in advance, so you have plenty of time for contacting outfitters and their references. Regardless of how meticulously you research your caribou bowhunt, the weather is still a critical and uncontrollable factor that neither you nor the best-intentioned outfitter can predict.

Central Barren Ground Caribou

The central barren ground caribou is the third most popular caribou species pursued by bowhunters and very similar in size to the barren ground and Quebec-Labrador. It is found in the Northwest Territories and northern Manitoba provinces, with by far the best bowhunting in the NWT in the unique and interesting town of Yellowknife. Bowhunting tactics for the central barren ground caribou are a combination of ambushing them on migration routes and spot-and-stalk hunting.

The migration is more of a slow-moving cross country trek, with scattered herds of caribou meandering in a southerly direction, following established routes around and across the thousands of various-sized lakes scattered in the rocky tundra. This seemingly haphazard travel gives bowhunters ample opportunity to glass moving herds of caribou and stalk them or get into position to ambush them as they circle around lakes or move along the narrow eskers (ridges or fingers of wind-blown sand) between the larger bodies of water.

I've been in many bowhunting camps, but Camp EKWO (which means caribou in the Dogrib Indian language), located on Humpy Lake and operated by Joyce and Moise Rabeska out of Yellowknife, NWT, is one of the best I've encountered. The fabulous food and ultra-comfortable and spacious tent accommodations are enhanced by the superb lake-trout fishing, nightly visits by local grizzlies, and the almost-constant passage of caribou on both sides of the strategically located camp. Camp EKWO has produced the world-record central barren ground caribou for archery, muzzleloader, and rifle. Not a bad accomplishment.

The main method of bowhunting the central barren ground is to cruise the extensive lake shores, glassing for caribou, or hike across the tundra to various lookout points and glass for feeding or moving groups. If the caribou are on the move, the guides usually know just where they are headed or will cross, and hustle the bowhunter into ambush position. Feeding or bedded caribou can often be successfully stalked across tundra that's broken by rock and boulder outcroppings and patches of willow, alder, and spruce.

I killed my first bull as they moved through a narrow bottleneck between two lakes, and missed the next two as they moved along the edge of a lakeshore. The largest bull that qualified for Boone and Crockett at the time I killed it was taken 400 yards from the main camp, as it and several other bulls moved along a narrow sandy esker.

Woodland and Mountain Caribou

According to Dave Widby, who experienced a successful woodland caribou bowhunt in the dense timber and brush country of Newfoundland, bowhunting these caribou is akin to whitetail deer spot-and-stalk hunting. Dave and his outfitter would cruise the logging roads and trapper trails through the dense woods on a four-wheeler, trying to spot a good bull. The woodland caribou use these trails and roads as the path of least resistance in their travels and are often spotted moving along or crossing these travel-ways.

Dave, a resident of Anchorage, Alaska, likened Newfoundland's tundra caribou country to the Alaskan bush. The heavy timber is interspersed with numerous open tundra and bog area, where the caribou feed, and allows bowhunters a decent opportunity to spot and stalk them. Spotting a caribou in one of these areas is just half the battle, as keeping them located amongst the willow- and alder dotted sloughs while stalking can be a problem. Walking up on and spooking an unseen caribou is a regular occurrence on these bowhunts. Binoculars are a woodland caribou bowhunter's best friend, and their judicious, constant use will often make the difference between success and failure.

Woodland caribou populations seem to fluctuate from year to year in different areas, so when planning your hunt, get the latest population information from your outfitter, provincial wildlife department, and bowhunting references before choosing a hunting area and outfitter.

Caribou migrations can vary from year to year, depending upon the weather. Book with an outfitter that can transport you to a new territory if the caribou have already passed through or are not in the immediate area.

Mountain caribou, as the name indicates, are found at the higher elevations in British Columbia and the Yukon and are bowhunted by the spot-and-stalk method. Binoculars and spotting scope are as essential to hunting these critters as your bow and arrow set. A good spotting scope can save you lots of boot-sole rubber by letting you judge and select your target from a distance. A spotting scope is invaluable in picking the best possible route for stalking within bow range of your chosen trophy.

Again the most valuable aspect of bowhunting a species such as mountain caribou, where an outfitter is required, is the time and effort spent in picking a primo area and the most capable outfitter you can afford. Start your planning well in advance of your bowhunt . . . you won't be sorry.

A prime bull caribou should be mandatory for any bowhunter's trophy room. The caribou's distinctive headgear, resplendent coloration, and unique habitat make it virtually impossible to have an unsuccessful caribou bowhunting experience. So start planning now.

43 Tips for Bowhunters

JOHN WEISS

Taking a deer with a compound or recurve bow is, to many, the ultimate accomplishment in hunting. These tips can help you do it.

1. Because arrows outfitted with hunting broadheads often fly differently from arrows outfitted with field or target tips, it pays to practice with the same broadheads you'll be hunting with. You'll occasionally have to replace the razor-blade inserts when they become too dull for hunting use, and you may have to replace the whole broadhead if it doesn't have inserts. If economy is important, practice with field tips during summer, then switch to broadhead practice as the season gets closer.

2. When you buy a new bow, fine-tune it by shooting through a large sheet of white paper tacked to a square wooden frame (place straw bales behind the wooden frame to stop the arrows). When you examine the tear holes, you can determine if your arrows are fishtailing or porpoising in flight. Ideally, you want to see a round shaft hole surrounded by perfect fletching cuts. If you're getting tail-high cuts, tail-left cuts, and so on, the remedy is to either slightly move the plunger button in or out, or adjust the arrow rest. Because every bow and each brand of arrow rest is different, consult the owner's guide for exact fine-tuning techniques.

To take bucks like this, you must spend a good deal of time prior to the season fine-tuning your equipment.

3. Strive for the most realistic shooting practice. Shoot arrows at life-sized 3-D foam deer targets, not at straw bales with bull's-eyes. And don't simply place the deer targets out in the open. Position them in shrubbery, under low-hanging tree branches, and in close proximity to other cover, to simulate actual shooting conditions.

4. The most common causes of an arrow wobbling in flight are an untuned broadhead, an untuned nock, or a bent arrow shaft. Use an inexpensive tabletop device called an Arro-Check to fix the problem. Lay the arrow on top of the device's opposing bearings, and spin it rapidly. If the tip of the broadhead scribes a wide circle, replace it with a new one. Now check the nock the same way, and replace it if necessary. If the arrow still wobbles in flight, the shaft has a minor bend that the naked eye cannot see. Either take the shaft to your pro shop, to have it straightened out or remove the broadhead and discard the defective shaft.

5. When a deer jumps the string, it instantaneously crouches to load its leg muscles with springed tension in preparation for flight. When it does this, the arrow frequently flies over its back. It never actually sees the arrow and attempts to duck it, however. Instead, it's reacting to the sound of the bowstring being released. Even though an arrow from a compound bow travels at an average of only 250 feet per second, sound travels at 1,088 feet per second, so the noise of your bowstring reaches the deer five times faster than the arrow itself. Dampen your

As a general rule, bowhunters take bigger bucks than those who use firearms, but not necessarily because they're better hunters. It's because most states' firearms seasons don't open until after the mating period when bucks are most vulnerable.

bow noise with string silencers, but also remember to aim slightly lower. To achieve the recommended lung shot, for example, the aiming point should be the heart.

6. When you engage in shooting practice, wear the same clothing you'll be wearing while actually hunting, not casual clothes. The hunting clothes will undoubtedly be heavier and bulkier, and this will slightly change the way you hold and draw your bow.

7. The cams and wheels of compound bows have an annoying habit of squeaking at precisely the wrong moment. Some hunters lubricate them with silicone spray, but this attracts dust and

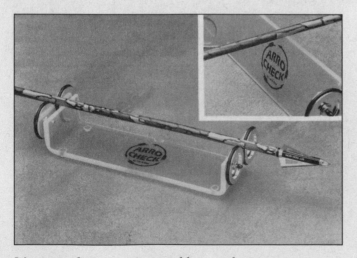

It's easy to diagnose arrow problems with an arrow spinner made for the purpose.

grit. It's better to use a small pinch of graphite powder. The cable guard may also squeak upon occasion, but due to the wear of the cables on the guard, graphite powder will quickly wear off. Keep a pencil stub in your pocket, and frequently blacken that part of the cable guard contacted by the cables.

8. How high should a bowhunting stand be? Let the shape of your chosen tree answer that question. If the tree looks like a straight, naked utility pole, a stand height of twenty-five feet or more may be in order. But if the tree has a multiple-forked trunk and many gnarled branches at a lower height—both of which will adequately break up your body outline— then hanging your stand at only eight or ten feet may be sufficient.

9. A bowhunter's ideal shot at a deer comes when the animal is standing broadside or quartering slightly away, which exposes the largest organ, the lungs. Don't settle for less or be too impulsive to shoot; deer tend to dawdle around, and in many cases they'll eventually offer the shot you want.

10. Even with a finely tuned bow, broadheads that have replaceable razor- blade inserts with cutout vents tend to fly more accurately than

This is your shot!

broadheads with solid-surface blades. The latter often plane a bit, especially in brisk breezes, causing the hunter to miss his point of aim.

11. If you know your shot at a deer was not as accurate as you would have liked, how long should you wait before following the blood trail? The rule of thumb is half an hour if the shot was in the front half of the animal, and three hours or more if the shot was toward the rear. An exception to this rule occurs during inclement weather. Then, you must take up the trail immediately, or rain or snow will quickly obliterate it and eliminate any chance for recovering the animal.

Turkey feathers are more forgiving— but plastic fletching is better in inclement weather.

12. What's the best type of arrow fletching, turkey feathers or plastic vanes? Both have benefits and shortcomings. Turkey fletching is more forgiving when you make mistakes such as not smoothly releasing the bowstring, but in inclement weather feathers tend to become matted. Plastic vanes won't correct even a slight bit of arrow wobble, but they're immune to moisture. Just bump the arrow shaft with your finger, and water droplets will fall away.

13. Many bowhunters hang a grunt tube and binoculars around their necks, but these can cause problems when you're attempting to draw. It makes more sense to stow these

items in large cargo pockets, so that they don't get in the way.

14. A peep sight on your string can shift after numerous shots if it's not permanently secured in place, and this will, of course, destroy accuracy. Many veteran bowhunters like to tightly wrap dental floss on the string immediately above and below the sight and then liberally paint the floss

Turkey feathers are more forgiving—but plastic fletching is better in inclement weather.

winding with clear nail polish or superglue to make it durable and prevent it from unraveling.

15. Buying a hunting bow from a department store or through a catalog is beneficial only from the standpoint of getting a good price. You need more than that, and it's rare to get a bow custom-fitted to your needs through such retail outlets. That's why many serious hunters prefer to deal with a local pro shop. You may pay a bit more, but the draw weight of the bow will be adjusted exactly as you want, arrows can be custom- cut in accordance with your measured draw length, a bow sight or custom arrow rest can be installed, and future tune-ups or repairs by a factory-authorized dealer are a breeze.

16. When you're shopping for a new bow at a custom archery shop, shoot several models and brands on their indoor target range (another service not offered by department stores and catalogs). High-tech compound bows are fitted with a wide variety of wheels and cams come

Put a dab of fluorescent paint on your sight pins to see them better in low light.

in too many designs to mention here. As a result, one bow model may draw easily and be perfect for target archery but be far too noisy and therefore unsuitable for deer hunting. Another bow's wheels may be dead quiet on the draw, but its breakover point—the point at which the draw weight suddenly lessens—may be unacceptable for your hunting purposes. You have to decide on these and other factors to satisfy your personal hunting needs, and the only way you can do this is by actually shooting and comparing numerous bows.

17. If you'll be bowhunting from a high tree stand, don't practice across level ground. Shoot from a stand hung in a tree in your backyard, from the roof of your garage, or from some other elevated vantage to master the acute downward shooting angles. Likewise, if you'll be hunting from a ground blind, practice while kneeling or sitting on a stool.

18. If you're commonly on stand at the crack of dawn or at dusk, and you have difficulty seeing your

metal sight pins in the low light, switch to plastic glow pins. Or dab a bit of fluorescent paint onto each metal pin. If you use lighted sight pins, be sure to change the battery at the beginning of each season and keep a spare in your fanny pack.

19. Which is better, a cutting-tip broadhead that you must sharpen, or a chisel-point broadhead with replaceable razor blades? Cutting-tip heads penetrate more easily because they begin severing hair and hide the instant the broadhead makes contact with the animal. Chisel-point broadheads, on the other hand, must push through the hair and hide before the razor blades can do their cutting work. Balance this against the fact that sharpening cutting-tip broadheads takes a good deal of time. Plus, they must be sharpened often because repeatedly pulling them out of a quiver and shooting them at targets quickly dulls them. Chisel-point broadheads need no time-consuming sharpening, though—just slip new ones in place.

20. Should your broadheads be turned in their arrow-shaft sockets until the blades are perfectly in line with the fletching? Engineers for broadhead companies say no. If, by coincidence, the blades end up perfectly aligned with the fletching, fine. But a less-than-perfect alignment is also fine; any effect upon arrow trajectory or flight will be so minimal that you'll never notice it.

21. Unless you practice throughout the year, it's wise to release the draw weight of your compound bow before putting it into off-season storage. Do this by making four to six turns of the limb bolts to lessen the stress on the limbs and reduce stretching of the string. Simply unstring a recurve or long bow after each day's hunt or practice session.

22. The risers and handles of compound bows are made of lightweight metal composite materials. If they come into contact with an aluminum or carbon arrow, a metallic clinking sound is created that will put nearby deer on full alert. Pad your arrow shelf, sight window, and handle with moleskin or felt that has a self-adhesive backing. The material also makes the handle warmer to hold in chilly weather.

23. Bow-tuning problems associated with erratic arrow flight can often be traced to a cheap arrow rest. It's false economy to spend $350 on a new bow and then slap on a $2 arrow rest. Check the catalog of the company that made your bow, and you'll undoubtedly find a wide array of arrow- rest options. The higher-quality rest you select, the better accuracy you can expect.

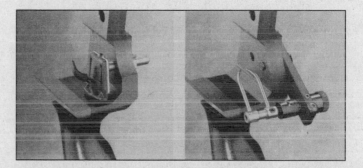

Buy a quality arrow rest. Two common styles are shown.

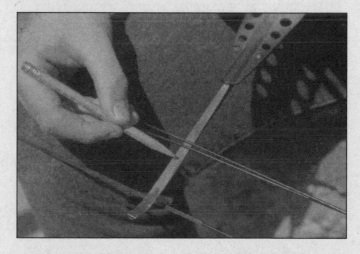

Graphite on cable and string guards prolongs their lives and eliminates squeaks.

24. In hot weather, never leave a long or recurve bow in an enclosed vehicle for long periods of time. These bows commonly have wood and/or fiberglass laminations, and excessive heat may cause the glue between the component layers to melt, ruining the bow. Some compound bows with solid-metal limbs and risers may also warp just enough to destroy accuracy.

25. The key to shooting accuracy is acquiring an intimate familiarity with your equipment, and this means regular practice throughout the year. Practice your shooting in small, untiring doses. It's far more beneficial to practice for twenty minutes every day of the week than to engage in a single four-hour marathon session on a Saturday morning.

26. How many pins do you need on your bow sight? Some hunters have only one, set at twenty yards. They then restrict themselves to shots of no more than thirty yards, which makes the slight aiming adjustment easy. Other hunters use four pins set at ten-yard intervals. It's a matter of individual preference.

27. Compound-bow hunters often own two identical bows, one of which is kept in camp as a backup. The reason is that it's very difficult to replace a compound bow's broken cable or string in the field; most such bows must be repaired at an archery shop with a bow press. Meanwhile, a backup bow set up exactly the same way as the damaged bow can save an otherwise ended hunt.

28. Wear an arm guard in cold weather when you're bulked up with heavier clothing. Otherwise, a released bowstring may slap against the sleeve of your bow arm and send the arrow flying wildly away.

29. A belt pouch can be used to support the lower limb and wheel assembly of your compound bow. When you're standing, you won't have to constantly strain your muscles by trying to hold your bow vertically, ready to draw and shoot. Moreover, when the moment of truth arrives, and a deer is within shooting range, the only movement necessary is raising the bow a few inches to clear the pouch. Such minimal movement will reduce the chances of alerting the deer to your presence.

30. Broadheads weighing 100 to 135 grains are recommended for most whitetail deer hunting situations.

31. As a rule, the best fletching twist for right-handed bowhunters is right helical; for left-handed bowhunters, it's left helical. In either case, a four-inch-long fletching is recommended for stabilizing a carbon arrow with a broadhead; five-inch fletching works best for aluminum arrows fitted with broadheads. Far less satisfactory results come from using straight fletching or fletching of less than four inches long and intended solely for competitive shooting with target points.

32. If your turkey-feather fletching becomes matted or bent due to exposure to moisture, allow it to dry thoroughly. Next, hold it briefly over the steam coming from a teakettle spout, which will allow the feather fronds to spring back to their original shape.

33. Many bowhunters think they can gain greater arrow speed—and thus a flatter arrow trajectory in flight—by increasing a bow's draw weight. This is true, but all bows have an upper draw-weight limit, and in all cases, the higher the limit selected, the more difficult the string is to draw and hold. One solution is to use an overdraw, a shelf that extends back from the bow handle. This shelf allows you to use arrows that are shorter and therefore lighter in weight, increasing your arrows' speed and flattening their trajectory without increasing draw weight.

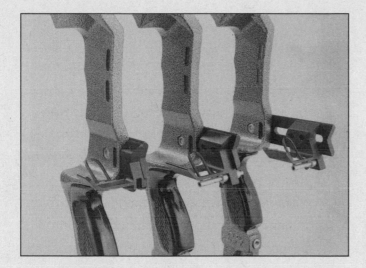

Overdraw shelves come in a variety of sizes.

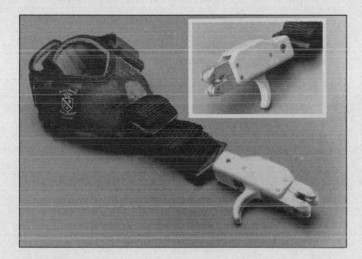

A mechanical bowstring release is generally smoother than shooting with a glove or tab, and it yields greater accuracy. But you must occasionally maintain it by removing grit and grime from the moving parts.

34. When you're using a recurve or long bow, deaden the twanging sound your bowstring makes upon release by tying two acrylic yarn puffs or rubber cat whiskers onto your string, one of them ten inches from the top limb and the other ten inches from the bottom. With an overly noisy compound bow, you may have to use four silencers: two on the string and two on the cable.

35. If you use a shooting tab or a three-fingered glove, small traces of perspiration and grime will eventually roughen the leather's surface, and this will begin to cause a stuttered string release that impairs accuracy. To cure this, place a teaspoon of unscented talcum powder in your hunting jacket pocket, and occasionally place your shooting hand in your pocket. A tab or glove with a fine coating of powder will give you the silkiest shooting release imaginable.

36. If you shoot with a mechanical shooting release, use a can of compressed air to blow out dust, pocket lint, and other debris that's sure to have accumulated in the trigger mechanism. Then, add one drop of unscented oil to the inner moving parts.

37. The weakest part of any bow is its string, because of minor but continual fraying. To prolong the string's life, rub it with beeswax several times each season. Put some on your fingertips, and then vigorously rub the string between them until you can feel heat being generated, which means the wax is softening and penetrating the strands. Whenever you have any doubt about the string's integrity, immediately replace it. You *do* have a spare on hand, don't you?

Get into the habit of applying beeswax to your bowstring several times a year.

38. One advantage that carbon arrows have over aluminum shafts is that they cannot be inadvertently bent; either they remain perfectly straight, or they break. Aluminum shafts become bent from shooting, penetrating a deer, or hitting the ground when a shot is missed. You should either discard damaged arrows or have your local archery shop put the shafts on an aluminum-arrow straightener.

39. If you plan to build one or more ground blinds, buy a roll of lightweight camouflage cloth. Inexpensive and available in all the popular patterns and colors, the cloth can be cut to length and thumbtacked between two trees. A few strategically placed branches help break up the blind's rectangular shape; all you have to add is a stool to sit on.

Carbon arrows won't bend; they're either straight, or they break.

40. What's the longest shooting distance a bowhunter should attempt? Only the distance that he has regularly practiced and at which he is confident he can execute the shot with accuracy.

41. Be aware of an important mechanical glitch that arises when shooting with sight pins—you have to hold your bow nearly vertical. If you try to cant your bow slightly to the right, you will shoot considerably low and to the right. And depending on whether you're a right- or left-hand shooter, you'll probably hit the animal too far forward or too far to the rear. That's why there is an increasing trend among bowhunters to no longer rely on sight pins, but to learn to trust instinctive shooting.

42. When using either a compound bow, recurve, or long bow, the bow arm should never drop the moment you release the arrow because this will cause the arrow to fly low to either the right or left, depending on whether you are right- or left-handed. This is called plucking, and it's detrimental to accuracy.

43. Once you become adept on the shooting range, continue your practice afield. The value of roving, as it is known, is learning to estimate distances. Using a judo head instead of a broadhead or field point, shoot at leaves, tiny patches of moss, or pinecones on the ground. It is equally important to shoot uphill, downhill, across ravines, through holes in cover, in brightly illuminated places, and in shadows.

Roving is an excellent way to fine-tune your shooting ability away from the target range.

Basic Types of Scent Reduction Products

RICHARD COMBS

Here is the thing: dogs can be trained to find an explosive material, sealed in plastic, buried in the ground, and untouched for years. They do it routinely in war-torn areas where land mines have been used indiscriminately. For that matter, I'm still impressed when my brittany goes dashing at full speed 15 or 20 yards past a small clump of cover, only to slam on the brakes, do a 180, and lock up on point. A single bobwhite quail might be in that clump of cover—a lone, non-smoking, non-perspiring little bird that did not wash with scented shampoo that morning, or eat garlic at dinner or bacon for breakfast, or stop to pump gas on his way to the field, or—well, you get the point. Everything produces some odor, and dogs, along with most of the animals we hunt, have incredible olfactory abilities. I will refrain from enumerating all the possible sources of odor on the human body. Are you skeptical that it is possible for a hunter to truly eliminate his scent, even for a short while? I am.

The real question, I believe, is not whether it is possible to entirely eliminate odor. The real question for bowhunters is whether or not it is possible to reduce odor sufficiently to give hunters an edge they would not otherwise have. Would you wash with unscented soap every time you went hunting if it meant that on one occasion you might slip within 35 yards of a bedded mule deer buck, instead of getting picked off at 55 yards? Would you wear an odor eliminating out-fit including hat and headnet day after day if it meant that sometime in the next three years a 160-class whitetail buck might stop for 3 seconds at 25 yards before running off, as opposed to turning and running without a pause when it got to 30 yards? Realistically, chances are you will never know for sure if the bear you just arrowed would have turned and run before offering a shot had you not sprinkled baking soda in your boots or used non-scented detergent to wash your parka.

It is difficult to be certain about the degree of effectiveness of these and other products in a given situation for several reasons. Little truly independent research has been done on the subject. Scent, as we have seen, is a matter of volatile (gaseous) molecules being carried through the air to the sensory organs, in this case nasal passages, of an animal. While the technology and methodology may exist to determine the concentration of these molecules in a given controlled area, few independent labs with the necessary resources have to date had sufficient motivation to conduct the kind of research that would provide useful information to hunters. Further complicating things, hunters are dealing with biology and uncontrolled conditions, not machines in a lab. A machine may indicate the concentration of various molecules in an enclosed space, but that does not tell us how those molecules behave in a forest or on a prairie.

It also doesn't tell us at what level of concentration a given species under given circumstances can detect those molecules, or how it will react to various concentrations of them.

What hunters have mostly relied upon, then, is common sense and anecdotal evidence accumulated by hunters in the field. I'll confess a bias: I'm highly skeptical of common sense. For thousands of years common sense told us the earth is flat and the sun circles it. Science came along to tell us the earth is round and it circles the sun, and I'm inclined to go with science. Having said, that I would nonetheless point out that I am sure I will smell my hunting partner more quickly, from further away, and with a more noticeable reaction, after a week in elk camp than was the case on the first day of the hunt. Is it unreasonable to suspect that the same is true for most game animals? Anecdotal hunting evidence is far from perfect, but it is evidence and should not be ignored, especially in the absence of other evidence. And anecdotal evidence suggests that scent reduction can make a difference. Virtually every consistently successful bowhunter I know makes some effort to reduce or control scent in some way.

Not all the anecdotal evidence available on the subject comes from hunters. Among the more convincing sources of evidence are trappers. Though I've done very little trapping personally, as a hunter I've long been fascinated by it. If hunters are concerned about odor control and the use of scent, successful trappers seem to be obsessed with it. Evidence from trappers strikes me as particularly convincing

for the reason that trapping by nature tends to reduce or eliminate many of the variables involved in hunting. For instance, if I'm hunting an elk wallow, a bull approaches, stops momentarily, then retreats into the brush, any number of things might explain the behavior. Did he catch my scent in the air? Did he come across scent I left on the ground as I approached the wallow? Did he see me? Hear me? Did another animal scare him off or warn him of my presence? I will probably never know. In the case of trapping, most of these variables would not apply. Some trappers run trap lines daily through the season, and almost all of them over the years experiment with a variety of locations and trap sets. Further, much as most of them enjoy trapping, trapping is hard work, and many trappers are looking for supplemental income. They tend to do what works, with as little wasted time and effort as possible. The fact that almost all of them are convinced careful scent control is a major factor in their success is telling.

Somewhere out there, perhaps, is a consistently successful bowhunter who pays no attention to scent control. I just haven't met him. Imperfect though the evidence may be, thousands upon thousands of hunters have logged countless hours in the field and have come to the conclusion that taking some measures to reduce scent while hunting is worth the effort and the expense.

Sources of Odor

When hunters talk about controlling odor, they are talking about two things. One involves the odors with which they or their clothing and gear may be contaminated, including soaps and shampoos, shaving creams, lotions, ointments, smoke, gas fumes, oils, mothballs, foods and beverages, cooking odors, and any other substance that hunters or their gear may come in contact with. For that matter, the clothing or gear may itself emit odor. The sources of most of these odors are clear enough. They are in our kitchens, our bathrooms, our garages, basements, and even storage sheds. When we leave home, they may be in our cars and trucks, in the diners we stop in for break-fast, in the gas stations where we stop for gas. Sometimes, they are just plain in the air around us.

Another type of odor is the one produced continuously by hunters' bodies and their breath, or more specifically by various secretions and the action of bacteria on these secretions. Most perspiration is produced by eccrine glands that cover the entire body, and has little if any odor, consisting primarily of water and a few salts.

Apocrine glands, however, produce perspiration that is much higher in fats and proteins. These fats and proteins, along with hair, dead skin, and other detritus form a rich medium for bacteria, and it is the action of these bacteria on the fats and other ingredients of perspiration that causes most body odor. In effect, apocrine glands are human scent glands. Most are located in the armpits and the pubic areas.(Interestingly, some of us have more apocrine glands than do others.Asian populations, for instance, have far fewer apocrine glands, and in some cases none at all. In Japan, body odor is considered a medical condition.) It is no accident, of course, that the areas of the body containing apocrine glands tend to be covered in hair. Hair contributes to an environment favorable for the formation of odor-causing bacteria,and holds odor. Laugh if you like at those hard-core trophy hunters out there who shave their underarms during hunting season—I know I do—but they may be on to something. I haven't yet got up the nerve to ask them if they shave their groin areas, also.

We can speculate about whether body odors or contaminant scents are more important, and which of these odors animals may or may not associate with humans or with danger, but the simplest and safest course of action for any hunter concerned about scent control is to try and keep all odors to an absolute minimum. Knowing how best to do this requires a basic understanding of how various scent reduction products work. Though manufacturers like to imply that their products will reduce or eliminate any form of scent, the fact ist hat some are better suited to reducing body odors at its source, while others are better suited for applying to clothing and other gear. At the time of this writing, scent control is a rapidly growing part of the hunting industry and new technology, much of it borrowed from medical and other applications, is developing so rapidly that it is difficult to stay abreast of it. Much of what follows is to some extent a sort of snapshot of the industry as it exists today.

Start Clean, Stay Clean

There is no scent reduction product that cannot be overwhelmed at some point. Scent control begins with getting clean and staying as clean as possible, and it only stands to reason that the cleaner the hunter, the less chance for any scent control product to fail. In fact, the scent-control regimen of some very successful hunters is as simple as washing themselves and their clothing thoroughly in scent-free soaps or detergents. Starting clean is easy enough, but staying clean is more challenging. What often happens is that hunters work up a sweat getting to their stand (or into their stand). Leaving off the parka or jacket until getting settled into a stand can alleviate that problem.Increasing numbers of bowhunters prefer ladder stands and ground blinds, partly because we bowhunters are an aging population. In the process, they are discovering that not only are ladder stands and ground blinds easier and safer, but getting into them is also quicker and quieter, and does not require working up a sweat, especially compared to climbers.

Whenever possible, keep hunting clothes in sealed containers until it's time to hunt. Apply scent reducers right before hunting.

The Chemistry behind the Products

Essentially, there are three types of commercially produced products intended to reduce odors. These are 1) antimicrobials, designed to prevent the formation of certain odors by killing or inhibiting the growth of bacteria that cause these odors, or by neutralizing acidity 2) products designed to prevent the formation of the gas molecules that form odors, or which create a chemical reaction such as oxidation, to destroy odors, and 3) products with materials such as activated carbon that adsorb odors. Some products combine two of these types of scent control, and by using various layers of clothing or different types of scent control products, many hunters simultaneously employ all three.

Sodium bicarbonate—more commonly referred to as baking soda—is famous for its ability to control odors by neutralizing acids, including the acids present in perspiration. It has some antimicrobial properties in that its presence creates a less inviting habitat for many types of bacteria, and it absorbs moisture, which creates an environment in which bacteria can thrive. It is the active ingredient in a number of the scent control products being marketed to hunters. If the product suggests you can gargle with it, there is a good chance its active ingredient is baking soda. The best way to use many of these products is to apply them directly to the skin after showering. Apply them everywhere, if you like, but pay special attention to the areas that perspire the most. Plain baking soda can be useful, either as a deodorant (mix it with a little corn starch to keep it from clumping), as a toothpaste, or a mouth rinse. For hunters who cannot (or prefer not) to line-dry clothes, a few tablespoons of baking soda in the dryer can reduce odors present in the dryer.

Most common deodorants are antimicrobials, including the unscented products marketed to hunters. Antiperspirants differ from deodorants in that they clog the pores to prevent perspiration, as opposed to acting on the perspiration. Though they might contain zinc or aluminum or other ingredients that have an antimicrobial effect, they prevent body odor primarily by preventing the perspiration on which bacteria thrive.

A number of herbs, minerals, and other substances are claimed to have deodorant effects, in some cases by acting as antimicrobials. Many people are interested in these because of allergies to ingredients often found in commercial deodorants, or because the commercial products cause irritation, or because they have concerns about the long-term health effects of deodorants. Determining the validity of claims made on behalf of "natural" deodorants is difficult if not impossible, and most of the evidence is purely anecdotal. The lack of scientific evidence supporting many of the claims may simply be an indication that there are no organizations sufficiently motivated to spend time and money researching the effectiveness of, for instance, coconut oil, as a deodorant. Coconut oil is among the substances sometimes touted as a deodorant, along with chlorophyll, sesame seed oil, aloe, and various "crystals" and minerals, often containing bauxite, alum, or zinc. Chlorophyll and zinc in particular have long been touted as natural deodorants, and we'll take a closer look at them in another chapter.

Another antimicrobial is silver, which is increasingly being used in clothing. The U.S. army has for some time issued to infantrymen socks with silver in the fabric to control the growth of bacteria that give rise to a number of foot ailments. In more recent years, several makers of hunting garments offer socks and undergarments incorporating silver.

The idea, again, is to prevent the growth of the bacteria that cause body odors.

Stopping odors by controlling the conditions that create them is one approach; another approach entails a chemical interaction with substances to prevent volatility, or destroying odors as quickly as they form through oxidation. As we have seen, odors are formed when substances release molecules into the atmosphere. Some substances are not volatile. Steel, for instance, is not volatile and normally has no odor. A chemical reaction that controls volatility—that is, one that stops the release of molecules into the air—prevents odors. Many of the scent reduction products that are sprayed onto the skin, clothing, or gear, operate by reducing volatility or creating other chemical changes that prevent the formation of odors.

Finally, there are the products that adsorb or absorb odors. Manufacturers like to point up the differences, but from the hunter's perspective it matters little. Technically, adsorption refers to a process in which molecules cling to the surface of other molecules. Absorption, on the other hand, refers to a process in which molecules are actually drawn into or contained within other molecules. Doubtless the best known of these products (in the hunting industry) exists in the form of carbon-impregnated clothing. Any bowhunter who has looked at an ad for these garments probably has a basic understanding of how they are supposed to work. Tiny carbon granules trap and hold odor molecules, preventing their release into the air. Eventually the granules are full up, and can contain no more odor molecules. An application of heat releases some, if not all of these molecules, freeing the carbon granules to trap odors again. The use of activated carbon has long had industrial and military applications, usually for controlling or neutralizing toxic substances of various kinds. The military often issues carbon clothing to personnel in areas where there is the threat of chemical weapons. It works.

The use of carbon clothing for odor control is more controversial. In industrial applications, carbon that has adsorbed its capacity and will be re-used is heated at temperatures that would destroy any garments. In military applications, carbon clothing is issued in airtight containers, and is intended to be used once, then discarded. The argument is often made that the temperatures to which carbon clothing is exposed in clothes dryer are insufficient to achieve the desired results. The case made by the manufacturers of these garments is that heat at these temperatures, while it may not entirely eliminate the scent molecules trapped by the carbon, will eliminate enough of them to enable the garment to work as intended. In addition, to some extent time may be substituted for temperature. By exposing carbon clothing to moderate temperatures for longer periods of time, we can achieve the same results as if we exposed it to higher temperatures for a short period of time.

Critics also suggest that to be effective, carbon must have scent molecules forced through it under pressure, or the scent molecules will simply find their way around the carbon molecules. Put an air filter in the middle of a room, as one argument goes, and it will have little if any effect. Put it in ducts or vents where air is forced through it, and it can work. This does not explain how carbon clothing protects military personnel from toxic chemicals, though it may be a simple matter of the concentration of carbon used. (That is, if the carbon particles are sufficiently concentrated that molecules cannot get around them, they can be effective.) The arguments about carbon clothing go back and forth. In recent years, lawsuits have been filed against the makers of carbon hunting clothing, and in at least one case, a ruling has been made. It was the kind of ruling that enables both sides to claim partial victory. In plain English, it seemed to suggest that some of the ads on the part of the carbon clothing companies had to be toned down. The implication is that the product may be useful, but claims of 100% effectiveness (as in "Forget the wind, just hunt") were excessive.

Cyclodextrins

Harnessing technology to control odors is a relatively recent phenomenon in the hunting community, but major industries ranging from the medical industry to companies involved in food, sanitation, household cleaners and detergents, and others have long experimented with technical means of reducing or eliminating odor. One fairly recent development along these lines has been the increasing use of cyclodextrins for odor control. (Probably the best known product currently using cyclodextrins is Proctor and Gamble's Febreze, a popular household odor eliminator.) In addition to reducing or eliminating odor, cyclodextrins can actually store and deliver odor (such as perfumes), and have also been used to release and store medications gradually into the body over time.

In layman's terms, here is how they work. Cyclodextrins are complex molecules, similar to sugars, and are shaped much like a doughnut. They tend to join together in strings that form tubes or hollowed out cones. The exterior is hydrophobic (repels water), while the interior is hydrophilic (attracts water). In addition, they can be ionically charged to create an electrostatic attraction with other molecules. The effect is that they attract and absorb other molecules (including the volatile molecules that are the source of odors), storing them in their hollow cavities. Eventually, of course, all the cyclodextrins are full of molecules. When this happens, additional cyclodextrins must be applied to the source of odor, at least in the case of sprays such as Febreze. In the case of clothing that contains cyclodextrins in the fabric, the odor molecules can be removed simply by washing and drying the garment.

Sound too good to be true? The scent control industry is highly competitive, and every product has its critics, many of whom make other products, or are on the payroll of those who do. There is a great deal of protective secrecy, rumors fly everywhere, and lawyers make a lot of money initiating or defending suits. Getting solid, unbiased information is difficult, and manufacturers often start to sound like politicians: "I'm sorry, but I can't discuss that while it's in litigation."

So far, the criticism sometimes heard regarding cyclodextrins is that they are good at containing certain odor molecules, not so good at containing others. So, for instance, cyclodextrins may be good at containing body odor, but may not eliminate odors of frying bacon. Or they might be good at eliminating the odor from the dog that rubbed against your leg on your way out the door, but not at eliminating campfire smoke. Dan River, the company that makes No-Trace hunting clothing, insists that the cyclodextrins in their clothing will effectively reduce body odor as well as external contaminants that may contaminate hunting clothes. Who is correct? It is true that a given cyclodextrin may attract and hold certain odor molecules, and not others. It is also true, however, that to some extent cyclodextrins can be tailored to work for a variety of molecules. It may be possible to make use of a variety of cyclodextrins to operate on a variety of odors. As a case in point, Proctor and Gamble claims that Febreze is effective on a wide range of household odors, from pet odors to cooking odors to cigarette smoke.

Just how much odor can cyclodextrins absorb? As of this writing, No Trace is the only brand of hunting garments making use of cyclodextrins. "If you sit for awhile in a truck that just smells strongly of gas fumes," concedes No Trace's Dewey Knight, "you could end up out in the woods hunting before the No Trace has an opportunity to absorb all the odor." Normally though, continues Knight, you can hunt up to a week before you'll need to wash the clothing to reactivate its scent reducing properties. "Of course that is under typical hunting conditions," Knight explains. "If you're very active and the weather is warm and you're sweating a lot, that time might be reduced." In any case, the same things can be said for most any odor reduction process on the market. All can be overwhelmed with very heavy odors, and the performance of all of them can be affected by activity levels, temperature, humidity, and other factors.

The fact that cylcodextrins have been used for some time, and continue to be used, in the medical and pharmaceutical industry as well as in other industries, suggests that they have some legitimacy. In fact, cyclodextrins have been tested by the scientific community, including specifically the use of cyclodextrins in clothing. Two tests I'm familiar with were conducted at the University of North Carolina, and by the Journal of Inclusion Phenomena and Macrocylic Chemistry. The limitation of these studies, and others like them, is that they examined the ability of cyclodextrins to increase the effectiveness of flame retardants, and to hold for release various kinds of perfumes or antimicrobials. Specific tests of their abilities to absorb odors were not to my knowledge conducted, although the tests

that were conducted yielded positive results and could be construed to indicate that cyclodextrins in clothing are—or at least have the poten- tial to be—effective odor reducers.

As always, hunters will doubtless conduct their own tests on these products, and will arrive at their own conclusions about whether or not this technology works. The tests will be less than scientific. On the other hand, they will be conducted in the only arena that truly matters to the hunter, which is out in the woods in the presence of game. And, scientific as any more formal tests might be, it is probable that the only way to know for certain if such a product can defeat the super sensitive noses of game animals is to wear them in the presence of game animals and observe their responses. For sure, what we can say at a minimum about cyclodextrins at this point is that they represent a promising technology for helping hunters with the most challenging aspect of big game hunting

Blinds

Blinds haven't traditionally been thought of as scent reduction products, so I've given them their own category. When I say "traditionally," I mean that few hunters would associate blinds with reductions in scent—but that's not to say the thought has never occurred to any hunters. In recent years, with the growing popularity of commercially produced, fully enclosed blinds, a number of hunters have suggested that these blinds could help contain scent. Use of such ground blinds is increasing in popularity, but they have not been commonly used long enough to accumulate the kind of anecdotal evidence that has built up around other scent reducing products.

Still, it doesn't seem inconceivable that blinds could afford some degree of scent control, if only because they block the wind, thereby preventing it from carrying at least some scent downwind. More recently, some blind makers have been offering in blinds the same carbon-impregnated fabrics that are offered in hunting garments. Short of that, hunters are well-advised to avoid contaminating blinds with foreign odors to the extent possible. Hunters generally prefer to set up blinds at least a few days prior to hunting from them, mostly to allow game to become accustomed to seeing them in the environment. It could be, though, that allowing the blinds to de-odorize, or the game to become accustomed to their odor, is at least as important as visual considerations. Many hunters also pile dirt, leaves, sticks, and other debris around the base of the blind, to aid in preventing the escape of odor from inside the blind. Whether blinds are designed with scent reduction in mind or not, it only makes sense for bowhunters using ground blinds to keep scent considerations in mind.

What Does Science Say?

Many readers aren't old enough to recall the controversy in the 1960s and 70s surrounding the health effects of smoking cigarettes. Suffice it to say that there was no shortage of scientists and even medical professionals willing to state for the record that there was no evidence supporting the notion that cigarettes increased the likelihood of contracting cancer. Sadly, many of them continued to maintain that position in the face of mountains of evidence to the contrary. Much of the public didn't know what to believe. That issue has been resolved by time, of course. Maybe a better comparison is the more current controversy surrounding global warming. Unless you happen to be a climatologist, you are more or less in the position of having to choose

which scientists you believe. The science of scent reduction— at least as it pertains to its practical applications in hunting situations—is still in its infancy. There are arguments and counter-arguments, with experts testifying for and against the efficacy of different scent reducing products.

In the only truly independent scientific study of scent control I have found—at least as it might have some relevance to a hunting situation—Dr. John Shivik of the National Wildlife Research Center extensively tested the ability of seven search dogs to find people wearing carbon-impregnated clothing, compared to their ability to locate people not wearing such clothing. The people were placed in blinds, the dogs were allowed to sniff a piece of fabric previously handled by the people in the blinds, and dogs and handlers were then given specified amounts of time in which to locate the subjects. In all but one of 42 trials, dogs found all the test subjects within the allotted time. Dr. Shivik found that persons not wearing carbon suits were detected from slightly greater distances, but did not find the differences in distance to be statistically significant. While noting that he believed it possible for individuals to put on sealed carbon suits in such a way as to remain undetectable to dogs, his overall conclusion was that for practical purposes, carbon suits are ineffective.

If you think that settles the issue once and for all, you are not a scientific thinker.

In fairness, if we are going to be truly scientific in our approach, we have to concede that the results of one test are never conclusive. It will be interesting to see if other researchers can duplicate these results, or if they arrive at different conclusions. As a side note, it is significant (though not surprising) that Shivik did observe significant differences in the time it took dogs to find subjects, and these differences were related to barometric pressure, humidity, and the variability of the wind. Shivik also speculated that one probable source of contamination of the suits was that wearers handled them in putting them on. Bowhunters using these suits might want to consider wearing rubber gloves when donning them.

Scent-Lok's Glenn Sesselman also makes an interesting point in regard to this study. Search dogs, he points out, are trained to detect a faint odor, then follow that odor as it grows stronger until they reach the source. A wild animal is not seeking the source of the odor, and if it is faint will not seek the source of it (assuming it isn't food or a female in heat). In most cases the animal will simply not react at all to a very faint odor.

Scent-Lok has funded several studies of their product, including at least one study in which it was compared to another product and found to be superior. The study was conducted by professors at the University of North Carolina, which is internationally renowned for its college of textiles. Laboratory testing indicated that Scent-Lok fabric was very efficient at adsorbing a wide range of odors and, perhaps most significantly, that it could in fact be regenerated sufficiently in an ordinary clothes dryer to remain effective for repeated use. The public has every right to be skeptical of studies that are not independently funded and conducted. In fairness, though, it should be pointed out that the academics conducting these studies are more than credible scientists, and that when they present their findings they put their reputations on the lines. Further, such studies are expensive. Few outside the industry are likely to invest the time, money, and human resources necessary to conduct a truly scientific study of this issue.

The criticism may be raised also that a study conducted in a lab is not necessarily a predictor of results outdoors. Fair enough, but this really only points to the limitations of science. A very large part of what defines scientific methodology is control of variables so that valid comparisons can be made. Laboratories offer a great deal of control. Operating in the outdoors makes control of variables such as temperature, wind velocity and direction, and humidity (to name only a few), extremely difficult or impossible.

In time, we may accumulate sufficient evidence to convince any rational, educated hunter that a given type of scent reduction product does or does not work. In the meantime, it would behoove hunters to keep an open mind on the subject. The more serious and consistently successful hunters I know tend to employ at least some of these scent-reduction products, and some use them all. They wash with unscented soaps, apply unscented deodorants, wear scent-reducing clothing of one type or another, or use scent reducing powders or sprays. None that I know totally ignore wind direction, and most take it seriously.

My own experiences, which I present here as neither less nor more valid than those of any other experienced hunter, are inconclusive. I am convinced that reducing scent is possible and that it makes a difference. How much of a difference is not clear. Depending on circumstances, I use some or all of these products. I have been detected by game when following a rigid scent control regimen. I have also had game downwind of me for extended periods of time, and remained undetected. In addition I have observed, as have many hunters, that game animals at times appear to detect an odor, but not to a degree that causes them to bolt. The head comes up, perhaps, and they appear to change from a relaxed state to a tense state. They look around, as if looking for the source of a faint odor. It could be that they detect an odor, but think it is at some distance, or are simply unable to locate the source of it. I've even had deer snort, or jump and run a short distance, only to stop. On more than one occasion I've had the opportunity to arrow animals that I'm sure were aware of my presence, but couldn't locate me. It is not unreasonable to speculate in these situations that keeping scent to a minimum is the difference between an animal that becomes alert to possible danger and remains in the area long enough to provide a shooting opportunity, and one that bolts instantly.

Based on all this, I am inclined to continue using scent reducing strategies unless and until more extensive scientific studies convince me they are ineffective. My feeling, which appears to be in accord with the thoughts of many experienced hunters, is that getting within bow range of mature big game animals is sufficiently difficult that I want any edge I can get.

Cover Scents

RICHARD COMBS

Behavioral scientists have observed that white-tailed deer can distinguish between as many as twenty different scents simultaneously, and it seems reasonable to assume that most of the species we hunt have similar capabilities. There is reason to wonder if it is even possible to fool a game animal's nose by attempting to cover one scent with another. Before you give up on the idea of cover scents, though, you might want to consider this question: Why do most dogs seem to delight in rolling in the foulest, rottenest, most disgusting carcasses or other sources of odors they can find? Biologists tell us this behavior is common to wild as well as domesticated canines, and many theorize that the behavior is an attempt to mask scent, as an aid in stalking prey. Along similar lines, why do canines, felines, and other critters often kick dirt over their droppings, if not to reduce or mask scent?

If it is true that animals engage in these behaviors to cover their scent, then thousands upon thousands of years of evolution would seem to support the notion that it is indeed possible to mask scent to a degree that will make a hunter less easily detected by his prey. While it seems unlikely that scent can be entirely eliminated in this manner, perhaps it can be reduced to such a degree that it cannot be detected for as great a distance, or as quickly, by a prey species. Or perhaps the mixture of aromas causes a momentary hesitation, giving

the predator a few extra seconds that can make the difference.

Native Americans were known to sometimes apply cover scents of one sort or another. Some tribes routinely sat in the smoke from campfires, convinced this cover scent gave them an edge when stalking into bow range of their quarry. They may not have understood scientific methodology, but they hunted almost daily all their lives, and for generation after generation depended on successful hunts for their very survival.

On a recent South African hunt, Wilhelm Greeff of Zingelani Safaris strongly urged me to burn cattle or zebra dung near my blind as a cover scent, insisting that it made a difference. Jim Litmer of Third Hand Archery products was in camp.

"We kept dung burning on and off all day outside our blind near a waterhole," Jim told me one night over dinner. "When the dung was burning, game came in. When the dung wasn't burning, no game came to the waterhole. At one point three rhinos came in and decided to stay awhile. They hung around until the dung burned up, and soon after that they spooked and ran off." My own experience was not quite so conclusive, but I can report that numerous species of game came to the waterhole I was watching while the dung was burning, including zebras, waterbuck, kudu, and numerous warthogs.

What Kind of Cover Scent to Use?

This is a more complicated question than it might at first appear to be. Typically, cover scents attempt to produce a strong smell that is common in the environment. Earth scent, pine scent, and the urine of common creatures such as foxes and raccoons are probably the most popular cover scents. Usually, earth and pine scents are sprayed on or attached to an item of clothing in the form of wafers or patches, while urines are usually applied a few drops at a time to boot soles before entering the woods, to prevent deer from readily discerning the trail. As in the case of food scents, some hunters feel it's important to use cover scents that are common to the area. Dirt would seem to be a common element, but, would a generic dirt scent closely resemble everything from the red clay of Georgia, to the sand of the South Carolina Low Country, to the fertile loam of the Midwest?

What about the use of urine from predators such as foxes? While some studies indicate that animals may react negatively to the urine of predators, even more studies suggest otherwise. Then too, although the urine of various species may have different odors depending on what they have eaten, urine does tend to break down quickly to the point at which, according to biologists, all mammal urine soon smells basically the same. More than a few successful deer hunters routinely apply fox urine to their boots before entering the woods.

Still other hunters scoff at the notion that an animal is put on the alert by, for instance, the scent of pines in an area where there are no pine trees. My own take on this is that since it is easy to use a scent that is common to the area being hunted, why not do it, just in case. Here is another consideration: If half the hunters in the woods are using earth scent (or pine scent, or fox urine), might not a deer learn to associate that scent with hunters? In the West, many hunters, especially elk hunters, hunt from spike camps, where they usually spend at least some time sitting around campfires. Like their Native American predecessors, some successful modern hunters are of the opinion that the smell of smoke acts as an effective cover scent. Most of us have heard stories about hunters who smoke cigarettes on deer stands, putting a smoking butt in the fork of a tree just long enough to shoot an approaching deer, then finishing the smoke before climbing down to take up the trail. Happily, I quit smoking years ago, but I can confirm the truthfulness of those stories, having done that very thing myself. Could cigarette smoke be a cover scent?

Assuming cover scents can work, whether or not smoke (or any other scent) can act as a cover would probably depend upon whether or not deer have learned to associate the smoke, or other scents, with humans, and more specifically with danger. It seems unlikely that animals in more-or-less remote areas would make that connection— although if they experience pain or a threat from one smoking hunter, the association could be made quickly. At

Did a cover scent encourage this bear to come into bow range? It's impossible to be certain, but positive results are hard to argue with.

the same time, deer that often come into contact with people, whether in heavily populated suburban areas, farm country, or areas where they are subject to heavy hunting pressure, would be quite likely to associate the smell of smoke with humans.

Cover Scents vs. Scent Reducers

I have spoken with one manufacturer that specifically recommends against using cover scents in conjunction with scent reducers. Most don't address the issue, while others insist that it makes perfect sense to do so. Many scent reducers work by absorbing scent, adsorbing scent, or chemically interacting with substances to prevent odors from forming. All these products have a capacity. Products that absorb or adsorb odor molecules at some point are filled up, and become ineffective until they are cleaned or reactivated in some manner, and products that oxidize or in some similar chemical reaction neutralize scent are in effect "used up" in the process. It would seem to make no sense to

invest in, for instance, a Scent-Lok suit, then spray pine scent all over it. The Scent-Lok will absorb the pine scent, counteracting its effectiveness. What's worse, the carbon particles in the Scent-Lok will reach capacity and then fail to adsorb any additional odors. In the case of some spray-on products, it is possible to reapply them frequently. Still, it would not seem logical to use a cover scent, then use a product that will attempt to neutralize that scent. If the scent reducer succeeds, the cover is not working. If the cover scent succeeds, the scent reducer is not working.

Some scent reducers, such as most soaps, detergents, and deodorants, work primarily as antimicrobials, preventing the formation of bacteria that cause body odor. In that case, the two products might be used in conjunction, since the cover scent would not prevent the scent reducer from killing bacteria and in this way preventing body odor. Another way to use cover scents involves placing them slightly downwind, where they can provide cover without fighting scent-reducing products.

Attractant Scents

RICHARD COMBS

The 140-class whitetail was more than 100 yards out when Kentuckian Jason Strunk first spotted it crossing a bean field. Though it was far-off and moving in the wrong direction when he lost sight of it, Jason cautiously stood up, lifted his bow from its holder, and turned in his tree stand. When the buck came around a bend in the logging road about two minutes later, Jason waited for the right moment, tooted on his hands-free grunt tube to stop the buck in a shooting lane, and loosed a perfectly aimed arrow. Not ten seconds later, he watched it drop. How did Strunk know that buck was headed his way? He had laid down a scent trail with a drag rag on his way into the stand less than an hour before, starting at the far edge of the bean field and circling carefully to his stand. When he saw the buck cross the field with its nose to the ground, he knew it was following his scent trail.

There are scents on the market designed to attract not only whitetailed deer, but mulies, sitkas, blacktail deer, elk, bear, wild hogs, moose, all the North American wild canines, bobcats, cougars, and even small game and furbearers such as rabbits, raccoons, and skunks. There is no question that game can be lured into shooting position with scents. What is equally clear is that scent doesn't always work. And when it does work, just why is a controversial issue.

Realistic hunters aren't really expecting to find something that always works. They're looking for something that gives them an edge—something that makes the odds against scoring on any given day a little lower. How many times would you use scent for one opportunity at a good buck?

The issues for hunters are what kind of scents work, when do they work, and when (and why) do they often not work? Attractant scents can be divided into several categories, though there may be some overlap. These are food scents, sex scents, and curiosity scents. Urine can also be a category of its own. Though it is often considered a sex scent, and might also be considered a curiosity scent, we'll explain why we list it as a category of its own when we get to it. Why do I say there may be some overlap among these categories? Until we can get inside an animal's head, we really have no way of knowing for certain what motivates it. Was it hungry and fooled by that bottled apple scent, or was it curious about a strange new smell it had never encountered before? Was that rutting elk fooled by the cow-in-heat scent, or was it curious about something that vaguely resembled the scent of a cow-in-heat but wasn't? Some would argue that any time animals respond to a bottled or synthesized scent, they are responding mostly from curiosity. And of course some hunters would say, "Who cares why they come in, just so they come in?" Manufacturers themselves recognize the overlap. Many refer to their scents as lures. The ingredients are something they prefer to keep secret, but they often indicate that the lure contains a mixture of ingredients designed to appeal to hunger or curiosity or both.

Food Scents

First let's distinguish between "food" and "food scents." In states such as Texas, where baiting deer is perfectly legal, hunters may put corn, apples, beets, or similar foods out as bait, and it seems reasonable to assume deer that encounter the bait for the first time are responding to smell. Bears, too, are hunted over bait in some states and Canadian provinces.

That is not what we are talking about, however. By "food scents," we are referring to bottled scents made from concentrates or synthetic odors, or solid mixtures that are volatile enough to produce food scents that can be detected from some distance, or various products that are heated or even boiled to produce scents intended to resemble foods. An interesting issue related to food scents is the oft heard caution about using the scents of foods that do not occur naturally in a given area. We'll examine this again in the chapter on animal intelligence, but essentially the idea is that a deer that suddenly detects the scent of, say, apples, in an area where there are no apple trees, will react with suspicion, or will sense in some way that something is not right and will avoid the area.

As in the case of similar concerns about cover scents, many biologists, and some hunters, scoff at that idea. In their opinion, the idea that a deer catches a whiff of corn in an area where there is no cornfield and is suddenly on the alert or suspicious that something is fishy, is just ridiculous. Deer are very wary, or so goes the reasoning, but they're not that complicated. They don't think that way. If it smells like something good to eat and they're hungry, they'll check it out. If the smell is unfamiliar but not threatening, they may or may not react with curiosity.

We can speculate about why animals respond to certain foods at certain times, and others at other times, but ultimately it's something only the animals themselves know for certain. It's probably often associated with seasonal factors, or the amount of sugar, protein, or other nutrients present in a given food source at a given stage of ripeness. The bottom line for many hunters, though, is that putting out a food scent is unlikely to do any harm, and can sometimes be the ticket to success.

Curiosity Scents

Most animals, especially deer, are curious to some degree, which is the idea behind curiosity scents. Animals investigate their environment, and one of their chief instruments of investigation is the nose. Whitetails have been referred to as one-hundred-pound noses that run around smelling everything in the woods. Given their curiosity and their reliance on their noses, it's not surprising that deer will, on occasion, approach the source of a strong, unusual, or unknown aroma to check it out.

What exactly are curiosity scents? In the case of commercially produced scents, that is a difficult question, since manufacturers are highly secretive about the formulas they have developed, if their ads are to be believed, after years of research. In a University of Georgia study involving the use of motion-activated cameras placed over a variety of scents, the numbers of deer attracted to car polish rivaled the numbers attracted to several kinds of urine and food scents. (Of course, who is to say the deer were not reacting to urine and food scents out of curiosity?)

Sexual Attractants

Sexual attractants don't just get game animals excited, they get hunters excited. No mystery there—when you consider that close to and during the rut is

More than one whitetail buck has followed a hot scent straight into the lap of a waiting bowhunter.

the one time, for many species, when even the most cautious, trophy-class animals allow their obsession with estrous females to make them vulnerable, it's not surprising that hunters would seek to take advantage of that vulnerability. Probably the most commonly used sexual attractant is doe-in-heat urine, which may be placed on the ground, used to saturate a rag or a wick and hung from a tree, or even sprayed into the air. Hunters also frequently use doe urine to lay down scent trails, saturating a rag that can be dragged, or a pad that can be worn on a boot sole.

Dominant buck urine, too, is popular. The idea is that bucks detecting the scent of another buck

in their area will feel challenged and will seek out the buck to chase it off. Still others theorize that dominant buck urine can attract and hold does in a given area. It has been demonstrated that does can determine the difference between subordinate and dominant bucks simply by smelling their urine. Though we tend to think of the bucks as seeking the does, does will frequent areas containing dominant bucks, and especially in those areas where the buck to doe ratio is in good balance, does may travel outside their home ranges to find dominant bucks.

Among the better trophy hunters I know are several who begin placing dominant buck scents in various forms throughout their hunting area, usually late in the summer, though sometimes earlier, and in one case year-round. The theory is that this brings more does in the area, and keeps them there, and in turn more bucks are drawn into that area as the rut approaches. (More about this approach in subsequent chapters.)

Earlier we suggested that urine could be considered a category in itself. Here is why: ungulates, including deer, tend to be fascinated by urine of any kind. It seems to be a means of communication within the species, but may also tell deer about other species, including predators, in the area. There is some controversy regarding how deer react to the urine of predators, but regardless of how they react, they do seem drawn to check out urine. Ordinary doe urine is a commonly used scent. Many hunters believe that it doesn't make sense to use doe-in-heat scent before any does are likely to be in heat, but there are some other reasons not to use it. One reason is that it tends to repel does. The hunter looking primarily to cull does from a local herd or put venison in the freezer probably doesn't want to repel does. Beyond that, some hunters theorize that does attract bucks, so why drive away does?

The whole issue of how deer react to human urine has generated the widest possible response from hunters. At one extreme are the hunters who use bottles or other devices to avoid contaminating their hunting location with the smell of human urine. At the other extreme are hunters who intentionally "contaminate" their stand sites with human urine, deposit human urine in scrapes, and even create mock scrapes with human urine, in the belief that it attracts deer. A number of more-or-less scientific studies in recent years have examined deer response to a variety of scents. The studies aren't always conclusive, but they do tend to point in a couple of interesting

directions. One of these is that deer herds confined in pens don't always react to smells the same way wild deer do. The other is that neither penned nor freeranging deer appear to have strong aversions to human urine, and may exhibit some curiosity about it. The bottom line is: Human urine may or may not attract deer to some degree, but it doesn't seem to repel them. Leave the urine bottles at home and let fly from your tree stand if you want.

Urine is not the only way deer convey sexual messages to one another—various glandular secretions, such as those deposited by bucks on rubs, may serve a similar function, along with the tarsal glands. A buck in rut can be smelled, even by the inferior noses of humans, for some distance under the right conditions, and any hunter who has picked a buck up by the hind legs to lift him into a pick-up truck, or who has ridden in an SUV with a buck behind the seat, is intimately acquainted with that aroma. Various commercial producers have attempted to bottle or mimic tarsal gland scent, and more than a few hunters like to trim off the tarsal glands of a tagged buck, to use as a lure. Many hunters freeze them in plastic bags for repeated use.

Pheromones

We can't address the issue of sexual scents without taking a look at pheromones. Pheromones are organic chemical substances used by various species to communicate with one another, or to produce any of a number of instinctive responses. Many insects, in particular, are known to use pheromones heavily. Pheromones may enable an ant to tell its community the location of a food source, for instance, or allow a colony of bees to coordinate an exodus from a hive to establish a new colony elsewhere. They also stimulate sexual activity. Insects aren't the only species that make use of pheromones. Mammals do, also.

Hunters became very excited about pheromones, more specifically the volatile substances produced by females in heat to produce sexual responses in males. A buck or a bull detecting these pheromones will instinctively react to them—every time. Hunters who first learned about pheromones thought that they had hit on the holy grail of deer hunting: A scent that would invariably cause any buck to come to the source of the pheromones. Their hopes were dashed, however, by another incontrovertible fact: After they're released by the deer, these pheromones last for anywhere from 15 seconds to, at most, six minutes. They work for animals in heat because animals in heat produce fresh pheromones continuously.

Does this mean that, as a practical matter, there is no such thing as doe-in-heat scent? Some experts would argue that that is indeed the case. Consider, though, that scientists have identified at least 93 substances in the urine of a doe in heat. It seems entirely possible that a buck can tell a doe is in heat even without the pheromones. Will a buck respond to a doe even if the pheromones aren't present? We can't say with any certainty, but experiences like those of Jason Strunk suggest that a buck will, at least sometimes, follow a trail of doe-in-heat scent, regardless of what the ingredients may be and regardless of whether or not it contains pheromones.

Timing

When is a good time to use scents? In the case of curiosity scents, arguably any time, since curiosity is not seasonal. It seems unlikely, though, that a buck eagerly seeking a hot doe—or a doe being pursued by a randy buck—would stray far from its route to check a smell out of curiosity. It also seems unlikely that a deer heading for a dinner of alfalfa, corn, or clover would delay getting dinner to check out a strange aroma. Nonetheless, any hunter who has spent time in the woods knows that deer aren't always chasing or being chased by other deer, nor are they always making a beeline for the nearest preferred food. Deer take their sweet time, most of the time, and tend to amble along slowly, browsing and grazing as they go.

When it comes to using food scents, timing raises some interesting and complex issues. As a general rule, most hunters, and even some manufacturers, recommend using food scents early in the season, pre-rut, and late in the season, post-rut. Why? Because the periods immediately before the rut, and during the peak of the rut, are the prime times for doe-in-heat scents or dominant buck scents.

To my knowledge, no one has done any sort of scientific (or, for that matter, unscientific) study to determine if doe-in-heat or dominant buck scents outperform food scents during the rut. Most manufacturers have little incentive to pursue such an inquiry; the status quo is that hunters use food scents on some hunts, sexual attractants on others. Why limit sales to one or the other?

How often have you heard that the best way to hunt bucks during the rut is to hunt where the does are? If that's sound advice, wouldn't it make perfect sense to attract does to your stand with food scents? Perhaps in some updated edition of this book, we'll have an answer to that question.

But the issue of when to use a given food scent is much more complicated than whether or not food scents are or are not more effective than sexual attractants at various times in the season. While it's true that deer like a variety of foods, it's also well documented that at any given time, deer have a preferred food and will often pass up other foods to get to it. Further, their priorities change, sometimes from one day to the next. Deer may pass up any food source available to get at alfalfa in late summer or early autumn. Later they might switch to soybeans, passing up alfalfa to get the beans. When the acorns fall, deer will abandon every other food source to get to them. Though they readily eat the acorns from red oaks, they seem to prefer the less bitter white oak acorn. Why these changing preferences? Availability has something to do with it, but in many cases, it's a matter of what is ripe. And some plants—especially broadleaf green plants such as the brassicas that are so popular these days in food plots—become sweeter after a frost or two. They may literally be ignored one day, and sought after to the exclusion of nearly everything else the next day.

What does all this have to do with food scents? Neither corn scents nor apple scents are likely to be at their most effective if acorns are dropping in the woods. And while all this might seem to suggest that acorn scents should be effective any time, there is the fact that deer seem to prefer foods with varying amounts of protein or sugars depending on the time of the year and whether they are bulking up with protein or seeking high-energy foods with more sugars.

Timing as it pertains to the use of sexual scents would seem to be a more straightforward matter. Though there is some evidence that the scents released by bucks can actually stimulate does to come into heat, the timing of the rut is fairly predictable. A doe, as every deer hunter knows, will run from a buck until she is good and ready to stand still for him. At the same time, it is unlikely that a buck would respond to a doe in heat if not for the increased level of testosterone that courses through his veins as the rut kicks in. That would suggest that the best time to use dominant buck or doe-in-heat

scent would be the period leading up to, and during, the time that the rut takes place, beginning when bucks begin frequently scraping, rubbing, and cruising for does, and very late in the season when testosterone levels have dropped.

Proper Use

Many bowhunters use an attraction scent in the hope that wandering deer will hit the scent stream and follow it to the source, where they are waiting to loose a well-aimed arrow. Others, though they would welcome such an occurrence, have more limited expectations. Their hope is that a deer passing by will stop to sniff or lick the source of the scent, pausing long enough and in a correct position to give them a perfect shot. In either case, it only makes sense to put the source of the scent in a spot that is comfortably within bow range, in the open, and likely to position the deer for a broadside shot.

It also makes sense to use the wind very carefully. It's a tricky situation— on the one hand, you want to position the scent source upwind of areas you expect deer to move through, while on the other hand you don't want them to get your scent. Obviously this is a situation in which scent control (reduction of the hunter's scent) is extremely important. In other circumstances, it is possible the target will be passing by upwind, but in the case of using attractant scents, game will be in a more-or-less downwind position. The trick here, aside from maximum personal scent control, is to position the scent source neither directly upwind nor downwind from the hunter, but crosswind. Ideally, game will hit the scent stream prior to being directly downwind of the hunter and follow it in without ever hitting the hunter's scent stream.

Hunters use a variety of media for conveying scent, including various wicks, drag rags, boot pads, liquids, gels, and homemade devices or concoctions. Which is the most effective may depend to some extent on current conditions. One consideration, according to Jamis Gamache of HeatWave Scents, is weather. "The use of liquid- based scent when it is raining or if temperatures are extremely cold is minimized greatly," explains Jamis, "because the scent is diluted with the rain or the liquid freezes. A better type [of] device would be a scentimpregnated wafer in which the scent is built into the device."

When conditions are favorable, Jamis believes aerosol sprays can disperse scent better than can a liquid on a wick. A few years ago, Jamis became sufficiently sold on heated scents that he formed his own company, HeatWave Scents. It's no secret that heat increases the volatility of most substances, which means, in effect, that it makes odors stronger. Not that you have to be a chemist to understand that fact.

"Think of it this way," says Jamis. "After a long day of hunting, you walk into the house and there is a hot pot of chili on the stove. You know right away when you walk in that something smells great. The next day you walk in and the leftover chili is still on the stove but is not heated. You practically need to stumble over it before you realize it is there. The same holds true for game scents. By heating or atomizing the scent, it produces a much stronger aroma, which is more apt to attract game to your hunting area."

At the beginning of this chapter, I made reference to laying down a scent trail with drag rags. Usually this is a rut-hunting strategy, and the attractant is doe-in-heat urine. I know at least one hunter who makes it a point to always step in deer droppings when he comes across them on his way to his stand, and claims to have taken a nice buck that followed that scent to his stand. Would food scents work? I know of no one who has tried it. I'd be inclined to think it could be very effective for bear hunters, but I, for one, would be leery of putting a food scent on any part of my body in bear country.

One technique that I see increasing numbers of deer hunters using involves soaking a drag rag with liquid scent, putting it on the end of a stick, and by that means laying down a trail that is not directly in their own footsteps. It can't hurt, and some hunters are convinced that it makes bucks less likely to detect the hunter's scent.

Earlier I made reference to some serious trophy hunters who begin making mock scrapes and putting out dominant buck scent in the summer, and sometimes year-round, in the belief that it attracts and holds does and bucks in an area. We'll take a closer look at that in the chapter about mock scrapes and rubs.

Natural vs. Synthetic Scents

RICHARD COMBS

On a hunt in the mountains of Virginia several years ago, I stepped out of a pickup truck, said good luck to my hunting companions in the backseat, and watched momentarily as the guide drove off down the logging road, leaving me in the predawn stillness of a crisp fall morning. It was the end of October and the perfect time, it seemed to me, to lay down a scent line to my stand using a drag rag with a little doe-in-heat scent. I removed the bottle of scent from my daypack and, in the darkness, attempted to squirt a little onto my drag rag. Nothing came out. I shook it a few times and squeezed again with my fingers. Still nothing. Finally, I squeezed with my whole hand. The entire top of the bottle burst open and doe-inheat scent sprayed all over me. I gathered my gear and began walking toward my stand, and soon heard something walking in the dry leaves behind me. I stopped and it stopped. I began walking and again I heard it, unmistakably following me. Eventually I was able to make out a forkhorn buck, following about 40 or 50 yards behind me. It left when I climbed into my stand, but later came back and hung around all morning. It ran off when I climbed down at lunchtime to make my way back to the logging road for the ride back to the lodge. The truck came along, with several other hunters inside, and stopped. I climbed in. The truck went about ten yards and stopped, the door flew open, and I flew out. I had to ride back to the lodge in the bed of the truck.

Being the scientific type that I am, I deduced several things from this experience. First, that the forkhorn buck sure was interested in something about me, and my best guess is that the doe-in-heat shower I took by the logging road had a lot to do with it. Second, you want to avoid contaminating yourself or your gear with that stuff if at all possible, but sometimes it is not possible.

I bring this up because it represents one of the arguments in favor of synthetic, as opposed to natural, scents. The near certainty of occasional contamination is definitely on the con side for natural scents, and on the pro side for synthetics, which tend to be easier to handle and less offensive, at least to humans.

Scents of nearly any kind can be synthesized in laboratories. Are these inferior or superior to natural scents? Contamination and convenience of handling aside, there are other issues to consider. On the pro side for synthetics, the argument is that certain natural substances, particularly urine, break down into other compounds, including ammonia. The ammonia smell is perfectly natural, and hence, arguably, a good thing. Soon after it is bottled, though, bacteria begin breaking urine down into unnatural compounds—unless special measures, including the use of preservatives, are used to prevent this. And preservatives, or so goes the argument, have their own unnatural scent. Synthetic scents, on the other hand, won't break down. And

Most camo is effective. Some patterns excel in one specific habitat while others, like the pattern above, are more all-purpose.

they're easier to use, since hunters needn't worry about when they were produced, or how they are stored, or how long they will be effective after the package is opened.

On the negative side for synthetic scents, some question whether or not it is possible to produce a synthetic scent that will fool an animal's nose. An animal will not have the same reaction, according to this line of reasoning, to a synthetic as opposed to a naturally produced scent. Animals that respond to a synthetic scent, according to this position, are reacting out of curiosity, and not because they are genuinely fooled.

Here is another controversial issue concerning the use of natural urines: Some products contain not deer, elk, or moose urine, but the urine of cattle or sheep. In fact, some cow- or doe-in-heat products actually contain the urine of cattle or sheep in heat. Hunters were scandalized to make that discovery, but it's not all that clear they should have been— for one simple reason: Target animals respond to them, and no scientific evidence to date proves that the urine from real does is more effective than the urine of other ungulates in heat. To further cloud the argument, recent studies indicate that the pheromones that get bucks and bulls (not to mention hunters) so excited are not present in urine, but in vaginal secretions. In a University of Georgia study, white-tailed bucks, when given a choice between vaginal secretions of estrous does and the urine of estrous does, ignored the urine and went in the direction of the secretions virtually every time.

Once again, we get into the motives of animals. Certainly the argument can be made that whether or not we truly fool an animal's nose, or whether it is reacting to a sexual stimulus or simply out of curiosity, doesn't matter. All that matters is, does it respond? To my knowledge, no scientific studies have been completed regarding how animals react to natural versus synthetic scents, or fresh urine deposited by animals in the wild as compared to urine bottled on a farm and used weeks or months later.

Part 4

Hunt Club and Land Issues

Introduction

JAY CASSELL

With hunting pressure heavy in densely populated states, especially in the Northeast, Midwest, and Middle Atlantic states, many hunters realize that they'd much rather be hunting private property, as part of a hunting club, then going it alone or with a group of buddies on public land. If you are able to joint an established club, great, go for it – after you've checked out the membership and have decided that you wouldn't mind spending time with these guys.

If you don't join an already existing club, perhaps you and your hunting buddies are able to get together and lease some property – from a private landowner, a timber company, whatever. Agreeing to lease land (after you have carefully checked it out) and form a club are the easy parts. After that, you've got some big decisions to make. And trust me, if anarchy rules, your club is not going to last. You need to have someone in charge, and you need to have rules --- on safety, guests, workdays, cabin clean up, game law violators, game you can and cannot harvest, ATV use, alcohol, firewood details -- the list goes on and on. In general, you don't want to have so many rules and regs that members feel handcuffed – but, if you don't have a basic plan, then you are going to run into problems. Wayne Fears' chapter on this issue is something well worth reading, for everyone.

Also covered in this section are such things as planting food plots and managing your property – topics worthy of books all by themselves. But if you have invested in property, or a hunting lease, or in building a cabin, then doesn't it make sense to plant food crops that will hold deer in your area, and will help them grow larger bodies and antlers? And, in many cases, it makes sense to have a six- or eight-point rule. Most clubs don't want to end up having property patrolled by spikes and forkhorns, I can tell you that. And when that 10-pointer steps out into the clover patch that you helped plant and manage (perhaps he was the six-pointer you let go last year), well, it will all be worth it.

Organizing a Hunting Club

J. WAYNE FEARS

Have you found a tract of land that you would like to lease for hunting but it's more than you can afford alone? You didn't like your old hunting club and would like to set up your own so it would be run right. You and your hunting buddies would like to organize a hunting club and find some land to lease. Whatever the reason, new hunting clubs are organized all the time and the good news is that if they are organized and managed correctly they stand a good chance of being around a long time.

Starting a hunting club is easy if the person doing the organizing is a strong leader and plans each step of the process. Some of the best clubs I have seen are small clubs with only four or five members. They had their organizational meeting around someone's dining room table. Getting the word out for workdays is easy. However, larger clubs are not that easy and require more organizational skills and effort.

Who and How Many Members

This is one of those chicken and egg questions. If you already have a tract of land selected, then the amount of dues money you need may dictate how many members you need. If you haven't already selected a tract of land, then you can get as many members as you want and find a tract of land large enough for the group.

Prospective members of a hunting club should have the same interests and goals in wildlife management that should be reflected in the bylaws.

Perhaps "Who" is more important than "how many." Anyone who has a serious interest in hunting the game for which the club is being organized, and who is congenial with the other members, is a potential member. However, it is best to start out with friends of a like interest as the founding

Forming a hunting club is easy when a core of like-minded hunters have been hunting together for years.

members and then slowly invite others to join after you are satisfied that their interest and intentions are the same as the founding group. Almost every hunting club goes through a weeding out process every now and then but you don't during the start-up if you can avoid it. Take your time and pick your members carefully.

The First Meeting

The first meeting is the most important meeting as this is usually when the officers are elected, club name chosen, bylaws adopted, fees set, and committees appointed. Make every attempt to get all prospective members to attend. Prepare meeting notices in the form of cards or letters and mail them to each person, inviting them to attend. Select a date and hour for the meeting that will be convenient for the majority of the prospective members. State the objectives and purposes of the club. If a tract of land has been selected, tell a little about the land. Also, serve refreshments and let it be known in the invitation.

Before the meeting, decide on a temporary chairman. He should be good on his feet in front of a group. He should call the meeting to order and get the proceedings under way promptly. He should state the purpose of the club, tell about the tract of land selected or what type of land the club will be searching. There is nothing like the possibility of an exclusive tract of land to hunt to generate excitement in a new club.

Next, the temporary chairman should open up the meeting for discussion. Then he will call for a vote to see if the group wants to form a hunting club. If so, then proceed with the actual formation of the club, which includes the election of officers and adoption of bylaws, selection of club name. and appointment of committees. Organize the fundamentals of the club at this first meeting and set plans in motion to lease that special tract of land. If land has already been selected, it may be possible to set the initiation fee and dues at that time. How much time has been spent preparing for this meeting will determine as to how much you can cover and not have the meeting go on for too long.

I have been to several organizational meetings where the club was formed and operational by the time the first meeting was over; however, these meetings were well planned.

Election of Officers

Hunting club officers may be president, vice president, secretary, treasurer, hunt master and safety officer. Acting together, they can constitute the Executive Committee. It is important that the officers be carefully selected to be good organizers, know how to maintain records, and have strong leadership skills. Particular care should be given to the election of the president since his contribution to the club goes beyond formalized duties such as presiding at meetings. He will meet with the landowner of the lease land, set standards for the club, and solve member disputes.

Club Name

Club names suggesting the sport of hunting are most commonly used but a name relating to some feature of the hunting land is a close second. Examples of club names include Bear Creek, Five Shot, Big Buck, Ten Point, Paradise Hill, and Hickory Ridge. Choose the shortest name that will best represent your group.

Initiation Fee and Dues

When considering the amount of initiation fee and annual club dues, the first thing to determine is what expenditures will be called for by the club's programs in a given year; and second, how large a membership your club will have. Expenses will include land rent, food plot seeds, fertilizer, boundary signs, possible clubhouse renovations, and utilities. The list could go on depending upon the goals of the club. Once you have made a realistic expenditure evaluation and a determination of the members, then the dues can be set accordingly. Be careful not to set them too high or too low. Decide upon a fee that will get the job done but will not be a burden to the club members.

Committees

A committee may be appointed to search for land to lease, get a wildlife management plan written for land already leased, or to design a base camp. By using committees, the president can get

The first meeting of a hunting club can determine the success or failure of the club.

club members involved with the club, thus keeping interest high while getting vital jobs done.

Arrange for the Next Meeting

Before adjourning the first meeting, a time, place, and date should be set for the next meeting. Plan the date for your next meeting so that each of your committees has time to gather the proper material and information, so that definite activities can be acted upon by the membership. Be careful not to extend the time so far into the future that the members lose interest.

Hunting Club Bylaws

A sample copy of hunting club bylaws is given in the Appendix of this book. Bylaws should govern the dayto- day operation of the club. Adapt the bylaws to local conditions that affect the club, its relationship with landowners, and its use of wildlife resources. Avoid overly burdensome bylaws. Many new clubs create too many bylaws and are unable to enforce them. Add bylaws as needed. Hunting club bylaws should address management of the lease property, safety, guest policy, hunting rules and regulations, operational committees, disciplinary procedures, and member-landowner relationships.

To Incorporate or Not

Your hunting club is engaged in an activity that has potential liability to third parties or to members; so there may be advantages to incorporation, especially if the club owns land or other valuable property.

A cooperation has such advantages as more freedom from personal liability than other forms of organization, continuity of existence, convenient method for members to join their resources and efforts together, and a background of legal and administrative precedents to help it operate properly.

A cooperation is a legal entity. All legal proceedings can be carried on by the cooperation as a body. It has a well-defined legal status with all rights spelled out by statute. The cooperation is founded on a legal structure, which makes clear what the organization can and cannot do. Members are less likely to be sued as individuals for damages, unless gross negligence or utter disregard for public society is present. Then only guilty members may be sued.

On the other hand, incorporation is usually not a requirement of most landowners leasing land and the advantages of incorporation are by no means conclusive. If the club has adequate liability insurance for the protection of its members and landowner, and wishes to operate on a relatively informal basis, the club may elect to operate as an unincorporated organization, as thousands of other clubs do. In fact, most of the hunting clubs I have worked with are unincorporated and have had no problems. When organizing a club you should seek the advice of an attorney concerning the need for incorporation.

Insurance

J. WAYNE FEARS

I t was the beginning of the perfect weekend. Ray had invited his new neighbor Jim to his hunting club for a weekend of deer hunting. While Jim was new to deer hunting, he was excited about spending the weekend hunting with Ray.

They arrived at the club cabin just before midnight on Friday night and unloaded Ray's two ATVs to be ready for leaving before daylight the next morning. Jim wasn't much help with the ATVs, as he had never ridden one before. Ray assured him that the unit he had brought for Jim to use was easy to ride, as it was fully automatic.

The following morning the two neighbors enjoyed a big camp breakfast and went out into the cold to start the ATVs for the ride to their stands. Ray gave Jim a few pointers about the ATV he was to ride and off they rode in the darkness.

At a fork in the road Ray gave Jim directions as to where his stand was located and they agreed to meet at the fork at 11:00 to ride back to camp for lunch. With that, they each disappeared into the darkness. Ray really liked his neighbor and was glad he wanted to learn more about deer hunting. In fact, Ray was working to get him a membership into the hunting club.

Later that morning Ray arrived at the fork in the road. He couldn't wait to tell Jim about the nine-pointer he saw but never got a shot at. He waited until 11:20 and when Jim never showed up Ray

A hunting club's insurance policy should take into consideration all type of potential liabilities such as a member's use of ATVs.

smiled thinking his neighbor just may be struggling with a big buck.

Ray cranked up his ATV and started down the road to where Jim was hunting. Rounding a bend in the road, his heart sank as he saw the ATV Jim was riding upside down in a deep ditch. He raced to the ditch to find Jim folded up under the machine barely able to talk. He had multiple fractures, a fractured spine, a concussion, and several deep cuts. He had been there since early morning and was near death.

Fortunately, Jim survived after a long hospital stay, several surgeries, and lots of physical therapy. He missed months of work and his medical expenses amounted to almost $500,000.

Who would pay all the medical bills? Who would support Jim's family while he was out of work? Who was responsible for the accident since Jim had no ATV riding instruction and it wasn't his unit? Would the club and Ray be sued? The list of unanswered questions went on and on. Fortunately, for Ray and his club, they had a general liability insurance policy that provided coverage for the club if they were found legally responsible for this accident. The same policy covered Ray as well.

Accidents of all types happen on hunting clubs every hunting season. Shooting, tree stand falls, ATV wrecks, fire, and falls in general are among the most common accidents that cause deaths or injuries on hunting leases. During the years I managed hunting leases, I saw these and other unusual accidents many times and usually the club couldn't believe it had happened on their lease. Fortunately, we required every club to carry a general liability insurance

Accidents can and will happen even in the best managed hunt club. Every club should have a comprehensive general liability insurance policy to protect its members and their investment.

policy and name the company I worked for as an additional insured in the policy.

Every hunting club needs general liability insurance for the protection of the club as well as for each of its members. In addition, for a small additional fee the landowner should be named as an additional insured, most lessors require it.

According to Dr. Ed Wilson, a hunting club insurance expert with the Davis-Garvin Agency, writing in *Quality Whitetails* magazine, "simplified, liability insurance is designed to provide coverage for hunting clubs and their members for acts which they could be held legally responsible. Thus, the insurance is designed to lessen the risk associated with occurrences caused by a negligent act of the

Even simple camp chores can be the potential source of litigation if proper insurance has not been purchased by the hunting club.

hunting club or members and guests. Clearly, all hunters and landowners should be aware of the risks they are taking by not having adequate liability insurance. It's simply not worth risking all of your personal assets or your family's security for unfortunate accidents or the acts of members of your hunting club."

What Coverage Should You Have?

The coverage package that is most recommended by the insurance agents contacted at this writing is one which has the following:

- $1 million per occurrence general liability coverage
- $2 million general aggregate

- $100,000 fire legal liability
- Member-to-member coverage
- Guest liability coverage
- Liability coverage for firearms, tree stands, ATVs, mobile equipment, limited watercraft, hunting dogs, and more

Policies of this type are available through organizations such as the Quality Deer Management Association and the Forest Landowners Association. In the Appendix of this book, I list a number of good sources of hunting club insurance.

How Much Does a Policy Cost?

The cost of a policy such as the one described above will vary from underwriter to underwriter and will vary depending upon the number of acres in your hunting lease. However, I shopped out hunting club insurance as I was writing this chapter, based on 1,000 acres, and the annual cost ranged from $222 to $360. A small price to pay for the peace of mind that comes from knowing you are protected in a case like Ray was in at the beginning of this chapter.

Drawing Up Club Rules

J. WAYNE FEARS

"The club's rules must spell out what is acceptable at the club and what is not…[and] the rules have to be enforced."

Rules are important if a hunting club is to offer a quality experience for its members, says Bernard Austin of Metairie, Louisiana. Austin is president of the Warrior Hunting Club and has served as president of the club for several terms. He gives the club's rules credit for the low turnover in members. "The club's rules must spell out what is acceptable at the club and what is not. Next, the rules have to be enforced," he says.

Elements of the Rules

Harvest. Warrior Hunting Club is primarily a deer-hunting club, so the rules begin by listing what deer can be harvested. Its members participate in a quality deer management program, and a number of doe tags must be filled each season. The rules explain how each member is responsible for keeping harvest data.

Guests. Club property is relatively small, just 1,000 acres, and the club lodge sleeps 10. Therefore, rules regarding guests must be explicit. Each member is allowed only four guests per season, at $30 per visit. No guest may visit the club more than twice during a season. Nonhunting guests must

Hunting club rules should include off-season use of the club property.

follow the same rules. The host is responsible for the guest and must be at the lodge as long as the guest is there.

Safety. A number of rules apply to safety. Each hunter must place a tack on a map, located in the lodge great room, showing where he is going to be hunting. This serves several purposes. If he doesn't return, other members know where to start the search. In addition, it keeps other members from hunting near the area. No member is allowed at the lodge alone. "We once had a member pass out, and if he had been alone he wouldn't have made it," Austin recalls. An orange line painted on trees a few hundred yards from the lodge reminds hunters to unload firearms at that point.

Consequences. "Our rules spell out what happens if a member or guest doesn't follow the rules," says Austin. All new members are on probation for one year. If a member is expelled from the club, there is no refund on his dues. "The rules must have teeth, or they aren't of much use," he says.

Miscellaneous. Because the club has a lodge to maintain, there are rules for keeping the building clean and in good condition.

A hunting club is just like any other group in a civilized society. If the members draw up a good set of rules and follow them, everyone will enjoy the hunting experience. It works at the Warrior Hunting Club.

This is just one of thousands of examples of how clubs use rules to keep the club run smoothly. Every situation is different and every club should tailor their rules to their goals and desires for good hunting.

Club rules should cover all aspects of use by the guests of club members. Each member should be required to be responsible for any guest he invites to the club.

Tips to Consider When Drawing Up Rules

Violation of Game and Fish Laws. It should be a club rule that no game and fish law violation will be tolerated and that the matter will be turned over to a conservation officer immediately. For this and many other reasons, invite the local conservation officer out to the club property and show him around. Inform him that your club has a zero tolerance toward game law violations and he will be called if there should ever be one.

Game to Be Harvested. Be specific about what game is to be harvested and when. Unless a club has a lot of land, it is best that only one game species be hunted during a season. Deer hunters don't want squirrel hunters walking under their stand shooting rimfire rifles. In addition, a hunter who has been trying to wait out an old buck for several days doesn't want a group of raccoon-hunting members running in his area all night. What about if a coyote runs through your area just at daybreak, does your club permit you to shoot legal varmints? This all needs to be spelled out in the rules.

Size and Sex of Game. If your club is in a quality deer management program there will be size restrictions on bucks and each member will be expected to help in the doe harvest. Some clubs do not permit the taking of bucks until each member has taken his share of does. Your rules should spell out how the deer harvest is to be conducted and what data the member must pull from each deer taken. Good recordkeeping is a must.

Hunting Methods. Club rules should state how members are expected to hunt, check-in rules and checkout rules, area restrictions, and any other expectations of the hunters. Many clubs are dedicated to still or stalk hunting and do not want man-drives. If so, state it in the rules. If you must stay on your stand or in your hunting area during certain hours, state it. Most hunters will hunt according to the rules if they know what is expected.

ATV Use. I once was a member of a club that permitted ATV use without any rules. Soon we had some hot rod members that were cutting "donuts" in all the food plots and running almost nonstop on the club roads all day. It quickly became an issue and almost destroyed the club. ATVs are a valuable tool to have in a hunting camp but their use must be regulated and the rules must stress common sense and courtesy for their use.

Litter. There should be rules concerning litter. Bring out of the field all that you took out with you, and this includes blinds. I have gone to duck and deer blinds that were akin to going to a garbage dump. Keep the woods and blinds clean. Also, address where deer entrails, hides, feet, and other waste parts are to be taken. This can be a major health hazard on clubs and it can attract every stray dog in the region, which can have a negative effect

Spelling out who can hunt what game and when is an important part of a hunting club's rules. As an example, some members hunting squirrels during deer season may drive members away from the club.

on hunting. Plan on how to handle waste parts of animals before the season opens and put the solution into the rules.

Dog Problems. During the years I worked with hunting leases I saw, on several occasions, people almost get into a shootout over the handling of dogs that strayed onto the club property, usually chasing deer. Free-ranging dogs whether chasing deer, hanging around camp, or strolling in front of your stand just before dark are not welcome guests. Develop, with some imput from the local conservation officer, how club members should handle the problem. Put it in the rules.

Camp Rules. If your club has a lodge, camp house or other type of structure, there needs to be a separate set of rules and we will discuss this later in this book. If you have a camping area, skinning

Club rules should be very specific about how the base camp is to be cared for and exactly who is responsible for cleanup.

shed, or general gathering area, some rules should be drawn up on how to keep the area clean. Spell out if firewood cutting is permitted or if it must be hauled in. State fire rules and what to do if there is a wildfire.

Rules Should Stress Safety. Have a well-thought out set of safety rules. Be strict with firearms especially in camp. If the club has a shooting range, have a separate set of rules posted at the range for range use.

Have Specific Rules for Alcohol Use. Some clubs forbid the use of alcohol on the club, others do not permit the use of alcohol until the hunt and all shooting activities are over for the day, and others say when you take a drink, gun handling is over for that day. We all know that alcohol and guns don't mix; so set your rules to have a safe hunt and camp.

Workday Requirements. Every club must have workdays to plant food plots, fertilize native food plants, clear roads, clean camps, etc. Rules are required to accomplish this and we will discuss this in a later chapter of this book.

We could go on for pages about rules but each club must set their own rules and enforce them.

Handling Rule Violations

The best clubs have a zero tolerance to those who break the more important rules one time or are a repeat violator of the minor rules. The quicker you weed out those people who choose to break the rules, the better the club environment will be.

Most clubs requires that a grievance or complaint against a club member must be reported to an officer or board member. Then a hearing is usually held so that all parties involved may speak their mind. The club bylaws should have a clause that permits the reviewing board to dismiss a member immediately if he is found guilty of not following the club rules. If it is truly a nonserious oversight, put the offender on probation; but if he is clearly one that cannot play by the rules, do the club a favor and ask him to leave.

In many cases, I have seen a strong, but fair, president dismiss a serious rule breaker the same day the offense occurred. Most agree the sooner you can solve these types of problems, the better. Think about these types of problems when you write your club's bylaws.

If the members draw up a good set of rules and follow them, everyone will enjoy the hunting experience.

Joining a Hunting Club

J. WAYNE FEARS

Joining a hunting club is a lot like getting married... you hope to stay together for the long term.

Jerry Dawson had just moved to a new town to become regional manager of his company. None of the people at work hunted and Dawson was making enough now that he could afford to join a hunting club. It was his dream to become a part of a great group of guys who had their own place to hunt. He looked forward to getting involved in the wildlife management on the club and someday when his son was old enough have their own club on which to hunt together.

Dawson asked around about hunting clubs but all he heard about were full with a waiting list. One Sunday just before deer season opened, he saw a short ad in the local newspaper, "wanted hunting club member" with a phone number. Excited, Dawson called the number several times before he got an answer. The voice on the other end told Dawson he had a group of trophy hunters and they leased 2,500 acres in the southern part of the county. There was plenty of deer and if he wanted to join the group he should send a check for $750 as quickly as possible as there were several hunters wanting to join. Dawson asked to visit the lease but the response was no one would be there until opening morning. Dawson committed and got instructions as to where to send the check and how to reach the lease.

Participating in a hunt with a prospective hunting club is a good way to see if this is a good club you want to join.

Opening morning at 4:30 a.m., Dawson drove up to the old tenant house that served as the club's base camp. As he walked into the dimly lit room, he was shocked at what he saw. Most members had a beer in their hand and all were talking at the same time. They were organizing a man-drive and those with AK-47s would be the drivers. "We get in more shooting when we are the drivers," a burly man in military camo told Dawson.

Someone offered the new member a beer and asked him how much ammo he brought. The club "president" assigned Dawson a pickup truck to get

Many hunting clubs recruit new members via posting an ad for members in local sporting goods stores.

A good way to get to know about the members of a hunting club and whether or not you would like to be a member of this group is to help them during a work weekend.

Locating Hunting Clubs

Dawson made many mistakes when he decided to join a hunting club. Don't make the same mistakes. First, start your search as early in the year as possible. Give yourself plenty of time to study the clubs you find which have membership openings.

One of the best places to start your search is to call the local conservation officer or county agricultural agent. Both have contact with hunting clubs as well as with landowners who lease land to clubs. If they recommend a club, it would be worth contacting.

Another good source is the local sporting goods store or gun shop. While you are talking to these people watch the local newspaper. Often under the heading of "hunting and fishing," you will find ads seeking members for hunting clubs.

Regardless of where you hear of a club with an opening, start your interview process with caution. While it may be a new club trying to fill its membership rolls for the first time, or just a club with an unexpected vacancy, be cautious as most good clubs have a waiting list for membership openings. A club having to search for members may have problems. Keep your ears and eyes open.

in the back of and soon a number of pickup trucks were speeding along logging roads in the cold dawn air.

That morning Dawson spent hidden behind a large log in fear of his life. The deer drive was a shooting and hollering contest. As the disorganized line of club members swung past Dawson, a doe passed by him and two shots were fired at her. Then a staggering driver came over to Dawson cursing the fact he missed every deer he had tried to shoot and wondered if Dawson had an extra "brew."

Dawson couldn't wait to get back to his truck so he could go home. His $750 was gone and he was considering taking up golf.

Look Carefully at Prospective Clubs

Joining a hunting club is a lot like getting married, you join up with the best of intensions, and you hope to stay together for the long term. Approach it with the same caution.

Before beginning your search, determine what you really want. What game is most important to you, what hunting methods do you enjoy most, do you want a lease that offers more than just one species of hunting, perhaps a place to shoot and hike during the nonhunting season?

Determine how much are you willing to spend for the initiation fee and an annual membership fee.

Once you have found a club or clubs to interview, set up a lunch with the president and find out the answers to these questions before you take the next step:

- Is the lease a year-round lease with all recreational rights or just for certain species or seasons. Is there a small shooting range on the property you can use?
- Find out how many members are in the club and how many acres it leases. From whom do they lease and what are the terms of the lease.
- What is the price of the membership and how much is the initiation fee. Does this include everything, or will the members be expected to pay for more add-ons later. Does your membership assure you a vote in how the club is run?
- What is the club's guest policy? Is there an additional fee for a guest?
- Is the club and its members insured and, if so, for how much?
- How are grievances settled?
- Does the club have a written wildlife management plan supervised by a wildlife biologist? Do they regulate their hunting according to the plan? Is data kept on the game taken? If the lease is to produce quality deer hunting for many years, these questions

must have a "yes" answer. If not, the membership should be considered a short-term investment.

- Ask for a copy of the property map, club's bylaws, harvest records, and rules. Study them carefully. Make sure you agree with the rules and that safety is stressed. Is the quality of game taken what you would be happy with?
- Find out who is in the club and see if you can get a membership roster. A few calls to other members can tell you a lot about the club. See if you can determine that they abide by game laws, how they hunt, what nights at camp are like, and how they feel about wildlife management on the lease. Take the time to find out who you will be hunting with.

Visit the Club

- If possible, visit the club lease while the members are there. The best way to do this and to really get to know them is to volunteer for a workday. Under these circumstances, you can get to know them much better and they you. Take a map and go over the property, look at their roads, food plots, stands, camp, etc. Be honest with yourself, do you like what you see?
- Attend a club meeting if possible and see how the business side of the club is run.
- In the end, the decision is yours. However, if you have gone through the process outlined above, you will be able to make an informed decision.

Joining the right hunting club can assure you of a quality hunting experience, provided it is done correctly. It can be a great way to avoid the crowds and to hunt with friends who hunt the way you enjoy.

Joining the right hunting club can guarantee a quality hunting experience …

Guest Policies

J. WAYNE FEARS

Everybody likes to hunt with a hunting buddy. It's just more fun. Because we all know that, most hunting clubs have a guest policy that allows the members to bring friends and family on hunts. On the surface, that sounds very good but it is often a privilege that brings down clubs, makes members turn on one another, and creates problems for all concerned. I have seen uninformed guests abuse poorly written rules in many ways.

A guest should know what is expected of him when staying at the club's base camp. Food and bedding arrangements should be made in advance of a guest's arrival.

- Often a member will keep bringing the same guest repeatedly. Soon it becomes apparent to the other members that the guest is simply avoiding the cost of initiation fee and dues, but using the lease as much as the members. I have noticed these types are never around as a volunteer on workdays.
- A common problem is the guest who doesn't fit in. He drinks too much, eats everyone else's food, is loud and obnoxious, never helps with camp chores or he knows how the club could be better run. One visit is too much, but these types usually keep coming back.
- Clubs that have liberal family guest privileges sometimes find their hunts are actually a mini-family reunion for one of the members. They can dominate a hunt or weekend. The paying members feel they are intruding. Then there is the member who brings his kids, who really wishes they weren't there, and depends upon the camp to help baby-sit them for the weekend.
- More than once I have seen clubs break up due to a member bringing his girlfriend to the camp for a weekend of romance. The other members are there to enjoy a hunt and camp life.
- Clubs with no guest limit will see the member who brings two or three guests, usually "very important people," and suddenly the property is crowded and many times these guests get the better hunting areas. I see this happen most often during the rut.

The list could go on for pages but the point is guest privileges can ruin an otherwise good hunting club quickly. Since the guest problems are usually

Guest policies should spell out exactly how a hunting club guest should conduct himself on the club property. Did this hunting club guest know he was not suppose to drive his ATV on food plots?

family, close friends, neighbors, or "the boss," the member who brings them is offended when it's brought to his attention and an internal war is started.

Stop the Problem before It Becomes a Problem

Since we all have friends and family we would like to share a hunt with, a guest privilege is important for most clubs. (I do know of some hunting clubs that do not permit guests.) To keep the guest privileges from getting out of hand and to be fair to all members of the club, it should be well thought out, with all members having input, and should be in writing. It should be a part of the club's bylaws, and a method of enforcement spelled out. Copies should be posted on the club bulletin board and each member should have a copy. It is most important that a new prospective member receives a copy before he becomes a member. Some clubs require a guest be given a copy to sign before he visits the club. He then knows that his visit is a privilege and knows beforehand what the club expects of him.

Hunting guest policies should always require that the host member of the club be fully responsible for the conduct of his guest.

The written guest rules with strong, swift, enforcement will solve most visitor problems before they become problems.

What to Include in a Guest Policy

While every club has special conditions and ideas about guests, here are some pointers to be considered when writing a new guest policy or rewriting one that may not be working in the best interest of the members:

- Charge a fee for each day a guest hunts on the club property. It costs just as much for a guest to kill a buck or gobbler as it does for a member. The guest usually doesn't help on workdays and doesn't pay dues. At this writing, the clubs I contacted charge from $25 to $70 per day for a guest. Two clubs I contacted charge an additional trophy fee if the guest takes a buck or gobbler. Remember, that buck or gobbler could have been taken by a hardworking club member. It should be the host club member's responsibility to pay the guest fee when the visit is made.

- Determine the number of guests the property can support in one day. What if every member showed up with a guest? The size of your property and overnight accommodations will dictate how many people, safely and comfortably, can hunt on the property. Don't have a guest policy so liberal that the property is overhunted or the clubhouse is overflowing. You may want to have a per day guest limit with advance notice being required. The number of guests the lease can accommodate may change from squirrel season to deer season to spring gobbler season.

- Since some members may want to bring a guest every time they come to hunt, you should limit the number of guest visits each member can have. Most clubs limit each member with three to five guest days per season. That varies with length of seasons and population of game. However, it is wise to set a limit.

- Be sure to limit the visits a specific individual can make to the club. I have seen people visit a club regularly, enjoy good hunting, and avoid the membership payments and workdays. Limiting an individual to two visits per hunting season will help stop freeloading.

- Have a family member policy. Keep it to immediate family members. Again, keep the size of the accommodations and property in mind when setting up this policy. A large hunting family can tax the facility. This is a touchy subject with some people so get all members involved in the decision. Also, keep in mind at some point children of members reach an age when they should purchase a membership.

- Have a youth policy even for family members. Many clubs require that a youth can only hunt after he has successfully passed a hunter education program. Consider having hunting youth hunt with an adult until they reach 16 years of age or so. That is a judgment call you need to make carefully. Nonhunting youth should be required to be with an adult at all times.

- Guests who eat and sleep at the club camp need food and a bed. Set up a policy to provide for this. When there are 10 bunks and 10 members spending the night, where are the two guests going to sleep? What about food and who is going to cook it? Guests are guests and should be treated with respect but, when they show up with no food and no cooking skills, who is going to take care of them. I have seen some serious problems in nice hunting club base camps when a host brought in guests and didn't plan on how to feed them or where they were going to sleep.

- Make sure all guests have a set of club rules and understand them before going out to hunt. Guests need to know what is expected of them, what the game harvest rules are, and how the hunts are conducted. Good rules usually spell this out.

- Consider having a guest ID card and a temporary guest pass for display on a vehicle or an ATV. This keeps confusion to a minimum with other members who may not know "this stranger" is a guest of the club.

- Require all guests to sign a liability waiver. This can help the club if a guest should be involved in an accident.
- The guest and his actions will be the responsibility of the host member.

Since we all have friends and family we would like to share a hunt with, a guest privilege is important for most clubs.

Enforcement

Guest policy and written rules are so that everyone hunting on the club lease will enjoy himself or herself. Most of the times enforcement of the rules is unnecessary; however, when the rules are broken, swift enforcement is necessary before the situation grows. Many clubs give enforcement power to any officer or board member. If it is a minor infraction, then a short talk with the host member is usually all that is needed. However, if it is a major violation of the rules, then discipline of the host member and dismissal of the guest are required.

The discipline of the host member should be in accordance with the club rules, and the guest should be removed from the welcome list. While this is an oversimplification, each case must be reviewed and handled based on the circumstances. Sometimes guests do things beyond the host's control and you can't blame the host member. Other times the host member is knowingly breaking the rules and the guest is simply doing as he is told. Listen to the facts and be fair in the action taken.

Guests should be expected to learn the boundaries of the hunt club property and to know the hunting methods of the club.

Managing the Clubhouse

J. WAYNE FEARS

It's a little slice of freedom, an escape from the "real world" and a place we all look forward to returning to year after year.

The heart of most hunting clubs is the "camp," be it a large lodge, converted school bus, mobile home, skinning shed, large tent, old tenant house, or log cabin. Throughout the country "camp" is a different structure to different clubs but what is the same is that it is where the meals are cooked, hunting stories told, hunters sleep, and traditions made. It's a little slice of freedom, an escape from the "real world" and a place we all look forward to returning to year after year.

Coming back to this special place is a lot less fun if when we return we find someone left a window open and your sleeping bag is soaked, several dishes of leftovers were left in the refrigerator several weeks ago, someone didn't turn the water off at the well and the pipes are all frozen, or the place looks like a fraternity party was held in the great room and it will take half a day to clean the place up. I have seen these and countless other acts of inconsideration at hunting club camps and it's a shame because with a little effort the camp could always be a reasonably clean, organized place to hang your hunting hat.

Small clubs usually have fewer problems with keeping the camp orderly than do large clubs. In

Hunting club base camps range from tent camps to farmhouses to repossessed mobile homes. This Iowa hunting club base camp is a restored farmhouse that offers all the comforts of home.

small clubs a simple Standard Operating Procedure (SOP) posted in the kitchen will usually get the job done. In larger clubs appointing a camp master to make sure the SOP is followed can be a good idea, especially if the camp is a nice lodge or cabin where the club has a financial investment.

Base camp rules should include policies on how to leave the camp when everyone goes home.

These are examples of the many types of base camps found at American hunting clubs.

My camp is a log cabin where eight of us hunt. It does not have running water or electricity. An outhouse is our toilet. We have designed an SOP that not only includes how to operate in the cabin but we incorporated the grounds care, shooting range, and outhouse in the SOP. Much of the SOP deals with how to leave the cabin when shutting down after a hunting trip. In 11 years of heavy hunting use, we have had no problems. A sample of this SOP is in the Appendix of this book.

Clubs that have a camp master usually select a member who likes to cook and spends a lot of time at the camp. It seems that those who like to cook have a knack for knowing how to keep a camp clean and they take pride in the kitchen, a source of many camp problems.

A lot of hunting club camps I have visited have the kitchen cabinets divided into small sections with each member getting a section for the storage of his kitchen supplies. The space in the refrigerator(s) is usually equally divided, and some members who come less often use an ice chest to store their perishables.

Garbage builds up fast in an active hunting club and where it can be correctly disposed is something a club should check out as soon as they lease the land. The camp master should appoint someone daily to take care of the garbage.

It should be up to each member spending the night to keep the sleeping quarters clean and in a reasonable orderly condition. Trashy camps become nasty, unhealthy, rat infested, and often a fire hazard.

Another area that can become a mess is the skinning shed or area where game is cleaned. Those who use it should be responsible for cleaning it and hauling off the waste after each use. The club rules should spell this out and those who want to leave a mess for others should find another club.

It is always a pleasure to be in a club where each member takes pride in the camp and without any organizational meetings or a camp boss; everyone knows what to do and pitches in to keep the camp clean and orderly. Members who have hunted together for years work as a team and the job of tending camp is easy and fun for all.

Choosing Land

MONTE BURCH

Before you can manage habitat for wildlife, you need to lease or own land. If you lease, be sure to get a long-term lease, because many wildlife habitat practices take a long time to show results. The dream of most people who enjoy hunting, fishing, or simply watching wildlife is to own property, but the old adage "They aren't making any more land" is even more applicable these days than when it was first said. With more land being gobbled up by urban sprawl, highways, and even big agriculture, less is available for wildlife. And not only is land for wildlife becoming more scarce, it's also becoming more costly. For instance, not too many years ago "rough"— hilly and unimproved— Ozark land went for $500 an acre. At the time of this writing, that same land goes for well over $1,000 an acre and the price is climbing! It seems that everyone wants a wildlife haven or their own acre in the country

Planning

If you dream of owning your own wildlife haven, first you must set goals and make a plan. How much can you afford? Will you live on the land? How much does land cost in your desired location? How much will insurance and taxes cost?

Then decide what type of wildlife you're interested in. In some cases you may be limited by existing habitat or topography, but often the habitat and management for one species may also be suitable for others. For example, managing a forest with openings for deer also benefits turkeys, quail, and numerous songbirds as well as small game such as squirrels and rabbits. And a pond or lake created and managed for fishing can also attract waterfowl and other wildlife.

We were very lucky when we purchased our farm back in the '70s. Located "where the Ozarks meet the prairie," as a nearby small town describes the area, the land is extremely diversified, with hardwood timber, open prairie, a creek, and a small marsh.

Proper habitat management is the key to hunters, anglers, and landowners desiring to attract and keep wildlife for hunting, the country, fishing, or just watching.

When looking at a property to buy, two tools are valuable in determining wildlife potential—a topographical map and an aerial photo. These can illustrate the topography—whether the land is flat, sloping, hilly, or mountainous— and whether it has streams, marshes, or other features. The aerial photo will also show vegetation types. In addition, a county plat map can tell you who owns land you're interested in. Other factors to determine are the average yearly rainfall, availability of water, soil types, and weather conditions, because some management practices can be successful only with proper rainfall and soil types. If you dream of having your own fishing lake, for example, the soil types and topography of the area will determine the suitability of lake or pond construction.

Can your land can be monetarily productive as well as managed for wildlife? Usually a well-managed farm, ranch, pine plantation, or timberland can be both a wildlife haven and a money-maker. In fact,

Tabletop planning is the first step whether in purchasing land or planning practices on existing land. A topographical map details the terrain.

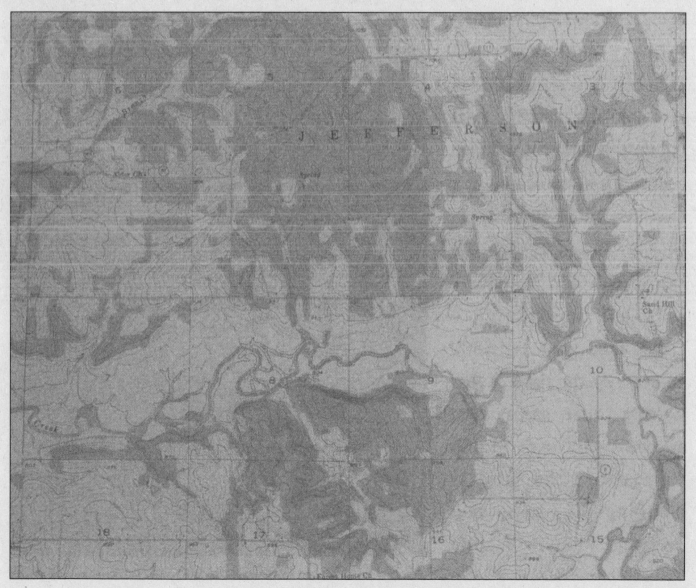

some studies show that well-managed timberlands can, over the long run, be more profitable than investing in the stock market. By managing timberlands you can make money selling such diverse products as chipwood, firewood, saw logs, and Christmas trees. Even unusual products such as grapevine wreaths, rustic furniture, mushrooms, ginseng, and other plants can be money-makers.

On prairie and agricultural lands, agricultural crops, hay, and livestock can all be managed along with wildlife. Even if you're not interested in doing these things yourself, leasing the land to a farmer or neighbor can benefit both parties. Or you may wish to sharecrop, allowing a neighbor to cut hay or plant and harvest corn or other crops. If you lease or sharecrop, make sure each party understands the agreement, and put it in writing. Also be sure that the other party knows that your primary interest is managing for wildlife, because some farming practices are not conducive to attracting wildlife.

Assessing Land

MONTE BURCH

Regardless of whether you've just purchased land or already own land you wish to improve for wildlife, it's important to assess the overall habitat management potential of the property. Follow this assessment with a management plan. Your aerial photo and topographical map can be used in planning sessions, but you'll also need to get out and walk the land. Don't hesitate to ask for help. Plenty of experts will give valuable free advice, and a number of federal and state wildlife habitat improvement programs offer funding. Begin by contacting your state fish and wildlife agency. You may also wish to contact the Natural Resources Conservation Service (NRCS), county Soil Conservation Service (SCS), county University Extension Service, and state and private foresters.

Identifying Habitat Types

Begin your assessment by identifying and marking six broad habitat types on the aerial photo:

1. **Upland woodlands:** Forests, or areas overgrown with trees with a canopy greater than ten percent.
2. **Bottomland hardwoods:** Forested bottomlands or wood swamps. This may also include tree-lined oxbows.
3. **Non-forested wetlands:** Potholes; marshes; sloughs; low, wet grassy areas; and shallow, water-logged depressions.
4. **Pasture and haylands:** Includes native prairies.

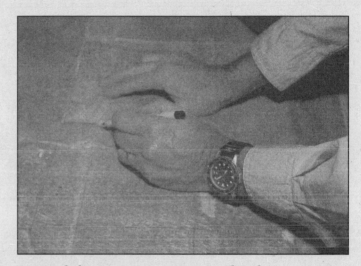

An aerial photo is a very important tool. It shows vegetation as well as other important features.

5. **Old fields:** Agricultural fields or pastures abandoned for more than two years and having less than ten percent canopy of overstory trees.
6. **Croplands:** Fields planted to row crops and small grains.

Once you've marked these areas on the aerial photograph, estimate the acreage of each habitat type. Now it's time for fieldwork. With a notebook, walk the property, examine the different areas, and make notes on the suitability of existing habitat for desired species as well as for possible improvement practices. Talking to an expert in the field can be a great help in this step. And before you make these evaluations, read the rest of this book to learn about management practices for different habitat types and the wildlife species you wish to attract.

Uplands

Concealment cover. Estimate the amount of dense or shrubby areas, brush piles, rock piles, fallen logs, and other cover. Include dense, shrubby draws extending into at least fifty percent of a field.

Edge. Examine the edges of fields or borders of the field. These include hedgerows, overgrown fencerows, and stops of vegetation between habitat types. Note whether the edges are straight or irregular. Determine the number of nest or roost trees (these include either dead or live trees of greater than six inches diameter at breast height [DBH] with cavities), including coniferous trees such as pine or red cedar. These are all used by doves.

Vegetative cover. Vegetative cover less than twenty percent will not supply enough cover and food for many species. Canopy coverage of shrubs and herbaceous vegetation that is six inches to four feet tall is preferred by white-tailed deer. Cover six to eighteen inches tall is preferred by other species, including quail, rabbits, and turkeys. If the area has more than sixty percent coverage of shrubs and herbaceous vegetation, however, it may be too thick for ground-nesting birds and small mammals to walk through. Note the types of cover—cool-season grasses, warm-season grasses, legumes, or a mixture of plants.

Past grazing or haying pressure. Determine past grazing or haying pressure on the area as well as past flooding or burning. Moderate pressure leaves three to six inches of cool-season grasses and eight to twelve inches of warm-season grasses over winter. Name and estimate the percentage of legumes, including clovers, in the grasslands. Finally, note the grassland species, including existing forbs.

Croplands

Determine the normal or past cropping rotations, including rotations into grass. Also determine land fertility.

Woodlands

Oak trees. Estimate the percentage of black and white oak groups in the forest, since they are the most important mast-producing trees.

Size class. Determine the size class of the woodlands, defined by the diameter at breast height (DBH). The size classes are:

1. *Old growth:* determine the percentage of trees greater than sixteen inches DBH.
2. *Saw timber:* trees greater than nine inches DBH.
3. *Pole timber:* two- to nine-inch DBH.
4. *Regrowth:* zero to two-inch DBH.

Canopy. An "open" canopy has less than fifty percent coverage. A "closed" canopy has greater than fifty percent coverage.

Nest and roost trees. Determine the percentage or number of nest and roost trees. These include either dead or live trees of greater than six inches DBH with cavities.

Understory. Determine the density and makeup of the forest understory. If there are more than four stems per square yard, walking through the forest will be difficult. These areas are, however, great for ruffed grouse.

Wetlands

Water availability. Determine the fall and winter water availability.

Flooding. Estimate the amount of land that can be flooded from one to eighteen inches deep either naturally by rainfall or manually by artificial means. If it is more than eighteen inches, puddle ducks can't tip up to feed.

Wetland plants. Determine the types and estimate the percentages of existing wetlands plants.

Winter cover. Estimate the percentage of winter cover, including woody vegetation and/or emergent plants that can provide protection from the weather.

Habitat Percentages

After you've assessed the habitat types on your property, it's useful to also determine the percentage of habitat types within a two-mile radius of your land. This allows you to manage for wildlife in conjunction with habitat surrounding you; perhaps you can offer something that is not already available.

Uplands. Estimate the percentage of native grasses within a two-mile radius and also the percentage of pasture and haylands within the same area.

Determining the types of habitat that surround your property will help you plan what you will plant, develop, or enhance on your land. Credit: Fiduccia Enterprises

Croplands. Determine former cropping practices and existing crops within a two-mile radius.

Woodlands. Estimate the amount of forest cover within a two-mile radius of the tract being examined. (Deer and turkey numbers are directly related to the amount of forest cover.)

Wetlands. Estimate the percentage of forested bottomlands and unforested wetlands within a two-mile radius of your field or wetland. (Ducks, such as mallards, are more attracted to large wetlands or groups of wetlands than to isolated ones.) Also determine the distance to the nearest large reservoir or waterfowl refuge.

Overall percentages. Determine the percentage of croplands, native warm-season grasses, woodlands, and wetlands within a two-mile radius of your property. The amount and types of upland habitat, including grasses and croplands, determines whether quail, rabbits, pheasants, prairie chickens, and doves will be attracted to the land. The amount and types of woodlands determines the suitability for white-tailed deer, turkeys, squirrels, and ruffed grouse. The amount and types of wetlands determines the suitability for waterfowl. As you can guess, diversity provides for more wildlife species.

With this assessment you will be able to determine what wildlife habitat management practices are suitable for your property. You may discover that some practices are not practical on your property. You may find that your land is capable of attracting or holding certain wildlife species, but the surrounding land is not. But you can, with the right property, money, and hard work, manage the habitat for a wide variety of species or manage for your preferred species.

Planning Food Plots

MONTE BURCH

Creating food plots (sometimes called "green fields" in the South) can be a very important facet of a landowner's wildlife management plan. Wildlife have four basic needs for survival: food, water, shelter from the elements and from predators, and space. These needs become increasingly important in winter, when animals need more energy to survive and food is often harder to find. Food plots can play a crucial role in winter survival, offering both food and shelter to a variety of wild animals. If you do nothing else in the way of management, providing food plots can attract wildlife to your land as well as provide food when it's most needed.

Although growing food plots is a relatively new idea to many hunters and landowners, I've been experimenting with them for about thirty years on our Missouri farm. Since I have a full, working farm, I've brought over many practices from my cow-calf and cash-crop alfalfa operation. I began with advice from Dave Pitts, then with the Missouri Department of Conservation, and planted green browse plots of ladino clover for deer and rabbits and annual plots of milo and soybeans for deer, turkeys, and upland birds. Each plot brought more wildlife. These days I'm constantly experimenting with new seeds, redoing plots and creating new ones. For example, I cleared four acres of nuisance trees—Osage orange

Food plots can be extremely important wildlife habitat for any number of species. Credit: Fiduccia Enterprises

and hardwood brush—and planted the area in a combination of warm-season grasses, the Whitetail Institute's Imperial Whitetail Clover, and Alfa Rack. Joan filled her antlerless tag the first day of the season from the spring-planted food plot and then took a ten-point buck— her first buck—from the same food plot the second day of the season.

Food plots can provide nourishment for a variety of wildlife. The wildlife attracted depends on the type of food in the plot. In recent years many landowners and hunters with leased land have planted food plots to attract and hold deer and, just as importantly, provide the supplemental nutrition to help the deer reach their optimum body and rack size. These food plots will attract wildlife other than deer as well.

"One reason for the growing food plot popularity is that more people are understanding nutrition as a manageable aspect," said biologist and deer expert Dr. Grant Woods from South Carolina. "We can manage three factors in a wild, free-ranging herd—age, sex ratio, and nutrition. The first two are totally dependent on the trigger finger. Nutrition is forest management—clear-cuts or thinning; prescribed fire or herbicide treatment; and agricultural practices including food plots. Food plots can be very important in many parts of the country. The average forage intake needed per deer per year is about two thousand pounds of dry matter. There's a wide variance, of course, with a fawn needing, say, eight hundred pounds, while a mature buck may require four thousand pounds, but the average is two thousand pounds per deer. Food plots can provide five thousand to ten thousand pounds of forage per acre per year, depending on the plants and the rainfall."

Steve Scott, with Whitetail Institute, the company that introduced Imperial Whitetail Clover, the first commercial deer food-plot product, in 1988, says his company has seen interest in food plots increase tenfold in the past few years. "We're finding that many people are having as much fun managing their land for deer and other wildlife as they are hunting."

You can't simply throw seed out on the ground and expect food plots to succeed. Successful plots require both time and money. Follow these eight steps and you'll be on your way to success: planning, land clearing or preparation, soil testing, liming, fertilizing, preparing the seed bed, seeding, and maintaining.

Planning

Location

Determine your food plot needs. What wildlife do you wish to attract and/or grow? Examine your property on an aerial photo and a topographical map to determine possible food plot locations. The aerial photo shows existing vegetation, while the topographical map illustrates where level areas exist that may be suitable for planting. Determine whether overgrown fields or areas of brush or low-grade timber could be cleared to create food plots. If the land is agricultural, identify areas that can be set aside to provide foods other than agricultural crops at different times of the year from when the agricultural crops are grown. Food plots can also be planted along logging and interior farm roads, but don't place them along public roads, because they may attract poachers and can also present a hazard to motorists. The best food plot locations are fairly accessible for tillage equipment, open, and tillable. Although open, they should also be close to good cover and escape routes. Good locations include along streams, timber edges, or timber clearings;

Food plots must be located near cover, but away from public roads and property boundaries. The size and shape can vary, but long and narrow plots of at least one-half acre are best.

near brushy draws; and in the corners of shrubby fencerows. If you plant them near timber edges, locate them at least twenty yards from the timber edge to reduce competition from trees and prevent overshading. The area between the food plot and the timber edge can be planted in shrubs to provide escape and cover for animals coming into the field.

If you have tracts of woodlands or timber, you can also create food plots in them. Woodland food plots offer the ideal situation for deer and turkeys: the woodlands have food and shelter and the food plots create diversity, more edge, and food. Both deer and turkeys love edge habitats, which are often called "wildlife openings" by biologists and wildlife managers. Old clearings, log loading yards, and other openings in timber may offer food plot possibilities. Abandoned homesteads are also great

food plot locations. Right-of-ways can also be used, but check with lessors about legal use of such areas.

In pine plantations, one method of creating a food plot is to make a "huband-spoke" clearing design. To do this, make a center opening of half an acre or larger and then run spokes from this center hub. The spokes are usually about thirty yards wide and up to one hundred yards long. Many people build a shooting house or tower in the center of the hub.

If you clear timberland, choose areas that have timber of poor value. Areas with firewood potential are good choices in some parts of the country. If you log timberland for sale or thinning, a spot used as a landing for loading logs can later be turned into a food plot.

If hunting is the major reason for the food plot, it's important to plant it in a huntable location.

Locate it not only for hunting success but also for safety. For instance, a food plot with the only stand location directed toward a public road or houses presents a safety problem, and plots that are unapproachable due to prevailing wind direction are difficult to hunt.

All of the food plots on our property are back some distance from neighboring fences and property lines. Food plots on or near property lines may tempt others to shoot onto your property, and if you shoot an animal and it then runs back onto the neighbor's property, you may have a problem.

Soil Type

Food plot soil should be tillable but not highly erodible. Bottomland, the flatter tops of ridges and hillsides, and along the contour of gentle slopes are all possible locations. Since good soil grows the most productive food plots, bottomland, alongside streams, and other areas with fairly deep soil are the best choices. You can plant on thin hilltop soils, but these areas tend to have problems in times of drought. Plant the plots on relatively flat terrain, not sloping hillsides, as tilling hillsides can cause serious erosion. You can add diversity in hillside clearings, however, by planting permanent vegetation such as warm-season natural grasses that will hold the soil in place. Deep, fairly heavy soil that holds moisture is best, but even marginal soils—those that are thin, rocky, semi-arid, or somewhat sandy—can grow food plots if you choose the correct seed and practice proper soil management.

Size, Number, and Shape of Plots

Size. The size of each food plot depends on the characteristics of your property, rainfall, deer density, and how large the suitable areas are. Food plots should be at least half an acre, and you may need to plant plots of one, two, three, or even more acres in areas with high deer densities. Deer can quickly overbrowse small plots, which lowers the attractiveness of the plot, causes problems with plant rejuvenation, and shortens the plot's lifetime. It is, however, better to have numerous small plots than one huge plot.

Number. The number of food plots depends on all of the above factors as well as the availability of other nearby food sources, both natural and agricultural. Many experts suggest a minimum of one food plot per forty acres in heavily timbered locations. I have a dozen or so plots on three hundred acres. Wildlife management consultant Larry W. Varner, Ph.D., from Texas, says the number of plots should be determined by the number of deer, the amount of rainfall, and the production potential of the species planted. "When deer density is one deer to twenty acres or more, I recommend that one to two percent of the total area be in food plots. With higher deer densities—one deer to ten acres or less—I recommend three to five percent. Another way to figure acreage is to go by average annual rainfall. In areas with thirty inches or more per year, I recommend about 0.15 acres per deer. In areas with twenty-five inches or less per year, you'll need 0.30 acres per deer."

Shape and orientation. The ideal shape of a plot is long and narrow, following the edge of the cover, rather than square and blocky. This allows a greater edge-to-interior ratio, providing more opportunities for wildlife to visit the plot yet have a quick escape into cover. Big square plots usually have visitation only around the edges except by turkeys and upland birds. The width of the opening into the food plot must be at least one and one-half times the height of any adjoining trees. This allows sunlight to reach most of the plot and encourages better growth. If possible, openings should also be oriented to face in an east/west direction to allow for maximum sunlight.

Field Work

Once you've determined the size, number, and location of your plots, visit the sites and evaluate their feasibility by examining the soil and determining how much clearing, herbicide application, and/or tillage will be needed. You should also plot roads or routes to reach the site for both planting and hunting. Take soil samples from each of the sites and have them analyzed at your local county extension office. Let them know what types of seed you'll be using, because different seeds have different soil requirements.

Costs

If you're planning your first food plots, you should know that successful food plots are not cheap. Once a plot has been established, including land clearing, initial liming, fertilizing, seeding, and so forth, the average annual cost to maintain it can run from $90 to $150 per acre. In areas of high deer density, you may also have to install an electric fence around the plots until they're established, at an additional cost.

Types of Food Plots

Food plots can be planted to provide a variety of winter, summer, spring, and fall foods or year-round foods, and several types of plants may be used. These include annuals such as wheat, oats, corn, milo, soybeans, and various pea species; and annual brassicas and perennial legumes such as clovers and alfalfa. Plots can be planted in the spring or fall, but fall planting is dependent on the species

selected and the availability of rain. Spring and fall plots offer wildlife different foods at different times of the year.

Larry Varner offers advice on how much to plant in spring and fall: "Another consideration is how much of the total food plot plan should be in summer vs. winter food plots. For each fifteen acres of food plot area, I would plant ten acres (sixty-six percent) in summer plots and five acres (33 percent) in winter plots. The reasons for this are twofold: (1) winter food plot species (wheat, oats, etc.) tend to be more productive than most spring-planted species and (2) improved nutrition in the spring and summer has the greatest impact on subsequent antler production and fawn growth."

Timothy E. Fulbright, Ph.D., with the Caesar Kleberg Wildlife Research Institute, Texas A & M University-Kingsville, says that cool-season food plots of oats, wheat, and triticale, along with legumes such as hairy vetch, Austrian winter peas, alfalfa, and clover, should provide nutritious forage from November through April. Warm-season crops such as lablab, cowpeas, soybeans, and milo should provide forage from early spring through late fall.

Annuals, of course, must be replanted each year, while perennials last for a number of years. In most instances a combination of perennials and annuals provides the best food plots. I use both annuals and perennials in my plots primarily because I test a lot of new products, but also because the different varieties offer wildlife a smorgasbord of food throughout the year.

Clover is one of the most popular food-plot seeds, especially for deer and turkeys. It has high palatability and provides good nutrition, and once established, the plot may stay for several years. One Imperial Whitetail Clover food plot on our property lasted for almost ten years. "Clover provides the best of both worlds," said Whitetail Institute's Steve Scott.

"There is no single 'magic bean,' including BioLogic," explained Grant Woods, one of the developers of the Mossy Oak products. "A good food-plot system matches the needs of the deer as their annual cycles change. In the spring deer need high protein and a lot of tonnage. As the summer develops into July and August, deer need moderate protein and a lot of energy. By late fall and carrying through the winter, they don't need quite so much protein, but they need a high amount of energy. Specific plants provide those nutrients at certain times.

"Small grains, such as wheat and oats, are medium for quality and their digestibility is not that good, but they are good for energy. Plant these small grains in the fall. The brassicas are the most drought-resistant group of plants, and they produce the most tonnage per unit of effort with their huge leaf surface area and very small stem surface. The ideal food plot would have brassicas in the fall for their high energy and nutrients. Mix in a legume such as alfalfa or clover. Clovers don't do as much in the fall, but they really shine in the spring and summer. Clovers are the first to green up, and turkeys and deer both love them. Clovers carry through that early season when there is nothing to eat in the woods—the acorns are all gone and the animals have browsed all the edible twigs.

"If you have a low deer density, some of the more progressive legumes, like soybeans or peas, are great forage. They have little browse tolerance, however, and a high deer density can wipe out a small plot before the plants can grow any tonnage. The bottom line is that you need a blend. Another advantage of blends is that if you have four, five, or six species or cultivars, and something fails because it is too wet or too dry, one weak cultivar is usually balanced out by something that is strong in

Food plots may be planted with annuals or perennials. Clover is one of the most popular perennial plants and it attracts all types of wildlife.

"You are not going to find anything that is more preferred year-round. We'd be the first to admit that when white oak acorns are falling, it doesn't really matter what you've got out, the deer are going to the acorns. But white oak acorns are available for a very short time. And clover provides the highest possible nutritional value at the right times of the year—the spring and summer months when you have antler development and third-trimester pregnant does."

that area. When you plant a monoculture, you are really exposing yourself to either the vagaries of the weather or pests."

Seeds

Any number of plants can be used for food plots for fall hunting, but some plants are at their best early in the hunting season or until the first frost. Other plants last into the winter months and provide an attractant during the late muzzleloading and bow seasons.

Annual seeds include spring-planted varieties such as peas, some clovers, rapeseed, brassicas, corn, beets, soybeans, and the sorghums. Most of these plants offer food from early summer until a hard freeze, although some are hardier and will last through a few freezes and several are hardy in southern zones. Some of the brassicas I've tested have done pretty well in Missouri even in hard winters. Other annuals include winter wheat, triticale, and oats. These are planted in late summer or early fall and some can provide green foods throughout the winter. Oats don't last all winter, but winter wheat provides food throughout the winter and deer are attracted to it when other plants have died back.

The perennials include alfalfa, most clovers, chicory, ryegrass, lespedeza, and deer tongue grass. Although there is no single best "all-around" plant, clover comes the closest. A wide variety of red, crimson, and white clovers is available. Some varieties are the first plants to green up in the spring, providing food throughout the summer and fall and into winter until a hard freeze. White clover and blends of ladino clover are some of the most popular perennials. The legumes—such as most clovers and lespedeza—do not have to be replanted each year,

and with proper maintenance, clover food plots can last several years. Legumes also attract turkeys that eat the many insects preying on these succulent plants.

You'll find many food-plot seeds available locally. Check with your county extension office or local seed dealers about the seeds that do best in your area. Some companies now sell seeds specifically designed for food plots. One of the first to market seeds for deer food plots was Whitetail Institute with its Imperial Whitetail Clover, a blend of seeds that includes early-starting varieties, varieties that germinate later, and varieties that are drought-resistant. Imperial Whitetail Clover is also preinoculated, eliminating the step of inoculating the seed to provide a better chance of success, a timesaver for first-time food plotters. I've been experimenting with Imperial Whitetail Clover for well over ten years with good luck except during extreme droughts.

Generic Food Plot Seeds

A wide range of generic agricultural seeds that can be used for food plots is available from local seed supply stores. The seeds go by a variety of names, so I won't attempt to enumerate them here. It's best to check with your county extension agent or local seed distributors about what works best in your area.

Corn. More than one hundred species of wildlife are known to eat corn. Deer, turkeys, and upland game love it. And small critters, such as raccoons and squirrels, can quickly reduce a corn patch to a barren field of green stalks. Corn is one of the best sources of carbohydrates and fat, but it's low in protein. For this reason corn provides good nutrition in fall and winter when other sources may be unavailable. An annual, corn is planted in the spring. Use field corn, not sweet or silage varieties. *Disadvantages:* Food plots for corn must be fairly large to prevent overeating. Corn is also somewhat more drought-prone than other food plot plants, and lots of fertilizer is needed for its production. It can be broadcast, but does best when row-planted.

Grain sorghum. Often called "milo," this plant is a close relative of corn. The leaves and stalks are relished by deer early in the season, and birds love the seeds the plant produces. Milo is also an excellent overwintering plant for many species of wildlife. It is an annual and is planted in the spring. *Disadvantages:* It has high fertility requirements, and it is usually drilled or row-planted.

Clovers. The clovers, including white, ladino, red, and crimson, are excellent food-plot seeds. The white, ladino, and red clovers are perennial. Red clover is fairly short-lived; it usually lasts two to three years. Some varieties of white or ladino clover can live for more than five years under the right conditions. Crimson clover is a fall-seeded annual. All the clovers are legumes, which means that they fix nitrogen in the soil. They are also primarily cool-season crops, which means that they produce forage in early spring and then again in the fall. Clover is fairly easy to establish. Broadcast-seeding on prepared food plots works best, although no-till planting on herbicide-killed or burned areas also works. Deer love the clovers, and turkeys, quail, and other birds not only eat the plants but relish the numerous insects they attract. Clovers can be planted in spring or fall. *Disadvantages:* The clovers tend to have shallow root systems and are affected by drought, some varieties are more drought-resistant than others.

Wheat. Wheat will grow almost anywhere in the United States and is one of the most important food-plot plants. A cool-season grass that grows up to 4 feet tall, it provides nutritious, tender forage in the fall, through the winter, and into spring. In late spring and summer the mature seeds in the seedheads provide high levels of protein. Wheat is an annual and is broadcast or drilled in early fall. Some experts like to combine wheat with legumes such as clovers or winter peas. *Disadvantages:* None.

Soybeans. A common agricultural legume, soybeans, especially the succulent young plants of summer, are loved by deer. Like all legumes, soybeans fix nitrogen in the soil and are often planted as a rotation crop with corn, which has high nitrogen requirements. Like corn, soybeans are high in carbohydrates. The soybean seeds are also readily eaten by turkeys, quail, and other upland game, especially during the winter months. Soybeans are annual and are usually drilled but can easily be broadcast-seeded. They are planted in late spring or early summer. *Disadvantages:* Soybeans have fairly high fertilizer requirements, and unless you plant a large plot, the deer will eat it to the ground before the plants have a chance to mature.

Alfalfa. Alfalfa is one of the most palatable, nutritious, and high-protein food-plot plants. Creeping or grazing alfalfa, which steadily renews itself and can last up to five years (longer with proper maintenance), has become increasingly popular for food plots. It has deeper roots than many other forage crops and can withstand drought better than the clovers. It can be planted in either spring or summer and is most commonly broadcast. It's fairly easy to seed, but it does require a well-tilled and prepared seed bed. *Disadvantages:* Plants are highly insect-prone (but this does attracts ground-feeding birds).

Other plants. Rapeseed, chicory, sugar beets, and plain old turnips are often used in hunt-attractant food plots for deer.

Commercial Food Plot Seeds Designed Primarily to Attract Deer

A number of commercially produced food plot products, designed primarily for deer but also used by other wildlife, are available. Many must be planted in the spring, although some are planted in the fall and some can be planted during either season depending on locale, temperature, and annual rainfall.

BioLogic. The BioLogic family of food-plot products was the result of the dedication of two individuals—Toxey Haas and Grant Woods—to managing white-tailed deer. Haas has a passion for chasing and raising whitetails, and Woods researches and manages deer herds.

• *New Zealand Premium Perennial Blend* provides a nutritious, highly palatable blend of forages throughout the growing season. The blend consists of perennial plants and annual brassicas. Plant in early fall in the South and in the spring in the North. As the brassicas die out in winter, broadcast BioLogic's Maximum, composed of one hundred percent New Zealand brassicas, directly onto the existing perennial crop during the early fall portion of the second growing season to maintain an optimum forage rotation.

• *Clover Plus* is a blend of New Zealand red and white clovers along with varieties of chicory. This blend produces high-quality forage, especially during the hot months of summer when other crops may be stressed. Plant in the early fall in the South and frost-seed or plant in the spring in the North.

• *Maximum* contains one hundred percent New Zealand brassicas that can be planted in either spring or fall. These brassicas yield as many as

Although local seed dealers carry most food plot seeds, a wide range of "specialty" food plot seeds are also available.

ten tons of forage per acre, with over thirty-eight percent crude protein. Planted in early fall, they will germinate in drier conditions than other fall food-plot crops. If planted in the fall, they must be planted thirty days before the first frost date; they can also be planted in the spring.

- *New Zealand Full Draw* is composed of a mixture of cultivars that offer nutrition from germination until the plot matures well after the hunting season. It is planted in early fall in the South or thirty to fifty days before the first frost date in the North.
- *Green Patch Plus* contains a blend of wheat, oats, clovers, and brassicas for large food plots. Plant it in the fall; it needs at least thirty days of growth before frost.
- *Biomass* produces high-quality protein through the spring and summer months, which maximizes antler growth and fawn development. Biomass requires daytime temperatures in the seventies or higher to ensure rapid germination, but it can be planted anytime during the spring after the last frost date and through the summer or in early fall as long as there is adequate soil moisture. When used as an early bow season attractant, plant it three weeks before bow season starts.

Whitetail Institute. Whitetail Institute was the first to design and distribute seed specifically for white-tailed deer, and they continue to produce a line of high-quality products for deer food plots, many of which are relished by other wildlife as well.

- *Imperial Whitetail* Clover does best in soils that hold moisture. It produces up to thirty-five percent protein year-round and lasts up to five years after a single planting. It's coated and preinoculated, is blended specifically for regional use, and may be planted in spring or fall.

- *Imperial Alfa* Rack is good for upland soils, hilltops, and hillsides. It provides up to thirty percent protein year-round and it also lasts up to five years after a single planting. It's preinoculated, specifically blended for regional use, and may be planted in spring or fall.
- *Imperial No-Plow* is for hard-to-reach areas or for landowners without farming equipment. It offers up to thirty-six percent protein, is an annual, and can be planted in spring or fall.
- *Imperial Power Plant* grows extremely fast, withstands heavy grazing pressure, and produces the high protein level that bucks need during the spring/summer antler-growing season. It contains a soybean and lablab and it can be planted through May in the South and as late as the end of June in the North. It lasts until the first frost, and even then it can provide some forage and good cover through the fall months.

Remington QuikShoots. Remington QuikShoots products are formulated to grow fast and provide a high-protein nutritional diet for deer, turkey, and upland species. QuikShoots blends can be planted in spring or fall and they have been tested in many areas of the United States.

- *Big Buck Blend* consists of sweet rapeseed and clover. Sweet rapeseed is an annual and the clover is a perennial.
- *Quik Clover Blend* consists of an annual rye and a special blend of perennial clover that will come back for three to five years.
- *No-Till Quik* Clover can be used to overseed an existing food plot.

Brier Ridge Wildlife. These seeds are blended by Olds Seed Solutions and seeds are available for both spring and fall planting.

- *Bucks Banquet* contains a mix of clover, leafy rapeseed, turnips, and chicory. Once cooler temperatures arrive, the mix becomes sweeter and more succulent.
- *Horn Honey Clover* contains a formula of high-quality clover seeds.
- *EZII Gro* is a low-maintenance perennial mix formulated to grow in areas where ideal preparation of the soil is difficult to achieve.
- *Rut N Ready* is a quick-grow mix designed to attract bucks during the rut. The mix contains high-energy turnips, rapeseed, and chicory.
- *Gobbler Gourmet* is a high-protein food source for turkeys. It attracts insects for spring and summer feedings and contains alfalfa, red clover, creeping red fescue, bird's-foot trefoil, Kentucky bluegrass, and white clover.
- *Rooster Relish* is a high-protein food source for pheasants. It contains buckwheat, early corn, black oil sunflower, early grain sorghum, and Japanese millet.
- *Fur & Feather Cover* Mix is formulated to provide deer, turkey, pheasants, and other wildlife with concealment cover. The mix contains early bird millet, early grain sorghum, huntsman millet, white proso millet, and Japanese millet.

Buck Busters. Buck Busters mixes have been field-tested under hunting conditions using a variety of soil types.

- *Fall Seed Mix* is very high in protein, with eighty-one percent digestible nutrients, and it includes three species of grass, winter peas, a mixture of brassicas, and crimson clover. Seed it from September 1 through October 15 in the Southeast, sixty days before the average frost date.
- *Summer Seed Mix* contains iron clay peas, forage soybeans, and hot weather corn varieties. Plant it

after the Fall Seed Mix (above) has gone to seed, usually in late May or early June.

Tecomate. Tecomate's Food Plot System includes a variety of seeds.

- *Lablab* is a good warm-season source of protein (up to forty percent), antlergrowing phosphorus, and other key ingredients. Basically a super cowpea, it is nutritious, drought-resistant, and productive, averaging over 12,000 pounds/acre. Plant it in spring or, for bowhunting plots, in early fall.
- *Lablab Plus* contains lablab, ebony pea (a fast-growing vining pea relished by deer), and other big-seeded peas. Plant in spring or, for bowhunting plots, in early fall.
- *Outback Legume Mix* is formulated for the Gulf and Atlantic Coast states. It will not withstand severe winters and consists of coated and preinoculated warm-season sub-tropical legumes.
- *HomePlace Wildlife Mix* with Wildflowers attracts butterflies, songbirds, hummingbirds, turkeys, deer, and other wildlife to backyards. It includes coated and preinoculated white and red clovers and a variety of wildflowers.
- *Chicory* contains a mix of chicory varieties that is fast-growing, high in protein, and drought-resistant. It produces lots of highprotein forage and lasts for three to five years. Frost-seeding works well, and the mix is good for fall hunting plots.
- *Longbeard Turkey Mix* contains coated and preinoculated white and red clovers, yellow sweet blossom clover, bird's-foot trefoil, vetch, and chicory. It's an ideal mix for small woodland food plots. Plant it in the fall in the South; in April through July in the Midwest; or frostseed.
- *Monster Mix* contains coated and preinoculated premium white and red clovers and chicory and

provides deer with food yearround. It can be planted in spring or fall.

- *Ultra Forage Mix* contains legumes (peas, vetch, and clovers), chicory, and brassicas, and includes a hybrid rape/turnip that provides both forage and a highly edible bulb. Plant it in fall.
- *Max-Attract 50/50* contains fifty percent peas, clovers, vetch and chicory and fifty percent premium grain. A forty-pound bag plants an acre. Plant it in the fall to attract bucks.

PlotSpike. PlotSpike, from Regan & Massey, Inc., offers a wide range of foodplot products and blends that contain no fillers and have no chemical coatings.

- *Chufas* are great for turkey food plots. They grow in a wide range of climatic and soil conditions. A warm-season perennial, chufa produces subterranean tubers that look like nuts and have high levels of protein and carbohydrates. Plant in spring.
- *Spring Wildlife Mix* is a blend of warm-season plants that attract a variety of wildlife including turkeys, deer, and hogs. If you plant it in spring after the last frost date, it will provide food until frost in the fall.

Premium Fall Blend contains perennial prairie bromegrass, which is very palatable and long-lasting and provides high protein. It also contains forage rape, forage clovers, and a chicory.

- *Clover Blend* contains clovers and chicory. Chicory adds longevity to food plots during drought conditions.
- *Quick Stand Mix* is blended for quick establishment in varying conditions and can be planted with minimum tillage.

- *New Zealand Blend* contains forage rape and kale and is high in phosphorus and calcium. Combined with the clovers in the blend, it provides winter-long grazing and reseeding.

Wildlife Nutritional Systems of Texas. This company produces a wide range of food-plot mixes and blends.

- *Blue Magic Winter Legume* does well in the southeastern United States on dry upland soils.
- *Winter Deluxe* is a traditional oat, wheat, and rye blend. It also contains triticale, a wheat/cereal rye cross that is very winterhardy and more palatable and disease-resistant than winter wheat.
- *Fall Blend* contains oats, triticale, Austrian winter peas, clover, and alfalfa. It is very easy to work with and does well on most soils.
- *Big Buck Xcellerator* is an economy version of the Fall Blend. It contains triticale, Austrian winter peas, and tyfon, a turnip/cabbage cross.
- *No-Till Buck Buster* is a fall-winter blend for those without access to farming equipment.
- *Spring-Summer Blend* consists of "Mr. Whitetail" Peas, browntop and pearl millet, white milo, and sunflowers. It is very fast maturing and can be double-cropped for spring planting in the North.
- *Upland Deluxe* is a mix for those whose primary concern is turkey, quail, doves, and other upland game birds. It consists of gamebird peas, browntop millet, white milo, hegari, and sunflowers and produces cover and a large seed crop. Plant it in the spring.
- *Alfagraze* is a perennial true grazing-type alfalfa developed in the United States specifically for food plots. Bred to tolerate the heavy grazing that is common in food plots, it may stay green year-round in some parts of the country.

- *No-Till Mr. Whitetail* Peas provide an easy method of establishing wildlife food plots. Simply seed the peas and then cut the grass and weeds. The peas create a spring/summer and early fall food plot for deer, quail, and turkeys.

Antler King Trophy. Antler King Trophy has a wide range of products.

- *Fall/Winter/Spring Food Plot Blend* continues to grow and provide more than twenty percent protein during the winter when other plants die or become dormant.
- *Mini-Max Food Plot Mix* is a mix of perennial and annual seeds that have been proven to thrive in minimum tillage and the lower pH of more acidic soils. This mixture contains seeds for both northern and southern plots.
- *Trophy Clover Mix* is a blend of four clovers designed to provide high-quality forage for deer.

Schuster Farms. Schuster Farms has a wide range of products including lablab, an annual warm-season forage legume.

- *Spring Mega Mass* is a mix of fourteen subtropical legumes that complement each other throughout the growing season.
- *Trophy Forage Mix* consists of a unique blend of triticale, wheat, oats and rye varieties developed specifically for forage production.
- *Forage Plus* is a mixture of wheat, oats, triticale, rye and winter peas. The winter peas add protein.
- *Double Deer Mix* is a mixture of oats, wheat, triticale, rye, alfalfa, clover, peas, and vetch that provides excellent protein and energy.
- *Fall Premium Perennial Mix* combines seven popular clovers with three alfalfas, six aggressive medics or leguminous herbs and one mystery ingredient.

- *Fall Mega Mass Mix* has all the nutritional ingredients of the Fall Premium Perennial Mix plus with oats, wheat, triticale, and rye.

Pennington. Pennington is one of the largest producers of food plot and wild game seeds. Check Pennington's website for their extensive listing of seeds and wild game products.

If you don't purchase a seed blend, you may wish to plant a variety of annual and perennial seeds of different species, which provides wildlife with different foods at different times of the year. Since some plants are more drought-resistant than others, planting a variety will also help to ensure that some food is available even during dry weather. I plant several food plots in this manner, keeping the annuals and perennials in separate strips. Many companies offer food-plot mixes that include rapeseed, brassicas, clovers, cowpeas, turnips, triticale, lablab, and others.

Regardless of the seed you choose, proper planting is important for success. Carefully follow the manufacturer's planting instructions. Some seeds are planted in the spring, some in the fall, and some can be planted in either spring or fall. Some seeds are "no-till," which means they can be broadcast without thoroughly working the soil. You must, however, kill competing vegetation before you broadcast the seeds.

Seeds for Wildlife Other Than Deer

Although most of the products and information available today are for creating food plots to attract white-tailed deer, combination plots can attract other wildlife as well. Created properly, food plots can be magnets for wild turkeys, quail, rabbits, and numerous non-game species. The secret is to use plants that provide different types of seeds and forage that can be used by different types of wildlife. Since deer are opportunists, they will also appreciate these combination plots.

For example, clovers and alfalfa used for deer food plots also provide great bugging areas for turkey poults and young quail because they are attractive to many insects. And because these plants are relatively short, they provide easy forage for small ground-feeding birds. Clovers and alfalfa can be planted in combination with other plants such as annual grains or warm-season grasses to provide cover, grains, and other forage.

One example of combination seed packages is the Mossy Oak BioLogic Turkey T.O.P. or Turkey Optimization Program. It allows you to create adult bird forage areas, poult bugging areas, and grain as food for both. A thirteen-pound bag plants one acre. The seeds come in separate bags and are planted in strips, with the poult bugging areas on the outside, adult forage areas inside the bugging area, and the grain production seed in the center. The instructions with the seeds also suggest creating a dusting area as turkeys dust frequently and will return daily to the same location to dust if the conditions are favorable. You can create a dusting area in or near an existing food plot by frequent tilling or raking with a sturdy garden rake to maintain an area of loose soil. Dusting sites should be shaded near midday and be near a food source turkeys like. An ideal location is at the edge of a food plot beneath overhanging tree limbs.

You can create your own combinations, but it's important to match seeds to specific areas and soils. For the most part different species should be kept separate rather than mixing them together in one large planting because different seeds require different planting techniques. Some require merely pressing into the soil, while others require a slight covering. When you're planning your seed plot,

consider that taller, spreading plants can prevent shorter plants from getting enough sunlight.

Strip Cropping Combination Food Plots

One of my favorite tactics is to strip-crop food plots. The more edge you create, the better the plot will be for all types of wildlife, and strip crops create a lot of edge. You'll need a plot of one acre or more; several of my plots are three to four acres. I prefer to create plots that are linear and that wind through cover such as timber rather than to create a large square block. One plan that has worked well is to place a strip of clover such as Whitetail Institute Imperial clover or Whitetail Institute Alfa Rack, which combines clover and alfalfa, along the outside of the plot. Then plant a strip of grain, such as milo combined with soybeans, next to the clover. Throw in some browntop millet as an added bird attractant as a separate strip. Deer will eat the soybeans to the ground, while the milo provides grain for turkeys and quail. Next leave a strip equal in size to the grain strip as open ground. This strip will grow up in ragweeds and other quail and dove foods with open ground beneath for ground-foraging birds. The clover is a perennial and will stay for several years. The grains are annuals and must be planted each year. You may wish to try alternating the open strip and grain strip each year to provide more versatility in the food plot. Or you could plant the third strip to green winter wheat or oats in fall for deer and turkeys and plant milo and soybeans in the spring. I've used all of these combinations with good results.

The strips should be twelve to fifteen feet wide and you can create as many as you desire. You can even add a wider sunflower strip on the outside of one edge to create your own mini-dove field. Or try a dual patch—seed one with spring-planted species

One simple method of establishing clover food plots is to over-seed with a legume in late winter.

and another with fall-planted species to create more versatility in attracting whitetails and other wildlife. Both Mossy Oak BioLogic and Pennington offer numerous spring, summer and fall planted seeds.

Since the annual portions of these fields require replanting each year, you may also wish to consider planting an entire field in perennials. An extremely effective combination is a plot with clover around the outside and warm-season grasses in the center. The native warm-season grasses such as switchgrass, big bluestem, little bluestem, and Indian grass are all bunchgrasses. This means that they grow tall and upright in bunches with bare ground between the plants, making them especially good at providing both cover and food for quail and turkey poults, pheasants,

and small mammals such as rabbits. The seed is relished by wildlife, while the foliage is an excellent deer food. Deer like to bed in the grass because it hides them well, and they especially like it if the area is close to another food source such as clover. The best method of managing warm-season grasses is with regular prescribed burns. The clover strip around the outside of the plot provides a natural firebreak, but it must be wide enough to create a good break; twenty feet should be adequate in most instances. (See Prescribed Burns.)

A very simple combination green browse food plot was recommended by the Missouri Department of Conservation over twenty years ago: Uniformly seed a one-acre plot with a half bushel of wheat and two pounds of orchard grass in early September. At the same time or in early winter, overseed half of the plot with two pounds each of ladino clover and red clover. During the following January through March, overseed the other half with ten pounds of Korean or Summit lespedeza. This legume plot with a thin stand of grass provides forage for turkeys, deer, and rabbits and also attracts insects for turkeys and quail. The lespedeza provides seeds for quail and green forage for other wildlife during summer periods when clovers may become dormant.

Disking Plots for Annual Weeds

One of the simplest methods of creating food plots, especially for turkeys and upland game such as quail, is disking and leaving the land fallow. This allows annual weeds, especially ragweed, to sprout. These weeds supply seeds and food without the expense of planting. One method recommended by many experts is to maintain a portion of a food plot in disked, fallow land each year. Then rotate, planting it the following year and disking another portion of the plot.

When to Plant

Timing is important when seeding food plots. Check the seeding times on the product bag and follow the times recommended for your state or zone explicitly—or check with your county extension office about recommended planting times. I like to make both spring and fall plantings—or rather cool and warm-season plantings. Doing this provides not only new growth and more food year-round, but also a better variety of foods and some drought protection. For example, I plant annuals such as corn, soybeans, milo, and peas in the spring, and I also plant perennials such as clover or alfalfa in the spring. The perennials can also be planted in the fall, and in some areas that's best because there's less chance of drought and less weed competition for the tiny seeds. In the fall I plant winter wheat or oats. In late fall I broadcast ladino clover over the wheat or oats, creating a perennial plot for the next year.

Advantages of fall planting. About the time the summer ends and cooler nights begin, many hunters start to think about the coming hunting season. I'm in the same mode at this time of year, but I'm also thinking about food plots. I've discovered that fall-planted food plots offer some advantages over spring-planted ones, especially plots of clovers and alfalfa such as Imperial Whitetail Clover and Alfa Rack.

Lack of weed competition. Clovers planted in the spring have to sprout and then come up through weeds and grasses that are usually already in place and have a jump on the tiny clovers. Even in a tilled food plot, they'll have some competition from sprouting grasses and weeds unless the weeds and grasses have been sprayed with an herbicide prior to planting.

Attractive food during hunting season. If all conditions are right, fallplanted food plots can offer extremely succulent new growth during the hunting season, attracting deer more readily than old growth food plots do.

One of the easiest food plots is made by simply disking the land and then leaving it fallow. The natural weeds that sprout will provide seeds and food for turkeys and quail. Credit: Plotmaster

Turkeys love clover and are often the first animals to frequent a food plot once it greens up in the spring.

Early spring establishment. Come next spring, plants in fall-seeded plot are already established, making it easier for them to compete with the weeds and grasses. This means that the fall-planted food plots will be at their prime during the spring months when whitetails need nutrition the most. Does in the last stages of pregnancy and bucks beginning antler regrowth require good nutrition at this time when there are few other food sources, and a new clover food plot is an excellent source.

More time available. It's easier for me to find time to plant in the fall than in the spring. Regardless of whether you're doing the work yourself or hiring someone to do it, spring is a busy time, especially for farmers trying to get their crops planted. Fall is not as busy for most farmers, so it's usually easier to hire someone or find time yourself.

More convenient liming. In order for clover and alfalfa to use the nutrients in the soil or the fertilizer you apply, the pH of the soil must be correct—between 6.5 and 7.0. It takes time for

lime to break down in the soil and work with the nutrients, and the time required depends on the type of lime applied. Because of the large amounts of lime often needed, commercial application is usually the best choice. This means applying the lime when food-plot areas are dry so the trucks won't get stuck. Late spring or early summer are good times for lime application for fall-planted food plots, and these are usually times when applicators and lime suppliers are not overbooked.

To have a successful fall food plot, several factors are important:

A good seedbed.

Getting seed in early. You must plant fairly early in the fall if you want to hunt over the food plot the same year.

Adequate rainfall. Regardless of whether you plant in the spring or fall, moisture is needed, and in many parts of the country rainfall is sometimes scarce in the fall.

It is important to choose seeds that are adapted to fall planting. Imperial Whitetail Clover is an excellent choice and my all-around favorite. I have about twenty-five acres planted in eight food plots scattered around my farm. The clover stays green here in Missouri until mid-winter, when the ground freezes solid. Then the clover dies back, but it's one of the first plants to rejuvenate in the spring. By late February or early March I see lots of wild turkeys in the clover plots, and their bright green droppings indicate where they're getting their first good nutrition after the long winter.

Unfortunately, not all soils are suited for clover. Well-drained, drier soils, particularly on hilltops, often do best with an alfalfa product. Most alfalfas tend to die back more quickly than clover and a

very hard frost can brown out some species. In fact, this can happen just before or during deer season, which can quickly change deer feeding patterns and, of course, hunting success. Whitetail Institute's Alfa Rack, however, is a clover-type creeping alfalfa blend that is less susceptible to early browning. Alfa Rack is a special blend suited to different parts of the country. It requires only six weeks to germinate, giving it a good start before winter hits.

Planting Steps

Following the proper planting procedure is important for both fall and spring food plots. Before you plant, take soil samples to determine the pH and soil nutrients your soil needs. Ideally, this should be

Clover seed is hardy enough to plant it in the fall, winter, or spring. It will lie dormant until it germinates with the warmer temperatures. Credit: Lee Hoard

done in late spring so that you can determine lime requirements and apply the lime. Then break ground. In central Missouri, where I live, I like to till the plot in early August. If I'm creating a new plot on an old field or a similar area, I first apply an herbicide to kill existing vegetation. Once the vegetation has died back, I apply fertilizer and till the soil.

You can plant clover seed anytime from fall through winter and into spring. The seed will lie dormant until there is enough sunlight and warmth to start to germinate it. If you're late getting your fall seed planted, plant winter wheat as a cover crop. This prevents soil erosion and keeps the tiny clover seeds from being washed away in case of heavy rains before germination takes place in the spring. I cleared a four-acre food plot two years ago and by the time I planted, it was too late for fall germination. Wary of erosion due to the bulldozer's action, I planted triticale over the plot as a cover crop. The triticale came up fine and I had lots of deer in the plot throughout the winter. The next spring I had one of the best Whitetail Imperial Clover germination successes I've experienced, and that plot, at this time, is one of my most productive.

One unusual but popular technique farmers and ranchers use to upgrade grass pastures is overseeding with legumes in the winter. I've done this with good success using ladino and red clovers to create food plots. Doing this also offers some of the advantages of fall planting. Overseeding is a great way to add quality nutrition to a grass stand without actually breaking ground. Imperial No-Plow is an excellent choice for this method and it is also extremely easy to use. For a total clover plot, rather than a mix of grasses and clovers, you must kill the weeds and grasses with herbicide before planting and then broadcast in mid to late winter. This works best when the ground is frozen. As the ground thaws in the spring, the seeds seep into the cracks in the soil created by the temperature changes. An even better idea is to spread the seed on snow cover. Not only does this allow you to see your seeds so you can keep your coverage even, but as the snow melts in the spring the seeds are distributed down into minute cracks in the soil. This method also provides an initial nitrogen boost. Legumes such as clovers add nitrogen to the soil. As the snow melts, it also adds nitrogen to the soil.

Three Steps to a Grand Scheme

TOM INDREBO

I've never believed that old saying, "It's better to be lucky than good." Far from it. I believe the harder you work, the luckier you get. Everyone can get lucky occasionally, but consistent success is no accident. Our accomplishments at Bluff Country Outfitters result from year-round planning, lots of work, never ending review and analysis, and trying to learn from our mistakes so we don't repeat them.

As I mentioned in Chapter 1, Laurie and I didn't come to Buffalo County in 1993 with a long-term plan and business blueprint to launch Bluff Country Outfitters. But this business didn't grow by itself, either. As we saw its potential grow and evolve, we kept feeding the fire while being sure it didn't consume us in the process.

Even today I don't keep a "recipe book" that lays out everything we accomplished since we moved here, or projects that we will accomplish in the years that follow. In fact, the book you're now reading is the first time I've sat down and turned my management thoughts and plans into the printed word. However, I keep my ears and eyes open at all times, and I pay attention to what works, what doesn't work, and how we can make things work even better. I've always been good at improvising and trying new ideas, and before I give up on an idea or expand it, I try to make sure it will work more than once and in different settings.

I also try to be patient. A quality deer-hunting operation can't be created in one or two years. It requires a long-term commitment that pulls you through the mistakes you're bound to make, and keeps things in perspective when a plan exceeds expectations. It's a day-to-day, week-to-week, month-to-month and year-to-year effort. You might not even see many differences each year, but when you look back five or 10 years, the differences are huge.

Meanwhile, you must remain flexible, adapt your plan to unexpected changes, and always blend those ideas into your state's deer- and wildlife-management rules and regulations. Sometimes you'll also need to work with neighbors, local conservation leaders, state wildlife biologists and maybe even local and state politicians. You won't always win disagreements and political skirmishes, and some partnerships end on sour notes, but win or lose, you must push on while complying with the state's larger, overall management programs.

STEP 1: Know the Land

So let's get started. At risk of simplifying our approach, I consider Bluff Country Outfitters' deer-, land- and hunting-management plan a three-step program. For Step 1, I stress the importance of knowing the land itself. Before you decide where you're going, you must know what your property is already producing and what's taking place in its every corner and hilltop. Study its terrain, its waterways and drainage patterns, property lines, ownership trends, access issues, local hunting culture, adjoining farming practices and woodland management.

With the Internet, it's easier than ever to develop a good library of topographical maps and aerial photos. Buy a county plat book every couple of years from the County Courthouse to watch land-ownership changes, and monitor how neighbors parcel up their lands when they sell out. It's not uncommon to see farmers sell their land by breaking it into 5-, 10-, 20- and 40-acre parcels. The smaller the holdings, the more landowners there will be, and the more complex your challenges will become.

BLUFF COUNTRY OUTFITTERS

Create a library of county maps, topographical maps, aerial photos and county plat books that show your hunting land. Nearby land-ownership patterns and the size of surrounding properties can have more impact on your management plan than your knowledge of your property's terrain and habitat.

Of prime importance, of course, is your own land and what it's producing. The more you know about its terrain, woodlands, logging operations and agricultural practices, the better you can predict how, where and when deer move about the area. This is especially crucial knowledge for bowhunters, who must take advantage of the deer's natural movements to increase their odds of success. Whether you're hoping to intercept a buck between his bedding and feeding areas, or to waylay him during the rut as he cuts cross-country to search for doe family groups and receptive partners, you'll do more guessing than bowhunting if you don't have a good grasp of what's taking place on the ground and how it affects deer activity.

That reminds me of "The Wishbone Buck," which Doug Hick of Phillips, Wisconsin killed nearby back in 1991. Doug was hunting along a rub line near the end of October, right before the rut really kicked in. At that time of year, bucks are back in the security of their home areas after leaving their summer hangouts and bachelor groups about a month before. Here in the Bluff Country, they lay up in October while the acorns and maple leaves are falling. They're almost nocturnal in their movements. They'll have a spot where they feel safe, where they'll see or smell you if you try to move in on them.

As October moves along, that buck will get up from his bed walk a route to a feeding area and rub trees every so often. If he lives a few years, you'll find where he's rubbed the same trees multiple times during those years. If you want a decent chance of shooting him, you must be familiar with that travel corridor and have an idea where he's bedding. At some point, his rutting urge will bring him out of his bedding area in daylight, but he will still be near his bed. If you're not familiar with this spot and stumble right into his bedding area, you'll bump him out and never see him in daylight.

To figure out how close you are to his bedding area, scout in the spring, find his rub line and unravel it back toward his bedding area. He will make a scrape every so often, and his end scrape will probably be about 50 to 60 yards from where he beds. Locate that final scrape, turn back in the direction you came from, and find the next-to-last scrape along his route and set up between those two scrapes.

The challenge is to figure out how to reach that spot and set up on it without alerting the buck when you're there in late October. This usually requires setting up your stand (or stands) before he returns from his summer range. The safest bet is to trim out the site in spring and get everything set. Things will grow in a bit during summer, so maybe in August or September go back in there, do the final preparations, and clear a little trail so you can slip in quietly in late October.

Then, once he's in there again in late September or early October, leave him alone for at least the first three weeks of October. He's not moving out soon enough in daylight to get a look at him. When it's time to go after him, don't force it. Wait for the right wind slip in there when it's right, and sit so you can watch that end scrape nearest his bedding area. If you've done your homework and you respected the wind you should be able to get that buck the first time you hunt him.

How will you know when the time is right? You'll have about a five-day window to take a buck on this kind of setup. That last scrape gets all torn up and dished out like a bowl because when that buck starts getting those rutting urges toward the end of October, he might get up and walk that short line from his bed every hour. The trouble is, most guys find that last scrape, get all fired up, and set up on it the first chance they get. They never see the buck because he knows they're there. They're too close to his bed and they made noise putting up their stand. Every time they show up, the buck knows it.

Doug Hick didn't blow his opportunity when he moved into place in 1991 to get the Wishbone Buck, but he had his doubts at first. After he got into his stand he pulled up his bow with his rope. As he lifted it, he accidentally banged the bow onto his tree steps. That buck came right in! Doug's stand was close to where the buck was bedded and the buck probably mistook the banging sound for deer messing around in his area. Doug had the right wind and the right situation, and he made the shot when the buck appeared.

We recognized the Wishbone Buck right away. I had seen him for a couple of years and had videotaped him quite a bit for our Monarch Valley tape. But I first encountered him when he was a 2½-year-old and running scrapes. In one memorable scene in the video, I filmed him as he walked all the way around me, trying to figure out what I was.

Doug shot him with his bow the following year in the situation we just described. The buck was an impressive 8-pointer that scored in the 140s when it was 3½ years old. We named him the Wishbone Buck in 1990 because the end of his beams looked like a turkey's wishbone. We never would have gotten him if we didn't know so much about that piece of ground and how, why and when bucks use setups like that to their advantage. Those kinds of details are usually the difference between hunting and just hoping.

STEP 2: Know the Deer

As the Doug Hick hunt illustrates, it's also important to know what deer are doing year-round on your land. Obviously, that means paying attention year-round not just when the hunting season is near or under way. Don't just note where you see deer. Try to figure out what draws them to particular sites and when you see them in different locations.

Don't expect to unlock all their secrets the first year or the first two years. Chances are, as long as you're hunting a particular piece of land, you'll always learn a little more about it year to year. Again, you might not realize how much you learn daily, weekly or monthly, but when viewed in three- or five-year increments, the knowledge you compile will be staggering. One reason I included the story about John Sligh and his 160-class bow-kill in September 2005 was to illustrate how easy it is to overlook a good spot for years. I was in my 13th year on our Bone Creek farm when the right circumstances finally coincided to steer me to that setup. Chances are, if I hadn't stumbled onto those two bedded bucks that summer, John never would have been sitting on that site after he arrived from Florida.

As you continue roaming, scouting and hunting your land, you'll learn a lot about the many ways deer use the terrain and cover to their advantage. You'll discover that some individual deer have habits that defy general rules. In some cases, those preferences vary by where you happen to be hunting. You can't discount something found in one place but not the other. In these bluffs, I've seen deer bed in little more than tufts of grass along a fence line where they can see far and wide, almost as if they were antelope. In most cases, though, they bed just over the top of ridges, along shelves in thicker cover where they can look out and down. They count on the wind to bring scent from over the ridge behind them.

Learn all you can about how winds swirl through your hills and valleys. Where do deer go to find relief from howling winds that make it difficult

to hear approaching threats? Pay attention to quiet zones downhill from ridgetops. The wind often comes up from our valleys with such force that it seems to blow right over the top, leaving calm air just beneath the ridgeline on the opposite side. It's not unusual for me to see trees bucking, groaning and popping above me in a stiff wind, even though the woods are quiet where I stand in a hollow below the ridgetop. Each ridge, valley and hilltop can create its own unique wind currents, depending on wind speed and direction, so the more time you spend in the woods, the better you'll know where to hunt under different conditions.

This hilltop shelf offers whitetails a safe place to rest, rub and monitor their surroundings for danger. Deer like to bed just over the top of ridges, along shelves in thick cover that lets them look out and down. They count on the wind to bring scent from over the ridge behind them.

I've also found that mature bucks tend to bed where they can see a decent distance. Some of them like to bed in more open cover than you might expect. I think they do whatever they can to avoid being surprised. In some ways, their behavior resembles that of wild turkeys. They want as much distance as possible between themselves and possible threats.

STEP 3: Combining Your Knowledge of Land and Deer

As you increase your knowledge of your land and the deer that live there, the real fun begins. The more you learn about both, the more you can use the ax, saw, tractor and plow to make your land even more productive for deer hunting.

Granted you can always hunt deer by relying solely on your knowledge of their habits and travel patterns. For some people, though, that's not enough. We also like to work with the land and create plans and projects that make deer hunting even more interesting and productive. As you're learning your land's features and how deer use them, it's time to place food plots and build waterholes, set up long-term forestry plans, learn the deer's food preferences, learn different plants' peak palatability stages, schedule plantings and harvests on your larger fields, and work with neighbors and experts to provide services you can't or won't tackle yourself.

In other words, it's possible to make good hunting sites even better by giving deer more reasons to be there. Again, though, you must know your land to recognize its potential and possibilities. For instance, not too far over the ridge from John Sligh's stand is a spot where we've had lots of luck over the years. Pat Reeve or his father sat there for several years, and the first year I guided hunters, I put a guy

in there. A big buck came through, the guy shot it, and I looked like I knew what I was doing.

That spot is a natural travel route that skirts a steep area right uphill from a stream. Deer bed along that hillside all the way out to a point where they can lay and watch everything below them. With good cover, the right terrain and lots of white oaks dropping acorns, deer were always bedding along there. I figured the bucks were always coming through that spot during the rut to look for does, and I wanted to make sure they had another reason to show up.

We'll cover this topic in depth later, but this is the site where I built one of our first woodland waterholes. We used a Caterpillar, built a clay-lined pond in there, and seeded the area around it. Why build a pond inside a thick bedding ground? During the rut, bucks run for hours and get thirsty. When they feel dehydrated they head for water, so I figured I would give them a water source right where they expect to find does.

That decision paid off. Bucks started flocking to that pond. Not only did they come there for water during the rut, they started coming there in September, especially during hot spells. The hotter the weather, the better action you'll have on woodland ponds. Twice now we've killed three Pope & Young bucks in one season off that pond which proves you can take a good spot and make it even better.

Not only that, but this example shows you don't need to be a mile from the nearest road to shoot big bucks. The spot is within a quarter-mile of our home. The experience also taught me how tolerant deer can become when they're hanging out near a great food source. During years of good acorn crops, deer bed near that pond and its white oaks, and they just watch us when we go past on the ATV. If they do run off, they seldom go very far.

The site where this woodland waterhole is located was already a good place to bowhunt before the pond was built. The pond's presence, however, makes the spot irresistible to whitetails, especially on hot days when a drink of water can lure them from their nearby bedding areas. Credit: SC

Adapting and Improving

By using your knowledge of deer and your land as building blocks, you'll never run short of ways to combine those elements to launch new management plans as you tweak, modify and overhaul previous projects and ideas. That's one of the great things about owning your own hunting property and realizing how much fun you can have with plants, axes and shovels during the off-season.

You learn something about yourself in the process. I know lots of people who never realized the satisfaction of planting seeds and seedlings, and then watching plants and trees grow in the years that follow. It adds a new dimension to deer hunting, and creates even more satisfaction when you see deer including your projects in their daily routines.

As you'll see in the next chapter, you'll find other ways to boost your overall hunting satisfaction as you become familiar with your woodlots and native plants. In some cases, you'll even discover how to make trees and long-range forestry plans pay dividends for you while improving and diversifying the deer's diet and nutritional needs.

Many bowhunters learn something about themselves while doing chores to improve their land's habitat for deer and other wildlife. That is, they find that using an ax, plow and shovel brings satisfaction and a sense of accomplishment as plants grow and deer habitat regenerates.

Knowing Your Land, Its Trees and Plants

TOM INDREBO

One aspect of deer and land management often overlooked in books and magazine articles is the importance of a forestry plan that includes your property's trees, shrubs and other naturally growing plants. Too many bowhunters and land-owning deer hunters concentrate on food plots and the latest and greatest seed varieties. Never forget that white-tailed deer in most regions have gotten along for eons without farmers and food plots, but they will always be a species that requires woodlands with lots of young growth, edge cover and thick understory.

Whitetails will never get by on food plots alone, yet when I drive around some regions, I'm amazed to see how many woodlands have become largely unsuitable for deer. I often see mature forests in such advanced stages of natural succession that little sunlight reaches the ground. As the woodland shrubs and bushes that create bedding cover disappear from lack of sunlight, deer move to more favorable habitats.

Mature woodlands support far fewer deer than younger, more diverse woods, and most of them desperately need chain-saw work. But before you jump in and make lots of noise and sawdust, make sure you know the age and health of your woodland, and how best to cure what ails it. Unless you have a sound understanding of forestry practices, it makes sense to hire the services of a trained forester to assess your woodlands. Be sure to ask for references

and work with someone with experience in your sort of property.

Explain what you want to achieve with your land to make it suitable for whitetails, and keep an open mind. Don't cringe and protest if he advises limited clear-cutting in some areas. Clear-cuts can jump-start deer habitat by opening the ground to sunlight and triggering dense regrowth. In my area, tree species like poplar (aspen) and oaks literally explode with new growth when given access to sunlight.

The secret for most of us is to perform several small clear-cuts in select spots to create more edge cover. Deer love these "new" areas because of their increased potential for bedding and food. Never forget, deer are browsers, not grazers. They seldom stand long in one spot, preferring to move every few bites to sample something new.

Work closely with your forester and walk along when he inspects your woodlands to assess their potential. Ask questions and make sure he grasps your goals—short-term and long-term. If you pay attention, you'll learn much about your own woodlands by seeing trees through a forester's eyes. You want diversity in your woodlot, not only in tree and plant species but in their ages.

I've found that when I enroll in a forestry program, the forester wants to cut everything with a trunk larger than 18 inches in diameter. Some older trees might look like prime specimens, but they're actually "overripe" and it might be best to harvest them before they reach the point of no return. Others are soft, hollowed by rot and age, and will topple in the first big storm. In the meantime, their trunks and decaying branches make good den trees and food sources for birds and small mammals, like raccoons and squirrels.

I also refuse to remove my best white oaks, especially those near bedding areas, staging areas and woodland ponds. Quality white oaks create prime food sources and often provide great sites for a portable stand. I make a point to get in there and fertilize them each spring to help them reach peak productivity.

Another thing to consider is the type of cover that lies between some of your known feeding and bedding areas. If much of this is fairly open woodland with little underbrush, you probably won't see much daylight deer activity. Also, what kinds of trees are in there? If it's an "early successional" section of woods, such as box elders that filled in long-forgotten fields or openings, you might want to create some extra year-round cover in obvious travel corridors to ensure a thicker understory. I've had good luck planting cedars, pines and spruce to increase this cover so deer feel more comfortable moving through during hunting hours.

The Logging Process

As you work with your woods and a trusted forester, don't be surprised when you learn logging isn't a one-time project. Depending on the size and composition of your property, you might want to log every year, every few years or every 10 years. As we discussed earlier in broad detail, many factors come into play when making forestry-related decisions.

Some decisions affect the here and now, but other efforts won't be noticed or appreciated until long after you're gone.

I conducted two logging operations on our 335-acre farm the first 12 years we lived here. And when my neighbors do some logging, I keep abreast of their work to help me understand how it might affect deer and their movements on our land. If there's one thing I've learned about logging it's this: It's difficult for loggers to take out too much! You might think they scalped your land, but that's seldom the case. Most of us can't handle fullblown clear-cuts, but it's often the lesser of evils. Far worse are some select cuts in which unethical loggers remove your prime trees and leave the junk standing. In worst-case scenarios, those trees simply grow more branches and quickly reshade the forest floor.

That's another reason you'll want to stay involved at every step. Not only does your presence keep everyone honest, you can intervene when needed. For instance, if you're considering pond construction, make sure those plans are not

Which trees should be logged off and which ones should be left alone? Sometimes it depends on their location. The author likes to build woodland ponds among mature maples and white oaks, knowing that acorns and fallen maple leaves help entice deer to a waterhole.

overlooked in your forestry/logging planning. And, unlike the woodlands, I want my ponds shaded as much as possible. The shade from surrounding trees helps slow evaporation from the ponds and makes deer feel a little more secure when taking a drink. So, although I insist that loggers leave all white oaks surrounding my woodland ponds or potential pond sites, I have them cut aggressively as they move farther back into the woods to improve nearby bedding grounds.

I also like to leave stands of maples nearby or around woodland ponds. Deer will gorge on white-oak acorns, obviously, but they also love to eat maple leaves shortly before and after they drop. That combination of ponds, white oaks and maples—with thicker underbrush and trees farther back into the woods—provides deer fresh browse, secure bedding areas, and quick access to water. In other words, ideal and diverse deer habitat.

Realize, too, that loggers often have different agendas than landowners and foresters. Unless they know you're watching every step, they'll focus on what's important to them, not you. Their goal is to get the work done quickly and efficiently. They want the wood, they want to remove it quickly, and they don't always care what kind of mess they leave behind. If they slice and dice your woodlands into a tangled pile of scrap branches and severed treetops, all those long-used deer travel corridors will be obliterated or confused beyond recognition.

To address such situations, I invite friends and neighbors to come in and buck that wood, cut firewood, and create or reopen travel corridors. This work must be done soon after loggers leave, however. If you wait for brush, brambles and young trees to spring up, that new growth will make clean-up and corridor-building and restoration a major headache.

Another vital responsibility to yourself is to continually track the cash value of wood leaving your property. This is yet another reason to work with trustworthy foresters and loggers who have strong references. Different woods—both in terms of the tree's species and the quality of its saw logs—bring vastly different prices. If there's significant lag time between the time your contract is signed and when the work is done, check to ensure lumber values didn't jump. Wood prices, especially for hardwoods, can be as volatile as oil!

Trees: The Long-Term Crop

No matter where you are in your planning efforts, another fun project is planting trees. I think of trees as a long-term crop. In many cases, I don't expect to be around when trees I plant pay big dividends for wood, deer and cash. On the other hand, you just might see some benefits faster than you expect.

Either way, success hinges on your forestry plans. You can't plant some trees just anywhere, and you don't want huge stands of the same species. That does deer no good. It's best to intermix your plantings with long-term goals in mind. If you're to maximize your land's qualities and account for its weaknesses, your plans must account for its topography, soil types, and orientation toward the sun. It's important to realize that not all hillsides, ridgetops and valleys are created equal. Some sites grow certain trees and shrubs better than others, and provide better bedding or feeding areas at different times of the year.

For instance, in northern climates it pays to notice which trees and shrubs can handle summer's extreme heat. Those that can't withstand moderate dry spells and hot summer suns will never grow

Trees are a long-term "crop," in that they can pay dividends in wood, deer and cash for many years if you follow a good forestry plan. This Bluff Country hillside provides a rich mix of oaks and aspen.

large enough to provide adequate cover when wintering deer seek those south-facing slopes for extra daytime warmth. Such areas are worth improving as bedding grounds. I've noticed several sites in my area where deer bed on sun-soaked ridgeline points. In fact, if you know of anyplace where deer spend lots of time bedding in winter, go there in winter and early spring to search for shed antlers. Deer often like these sites in autumn, too, and bask there in the morning sun.

Tree plantings can serve many purposes, of course. As we mentioned earlier, they can be planted in select numbers and places to increase cover in travel corridors and bedding areas. Also look for areas where you can plant trees to create more borders and edge cover. I often create shelterbelts of spruce and pine, and then I mix in ash, oaks and more pine behind them for every other row. You might want to encircle some fields, create windbreaks or divide a field into several irregularly shaped sections that you let revert to brush and trees. As you create these new woodlands, you make some fields more secluded and private, which encourages daytime feeding activity.

In still other cases, though, I've converted entire fields into wooded cover. That's why I view trees as a long-term crop. No matter what I plant or the purpose for the plantings, I try to learn all I can about the different tree species that grow well in my region and learn how deer abuse or make use of them.

For instance, it's easy to get poplars to regenerate along field edges. Simply plow or roto-till the soil, and poplar shoots start "suckering" within weeks. Within a couple of years you'll have dense poplar stands that deer and ruffed grouse covet.

Although deer will browse on poplars, they simply hammer white cedars during winter. Deer browse white cedar so aggressively that I must protect them with fencing materials until they grow beyond the deer's reach and maintain themselves. When I first planted cedars around my ponds, they didn't last long. The deer tore them up. I even had trouble with white pine. Deer tear them up early and often by rubbing in autumn and browsing in winter.

When I'm trying to create thermal cover where deer can bed, I often plant Colorado blue spruce because deer pretty much leave these trees alone. In fact, spruce trees, in general, don't suffer much abuse from deer.

Again, stay involved with your forester. I've learned a lot from state and county foresters about how to better plan my tree plantings for diversity. I want oaks, white ash, cedars, various spruce species, Norway pines, red pines and white pines on my land. In one case we planted 87 acres in trees, which required 800 trees per acre to ensure we got enough survival to maintain the stand. We probably planted 100,000 young trees on that site. When big numbers die off in dry years we go back in and replant.

As you draw up your plans, figure in some expenses for replanting, and look ahead a few years to ensure you spend your money wisely and efficiently. In Wisconsin, for example, the state pays up to half the cost of converting certain fields into woodlands if you maintain your reforesting plan a minimum of 15 years. By keeping the land out of agricultural production that long, you pretty much let trees take over while letting the state help you recoup the costs. This benefits the state because well-established woodlands make it difficult for someone to come along later and turn it back into croplands.

Also look into government nursery programs. In many cases you can buy your tree stock in bulk at great prices from your state or county nursery. In addition, you can usually tap into their expertise and advice on how to buy the best trees at the best price, and find out ways to do your plantings as cheaply and easily as possible.

Beyond—and Beneath—Trees

As you talk to foresters and deal with nurseries, don't forget to discuss options for underbrush that benefit deer and other wildlife. For instance, I like to encourage the growth of wild raspberries and blackberries. Sometimes it's just a matter of opening the woodland canopy and roughing up the topsoil—a process called scarifying—and let sunlight and rain do the rest. Not only can these thick brambles provide dense, thorny cover for deer, their leaves also provide good nutrition in fall for whitetails. Whenever possible, look for ways to offer deer a variety of naturally produced annual foods. That way, if one crop isn't producing in a particular year or place, you'll be better able to focus your attention when it's time to hunt.

Realize, too, that trees don't have to produce mast crops to benefit deer. Although deer key on white oaks

first when they start dropping acorns, they'll hit falling maple leaves next. Red-oak acorns are seldom much of a factor early, and they're easy to identify because they're the last trees to lose their leaves.

I mention maple leaves because I've learned that whitetails gorge on them for a few days each year in early autumn. I think deer like maple leaves because they hold much of the sugar that flowed into them just before dropping. In fact, if you clear shooting lanes in early fall and cut maple branches still carrying leaves, deer never take long to strip every leaf from the cuttings. Whenever possible, I make sure to get out there and do some final

It's difficult to cut down too many trees. The author likes to generate thickets of raspberries and blackberries by using a chainsaw to create a small opening and then roughing up the topsoil. These plants and young trees also provide good browse for wintering whitetails.

trimming on my stands. Usually the peak color in our region is the first week of October and, soon after, the maples shed their colorful leaves.

Maple leaves start falling—usually in mid-October around here—right about when the first does come into heat. When this happens, those does are often in the maple stands eating fallen leaves. It's only a short time frame, though; maybe a five-day window when you can count on whitetails hitting those leaves. Obviously, if you know it's going to happen, it's a great time to be out there.

That's another example of how the hunting season and the deer's world are made up of many different steps. If you're not in step with the deer, you could be missing your best bet by one or two days nearly every day of the hunting season! That's the downside of creating diverse habitat and food sources. The more you produce, the more you must plan, scout and perform maintenance. Even so, I keep planting, cutting, clear-cutting and scarifying the soil in order to diversify my land's plant and food communities.

That also means keeping track of all the fruit trees scattered about our lands. Many long-forgotten farmers in our region planted apples, plums and other fruit trees throughout their properties. Even though people no longer rely on these trees for fruit, deer have never forsaken them. So, between apples, plums, white oaks, red oaks, maple leaves, poplar buds, maple buds, white-pine needles, white-cedar fronds, and raspberry and blackberry leaves, deer on our farm have no trouble finding a smorgasbord of woodland foods.

Pay attention to all these natural food sources as autumn moves along. If you ignore them and concentrate all your efforts on food plots and agricultural fields, you'll miss some of the hunting season's best action.

Choosing the Right Equipment

PETER FIDUCCIA

If you believe you can plant food plots that will grow healthy plants with high nutrition and tonnage for deer and other wildlife by simply tossing seeds over unprepared ground, you've been misinformed! Anyone undertaking a land and deer management program must recognize that a crucial element of food plot planting success is using the correct tools for the job at hand. For instance, using a large tractor with heavyduty attachments to plant a small plot in the middle of a woodlot—or a quarter- to half-acre plot in a field—is overkill and not practical. It also wouldn't be realistic for you to use a hand rake and hand seeder to plant an acre field of clover!

The type and size of equipment needed to plant successful food plots should almost exclusively be coordinated to the total amount of acres to be planted. Therefore, the equipment needs of each manager will differ considerably and must be carefully selected to match the size of your food plot agenda and should follow general recommendations. Before you buy a single piece of equipment, realistically evaluate the limitations of your budget. Only buy what you can afford to purchase and you'll avoid the piggy bank before you even get started.

Miniature Properties

Food plot planters who plant mini-sized food plots often get frustrated or give up because the equipment they use isn't well tailored to the size of their property and the food plots they want to grow. This leads many managers to go back to broadcasting seed by hand over improperly prepared ground, which is a plan destined for failure. The "throw and grow" plan never works as well as preparing

Using a tractor to plant a woodlot food plot strip like this would be highly impractical for most food plot managers.

When planting tiny plots, particularly in woodlots, hand tools may be the only practical choice.

the ground properly using well-matched planting implements for the job.

If you're planting small food plots, strip areas of about 12 x 50 feet in the woods, or a plot measuring about onetenth of an acre in fields, and understand there will be plenty of planting by hand and physical labor involved. In some instances, the hard work put into some plots can be downright back-breaking. It should be noted that the more work put into a hand-worked plot, the more you will get out of it—and that is a hardcore fact.

These types of plantings begin by thinking through everything you will need to make the plot grow to its maximum potential. A selection of necessary and sturdy tool choices include a:

• strong leaf rake
• sturdy garden rake with iron teeth
• heavy four-pronged pitchfork
• sharp, pointed spade shovel

• large pair of pruning shears
• small handheld pair of pruning shears
• chainsaw
• handheld or two-wheel seeder
• seed compacter (something as simple as a piece of fence with a cinderblock and rope to pull over the planted area to smooth it out)
• a handheld weed killer
• fertilizer spreader
• soil test kit

I strongly recommend a hand-plating plan only if there is absolutely no other equipment option you can afford to purchase.

Small to Medium Properties

Small- to medium-sized properties can be realistically and effectively planted with an ATV as long as the ATV used has enough power to pull implements without straining the engine. If you don't already own an ATV, consider buying one with a lot of horsepower, such as a 650cc machine. Small 25 to 35 horsepower tractors will also do the job, but often don't work as efficiently as an ATV does in woodland or other tight places. The first important decision you must make is whether you need an ATV and ATV implements or a small tractor and tractor-sized implements. Therefore, it is particularly important to carefully plan what types of equipment are needed to grow quality crops and require the least amount of labor, and then determine what equipment is realistically affordable. Once again, this requires a frank evaluation with yourself about what you can afford to spend on the equipment without spending a large portion of the overall budget or, more importantly, getting a divorce.

ATVs

Today almost anyone who owns land also owns a 4x4 ATV to begin with. They are affordable, reliable, useful machines that are regularly used for multiple purposes including hunting, fishing, recreational riding, and as effective, practical pieces of equipment for food plot planting. Over the last several years some, ATV makers have manufactured a line of planting implements to compliment their ATVs. Pragmatically, buying an ATV and their planting attachments will often than not be the most affordable choice for an overwhelming number of land managers.

Depending on the manufacturer, the line of implements available range from meager to complete. For instance, I own Arctic Cat ATVs. Arctic Cat offers a complete line of well-suited farm planting implements, including cultivators, two and four point seeders, rackmounted sprayers with 10-foot-long folding boom spray bars, four row planter/dill seeders, rakes, tandem discs, drag harrows, landscape rakes, rear blades, box scrapers, moldboard plows, single discs, brush movers, and finish mowers.

Other ATV manufacturers also offer a line of implements, but do not offer as many different types or machines as well-built as Arctic Cat's line. For the average food plot planter, the amount of ATV implements that are available within the marketplace will definitely fulfill any planting need for small- to medium-sized properties. I mention

Cody removes his rifle from its case for an afternoon hunt from his favorite deer blind on our farm.

Every year we plant about 25 food plots ranging from 1/10 of an acre to an acre or more. About 95 percent of our plots are planted with an ATV and ATV implements. Credit: Arctic Cat.

A 45hp tractor and corn planter preparing to plant a 4-acre field of corn.

Make sure you have an ample supply of anti-freeze, fuel stabilizers, fluids, sprays, and chargers in your shed. This will pay big dividends when preparing your equipment for storage or spring plantings.

Arctic Cat because I have personal experience with the brand and can vouch for them; I have put the ATV and planting tools to the test and they have performed flawlessly for many years (as long as they are maintained properly, as any piece of equipment should be).

On properties where food plots range from one-tenth of an acre to three acres or more, an ATV matched up with compatible farm ATV implements is the way to go. ATVs are much more appropriate to planting less accessible areas of land or when used to plant in hard-to-navigate woodland areas where the plot more often than not has to be shaped around trees and other natural woodland structures. This is particularly true in spots that require a lot of tight-tuning.

For those with deeper pockets, a small tractor will also fit the bill when it comes to planting small- to mediumsized land. A 4x4 25 to 35 horsepower tractor is a practical choice. Once you decide on a tractor, the implements you purchase should be matched to the tractor as well. They will be more expensive than ATV implements and, like the tractor, they will require more storage room. Implements needed for tractors this size include:

- heavier multi-tined plows
- double-row, hydraulic disk harrow seeders
- heavy-duty PTO driven three-point seeder spreaders
- multi-nozzle herbicide boom-arm sprayers
- subsoilers
- cultipackers
- PTO driven rotovators

Tractors are also prone to turning over if not used properly. Therefore, if you are unfamiliar with operating a tractor, you should plan to use one first before making your decision. I know several land managers who after attempting to drive a tractor decided to abandon that choice and use an ATV instead to do their planting.

Large Properties

I define large properties as those with land over 500 acres and with total planting acreage that exceeds 50 acres. When it comes to planting and tilling large acreage of this size, the most logical choice of equipment is traditional farm machines and planting equipment.

Before storing our equipment over the winter, each tractor and ATV gets a complete maintenance inspection and oil and fluid replacement.

Tractors

A large tractor and heavy-duty implements are the best choice when a manager's deer and food plot plan includes planting 50 or more acres of food plots. Turning under old, dormant fields into crop-producing pastures, or other types of farm work on large acreage, requires land managers to invest in 50 horsepower or larger tractors. This type of heavy-duty planting equipment makes the job quicker and easier to accomplish when planting really big properties. They're big-farm friendly and will enable land managers to develop and grow the very best possible food plots. Big tractors basically need the heavy-duty three-point versions of all the same type of attachments including:

• disc harrows
• hay and brush cutters
• large multi-blade plows
• rotary cutters
• spraying rigs
• primary seeders
• compactors
• back-blades

A quality front-end hydraulic bucket loader is also a necessary piece of equipment for large parcels of land that will be planted. They will be regularly used to move mounds of dirt or gravel quickly and easily or remove large, heavy rocks from fields. They will also be used to bring bucket loads of fertilizer, manure, or bags of seed from place to place and for hauling 5- to 12-foot trees to planting locations.

A hydraulic rear-mounted back-blade attached to a larger type of tractor will also make short work of grading farm roads and other trails. They are also handy when filling deep ditches created by run-off, holes, ruts, and much more.

The wise maintenance manager always checks all the manufacturers' manuals before storing them for the winter.

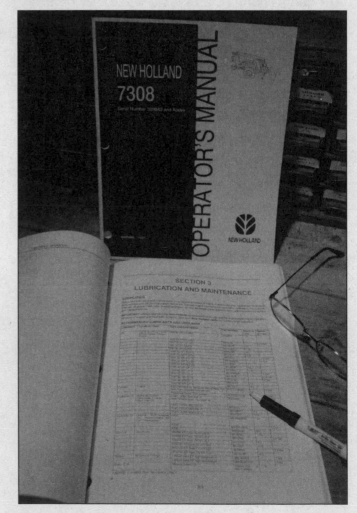

Maintenance

We store our ATVs in our heated shed through the winter.

Finally, when it comes to ATVs, tractors, and their planting implements, providing many years of reliable service requires basic upkeep. One of the chief causes of farm equipment failure is lack of general maintenance. A good maintenance program starts with storing your equipment out of the weather, particularly during the winter months, when it is not in use. Before storing equipment for long periods of time, it is important to include the following procedures to ensure the equipment will be ready for use in spring:

- Add proper fuel line anti-freeze and stabilizers to the gas
- Add diesel fuel supplements (for diesel equipment only).
- Check levels of other fluids and replenish additives as needed.
- Keep the battery on a low trickle charge with a 1.5A batter charger that allows safe charging of most batteries during long storage periods.
- Clean the battery's post and terminals and coat with a terminal protective spray or gel.
- Cover ATVs, tractors and planting implements with a tarp.
- Lubricate all grease point fittings.

Keep in mind that owning a large tractor and implements requires a land manager to be mechanically inclined, as needing to make routine maintenance and minor repairs to larger equipment is inevitable. In the end, however, big tractors and implements will make short work of planting large acreage.

The importance of purchasing the right planting equipment for the size of acreage and the number and size of the food plots to be planted is a crucial first step in developing a deer and land management program. Having the correct type of equipment comes before planting a single seed. Using effective equipment will not only make the overall undertaking of developing food plots quicker and easier, but will also make the process much more enjoyable and satisfying!

During the planting season, be sure to develop a general maintenance and checklist program and chart. It should include daily, weekly, and monthly maintenance and verification of the following:

- Regular oil changes
- Check transmission and hydraulic levels
- Clean or change spark plugs
- Clean or replace all filters as necessary

It's a good idea to remove the batteries on equipment that will not be used during the winter and place them on trickle chargers to keep them fully charged and ready to go in spring.

Although we live on our farm, we still remove the ignition keys from our ATVs and tractor when leaving them out overnight.

- Replace worn hoses
- Check water levels frequently
- Check all fluid levels (brake, power-steering, battery, etc).
- Regularly inspect of all belts and hoses
- Grease all fittings properly and completely with a multi-purpose lithium-based lube grease each time the equipment is used.
- Add fuel enhancers as a water remover and injector cleaner
- Sharpen all blades as needed or warranted (plow, disc blades, or other implements that may require sharpening

IMPORANT NOTE : Always check the manufacturer's manual before doing any maintenance to your equipment. Follow their guidelines and recommendations regarding all levels, types of oil to use, etc., over any other suggestions. Keeping up a wellplanned maintenance program up for your equipment will ensure that the equipment will provide reliable service season after planting-season.

Safekeeping Tips for Equipment

No matter what type of planting equipment you purchase or already own—be it a tractor, an

ATV, or other farming implements—the gear can be a substantial financial investment for most land managers. To keep your investment safe, consider taking some basic precautions.

Storage, Theft, Foul Weather, and Insurance

- When storing equipment over long periods, particularly over the winter months, it is best to keep it in a barn, shed, or garage that is heated if possible. All the equipment should be covered with a tarp secured with tie-downs.
- Use trickle chargers to keep all of the batteries fully charged during long periods of storage. This is especially important during the winter months.
- If you are an owner who doesn't live on your land full-time, it is crucial that your storage building has a high-quality, heavy-duty security lock to discourage would-be thieves from stealing your equipment. It's a sad state of affairs, but a reality of our times.
- Never leave your equipment in the field even for short periods of time without removing the key.
- If equipment must be left outside, particularly overnight in unprotected areas, remove the ignition key and the spark plug.
- Never make the mistake of not purchasing insurance for your valuable equipment. Insurance for ATVs, tractors, and implements is surprisingly affordable and easy to purchase. Ask your insurance agent if you can add a rider to your existing homeowner's insurance policy

Food Plot Placement

PETER FIDUCCIA

This chapter provides information about where to plant wildlife food plots in relation to the plants receiving the most advantageous direct sunlight and soil fertility. This is an element of planting that

A woodlot plot of subterranean clover. Studies have shown subterranean clover can reach over 90 percent of its potential growth when receiving 50 percent shade and it will even do well in plots with 75 percent shade!

shouldn't be overlooked by novice or season veteran food plot managers. In reality, selecting the right planting location is an important aspect of growing quality, high-yielding crops. To maximize a plant's growth success, it is important to provide the plant with the proper daily length of direct sunlight it requires. It is also important and advantageous to match a particular plant to the correct soil type it needs whenever it is possible or practical. For instance, place plants that thrive in moist soils in wet sites and plants that do best in well-drained soils in soils that stay mostly dry.

Fields

The *best* planting locations for growing healthy crops is unquestionably in existing agricultural fields, reclaimed openings, or overgrown pastures that have been out of cultivation and are in need of some work to make them amenable to wildlife food plot plantings. What all three of these locations have in common is they will all provide maximum daily sunlight and good soil conditions for the crops planted in them.

Other Locations

Other potential food plot planting sites include along the banks or edges of logging roads; along right-of-ways; old hiking, horse, or ATV trails;

This tiny clover plot required 250 pounds of lime to raise its pH from 5.3 to 6.2. I fertilized the plot two weeks after this picture was taken with 200 pounds of T-19.

firebreaks; and cleared sections of woods. The latter group will *only* produce healthy food plots if the plantings receive enough *daily* sunlight, have the correct pH levels, and are fertilized accordingly. Historically, these locations don't provide more than four to six hours of sunlight, which may be problematic. Sometimes it is necessary to either plant crops that are shade-tolerant or remove over-story to allow more sunlight to reach the plantings. Keep in mind many plants can be placed in nearly any plot, on practically any site, as long as the soil is *properly* prepared for the planting *beforehand*.

Woodland Clearings

Not all pieces of property include openings to plant their food plots. Some properties may have open land to plant, but the food plot managers may also want to create a plot in a hidden area in the woods. In either case, it is necessary to create

This plot of mixed clovers was planted in a field that received a minimum of eight hours of direct sunlight.

This brassica plot of forage rape was planted in a field that received a maximum of 10 to 12 hours of sunlight each day.

an opening for such plots. By carefully choosing the best quality soils to create the plot, you will substantially reduce the amount of lime and fertilizer needed on these types of sites. Inevitably, plots made in wooded clearings require lots of lime and fertilizer. This is best accomplished by taking some pH samples and sending them out to be analyzed *before* finally clearing an area for a woodland planting.

Clover and Other Legumes

When planting any of the variety of clovers—bird's-foot trefoil, Lablab, cowpeas, lupines, and other legumes—it is important to remember that this entire group grows best when it receives at least six to eight hours of full sunlight. Managers also need to ensure the proper pH levels are met *and* the correct fertilizer is applied for their plantings. When this group receives the required amount of daily sunlight, you can be assured your plots will grow much better. Some legumes are sold as being shade-tolerant and only require four to five hours of sunlight each day; if the pH is correct and the suggested type of fertilizer is used, they, too, will produce dandy food plots.

Grains

This group is classified as small and large grains. They include Grain Sorghum, oats, wheat, triticale, rye (*Secale cerale*), and corn. These plants need a lot of direct sunlight per day to grow. Before selecting a site, keep that in mind if you wish to have the best production and nutrition from grain crops.

Behind the row of pines is a 1-plus-acre field. Because the woods border it on three sides, it makes it an ideal inside corner. I planted the row of pines to partially obstruct the view of a 5-acre field above and make the 1-plus-acre field seem more secluded (for deer).

Brassicas

Plants that fall into the brassica family consist of forage rape, turnip, forage kale, canola rapeseed, radish, rutabaga, cabbage, and cauliflower. For the deer and food plot manager, the most common brassica plants are turnips, kale, rape, and radishes. Another critical consideration with brassicas is that they do best in colder climates, particularly after a few hard frosts.

Brassicas are by far the easiest plants to grow. It is important, however, to pay specific attention to site location areas where brassicas will be planted. Brassicas are finicky plants and as such they require *a lot* of sunlight to grow well. In fact, they need much more sunlight than the clovers and other legumes do. Therefore, when planting brassicas, it is crucial to select planting sites that will receive direct sunlight from sunrise to sunset or about twelve to fifteen hours of daylight.

Inside Corners

Another good place to plant food plots is near inside corners (see more about inside corners in the *Shooter's Bible Guide to Whitetailed Strategies* available on our website at www.deerdoctor.com). An inside corner, which is often referred to as an "interface," is where existing terrain features meet thicker inside corners and provide more security for deer as they enter the food plot. Not surprisingly, inside corners make deer feel much more comfortable and safer than more food plots placed in fields or other more open areas do. A food plot that takes full advantage of interface areas where the plot actually meets or borders thicker cover is a prime plot to see and bag more deer during daylight hours, particularly a mature buck.

As I have mentioned in previous writings, to encourage deer to use plots in large fields during

This plot of Subterranean clover was intentionally planned as a woodlot planting because it is tolerant of shade.

midday, I often break up a 5-acre field with a few rows of pines. It gives the deer the illusion that the 5-acre field is much smaller than it actually is. The rows of pines block off the view of the rest of the field, creating a few plots that appear to the deer to be more concealed-type plots, allowing them to feel that it is safe to enter the plots even during midday.

You can create land features that are used to maximize inside corners using your chainsaw or by employing specific habitat management land feature practices. On some properties, land features are a gift of Mother Nature and are naturally available. A thick row of tall pines, an island in the middle of the plot, a long section of manmade blow downs, or any other type of natural or manmade obstruction to block off a large view from a food plot will create an illusion of safety for a wise old buck. This will lure him from the edge of the woodlot into your food plot!

Irregularly shaped food plots also help to create a false illusion of safety for nervous bucks.

Many of my irregularly shaped food plots are intentionally small and narrow down considerably from the wider points of the plot. Interface-type plots are easy to create in secluded woodlot areas where the cover is naturally thick all around the plot. Deer instinctively feel they can access the plot from all points of the

compass without revealing themselves. Mature bucks will often use this type of plot at even midday to check out potential does that may be near or in estrus.

Conclusion

The ideal way to become a consistently successful wildlife manager and food plot planter is to plan each step in the process carefully beforehand—I know I have mentioned this before, but it can't be emphasized enough. If you lack the proper preparation, your food plots are destined at best for mediocrity and at worse for total failure. Those who believe they can simply spread some seed on the soil and expect to grow successful crops that will enhance the antler size of the bucks on their lands are in for a rude and expensive awakening.

Many of the other plants used for wildlife food plots have specific requirements and therefore benefit from a food plot manager selecting the proper planting sites. The savvy deer manager understands the nuances of the importance of site selection related to each plant and keeps that uppermost in his mind before arbitrarily planting a crop in a location where it will not achieve its maximum growth potential. Your food plots will not benefit from randomly selecting planting sites without taking into consideration the plants' soil and sunlight needs before hand.

Plots and Planting Techniques

PETER FIDUCCIA

This is a short but vital chapter. The advice here will help you to grow more successful food plots and should not be ignored. One of the most overlooked aspects of planting food plots is to precisely measure the size of each plot. Knowing what a particular plot's measurements are will help you quickly establish the accurate amounts of lime, fertilizer, herbicide, and seed that you will need to apply. To get the exact measurements of a food plot doesn't require managers to be rocket scientists. Determining a plot's accurate dimensions can be done quickly and easily using a handheld calculator, range finder, GPS unit, or even a pad and pencil.

Cody uses a Swarovski range finder to measure the total square footage of one of our food plots.

Measure Each Plot Accurately

One of the chief causes of a food plot failing or not growing to expectations is that many times they suffer from too little or too much application of lime, herbicide, fertilizer, and *most often* too much seed. This happens simply because the food plotter either didn't think measuring the plot was important or didn't realize it was a necessary step to successful plot management.

The reality is that over-seeding a food plot is most often worse than under-seeding it! As the old adage goes, "Everything in moderation." This is particularly valid when it comes to preparing and planting a food plot. If too much herbicide is applied to a food plot, for example, the excess herbicide can either result in the plot's inability to grow a crop properly or, worse yet, render the soil of the plot dormant for long periods of time.

Placing either too much or too little lime in a plot inadvertently throws the pH levels off one way

Some food plots fail because of drought, over-browsing, flooding, or other natural elements. They shouldn't fail because they weren't measured before they were planted.

or the other. Putting too much fertilizer down can end up burning the plants. Not applying enough fertilizer can result in not providing the plants with the sufficient amount of minerals needed for maximum growth. If you neglect to accurately determine the overall dimensions of each food plot, not only will the plantings suffer, but you will also waste quite a bit of valuable time, work, and money. It will also result in frustration when the plots don't perform as expected. I strongly suggest that you take the time to measure each plot accurately and don't skip this very important step if you hope to grow better food plots.

An important figure to remember about food plot planting is that the overall dimensions of an acre of land measures out to be 43,560 square feet. Since a majority of plots are more or less square or rectangle in shape, simply measure the length of the plot by the width of the plot to get the plot's precise overall size. To determine what percentage the plot size is as it relates to an acre, take the plot's overall dimensions and divide it by 43,560 (the total number of feet in one acre). This will provide you with the fraction figure or percentage of an acre that is related to each plot.

For example: Let's say your plot is 75 feet by 120 feet. Multiply 75 by 120 and you'll get a figure of 9,000 square feet. Divide 9,000 by 43,560, and you get 0.20 or two-tenths (2/10) of an acre.

If you don't have a range finder or a surveyor's measuring wheel, use a 100-foot tape measure. They are readily available and inexpensive.

I want to emphasize again how important it is to know the exact size of each food plot so you will know *exactly* how much seed to plant or how much lime or fertilizer is needed.

This formula can be used to determine the size of irregularly shaped plots as well. It takes a little more math work in measuring and calculating asymmetrical plots, but it is still an *essential* step in the overall land manager's food plot program. It is worth the extra effort it takes to get the accurate dimensions of uneven food plots. Measure all sides of lopsided plots individually, then apply the same calculations to reach a close approximation of the overall size of the plot.

To eliminate having to recalculate food plots every season, store the dimension information either on a computer or in a handwritten log book for future reference. It will help eliminate unnecessary work the following spring, leaving you only to calculate the size of new plots that are created. To eliminate confusion, each food plot should be given a name or number. The dimensions should then be applied to that particular plot in your computer or handwritten log to prevent the final measurements from being confused with another plot. Obviously, if the size of a plot is extended or reduced, the plot needs to be measured again and the new dimensions re-entered into a log.

Knowing the exact dimensions of all your plots will save you lime, herbicide, fertilizer, seed, money, time, and, most important, the frustration and grief of a plot not growing as well as you hoped it would.

Weed Management

PETER FIDUCCIA

Weeds are to a wildlife food plot what water is to the "Wicked Witch of the West"—*deadly*. Weeds will ultimately "snuff out" or at least severely limit a food plot plant's growth and the nourishment it provides wildlife. When a food plot fails, an overwhelming majority of the time they are lost to the presence of obnoxious weed growth within the plot. Weeds effectively compete with plot plantings for nutrients, light, and, most critically, water.

Controlling weeds from overtaking a food plot can be a very a difficult problem to overcome.

The reality of weeds is that they are found everywhere. For the food plot manager, the element that helps weeds to grow in their plots is by the disturbance of the soil when cultivating a food plot. The more the soil is disturbed and the deeper the ground is turned over, the more the weeds will grow in the food plot.

This field is choked with dandelion, a broadleaf perennial. In spring, sprouts emerge from the soil. The yellow flowers turn into white puffballs containing seeds that spread by wind into other food plots. The taproot survives deep in the soil, making it hard to kill. I use Big N' Tuf herbicide to eliminate the taproots of dandelions.

In a test conducted on our farm, we selected a few half-acre plots that were individually planted with forage radishes, turnip, or forage rapeseed. We did not use herbicides to prepare the plots and instead we allowed the weeds to grow naturally in each of the three plots. We wanted to compare how well our herbicide treatments were actually working to either eradicate weeds or severely limit their growth in our food plot program. The experiment did not have a surprising result, to say the least, but with the price of herbicide we felt it was worthwhile to conduct on a small scale.

What we learned was mostly what we expected to find out. Using the correct herbicides did, in fact, eliminate, or at least substantially reduce, the overall volume of weeds in our food plots. The plants in the food plots we used without herbicides grew taller, were greener, and more robust than the plants in the experimental plots were. What the test revealed was not a surprising result.

The real discovery came as we watched deer feed in our food plots throughout the summer and into late fall and winter. As usual, they ate the offerings of the food plots where the weeds had been controlled with herbicides as eagerly as they normally do.

In the three plots where the weeds grew unchecked and aggressively and competed with the plantings, however, the use of the plots by deer to feed in were significantly less throughout spring and summer. In fall, after the weeds died, the plantings were being ignored by the deer and other wildlife. Even though the turnips and radishes were visibly abundant, the deer refused to eat them. Instead, they casually walked through the three plots to get to other food plots.

Disking a plot too deeply will always disturb the weed bank and encourage weed growth.

Big N' Tuf is an affordable and effective herbicide that kills both grass and broadleaf weeds. It can be found in most farm supply stores.

It took some time but finally the light came on and we realized the weeds had sucked the very *life juices* from the turnips, rape, and radishes. They significantly reduced the nutritional value. It eventually, albeit unexpectedly, became as plain as the noses on our faces that the deer not only found the plants to be much less nutritious they also found them to be much less flavorful. The weeds had changed the palpability of each of the three plantings so much that the deer treated them as non-food items! Needless to say, our test clearly demonstrated the importance of controlling weeds in our food plots.

Eradicating or even reducing weed problems in food plots is a never-ending battle and it is rarely

This plot was first sprayed to kill the weeds. Seven days later. we top-seeded turnips in a totally weed-free plot.

an easy problem to control. Basically, you can get an upper hand on weed management by mowing or using the correct herbicides. The use of chemicals is by far *the most effective way to control weeds in food plots.* Be forewarned, however, that it is essential to completely understand what a particular herbicide is capable of controlling and what type of weeds it is meant to kill. No matter what type of weed, grass, or broadleaf plant you want to eliminate, there is a chemical made to control or kill it. Whenever herbicides are used to kill or control weeds, it is a must to first *read the entire label slowly and carefully* before applying the herbicide to the ground. I know that sounds like common sense, but I can assure you many times the warning is disregarded or overlooked.

Another important factor in effective weed control is best achieved by using the right equipment to manage or eliminate weeds. The quickest way to apply herbicides is by hiring a sprayer truck from a local farm supply company or co-op service. It is more costly, but in the end saves a lot of time and effort on your part. You can also effectively apply herbicides using a wick-bar arm applicator, a backpack sprayer, or a sprayer mounted on the back of an ATV or tractor. The longer the arms of the sprayer, the quicker the job will get done. *Before using any type of sprayer, however, it is imperative to first calibrate the sprayer.* This is an absolutely crucial procedure to managing weeds effectively, therefore do not ignore this step.

The management or elimination of weeds using herbicides is a complicated matter. It requires a serious understanding of how to use chemical herbicides safely and effectively. It also requires a detailed knowledge of the weeds on your land. The more you know about the weeds that are indigenous to your area, the better you will be able to control your weed problem. There are many free guides available on the web. Knowing what herbicides kill what weeds will save you time and money. It will also help to ensure the successful growth of the plantings in your food plots.

Managing weeds in food plots is a combination of different types of methods, including, mowing, handweeding, light tilling, choosing the best plot sites, preparing the site for planting correctly, and using chemical herbicides safely, wisely, and exactly as instructed by the label. The most successful elimination of weeds is accomplished by combining a few of these methods rather than using just one of them.

I strongly recommend reading all you can on weed control and the identification of weeds. I found the following books to be information sources on this subject: *Invasive Plants* by Sylvan Ramsey Kaufman and Wallace Kaufman; *Weeds of the Northeast* (Comstock books) by Richard H. Uva; *Common Weeds of the United States* by the U.S. Department of Agriculture; and, for the more "green-minded" food plot planter, *Weeds: Control without Poisons* by Charles Walters—all available on Amazon.

This is "Mr. Big." He's standing in front of a failed rape crop overtaken by weeds before moving off to a more appealing planting.

The web is also a terrific source for more detailed information on weeds and their control. It is also an excellent place to get further information on the safe and effective use of all types of chemical herbicides.

More Weed Control Tips

- Avoid using untreated manure as fertilizer in food plots. Untreated manure contains the seeds of many weeds. If you want to buy bulk manure as fertilizer, purchase commercially treated manure. It is more expensive but has been treated to reduce weed seeds in it.
- Prevent weeds from establishing themselves.
- Don't use contaminated seeds; they contain weeds. Instead, use only certified seeds, which state the contents are weed-free.

- If you use your mower to cut weeds or other obnoxious plants, wash it down from top to bottom before using it to mow clovers or other plantings in your food plots.
- Try to treat weeds prior to them going to seed.
- Pull weeds when practical and/or necessary.
- Other than herbicides, employ other weed-controlling methods such as mechanical weed control via mowing, mulching, or burning.

Not All Weeds Are Wicked or Evil!

It should be noted, however, that not all weeds have to be eradicated from your land. Many weeds are an important element within a deer's overall diet. Deer feed four to six times per day (every four to six hours), actively seeking out a wide variety of food sources. They mostly eat browse (leaves, twigs, shoots, vines, etc.). They include all types of soft and hard mast (fruits and acorns), flowering plants, grain crops, legumes, clovers, vegetables, and some grasses in their diet. Grass compromises a very small amount of a deer's overall diet, less than 10 percent. They also actively seek out a large variety of weeds including sumac and poison oak! My point is, while weeds are evil in a food plot, they do play a vital role in a deer's diet, making them an important food source when they grow *outside* of your food plot planting!

Part 5

Cooking

Introduction

JAY CASSELL

And now comes the fun part – or, I should say, more of the fun – and that's cooking what you have taken. In this section you'll find so many good venison recipes that you'll want to try them all – and if you keep hunting and keep taking deer every year, hopefully you will. But here you'll find prime recipes from renowned game chef Kate Fiduccia (information on her cookbooks is on page 625) as well as John Weiss, who contributed so many other sections on hunting in this book. All I can say is, enjoy!

Main Meals

KATE FIDUCCIA

Its an ill cook that cannot lick his own fingers

William Shakespeare, Romeo & Juliet (1597)

Fall is the time of year when hunters are itching to be out of the office and in the woods. For us, the fall is our spring, our renewal. The woods come alive with vivid yellows, reds and oranges, and we savor the crisp, cool morning air as we inhale the unmistakable aroma of the woods that is never more pungent or exceptional than at this time of year.

How many times have you become enveloped by these moments and thought of the frontiersman or pioneer and what he must've felt and sensed during this time of year? Was he daydreaming of which route he'd take to his stand, what technique he would use to either rattle or call in a deer, or what game he might see on an upcoming elk or bison hunt? If you think about it, hunting's natural progression and our thoughts about the pursuit of game haven't changed much. After all, hunting season brings us in tune with Mother Nature as we strain to become one with the woods, fields and earth around us.

In the end, the heart of hunting revolves around its finale: the consumption of the game we take. For thousands of years, venison has served as a main meal for families across the globe. Venison satisfies our yearning for self-sufficiency by allowing us to take pride in our ability to hunt, clean, care for, preserve and cook our own food. It ignites the flames of tradition. Venison is a versatile meat that can be featured in elaborate gatherings, traditional holiday meals or quick dinners for the family. It also adapts well to international cuisines. The recipes that follow offer you a range of these choices, from simple to fancy, using ingredients you'll find right in your kitchen. The recipes are organized by the cuts of meat, starting with roasts, steaks and chops, and ending with ground venison and sausage.

Roast Mustard Loin of Venison

*Serves: 8 to 12 * Prep Time: 10 minutes * Marinating Time: 1 to 2 hours * Cooking Time: 30 minutes*

- 4- to 5-lb. venison loin, well trimmed (you may also use 2 smaller portions)
- 2 to 3 cups Simple Marinade*
- ¼ cup plus 1 tablespoon olive oil, divided
- 1 cup Dijon mustard
- ⅓ cup chopped scallions
- ⅓ cup dry white wine
- ¼ cup bread crumbs
- 4 large cloves garlic, minced
- 1 teaspoon sea salt
- ½ teaspoon crumbled dried sage
- ½ teaspoon crumbled dried thyme
- ¼ teaspoon pepper

Measure venison loin against a large skillet, and cut into halves if necessary to fit skillet. Place venison in nonaluminum pan or bowl; pour marinade over and turn to coat. Cover and refrigerate for 1 to 2 hours, turning occasionally. Remove venison from marinade and pat dry; discard marinade.

Heat oven to 375°F. In large skillet, heat 1 tablespoon of the oil over high heat until it is hot but not smoking. Add venison and quickly sear on all sides. Transfer venison to roasting pan; set aside.

In blender or food processor, combine remaining ¼ cup oil with the mustard, scallions, wine, bread crumbs, garlic, salt, sage, thyme and pepper. Process until smooth; the coating should be thick. Spread coating evenly over venison. Roast to desired doneness, 15 to 17 minutes for medium-rare. Remove venison from oven when internal temperature is 5° less than desired. Tent meat with foil and let rest for 10 to 15 minutes before slicing.

I sometimes like to use Myron's 20-Gauge Venison Marinade instead of the Simple Marinade. It is a very versatile, all-natural cooking sauce whose ingredients include soy sauce, garlic, red wine, rice wine vinegar, olive oil and spices. It has a rich, slightly malty flavor base, a pungent and peppery bite and subtle juniper flavor points, and works well for a variety of game and fish.

Spit-Roasted Leg of Venison

*Serves: 25 to 30 * Prep Time: 10 minutes * Marinating Time: 24 hours * Cooking Time: 2 to 3 hours*

*H*ere's a recipe for a deer camp full of hungry hunters. We enjoyed this at the Turtle Greek Camp in the Adirondack Mountains many years ago. While it was cooking , the aroma permeated the woods outside the lodge, where the younger hunters were prompted by the cook to maintain a vegilant watch over that fire!

Marinade:

- 4 to 5 gallons white wine (enough to cover the venison)
- 4 carrots, sliced
- 3 onions, sliced
- 2 heads of garlic, peeled and sliced
- 1 tablespoon dried juniper berries
- 1 tablespoon whole black peppercorns
- 1 whole leg of venison (18 to 20 lbs.), trimmed of as much fat as possible
- Salt and pepper
- 1 lb. butter, melted
- Hunter s Sauce for serving, optional

In a nonaluminum container large enough to hold the venison leg, combine 4 gallons of the wine with remaining marinade ingredients. Add leg of venison, and pour in additional wine as needed to cover leg. Refrigerate for 24 hours, turning several times.

When you're ready to cook, prepare a hot wood fire. Remove leg from marinade and pat dry. Secure leg to a spit and season generously with salt and pepper. Strain marinade into large saucepan and heat to boiling; keep warm during cooking to prevent bacterial growth. Place spit over fire and cook for 2 to 3 hours, or until desired doneness, basting often

with the melted butter and reserved marinade. The venison should remain slightly rare. Serve with Hunter's Sauce.

Christmas Venison Roast with Baby Mushrooms

*Serves: 8 to 10 * Prep Time: 40 minutes * Cooking Time: 1 ¼ to 1 ½ hours*

- ¾ cup unsalted butter (1½ sticks), divided
- ½ cup minced shallots, divided
- ¾ lb. fresh spinach leaves
- ¼ lb. fresh baby portobello mushrooms, washed
- ½ lb. grated Swiss cheese
- 5 slices bacon, cooked and crumbled
- Salt and pepper
- 4-lb. boneless venison roast*
- 1 lemon
- 4 cups brown sauce
- 1½ cups red wine

First, prepare the stuffing. In large saucepan, melt 6 tablespoons of the butter over medium heat. Add ¼ cup of the shallots. Saute until translucent. Add spinach and mushrooms; cook about 3 minutes longer. Mix in grated cheese and crumbled bacon. Cook, stirring constantly, until cheese melts and mixture is well blended. Season to taste with salt and pepper. Transfer to medium bowl and place in refrigerator to cool.

Heat oven to 350°F. Butterfly roast, trying to achieve uniform thickness throughout. Season with salt and pepper; squeeze lemon juice liberally over inside of roast, picking off any lemon pips. Spread cooled stuffing evenly over roast. Roll up roast jelly-roll style, rolling with the grain of the meat. Tie roast at 1-inch intervals, using kitchen string.

Melt 4 tablespoons of the remaining butter in large stockpot over medium-high heat. (While a large skillet will also work, the sides of this larger pot will prevent grease from splattering on your stovetop.) Add roast and sear on all sides. Transfer to roasting pan. Roast to desired doneness, 15 to 20 minutes per pound. Remove roast from oven when internal temperature is 5°F less than desired; I prefer rare, so I remove it when the temperature is 125°F. Transfer roast to serving dish and tent loosely with aluminum foil; let rest while you prepare sauce.

In medium saucepan over medium heat, melt remaining 2 tablespoons of butter. Add remaining ¼ cup shallots and saute for about 2 minutes. Blend in brown sauce and red wine. Reduce heat and simmer, stirring frequently, for about 15 minutes. Check seasoning and adjust as necessary. Pass through fine strainer (or china cap) and serve with roast.

Since you will be butterflying the roast, you need to start with a boneless roast that is in one piece (not a tied-together roast). Rump or round roasts work well in this recipe.

Adirondack Spinach Venison Roast

Serves: 8 to 10 ∗ Prep Time: 25 minutes ∗ Cooking Time: 1 ¼ to 1 ½ hours

- ½ cup unsalted butter (1 stick), room temperature, divided
- 4 cloves garlic, minced, divided
- 10 oz. fresh spinach leaves
- ½ lb. shredded Gruyere cheese
- Salt and pepper
- 4-lb. boneless venison roast*
- 2 tablespoons lemon juice
- 3 slices dry white bread, torn into small pieces
- 2 bay leaves, crumbled
- 1 teaspoon ground sage
- 2 slices uncooked bacon, chopped
- Half of a medium onion, chopped

In large skillet, melt 2 tablespoons of the butter over medium heat. Add half of the minced garlic and saute until golden. Add spinach and saute until wilted. Add cheese, and salt and pepper to taste. Cook for about 2 minutes longer, stirring constantly. Remove from heat and let cool to room temperature.

Heat oven to 350°F. While the spinach mixture is cooling, butterfly the roast, trying to achieve uniform thickness throughout. Season with salt, pepper and lemon juice. Spread cooled stuffing evenly over meat, keeping an inch away from edges. Roll up roast jelly-roll style, rolling with the grain of the meat. Tie roast at 1-inch intervals, using kitchen string. Place roast on rack in roasting pan. Sprinkle with salt and pepper, and rub remaining 6 tablespoons butter over entire roast.

In food processor or blender, combine bread, bay leaves, sage, bacon, onion and remaining garlic. Pulse on and off, or blend at medium speed, until all ingredients are mixed thoroughly, 30 to 60 seconds. Pat bread-crumb mixture firmly over top and sides of roast.

Roast to desired doneness, 15 to 20 minutes per pound. Remove roast from oven when internal temperature is 5°F less than desired; I prefer rare, so I remove it when the temperature is 125°F. Let roast rest for 10 to 15 minutes before slicing.

Since you will be butterflying the roast, you need to start with a boneless roast that is in one piece (not a tied-together roast). Rump or round roasts work well in this recipe.

Venison Filet Wellington

*Serves: 5 to 8 * Prep Time: 45 minutes **
Cooking Time: 10 to 15 minutes

Here's an elegant dish that will knock the socks off your deer-camp buddies. It may look complex, but it really is quite simple. From start to finish, Venison Filet Wellington will take about an hour. Read *the direction at least once before preparing this dish, and you will see how quickly it comes together. Have all your ingredients ready, to make the assembly smooth and quick. Don't miss trying this recipe; it is well worth the effort.*

- 2-to 3-lb. venison loin, well trimmed
- 2 tablespoons clarified butter, room temperature
- 2 to 4 slices bacon
- 2 tablespoons butter
- 3 tablespoons olive oil
- 2 tablespoons chopped shallots
- ½ lb. fresh white or straw mushrooms, finely chopped
- 1 egg, separated
- 2 tablespoons cold water
- 1 sheet (half of a 17¼-OZ. pkg.) frozen puff pastry, thawed per package directions
- Flour for rolling out pastry
- 1 cup shredded fresh spinach leaves
- ½ cup shredded Swiss cheese
- Hunter's Sauce

Heat oven to 325°F. Heat a large, heavy-bottomed skillet over medium high heat. While skillet is heating, rub venison with clarified butter. Add loin to hot skillet and sear to a deep brown color on all sides. Transfer loin to dish and set aside to cool to room temperature. Meanwhile, add bacon to same skillet and fry until cooked but not crisp. Set aside on paper towel-lined plate.

While the loin is cooling, prepare the filling. In medium skillet, melt the 2 tablespoons butter in the oil over medium heat. Add shallots and saute until golden, stirring constantly; don't let the shallots brown or they will become bitter. Add mushrooms and saute until most of the liquid evaporates. Set mushroom mixture aside to cool.

Beat egg white lightly in small bowl. In another small bowl, lightly beat egg yolk and water. Set both bowls aside.

To prepare the shell, roll out pastry on lightly floured surface to a rectangle 1 to 2 inches larger on all sides than the loin. Spread cooled mushroom mixture over the pastry, leaving 1 inch clear around the edges. Layer the spinach, cheese and bacon in a thin strip over the center; the strip should be about as wide as the loin. Place loin on top of bacon. Brush edges of pastry with egg white; this will help hold the pastry shell together while it is baking. Wrap pastry around loin and crimp edges very well to seal. Turn pastry-wrapped loin over so the seam side is down. Place onto baking sheet. Brush pastry with egg yolk mixture; this will provide a beautiful glaze to the Wellington.

Bake for 10 to 15 minutes, or until pastry is golden brown. The loin should have reached an internal temperature of 130°F. Remove from oven. Slice into individual portions and serve immediately with Hunter's Sauce.

Kate's Cooking Tips

Clarified butter is regular butter from which the milk solids have been removed. Unlike regular butter, it won't burn even at high temperatures, so it is ideal for searing the venison in this recipe. To make clarified butter, melt a stick (or more) in the microwave, or in a small saucepan over low heat. Skim off and discard any foam from the top. Pour the clear yellow liquid into a bowl, leaving the milky residue behind. Cool to room temperature, then chill until hard. If there is any trace of milky residue in the chilled butter, re-melt and pour the clear yellow liquid through cheesecloth.

Here's a handy chart for internal temperatures of meat at various stages of doneness:

Amount of Internal	Doneness Temperature
RARE	130° TO 135°
MEDIUM-RARE	135° TO 140°
MEDIUM	140° TO 145°
MEDIUM-WELL	145° TO 155°
WELL DONE	155° TO 160°

Venison Tenderloin Siciliano

*Serves: 4 * Prep Time: 10 minutes * Cooking Time: 10 minutes or less*

Peter and I were hunting Rocky Mountain elk in northern New Mexico and stopped one evening in the beautiful town of taos for dinner. We dined on a version of this dish, and were fortunate enough to have the chef share the recipe with us. Although I have altered it over the years, this recipe is simple yet offers a deliciously rich flavor. Marsala, a sweet, fortified wine from sicily, can be found in your local liqour store.

- 1 cup flour
- Salt and pepper
- 1 lb. venison tenderloin, cut into ½-inch-thick medallions
- 2 tablespoons butter
- 2 tablespoons canola oil
- 1½ cups mushrooms, sliced
- 3 tablespoons minced shallots
- ½ cup Marsala wine
- 1½ cups brown sauce or beef gravy
- 1 tablespoon chopped fresh parsley

Place flour in large plastic food-storage bag; add salt and pepper to taste and shake well to mix. Add medallions, 2 at a time, and shake to coat. Transfer medallions to a plate as they are coated.

In large skillet, melt butter in oil over medium-high heat. Add medallions and cook until browned on first side. Turn medallions; add mushrooms and shallots. Cook for about 2 minutes longer. Add Marsala and heat to simmering. Add brown sauce and parsley and heat to simmering again. Simmer for 2 minutes longer. Serve immediately.

Chicken-Fried Venison

*Serves: 6 * Prep Time: 10 minutes *
Marinating Time: 2 hours * Cooking Time: 15 minutes*

Serve this classic southern - style dish with a brown sauce and garlic mashed potatoes.

- 2 lbs. venison loin, cut into ½-inch-thick medallions
- 2 cups milk
- 4 cloves garlic, minced
- 1 tablespoon cayenne pepper, divided
- 1½ teaspoons black pepper
- ½ teaspoon onion salt legg
- ¼ teaspoon salt
- 1 cup all-purpose flour
- ¼ cup canola oil (approx.), divided

With flat side of a meat mallet or the bottom of a saucepan, pound medallions to flatten slightly. In bowl, combine milk, garlic, 1½ teaspoons of the cayenne, the black pepper and onion salt. Add medallions; cover and refrigerate for 2 hours.

When ready to cook, transfer medallions to a plate and set aside. Add egg to milk mixture and beat together. Return medallions to milk mixture. In large bowl, mix remaining 1½ teaspoons cayenne and the salt with the flour. Dredge medallions in flour.

In cast-iron skillet, heat 1 tablespoon of the canola oil over medium-high heat until hot but not smoking. Place 1 or 2 medallions at a time into skillet and cook for 2 to 3 minutes per side, until golden brown. Transfer to heated platter and repeat with remaining medallions, adding additional oil as necessary.

Kate's Cooking Tips

When roasting venison, make sure that the roasting pan is slightly larger than the roast, but not too much larger. If the pan is too large, the drippings will spread out and burn.

Make sure that large cuts of venison are at room temperature before cooking. This way they will cook more uniformly.

When time allows, after cutlets are breaded, place them in the refrigerator for 2 to 3 minutes. I like to do this to "set" the breading before frying.

Blackened Cajun Medallions of Venison

*Serves: 4 * Prep Time: 10 minutes *
Cooking Time: 10 minutes or less*

Open the windows or turn on a powerful vent fan when you're cooking this, as it will produce a lot of smoke! This dish is excellent served with the Wild Rice Casserole.

Blackened Seasoning Mix

- 2 teaspoons paprika
- 2 teaspoons crumbled dried thyme
- 1 teaspoon black pepper
- 1 teaspoon garlic powder
- 1 teaspoon cumin
- 1 teaspoon crumbled dried oregano
- 1 teaspoon sugar
- ½ teaspoon cayenne pepper
- ½ teaspoon salt
- 4 venison loin medallions (4 to 6 oz. each), ¾ to 1 inch thick

- 2 tablespoons unsalted butter, melted
- 1 tablespoon butter

In small bowl, stir together all seasoning mix ingredients. Pat medallions dry. Brush each side with melted butter. Sprinkle generously on both sides with seasoning mix, and pat to help seasonings adhere.

Heat large cast-iron skillet over high heat. When hot, add the tablespoon of butter. When butter just stops foaming, add medallions and cook for 2 to 3 minutes on each side, depending upon the thickness of the steaks. Serve immediately.

Applejack Venison Medallions

*Serves: 6 * Prep Time: 10 minutes *
Cooking Time: 20 minutes*

I like to serve this with an gratin potatoes, and a dish of green peas garnished with pearl onions.

- 6 venison loin medallions (4 oz. each), ¾ inch thick
- Salt
- ½ cup clarified butter, divided
- 3 tablespoons applejack brandy, preferably Calvados
- 1 large shallot, minced
- 1 teaspoon crushed black and red peppercorn blend

- ½ teaspoon cornstarch
- 2 cups beef broth (prepared from beef bouillon granules)
- 1 cup heavy cream, room temperature

Pat medallions dry and sprinkle both sides with salt to taste. In large skillet, melt ¼ cup of the clarified butter over medium-high heat. Add medallions in a single layer and sear on both sides. Transfer medallions to a plate; pour excess butter from the skillet and lower heat to medium. Return medallions to skillet and add brandy. Cook until brandy is warm. Remove skillet from heat and carefully ignite brandy with long-handled match. When flames die out, transfer medallions to plate; set aside and keep warm.

Melt remaining ¼ cup butter in same skillet over medium heat. Add shallot and peppercorns, and saute until shallot is translucent. Meanwhile, blend cornstarch and broth in measuring cup or small bowl. When shallot is translucent, pour broth mixture into skillet, stirring constantly. Cook until broth is reduced to about half, stirring frequently. Add 2 tablespoons of the reduced sauce to the cream and mix well (leave the cream in its measuring cup, or place in a small bowl); this raises the temperature of the cream to prevent curdling when cream is added to the sauce. Reduce heat under skillet to low and add cream mixture. Simmer until the mixture is reduced to saucelike consistency, stirring frequently. Return medallions to skillet and re-warm them briefly before serving.

Venison Medallions with Herbed Cheese Sauce

*Serves: 2 * Prep Time: 5 minutes *
Cooking Time: 15 minutes*

Serve these tasty medallions with twice - baked potatoes and steamed broccoli.

- 1½ cups all-purpose flour
- Salt and black pepper
- ½ cup Boursin herb cheese, or any soft herbed cheese
- ¾ cup heavy cream
- 2 tablespoons olive oil
- 6 venison loin medallions (3 oz. each), ½ inch thick
- ½ cup white wine
- Cayenne pepper

Place flour in large plastic food-storage bag; add salt and black pepper to taste and shake well to mix. Set aside. In small bowl, blend herbed cheese and heavy cream with whisk or slotted spoon; set aside.

Heat oil in heavy-bottom skillet over medium-high heat. Dredge medallions in seasoned flour. Add to skillet and sear well on both sides. Transfer medallions to warm plate; set aside and keep warm. Add wine to skillet and cook for about a minute, stirring to loosen any browned bits. Add cream mixture. Stir well to blend, and season with salt, pepper and cayenne to taste. Cook over medium heat, stirring frequently, until sauce thickens

slightly; do not boil. Pour sauce over medallions and serve.

Canadian Barren-Ground Caribou Tenderloin

*Serves: 2 * Prep Time: 10 minutes * Cooking Time: 10 to 15 minutes*

- 3 tablespoons canola oil, divided
- 3 medium yellow onions, thinly sliced
- 4 caribou or venison tenderloins (3 oz. each), well trimmed
- 3 tablespoons minced shallots
- ½ cup thickly sliced fresh mushrooms
- 1 cup heavy cream, room temperature
- ½ cup Madeira wine
- ¼ cup unsalted butter
- Salt and white pepper

In medium skillet, heat 1 tablespoon of the oil over medium-high heat until it is hot but not smoking. Add onions and saute until browned. Remove from heat; set aside and keep warm.

While onions are cooking, pound each of the tenderloin pieces with flat side of meat mallet until very thin. In large skillet, heat the remaining 2 tablespoons oil over high heat until it is hot but not smoking. Saute flattened tenderloins for about 1 minute on each side. Transfer to a warmed platter; set aside and keep warm.

Add shallots to same skillet and cook over medium-high heat, stirring constantly, for about 1 minute. Add mushrooms and saute until tender. Add cream, wine and butter. Cook until slightly thickened, stirring constantly. Add salt and pepper to taste.

To serve, divide onions between 2 dinner plates. Top each with 2 cutlets. Pour mushroom sauce over the top.

Sweet Moose Loin Roast

*Serves: 12 to 14 * Prep Time: 15 minutes * Cooking Time: 1 to 1 ½ hours*

- ½ cup light molasses
- 1 tablespoon dark brown sugar
- 1 tablespoon sesame oil
- 4 cloves garlic, minced
- 3 tablespoons canola oil
- 4-lb. moose loin portion, well trimmed
- 1 teaspoon sea salt
- 1 teaspoon freshly ground pepper
- Horseradish Cream Sauce

Heat oven to 425°F. In small bowl, combine molasses, brown sugar, sesame oil and garlic. Mix well and set aside.

In large skillet, heat canola oil over high heat until it is hot but not smoking. Add moose loin and quickly sear on all sides; if the loin is too large for the skillet, cut it into halves and sear in 2 batches.

Place seared loin on rack in large roasting pan. Season with salt and pepper on all sides. Spread molasses mixture all over loin. Place in oven and reduce temperature to 350°F. Roast to desired doneness, 13 to 18 minutes per pound. Remove roast from oven when internal temperature is 5° less than desired; I prefer rare, so I remove it when the temperature is 125°F. Let meat rest for 10 to 15 minutes before slicing. Serve with Horseradish Cream Sauce.

Roast Venison with Green Peppercorn Sauce

*Serves: 6 to 8 * Prep Time: 5 minutes * Cooking Time: 1 ¼ to 1 ½ hours*

- ¼ teaspoon salt
- ⅛ teaspoon pepper
- ⅛ teaspoon garlic powder
- 3-lb. venison roast, preferably boneless
- 2 tablespoons butter
- 2 tablespoons olive oil
- ⅓ cup canned or bottled green peppercorns, drained
- 2 cups light cream
- 1 cup beef bouillon

Heat oven to 325°F. Mix the salt, pepper and garlic powder, then rub over entire roast. In Dutch oven, melt butter in oil over medium-high heat. Add roast and brown on all sides. Place in oven and roast, uncovered, to desired doneness, 15 to 20 minutes per pound. Remove roast from oven when internal temperature is 5° less than desired; I prefer rare, so I remove it when the temperature is 125°F. Transfer roast to serving dish and tent loosely with aluminum foil; let rest while you prepare sauce.

Remove excess fat from Dutch oven. Place pan over medium heat on stovetop. Add green peppercorns, slightly crushing some of the grains. Add cream and bouillon. Heat to boiling, then cook until liquid is thickened and smooth. Season to taste with salt and pepper. Slice roast and serve with green peppercorn sauce.

Venison Cutlet Delight

*Serves: 4 to 6 * Prep Time: 20 minutes *
Cooking Time: 15 minutes*

- 1 cup all-purpose flour
- Salt and pepper
- 2 eggs
- ½ cups milk
- 1 cup Italian-seasoned bread crumbs
- ¼ cup grated Parmesan cheese
- 1 teaspoon garlic powder
- 8 venison cutlets (about 4 oz. each),
- pounded to ¼-inch thickness
- ½ cup canola oil (approx.)
- 1 can (10 oz.) whole asparagus, drained
- ½ lb. bacon, cooked and crumbled
- ½ lb. Swiss cheese, sliced

Heat oven to 400°F. Place flour in large plastic food-storage bag; add salt and pepper to taste and shake well to mix. In medium bowl, beat together eggs and milk. In large bowl, mix together bread crumbs, Parmesan cheese and garlic powder.

Pat cutlets dry. Flour each cutlet, dip into egg mixture, then coat with bread crumb mixture; transfer to plate in a single layer as each is coated.

In large skillet, heat about ¼ inch of the oil over medium heat until hot but not smoking. Fry cutlets in small batches until just browned on both sides, adding additional oil as necessary. Transfer browned cutlets to paper towel-lined plate.

When all cutlets have been browned, arrange in single layer on large baking sheet. Place 2 asparagus spears on each cutlet. Top each with a little crumbled bacon, then place a slice of Swiss cheese over each. Place in oven just until cheese melts, 1 to 2 minutes. Serve immediately.

Steak with Caper-Mustard Sauce

*Serves: 4 * Prep Time: 10 minutes * Cooking Time: 20 minutes*

- 1 cup all-purpose flour
- ½ teaspoon salt
- ½ teaspoon pepper
- 4 boneless venison steaks (about 6 oz.
- each), well trimmed
- 2 tablespoons canola oil
- 1 medium onion, finely chopped
- 1 shallot, minced
- 2 tablespoons red wine vinegar
- ¼ cup beef broth (prepared from beef bouillon granules)
- ¼ cup nonfat plain yogurt
- 2 tablespoons drained and rinsed capers
- 1 tablespoon Dijon mustard
- 2 tablespoons chopped fresh parsley

Place flour in large plastic food-storage bag; add salt and pepper and shake well to mix. Pat steaks dry, and dredge steaks in seasoned flour.

In heavy-bottomed skillet, heat oil over medium-high heat until hot but not smoking. Add steaks and cook for about 2 minutes on each side for medium-rare, or as desired. Transfer steaks to platter; set aside and keep warm.

Add onion, shallot and vinegar to same skillet. Saute until vinegar has cooked away. Lower heat to medium and add broth, then yogurt. Simmer until mixture is reduced by half; do not allow mixture to boil.

Remove skillet from heat. Stir in capers and mustard. Blend together thoroughly, then pour over steaks. Sprinkle with parsley and serve.

Curry Grilled Venison Steaks

*Serves: 4 * Prep Time: 5 minutes *
Cooking Time: 10 minutes or less*

- 2 teaspoons salt
- 1 teaspoon coarsely ground pepper
- 1 teaspoon curry powder
- ½ teaspoon garlic powder
- 2 tablespoons red wine vinegar
- 4 boneless venison steaks (about 6 oz. each), ¾ inch thick, well trimmed

Heat broiler, or prepare grill for high heat by lighting coals or preheating gas grill. In small bowl, mix together salt, pepper, curry powder and garlic powder. Add vinegar to glass baking dish. Add steaks, turning to coat both sides. Sprinkle steaks with half of the curry mixture; turn and sprinkle with remaining curry mixture.

If broiling indoors, place steaks on lightly greased rack in broiling pan. With oven rack at closest position to heat, broil steaks for 2 minutes. Turn steaks and continue broiling for 2 or 3 minutes for medium-rare, or until desired doneness.

If grilling outdoors, grill for 2 to 3 minutes on each side for mediumrare, or until desired doneness.

Venison Steak with Red Currants

*Serves: 4 * Prep Time: 30 minutes *
Cooking Time: 10 minutes or less*

While hunting red stag at a 5,000-acre ranch owned by the German baron Josef von Kerckerinck, I learned about the European fondness for pairing fruit with wild game—something I'd not encountered very frequently here in the States. Since then, I've created many delicious variations on this theme. If you're fond of such a flavor combination, I'm sure you'll enjoy this recipe as much as I do. If this pairing is new for you, give it a try; it will give your game a delicious new taste. As it turned out, I took a 16-point stag on that hunt; the meat was delicious with this recipe.

- 2 cups red wine
- ½ cup sugar
- 2 pears, peeled, halved and cored
- 4 venison steaks (8 oz. each), well trimmed
- Salt and pepper
- 2 tablespoons butter
- 2 tablespoons canola or corn oil
- 2 shallots, chopped
- ¼ cup red wine vinegar
- 1 cup beef broth
- ¼ cup heavy cream
- ⅓ cup red currants*

In medium saucepan, combine wine and sugar and cook over medium heat, stirring constantly, until sugar dissolves. Increase heat slightly and cook until mixture is steaming but not bubbling. Add pears and cook for about 3 minutes. Remove pan from heat; set aside and keep warm.

Pat steaks with paper towel; season to taste with salt and pepper. In medium skillet, melt butter in oil over medium-high heat. Add steaks and sear on both sides. Cook until medium-rare, about 2 minutes per side. Transfer to dish; set aside and keep warm.

Add shallots to same skillet and saute over medium-high heat until fragrant; do not burn. Add vinegar, stirring to loosen browned bits, and continue cooking until liquid has cooked almost completely away. Add broth and boil until reduced by about half. Reduce heat to medium, stir in cream and simmer until reduced to saucelike consistency; stir frequently and remove skillet from heat temporarily if sauce begins to boil over. Add salt and pepper to taste. Add red currants to sauce and cook, stirring gently, until heated through. Serve steak with red currant sauce, garnishing each with poached pear half.

Available in most gourmet markets and specialty food stores. Black currants, not as prominent in the food markets, also work well here. Just increase the amount to ½ cup.

Steak Au Poivre

*Serves: 4 * Prep Time: 10 minutes **
*Marinating Time: 2 to 6 hours * Cooking Time: 15 minutes*

This dish is a favourite of mine; I serve it frequently when we have dinner guests.

- 2 tablespoons coarsely crushed black peppercorns
- 2 tablespoons coarsely crushed white peppercorns
- ⅛ teaspoon hot red pepper flakes
- 8 venison loin medallions (3 oz. each), ½ inch thick
- 1 tablespoon canola oil
- 2 tablespoons chopped shallots
- 2 tablespoons brandy
- 1 cup beef broth
- 2 tablespoons Dijon mustard
- ⅛ teaspoon Worcestershire sauce
- ½ cup heavy cream, room temperature

In small bowl, mix together the peppercorns and red pepper flakes. Press peppercorn mixture into both sides of the steaks. Place on plate; cover and refrigerate for 2 to 6 hours. Bring steaks to room temperature before cooking.

In large skillet, heat oil over medium-high heat until hot but not smoking. Add medallions and sear on one side. Turn medallions, then add shallots to skillet and cook until steaks are seared on second side. Carefully add brandy. Allow to warm for a moment. Remove from heat and carefully ignite with long-handled match. When flames die out, transfer medallions to platter; set aside and keep warm.

Add broth, mustard and Worcestershire sauce to skillet. Heat to simmering over medium heat; cook for about 1 minute, stirring constantly. Add cream and heat to simmering. If the steaks are warm, serve immediately with the sauce ladled over the top of the steaks. If they have cooled slightly, add the steaks back to the skillet to heat through; serve immediately.

Venison Parmigiana

*Serves: 6 * Prep Time: 10 minutes *
Cooking Time: 25 minutes*

Serve with a side of hot linguini, fresh romaine salad and garlic bread with "the works"!

- ¼ cup all-purpose flour
- Salt and pepper
- 2 eggs
- ½ cup milk
- 3 cups seasoned bread crumbs
- ¼ teaspoon garlic powder
- 12 venison cutlets (3 to 4 oz. each), pounded as needed to even thickness
- ½ cup olive oil (approx.)
- 4 cups tomato sauce
- 1 lb. mozzarella cheese, shredded
- 1½ cups grated Parmesan cheese

Place flour in large plastic food-storage bag, add salt and pepper to taste and shake well to mix. In medium bowl, beat together eggs and milk. In large bowl, mix together bread crumbs and garlic powder.

Pat cutlets dry. Flour each cutlet, dip into egg mixture, then coat with bread crumb mixture; transfer to plate in a single layer as each is coated. Heat broiler. In large skillet, heat about ¼ inch of the oil over mediumhigh heat until hot but not smoking. Fry cutlets in small batches until just browned on both sides, adding additional oil as necessary. Transfer browned cutlets to paper towel-lined plate.

Spread a thick layer of tomato sauce on the bottom of a large rectangular baking dish (the dish needs to be large enough to hold all cutlets in a single layer; use 2 smaller dishes if necessary). Place browned cutlets on sauce in a single layer. Top each cutlet with about ¼ cup tomato sauce, some mozzarella cheese and 2 tablespoons Parmesan cheese. Place dish under broiler and broil until cheeses melt and bubble. Serve immediately.

Western Style Bar-B-Que Venison Chops

*Serves: 6 * Prep Time: 30 minutes * Marinating Time: 1 to 4 hours * Cooking Time: 10 minutes or less*

I was practicing shooting my five arrows for the day, when out of the corner of my eye I thought I saw a deer bolt across our food plot. I slowly put my bow down and glanced across the clearing, resting my gaze momentarily on each apple tree to see if there were any hungry customers munching away. Suddenly, another deer jumped out from the thick cover and darted across. I patiently watched these two young bucks run in and out of the woods, quickly grabbing apples and flicking their tails nervously. As I moved uphill to see what might be spooking them, I spotted a small black bear cub just down the hill. Not knowinf where the snow was, I retreated to the safety of my deck, just before the cub bawled out to the sow. Had it been deer season at the time, I probably would not have ever seen the bear cub, as the 5-pointer would not have gotten away from my arrow.

This leads me to a pointer for deer chops. If your chops are from a young deer, they will probably be so tender that they won't need much marinating; in fact, you could probably just sprinkle the trimmed chops with pepper and grill them. In the recipe below, use the shorter marinating time for young chops, just for a flavor boost. If your chops are from a more mature deer, use the longer *marinating time, which will help tenderize the meat. Serve with a potato salad and grilled corn on the cob.*

- ½ cup white wine vinegar
- ¼ lemon, diced
- 1 teaspoon ground coriander seed
- ½ teaspoon cumin
- ¼ teaspoon cayenne pepper
- ⅛ teaspoon paprika
- Hot red pepper flakes and black pepper to taste
- 6 venison chops (6 oz. each), about ½ inch thick, well trimmed

To prepare the sauce: Combine all sauce ingredients in small nonaluminum saucepan. Simmer over medium-low heat for about 20 minutes. Let cool.

Place chops in glass pan and cover with cooled sauce. Cover and refrigerate for 1 to 4 hours.

When you're ready to cook, prepare grill for high heat; light coals or preheat gas grill (high heat is necessary to sear the chops while still maintaining medium-rare doneness). Remove chops from marinade. Place on grate and grill for 2 to 4 minutes on each side; the length of time will depend upon the thickness of the chops and desired doneness.

Pan-Fried Venison with Creamy Peppercorn Sauce

*Serves: 8 * Prep Time: 10 minutes * Cooking Time: 30 minutes*

- ¾ cup white wine vinegar
- ¾ cup sauterne or sweet white wine
- 1 tablespoon whole black peppercorns
- 1 tablespoon dried whole green peppercorns*
- 1 tablespoon dried whole pink peppercorns*
- 2 cups heavy cream, room temperature
- 2 cups all-purpose flour
- 1 teaspoon salt
- 1 teaspoon pepper
- ¼ teaspoon garlic powder
- 3 lbs. venison steaks
- 2 tablespoons canola oil

In heavy nonstick saucepan, stir together vinegar, sauterne and peppercorns. Heat to boiling over medium-high heat. Boil until liquid is reduced to about half, about 10 minutes, stirring frequently. Reduce heat to medium, stir in cream and simmer until liquid is reduced to about 1¼ cups; stir frequently and remove pan from heat temporarily if sauce begins to boil over. Keep sauce warm over very low heat.

Place flour in large plastic food-storage bag; add salt, pepper and garlic powder and shake well to mix. Add steaks and toss to coat. In large, heavy skillet, heat oil over medium-high heat until hot but not smoking. Add steaks and cook for about 2 minutes on each side, or until desired doneness. Serve steaks with peppercorn sauce.

*Available at specialty foods shops and some supermarkets and also from Specialty World Foods. The green and pink peppercorns add color and contribute

subtle flavors to the sauce; however, you may prepare the sauce using black peppercorns only.

Venison Steak Forestiere

*Serves: 8 * Prep Time: 10 minutes * Cooking Time: 15 minutes*

- 1½ cups all-purpose flour
- Salt and pepper
- 8 boneless venison steaks (4 to 6 oz. each), well trimmed
- 2 tablespoons canola oil
- 1 cup sliced mushrooms*
- ½ cup crumbled cooked bacon
- 1 tablespoon minced garlic
- 1 tablespoon chopped fresh parsley
- ½ cup red wine
- ¾ cup brown sauce or beef gravy

Place flour in large plastic food-storage bag; add salt and pepper to taste and shake well to mix. Pat steaks dry, and dredge in seasoned flour.

In large skillet, heat oil over medium-high heat until hot but not smoking. Add steaks, and cook for

2 to 3 minutes on each side. Transfer steaks to plate; set aside and keep warm.

Add mushrooms, bacon, garlic and parsley to skillet; stir well. Add wine, stirring to loosen any browned bits. Add brown sauce and stir well. Return steaks to skillet; simmer for 5 minutes.

To add flavor, try using half baby portobello mushrooms.

Venison Steak Fajitas

*Serves: 5 * Prep Time: 20 minutes * Cooking Time: 7 to 8 hours, largely unattended*

When the summer days are getting longer, most of us want to spend our time outdoors on a bass pond rather than in the kitchen. This is one of my favorite dishes for times like that. You can start it in the slow cooker at noontime, or a little before, and you'll have a late, quick meal to enjoy while you discuss how "the big one" got away!

- 2 lbs. boneless venison steak
- 2 limes, halved
- 1½ cups tomato juice
- 3 cloves garlic, minced
- 1 tablespoon minced fresh parsley
- 2 teaspoons chili powder
- 1 teaspoon crumbled dried oregano
- 1 teaspoon ground cumin
- ½ teaspoon ground coriander seed
- ½ teaspoon salt
- ¼ teaspoon pepper
- 1 medium onion, sliced
- 1 green bell pepper, sliced
- 1 red bell pepper, sliced
- 1 jalapeño pepper, thinly sliced
- 10 flour tortillas
- Accompaniments: Sour cream, chopped tomatoes, guacamole, salsa or grated cheddar cheese

Slice venison thinly across the grain. Place slices in medium bowl. Squeeze limes over venison slices, picking out any seeds. Toss to coat well. Place venison in slow cooker. Combine tomato juice, garlic, parsley, chili powder, oregano, cumin, coriander, salt and pepper; stir to mix well. Pour over venison. Cover and cook on LOW for 6 to 7 hours.

Add the onion, bell peppers and jalapeno. Re-cover and cook for 1 hour longer. Warm the tortillas in the microwave. With a slotted spoon, put about ½ cup of the venison mixture in each flour tortilla. Add one or more accompaniments as desired; roll up tortilla.

Hunter's Venison Stroganoff

*Serves: 4 * Prep Time: 10 minutes **
Cooking Time: 30 minutes

When time is short but it's just the right weather for a hearty meal, try this simple version of the classic main course. Serve it over egg noodles, to catch all of the savory sauce.

- 1 to 1¼ lbs. boneless venison sirloin steak, cut into ¾-inch strips
- Salt and pepper
- 2 tablespoons vegetable or canola oil
- 1 lb. button or baby portobello mushrooms, sliced
- 1 large yellow onion, thinly sliced
- 1 tablespoon all-purpose flour
- 1 cup beef broth
- ½ cup dry red wine
- ¾ cup sour cream, room temperature
- 1½ teaspoons paprika

Sprinkle venison strips with salt and pepper to taste. In large nonstick skillet, heat oil over high heat. Add venison strips in batches and cook, stirring frequently, until browned on all sides. Use slotted spoon to transfer browned strips to large bowl after each batch. When all venison has been browned and removed from skillet, add mushrooms and onion to skillet. Saute until browned, about 12 minutes. Sprinkle flour into skillet, stirring constantly. Add broth and wine. Reduce heat to medium and simmer, stirring frequently, until sauce thickens and coats spoon, about 5 minutes. Reduce heat to low. Return venison and any accumulated juices to skillet. Mix in sour cream and paprika. Cook, stirring frequently, until heated through, about 3 minutes; do not boil or the sour cream may separate. Check for seasoning, and add salt and pepper as necessary.

Grilled Elk Steak Florentine

*Serves: 4 * Prep Time: 10 minutes **
Cooking Time: 15 minutes

- 2 elk steaks (1½ lbs. each), about 1½ inches thick
- 2 tablespoons coarsely crushed black peppercorns
- 1 tablespoon plus 1½ teaspoons crumbled dried sage
- 1 tablespoon crumbled dried thyme
- 1 tablespoon crumbled dried rosemary

- 1½ teaspoons garlic powder
- 2 tablespoons sea salt
- ½ cup olive oil plus additional for brushing steaks
- 8 cloves garlic, thinly sliced
- 3 lbs. fresh spinach leaves
- 2 tablespoons lemon juice
- Salt and pepper
- Grated Parmesan cheese for garnish

Prepare grill for high heat; light coals or preheat gas grill. Trim steaks of all fat and connective tissue. Pat dry. In small bowl, combine crushed peppercorns, sage, thyme, rosemary, garlic powder and sea salt. Press mixture evenly into both sides of steaks. Brush steaks gently with oil. Place on grate directly over hot coals and sear both sides. Cook for 3 to 5 minutes on each side, or until internal temperature is about 125°F (rare). Transfer to plate; cover loosely with foil and let stand for 5 minutes.

In large skillet, heat ½ cup oil over high heat. Add sliced garlic and cook, stirring constantly, until golden. Add spinach to pan and cook, stirring constantly, until just limp, about 30 seconds. Remove from heat and season with lemon juice and salt and pepper to taste. Toss to coat well.

Divide spinach among 4 plates. Slice steaks into ¼-inch thick strips and arrange on plates. Sprinkle lightly with Parmesan cheese; serve immediately

Thai Marinated Venison Ribbons

*Serves: 4 * Prep Time: 10 minutes **
*Marinating Time: 4 hours * Cooking Time: 15 minutes*

*T*hank goodness for Chinese take-out! As our schedules become busier, ready-to-eat meals play a bigger role in our daily lives, and Chinese food is comfortingly similar at small take-out restaurants across the country. My experience with Chinese food began when I was still in grade school. Every Friday, Dad came home with a take-out Chinese meal. My sister and I loved to giggle over our favorite, the PuPu Platter. I can still envision Chrisi looking at me with her silly grin and snickering, "Please pass the PuPu."

As I look back on many marvelous years of Chinese food indulgence, I can appreciate its reliable convenience with my family. It's a comfort to know that all members of our household will vote "yes" when it comes to Chinese take-out as a last minute dinner decision. The best part, however, is hearing my twelve-year-old son snicker, "Mom, please pass the PuPu."

Here's one of my favorite Asian-style venison recipes. It's quick and delicious. Serve with a salad or marinated cucumbers. Good eating!

Marinade:

- ½ cup fresh basil leaves, chopped
- ¼ cup reduced-sodium soy sauce
- 2 tablespoons crushed red pepper flakes
- 2 teaspoons sugar
- 2 teaspoons vinegar
- 1 teaspoon minced garlic
- 1 lb. boneless venison cutlets, well trimmed
- 2 tablespoons peanut oil (approx.)
- 2 cups water
- 1 cup no-salt beef broth
- 2 tablespoons reduced-sodium soy sauce
- 2 cups cooked, unseasoned ramen or cellophane noodles*
- Chopped green onions for garnish

In large zipper-style plastic bag, combine all marinade ingredients. Thinly slice venison diagonally across the grain into ¼ inch-wide strips (partially frozen meat is easier to slice). Add venison strips to bag with marinade. Seal bag well and shake until strips are thoroughly coated with marinade. Refrigerate for about 4 hours, turning bag occasionally.

Remove meat from marinade and place on paper towels to drain. Add 1 teaspoon of the oil to wok or large skillet. Heat over medium-high heat until very hot. Stir-fry venison in batches for 3 to 5 minutes per batch, transferring to warm platter as it is cooked; add additional oil as necessary for subsequent batches. When all venison has been cooked, return all to the wok. Add water, beef broth, soy sauce and pre-cooked noodles. Cook, stirring constantly, until entire mixture is heated through. Place on platter, garnish with green onions and serve immediately.

* Reserve ¼ cup of the cooking water and mix with cooked noodles to prevent them from sticking together.

Kate's Cooking Tips

It's good to note here that you don't need a wok to cook a stirfry meal. Any large skilletpreferably one that's coated with a non-stick finish-will do. I like to use peanut oil for stirfrying, as it imparts a slightly different flavor to the meat and has a higher smoking point than regular corn oil. Watch the temperature of the oil when you're adding meat to the pan; if the oil is too hot, the meat will clump together when you begin cooking it.

When using fresh garlic, place the cloves on a cutting board. Place the side of a chef's knife on top of the cloves. With the palm of one hand, whack the side of the knife to crush open the clove. The peel will come off easily, and the crushed clove is ready to be chopped or added whole to your dish.

Broccoli-Venison Stir-Fry

Serves: 2 * Prep Time: 15 minutes * Cooking Time: 10 minutes

- ½ lb. boneless venison, preferably rump or loin meat
- 1 tablespoon plus 1 teaspoon soy sauce, divided
- ½ cup peanut oil or vegetable oil, divided

- ¼ teaspoon pepper
- ½ cup no-salt beef broth
- ½ lb. fresh broccoli heads, cut into small flowerets
- ½ cup thinly sliced bok choy or celery
- ½ cup fresh chives, cut into ½-inch slices before measuring
- ¼ cup sliced water chestnuts
- ¼ cup canned baby corn ears
- Hot cooked white rice
- Fried Chinese noodles for garnish

Slice venison across the grain into very thin strips. In medium bowl, mix together 1 tablespoon of the soy sauce, 2 teaspoons of the oil and the pepper. Add venison strips and toss to coat.

In wok or large nonstick skillet, heat remaining oil over medium-high heat until hot but not smoking. Add venison strips, keeping them separated as you add them to prevent them from clumping together. Cook for 1 to 2 minutes, stirring constantly. With slotted spoon, transfer venison to paper towel-lined plate; set aside and keep warm.

Remove all but 2 tablespoons oil from wok; increase heat to high. Add remaining 1 teaspoon soy sauce, the beef broth and broccoli to wok. Cook for about 3 minutes, stirring frequently. Add bok choy, chives, water chestnuts and corn to wok; return drained venison to wok. Stir-fry for 2 minutes longer. Serve hot over a bed of white rice, with a decorative topping of fried Chinese noodles.

Venison Steak Heroes

Serves: 4 * Prep Time: 15 minutes * Cooking Time: 10 minutes

- ¼ cup A-1 Steak Sauce
- 1 tablespoon brown sugar
- 1 tablespoon soy sauce

- ½ teaspoon ground ginger
- 1 tablespoon peanut oil
- 1 lb. venison loin, cut into ½-inch strips
- 1 medium red bell pepper, thinly sliced
- 1 medium yellow bell pepper, thinly sliced
- 1 medium onion, thinly sliced
- 1 cup sliced fresh button mushrooms
- 2 cloves garlic, minced
- 4 hero rolls, split and toasted

In small saucepan, combine steak sauce, brown sugar, soy sauce and ginger. Heat over low heat, stirring constantly, until sugar dissolves. Remove from heat and set aside.

In wok or large nonstick skillet, heat oil over high heat until hot but not smoking. Add venison strips and stir-fry for about 1 minute. Add red and yellow peppers, onion, mushrooms and garlic. Stir-fry for 3 to 4 minutes. Stir in steak-sauce mixture. Cook for 5 minutes longer, stirring constantly. Spoon hot mixture onto split rolls.

Venison and Vegetable Kabobs

*Serves: 4 * Prep Time: 20 minutes * Marinating Time: 4 to 6 hours * Cooking Time: 10 minutes or less*

Meat Marinade:

- ¾ cup olive oil
- ¾ cup red wine vinegar
- 1 tablespoon chopped fresh parsley
- 1 teaspoon cumin
- ⅛ teaspoon crumbled dried oregano, preferably Mexican
- Salt and pepper to taste
- 4 cloves garlic, chopped
- 1½ lbs. boneless venison loin or top round, well trimmed and cut into 1-inch cubes

Vegetable Marinade:

- ½ cup soy sauce
- ¼ cup sesame oil
- 2 tablespoons lemon juice
- 1 tablespoon shredded fresh gingerroot
- 5 cloves garlic, chopped
- 8 fresh button or small portobello mushrooms, cut into 1-inch chunks
- 1 large onion, cut into 1-inch chunks
- 1 red bell pepper, cut into 1-inch chunks
- 1 green bell pepper, cut into 1-inch chunks
- 1 yellow bell pepper, cut into 1-inch chunks

In large zipper-style plastic bag (or nonreactive bowl), combine all meat marinade ingredients. Add venison cubes. Seal bag well and shake until cubes are thoroughly coated with marinade. In another large zipper-style plastic bag, combine all vegetable marinade ingredients. Add mushrooms, onion and bell pepper chunks. Seal bag well and shake until vegetables are thoroughly coated with marinade. Refrigerate both bags for 4 to 6 hours, turning bags occasionally.

Bring venison and vegetables to room temperature prior to grilling. Prepare grill for high

heat; light coals or preheat gas grill. Drain venison and vegetables, reserving venison marinade. Thread mushrooms, peppers, onions and venison onto metal skewers. Grill for 5 to 10 minutes, turning skewers and basting with the venison marinade several times.

Chinese Venison Steak with Mushrooms

*Serves: 6 * Prep Time: 15 minutes * Marinating Time: 30 to 60 minutes * Cooking Time: 10 minutes or less*

- 1½ lbs. boneless venison steak, well trimmed
- 2 tablespoons soy sauce
- 2 tablespoons sherry
- 1 tablespoon Worcestershire sauce
- 2 teaspoons cornstarch
- 1 teaspoon sugar
- 1 teaspoon sesame oil
- ½ teaspoon pepper
- ½ cup peanut oil
- ½ lb. mushrooms, quartered
- 4 scallions, cut into ½-inch lengths
- 1 can (8 oz.) whole water chestnuts, drained
- 1 package (10 oz.) frozen snow peas, thawed
- 3 tablespoons water
- 2 tablespoons sesame seeds
- Hot cooked white rice

Cut steak into 1½-inch cubes. Pound cubes with meat mallet to flatten to about ¾ inch thick. In nonreactive bowl, combine soy sauce, sherry, Worcestershire sauce, cornstarch, sugar, sesame oil and pepper. Add flattened venison, stirring to coat. Cover and refrigerate for 30 to 60 minutes.

Remove venison from marinade; discard marinade. Let venison stand until room temperature.

Set a colander inside a pot or large bowl; set aside. In wok or large nonstick skillet, heat oil over high heat until hot but not smoking. Add venison and stir-fry for about 2 minutes (if using smaller skillet, cook venison in batches). Transfer venison to colander to drain.

Remove all but 2 tablespoons oil from wok. Add mushrooms and scallions; stir-fry for 2 minutes. Add water chestnuts and snow peas, stir-fry for 30 seconds longer. Return drained venison to wok and stir well. Add water and cook for 30 seconds longer. Sprinkle venison mixture with sesame seeds. Serve immediately with hot white rice.

Gunnison Venison Goulash

*Serves: 4 to 6 * Prep Time: 10 minutes *
Marinating Time: 8 hours * Cooking Time: 1¾ hours*

The mountains surrounding Crawford, Colorado harbor large numbers of elk. One year, Peter and I were hunting that area during early October when the rut was in full swing. We had summited one peak, which Peter had affectionately nicknamed "Zit-Zit Mountain" (due to its propensity to be struck by lightning), and were glassing the clearing below. My heart nearly skipped a beat when I spotted a dandy 5x5 elk just on the edge of the forest. It was grazing with a harem of four cows. Peter and I planned our route to get closer to the bull and lure it in with a few seductive cow calls.

Forty minutes later, we set up behind a large fallen tree and started with a few soft mews. What happened next still sends chills down my spine. The big 5x5 lifted its head and answered with a bellowing bugle. In the middle of the bugle, from just to the elk's right, out stepped another bull, with a massive 6x5 rack. The pushing, shoving, grunting and fighting that ensured was awe-inspiring! When they finally broke, I got an opportunity to rest my gun and take one well-placed shot. The bullet from my .308 single-shot rifle put plenty of elk

vension in our freezer that season. Here's one recipe that I used to take advantage of that bounty. The recipe can be doubled if you're serving a large group. Serve this with hot buttered noodles.

Marinade:

- 3 cups dry red wine
- 2 medium onions, diced
- 4 cloves garlic, crushed
- ½ teaspoon whole black peppercorns
- ¼ teaspoon crumbled dried rosemary
- ¼ teaspoon crumbled dried thyme
- 2 lbs. boneless venison stew meat (shoulder), well trimmed and cut into 1-inch cubes
- Salt and pepper
- 3 tablespoons canola oil
- 1 tablespoon flour
- 1 carrot, diced
- ¼ teaspoon cinnamon
- ¼ teaspoon cloves
- ½ cup sour cream

Combine all marinade ingredients in large nonreactive saucepan and heat to boiling. Remove from heat and let cool. Place venison cubes in marinade. Cover and refrigerate for 8 hours or overnight, stirring occasionally.

Remove the venison from the marinade; reserve marinade. Pat venison dry, and season to taste with salt and pepper. In large Dutch oven, heat oil over medium-high heat until hot but not smoking. Add venison cubes and brown on all sides, cooking in batches if necessary. Transfer venison to bowl as it is browned; set aside.

Add flour and carrot to pan. Cook over medium heat, stirring constantly, until oil is absorbed into flour, 2 to 3 minutes. Stir in reserved marinade, cinnamon, cloves and browned venison.

Heat to boiling. Lower heat; cover and let simmer for about 1½ hours, or until venison is very tender. Remove venison from pan. Stir sour cream into pan juices and cook, stirring constantly, for about 5 minutes; don't let the mixture boil or the sour cream will curdle. Add salt and pepper to taste.

Wild Game Lasagna Italiano

*Serves: 8 to 10 * Prep Time: 1¼ hours, mostly for sauce preparation * Cooking Time: 50 minutes*

For those who love lasanga but prefer it without all the mozzarella cheese, this is a tasty alternative. This dish is based on a recipe from a long-time friend of Peter's who served us a delicious meal while we were fishing salmon in Alaska many years ago. It was prepared compliments of an Alaskan moose that had made its way into camp—through many feet of slow— the previous hunting season.

- 1 quantity of Venison Bolognese Sauce
- 1 quantity of Bechamel Sauce
- 1 package (16 oz.) lasagna noodles
- 1¼ cups grated Parmesan cheese

Prepare sauces according to recipe directions. While sauces are simmering, cook lasagna according to package directions; drain well. Arrange drained lasagna noodles on wax paper to prevent them from sticking together.

Heat oven to 350°F. Pour a layer of Venison Bolognese Sauce into 13x9x2-inch baking dish. Top with a layer of lasagna noodles; they should touch but not overlap. Next, top with another layer of Bolognese Sauce. Follow with a thin layer of Bechamel Sauce. Sprinkle some of the Parmesan cheese over the Béchamel.

Repeat layering order until pan is almost full, ending with a layer of Parmesan cheese. Cover with foil and bake for about 30 minutes, or until bubbly. Remove foil and bake for 10 minutes longer to lightly brown the dish. Let stand for 10 minutes before serving.

This can be assembled a day ahead and refrigerated before baking. Cover with plastic wrap, then foil. Bring to room temperature, remove plastic wrap and re-cover with foil before baking.

Venison Bolognese Sauce

*Serves: 4 * Prep Time: 5 minutes *
Cooking Time: 1¼ hours*

Serve over a bed of hot linguini, topped with freshly grated Parmesan cheese and red pepper flakes. A green salad and garlic bread go well on rhe side.

- 2 onions, chopped
- 3 garlic cloves, minced
- 3 tablespoons olive oil
- 1 lb. ground venison
- 1 can (28 oz.) plum tomatoes, drained and chopped
- 1 can (6 oz.) tomato paste
- 1 teaspoon salt
- ½ teaspoon pepper
- ½ teaspoon sugar
- ½ teaspoon crumbled dried oregano
- 1 bay leaf, crumbled

In large skillet, cook onions and garlic in oil over medium heat until soft. Add venison and cook until meat is no longer pink, stirring to break up. Add tomatoes and tomato paste, and simmer for about 30 minutes. Add seasonings and cook for 30 minutes longer. Remove bay leaf before serving.

Meatloaf Parmentier

*Serves: 6 to 8 * Prep Time: 15 minutes *
Cooking Time: 1¼ hours*

*T*his is an easy meal to put together, because the potatoes roast in the same dish as the meatloaf. Pop in the Broccoli Casserole for the last hour the meatloaf bakes, and you've got the entire meal in the oven at once.

- 2 lbs. ground venison
- ⅓ cup chopped onion
- ¼ cup minced green bell pepper
- 2 cloves garlic, minced
- 1 teaspoon salt
- ½ teaspoon cumin
- ¼ teaspoon pepper
- 2 eggs
- 3 tablespoons beef broth
- 2 tablespoons Worcestershire sauce
- 1 tablespoon green Tabasco sauce
- 2 lbs. tiny new potatoes, scrubbed but not peeled
- 2 teaspoons canola oil, optional

Heat oven to 350°F. In large bowl, mix together the venison, onion, green pepper, garlic, salt, cumin and pepper. In another bowl, beat together the eggs, broth, Worcestershire sauce and Tabasco. Pour egg mixture into meat mixture, and mix gently but thoroughly. Shape into loaf and place in roasting pan that has enough room for the potatoes as well.

Peel a narrow band around each of the potatoes; this prevents the skin from splitting during roasting. If you like crisp skins, place them around the meatloaf

with no further preparation. If you like softer skins, toss potatoes with oil to lightly coat them first. Bake meatloaf and potatoes for about 1 hour. When the meatloaf is done, transfer to serving platter and let stand for about 10 minutes. If the potatoes are not quite done yet, depending upon their size, put the pan back in the oven for another 10 minutes or so.

Sicilian Venison Burgers

*Serves: 4 * Prep Time: 10 minutes *
Cooking Time: 10 minutes*

*T*hose burgers are a little smaller than my other burger recipes because they are not stuffed. Here, the delicious accompaniments go on top.

- 1¼ lbs. ground venison
- ⅓ cup fresh bread crumbs
- 2 oz. pitted black olives, finely chopped
- Salt and pepper
- 2 teaspoons canola oil*
- 2 teaspoons butter,* cut into 4 equal pieces
- 1 tablespoon olive oil
- 1 medium red onion, thinly sliced
- 1 clove garlic, minced

- 1 jar (10 oz.) artichoke hearts in oil, drained and chopped
- ¼ cup sun-dried tomato paste
- 1 teaspoon Italian herb blend
- 4 slices mozzarella cheese (1 oz. each)
- 4 club rolls, optional

In medium bowl, combine venison, bread crumbs, olives, and salt and pepper to taste. Mix gently but thoroughly, and shape into 4 flat patties (flat patties cook more evenly than rounded ones).

Heat broiler. In large skillet, heat canola oil over medium-high heat until hot but not smoking. Add patties and fry first side for about 3 minutes.

While first side is cooking, place 1 piece of the butter on top of each patty. Flip and cook the other side for about 3 minutes. While second side is cooking, heat olive oil in medium skillet over medium-high heat. Add onion and garlic and sauté until onion is soft. Add artichoke hearts and stir until they are warm.

Transfer patties to rack of broiler pan. Spread each patty with 1 tablespoon of the sun-dried tomato paste. Divide onion mixture into 4 even portions and spoon on top of patties. Sprinkle with herb blend. Place 1 cheese slice on top of each patty. Broil until cheese melts. Serve on club rolls, or sans bun.

If you are using ground venison with some type of fat added, ignore the oil and butter suggestions as you will have enough from the mixture for the pan-frying

Grilled Moose Burgers

*Serves: 4 * Prep Time: 5 minutes **
Cooking Time: 10 minutes or less

When I grill burgers, I like to use a long-handled, hinged grill basket that holds four burgers at once. These racks allow you to flip the burgers without breaking them or losing them between the grill slats.

- 1½ lbs. ground moose or venison
- 8 slices bacon, cut in half
- 4 hamburger buns, split
- Salt and pepper
- Herbed Butter or Garlic Butter for serving

Prepare grill for medium-high heat; light coals or preheat gas grill. Shape the ground venison into 4 thick patties. Place 2 half-strips of bacon on each patty and place them, bacon-side down, in hinged grill basket. Place two more half-strips on each patty and close the basket.

Grill about 4 inches from coals until bacon is crisp and burgers are done to taste, 7 to 9 minutes per side. Remove from rack. Place on buns, season with salt and pepper and top with a pat of Herbed Butter or Garlic Butter.

Grilled Stuffed Venison Burgers

*Serves: 4 * Prep Time: 5 minutes **
Cooking Time: 15 to 20 minutes

Here's a fun recipe for burgers. I like to serve them with fresh Jersey tomatoes, sans bun.

- 2 lbs. ground venison
- 1 teaspoon salt
- ¼ teaspoon pepper
- 1 small yellow onion, minced
- 2 tablespoons pickle relish
- 4 thin slices Cheddar cheese
- 2 teaspoons canola oil (approx.)

Prepare grill for medium-high heat; light coals or preheat gas grill. Season venison with salt and pepper. Mix gently but thoroughly, and shape into 8 flat patties. In small bowl, combine onion and relish. Divide onion mixture evenly among 4 of the patties, spreading out but keeping away from edges. Top each with 1 cheese slice, then with remaining patties. Seal edges well with wet fingers. Lightly brush each patty with canola oil; this will prevent them from sticking. Place in hinged grill basket and grill to desired doneness, 8 to 10 minutes per side.

Savory Doe Burgers

*Serves: 4 * Prep Time: 5 minutes *
Cooking Time: 15 to 20 minutes*

*B*efore beginning preparation of this recipe, bring all ingredients to cool room temperature. This will ensure even cooking of the burgers.

- 2 lbs. ground venison
- 4 slices bacon, cooked and finely crumbled
- ½ teaspoon salt
- ¼ teaspoon pepper
- 4 oz. Roquefort or blue cheese, room temperature
- Heavy cream as needed (1 to 2 tablespoons)
- 2 teaspoons canola oil (approx.)

Prepare grill for medium-high heat; light coals or preheat gas grill.* In medium bowl, combine

venison, bacon, salt and pepper. Mix gently but thoroughly, and shape into 4 patties.

In another small bowl, beat cheese until it reaches a smooth consistency, adding a little cream if need be. Split each patty almost in half, as though butterflying. Place ¼ of the cheese in the middle of each patty and fold back together. Seal edges well with wet fingers.

Lightly brush each patty with canola oil; this will prevent them from sticking. Place in hinged grill basket and grill to desired doneness, 8 to 10 minutes per side.

* If you prefer, you may pan-fry these burgers in a small amount of canola oil.

Venison Lasagna De Katarina

*Serves: 6 to 8 * Prep Time: 1 hour *
Cooking Time: 1 hour*

*A*nyone who has gone deer hunting with Italians knows that hunting is but a small part of the overall experience. My Italian deer-hunting husband, Pietro, introduced me to this facet of hunting early on in our relationship.

We were hunting small game with a few of his relatives. After only an hour or so of chasing rabbits, Cousin Anthony announced it was time for a break. In perfect synchronization, shotguns were unloaded and we headed back to the vehicles. As I rounded the back of one car, I detected a peculiar odor. Just then, Cousin Guido and Uncle Nunzio popped open the trunk, and to my utter surprise, they began to unpack a feast of Italian cheeses, frutti di mare (seafood salad), prosciutto, fried calamari, backed ziti, lasanga, pasta and meatballs, and shortribs and gravy. It was the longest and most delicious lunch I've had afield!

In the tradition of my family by marriage, here's a tasty vension dish that you can prepare and freeze ahead of time to take to camp.

- 3 tablespoons olive oil
- ½ cup chopped onion
- 4 cloves garlic, minced
- 1 to 1½ lbs. ground venison
- 1 can (16 oz.) plum tomatoes, undrained
- 1 tablespoon crumbled dried basil
- 1 teaspoon crumbled dried oregano
- 1 teaspoon pepper
- ½ teaspoon salt
- ¾ lb. lasagna noodles
- ¾ lb. ricotta cheese
- ¾ lb. fresh spinach leaves, cut into bite-size bits
- ½ lb. shredded mozzarella cheese
- ½ cup grated Parmesan cheese

In large skillet, heat oil over medium heat. Add onion and garlic; cook until golden, stirring occasionally. Use slotted spoon to transfer onion and garlic to bowl; set aside. Add venison to skillet and cook until no longer pink, stirring to break up. Return onion and garlic to skillet.

Place tomatoes in food processor and pulse a few times to puree them; do not let them get foamy. Add to skillet with venison. Simmer for about 15 minutes over low heat. Add basil, oregano, pepper and salt; simmer for 20 minutes longer. While sauce is simmering, cook lasagna according to package directions; drain well. Arrange drained lasagna on wax paper to prevent them from sticking together. Heat oven to 350°F. Pour a thin layer of the venison mixture into 13x9x2-inch baking dish. Top with a layer of lasagna noodles; they should touch but not overlap. Spoon one-third of the ricotta cheese onto noodles and spread evenly. Scatter half of the spinach over the ricotta. Sprinkle with one-third of the mozzarella and one-quarter of the Parmesan cheeses.

For the second layer, top cheeses with another layer of lasagna noodles. Spread half of the remaining meat sauce over the noodles. Spoon half of the remaining ricotta cheese over the sauce. Top with half of the remaining mozzarella, and one-third of the remaining Parmesan.

For the third layer, top cheeses with another layer of lasagna noodles. Top with remaining ricotta cheese, then with remaining spinach. Sprinkle with the remaining mozzarella cheese and half of the remaining Parmesan cheese. Top with a final layer of lasagna noodles. Spread remaining meat sauce over the noodles, and sprinkle with remaining Parmesan cheese. Bake for 30 to 45 minutes, or until browned and bubbly. Let stand for 10 to 15 minutes before serving.

This can be assembled a day ahead and refrigerated before baking. Cover with plastic wrap, then foil. Bring to room temperature, remove plastic wrap and re-cover with foil before baking. You may also freeze the assembled lasagna; thaw and bring to room temperature, remove plastic wrap, recover with foil and bake.

Venison Chili Tostadas

*Serves: 6 to 8 * Prep Time: 20 minutes *
Cooking Time: 20 minutes*

These are fabulous when served with a pitcher of Sangria and a side of Spanish rice.

- 1 tablespoon canola oil, divided
- 1 small onion, chopped
- ¾ lb. ground venison
- 1½ teaspoons chili powder
- ½ teaspoon cumin
- ¼ teaspoon salt
- ⅛ teaspoon pepper
- ¼ cup water

- ¼ cup retried beans
- 4 flour tortillas (6 to 7 inches in diameter)
- ¼ cup shredded Monterey Jack or sharp cheddar cheese
- ¼ cup sour cream
- 1 cup shredded fresh spinach or lettuce
- 1 cup chopped tomatoes
- 1 red onion, thinly sliced and separated into rings

Heat oven to 375°F. In medium skillet, heat 1½ teaspoons of the oil over medium heat. Add onion and saute until translucent. Add venison and cook until meat is no longer pink, stirring to break up. Drain grease. Add chili powder, cumin, salt and pepper. Mix well and cook for 1 minute longer. Add water and cook until mixture is almost dry. Add beans and mix well. Remove from heat, set aside and keep warm.

Brush tortillas lightly with the remaining 1½ teaspoons oil. Place on baking sheet and bake until crisp and golden, 8 to 10 minutes. Remove from oven.

Re-warm venison mixture if necessary; it should be hot. Divide venison mixture evenly between tortillas, spreading it evenly. Sprinkle 1 tablespoon of cheese over each. Return tortillas to oven and bake until cheese melts, about 3 to 4 minutes. Transfer tostadas to individual serving plates.

Spread 1 tablespoon sour cream in the middle of each tostada. Sprinkle shredded spinach around outside of sour cream circle. Sprinkle chopped tomatoes on top of spinach and top with red onion rings. Serve immediately.

Kate's Cooking Tips

If you've never made cabbage rolls before, here's a tip for preparing the cabbage leaves. Cut the stem off a large head of cabbage. Cut out just enough of the core so the leaves begin to separate. Gently place the head in a large pot of boiling water. Peel the leaves off as they begin to loosen. When you've peeled off enough leaves, remove the head from the water. Place the peeled leaves back in the boiling water for no more than 2 minutes. Remove and rinse under very cold water to stop the cooking. Pat dry.

Venison-Stuffed Cabbage

*Serves: 4 * Prep Time: 10 minutes *
Cooking Time: 1 hour*

My mom used to prepare this for us using a combination of ground beef, pork and veal; she even found a good use for leftover rice with this dish. Over the years, I have prepared this with straight ground venison and even a mix of venison and ground pork. Either way, it is always a delicious, filling meal with an attractive presentation.

- 1 lb. ground venison
- ¾ cup leftover cooked white rice
- 4 tablespoons minced onion
- 2 tablespoons chopped fresh parsley
- ¼ teaspoon salt
- 1/8 teaspoon cayenne pepper
- 1 clove garlic, minced
- 8 large cabbage leaves, par-blanched

- 4 teaspoons butter
- ¾ cup tomato juice, heated

Heat oven to 375°F. In medium bowl, combine venison, rice, onion, parsley, salt, cayenne and garlic; mix gently but thoroughly. Divide into 8 equal parts. Place 1 part at the base of each cabbage leaf and roll up, folding in the sides before the last turn. Secure with long wooden toothpicks.

    Place rolls in buttered baking dish. Dot each roll with ½ teaspoon butter. Pour tomato juice around rolls. Cover and bake for about 50 minutes, basting with tomato juice several times; internal temperature must be above 140°F. Remove from oven and let stand for 10 minutes before serving.

Venetian Venison Pizza Pie

*Serves: 4 ∗ Prep Time: 10 minutes ∗
Cooking Time: 15 minutes*

A few years ago, Peter and I owned an Italian restaurant with a fine dining section in the back and a unique pizza area in the front. We introduced many new pizza toppings to the community. We served 24 different types of international pizza pies including Russian pizza (with vodka sauce and peas), Polish pizza (with Kielbasa and sauerkrant) and even the All-American Pie (with sliced franks and beans). They were a hit! One of the most popular pies was the Venetian Italian Pie. On it, we had Italian suasage and a saitied Italian vegetable known as braccoli rabe, a bitter version, of the more common broccoli. If you can't find it in your grocery store, you can substitute Chinese broccoli, which has a similar flavor. Try this version of our Italian Pizza Pie—with vension!

- 1 to 2 tablespoons olive oil
- 1 clove garlic, minced
- ½ lb. broccoli rabe, trimmed
- Dough for 1 pizza crust
- ⅓ cup tomato sauce
- 1 cup shredded mozzarella cheese
- ¼ lb. venison garlic sausage or spicy venison sausage (remove casings if using links)
- 1 tablespoon grated Parmesan cheese

Heat oven to 450°F. In medium skillet, heat oil over medium-high heat. Add garlic and saute until golden. Add broccoli rabe and saute for 1 to 2 minutes. Transfer broccoli rabe to paper towel-lined plate; blotto remove excess oil. Chop coarsely.

    Place dough on pizza pan or baking sheet, shaping to fill to edges. Spread tomato sauce over dough. Top with mozzarella cheese. Crumble sausage over the cheese. Arrange broccoli rabe evenly over all. Sprinkle with Parmesan cheese. Bake for 12 to 15 minutes.

Venison Sausage

*Yield: 2¾ lbs. ∗ Prep Time: 20 minutes ∗
Cooking Time: 30 minutes*

- 2 lbs. venison meat, trimmed of all fat and connective tissue, cut into ½ x 3- inch pieces

- ¾ lb. unsalted pork fat, cut into ½ x 3- inch pieces
- 1 tablespoon brown sugar
- 2 teaspoons sea salt
- 1½ teaspoons crumbled dried sage
- ½ teaspoon black pepper
- ½ teaspoon hot red pepper flakes
- ½ teaspoon nutmeg
- ½ teaspoon cayenne pepper
- ¼ teaspoon crumbled dried rosemary
- ¼ teaspoon allspice

It will be easier to work with the fat and venison if they are well chilled. In large bowl, combine venison and fat cubes, tossing to mix. Chop or grind to coarse consistency. Return ground mixture to bowl. Add remaining ingredients. Mix with your hands until thoroughly combined.

Form sausage into patties, or use in bulk for pizza, casseroles, etc. Sausage should be kept refrigerated no longer than 3 days. If you make more than you will be using in that time, freeze bulk sausage or patties (layered with wax paper) immediately after chopping.

To prepare patties, pan-fry in nonstick skillet over medium heat until cooked completely through; if patties are frozen, thaw in refrigerator before cooking. *Note: When making sausage, everything must be as clean as possible. Wash your hands and equipment very carefully before you begin and again when you're finished. And because home-ground meat can harbor bacteria, wear clean plastic kitchen gloves if you have any abrasions or cuts.*

Sausage and Peppers Skillet

*Serves: 4 * Prep Time: 15 minutes * Cooking Time: 30 minutes*

- 1 lb. spicy venison sausage links, cut into 1-inch chunks
- 1 tablespoon canola oil, if needed
- 1 medium yellow onion, cut into 1-inch chunks
- 1 large red bell pepper, cut into 1-inch chunks
- 1 large green bell pepper, cut into 1-inch chunks
- 1 lb. small new potatoes, cut into ¼ -inch cubes
- ¾ cup water
- ⅛ teaspoon pepper

In deep skillet, cook sausage over medium heat for about 5 minutes. Remove all but 2 tablespoons fat from skillet. If you have lean sausage and don't have 2 tablespoons fat remaining, add canola oil as needed and let it heat up before proceeding.

Add onion, red and green peppers, potatoes, water and pepper to skillet. Reduce heat to low; cover and simmer for 20 to 25 minutes or until potatoes are tender, stirring occasionally. *Note: For a special presentation, serve in roasted red peppers. Cut off stems of peppers and remove seeds. Place under broiler for 5 to 7 minutes to blacken peppers while vegetables are simmering.*

New Year's Eve Rack of Venison Ribs

*Serves: 4 * Prep Time: 45 minutes *
Cooking Time: 40 minutes*

The winter holiday season is my favorite time to prepare wild game. At that time of year, I have a wide variety of vension to choose from and plenty of opportunities to prepare decorative and festive-looking wild-game dishes for family and friends.

My family's traditional meal for New Year's Eve was laden with all kinds of seafood—breaded, fried or swimming in aromatic tomato sauce. One year, however, I decided to experiment with a vension dish for the main course. Keeping with tradition, I prepared an appetizer dish with an assortment of fishes and let everyone wonder what I was going to present for the main dish.

While the vension was cooking in the oven, the piquant aroma permeated the house and I could see the anticipation growing—or was it that I heard stomachs growling!? Scrumptions is hardly the world for this mouth-watering dish, which was such a hit that we have made it an annual tradition since. I always serve this with the Rummied Sweet Potato Casserole; green peas with pearl onions add a splash of color.

- 2 racks of venison ribs (about 8 ribs each)
- 4 cups cubed white bread (you might need a little more)
- 2 cups heavy cream (you might need a little more)
- 3 tablespoons Dijon mustard
- 2 tablespoons chopped fresh parsley
- 2 tablespoons snipped fresh chives
- 2 tablespoons chopped garlic
- 1 tablespoon prepared horseradish
- Salt and pepper

Heat oven to 350°F. "French" the ribs by trimming away the scant amount of meat that surrounds the tips of the rib bones. Trim and discard all fat from the ribs as well. Cover rib tips with foil to prevent burning. Combine bread cubes, cream, mustard, parsley, chives, garlic, horseradish, and salt and pepper to taste in food processor. Process until mixture is soft and smooth. It should be neither runny nor too firm; add a little additional bread or cream as necessary to adjust texture. Coat meat side of ribs with the mixture.* Place ribs in a single layer, coating-side up, in baking dish. Bake for 30 to 40 minutes, or until internal temperature reaches about 125°F. Remove foil from rib tips. Cut ribs into portions and serve with pan juices.

*Because venison is such lean meat, the coating must cover the meat side of the ribs completely to ensure that the heat does not dry out the meat. The coating will impart a delicious seasoning to the meat as well.

Baked Moose Ale Ribs

*Serves: 4 * Prep Time: 10 minutes * Marinating Time:24 hours * Cooking Time: 2 to 2½ hours*

- 4 lbs. moose ribs
- Spicy Beer Marinade

Trim and discard all outer fat from ribs. Place ribs and marinade in large plastic container or large zipper-style plastic bag. Cover or seal, and refrigerate for 24 hours, turning ribs occasionally.

Heat oven to 275°F. Place ribs and sauce in shallow roasting pan or 9x13-inch baking dish (choose a pan that will hold ribs in single layer). Cover pan with foil and bake for 2 to 2½ hours, until the venison begins to fall off the bone.

Mouthwatering Venison

KATE FIDUCCIA

In all of the *Whitetail Strategies* books I have written, I have always included a chapter with my favorite wild game recipes prepared by my wife and hunting partner Kate. As many of you know, Kate is not only an excellent big game hunter she is also a heck of a wild game chef.

Kate has written four wild game cookbooks and is finishing two more. The recipes I selected in this chapter have been quality-controlled by yours truly and have passed my venison palate with flying colors!

They are all quick and easy to prepare and will make you the hit of deer camp or at home when you make them for family or friends. Remember that you can visit our website at www.woodsnwater.tv to get more of Kate's free wild game recipes and her gourmet sauces to share with your family or friends. Good eating!

Tex-Mex Egg Rolls

Serves: 8 (2 egg rolls each)
Prep Time: 10 minutes
1 pound ground venison
1 medium onion, finely chopped
2 cloves garlic, minced
½ cup medium salsa (preferably a smoother type such as Pace Picante)
½ teaspoon chili powder
¼ teaspoon cumin
Salt and pepper
⅔ cup shredded cheddar cheese
1 package egg-roll wraps
Vegetable oil
Sour cream and guacamole for serving, optional

In large skillet, cook venison, onion and garlic over medium heat until venison is no longer pink and onion has softened, stirring occasionally to break up meat. Drain grease. Add salsa, chili powder, cumin, and salt and pepper to taste. Simmer for about 5 minutes. Add cheese and stir until mixed thoroughly. Lay 1 egg-roll wrap on work surface; cover remaining wraps with plastic to keep them from drying out. Place a large spoonful of venison mixture on center of wrap and roll as directed on package. Place filled egg roll on platter and repeat with remaining ingredients.

Heat 2 inches oil to 375°F in deep fryer or large pot. Fry egg rolls, two at a time, until golden brown, about 2 minutes. Drain on paper towel–lined plate. Serve with sour cream and guacamole.

"Too Late" Venison Cutlet Gruyère

Serves: 6
Prep Time: 10 minutes
Cooking Time: 10 to 15 minutes

One of the fun parts of hunting is naming deer stands. We have one we call "Torn Shirt" because Peter tore his shirt while putting it up. Another is named "Big View" because the stand overlooks several fields and has a . . . big view! The "Too Late" stand is near a pine-covered ridge and got its name because once the deer reach the peak of the ridge and come out from the cover to cross to the other side, it's too late. I first prepared the following tasty recipe with a buck taken from this stand.

¼ cup all-purpose flour

Salt and pepper

2 eggs

½ cup milk

3 cups seasoned bread crumbs

¼ teaspoon garlic powder

12 venison cutlets (about 4 ounces each), pounded as needed to even thickness

½ cup olive oil (approx.)

1½ cups seasoned tomato sauce

2 large beefsteak-type tomatoes, thinly sliced

12 slices Gruyère or Swiss cheese

Heat broiler. Place flour in large plastic food-storage bag; add salt and pepper to taste and shake well to mix. In medium bowl, beat together eggs and milk. Combine bread crumbs and garlic powder in wide, flat dish and stir to mix. Blot cutlets with paper towel.

Working with one cutlet at a time, add to bag of flour and shake to coat. Tap off excess flour, then dip floured cutlet into egg mixture. Dredge in bread crumb mixture; set aside on a plate. Repeat with remaining cutlets.

In large skillet, heat about ¼-inch of the oil over medium heat until it is hot but not smoking. Fry cutlets in batches, adding additional oil as necessary, until cutlets are golden brown on both sides and not quite done to taste; transfer cutlets to sheet pan as they are browned.

In small saucepan, heat tomato sauce over low heat; cover and keep warm. Place 1 or 2 tomato slices and 1 cheese slice on top of each cutlet. Place sheet pan under broiler just long enough to melt the cheese.

Ladle about ¼ cup warm tomato sauce on each of 6 plates and place 2 cutlets on top; or, place 2 cutlets on each plate and drizzle tomato sauce around the cutlets. Serve hot.

Venison Tamale Pie

Serves: 6
Prep Time: 20 minutes
Cooking Time: 40 minutes

Here's a dish that takes a little bit of extra time because of the cornmeal crust. But it's well worth the effort! It was during a whitetail hunting trip to south Texas that I first tasted true tamales. We were hunting at the Lazy Fork Ranch and the cook prepared many dishes native to her Mexican homeland. Although I wasn't able to get the exact recipe from her, this one comes close—and I haven't had any complaints on the receiving end when I serve it!

Filling

1 tablespoon canola oil

1 pound ground venison

4 scallions, chopped

1 can (8 ounce) tomato sauce

1 cup whole-kernel corn, drained

¼ cup chopped Anaheim peppers

¼ cup cornmeal

1 teaspoon chili powder

1 teaspoon salt

½ teaspoon pepper

½ teaspoon cumin

¼ teaspoon crumbled dried oregano leaves

Cornmeal Pie Crust

1 cup all-purpose flour, plus additional for rolling
    out crust
2 tablespoons cornmeal
⅓ cup vegetable shortening
3 to 4 tablespoons cold water

Topping

1 egg, lightly beaten
¼ cup evaporated milk
½ teaspoon dry mustard
1 cup shredded Monterey Jack cheese
1 cup shredded cheddar cheese
6 pitted black olives, sliced
Heat oven to 425°F.

To prepare filling: In large skillet, heat oil over medium heat. Add venison and cook until no longer pink, stirring to break up. Drain. Mix in remaining filling ingredients. Let simmer for 5 minutes, then remove from heat.

To prepare crust: In small bowl, blend together flour and cornmeal. Cut in shortening with pastry blender or two knives. When mixture resembles coarse meal or very small peas, add water a little at a time, mixing with fork until dough is formed. Roll out pastry on floured surface until it forms a 15-inch circle. Fit pastry into deep-dish 9-inch pie pan and crimp edges.

Spoon filling into pie crust. Place pie pan on baking sheet and bake for 25 minutes. While it is baking, prepare the topping for the pie: Combine egg, milk and mustard in medium bowl; mix well. When pie has baked for 25 minutes, remove from oven, sprinkle cheeses over filling and pour milk mixture on top. Decorate with sliced olives. Return to oven and bake for an additional 5 minutes. Let stand for 10 minutes before serving. Serve with sour cream and chopped tomatoes.

Escarole Soup with Venison Meat-a-Balls

Serves: 6
Prep Time: 15 minutes
Cooking Time: 45 minutes

My mother, Lucy, introduced Kate to many different Foodstuffs—escarole, broccoli rabe, scungilli and calamari, to name a few. She often reminded her about the way many Italian dishes are prepared: "Use garlic, garlic and more garlic." Both her escarole and broccoli rabe dishes started by sautéing plenty of garlic; the greens were added as the garlic was cooking. After this, chicken broth was added to finish cooking the greens.

When Kate shared with her this venison version of her Meatball Escarole Soup, she was quite pleased, and Kate was happy that she had passed her test. Then she cautiously whispered in her ear, "But next time, use a little more garlic!"

½ cup bread crumbs
½ cup milk
1 pound ground venison
1 egg, beaten
2 tablespoons grated Parmesan cheese, plus
    additional for serving
1 tablespoon chopped fresh parsley
7 cloves garlic, minced, divided salt and pepper
3 tablespoons olive oil
1 pound escarole, washed and chopped
4 cans (14½ ounces each) chicken broth
Italian bread for accompaniment, optional

In medium bowl, mix together bread crumbs and milk; let stand for about 5 minutes. Add venison, egg, Parmesan cheese, parsley, half of the garlic, and salt and pepper to taste. Mix well. Shape into small meatballs (small enough to fit on a spoon and pop into your mouth) and place on a plate. Cover and refrigerate while you prepare the rest of the soup mixture.

Kate takes a break in our kitchen where she often "Goes Wild" with her delicious cooking!

In large saucepot or Dutch oven, heat oil over medium-high heat. Add remaining garlic and sautl until golden; do not let it brown. Stir in escarole and continue sautleing until escarole has wilted down. Add chicken broth. Cover pot and simmer for about 30 minutes. Gently add meatballs to the simmering broth. Leave them untouched for a few minutes so they can set, then stir gently and continue simmering for 7 to 10 minutes longer, until the meatballs are cooked through. I always sample a meatball at about 7 minutes to see if it's done yet.

Serve hot, with grated Parmesan cheese and Italian bread.

Horseradish Cream Sauce

Yield: 1 cup
Prep Time: 10 minutes
Chilling Time: 1 hour or longer

This makes a great dipping sauce for fondue, and also works well as a side for roasts or steaks.

1 cup heavy cream
2 scallions, minced
2 tablespoons fresh
grated horseradish
¼ teaspoon paprika
⅛ teaspoon salt

In large bowl, whip cream until soft peaks form. Stir in scallions, horseradish, paprika and salt. Transfer to glass bowl and chill for 1 hour or longer to allow flavors to blend before serving.

Hunter's Sauce

This classic sauce is delicious with venison roasts and pan-fried steaks.

Yield: 2 cups

Prep Time: 35 minutes

3 tablespoons butter

1½ teaspoons vegetable oil

10 ounces fresh mushrooms, cut into quarters

3 shallots, minced

2 tablespoons all-purpose flour

1 tablespoon finely chopped scallion

2 tablespoons brandy

Salt and pepper to taste

½ cup dry white wine

1 cup brown sauce or canned beef gravy

2 tablespoons tomato sauce

1 teaspoon finely chopped fresh parsley

In small saucepan, melt butter in oil over medium heat. Add mushrooms and shallots and sauté until golden brown. Stir in the flour to absorb the juices. Add scallion, brandy, and salt and pepper to taste. Cook over low heat for 2 minutes. Add wine and simmer until liquid is reduced by half. Add brown sauce, tomato sauce and parsley. Heat until sauce starts to bubble, stirring occasionally. Pour into serving dish and serve hot.

Memorable Meals from Premier Wild Chefs

KATE FIDUCCIA

Over the eighteen years that l have been co-host of the Woods N' Water Outdoorsman's Edge television series, I have been fortunate enough to travel throughout North America to hunt a variety of big game. Not only have I been able to enjoy some of the most exhilarating hunting opportunities a hunter could hope for, but I have been exposed to an added bonus as well: the home-cooked wild-game dishes of each outfitter I hunted with.

Some of these memorable meals were prepared by seasoned wild-game chefs in unique, five-star lodges, and some equally as unforgettable were prepared by camp chefs in cook tents located hours by horseback from civilization. Whether in a commercial kitchen or with the barest of essentials, each chef showed the same inspiration in preparing wild- game meals for their guests.

The meals I enjoyed on these hunts have proved, to me, to be as important as the hunt itself, and they solidified in my mind that for most hunters, preparing and eating wild game is as much a tradition as the hunt itself. Wild game cooking is—in the end—the element that binds the hunt and the eating of game together. Both would be less without the other. Following are some of my favorite outfitter recipes.

> *Any sportsman who can kill his deer without the tingling spine, the quick clutch at his heart, the delicious trembling of nerve fibers when the game is finally down, has no place in the deer woods.*
> —*Lawrence R. Koller,* Shots at Whitetails *(1948)*

Anticosti Outfitters Braised Deer

Serves: 12 to 15

Prep time: 15 minutes

Cooking Time: 2¾ hours

The recipe for this delicious braise was graciously provided by the chef at Anticosti Outfitters, and reflects the fine culinary tradition of this lodge.

5-lb. venison roast

¼ cup butter

2 carrots, chopped

1 large onion, chopped

Salt, pepper and garlic powder

1 can (14½ oz.) beef broth

⅓ cup red wine

2 tablespoons all-purpose flour

Heat oven to 325°F. Pat roast dry. In Dutch oven, melt butter over medium-high heat. When it stops sizzling, add roast and brown well on all sides. Transfer roast to plate; set aside.

Add carrots and onion to Dutch oven and cook for 3 to 4 minutes. Season roast with salt, pepper

Safari Anticosti Outfitters

Emerging from the prehistoric Champlain Sea, the 3,200-square-mile Anticosti Island spreads across the entry to the majestic Gulf of St. Lawrence. In 1895 the French chocolate magnate Henri Menier bought Anticosti Island for $125,000. He went on to invest another 5 million dollars to turn his island into a paradise. In 1974 it was sold to the Quebec Government for 26 million dollars. In 1984 Anticosti Outfitters Inc., which is owned by Jean Gagnon, obtained an exclusive lease of 400 square miles on the southeastern sector of the island from the government. This area has an estimated population of 15,000 white-tailed deer! The rest is history. Safari Anticosti Outfitters has developed the most prestigious deer-hunting grounds in the province of Quebec, investing over 12 million dollars along the way to accomplish its goal.

I was first invited to hunt at Safari Anticosti Outfitters in 1990. Besides getting my two whitetails, I also had the rare opportunity to see seals, whales and uncountable numbers of birds in a variety of colors. The accommodations were top-shelf, but what really impressed me was the food. After each day's hunt, the guests would gather at the log lodge, which was perched on the edge of a sandy cliff overlooking the Atlantic Ocean and mouth of the St. Lawrence Seaway. There, with white-linen table service, we dined on five-course French gourmet cuisine including smoked salmon and oyster appetizers, fine French wine, melon soup, prime rib and mouth-watering homemade desserts. Peter has hunted with Anticosti Outfitters several times since and assures me that with each passing year the hunting, service, and food only get better.

(450) 359-1113

www.safarianticosti.com

and garlic powder to taste, and return to Dutch oven. Add broth. Cover and bake for 1½ hours.

Add wine and bake for about 1 hour longer, or until roast is cooked to your liking. Transfer roast to serving plate; tent with foil and set aside for 10 to 15 minutes. Meanwhile, sprinkle flour into juices in Dutch oven, whisking constantly; cook over medium heat until thickened. Serve gravy with roast.

Jean-Marie Chretien, General Manager
Safari Anticosti

Sun Canyon Ranch Crock-Pot Pepper Steak

Serves: 6 to 8
Prep Time: 15 minutes
Cooking Time: 10 to 11 hours
For a great meal, serve this stew over grilled polenta slices or corn bread.

2 lbs. venison steak (deer or elk)
½ cup all-purpose flour
2 tablespoons canola oil (approx.)
1 can (14½ oz.) tomatoes, undrained
2 green bell peppers, sliced
1 large onion, sliced
6 oz. fresh mushrooms, sliced
3 tablespoons soy sauce
3 tablespoons molasses
Salt and pepper

Cut steak into strips and dredge with flour. In medium skillet, heat oil over medium-high heat until hot but not smoking. Brown venison strips in small batches, transferring to slow cooker as they are browned.

In small bowl, combine tomatoes, peppers, onion, mushrooms, soy sauce, molasses, and salt and pepper to taste. Mix well. Pour mixture over venison. Cover and cook on HIGH for 1 hour, then reduce heat to LOW and cook for 9 to 10 hours longer.

Susan and Lee Carlbom
Sun Canyon Lodge, Augusta, MT

Lucky Star Ranch Venison Stew

Serves: 6
Prep Time: 20 minutes
Cooking Time: 2 hours

Sun Canyon Ranch

I first met Lee and Susan Carlbom in 1987. Their outfit is uniquely western, invoking a true feeling of wilderness hunting. Located in the eastern gateway to the Lewis and Clark Forest and the unique Bob Marshall Wilderness Area, Sun Canyon Ranch provides excellent hunting opportunities for both mule deer and elk. It also gives clients a chance to revitalize their spirit as they venture into the last of the true mountain wilderness areas of the continental United States. What struck me most about this facility is that no matter where we were, either at the lodge or in the wilderness, Lee and Susan somehow managed to prepare delicious meals indigenous to the West.

1-888-749-3654

www.suncanyonlodge.com

Tuckamore Lodge Salisbury Moose Steak with Mushroom Sauce

Serves: 4

Prep Time: 15 Minutes

Cooking Time: 15 Minutes

With this recipe, Peggy Mitchelmore turns what seems like just another Salisbury steak recipe into something quite memorable. Serve this with baked potatoes and green beans or steamed broccoli.

We serve this stew with sour cream, baguettes and a nice fresh green salad. It is an ideal menu for a large crowd, because the stew can be prepared beforehand and gently reheated just before serving.

2 lbs. venison stew cubes

1½ cups all-purpose flour

1 tablespoon butter

1 tablespoon oil

Salt, pepper, paprika and chili powder

4 onions, cut into quarters

1 or 2 cans (14½ oz. each) tomatoes, undrained

1 cup heavy cream, or a little more as needed

½ cup ketchup

½ cup red wine, or a little more as needed

1 package (2.4 oz.) Knorr goulash mix, optional

Tomato juice, optional

Pat venison cubes dry; dust with flour. In large skillet, melt butter in oil over medium-high heat. Brown venison cubes in small batches, transferring to Dutch oven or stockpot as it is browned. Season browned venison with salt, pepper, paprika and chili powder to taste. Add onions, tomatoes, cream, ketchup and wine, and goulash mix if using. Cover Dutch oven. Simmer for 2 hours, stirring every 30 minutes; make sure stew meat is always covered with liquid, adding more cream (at room temperature), wine or tomato juice, depending upon your taste.

Baron Josef von Kerckerinck

Lucky Star Ranch, Chaumont, NY

Lucky Star Ranch

As the founder of the North American Deer Farmer's Association, Baron Josef von Kerckerinck knows a lot about deer. On his stately 5,000-acre Lucky Star Ranch in upstate New York, Josef has raised and managed all types of game—European red stag, fallow deer and a host of other non-native deer. Over the last several years, he has been steadily convening the ranch to a strictly white-tailed deer hunting ranch. A native of Germany, Josef brings the European aspect to all his client's hunts with true European shooting houses for the hunt and, most importantly, European-style meals for the guests.

There are few that can come close to Josef's hospitality at his multi-faceted facility. He has always made my family and me feel more than welcome whenever we visit. Over the years, Peter and I have enjoyed great deer hunting at the Lucky Star, and it was here that my son Cody, at the age of nine, shot his first deer—a memory we'll cherish forever.

(315) 649-5519 at www.luckystarranch.com

Patties

1 lb. ground moose
¾ cup cracker crumbs
1 tablespoon Worcestershire sauce
½ teaspoon onion powder
½ teaspoon steak spice
½ teaspoon salt
¼ teaspoon pepper
¼ teaspoon garlic powder

Sauce

2 tablespoons butter
1 can (8 oz.) mushrooms, drained and chopped
2 tablespoons all-purpose flour
1 teaspoon curry powder
1 cup hot water
1 beef bouillon cube

In a bowl, combine all patty ingredients. Mix gently but thoroughly. Divide evenly and shape into 4 patties.

In small saucepan, melt butter over medium heat. Add mushrooms and sauté for 2 to 3 minutes. Blend in flour and curry powder. Add hot water and bouillon cube. Cook, stirring constantly, until smooth and thickened.

While sauce is thickening, either pan-fry or grill the patties for 2 to 3 minutes per side. Pour sauce over each patty and serve.

Peggy Mitchelmore
Tuckamore Lodge
Main Brook, Newfoundland

Conklin's Lodge Venison Roll-Ups

Serves: 8 to 10 as appetizers, 4 to 6 as main dish
Prep Time: 15 Minutes
Cooking Time: 10 Minutes
2 lbs. boneless venison steaks

Barb Genge is the president and owner of Tuckamore Lodge, a first-class operation with Scandinavian-style accommodations in the heart of rugged Newfoundland wilderness. Whether you are there to whale-watch, observe towering icebergs, visit the ancient Viking settlements, or, as we were, to hunt moose, you will experience Tuckamore's hospitality and professionalism. This facility is world renowned in adventure tourism and is recognized as one of the six best lodges in all of Canada. Guests are treated to three sit-down meals a day in the luxurious comfort of the main log cabin lodge. Prepared by a culinary staff headed by Peggy Mitchelmore, each meal, especially dinner, is exquisitely prepared and scrumptious. During our stay, we dined on meals fit for a king, as well as a wide array of fabulous desserts like Death by Chocolate and Gooseberry Pie. Peter and I hunted moose with Barb on two occasions and came home with enough moose meat to try many of the moose recipes the staff so generously shared with us.

1-888-865-6361

www.tuckamore-lodge.nf.net

Garlic powder, salt and pepper
1 lb. sliced bacon

Slice steaks across the grain into ¼-inch-thick strips. Arrange strips in a single layer on work surface. Sprinkle the tops with garlic powder, salt and pepper to taste. Roll each slice jelly-roll-style with the seasoned side in. Wrap each roll with a portion of bacon, trimming bacon according to the thickness of the roll, and secure with a wooden toothpick. Cook rolls in skillet over medium heat

Conklin's Lodge and Camps

Located in the gorgeous deep woods at the north entrance to Baxter State Park (which boasts nearly 205,000 acres of wilderness), Conklin's Lodge and Camps offers excellent year-round hunting, fishing and outdoor activities. Registered Maine Guide Lester Conklin and his wife, Marie, have been operating their lodge since 1987. In addition to highly successful guided bear and white-tailed deer hunts, guests of Conklin's also enjoy pursuing grouse, woodcock, snowshoe hare or even winter coyotes, with or without a guide. Whether you're with a top-notch guide or you adventure out on your own, you'll feel the true spirit of the deep northern backwoods in this area. While on stand, you may see moose, bobcat, lynx, red fox, marten or even a fisher. When you return to camp, you'll be treated to one of Marie's delicious meals, which include favorites such as glazed baked ham, roast pork with gravy, homemade lasagna and stuffed Cornish hen.

(207) 528-2901 at www.conklinslodge.com

until bacon is cooked, turning to cook evenly. Remove toothpicks before serving.

Marie Conklin
Conklin's Lodge and Camps, Patten, ME

Cedar Ridge Outfitters Red Stroganoff

Serves: 8 to 10
Prep Time: 10 minutes
Cooking time: 3 to 4 hours
Here's one of Debbie Blood's camp favorites. Serve it with a heaping bowl of hot white rice.
3 tablespoons vegetable oil (approx.)
3 lbs. boneless venison, cut into ¾-inch cubes
2 cans (14½ oz. each) whole tomatoes, drained, juices reserved

Cedar Ridge Outfitters

Hal and Debbie Blood own Cedar Ridge Outfitters. They have been successfully guiding deer, moose and bear hunters in the woods around Jackman, Maine for 20 years. Deer hunting at Cedar Ridge is typical of Maine. You don't see a lot of deer every day, nor bucks in a week. But when you do see a buck, more often than not it's a dandy!

Peter and I first met Hal in the mid-'80s, and later got to know his wife, Debbie. She is a licensed and expert Maine guide who also commands the base operation. On our last visit, we thoroughly enjoyed both the Bloods' hospitality and some of the finest home-cooked meals I have had the pleasure of eating. All meals are served family-style, and Debbie always makes sure they're served piping hot and delicious.

(207) 668-4169 at www.cedarridgeoutfitters.com

Cedar Ridge Outfitters Red Stroganoff

2 cans (14½ oz. each) beef consommé

4 cans (8 oz. each) tomato sauce

2 cups sliced fresh mushrooms

1 large onion, sliced

1 green bell pepper, sliced

Heat oven to 350°F. In large skillet, heat 1 tablespoon of the oil over medium-high heat until hot but not smoking. Brown venison cubes in small batches, adding additional oil as necessary. Transfer venison to a Dutch oven as it is browned.

When all venison has been browned, slice drained tomatoes and add to Dutch oven with venison. Add remaining ingredients including reserved tomato juice; stir gently. Cover and bake for 2 hours, then check consistency. If the mixture seems to have too much liquid, remove the lid before continuing; if the mixture seems too thick, stir in a little water and recover. If the venison is tender at this point, bake for 1 hour longer; if it is a little tough, bake for 2 hours longer, or until venison is tender.

Debbie and Hal Blood

Cedar Ridge Outfitters, Jackman, ME

Legends Ranch Herbed Venison Rolls

Serves: 5 to 8

Prep Time: 1¼ Hours

Cooking Time: 30 Minutes

When we visited, the side dishes served with this entrée included basil pesto-stuffed tortellini with tomato sauce, fresh steamed asparagus spears and a fresh garden salad. The recipe below has been halved for home use.

Cheese Filling

8 oz. cream cheese, softened

3 large cloves garlic, minced

1½ teaspoons Italian herb blend

¾ cup shredded mozzarella cheese

2 small eggs, beaten

Jalapeno pepper, minced

2- to 3-lb. boneless venison sirloin tip or tender rump roast, well trimmed

Breading

3 cups all-purpose flour

¼ cup seasoning blend of your choice (if using seasoned salt, use a lower-sodium type)

1½ cups Italian-seasoned bread crumbs

4 eggs, beaten

½ cup milk

Make the cheese filling: in glass bowl, combine cream cheese, garlic and herbs; mix well. Add remaining filling ingredients; mix until creamy. Reserve in refrigerator.

Prepare the venison: Cut roast across the grain into ¾-inch-thick steaks. You should get 5 to 8 steaks, depending upon the size of the roast. Place steaks on lightly oiled work surface (the oil prevents the meat from sticking). Place plastic wrap over steaks to prevent splattering. Gently pound steaks with tenderizing mallet to about ⅛-inch thickness. At this point, each steak should be about 6 inches in diameter.

Place a large spoonful of the chilled cheese filling on a steak, an inch from the edge nearest you; use only as much filling as the steak can hold. Fold the sides of the steak over the filling. Then, roll up the steak jelly-roll-style and place, seam-side down, in a single layer on a sheet pan. When all rolls are complete, place in freezer for about 20 minutes to harden the cheese.

While rolls are in the freezer, combine flour and seasoning in food processor and pulse to mix well; alternately, stir together in large bowl. Place flour mixture in large pan. Place bread crumbs in a separate pan. Mix eggs with milk and place in shallow container.

Heat oven to 275°F. Remove venison rolls from freezer and let stand for about 5 minutes, which will allow the meat to "sweat" prior to being breaded. Coat each venison roll with the flour mixture, then place in egg wash and coat well. Roll in bread-crumbs and set aside.

In deep skillet over high heat, melt enough shortening to cover several rolls; heat shortening to 350°F. Fry rolls, a few at a time, for about 1 minute each. This will seal the meat and turn the crust a light golden brown. Transfer rolls to a jelly-roll pan (large baking sheet with sides) as they are fried. When all have been fried, place pan in oven for 10 to 15 minutes, until rolls are a rich brown.

John Eye
Legends Ranch, Bitely, MI

Legends Ranch

Legends Ranch is owned and operated by Skipper Bettis and Keith Johnson. Between them, they have nearly 75 years of deer-hunting experience. The deer hunting at this ranch is truly legendary. My son, Cody (who was 11 at the time), and I were invited to hunt at Legends Ranch in 2000. We both shot terrific 8-point bucks and saw some real wall hangers during our hunt, too.

Lodging and meals at the Legends Ranch are as outstanding as the hunting. Chef John Eye treats all guests to gourmet meals you would normally find at the finer restaurants across the country. During our stay, Chef Eye and I had many conversations about his experiences as a professional chef, and his love for preparing wild game. During these conversations I decided that one of John's wild-game recipes would be a valued addition to this book.

(231) 745-8000 at www.legendsranch.com

Whale River Lodge Caribou Stroganoff

Serves: 4
Prep Time: 10 Minutes
Cooking Time: 2 hours

The head chef at Whale River shared many caribou recipes with me, and I have used them to prepare meat from the two trophy-class bulls I took at the camp. The recipe that has received the most acclaim is this delicious caribou stroganoff. Serve over cooked rice or noodles, accompanied by a salad.

2 lbs. caribou steak
2 tablespoons butter
4 cups water
1 package (1 oz.) onion soup mix
2 tablespoons chopped fresh parsley

1½ teaspoons garlic powder
¼ teaspoon crumbled dried oregano
Pepper
½ cup sour cream
¼ cup cornstarch

Cut steak into 1-inch cubes. In Dutch oven, brown cubes in butter over medium-high heat. Add water, onion soup mix, parsley, garlic powder, oregano, and pepper to taste; stir well. Heat to boiling. Reduce heat to low and cook for about 1½ hours, stirring occasionally. When caribou is tender, remove about 2 tablespoons of the liquid from the Dutch oven and stir into the sour cream, along with the cornstarch; this raises the temperature of the sour cream to prevent curdling. Stir sour cream mixture into liquid in Dutch oven and cook, stirring frequently, until sauce thickens.

Alain Tardif
Whale River Lodge Outfitters, northern Quebec, Canada

Midwest Venison Casserole

Serves: 6 to 8
Prep Time: 15 minutes
Cooking Time: 1¼ to 1¾ hours

The home-cooked meals at Midwest USA are just as memorable as the hunting. I have made this recipe several times for family and guests. Every single guest has asked me for the recipe. So, here it is.

2 lbs. ground venison
One-quarter of a medium onion, diced
4 cans (10¾ oz. each) condensed cream of
    mushroom soup
1 bag (24 oz.) frozen vegetable of your choice
1 bag (32 oz.) frozen Tater Tots

Whale River Lodge

The vast openness of the northern Canadian tundra is both beautiful and stark. Across thousands of miles each year, a distant cousin of the white-tailed deer makes its annual trek. Alain Tardif, owner of Whale River Lodge, has been in the caribou outfitting business for 30 years and has mastered the secret of bringing clients to the areas where the caribou are. On top of that, he has built and staffed lodges that cater to every hunter's needs in areas that are so remote, the only population is native Inuits. I knew we would be traveling far into northern Quebec, but it wasn't until we traveled by jet plane for 2½ hours north of Montreal, then flew by floatplane for another 2 hours, that I realized how far north we were really going! How they get the equipment needed, especially for the kitchen, to these remote places is mind-boggling. But, according to Alain, having the comforts of home is all-important to the hunt, especially when it comes to mealtime.

(800) 463-4868 at www.whaleriverlodge.com

Midwest USA

As most deer hunters know, Iowa is among the top states in the nation for bagging a trophy-class whitetail buck. Rod Hughes owns Midwest USA Outfitters in Cantril, in the southeastern portion of the state. The whitetail hunting here is exciting because a hunter never knows when the next Iowa Boone & Crockett record-book buck will walk into the sights. I always enjoy hunting in Iowa because of this anticipation.

(888) 530-8492

Heat oven to 375°F. In large skillet, cook venison and onion over medium heat until venison is no longer pink and onion has softened, stirring occasionally to break up meat. Drain any fat. Spread venison on bottom of 9 x 13 x 2-inch baking dish. Spread 2 cans of the undiluted soup over venison. Next, distribute frozen vegetables on top. Spread remaining 2 cans of undiluted soup over vegetables. Finally, top with frozen Tater Tots. Cover with foil and bake for 45 minutes. Uncover and bake for 15 to 30 minutes longer. Let sit for about 10 minutes before serving.

Rodney Hughes
Midwest USA Outfitters, Cantril, Iowa

Hunter's Sauce

Yield: 2 cups
Prep Time: 35 Minutes
This classic sauce is delicious with venison roasts
    and pan-fried steaks.

3 tablespoons butter
1½ teaspoons vegetable oil
10 oz. fresh mushrooms, out into quarters
3 shallots, minced
2 tablespoons all-purpose flour
1 tablespoon finely chopped scallion
2 tablespoons brandy
Salt and pepper
½ cup dry white wine
1 cup brown sauce or canned beef gravy
2 tablespoons tomato sauce
1 teaspoon finely chopped fresh parsley

In small saucepan, melt butter in oil over medium heat. Add mushrooms and shallots and sauté until golden brown. Stir in the flour to absorb the juices. Add scallion, brandy, and salt and pepper to taste. Cook over low heat for 2 minutes. Add wine and simmer until liquid is reduced by half. Add brown sauce, tomato sauce and parsley. Heat until sauce starts to bubble, stirring occasionally. Pour into serving dish and serve hot.

Game Accompaniments

As a lifelong lover and reader of cookbooks, I am always trying the latest recipes, experimenting with new ingredients or tweaking old recipes. Sometimes, when I'm trying to come up with a side dish for a new recipe, nothing hits me right away. That's why I like those cookbooks that include a section on side dishes. I often think, "Well, if this is one of the author's favorites, it should be good enough for me!"

So, here are some of my favorite side dishes to serve with venison. Some, such as the Wild Rice Casserole or the Broccoli Casserole, can be placed

Oh give me a home where the buffalo roam, Where the deer and the antelope play, Where seldom is heard a discouraging word, and the skies are not cloudy all day.

—Dr. Brewster Higley (19th Century)

in the oven alongside a roast; others, such as the Brown Rice Salad or Corn Relish, can be made in the morning to be served at lunch or dinner time.

Fusilli Salad

Serves: 6
Prep Time: 15 Minutes
Cooking Time: 15 Minutes
1 tablespoon plus 1½ teaspoons salt
1 lb. fusilli pasta
1½ lbs. plum tomatoes, seeded and chopped
1 small red onion, minced
3 fresh basil leaves, chopped
2 cloves garlic, minced
12 black olives, sliced
1 cup julienned romaine lettuce
½ cup olive oil
Salt and freshly ground pepper
2 tablespoons grated Parmesan cheese

In stockpot or Dutch oven, combine salt and 4 quarts cold water. Heat to boiling over high heat. Add pasta and cook until al dente according to package directions; stir frequently to prevent sticking.

While pasta is cooking, combine tomatoes, onion, basil, garlic, olives, lettuce and olive oil. Toss to coat well. Season to taste with salt and pepper.

Kate's Grilling Tips

My favorite way to grill corn is to remove some of the outer corn husks and slightly open the inner husks to remove the silk. Then I spread butter (or margarine) on the corn and close the husks around the corn again. I wrap each ear of corn in heavy-duty aluminum foil and twist the ends.

Then I place the ears on the grill for about 20 to 30 minutes, turning frequently. I season with salt and pepper once they are cooked and the husks are removed.

* * * *

If you love eggplant, try this grilled recipe. Peel eggplant (small ones are more tasty than larger ones) and cut off the ends. Cut into slices about 1 inch thick, but don't cut all the way through the bottom (as you might slice a loaf of garlic bread). Between the slices, add a little butter, salt, pepper, oregano and thin slices of mozzarella cheese and tomato. Wrap tightly in foil. Grill for about 20 minutes, turning every 5 to 7 minutes.

When pasta is al dente, drain in colander and rinse with cold water; drain well. Combine with vegetable mixture and toss to mix thoroughly. Garnish with Parmesan cheese and serve immediately.

Broccoli Casserole

Serves: 6
Prep Time: 10 Minutes
Cooking Time: 55 Minutes

I usually serve this side dish with roasts, since it can cook in the same oven as most roast recipes.

3 eggs

1½ cups light cream

½ teaspoon dry mustard

½ teaspoon salt

¼ teaspoon pepper

2 cups chopped cooked broccoli

1 cup shredded cheddar cheese

Heat oven to 350°F. Lightly grease medium casserole or glass baking dish; set aside. In medium bowl, lightly beat eggs. Add cream, mustard, salt and pepper; mix well. Add broccoli and cheese; stir to combine. Pour broccoli mixture into prepared baking dish. Place baking dish into a larger baking pan. Pour hot water into larger pan to reach halfway up sides of baking dish. Bake for 45 to 55 minutes, or until mixture is set. Serve warm.

Pungent Caramelized Onions

Serves: 12

Prep Time: 5 Minutes

Cooking Time: 2 ½ hours

These go well with steaks, medallions and roasts.

¼ cup plus 1 tablespoon olive oil, divided

7 large onions (about ½ lb. each)

½ teaspoon salt

2 tablespoons red wine vinegar

Heat oven to 325°F. Brush 1 teaspoon of the oil on shallow-sided baking sheet. Slice onions into quarters, leaving skin on. Place onions, skin-side down, on prepared baking sheet. Brush with one-quarter of the remaining oil, and sprinkle with the salt. Cover baking sheet with foil and bake for 30 minutes.

---

*You don't have to use white pepper. I use it to make the dish look nicer. Black pepper will work just as well.

Uncover; brush onions with one-third of the remaining oil, and sprinkle with the vinegar. Turn onions so the outside is down. Bake for 1 hour longer. Brush with half of the remaining oil and turn onions again. Bake for 1 hour longer; brush with remaining oil before serving.

Cheesy Garlic Mashed Potatoes

Serves: 6 to 8

Prep Time: 15 Minutes

Cooking Time: 25 Minutes

1 head garlic

3 lbs. baking potatoes, peeled and quartered

1½ teaspoons salt, divided

½ cup unsalted butter (1 stick), melted

1 cup shredded cheddar cheese

½ cup heavy cream, room temperature

1 teaspoon white pepper*

Separate and peel the garlic cloves, then crush them gently with the side of a large, heavy knife. In large saucepan or Dutch oven, combine potatoes, garlic, and 1 teaspoon of the salt. Add water to cover. Heat to boiling over high heat; reduce heat and simmer until potatoes are tender, about 20 minutes. Drain in colander. Press potatoes and garlic through ricer or food mill.

Place hot potatoes in large bowl and beat in butter and cheddar cheese.

Gradually mix in cream, pepper and remaining ½ teaspoon salt. Serve hot.

Corn Relish

Serves: 6

Prep Time: 10 Minutes

Chilling Time: 2 hours

I like to serve this as a side dish with burgers during the late summer when corn is at its peak!

3 tablespoons white wine vinegar

2 tablespoons sugar

1 teaspoon salt

½ cup canola oil

1½ cups cooked whole-kernel corn, prepared from
    fresh or frozen

½ cup sliced celery

¼ cup pickle relish, drained

¼ cup diced red bell pepper

¼ cup chopped scallions

In small jar with lid, combine vinegar, sugar and salt. Cover and shake until salt and sugar dissolve. Add oil; re-cover and shake well to blend.

In medium bowl, combine corn, celery, pickle relish, pepper and scallions. Mix well. Pour dressing over the top and mix again. Cover and refrigerate mixture for at least 2 hours. This relish can be made a day ahead.

Brown Rice Salad

Serves: 6
Prep Time: 10 Minutes
Cooking Time: 1 hour
Chilling Time: 1 hour

> **Kate's Cooking Tips**
>
> *When preparing a large meal with many side dishes, get your serving dishes out ahead of time and label them accordingly. I write "potatoes," "gravy," "mushrooms," "venison roast," etc., on small pieces of paper and place them into each dish. This way, all my serving dishes are out and ready when the time comes to plate. There is no confusion (amidst entertaining your guests) as to what goes where when it's hot and ready to be served.*
>
> *Remember to taste your dish just before serving. This is the last time you can adjust the seasoning.*

1 cup brown rice

2¼ cups water

1 teaspoon butter

¼ cup canola oil

¼ cup red wine vinegar

1 teaspoon balsamic vinegar

1 teaspoon salt

¾ teaspoon sugar

½ teaspoon dried dill weed

1 cup cooked whole-kernel corn, prepared from
    frozen

1 cup cooked peas, prepared from fresh or frozen

Combine rice, water and butter in medium saucepan. Heat to boiling; stir once and cover. Reduce heat and simmer for 45 minutes. Remove from heat and let stand, covered, for 5 to 10 minutes. Fluff with fork and transfer to large bowl. Let stand until cool.

In small bowl, combine oil, vinegars, salt, sugar and dill. Mix well. When rice has cooled, add corn and peas to rice and toss to mix well. Pour dressing over mixture and toss to mix well. Cover and refrigerate mixture for at least 1 hour. This salad can be made a day ahead.

Rummed Sweet Potato Casserole

Serves: 4
Prep Time: 15 Minutes
Cooking Time: 40 Minutes
1½ cups thinly sliced apples
4 cooked medium sweet potatoes, thinly sliced
½ cup light brown sugar
Cinnamon and allspice to taste
¼ cup butter, cut up
¼ cup light rum
¼ cup water

Heat oven to 350°F. Heat medium saucepan of water to boiling. Add apple slices and cook for about 2 minutes. Drain and rinse with cold water. Lightly grease medium casserole or glass baking dish. Fill dish with alternating layers of potatoes and apples, sprinkling each layer with brown sugar, cinnamon and allspice. Dot top with butter. Mix rum and water and pour over the top. Cover casserole with foil and bake for 40 minutes. Serve warm.

Wild Rice Casserole

Serves: 6
Prep Time: 10 Minutes
Cooking Time: 2 hours
¾ cup uncooked wild rice
¼ cup uncooked brown rice
2 stalks celery, chopped
¼ cup chopped onion
1 quart chicken broth
½ cup white wine
2 tablespoons butter
Salt and pepper

Heat oven to 350°F. In medium bowl, mix together the rices, celery, and onion. Transfer to casserole. Add chicken broth, wine, butter, and salt and pepper to taste; stir gently to combine. Cover and bake for 2 hours.

Roasted Herbed New Potatoes

Serves: 8
Prep Time: 10 Minutes
Cooking Time: 1 hour
2 lbs. small new potatoes (red bliss, fingerling, banana)
2 onions, out into chunks
⅓ cup olive oil
¼ cup butter, melted
¼ teaspoon crumbled dried thyme
¼ teaspoon crumbled dried rosemary
¼ teaspoon crumbled dried marjoram
½ teaspoon salt
¼ teaspoon pepper

Heat oven to 425°F. Combine all ingredients except salt and pepper in medium mixing bowl. Toss to coat. Transfer to large roasting pan and bake until potatoes are done, about 1 hour, turning potatoes every 15 minutes with wooden spoon. Season with salt and pepper before serving.

Summertime Vegetable Pie

Serves: 6
Prep Time: 25 Minutes
Cooking Time: 45 Minutes

When vegetables are fresh from the garden, this dish is at its most piquant. My grandmother used to prepare this, and I now serve it with venison burgers, grilled steaks or shish kabobs.

1 medium eggplant, peeled and cubed*
2 medium zucchini, cubed*
1 large onion, chopped
¼ cup canola oil
4 medium tomatoes, peeled, cored, and chopped
3 large eggs
1 cup grated Parmesan cheese, divided
1 tablespoon minced fresh parsley
½ teaspoon crumbled dried basil
½ teaspoon crumbled dried oregano
Salt and pepper
⅓ lb. shredded mozzarella cheese (about 1⅓ cups)

Heat oven to 350°F. Lightly grease a pie plate or baking dish; set aside. In large skillet, sauté eggplant, zucchini and onion in oil over medium heat until vegetables are soft. Add tomatoes; cover and simmer for about 15 minutes. Transfer to large bowl; set aside to cool.

In medium bowl, combine eggs, ⅓ cup of the Parmesan cheese, the parsley, basil and oregano. Beat with fork until well blended. Add to vegetables, along with salt and pepper to taste; stir to combine. Pour half of mixture into prepared pie plate. Top

with half of the remaining Parmesan cheese. Top with remaining vegetables and Parmesan cheese. Sprinkle the top evenly with the mozzarella cheese. Bake for 40 to 45 minutes, or until mixture is set. *For a pretty presentation, eggplant and zucchini can be sliced length-wise into thin ribbons, as shown in photo.

Super Herbed Italian Bread

Serves: 8 to 10
Prep Time: 10 Minutes
Cooking Time: 10 Minutes

Having grown up in a non-Italian household, I often ate garlic bread that was dressed to the hilt. Mom used all sorts of toppings: garlic, Parmesan or mozzarella cheese, oregano, paprika, butter, and even mayonnaise. Later, when I came to know

Summertime Vegetable Pie

Peter's Italian family, I realized that while bread was included with the pasta in a true Italian meal, it was usually served hot and plain, or with butter on the side. As a lover of all types of bread, I found this acceptable, but not quite as desirable as what I grew up with. So, here's a recipe for Italian bread with the works. This goes well with Venison Bolognese, charbroiled steaks, or chops.

½ cup butter (1 stick), preferably room temperature
4 cloves garlic, minced
½ cup mayonnaise
½ cup grated Parmesan cheese
1 loaf Italian bread, split lengthwise
½ teaspoon crumbled dried oregano
½ teaspoon paprika

Set oven to broil and/or 550°F. Melt butter in small saucepan over medium heat. Add minced garlic and cook for about 5 minutes (longer won't hurt); do not let the garlic brown. While that is cooking, combine mayonnaise and Parmesan cheese in small bowl; mix well and set aside.

Place halved Italian bread on baking sheet, crust side down. Drizzle garlic butter over bread. Place bread under broiler and let it brown slightly. Remove from broiler. With spatula, spread mayonnaise mixture on bread. Sprinkle oregano and paprika over mayonnaise mixture. Return bread to broiler and cook until edges are nicely browned. To serve, slice bread into 2-inch-wide strips.

Steaks, Chops, and Roasts to Brag About

JOHN WEISS

Every serious hunter should have a collection of wild game cookbooks. I've written five myself and have more than forty others in my kitchen library that I regularly consult. Understandably, I've experimented with, refined, and even created hundreds of venison recipes over the years. One interesting thing I've learned is that it's more often the cooking method, not the particular selection of ingredients, that determines the outcome.

Serious hunters who take at least one deer every year, plus assorted other species, should have a library of game cookbooks. This is Jackie Bushman, founder of Buckmasters.

With that in mind, I'll first describe cooking methods for various cuts of venison, with the actual recipes that follow being of less importance to the outcome. That way, no matter which recipe is selected, the meat should turn out tender, flavorful, and delicious.

Roasting is a technique in which a venison roast is placed (fat-side up if draped with bacon or other fat) on a rack in an open, shallow roasting pan. The rack holds the roast out of the grease, and the bacon or other fat dribbles down slowly and bastes the roast as it cooks.

Roasts such as rolled shoulder roasts should be cooked only until medium-rare with a blush of pink in the middle. Cook beyond this point, and the venison steadily becomes tougher.

In such cooking, it is imperative that a meat thermometer be used to monitor the progress of the roast. Insert the thermometer so the bulb is in the center of the thickest part of the meat, and make sure that the bulb does not touch bone or the bottom of the pan. A venison roast should be cooked only until it is medium-rare to medium on the inside, with a blush of juicy bright pink to the meat's color. Forget that you may like your beef roasts well done. Venison is not beef!

If you look at your meat thermometer, you'll see a graduated temperature scale paired to the desired "doneness" of various types of meat such as beef, pork, and fowl. Venison won't be listed on the scale, meaning that you have to go by temperature alone, and to achieve a roast that is medium-rare to medium you should cook it until its internal temperature registers 140° to 150°F (by comparison, a well-done beef roast has an internal temperature of 160° to 170°F).

Ideally, your roasting pan should sit on the middle shelf-rack in your oven, and the temperature dial of the oven should be set at 300° to 350°F, depending upon the size of the roast. Very large roasts (more than six pounds) should be cooked at the lower temperature and mid-size roasts (two to five pounds) at the higher temperature. You should never use a dry-heat cooking method with roasts smaller than two pounds because they will turn out tough and dry, so always use a roast of ample size; if it's larger than what your family can consume at one meal, the leftovers can be served in sandwiches, soups, or stews.

Broiling is another dry-heat cooking method, but this technique is generally reserved for tenderloin steaks, backstrap steaks, or sirloin tip steaks. Steaks to be broiled should be at least three-quarter-inch thick, but not more than one and one-half inches

When broiling, as with sirloin tip steaks, whether over coals or under the oven's broiler, use high heat to briefly sear both sides, never allowing the inside to go beyond medium-rare.

thick. Turn your oven's regulator dial to broil, or to its highest setting (generally, 500°F), and remember that the oven door should be left slightly ajar.

Place your venison steaks on the rack of your broiler pan so the juices can drain away (otherwise, they may flame up) and situate the pan so the meat will be from two to five inches from the heat source. Here is where each cook will have to temper his decisions with good judgment because the heat output of gas broilers, compared to electric, can vary quite a bit; also, thicker steaks should be placed farther away from the heat than thin ones.

Broil the steaks just until their top sides begin to brown, then flip them and broil on the other side for about one-half the previously allotted time. You may wish to barely slice into one of the steaks to check its progress. Those who broil beef steaks claim this heresy, that cutting into them will allow their juices to escape. True, but in the case of venison this small loss is better than relying purely upon guesswork and perchance allowing the steaks to broil just one minute too long and become overdone.

I advise against cooking a venison steak beyond the point of medium-rare, as this stage is when it's at its best. In cooking outdoors over a propane or charcoal grill, simply use the same method as with beef steaks but, again, never permit the meat to cook beyond medium-rare.

Pan-broiling is a splendid method of cooking steaks, but few people are familiar with it. A heavy, cast-iron skillet or griddle is necessary; it should be sparingly brushed with just a bit of cooking oil. One-half teaspoon of oil should be plenty to prevent the meat from sticking; if you add more than this you are no longer pan-broiling but panfrying.

Lay your steaks in the pan and then cook them over very low heat. Since the meat is in direct contact with the skillet or griddle, it is essential to turn the meat occasionally to ensure even cooking. The steaks are ready to serve when they are slightly brown on both sides and pink and juicy in the middle.

Panfrying is similar to pan-broiling in that a heavy skillet or griddle is used. However, substantially more cooking oil is used and the meat is cooked at a much higher temperature. While pan-broiling is ideally suited to thick steaks, panfrying is best accomplished with thinner steaks that have been floured or breaded.

Panfrying typically results in the outer surfaces and edges of steaks achieving just a bit of crispness, which, depending upon the recipe ingredients in the breading, enhances the flavor of the meat. In

Pan-broiling (or pan-frying), which can also be done on a griddle, is best reserved for sirloin tip or backstrap steaks. Sprinkle just a bit of salt on the cooking surface and you can reduce the amount of cooking oil by half.

achieving this desirable result, there may be some sacrifice of tenderness. So, beforehand, you may desire to treat your meat (especially sirloin tip steaks) to a dose of commercially prepared meat tenderizer.

One thing to guard against in panfrying is a burner temperature that becomes so hot your fat or grease begins to smoke. Another axiom of panfrying is to turn the meat frequently to ensure even cooking but, still again, venison steaks should never be cooked beyond medium.

Finally, one trick that ensures success, no matter which cooking method you decide to use, is that your intended serving platter and dinner plates be preheated. I like to simply slip them into the oven for five minutes before the meal is served.

The necessity of hot dinnerware has to do with the fat content in venison compared to beef. Remember that beef has a good deal of interstitial fat, or marbling, which gets extremely hot during cooking and therefore helps to retain the temperature of the meat long afterwards. Because venison does not have much fat woven between its tissue fibers, it cools quickly.

As a result, if you remove a venison roast from the oven, or steaks from the broiler or skillet, and place the meat on a cold platter straight from the cupboard, and then those seated transfer meat from the platter to their cold dinner plates, you're in for an unpleasant experience. Before anyone is even half finished eating they'll begin remarking upon how their venison is becoming colder and tougher with each bite. A hot serving platter and preheated dinner plates are the answer.

Now let's look at a number of recipes that call for roasting, broiling, panbroiling, or panfrying the tender cuts of venison. Keep in mind that you can vary any of the following recipes, especially those calling for roasts, by first soaking your venison in a marinade.

The tenderloins and backstraps are also perfectly suited to being cubed and then grilled or broiled as shish-kabobs.

Pan-Broiled Venison

Sautéed Steaks or Chops

¼ cup butter (½ stick)
1 teaspoon Lawry's Seasoned Salt
4 inch-thick steaks or chops

Melt the butter in a skillet, then blend in one teaspoon of the seasoned salt. Place the steaks in the pan and cook them slowly over medium heat until they are browned on all sides and pink and juicy in the middle. Serves four.

Spicy Deer Steaks Marinade

flour
3 tablespoons butter
3 tablespoons cooking oil
4 inch-thick steaks or chops

Use a marinade that contains wine, vegetable juice, or citrus juice, pour it over the steaks in a bowl, and refrigerate overnight. Drain and pat dry with paper towels. Flour the steaks well, then panfry in a skillet over medium heat containing the butter and cooking oil. Serves four.

Georgia-Style Steaks

4 steaks or chops
1 cup ketchup
1 tablespoon salt
1 tablespoon chili powder
2 tablespoons tarragon
1 onion, chopped
⅓ cup A-1 Steak Sauce

In a skillet, sear the steaks in just a bit of cooking oil on medium-high heat. Meanwhile, in a saucepan, bring all the remaining ingredients to a boil, stirring continually. Transfer the steaks to a shallow roasting pan, pour the sauce over the top and bake for one and one-half hours at 350°F. Serves four.

Venison Teriyaki

2 pounds tenderloin steak

3 tablespoons olive oil

3 tablespoons soy sauce

½ teaspoon garlic powder

1 tablespoon lemon juice

1 tablespoon brown sugar

2 cups uncooked Minute Rice

1 green bell pepper, sliced into strips

1 sweet white onion, sliced

1 cup sliced mushrooms

1 cup beef broth or bouillon

Slice the tenderloin into thin strips. Add the olive oil and soy sauce to a wok or high-sided skillet, then stir in the garlic, lemon juice, and brown sugar. Heat the wok or skillet on medium-high heat until the liquid begins to steam. Add the tenderloin strips and stir-fry them until they are almost cooked. Meanwhile, prepare the Minute Rice according to the package instructions. Now add to the wok or skillet the green pepper, onion, mushrooms, and broth. Turn the heat down to medium, cover, and slowly cook until everything is steaming. Ladle over a bed of the rice. Serves four.

High-Country Buttermilk Venison

4 backstrap or sirloin tip steaks

1 cup buttermilk

cooking oil

flour

Cut the steaks into one-inch cubes, then pound each with a meat hammer to about one-half-inch thick. Place the meat in a bowl, cover with the buttermilk, and allow the steak to soak for two hours. Then dredge the pieces in flour and panfry. Serves four.

Pepper Steak

4 backstrap or sirloin tip steaks

black pepper

2 tablespoons butter

2 tablespoons olive oil

4 teaspoons brandy

Sprinkle a bit of the pepper on both sides of the steaks and then gently pound it into the meat with a meat hammer. Add the butter and olive oil to a skillet and quickly sear the steaks on both sides. Turn the heat down to low and continue cooking until they are medium-rare. Meanwhile, warm the brandy in a small saucepan. When the steaks are ready, transfer them to a preheated platter. At tableside, pour the brandy over the steaks and ignite it. It will briefly flare up and then burn out. Serves four.

Kate's Venison Cutlets

2 pounds steak meat, ¼-inch thick

1 cup seasoned (salt & pepper) flour

2 eggs

1-½ cups milk

1 cup Italian-seasoned bread crumbs

¼ cup Parmesan cheese

1 teaspoon garlic powder

olive oil

1–10-ounce can whole, cooked asparagus

½ pound crisp bacon, crumble

½ pound sliced Swiss cheese

Preheat oven to 400°F. Dredge the cutlets in the seasoned flour. Dip each into a bowl of blended eggs and milk, then coat with a mixture of the bread crumbs, Parmesan cheese, and garlic powder. Heat one-half inch of olive oil in a skillet and fry the cutlets for one minute on each side. Transfer to paper toweling to briefly drain. Place on a cookie sheet. Place two whole asparagus spears on each cutlet, top with bacon bits and one slice of Swiss cheese. Place in the oven until the cheese melts. Serves six.

–Kate Fiduccia

Cracker-Fried Steaks

4 backstrap or sirloin tip steaks
2 eggs, beaten
1 cup saltine crackers, finely crushed
    cooking oil

Dip each steak into the beaten egg, roll in the cracker crumbs, then pound gently with a meat hammer. Dip the steaks a second time in the egg, then roll again in the cracker crumbs. Fry in the cooking oil until the cracker coating has a toastlike color and appearance, no more! Serves four.

Sirloin Tip Roast

1 - 2½-pound sirloin tip roast
2 cloves garlic, slivered
2 tablespoons Dijon-style mustard
1 tablespoon chopped fresh thyme
½ teaspoon black pepper

Preheat oven to 325°F. Using the tip of a knife, cut small, evenly spaced slits in the roast and insert the garlic slivers. Rub the roast with the mustard, then sprinkle with the thyme and pepper. Place on a roasting pan, then place in the oven until the temperature reads 140° to 145°F. Transfer to a warm serving platter, remove the string ties, and slice thinly. Serves six.

Iron Range Venison Roast

1 3-pound rolled rump or shoulder roast
1 teaspoon fennel seed

1 teaspoon sage
1 teaspoon sugar
1 teaspoon salt
½ teaspoon black pepper

Carefully remove the string ties so you can open the roast. Spread the venison out as much as possible and make numerous scoring cuts across the meat with a knife. In a bowl, blend all the remaining ingredients, then sprinkle evenly over the meat. Roll the meat back up into its original shape and make new string ties. Insert a meat thermometer, drape the roast with bacon, and set in a roasting pan. Roast at 325°F until the internal temperature registers 145°F. Serves six.

Steak Sandwiches

1-½ pounds loin steak meat
cooking oil
1 green bell pepper, sliced
1 sweet white onion, sliced

Slice the tenderloin or backstrap meat thinly, then briefly sear in a frying pan containing a small amount of hot oil. Add the pepper and onion slices, cover, and continue cooking over low heat until the vegetables are cooked but still crisp. Toss briefly and then serve on hard-crusted sandwich rolls or warmed tortilla-fajita wraps. Serves four.

Terrific Pot Roasts and Braised Venison

While the dry-heat cooking methods described in the last chapter are designed chiefly for very tender cuts of venison, moist-heat cooking methods work best for not-so-tender cuts that need a bit of help if they are to provide toothsome fare.

We're referring here to venison cuts from the front legs, such as rolled shoulder roasts, blade roasts, and arm roasts. But we can also include rolled roasts from the neck, and even venison from the otherwise tender rear legs but when taken from an old, grizzled buck that is likely to be on the tough side.

These meals traditionally are done in a pot or deep pan on top of the stove, in the oven, or even in a vessel such as a Crockpot. In any of these cases, the idea is to cook the meat in a closed environment so that steam is trapped and softens the meat's connective tissue. The steam comes from a small amount of liquid added to the cooking vessel in accordance with the particular recipe you're following. Generally the liquid is water, vegetable juice, soup, or wine.

What I especially like about cooking pot roasts or using a braising recipe is that you can often put potatoes, vegetables, and other items right in with the meat, which vastly simplifies meal preparation. And, depending upon the recipe, you frequently obtain a rich, sumptuous gravy as a special bonus. Still other times, only vegetables are added to the meat while it cooks, and the mixture is then served over a bed of potatoes, rice, or noodles.

Five-Minute Pot Roast

1 2-pound shoulder or neck roast
1 cup water
1 envelope dry onion soup mix

This is the fastest, easiest pot roast I know of and, happily, one of the most delicious. Place your roast in the center of a square sheet of heavy-duty aluminum foil and bring the edges up and around the sides to form a pouch. Pour one cup of water over the top of the roast, then sprinkle on the dry soup mix. Now pinch together the edges of the foil to form a tight seal to trap steam, and

Virtually any cut of venison from the front or back legs, or from the backstraps, is suitable for braising. These are backstrap steaks that have been cooked to tender perfection.

place the pouch in a shallow roasting pan. Place in a 325°F oven for one and one-half hours. When you open the pouch to slice the meat you'll find it tender beyond belief and, as a special surprise, you'll have a good quantity of perfect gravy you can ladle over noodles or potatoes. As with all venison, remember to serve on a hot platter. Serves four.

German Pot Roast

1 3-pound shoulder or neck roast
2 onions, chopped
1 teaspoon garlic powder
4 tablespoons butter
¼ cup vinegar
1 cup tomato sauce
½ teaspoon poultry seasoning
¼ teaspoon nutmeg
1/4 teaspoon cinnamon
1/4 teaspoon allspice

In a skillet, sauté the onions with the garlic powder in the butter, then transfer to a plate where they will stay hot. In the same skillet, sear the roast until it is

As a rule, pot roasts usually are first browned over high heat in a skillet.

The pot roast is then transferred to a pot along with seasonings and the other ingredients a recipe may call for.

The pot is then covered and transferred to a pre-heated oven, or it can slow-cook on a stovetop burner.

brown on all sides. Transfer the meat to an oven-proof pot, spoon the onions over the top, pour the vinegar and tomato sauce into the pot, then sprinkle the seasonings on top of the meat. Cover the pot with a lid and cook slowly in a 300°F oven for two hours. After placing the meat on a hot platter and slicing it, pour the juices from the pot over the meat. Serves four (with leftovers for sandwiches the next day).

Pot Roast Elegante

1 2-pound shoulder or neck roast
salt and pepper
1 medium can condensed cream soup
1 onion, sliced

In a skillet, brown the roast on all sides in a bit of cooking oil. Transfer the roast to a pot or oven-tempered glass casserole dish and sprinkle with a bit of salt and pepper. Pour on top of the roast and around the sides a can of condensed soup (cream of mushroom, cream of celery, or some other favorite). Lay the onion slices on top, cover, and slow-cook at 325°F for one and one-half hours. Transfer the roast to a hot platter, slice, then pour the cream gravy from the cooking pot over the top. Serves four.

Pot Roast Italiano

1 2-pound shoulder or neck roast
1 medium can condensed cream soup
½ cup dry red wine
2 tablespoons parsley flakes
½ teaspoon thyme
1 bay leaf, crumbled
salt and pepper

In a skillet, brown the roast on all sides in cooking oil. Transfer the roast to a pot or oven-tempered casserole dish. In a bowl, blend the soup (I like cream of mushroom) with the wine and then

The beauty of pot roasts is that you can throw potatoes and other vegetables right in with the meat to produce a one-pot meal. This one is being prepared in a cast-iron Dutch oven over campfire coals.

pour the mixture over and around the roast. Sprinkle the seasonings on top of the roast, cover, and place in a 325°F oven for one and one-half hours. Transfer the meat to a hot platter, slice, and pour the sauce over the top. Serves four.

Hungarian Pot Roast

1 3-pound shoulder or neck roast
1 large clove garlic
salt and pepper
1 onion, chopped
2 carrots, sliced thick
½ teaspoon oregano
½ teaspoon parsley flakes
1 stalk celery, chopped

1 cup beef broth or bouillon
1 teaspoon Hungarian paprika
½ cup sour cream

Slice the garlic clove into thin slivers, then insert them into thin knife slits made into the roast. Rub the roast with salt and pepper, then brown the roast in a skillet using a bit of oil. Place the roast in a pot and add all the remaining ingredients except the sour cream. Cover the pot and with the stove burner on low heat slowly simmer the roast for one and one-half hours or until it is tender. Transfer the roast to a hot platter and slice, then ladle the vegetables over the meat, using a slotted spoon. Add the sour cream to the broth in the pot, turn the heat up, and cook until the sauce is steaming, then pour over the sliced pot roast. Serves four to six.

All-in-One Pot Roast

1 2-pound shoulder or neck roast
salt and pepper
4 potatoes, cut into large chunks
4 carrots, cut into large chunks
1 can green beans, drained
flour or corn starch, as needed

In a skillet or deep pan, sear the roast on all sides until it is brown, then transfer to a pot. Pour hot water into the pot until it comes up halfway on the side of the roast. Sprinkle with salt and pepper, cover the pot with a lid and begin slow cooking with the stove burner heat turned on low. After forty-five minutes of simmering, place the potato chunks in the pot. After another thirty minutes, add the carrots and green beans. Continue to simmer until the vegetables are tender. Transfer the meat to a hot platter and slice. Use a slotted spoon to transfer the vegetables to a hot dish. Then thicken the gravy with just a bit of flour or cornstarch and pour over the pot roast slices. Serves four.

Creamed Sirloin Tips

2 pounds sirloin tip steak
meat tenderizer
1 onion, finely chopped
2 tablespoons butter
½ cup water
2 tablespoons flour
½ cup sour cream
1 4-ounce can mushrooms

In braising venison, the meat is first seared on both sides in a pan. The temperature is then reduced to a slow-bubble, other ingredients are added, and then the pan covered and allowed to simmer on low heat.

Sprinkle meat tenderizer over the steak meat, then gently pound it into the meat with the sharp edge of a meat hammer. In a skillet, sauté the onions in the butter until they are clear. Now use a knife to cut the sirloin tip steaks into triangular- shaped wedges and sear these in the skillet, over medium heat, with the onion until the venison is brown on all sides. Reduce the heat to low, add one-half cup water, cover the pan, and slowly simmer for half an hour. Meanwhile, stir the flour into the sour cream. When the meat is tender, add the cream mixture and mushrooms to the skillet, cover, and allow to slowly bubble for another twenty minutes. The creamed sirloin tips can be served as-is, or ladled over a bed of noodles. Serves four.

Venison Scaloppini

2 pounds round steak
6 tablespoons olive oil
2 teaspoons garlic powder
1 12-ounce can tomatoes
1 teaspoon oregano
1 teaspoon parsley flakes
1 teaspoon salt
½ teaspoon black pepper
4 slices mozzarella cheese

Cut the round steaks into four equal portions. In a skillet, blend the garlic power into the olive oil,

then brown the steaks on both sides over medium-high heat. Add the tomatoes and sprinkle the seasonings over the tops of the steaks. Reduce the heat to low, cover the pan, and slowly simmer for forty five minutes. Spoon the tomatoes and juices into an oven-proof platter, arrange the steaks on top, then lay a slice of mozzarella cheese on top of each of the steaks. Slide the dinner platter into an oven preheated to 400 °F until the cheese is melted and just beginning to brown. Serves four.

Venison Swiss Steak

½ teaspoon salt
¼ teaspoon black pepper
flour
2 pounds round or sirloin tip steak
1 cup cooking oil
1 green pepper, chopped
2 onions, sliced
1 8-ounce can tomatoes with liquid

Blend the salt and pepper with flour, then gently pound the mixture into both sides of your steak with a meat hammer. Now cut the meat into four equal portions. In a skillet containing several tablespoons of oil, brown the meat on both sides. Add the pepper, onion, and tomatoes (with packing juice), cover the pan, reduce the heat to low, and slowly simmer for one hour. Check after one-half hour and add a bit of water to the pan if necessary. Serves four.

Barbecued Round Steak

2 tablespoons butter
2 tablespoons cooking oil
1 onion, chopped
2 stalks celery, chopped
2 pounds round steak
barbeque sauce
1 cup beef broth or bouillon
2 tablespoons brown sugar
4 tablespoons Worcestershire sauce
1 medium can tomato soup

Blend the butter and cooking oil in a skillet and sauté the onion and celery, then set aside briefly. In the same skillet, brown the round steak. In a separate saucepan, add all the remaining ingredients and simmer for 15 minutes. Place the browned steak in a deep casserole dish, spoon the sautéed onions and celery over the top, then pour the barbecue sauce over all. Cook, uncovered, for one and one-half hours in a 350°F oven. Serves four.

Sumptuous Soups, Stews, and Casseroles

Soups and stews with venison as the main ingredient undoubtedly date back to the first primitive uses of fire and food cooked in clay vessels. However, it wasn't until the medieval 14th-century reign of King Henry that "stuwe" acquired its official name to identify the nature of the feast.

Some cooks proclaim that a stew is nothing more than a thick soup. Others say soup is nothing

more than a thin stew. But there are differences worth noting. There are also many similarities, and there truly is no such thing as an original or secret recipe. By simply adding a pinch of thyme, subtracting the celery, splashing the pot with just a hint of sherry, or doing any number of countless other small things, we could concoct supposedly "new" recipes until the end of time.

Incidentally, casseroles loosely fit into the category of stews, and so they'll also be included in this chapter. By definition, a casserole is a very thick stew with a basis of rice, noodles, or potatoes, but unlike a stew, which is generally prepared in a pot on a stove burner, a casserole is prepared in a glass or earthenware vessel and baked in one's oven.

But let's first get back to soups and stews and the main differences between them. For one, the typical assortment of vegetables comprising a soup are generally diced while those going into stews are generally cubed or chunked. The reason for this is that soups traditionally are made on short notice and

Is a stew really only a thick soup, or is a soup really only a thin stew? The debate goes on, but in either case venison is one of the most popular main ingredients.

Casseroles generally are stew-like concoctions baked in the oven, often with a topping of breadcrumbs or biscuits. Hearty stews are terrific one-pot meals. Leftovers re-heat easily and freeze well.

designed to be eaten just as quickly. Hence, you want to speedily combine all of the ingredients.

Stews, on the other hand, are long-term love affairs that are best eaten only after hours of slow simmering. Consequently, the use of small, diced vegetables, as in soups, would see the stew transform itself into mush; thick hunks of vegetables hold together longer to give the stew body and integrity.

Another difference between soups and stews is that soups typically have a broth color ranging from semi-clear to amber, while stews usually reveal a rich, dark, gravy-like color. The reason for this is that in preparation of soup the venison chunks are either placed in the soup pot raw to steamcook, or they are just briefly seared in a bit of cooking oil before going into the pot. But in preparation of stew, the venison chunks are usually first dredged with seasoned flour and then browned in a skillet.

Finally, don't make the mistake of using your most tender cuts of venison in soups or stews.

The lengthy cooking period, especially with stews, which is necessary to harmonize the flavors of their various components, will turn already tender cuts of venison into soft, limp meat lacking any substance. Instead, use tougher cuts that will hold together through the duration of the cooking and only later become tender.

Last, there are two other important points. Never allow a soup or stew to come to a rolling boil because this will cause the meat to shrink, the vegetables to wilt, and the spices to commit suicide. What you want is an almost arthritic simmer, which reveals faint wisps of steam as tiny bubbles barely pop on the surface. And never allow soups or stews to cook so long that their liquid content begins to evaporate significantly. If this happens, adding a bit of water, stock or wine is the usual remedy.

Hearty stews are terrific one-pot meals. Leftovers re-heat easily and freeze well.

Virtually any combination of vegetables can be used to create a soup or stew. As a rule, stews cook longer, so vegetables should be cut into chunks; soups are cooked more quickly, so vegetables should be diced.

Stormy Weather Soup

1 pound venison, cubed

3 carrots, diced

4 potatoes, diced

2 onions, diced

2 bell peppers, diced

1 large can tomatoes

3 celery stalks, diced

1 large can ⅛ Juice

2 tablespoons Worcestershire sauce

2 teaspoons Tabasco sauce

salt and pepper to taste

In a skillet, brown the venison cubes in a bit of oil, then transfer to a large pot. Cover the meat with cold water, then add the remaining ingredients and slowly simmer for one hour. Serves four.

Don't use your most tender cuts of venison for soup or stew because they'll fall apart. Use the tougher cuts from the front legs and neck; the slow-cooking process will tenderize them and their coarser texture will hold them together. The first step with nearly all recipes is to dust the meat chunks with flour and then brown them in a skillet.

Venison Minestrone

4 cups dry pinto beans

water 1-½ pounds venison, cubed

1 large onion, chopped

6 carrots, chopped

6 stalks celery, chopped

6 tablespoons olive oil

1 large can tomatoes

3 potatoes, cubed

2 teaspoons garlic powder

Stews are traditionally served as complete evening meals while soups are usually served as quick, high-energy lunches accompanied by breads or crackers. But it's not necessary to become a conformist; do as you like.

2 tablespoons basil
½ cup parsley, chopped
½ cup macaroni, cooked
½ head cabbage, chopped
Parmesan cheese

Place the beans in a deep bowl, completely cover with cold water, and allow to soak overnight. Simmer the meat in one quart of cold water until it is tender, then refrigerate overnight. The following day, drain the beans and add them to the pot containing the venison and broth and simmer two hours or until the beans are tender. Meanwhile, in a deep skillet, sauté the onion, carrots, and celery in the olive oil. When the vegetables are fully cooked, add the can of tomatoes and simmer until the liquid is almost evaporated, then add this skillet of vegetables to the soup pot along with three quarts of water. Allow the soup to simmer for one hour, then add the potatoes, garlic, basil, and parsley and allow to simmer for one hour longer. Just before serving, stir the macaroni and cabbage into the soup, cover and let sit for at least five minutes. After ladling the soup into bowls, sprinkle about one tablespoon grated Parmesan cheese on top of each. Serves four (with plenty left over that can be frozen for another meal).

Savory Bean Soup

1 pound venison, cubed
1 8-ounce can tomato sauce
1 large can tomatoes
2 tablespoons dried onion flakes
10 cups water
1 medium can red kidney beans
½ teaspoon chili powder
2 teaspoons salt
½ cup uncooked Minute Rice
½ cup shredded American cheese

Add all of the ingredients, except the rice and cheese, to a deep pot and simmer on low heat for one hour. Five minutes before serving, stir in the rice. Ladle the soup into bowls, then sprinkle the cheese on top of each. Serves four generously.

Venison Cider Stew

2 pounds venison, cubed
1 teaspoon dried onion flakes
2 teaspoons salt
¼ teaspoon thyme
¼ teaspoon nutmeg
3 potatoes, cut into chunks
4 carrots, cut into chunks
1 apple, chopped
1 cup apple cider

Brown the venison in a skillet in a bit of oil, sprinkling on the onion, salt, thyme, and nutmeg while stirring continually. Transfer the seasoned meat to a crockpot or stew pot, add the vegetables and apple, then pour the cider over the top. Slow-cook on low heat for at least three hours. If too much of the liquid begins to evaporate, replenish it with a mixture of one-half cup water blended with one-half cup cider. Serves four.

Venison-Mushroom Stew

1-½ pounds venison, cut into chunks
seasoned flour
2 tablespoons olive oil
1 teaspoon salt
½ teaspoon black pepper
2 medium onions, quartered
5 potatoes, cubed
3 stalks celery, cut into wide slices
2 green peppers, sliced
2 carrots, cut into wide slices
3, 4-ounce cans of mushrooms, liquid discarded
1 can mushroom soup

Toss the venison chunks in seasoned flour and brown in a skillet with olive oil. Place the meat in a crockpot. Add the remaining ingredients, except the mushroom soup. Cover the ingredients with water and cook for three hours. If the water begins to evaporate, add a little more. About thirty minutes before done, add the mushroom soup and stir in thoroughly. Serve over hot white rice or buttered noodles.

–Kate Fiduccia

Winter Day Stew

2 pounds venison, cubed
¼ cup bacon drippings
1 onion, cut into chunks
2 carrots, cut into chunks
2 stalks celery, cut into chunks
1, 4-ounce can mushrooms
3 potatoes, cut into chunks
2 medium cans beef or chicken broth
1 cup port wine
2 tablespoons Worcestershire sauce
1 teaspoon brown sugar
½ teaspoon cloves
½ teaspoon cinnamon

In a skillet, brown the venison and onion in the bacon drippings. Transfer the onion and venison to a stew pot, add the remaining ingredients and simmer three hours. If the stew becomes too thick, add more broth or wine. Serves five generously.

Deer-Me Casserole

2 pounds venison, cubed
1 medium can condensed cream of mushroom soup
1 cup canned tomatoes, with juice
1 envelope dry onion soup mix
½ cup seasoned bread crumbs

Arrange the meat cubes in the bottom of a casserole dish, then pour the mushroom soup (undiluted) over the top. Sprinkle the onion soup mix, then pour the tomatoes and juice over the top. Cover the dish and bake at 325°F for two hours. During the final fifteen minutes of cooking, remove the cover from the dish and sprinkle the top of the casserole with the breadcrumbs. Continue baking until the breadcrumbs are nicely browned. Serves four.

Venison Stroganoff

½ cup butter
1 teaspoon garlic powder
1-½ pounds venison, cubed

1 cup flour

1 onion, chopped

1 tablespoon salt

¼ teaspoon black pepper

1-½ cups water

1 cup fresh mushrooms

1-¼ cups sour cream

In a skillet, melt the butter and then stir in the garlic powder. Flour the venison chunks and then brown them in the skillet. Add the onion, salt, and pepper, then stir in the water, cover the pan, and simmer slowly for forty-five minutes. Now add the mushrooms and sour cream and continue to cook another fifteen minutes, but do not allow the sauce to come to a boil. Traditionally, stroganoff is served over a bed of thick Pennsylvania Dutch noodles, but for variety you can use thin oriental noodles or rice. Serves four.

West Texas Venison Casserole

2 pounds round steak or sirloin tip steak

¼ cup flour

1 teaspoon salt

½ teaspoon black pepper

¼ cup bacon drippings

1 stalk celery, chopped

3 onions, sliced

2 tablespoons Worcestershire sauce

2 cups tomatoes, with juice

1 8-ounce package wide noodles

Cut the venison into four or six equal pieces, then dredge in a mixture of the flour, salt, and pepper. Brown the meat on all sides in a high-sided skillet containing the bacon fat. Add the celery and onions and continue cooking over low heat until the onions are clear. Add the other ingredients,

except noodles, cover the pan, and cook slowly for one and one-half hours or until the meat is tender. Prepare the noodles according to the package instructions. Then place the noodles on a hot serving platter, carefully lay the venison pieces on top, then pour the sauce from the pan over the top. Serves four.

Cheddar-Noodle Casserole

1 pound venison, cut into cubes

1 stick margarine

1 small onion, minced

1 4-ounce can mushrooms, with liquid

1 teaspoon Worcestershire sauce

1 bay leaf, crumbled

1 8 ounce package noodles

1 cup milk

1 teaspoon salt

¼ teaspoon black pepper

½ cup grated cheddar cheese

1 cup seasoned croutons

In a skillet, brown the venison cubes in two tablespoons of the margarine, then stir in the minced onion and cook over low heat until it is clear. Drain the mushrooms and set aside, pouring the packing juice from the mushroom can into the skillet with the meat and onions. Add the Worcestershire sauce and bay leaf, stir well, cover the pan, and simmer on low heat for thirty minutes. Prepare the noodles according to the package instructions, then drain. Stir the remaining margarine into the hot noodles until it is melted, then add the venison cubes, pan juices, milk, salt, and pepper. Transfer to a buttered casserole dish, then sprinkle the cheddar cheese on top. Now sprinkle the croutons on top. Bake at 325°F for one hour. Serves four.

Although casseroles are stew-like concoctions, they're unique in that venison burger is usually used instead of meat chunks, and some type of pasta is added such as rice or noodles.

Hunter's Favorite Pie

2 pounds venison, cubed

2 tablespoons butter

2 onions, diced

1 teaspoon garlic powder

1 large can tomatoes

1 tablespoon paprika

½ teaspoon red cayenne pepper

1 bay leaf, crumbled

¼ teaspoon thyme

1 cup beer

3 carrots, sliced thinly

1 package frozen peas

1 tube biscuits

In a skillet, brown the venison in the butter. Then stir in the onions, garlic powder, tomatoes, seasonings, and beer. Cover the pan and simmer slowly for one hour. Stir in the carrots and peas, cover, and simmer fifteen minutes longer. Transfer the mixture to a deep casserole dish and arrange biscuits on top. Now bake at 400°F for fifteen minutes or until the biscuits are nicely browned. Serves four.

What to Do With All That Burger and Sausage

Of all meat products grown in this country, hamburger is the most widely consumed. According to the American Beef Council, every adult consumes an average of thirty-one pounds of hamburger per year in one form or another. Deerburger is equally versatile. And because it's lower in fat and cholesterol than beef, it's more healthy. Use deerburger in any manner in which you'd use hamburger.

Although not as widely used as burger, bulk venison sausage and links also are popular in hunting households. Our favorite uses for them are included in this chapter, as well.

Before offering specific burger recipes, we should point out a few important aspects of using this particular ground meat. First, because of its fat content (which we added at grinding time, usually in the form of suet), it is not necessary to add any cooking oil to a skillet or griddle before frying burgers. It is wise, though, to sprinkle just a bit of salt onto your cooking surface, as this will prevent the meat from sticking and scorching until the fat in the meat has had a chance to render-out slightly for the remainder of the frying.

Second, most grocery stores and meat markets that grind burger use the tougher cuts of beef. Likewise, hunters commonly use scraps, trimmings, and tougher cuts in their burger. But many hunters also commonly use their most tender cuts of venison, throwing into the burger-to-be pile pieces of rump meat and end-cuts from backstraps. This can result in burger that is so tender it may begin to fall apart in the pan. This poses no problem if you're merely browning the meat before adding it to spaghetti sauce, chili, and the like, but it's annoying when you're trying to fry deerburgers.

The solution is to add some type of flavorless binder to the burger just before forming the burger patties with your hands. The best binder combination I've come across is one slice of fresh,

Some hunters have been known to push their entire deer through a meat grinder. But even if you grind only the tougher cuts, scraps, and trimmings, you'll still have upwards of forty pounds of burger and sausage.

Venison burgers, especially when a fancy recipe such as Burgers Al Fresco is used, produce eventful meals to be proud of.

crumbled bread, an egg, and a bit of cold water for every one pound of burger. Add the burger and binding ingredients to a bowl and knead them together with your hands; then make each individual burger patty in the usual way.

If your family begins to tire of deerburgers prepared in the customary manner, try adding a little flare to your burgers. Before forming them into patties ready for the skillet, add a splash or two of Worcestershire sauce, A-1 steak sauce, or barbecue sauce, kneading it thoroughly into the meat. For still different variations of burgers, knead into the ground meat a bit of finely chopped sweet onion and garlic powder, or a combination of sweet basil and thyme. One of the simplest and yet most delectable ways to enjoy your burgers is to sprinkle them with nutmeg while they're frying for a unique nutty flavor.

Other popular uses for all that deerburger you've created include the following:

Venison Burgers Al Fresco

1 pound deerburger

1 egg, slightly beaten

½ cup sharp cheddar cheese, shredded

¼ cup fresh broccoli, finely chopped

1 teaspoon Worcestershire sauce

1 clove garlic, finely chopped

1 tablespoon onion, finely chopped

Mix all ingredients together and make into four patties and fry or grill for five to six minutes per side. Serves four.

–Kate Fiduccia

Venison Meatloaf

1-½ pounds deerburger

2 slices fresh bread, crumbled

2 eggs

1 8-ounce can tomato sauce

1/2 cup onion, chopped

1-½ teaspoons salt

1 medium bay leaf, crumbled

dash thyme

dash marjoram

In a bowl, combine all ingredients and knead together with your hands. Dump the works into a bread pan and tap to settle the contents. Bake at 350°F for one hour. Serves four.

Deerburger Chili

2 pounds deerburger

1 green pepper, chopped

2, 16-ounce cans red kidney beans, with liquid

2, 12-ounce cans whole tomatoes with liquid

1 tablespoon red cayenne pepper

2 tablespoons garlic powder

1 teaspoon ground cumin powder

4 tablespoons chili powder

2 bay leaves, crumbled

Brown the deerburger in a skillet, then spoon off the grease. Add the burger and remaining ingredients to a deep pot along with one quart of cold water. Slowly simmer on low heat for two hours. Serves eight.

Venison Meatballs, Noodles, and Gravy

1-½ pounds deerburger

3 slices fresh white bread

2 teaspoons salt

¼ teaspoon black pepper

⅛ teaspoon basil

⅛ teaspoon oregano

⅔ cup chopped onion

¼ cup butter

1 10-ounce package wide noodles

1 cup milk

1 tablespoon flour

Crumble the bread and knead it into the deerburger with the salt, pepper, basil, oregano, and onion. Now form one-inch-diameter meatballs with your fingers. Place the meatballs on a cookie sheet and chill in your refrigerator for one hour, then brown the meatballs in a skillet containing the butter, turning them frequently. Reduce the heat under the skillet to low, cover with a lid, and let the meatballs continue to cook slowly for another fifteen minutes. Meanwhile, cook the noodles according to the package instructions, then drain. Transfer the meatballs from the skillet to a plate in your oven to keep them hot. Add to the drippings in the skillet the milk and just a pinch of the flour at a time, constantly stirring on medium-high heat until it turns into a rich gravy. Add the meatballs to the gravy, stir gently, then ladle over the top of the bed of noodles on a hot platter. Serves four generously.

Venison Goulash

1 4-ounce package wide noodles
1 pound deerburger
1 onion, chopped
½ cup ketchup
3 stalks celery, chopped
1 4-ounce can sliced mushrooms
1 14-ounce can tomatoes, with liquid
2 teaspoons salt
½ teaspoon black pepper

Cook the noodles according to the package instructions. Meanwhile, brown the deerburger in a skillet. Drain off the grease, then add the onions and continue cooking until they are clear. Stir in the cooked, drained noodles, ketchup, celery, mushrooms, tomatoes, salt, and pepper. Cover the skillet with a lid and simmer on very low heat for one-half hour. Serves four.

Grill venison sausages the same way you would those made of beef or pork. They're also terrific when added to casseroles.

Chicago!

1 pound deerburger
2 teaspoons butter
2, 8-ounce cans tomato sauce
½ teaspoon salt
½ teaspoon Worcestershire sauce
1 8-ounce package cream cheese
1 8-ounce carton small-curd cottage cheese
¼ cup sour cream
1 green pepper, chopped
¼ cup scallions, minced
1 6-ounce package wide noodles

In a skillet, melt the butter over medium heat and brown the deerburger, then spoon off grease. Stir in the tomato sauce, salt, and Worcestershire sauce, and allow to simmer on very low heat. In a separate bowl, blend the cream cheese, cottage cheese, and sour cream, then stir in the green pepper and a bit of the scallions. Prepare the noodles according to the package instructions, then drain. Stir the noodles into the cheese blend. Butter the inside of a casserole dish, then spread the noodle-cheese mixture in the bottom. Spoon the meat and tomato sauce on top of the noodles and sprinkle with the remaining scallions. Bake at 350°F for forty-five minutes. Serves four generously.

Favorite Ways to Cook Sausage

Venison sausage, whether in bulk form, links, or rings, can be cooked and served exactly the same as you would their beef or pork counterparts purchased at your grocery store.

To make sausage sandwiches, form patties from bulk sausage and fry as you would burgers, then serve on sandwich rolls. As a pleasing variation of this, melt two tablespoons of butter in a skillet. Then knead into the equivalent of each intended sausage patty one egg, one teaspoon of water, and one-quarter teaspoon parsley flakes. Form into patties and fry in the usual way. When the sausage patties are almost done, top each with a slice of mild cheddar cheese and cover the pan briefly. When the cheese is melted, serve each sausage patty between two slices of buttered rye toast.

When using sausage links or ring sausage for sandwiches, I like to fry them slowly on low heat and, when they are cooked all the way through, slice them lengthwise and serve in Italian buns with a heap of green pepper strips and onion slices that have been seared in a bit of olive oil.

Link and ring sausage can also be slow-cooked in a skillet, refrigerated, sliced thin, and served as hors d'oeuvres with assorted cheeses and crackers.

Try these favorite recipes:

Sausage Supreme

1 pound bulk sausage

1 onion, chopped

2 teaspoons Worcestershire sauce

1 teaspoon garlic powder

3 carrots, grated

1 8-ounce package "curly" noodles

1 can condensed cream of mushroom soup

½ cup Parmesan cheese

In a skillet, brown the sausage, pour off the grease, then stir in the onion and Worcestershire sauce. When the mixture begins to bubble, stir in the garlic powder, then turn off the heat. Prepare the noodles according to the package instructions, then drain. Now stir the noodles, sausage mix, carrots, and soup together until they are well blended. Pour into a buttered casserole dish and bake in a 350°F oven for twenty minutes. During the final four minutes of cooking, sprinkle the Parmesan cheese over the top. Serves four.

Country Casserole

1 pound bulk sausage

1 onion, chopped

1 green pepper, chopped

1 16-ounce can baked beans

1 8-ounce package elbow macaroni

½ cup tomato juice

½ teaspoon salt

½ cup grated mild cheddar cheese

In a skillet, brown the sausage in a bit of cooking oil, spoon off grease, then stir in the onion and green pepper and continue to cook on low heat until they are tender. Meanwhile, cook the macaroni according to the package instructions, and drain. Blend the macaroni and sausage mix, then transfer to a large casserole dish. Stir in the beans, tomato juice, and salt. Mix thoroughly. Bake in a 400°F oven for twenty minutes until the casserole begins to bubble. Then sprinkle the cheddar cheese on top and bake five minutes longer. Serves four.

Espagnole

8 large sausage links

3 cups white rice, cooked, keep warm

¼ cup chopped onion

¼ cup chopped green pepper

1 12-ounce can tomatoes, drained

1-½ teaspoons salt

½ teaspoon black pepper

Fry the sausage links in a skillet containing a bit of oil until they are thoroughly cooked. Remove the sausage links from the pan and slice them into half-inch thick "rounds." Add the onion and green pepper to the drippings in the pan and cook until the onion is clear. Now stir in all the remaining ingredients and cook, uncovered, over low heat for fifteen minutes. Serves four.

Venison Ragout

8 large sausage links

1 cup chopped onion

½ teaspoon garlic powder

1 green pepper, cut into half-inch strips

1 12-ounce can tomatoes, drained

2 tablespoons paprika

¼ teaspoon black pepper

½ teaspoon salt

Gently fry the sausage links until they are thoroughly cooked, then cut them into one-half-inch thick "rounds." In the same pan, sauté with the onions and garlic powder until the onions are clear. Add the green pepper, tomatoes, sausage pieces, and seasonings. Cover and simmer over low heat for thirty minutes. Meanwhile, prepare a bed of boiled new potatoes, white or brown rice, or noodles, and transfer to a hot serving platter, then ladle the ragout on top. Serves four.

I hope you will find butchering and preparing your own venison to be a satisfying way to enjoy nature's bounty. May it bring many scrumptious meals to your family and friends.

Part 6

Favored Reads

Introduction

JAY CASSELL

Most of the material in this section consists of various magazine articles I've written over the years – with the exception being "Trail's End," by the renowned naturalist Sigurd Olson. His story on a big buck surviving hunting season in the north woods has always rung a bell with me – the buck's point of view. Whew. Put yourself in his shoes, or hooves.

The other stories, all by yours truly, are some of my favorites, ones I done over the past twenty years or so. "Work Weekend," about getting our old hunting camp ready for another season in New York's Catskill Mountains, is just a special story about a special place. Sadly, the landowner passed away recently, and the land is for sale. We don't know if we'll get another hunting season out of that camp this year or not – needless to say, this is a tough one.

But I hope you enjoy this section. These stories are from the heart.

Trail's End

SIGURD OLSON

It was early morning in the northern wilderness, one of those rare, breathless mornings that come only in November, and though it was not yet light enough to see, the birds were stirring. A covey of partridge whirred up from their cozy burrows in the snow and lit in the top of a white birch, where they feasted noisily upon the frozen brown buds. The rolling tattoo of a downy woodpecker, also looking for his breakfast, reverberated again and again through the timber.

They were not the only ones astir, however, for far down the trail leading from the Tamarack Swamp to Kennedy Lake browsed a big buck. He worked his way leisurely along, stopping now and then to scratch away the fresh snow and nibble daintily the still tender green things underneath. A large buck he was, even as deer run, and as smooth and sleek as good feeding could make him. His horns, almost too large, were queerly shaped, for instead of being rounded as in other deer, they were broad and palmate, the horns of a true swamp buck.

The eastern skyline was just beginning to tint with lavender as he reached the summit of the ridge overlooking the lake. He stopped for his usual morning survey of the landscape below him. For some reason, ever since his spike-buck days, he had always stopped there to look the country over before working down to water. He did not know that for countless generations before him, in the days when the pine timber stood tall and gloomy round the shores of the lake, other swamp bucks had also stopped, to scent the wind and listen, before going down to drink.

As he stood on the crest of the ridge, his gaze took in the long reaches of dark blue water far below him; the ice-rimmed shores with long white windfalls reaching like frozen fingers out into the shallows, and the mottled green and gray of the brush covered slopes. His attention was finally centered on a little log cabin tucked away on the opposite shore in a clump of second growth spruce and balsam. Straight above it rose a thin wreath of pale blue smoke, almost as blue as the clear morning air. The metallic chuck, chuck of an axe ringing on a dry log, came clearly across the water, and a breath of air brought to him strange odors that somehow filled him with a vague misgiving.

He was fascinated by the cabin and could not take his gaze from it. On other mornings, it had seemed as much a part of the shoreline as the trees themselves, but now it was different. A flood of almost- forgotten memories surged back to him, of days long ago, when similar odors and sounds had brought with them a danger far greater than that of any natural enemy. He rubbed the top of a low hazel bush and stamped his forefeet nervously, undecided about what to do. Then, in a flash, the full realization came to him. He understood the meaning of it all. This was the season of the year when man was no longer his friend, and it was not safe to be seen in the logging roads or in the open clearings near the log houses. He sniffed the air keenly a moment longer, to be sure, then snorted loudly as if to warn all the wilderness folk of their danger, and bounded back up the trail the way he had come.

Not until he had regained the heavy protecting timber of the Tamarack Swamp, north of Kennedy Lake, did he feel safe. What he had seen made him once again the wary old buck who had lived by his cunning and strength through many a hunting season. Although he was safe for the time being, he was too experienced not to know that before many days had passed, the Tamarack Swamp would no longer be a haven of refuge.

As he worked deeper into the heavy moss-hung timber, he stopped frequently to look into the shadows. The trail here was knee-deep in moss and criss-crossed by a labyrinth of narrow rabbit runways.

Soon his search was rewarded, for a sleek yearling doe met him at a place where two trails crossed. After nosing each other tenderly, by way of recognition, they began feeding together on the tender shoots of blueberries and still green tufts of swamp grass underneath the protecting blanket of snow.

All that morning they fed leisurely and when the sun was high in the heavens, they worked cautiously over to the edge of the swamp. Here was a warm sunny opening hedged in by huge windfalls grown over with a dense tangle of blackberry vines. They often came here for their afternoon sunning, as the ice-encrusted ovals in the snow attested. Leaping a big windfall that guarded the entrance to the opening, they carefully examined the ground, then picked their beds close together. There they rested contentedly with the warm sun shining upon them, little thinking that soon their peace would be broken.

The snow had fallen early that autumn and good feed had been scarce everywhere, except in the depths of the Tamarack Swamp, where the protecting timber had sheltered the grass and small green things. The plague had killed off most of the rabbits, and the few that survived were already forced to feed upon the bark of the poplar. The heavy crust, forming suddenly the night after the first heavy snow, had imprisoned countless partridge and grouse in their tunnels. As a result, small game was scarce and the wolves were lean and gaunt, although it was yet hardly winter. The stark famine months ahead gave promise of nothing but starvation and death, and the weird, discordant music of the wolf pack had sounded almost every night since the last full moon.

The swamp buck and his doe had not as yet felt the pinch of hunger, but instinct told them to keep close to the shelter of the Tamarack Swamp, so except for the morning strolls of the buck to the shore of Kennedy Lake, they had seldom ventured far from the timber. They had often heard the wolf pack, but always so far away that there was little danger as long as they stayed under cover.

Several days had passed since the buck had been to the shore of Kennedy Lake. As yet the silence of the swamp had been unbroken except for the crunching of their own hooves through the icy crust on the trails, and the buck was beginning to wonder if there was really anything to fear. Then one day, as they were again leisurely working their way over to the sunning place in the clearing, they were startled by the strange noises far toward the east end of the swamp. They stopped, every nerve on edge. At times they could hear them quite plainly, then again they would be so faint as to be almost indistinguishable from the other sounds of the forest.

The two deer were not much concerned at first. After satisfying themselves that there was no real danger, they started again down the trail toward the clearing. They could still hear the noises occasionally, but could not tell whether they were coming closer or going further away.

Then just as they neared the edge of the swamp, the sound of heavy footsteps seemed suddenly to grow louder and more distinct. Once more they stopped and stood with heads high, ears pricked up, listening intently. This time they were thoroughly alarmed. Closer and closer came the racket. Now they could hear distinctly the crunching of snow and the crackling of twigs, and then the whole east end of the timber seemed to be fairly alive with tumult, and the air reeked with danger.

The buck ran in a circle, sniffing keenly. The same scent that had come to him from the cabin now rankled heavily in the air, and he knew the time had come to leave the shelter of the Tamarack Swamp. He hesitated, however, not knowing which way to turn. Back and forth he ran, stopping now and then to paw the ground, or to blow the air through his nostrils with the sharp whistling noise that all deer use when in danger.

A branch cracked sharply close at hand, and the scent came doubly strong from the east. With a wild snort the buck wheeled and led the way toward the western end of the swamp followed closely by the doe. Their only hope lay in reaching a heavy belt of green hemlock timber which they knew was separated from the western end of the Tamarack Swamp by a broad stretch of barren, burned-over slashing. As they neared the edge of the swamp they stopped, dreading to leave its protection. From where they stood they could see the dark wall of timber half a mile away. A brushy gully ran diagonally toward it across the open slashing, offering some protection, but the hills on either side were as stark and bare as an open field.

Again came the crack and crunch, now so close that the very air burned with danger. It was time to go. They bounded out of the timber, their white flags waving defiance, and were soon in the brush gully, going like the wind. Just as they sailed over a windfall, the buck caught a glimpse of something moving on a big black pine stump on top of the ridge to their right. Then the quiet was shattered by a succession of rending crashes, and strange singing and whining sounds filled the air above them.

Again and again came the crashes. Suddenly the little doe stopped dead in her tracks. She gave a frightened baa-aa a of pain and terror as the blood burst in a stream from a jagged wound in her throat. The buck stopped and ran back to where she stood, head down and swaying unsteadily. He watched her a moment, then, growing nervous, started down the trail again. The doe tried bravely to follow, but fell half- way across a windfall too high for her to clear. Again the buck stopped and watched her anxiously. The snow by the windfall was soon stained bright red with blood, and the head of the little doe sank lower and lower in spite of her brave efforts to hold it up.

Hurriedly the buck looked about him. Several black figures were coming rapidly down the ridge. He nosed his doe gently, but this time she did not move. Raising his head he looked toward the approaching figures. Danger was close, but he could not leave his mate.

A spurt of smoke came from one of the figures, followed by another crash. This time the buck felt a blow so sharp that it made him stumble. Staggering to his feet, he plunged blindly down the gully. His flag was down, the sure sign of a wounded deer. Again and again came the crashes, and the air above him whined and sang as the leaden pellets searched for their mark. The bark flew from a birch tree close by, spattering him with fragments. In spite of his wound, he ran swiftly and was soon out of range in the protecting green timber. He knew that he would not be tracked for at least an hour, as his pursuers would wait for him to lie down and stiffen.

He was bleeding badly from a long red scar cutting across his flank, and his back trail was sprinkled with tiny red dots. Where he stopped to rest and listen, little puddles of blood would form that quickly turned bluish black in the snow. For two hours he ran steadily, and then was so weakened by loss of blood that at last he was forced to lie down.

After a short rest, he staggered to his feet, stiffened badly. The bed he had melted in the snow was stained dark red from his bleeding flank. The cold, however, had contracted the wound and had stopped the bleeding a little. He limped painfully down the trail, not caring much which direction it led. Every step was torture. Once when crossing a

small gully, he stumbled and fell on his wounded leg. It rested him to lie there, and it was all he could do to force himself on.

While crossing a ridge, the wind bore the man scent strongly to him, and he knew that now he was being trailed. Once, he heard the brush crack behind him, and was so startled that the wound was jerked open and the bleeding started afresh. He watched his back trail nervously, expecting to see his pursuer at any moment and hear again the rending crash that would mean death.

He grew steadily weaker and knew that unless night came soon, he would be overtaken. He had to rest more often now, and when he did move it was to stagger aimlessly down the trail, stumbling on roots and stubs. It was much easier now to walk around the windfalls than to try to jump over as he had always done before.

The shadows were growing longer and longer, and in the hollows it was already getting dusk. If he could last until nightfall he would be safe. But the man scent was getting still stronger, and he realized at last that speed alone could not save him. Strategy was the only course. If his pursuer could be thrown off the trail, only long enough to delay him half an hour, darkness would be upon the wilderness and he could rest.

So waiting until the trail ran down onto a steep ravine filled with brush and windfalls, the buck suddenly turned and walked back on his own trail as far as he dared. It was the old trick of back tracking that deer have used for ages to elude their pursuers. Then stopping suddenly, he jumped as far to the side as his strength would permit, landing with all four feet tightly bunched together in the very center of a scrubby hazel bush. From there, he worked his way slowly into a patch of scrub spruce and lay down, exhausted, under an old windfall. Weakened as he was from loss of blood and from the throbbing pain in his flank, it was all he could do to keep his eyes riveted on his back trail, and his ears strained for the rustling and crunching that he feared would come, unless darkness came first.

It seemed that he had barely lain down, when without warning, the brush cracked sharply, and not 100 yards away appeared a black figure. The buck was petrified with terror. His ruse had failed. He shrank as far down as he could in the grass under the windfall and his eyes almost burst from their sockets. Frantically he thought of leaving his hiding place, but knew that would only invite death. The figure came closer and closer, bending low over the trail and peering keenly into the spruce thicket ahead. In the fading light the buck was well hidden by the windfall, but the blood-spattered trail led straight to his hiding place. Discovery seemed certain.

The figure picked its way still nearer. It was now within 30 feet of the windfall. The buck watched, hardly daring to breathe. Then, in order to get a better view into the thicket, the hunter started to climb a snow covered stump close by. Suddenly, losing his balance, he slipped and plunged backwards into the snow. The buck saw his chance. Gathering all his remaining strength, he dashed out of his cover and was soon hidden in the thick growth of spruce.

It was almost dark now and he knew that as far as the hunter was concerned, he was safe. Circling slowly around, he soon found a sheltered hiding place in a dense clump of spruce where he could rest and allow his wound to heal.

Night came swiftly, bringing with it protection and peace. The stars came out one by one, and a full November moon climbed into the sky, flooding the snowy wilderness with its radiance.

Several hours had passed since the buck had lain down to rest in the spruce thicket. The moon was now riding high in the heavens and in the open places it was almost as light as day. Although well hidden, he dozed fitfully, waking at times with a start, thinking that again he was being trailed. He would then lie and listen, with nerves strained to the breaking point, for any sounds of the wild that might mean danger. An owl hooted over in a clump of timber, and the new forming ice on the shores of Kennedy Lake, half a mile away, rumbled ominously. Then he heard a long quavering call, so faint and far away that it almost blended with the whispering of the wind. The coarse hair on his shoulders bristled as he recognized the hunting call of the age-old enemy of his kind. It was answered again and again. The wolf pack was gathering, and for the first time in his life, the buck knew fear. In the shelter of the Tamarack Swamp there had been little danger, and even if he had been driven to the open, his strength and speed would have carried him far from harm. Now, sorely wounded and far from shelter, he would have hardly a fighting chance should the pack pick up his trail.

They were now running in full cry, having struck a trail in the direction of the big swamp far to the west. To the buck, the weird music was as a song of death. Circling and circling, for a time they seemed to draw no nearer. As yet he was not sure whether it was his own blood-bespattered trail that they were unraveling, or that of some other one of his kind. Then, suddenly, the cries grew in fierceness and volume and sounded much closer than before. He listened spellbound as he finally realized the truth it was his own trail they were following. The fiendish chorus grew steadily louder and more venomous, and now had a new note of triumph in it that boded ill for whatever came in its way.

He could wait no longer and sprang to his feet. To his dismay, he was so stiffened and sore, that he could hardly take a step. Forcing himself on, he hobbled painfully through the poplar brush and clumps of timber in the direction of the lake. Small windfalls made him stumble, and having to walk around hummocks and hollows made progress slow and difficult. How he longed for his old strength and endurance. About two-thirds of the distance to the lake had been covered and already occasional glimpses of water appeared between the openings.

Suddenly the cries of the pack burst out in redoubled fury behind him, and the buck knew they had found his warm blood-stained bed. Plunging blindly on, he used every ounce of strength and energy that he had left, for now the end was only a matter of minutes. The water was his only hope, for by reaching that he would at least escape being torn to shreds by the teeth of the pack. He could hear them coming swiftly down the ridge behind him and every strange shadow he mistook for one of the gliding forms of his pursuers. They were now so close that he could hear their snarls and yapping. Then a movement caught his eye in the checkered moonlight. A long gray shape had slipped out of the darkness and was easily keeping pace with him. Another form crept in silently on the other side and both ran like phantoms with no apparent effort. He was terrorstricken, but kept on desperately. Other ghost-like shapes filtered in from the timber, but still they did not close. The water was just ahead. They would wait till he broke from the brush that lined the shore. With a crash, he burst through the last fringe of alders and charged forward. As he did so, a huge gray form shot out of the shadows and launched itself at his throat. He saw the movement in time and caught the full force of the blow on his horns. A wild toss and the snarling shape splashed into the ice rimmed shallows. At the same instant the two that had been running alongside closed, one for his throat and the other for his hamstrings. The first he hit a stunning blow with his sharp front hoof, but as he did so the teeth of the other fastened on the tendon of his hind leg. A frantic leap loosened his hold and the buck half-plunged and half-slid over the ice into the waters of Kennedy Lake. Then the rest of the pack tore down to the beach with a deafening babble of snarls and howls, expecting to find their quarry down or at bay. When they realized that they had been outwitted, their anger was hideous and the air was rent with howls and yaps.

The cold water seemed to put new life into the buck and each stroke was stronger than the one before. Nevertheless, it was a long hard swim, and before he was halfway across, the benumbing cold had begun to tell. He fought on stubbornly, his breath coming in short, choking sobs and finally, after what seemed ages, touched the hard sandy bottom of the other shore. Dragging himself painfully out, he lay down exhausted in the snow. All sense of feeling had left his tortured body, but the steady lap, lap of the waves against the tinkling shore ice soothed him into sleep.

When he awoke, the sun was high in the heavens. For a long time he lay as in a stupor, too weak and sorely stiffened to move. Then with a mighty effort he struggled to his feet, and stood motionless, bracing himself unsteadily. Slowly his strength returned and leaving his bed, he picked his way carefully along the beach, until he struck the trail, down which he had so often come to drink. He followed it to the summit of the ridge overlooking the lake.

The dark blue waters sparkled in the sun, and the rolling spruce covered ridges were green as they had always been. Nothing had really changed, yet never again would it be the same. He was a stranger in the land of his birth, a lonely fugitive where once he had roamed at will, his only choice to leave forever the ancient range of his breed. For a time he wavered torn between his emotions, then finally turned to go. Suddenly an overwhelming desire possessed him, to visit again the place where last he had seen his mate. He worked slowly down the trail to the old Tamarack Swamp and did not stop until he came to the old meeting place deep in the shadows where the two trails crossed. For a long time he did not move, then turned and headed into the north to a new wilderness far from the old, a land as yet untouched, the range of the Moose and Caribou.

Work Weekend

JAY CASSELL

Joey peered through the scope carefully, took a long breath, settled in, and slowly began to squeeze the trigger. As I watched the target downrange, 1 heard the sharp crack of the .22. A split second later the aluminum can flew off the downed log, 50 yards away. "Yessss," cried Joey. "Got another one!"

At that, Joey and his cousin, Steven, showed us that the bolts on their .22s were both open, then put the rifles down and sprinted down the range, where they quickly put all of the cans back on the log, then came racing back so they could reload and start shooting again.

The boys had worked for their reward of shooting the rifles. We were at our deer hunting camp, The Over The Hill Gang, deep in New York's Catskill Mountains, on our annual summer work weekend to tackle the chores that must be done to keep a hunting camp functioning. Dan Gibson, his 21-year-old son Keith and I unhitched the splitter from my truck and started splitting the logs we had piled up earlier in the summer. Keith, who's in the Army Reserve, may ship off to Iraq before the season, although I know he'd like to get in a bit of deer hunting before he goes. Kevin Kenney, meanwhile, was down the road about a quarter mile chainsawing a black cherry that came down in a late-spring windstorm. Last hunting season was an especially cold one, with temperatures consistently below 20 degrees. We came close to running out of wood

for our two woodstoves—one in the kitchen, the other in the bunkroom—so we were making doubly certain that we had enough for the upcoming season.

While all this was going on, Vin Sparano was out behind the cabin, installing a new floor in the outhouse. Every couple of years the local porcupine population decides it's time to feast on our outhouse, and then we have to rebuild it. It's an ongoing battle, with us staying about one step ahead. Rod Cochran, out in front, was replacing rotted planks on the front deck, while Matt Sparano, Steven's dad, grabbed a bucket of paint and began touching up the cabin's trim.

When Ken Surerus and his son, Raymond, showed up, they started stacking all of the firewood that Dan, Keith and I had been splitting.

By the end of the day, the old camp—it was built in the 1940s—was in pretty good shape. A new American flag was up on the roof, all of the weeds and brush around the building had been cut back, and the inside had been swept clean. Before the season, we'd all be back again, sighting in our rifles and doing last-minute chores such as getting the propane tank filled and stocking up the kitchen with food for the season. I also have two tree stands that need to be shored up before November. They're about two miles apart; one has a rotting floor, the other needs new rungs on the ladder.

Author Rick Bass, who wrote *The Deer Pasture*, once said this about his hunting camp: "For a place we visit only one week out of the year, we worry about it far too much."

I don't know about you, but that's the way all of the guys in my camp feel. We think about that place all the time. We do go there more than one week a year, but we'd all go there more often if we could. It's tough to explain, but a good deer camp becomes a part of you. The years go by, and members come and go, some to that hunting ground in the sky, but you come to realize that part of you is always in deer camp. I don't even see some of the guys except during work weekend and in deer season, but that doesn't matter.

What matters is that they all show up every year to take part in the ritual of deer camp. What matters is that the pulse of the camp keeps beating from year to year, generation to generation. So you bring the youngsters along and teach them about the woods, you instill proper gun handling and safety in them, you make them understand the importance of respecting the game we hunt. And when they get old enough, as Keith and Raymond have, then you let them into the camp as full members, sharing in the work, in the fun, in the good times and, when they happen, the tough times too.

Work weekend—it's the beginning of another cycle of hunting seasons. Before you know it, it'll be opening day, I'll be in my tree stand with its new floor, the sky will have a hint of light to the East, and I'll be watching the trail on the ledge down below. And life will be as good as it possibly can be.

Gearing Up

JAY CASSELL

Around about this time, it suddenly hits me: Deer season is right around the corner! Excellent—and then I remember all the things I need to fix, or tune up or replace. That's when I pull out a Cabela's or Bass Pro catalog and start looking for all those items I absolutely have to have this year

Bow season opens in mid-October here in New York, so tuning up my six-year-old bow is first priority. Sometimes I think I should get a new, lighter weight bow, but I've spent too much time in the woods with this one. I'll readjust the fiber-optic sights to make sure I'm dead on at 20 yards, then I'll wax the strings, oil the pulleys and the trigger, sharpen half a dozen broadheads, and I'll be ready for the season.

That reminds me; I need to buy a new block target— my old one is too beat up. For that matter, I also need camo netting for my tree stand down by the swamp. A new foam seat wouldn't be a bad idea, either, since someone stole mine out of my stand last year. I should buy a dozen new screw-in tree steps, too. And I'd better add some six-hour hand warmers to the list.

For rifle season, which starts before Thanksgiving, I first take my 12-year-old Browning .30-06 bolt-action out to the range and run some rounds through it to make sure it's about two inches high at 100 yards. I shoot during the year, but checking to make certain it's on before the season is critical.

My old Leupold scope is all scratched up, with some dings, but it's still as sharp as ever. That 3-9X has been on my '06 ever since I bought them both, and there is no way I could replace it. I've got new scopes on some of my other rifles, but this marriage of scope and rifle isn't getting a divorce so long as I'm in charge.

Rifle, scope, clothes are still fine, boots got new soles last year, coat, hat, gloves—gloves could be a problem. I have woolen half-finger gloves, with the fold-over mitten when you want to cover up your fingertips. I lost one of them on a deer drive last year.

I've got enough scents—attractants, masking scents, odor neutralizers—to last the rest of my life. Scentless detergent for my clothes should go onto the shopping list, now that I think of it. I put camo duct tape on my day- pack last year after mice chewed through it to get at a Snickers bar, but there's no need to replace it.

The walkie-talkies need nickel cadmium batteries, and they're not cheap. But we use our radios for safety checks, coordinating drives, all sorts of things. Four batteries go onto the list, $35 a pop. Now I'm ready. No, wait, I need fuel for my lanterns.

Mantles, too. I have a propane lantern, so I'd better get more canisters while I'm at it.

At least this year I've got something new, something that won't cost a dime to repair. This summer I bought an ATV, a purchase I've put off because I like to walk, not ride, plus it always killed me to think I'd go blasting off in the morning while a monster 10-pointer stood right there, watching me fade over the hill. But quads are worth the expense. I don't know about you, but dragging deer for a couple of miles uphill is not my idea of a good time. Nor is carrying 2x4s and sheets of plywood out to new stand sites. And in the morning, you can stay at the breakfast table and drink your coffee without rushing because you can drive to within range of your stand instead of leaving 40 minutes early to get there. At night, I can just pile my backpack and other gear on the quad and get back to camp in a hurry.

Come to think of it, I need to get a storage basket to put on the back of my quad. A rifle holder seems like a good idea, too. I also need warmer gloves for riding. And the quad's trailer—I'd better get a spare tire for that, plus a bracket to hold it. I hope I remembered to renew the registration.

I can't wait for deer season to start. This preseason stuff is wearing me out.

Opening Day

JAY CASSELL

The night before opening day of deer season is always a special one, filled with hope and anticipation. In our hunting area in New York's Catskill Mountains, the opener has traditionally been the third Monday of November. It's the best Monday of the year.

Camp members usually start showing up on Saturday to help with the grocery shopping and do any camp chores that have been put off until the last minute. By Sunday afternoon everyone is in camp, working a bit on the cabin, perhaps doing some last-minute sighting in at the rifle range or hammering in a few more nails into tree stands. Come nighttime, with all the work done, everyone gathers in the kitchen to catch up and talk deer hunting.

"Where you going in the morning?" someone will ask, and before too long, plans will be laid out. "I'm going to the Living Room stand, at least for the morning," I'll chip in, adding that I'll stay all day if the weather isn't too cold and if I've got a good feeling about things.

Inevitably talk will make its way to Kenny, who has taken a buck 31 out of the past 32 opening days. I used to wonder whether Kenny was full of it or not, but I've spent enough time in the woods with him over the years to know that he's the real deal. He'll spot deer that I can't even see until they put up their white flags and flee. His 20-10 vision helps immeasurably, but he does his preseason

scouting—knows what to look for and where. And he can shoot.

"What do you think, Kenny?" I'll ask nonchalantly. "See any bucks down by the Living Room this year."

Kenny will get that smile on his face, then lower his voice and look me in the eye, furtively glancing left and right to make sure that no one else can hear. "I've seen a really nice eight-point running that ledge you like to watch," he'll confide. "I saw him there three weeks ago, and there are some rubs down below. You sit in that stand all day, and you'll see him. There's a nice five in there, too."

The alarm goes off at 4:15 in our camp, though some of the guys are up before then, too restless to sleep; no matter how old you are and how many opening days you've seen, the next one is always the one you've been waiting for.

Dan is the first one out of bed, and he'll turn on the propane lights, start the coffee and begin frying bacon and eggs. Soon, everyone has filtered into the kitchen, in long johns, shorts, camo clothes. Most of the guys eat silently, thinking about the hours to come. Then dishes will be put into the sink and we'll all be getting into our hunting clothes. Outside, a quad is started up, its low, staccato hum a reminder that the sun will be rising soon, that it's time to go.

I'm always out of sync on opening morning, as I don't have my routine down yet. But I'll go out to my car, put on my jacket and hat—I keep most of my clothes in the car so they don't absorb camp odors—then load up my '06, wish everyone luck and head down the wilderness trail well before light.

Some mornings, if it's cold, my footsteps crunch as I go, so I have to move slowly and carefully, trying not to make noise. It's about a mile to my stand from camp, though, so I have to move as quickly as I can.

Eventually I'll veer off the main path and take the old jeep trail down the ridge, moving through the hemlock grove and along the stream, keeping my eyes open, as by now dawn is coming fast, with the woods changing from blackness to an eerie gray.

When I reach the stand, I take the rifle off my shoulder, tie it to a drawstring, then climb up as quietly as possible. Getting into the stand, I'll quickly pull up my rifle and sit down, letting the woods settle down after my intrusion. Soon, the sounds of the awakening woods overwhelm me as squirrels start foraging, and woodpeckers, sparrows, cardinals and chickadees all begin flitting about, welcoming the day.

I concentrate on not moving, on listening through the bird noise for possible hoofsteps in the leaves. If it's cold and the forest floor is crunchy, I can hear things coming from a mile away. Warm, moist mornings are different, as deer could almost walk under my stand without my hearing them. Those mornings, I have to rely on my eyes.

At 6:30, I hear a gunshot off to the north, way on the far side of the property. I smile and shake my head. Kenny just took number 32. It never fails. I wonder if it's a nice buck. But who else? Will this be my morning too? It's happened before.

The View from Above

JAY CASSELL

My latest tree stand is called the Living Room stand. Measuring eight feet by eight feet, it's the largest stand I've ever hunted from. I found it three years ago, hiking down some ledges that I'd never explored. Pussyfooting my way along a rivulet coming off the ridge, I first saw an old ladder and then, looking up, spied this huge, abandoned stand. A perfect square, wedged between three live trees and one 2x4 shoring up the last corner, the stand looks down over two steep ledges. Deer runways cross both; to the left is a large open hardwood flat, to the right is a stream and funnel that lead down to the Neversink River below.

It took a day to patch up that old stand. I had to rebuild the supports and the ladder, and replace the floor that porcupines had been feasting on, but that stand is now ready to last another 10 years. I've spent the past two opening days there, and it's been worth it...sort of.

The first year, I had a buck pass by, 40 yards downhill, right at dark. I saw him, raised my .30-06—and he was gone. And last year I had a sixpointer and a doe sneak in behind me. They came down from above, their sounds muffled by the stream. The first time I knew they were there was when I heard a snort; whirling around, I saw two tails bounding through the woods, already too far, too obscured, for a shot.

If you're like me, you've paid your dues in tree stands, and I remember all of my old stands because I learned things at each—from the wildlife I saw, the game I took, and *especially the game I missed.*

One stand that really sticks in my memory is a portable I had on property near my home in suburban New York. The stand was in a tree on the side of a knoll, with a dropoff to the right and another knoll to the left. A major deer trail came through an old rock wall 25 yards above me and then snaked down between both knolls. Deer used that trail every day, moving from the fields below to bedding areas in the woods in the morning, and doing the reverse in the evenings.

I took some does and small bucks there, but nothing major. Fact is, the big bucks never did come through the break in that wall. They'd always come sneaking around the side, or jump the wall, then test the wind, moving cautiously. *I saw two Pope & Young-class bucks* out of that stand, and they both made me before I had shots, thanks to the prevailing thermals. 1 learned about using the wind to my advantage from those encounters, though. To this day I know that thermals come up in the morning, down in the evening, and local structure can push them all over. I also saw, up close, how big bucks operate on a totally different level than smaller bucks.

Wind also ruined my chances at a monster buck in the *Catskills*. I was in another old stand 1 had fixed up. This one, built into three maples, overlooked a huge, 250- *yard-long flat, filled with mixed hardwoods*, deadfalls and heavy brush. On opening day, eight o'clock, I saw a doe and a buck moving along the far edge of that flat. Eventually, they turned and started in my direction, the doe in the lead, always right in front of the buck. I watched and waited, knowing I'd have a shot when they emerged into a small clearing in another 10 yards. They never made it. A slight breeze from behind me sent my scent in their direction, and that doe just about turned inside out when she smelled it. She took off fast, with the buck dutifully following right behind. I never had a clear shot at that buck, a 10-pointer with two drop tines on his left side.

Some stands you remember not for the game you see but for other wildlife. There's one bow stand I built in a swamp near my home. I've seen deer, coyotes, foxes and turkeys out of that stand, but it's the barred owl I remember most. He came hooting through the darkness, just as I was getting down for the evening. With a rush of wind and a crash of branches and wings, he landed on a thick branch just five feet away and spooked the hell out of me. He was spooked, too, because the moment he saw me he hopped off that branch and took off, a ghostlike apparition winging away into the night.

Tree stands—each day you climb into your stand could be the day you experience something you'll remember for the rest of your life.

Hunting the Burbs

JAY CASSELL

Driving down Route 138 with my 17-year-old daughter, Katherine, behind the wheel, I leaned back and stared out at the darkness passing by. A typical weekday night, we were headed to town to grab some Chinese takeout. It was October, and Katherine knew to keep an eye out for deer. The pre-rut was close, and this time' of year is when the whitetail frequently encounters its primary suburban predator: the automobile. Sure enough, there was a white flicker off the right headlight. "Slow down," I said. With no cars behind us, my hunter instincts took over, and I asked Katherine to put it in reverse so we could take a look.

Backing up 20 yards, we peered into the woods. "Dad, that's the biggest buck I've ever seen," Katherine whispered, as if the deer might hear us over the engine note. But she was right. There, by the side of the road, grazing at the edge of someone's lawn, was a massive 12-pointer, the kind of buck you might see on the cover of *Petersen's Hunting*. We saw approaching headlights, so we took off, hoping that buck wouldn't decide to cross the road.

It was probably the buck that my friend Bruce missed the year before. He'd been hunting in woods behind somebody's backyard when a massive buck came running by. He whistled, got it to stop, then was shaking so hard that he missed it at 10 yards.

So it goes when you hunt in suburbia—lots of huge bucks living near houses, and minimal hunting pressure. I live 50 miles north of New York City, and the deer population is out of control, but getting permission to hunt is tough. Last year I asked one neighbor, who has five wooded acres, if I could hunt at the edge of his property, and he flat out told me no. He was afraid I'd shoot his kids.

Getting hunting permission is tough, but persistence will pay off. Eventually, you do get lucky.

One of my favorite spots was a 100-acre farm a mile from my home. The land hadn't been farmed in years. It was owned by an elderly woman, and her caretaker let me onto the property. "There are so many deer around here it's ridiculous," he told me. "*Shoot 'em all.*"

I set up a stand overlooking two major game trails and took a good number of deer there for five years ranning. The best time of day was when the school bus came down the road at three o'clock. The kids would get off, walk the road making all sorts of noise and unknowingly drive deer to me. The only problem was that the deer would often come running by me at warp speed, too fast for a shot.

Another favorite spot is at my buddy Dan's. His house is on six acres that slopes down to a swamp. Neighbors on both sides have given us permission to hunt because they are tired of the deer eating their shrubs.

I set up on a knoll that overlooks a generational trail skirting the swamp. Dan sets up along an old rock wall halfway up the property, while his son Keith has a stand up near the top. The best trail leads down through the middle of Dan's property, past the swimming pool and barbecue, then down into the woods.

Then there's my stand at Ellen's house. Ellen lives on the edge of a deer funnel that leads from dense, posted woods, down through two neighborhoods. The deer go up that funnel in the morning, down it in the evening. My stand? An old wooden play cabin, with shutters and a door. I've got a swivel chair in there, and I can rotate to shoot out of any window. They aren't suspicious of it, but you have to sneak down the patio, then cross the lawn without being seen by the neighbor's dog. If it spots you, you can bet it's going to bark for 20 minutes, scaring off incoming deer.

Hunting the burbs—it's what hunting is all about in 2014 in many parts of the country, and while it's not the wilderness experience we all long for, it's still hunting and it's still challenging.

The difference is that you have to be creative to get a buck. Now that I'm thinking about it, maybe I'll develop a new line of camo clothing, perhaps resembling gas grill covers, or something with rhododendron patterns. Then all I need is a special cover scent—Citronella candles might work, or maybe a barbecue sauce scent. Then those bucks are cooked.

Way North

JAY CASSELL

There's a bookcase in my living room that stretches from the floor to the ceiling. Books are crammed into every conceivable space—old ones, new ones, hunting, fishing, history—there's a lot of good reading on those shelves. I was looking at them the other day, and my eyes strayed to the top shelf. There, wedged between two old volumes, is the scapula of a caribou. On it is inscribed "Mulchatna River, Alaska, 8/27-9/2, 1997." 1997. It seems like just last year.

I flew to Anchorage and met up with my hunting buddy Chris at the floatplane docks on Lake Hood. We stashed our gear in our chartered twin Otter and took off, heading southwest through the majestic landscape of Lake Clark Pass, en route to the Mulchatna River. I gazed out the window at the sun glinting off the mountain glaciers and clouds scudding across snow-capped peaks that stretched as far as the eye could see.

We flew out over the Mulchatna flats, eventually landing on a stark, five-acre lake. We unloaded our gear into a big pile, said goodbye to our pilot, and watched as he taxied, turned into the wind, then blasted across the water in a whirlwind of spray—getting airborne and banking east, back to Anchorage, two hours away. We were on our own, deep in Alaska, for five days.

Our surroundings consisted of low mountains and knolls, grass and scrub brush. A low breeze blew across the flats, drowning out the silence of the wilderness, a silence so pervasive that it can ring in your ears when the wind stops. We set up camp and went scouting.

It took less than a day to find the bull I wanted. We spotted a herd of about 100 head moving in our direction at a steady pace from the east. The herd undulated with the landscape, the racks of the three main bulls dipping up and down as they walked. At times the caribou would drop down into a gully, then flow out the other side, a land-based wave. Suddenly Chris pointed to a gully a mile away. "They're headed for that gully and the flat beyond," he said. If we want at shot at that big herd bull, we gotta move.

We reached our destination in half an hour, sucking wind but knowing we had beaten the herd. Then it was a waiting game. I watched through my binoculars as the herd stopped to rest, the bull lying down. Finally, after another hour, they got up and came in our direction. With my .30-06 steady on a daypack, I waited until the bull was clear of other animals. The shot echoed across the land like a roll of thunder, the other caribou scattering like quail in a flushed covey, and the bull collapsed where he had stood, his great body crashing to earth.

We sprinted to the bull and, after congratulations, handshakes and back-slapping, got to work, removing the hide from the carcass, then carving away the meat—all done in warming temperatures amid a swirl of black flies and mosquitoes, loaded rifles at the ready, both of us on constant lookout for grizzlies.

We loaded the frame packs and humped the quarters back to camp a mile away, then returned for the rest of the meat and the antlers—always approaching the carcass carefully, making sure that the pole with the red handkerchief on top was still standing, signaling to us that no large, unpleasant creatures had moved in on our kill.

That night was a festive one. Chris dug some Yukon Jack and two tin cups out of his pack, and we toasted the herd bull, our 20-year friendship and the wilderness that is Alaska. With Orion soaring overhead and the temperatures plummeting into the 30s, it was a perfect way to end a magnificent day.

Chris got his caribou on the last day, a huge, older bull with massive antlers shed of their velvet. We were hauling the meat back to camp when we heard the Otter in the distance, first a faint buzz, then a roar as the plane appeared over a low mountain, flew overhead, then circled and landed. Then it was back to Anchorage, back to New York and daily existence

I think of all this when I see that scapula on the shelf. I found it one day near camp, and I've always wondered if that animal died a natural death or was ambushed by something. And now one of its bones is on a shelf in a home in suburban New York. Up in my cabin in the mountains, in the whitetail woods, my bull's rack hangs over the door, welcoming visitors, a vestige from a wilder place, a slice of my lifetime, another September hunt.

The Rack

JAY CASSELL

"I found his antler, Dad," the throaty voice of my six-year-old son, James, crackled over the telephone. "I saw it in the woods when Mom was driving me home from school, right near where we went hunting! Are you coming home tonight?"

When I told him that my flight wouldn't get in until 11:00, and that I wouldn't be home until midnight, there was a disappointed silence over the phone. Then, "Well, okay, but don't look at it until morning, so I can show you. Promise?"

I promised. We had a deal. I told him I'd see him soon, then asked to talk with his mother.

"Love you, Dad."

"Love you too, James."

Unbelievable. My son had found the shed antler of the buck I had hunted, unsuccessfully, all season. The big ten-pointer I had seen the day before deer season, the one with the wide spread and thick beams. He had seen me that day, having winded me as I pussyfooted through some thickets for a closer look. I think he somehow knew that he was safe, that he was far enough away from me.

I had scouted the 140-acre farm and adjoining woods near my home in suburban New York, the farm that I had gotten permission to hunt after five years of asking. "You can hunt this year," Dan the caretaker had said to me during the summer, when I asked my annual question. "I kicked those other guys off the property. They were in here with ATVs and Jeeps, bringing two and three friends every day they hunted, without even asking. Lot of nerve, I thought. Got sick of 'em, so I kicked 'em off. Now I'll let you hunt, and your buddy John, three other guys, and that's all. I want some local people on here that I know and trust."

When Dan had told me that, I couldn't believe it. But there it was, so I took advantage of it. Starting in September, I began to scout the farm. I had seen bucks on the property in previous years while driving by, but now I got a firsthand look. There was sign virtually everywhere: rubs, scrapes, droppings in the hillside hayfields, in the mixed hardwoods, in the thick hemlock stands towering over the rest of the woods. I found what were obviously rubs left by a big deer. In a copse of hemlocks near the edge of the property, bordering an Audubon nature preserve, were scrapes and, nearby, about five or six beech saplings absolutely ripped apart by antlers.

With James's help, I set up my tree stand overlooking a heavily used trail that seemed to be a perfect escape route out of the hemlocks. James and I also found an old permanent tree stand, which he and I repaired with a few two-by-fours and nails. This would officially be "his" tree stand—or tree house, as he called it.

Opening day couldn't come fast enough. James and I talked about it constantly. Even though he's only six, and can't really hunt yet, he couldn't wait for deer season. He knows what deer tracks and droppings look like; can tell how scrapes and rubs are made; can even identify where deer have passed in the leaf-covered forest floor. My plan was to hunt the first few days of the season by myself while James was in school, and then take him on a weekend. If luck was with me, maybe I'd take the big buck and could then concentrate on filing my doe tag with my son's help.

Opening day came and went, with no trophy ten-pointer in sight, or any other bucks, for that matter. A lot of other days came and went too, most of them cold, windy and rainy. Three weeks into the two-month-long season, on a balmy Sunday in the 50s, James and I packed our camo backpacks with candy bars and juice boxes, binoculars and grunt calls, and at 2:00 p.m. off we went, on our first day of hunting together. When we reached the spot where I always park my car, on a hillside field, I dabbed some camo paint onto James's face, which he thought was cool. Then we started hiking up the field and into the woods, toward the hemlocks.

We saw one white tail disappear over a knob as we hiked into James's stand. I didn't really care, though. This was the first time I was taking my son hunting! It would be the first of many, I hoped. I wouldn't force it on him, just introduce him to the sport, and keep my fingers crossed.

At James's stand, we sat down and had a couple of candy bars. "Can I blow on the deer call now, Dad?" I said yes, and he proceeded to honk away on the thing like a trumpet player.

"Do it quietly," I advised. "And remember, always whisper, don't talk loudly. And don't move around so much!"

What with James honking on the call and fidgeting—checking out my bow, looking around, pointing to the hawk soaring overhead, crumpling up his candy bar wrapper and stuffing it into his pocket—I was sure no self-respecting deer would come within a mile of us. None did, not to my son's stand, or to mine, or to the rocks where we later sat, overlooking a trail and those ripped-up beech saplings, until darkness finally settled over the woods. But that was okay.

Hiking out of the woods, we met my friend John coming from his tree stand.

"I saw that ten-pointer today," he began, giving James a poke in the ribs with his finger.

"Where?"

"Up near those hemlocks, the same area you and I have been hunting. We were probably 100 yards away from each other."

"Well, what happened?" Part of me was saying, *Great, he got the buck!* The other part of me was saying, *Pleeeease tell me you didn't shoot him.* John looked at me sheepishly.

"I was watching that trail, and I saw a doe headed my way, right where I always put my climbing tree stand. Then, right behind her, I saw a buck—you know that six-pointer we've seen over by the lake? Well, I started to draw back on him—he was only 30 yards away—but then I saw some movement to my left. It was HIM! Cutting through the hemlocks. That six-pointer and doe got out of there fast, and the ten-pointer got to within ten yards of my stand, stopped broadside to me, and then looked up straight at me!"

"Did you shoot? Did you shoot?"

"I couldn't. I was shaking too much. I mean, I could even hear the arrow rattling against the rest. Eventually, he just took off down the trial. Man, he was something. Must weigh 200 pounds!"

Later, driving the short ride home, James said, "Hey, Dad, how come John didn't shoot that deer?"

"Shooting a deer is a lot harder than many people think. Even if everything else is right, sometimes you can get so nervous that you just can't shoot, no matter how much you want to. John's time will come, though. He works at it."

I didn't see the buck until two days after Christmas. Hunting by myself, I left my normal tree stand and circled around to the backside of the hemlocks. At 4:00 p.m., I was wedged between some boulders that overlook a well-used trail. It was 20oF, getting dark, and I was cold and shivering uncontrollably. But I kept hearing a rustling behind me. *Another squirrel.* But it wasn't. Suddenly, 60 yards through the trees, I could see a big deer headed my way. It was moving with a purpose. It stopped at what appeared to be a scrape, and I could see a huge symmetrical rack dip down as the buck stuck his nose to the ground. Then he stood up, urinated into the scrape, turned, and headed back into the hemlocks. If he had kept coming down the trail, I would have had a clean 15-yard shot. It wasn't meant to be.

That was my season. I didn't see that ten-pointer again, and I missed my only shot of the year, a 35-yarder at a forkhorn that sailed high. Such is deer hunting.

So now I was returning home from my trip. I walked in the door at midnight, quickly read through some mail on the counter, soon slipped into bed. My wife rolled over and whispered, "Don't forget to wake up James before you go to work. He really wants to show you that rack."

The alarm went off at 6:30, and I got up to take a shower.

"Psst, Dad, is that you?" came a sleepy voice from my son's room.

"Yes, buddy, how are you?"

"Wait here, Dad!"

Before I could say another word, he jumped out of bed, put on his oversized bear-paw slippers, and went padding down the stairs to the basement. When he returned, he had the biggest grin on his face that I've ever seen.

"Look, Dad!"

And there it was, half of the ten-pointer's rack. A long, thick main beam, four long, heavy points, the back one eight inches. Amazing. And that buck will be there next year.

"Dad, can I put it on my wall?"

"Of course."

"And can we go look for the other half of his antlers tomorrow, because tomorrow's Saturday, and I don't have school, and you once told me that their antlers usually fall off pretty close together. Please?"

"Sure, James. If you're good in school today."

The deal was made. We never found the other half of the shed, though. It snowed, and we couldn't really look. Mice probably ate the other half.

But you know what? I think maybe my future hunting companion was born this past season.

A Dangerous Game—Hunting at a Higher Level for Trophy Blacktails

JAY CASSELL

The concepts of fear and hunting have always seemed incongruous to me. No matter where I hunt, I always know I'm the most dangerous creature in the woods. Whether I'm hiking back to deer camp in the dark, with coyote song pulsing through the darkness; or I'm walking across a field on my buddy's upstate farm, bow in hand, headed to my treestand in the predawn darkness; no matter where I go, I know that other creatures will shy away at my coming. I am armed; I have nothing to fear.

With that imperious view of the natural order of things, I stepped ashore on Kodiak Island last fall, and faced a new reality. It didn't make any difference that I had a Remington Model 700 .300 Ultra mag, loaded with 200-grain Swift A-Frame bullets, over my shoulder; that I had some of the best optics available; that I had a topo map, GPS unit, and compass with me; or, finally, that I had a can of bear repellant (range – 10 yards; spray duration – 5 seconds). What made a difference was this: I was not the top-of-the-line predator here. That title belonged to the many Kodiak bears that inhabit this 150 – by 50-mile-long island in the Pacific Ocean, 20 miles across the Shelikof Strait from mainland Alaska. And that made all the difference in the world.

On the beach, looking at the 12-inch-long bear tracks in the black gravel, gazing at the head-high grass thickets I had to hike through to get up the mountain, toward the snowline, I knew that I could be the prey at any moment. Some hunters have been mauled on this island, others have been charged by bears intent on either stealing a dead deer or fending off perceived danger to their cubs. Could I be next? What would I do if a bear charged? Would a bullet really stop an oncoming, enraged brown bear at 10 yards? Could pepper spray do anything other than piss a bear off? I might find out.

Planning a Hunt Like No Other

The pieces for this trip started to come together two years earlier, when Doug Jeanneret of the U.S. Sportsmen's Alliance and Joe Arterburn of Cabela's asked if I'd like to join them on their annual blacktail hunt on Kodiak. There would be eight of us (six hunters, the captain and mate) living on a houseboat based in Larsen Bay at the southwestern tip of the island. We'd each have two deer tags. Bonus hunting would be jump shooting for ducks, including mallards, buffleheads, and gaudily colored harlequins. We could also fish for halibut and go crabbing for Dungeness and Tanner crabs.

I'd have to take a long flight from New York to Anchorage and then on to Kodiak; live on a cramped boat for a week with a bunch of guys and what might generously be called a shower; hunt on a island with approximately one brown bear per square mile, at a time when they are all feeding heavily in preparation for the upcoming winter; plus, hike and climb every day until I become aware of muscles I didn't even know existed. I told them to count me in.

Time flew, and before I knew it, I was packing my gun and gear and confirming airline reservations. In late October, our group of six convened at the Best Western in the city of Kodiak, where a 1200-pound-plus stuffed brown bear lords over the lobby, dined at a local steak and burger joint, then flew on down to Larsen Bay the next morning, in a crammed Turbo Beaver.

Flying over Kodiak was worth the trip by itself. Snow-covered, jagged peaks soared into the azure blue sky, while frozen-over lakes and tributaries dominated the valleys. The shadow of our plane etched its way across the whiteness below. ("This is my office," our pilot confided to me with a knowing grin.) In time, we came out of the mountains, crossed an unusually tranquil bay, then began our approach to the dirt strip at Larsen Bay. The landing went smoothly, we piled our gear into a waiting F250, then drove the mile to the docks, where the 56-foot houseboat, "The Sundy," was moored. Our home for a week, the boat had a cabin up front with six bunks, three to a side; a kitchen and dining area with two tables; and a large open area to the stern, where we would grill meals, hopefully hang deer, and socialize. The cabin up top,

The author in the Kodiak Holiday Inn lobby. Kodiak bear in the background was a haunting reminder of what lay ahead.

Loading up the plane for the flight to camp.

The flight to our destination, Larsen Bay, took us over beautiful and desolate land.

Once on the ground, the first order of business was making sure that our rifles were still zeroed.

Our home for a week – the Sundy.

Our taxi – a Zodiak inflatable.

the domain of Capt. Al Henderson, was equipped with a GPS-depthfinder and a sat phone, should anyone need to make calls. We were on our way.

After a stop on a deserted beach to sight in rifles, we cruised down a jagged coast lined by snow-capped mountains that rose from the beach to almost 5000 feet. After an hour, the engines cut out and Capt. Al started barking orders. "I need two men up front to man those crab pots," he yelled. "And a third down here to pass up more of them."

I liked this concept – potential surf (crabs) and turf (venison). With fish heads and skeletons for bait, we tossed five large traps overboard, spaced but 100 yards apart, then proceeded down the bay. Another half hour, and the boat slowed again. This time, word came that it was time for two hunters to get in the skiff and head to shore. This would be a short hunt, as we only had about three hours until dark, but it made sense to try for something. Jeanneret and I were soon in the inflatable skiff, headed toward shore. Show time.

On the Ground

Once ashore, my pent-up bear fears from the past two years somewhat in check, Jeanneret and I headed uphill, toward an area where he'd

seen blacktails on previous hunts. As I climbed, I thought things through. Being bear-scared 100 percent of the time was not an option. Better to channel that fear inward, make it work for me, not against. Better to be on total alert 100 percent of the time, to be the best hunter I could be. As I was to discover, hunting with this frame of mind, your adrenalin always pumping, is a form of elevated consciousness, one that you start to thrive on. At the end of the day, when you relax, you feel completely exhausted.

Jeanneret and I hiked halfway up a ridge above Uyak Bay that afternoon, gaining vantage points where we could, glassing a ravine, watching a well-used bowl like any deer hunters would do. By dusk, we had seen five does and one spike, none of the trophy blacktails that some say literally hide behind every bush on the island. This hunt, I thought to myself as we rode the skiff back to our houseboat, this hunt was going to be a tough one. This would be a test.

Onboard, we wolfed down burgers from the grill, and chased them with a couple of beers. It had been a long day, and I could barely stay awake. I scrambled into my upper bunk, slipped into my sleeping bag, and put my head on the pillow. The sounds of waves gently lapping against the hull soon had me sound asleep.

Glassing high, glassing low – you keep looking until you see something. Good high-power binoculars are a must.

Next morning, hunting partners remained the same, and Jeanneret and I headed back toward the same area, planning to hike way above where we had been the previous evening. It was a straight 45-degree climb from the beach to the top; at one point I remember thinking I was glad I had spent time at the gym, preparing for this hunt.

Bulling our way through head-high grass, we paused to watch a thick clump of brush that opened out into some hardwoods. In time, a doe emerged from the brush, headed uphill. There was more movement in that thick stuff, and I slowly raised my rifle, hoping this second deer might have antlers. It didn't; we kept climbing.

Two hours later, we crested the ridge, crossed a 500-yard-long open area, and reached a bowl Jeanneret had been talking about. Fresh deer tracks crisscrossed the snow in every direction. It looked promising, but with 50-mph gusts whipping in off the Pacific, we lasted about half an hour, then had to retreat into the lee of the ridge. We eventually set up by some thick brush and glassed a lake below. Deer trails lead from the lake up the mountain on its far side, stretching up onto the snowline and beyond. Somewhere in the distance, cutting through the howling wind, I thought I heard a gunshot. I wondered if one of our group had shot.

When darkness started to enshroud the mountain, we slowly made our way downhill, not wanting to hike out in the dark in the middle of bear country. Below, out in the bay, we could see the spec that was the Sundy, anchored, waiting for her hunters to radio in for a pickup. Soon we were back in the Zodiak, motoring over whitecaps as the bay started to churn with the wind. The lights of the boat in the distance beckoned with warmth, camaraderie, and good food.

First Blood

Onboard, one of our group, Luke, had a heavy-bodied, wide-racked 9-point buck hanging near the stern. The mood was festive, beers were opened, and everyone congratulated Luke, whose smile beamed that this was a day he'd never forget.

"Joe and I hiked up this ravine, then cut inland for maybe half a mile before setting up to watch a game trail. In time, this guy came ambling by, head to the ground, obviously looking for does. I took him at 48 yards.

"That was the easy part," Luke continued. "Getting him out of that thick stuff, then down the ravine, that was work. I'm still sweating."

What went unsaid was that both he and Joe had been dragging as hard as they could. It's not that the bears are always attracted to the sound of gunshots, as is popularly believed. In truth, the bears also zero in on all the jays and magpies that flock to the gut pile, once you've field-dressed your animal. The trick is to dress your deer and then get out of there fast. "There were so many downed trees and hummocks, the drag took forever," Luke concluded.

Later, Arterburn pulled me aside and said, "Listen, that's a good spot where Luke took that deer. There are always deer up there. You and I should go there tomorrow."

After a venison and salmon dinner, and celebratory cigars all around, we piled into our respective bunks. As happened every night for the whole week, I was asleep the minute my head hit the pillow. I slept the sleep of exhaustion, and didn't wake until the sun was coming up.

My Turn

Arterburn and I hiked up the same ravine that Luke and he had the day before. The temperatures

The author checking a rub at treeline.

were in the 40s, but this was a straight-up climb, over mud and rocks made all the more slippery from spray from a nearby waterfall. Even stopping every 20 yards, it was tough work. Soon I was stripping off outer layers, trying to cool down. My glasses kept fogging up. I was gasping for air. If a bear or deer had come out of the thickets that clawed at us from either side of the trail, I wouldn't have been able to see it anyway.

An hour went by before we reached the top, coming out into a bowl edged by a jagged cliff on one side and a sloping ridge on the other. Arterburn pointed the muzzle of his rifle at bear track in the mud.

"It's old," he said. "Probably a couple of days."

Now we went into hunting mode, easing up the trail, stopping only near trees or rocks, moving slowly, glassing. At this point I was focused on deer, watching for movement, looking for brown horizontal lines or satellite dish ears hidden in brush.

"There's one," Joe whispered, pointing up the side ridge. I looked and there, silhouetted against the sky at the top of the cliff, stood a large-bodied blacktail. I pulled out my 8x42s. Spike.

"I've got two tags," I whispered, "so I could shoot him. But we're so far from the coast that the only thing I'd want to drag out of here is a trophy."

Which is what happened. Coming into an open park, we eased along a game trail that sidehilled up the ridge, then settled back into some thick grass. We agreed to sit there for at least an hour, glassing and watching. I wolfed down a sandwich and water as we waited, then saw movement in the brush on the opposite side of the park, 100 yards away. I eased my .300 Ultra Mag onto my lap, then froze. Now I could see a big, racked buck emerging from the thicket and moving down the trail. Even without my glasses, I could tell he was a keeper: big body, 8 or 10 points.

"Joe," I whispered. "I'm seeing a nice buck right now."

"Shoot him," Arterburn growled as he looked through his glasses. He passed me his shooting stick.

The buck was now out in the open, moving with a purpose across the meadow, directly toward us. The wind blew in my face—perfect—as I eschewed the shooting stick and instead got down on my belly and crawled 8 yards to a lip by the trail we had just come up.

The buck disappeared, out of my view, but then I saw a small tree 40 yards away thrashing back and forth, and watched with delight as the 10-pointer raked it with his antlers. Now he started coming toward us again. He had no idea we were there. At 30 yards, he veered to his right, heading up the meadow. I had a broadside shot.

"Shoot him now!" Arterburn pleaded. He hadn't finished before my rifle boomed, and the buck hunched over and ran, heartshot. He went 15 yards, and piled up in some hummocks. My tag was filled with the blacktail buck I had been hoping for.

After the Shot

Walking over to the deer, the two of us slapped each other's backs, shook hands, and did all the

The author with a heavy-bodied 10-pointer, the result of a slow still hunt.

rejoicing that successful hunters do. But we also knew we had a job to do, and we had to do it quickly.

After admiring the buck, a thick-bodied deer with a rut-swollen neck, chocolate antlers, the double throat patch typical of the species, plus a distinctive black crown, we started in with the field dressing, making sure our loaded rifles were within arm's reach. One man stood guard, the other man worked, and within a few minutes the guts were out, the photos taken, the drag rope affixed to antlers. As we pulled the deer, all 200 pounds of him, the first magpie came soaring in, squawking all the way. Others were right behind him.

"We need to get out of sight of the gutpile," Arterburn said as we pulled the dead weight around hummocks, through water, up and over deadfalls, then onto the game trail. The work was excruciating, with each pull harder than the previous. We were both sweating, both watching our backtrail constantly, both pulling as far as we could before stopping to catch our breaths. It took 20 minutes to get away from the gutpile, which by now had become a feeding frenzy for every bird within a mile. Soon we had the deer in the stream, where the dragging was easier except for all the deadfalls and rocks. Twenty minutes more brought us out of the park, into the ravine. Now we were at the top of the waterfall. We went over the edge, headed down the falls. At times we had to hold the deer to prevent it from falling. Other times we had to hold the drag rope with one hand while grasping at saplings to keep ourselves from sliding down, a long drop to the beach below.

As we neared the bottom, we stopped, panting for breath, muscles screaming. Arterburn pulled out the radio and called the ship.

"Two hunters ready for pick up," he huffed into the radio. "Plus one extra passenger."

"Roger that," came the reply. "We'll come and get you."

We pulled the deer down to the beach and waited, rifles loaded, keeping an eye behind us. There would be no place to go were a bear to come down the trail, following our scent, as the beach was short, and blocked at both ends by rockpiles. I had heard a hunter back in town telling a colleague that a bear had stolen a buck from him at the end of a long drag, right on the beach. "Picked it up the way a Lab picks up a duck," he'd said.

After a mile-long drag through all that thick stuff up above, I'm not sure I was ready to give up my deer to any bear. Fortunately, I didn't have to make that decision, as we heard and then saw the Zodiak headed our way. A few more photos, then we were back in the boat, headed to the mother ship. My trip was a success, and it wasn't over.

A Fitting Finale

The next four days were spent doing all the things you'd ever want to do in Alaska. The following day, a soggy, windy mess, was spent jump shooting mallards, buffleheads, and harlequin ducks, an oddly beautiful bird found mostly in the Pacific Northwest. At the end of the day we picked up our crab traps, by now overflowing with Dungeness and Tanner crabs. That night, we cleaned and boiled all the keepers in Old Bay seasoning, then had a once-in-a-lifetime feast

Tanner crabs – part of the game smorgasbord.

Along with halibut.

of fresh crabs, venison, and red wine, eight grubby men in camo eating a natural, wild meal you couldn't get at the finest restaurant in New York.

The week passed quickly: hunting low along the coastline for blacktails one day with Len Nelson; then high, up above the snowline, the next day with buddy Skip Knowles; then finally, on the last day, catching halibut, skinning deer, cutting meat into steaks, fillets, and roasts, then grinding the rest into hamburger. With a vacuum packer on board, we bagged everything and divvied it up into freezer boxes, ready for the plane rides home.

In time, we were steaming out of Uyak Bay, headed to Larsen, where we loaded everything into a waiting pickup and drove to the landing strip. Snow was falling and the wind was starting to really blow as the Beaver burst out of the clouds, ready to take us back to civilization. We took off into the wind and headed out over the mountains as the squall moved in, bouncing the plane up, down, and sideways, the windows obscured by snow. But we made it – back to the airport, back to the Kodiak Best Western, then back to Anchorage and on home.

It's a strange feeling, sitting here at a computer, poring over my trip notes, remembering an adventure that I had looked forward to for so long, and which went by so quickly. But, it was one of those trips you'll always remember, along with your hunting colleagues who now hold a special place in your memories.

Packing for a Kodiak hunt requires some thought. You don't want to overpack, yet you need to be prepared for different situations. The weather, for example, can change in a heartbeat. In the week I was there, we had one day that was sunny and in the 50s; the next it was snowing; and the next it was raining and blowing 50-mph gusts. You've got to be ready for all of it.

For firearms, a deer sized caliber is fine, although you do want something that packs enough power should you find yourself in a situation with a 1200-pound guy in a brown suit. Following is a partial list of some of the gear I took along.

- .300 Remington Ultra Mag, Model 700, topped with a Cabela's Alaskan Guide riflescope, 3 – 10x40, duplex reticle.
- .300 Remington Ultra Mag cartridges with 150-, 200-grain Swift A-Frame bullets
- Cabela's Alaskan Guide full-size binoculars (8x42)
- Bushnell Legend rangefinder
- Shockey Fannin caping knife
- Remington skinning knife
- Surefire E2L AA Outdoorsman flashlight
- Saint Minmus white LED headlamp
- Cabela's MTO 50 jacket, pants (this raingear is the bomb: it's quiet, comfortable, and kept me dry no matter what the conditions.
- 2 pair gloves
- Two pair Cabela's Alaskan Guide Microtex shirts & pants
- Fleece pullover, pants
- Polartec watch cap
- 3 pair base layers, different weights.
- 2 pair boots (Cabela's Meindl Perfekt boots, Columbia Omni-Heat boots)
- Cabela's Elite Scout Hunting Pack
- Cabela's XPG backpacker sleeping bag
- 3 pair socks, liner socks.
- Scent Killer body soap, field wipes, antiperspirant (Wildlife Research)

I ran into four members of our group at a recent trade show. We all went out for a few beers, to relive old times. Len told about the bear, always out of sight, that kept growling at he and Jeanneret on the day they hunted together. It followed them for more than 400 yards, crunching through the snow, snarling, roaring, keeping pace with the two hunters. They eventually called the skiff to get them out of there.

Skip and I reminisced about hunting above the snowline together, and glassing a draw where a forkhorn practically walked over me as I stood motionless behind a tree. Twenty yards from there, we came upon sow and cub tracks, prints so fresh that the snow was still tumbling from the rims down into the prints. I remember being glad I hadn't shot that small buck with bears obviously close by. We went in the other direction.

Luke was still beaming about the trophy buck he took, and kept talking about the "best day of his life."

Looking back, it was the best week for all of us.

The Men That Don't Fit In

By Robert Service

There's a race of men that don't fit in,
　A race that can't stay still;
So they break the hearts of kith and kin,
　And they roam the world at will.
They range the field and they rove the flood,
And they climb the mountain's crest;
Theirs is the curse of the gypsy blood,
　And they don't know how to rest.

If they just went straight they might go far;
　They are strong and brave and true;
But they're always tired of the things that are,
　And they want the strange and new.
They say: "Could I find my proper groove,
　What a deep mark I would make!"
So they chop and change, and each fresh move
　Is only a fresh mistake.

And each forgets, as he strips and runs
　With a brilliant, fitful pace,
It's the steady, quiet, plodding ones
　Who win in the lifelong race.
And each forgets that his youth has fled,
　Forgets that his prime is past,
Till he stands one day, with a hope that's dead,
　In the glare of the truth at last.

He has failed, he has failed; he has missed
　his chance;
　He has just done things by half.
Life's been a jolly good joke on him,
　And now is the time to laugh.
Ha, ha! He is one of the Legion Lost;
　He was never meant to win;
He's a rolling stone, and it's bred in the bone;
　He's a man who won't fit in.

Part 7

Contributors and Their Works

All short stories, articles, recipes, and other works appearing in this compendium have been reprinted courtesy of the authors listed below. To buy any of their books, go to the websites indicated.

Hal Blood (bigwoodsbucks.com)

*Hunting Big Woods Bucks: Secrets of Tracking and Stalking Whitetails**
Hunting Big Woods Bucks, Vol. 2

Monte Burch (monteburch.com)

Backyard Structures and How to Build Them
Black Bass Basics
Building Small Barns, Sheds & Shelters
Cleaning and Preparing Gamefish
Country Crafts and Skills
Denny Brauer's Jig Fishing Secrets
Field Dressing and Butchering Upland Birds, Waterfowl and Wild Turkeys
Lohman Guide to Calling & Decoying Waterfowl
Lohman Guide to Successful Turkey Calling
Making Native American Hunting, Fighting and Survival Tools
Mounting Your Deer Head at Home
Monte Burch's Pole Building Projects
Pocket Guide to Bowhunting Whitetail Deer
Pocket Guide to Field Dressing, Butchering & Cooking Deer
Pocket Guide to Old Time Catfish Techniques
Pocket Guide to Seasonal Largemouth Bass Patterns
Pocket Guide to Seasonal Walleye Tactics
Pocket Guide to Spring and Fall Turkey Hunting
Solving Squirrel Problems
*The Complete Guide to Sausage Making**
*The Complete Jerky Book**
*The Hunting and Fishing Camp Builder's Guide**
*The Joy of Smoking and Salt Curing**
*The Ultimate Guide to Growing Your Own Food**

The Ultimate Guide to Making Outdoor Gear and Accessories
The Ultimate Guide to Skinning and Tanning

Jay Cassell (http://www.amazon.com/s/ ref=ntt_athr_dp_sr_1?_encoding=UTF8&field-author=Jay%20 Cassell&ie=UTF8&search-alias=books&sort=relevancerank)

North America's Greatest Big Game Lodges & Outfitters: More Than 250 Prime Destinations in the U.S. & Canada
North America's Greatest Whitetail Lodges & Outfitters: More Than 250 Prime Destinations in the U.S. & Canada (with Peter Fiduccia)
*Shooter's Bible: The World's Bestselling Firearms Reference**
*The Best Hunting Stories Ever Told**
*The Gigantic Book of Hunting Stories**
*The Little Red Book of Hunter's Wisdom (with Peter Fiduccia)**
The Quotable Hunter
*The Ultimate Guide to Fishing Skills, Tactics, and Techniques: A Comprehensive Guide to Catching Bass, Trout, Salmon, Walleyes, Panfish, Saltwater Gamefish, and Much More**
The Ultimate Prepper's Guide
The Ultimate Guide to Self-Reliant Living

Richard P. Combs (http://www.amazon.com/ Richard-Combs/e/B001KMGYQQ/ref=sr_ntt_srch_ lnk_1?qid=1341340136&sr=1-1)

Canoeing and Kayaking Ohio's Streams: An Access Guide for Paddlers and Anglers
*Guide to Advanced Turkey Hunting: How to Call and Decoy Even Wary Boss Gobblers into Range**
Turkey Hunting Tactics of the Pros: Expert Advice to Help You Get a Gobbler This Season

Judd Cooney (http://www.juddcooney.com/)

Advanced Scouting for Whitetails

Decoying Big Game: Successful Tactics for Luring Deer, Elk, Bears, and Other Animals into Range

How to Attract Whitetails

The Bowhunter's Field Manual

Kathy Etling (www.amazon.com/Kathy-Etling/e/B001K8D1XE)

Bowhunting's Superbucks: How Some of the Biggest Bucks in North America Were Taken*

Cougar Attacks: Encounters of the Worst Kind

Denise Parker: A Teenage Archer's Quest for Olympic Glory

Hunting Bears: Black, Brown, Grizzly and Polar Bears

Hunting Superbucks: How to Find and Hunt Today's Trophy Mule and Whitetail Deer

The Art of Whitetail Deception

The Quotable Cowboy

The Ultimate Guide to Calling, Rattling, and Decoying Whitetails*

Thrill of the Chase

J. Wayne Fears (http://www.jwaynefears.com/)

Backcountry Cooking

How to Build Your Dream Cabin in the Woods: The Ultimate Guide to Building and Maintaining a Backcountry

Getaway*

Hunting Club Guide

Hunting North America's Big Bear: Grizzly, Brown, and Polar Bear Hunting Techniques and Adventures

Hunting Whitetails East & West

Scrape Hunting from A to Z

The Complete Book of Dutch Oven Cooking*

The Field & Stream Wilderness Cooking Handbook: How to Prepare, Cook, and Serve Backcountry Meals

The Pocket Outdoor Survival Guide: The Ultimate Guide for Short-Term Survival*

Kate Fiduccia (www.amazon.com/Kate-Fiduccia/e/B001K8AD58)

Cooking Wild in Kate's Camp

Cooking Wild in Kate's Kitchen: Venison

Grillin' and Chili'n: Eighty Easy Recipes for Venison to Sizzle, Smoke, and Simmer

The Quotable Wine Lover

The Venison Cookbook: Venison Dishes from Fast to Fancy*

Peter Fiduccia (http://www.woodsnwater.tv)

101 Deer Hunting Tips: Practical Advice from a Master Hunter

North America's Greatest Whitetail Lodges & Outfitters: More Than 250 Prime Destinations in the U.S. & Canada (with Jay Cassell)

The Little Red Book of Hunter's Wisdom (with Jay Cassell)

Whitetail Strategies: A No-Nonsense Approach to Successful Deer Hunting

Whitetail Strategies: The Ultimate Guide

Whitetail Strategies, Vol. II: Straightforward Tactics for Tracking, Calling, the Rut, and Much More

Dave Henderson (http://www.hendersonoutdoors.com/)

Campsite to Kitchen Cookbook

Gunsmithing Shotguns: A Basic Guide to Care and Repair

Modern Shotgunning

Shotgunning for Deer: Guns, Loads, and Techniques for the Modern Hunter*

The Ultimate Guide to Shotgunning: Guns, Gear, and Hunting Tactics for Deer and Big Game, Upland Birds, Waterfowl, and Small Game

White Tails: A Modern Look at Deer Hunting

Tom Indrebo (http://www.amazon.com/Tom-Indrebo/e/B002EID7K6)

Growing & Hunting Quality Bucks: A Hands-On Approach to Better Land and Deer Management*

Dr. Todd A. Kuhn (http://www.amazon.com/Shooters-Bible-Guide-Bowhunting-Todd/dp/1620878127/ref=sr_1_1?s=books&ie=UTF8&qid=1404409989&sr=1-1)

The Shooter's Bible Guide to Bowhunting

Jeff Murray (http://www.amazon.com/Jeff-Murray/e/B001K8Z7UO/ref=sr_tc_2_0?qid=1404409535&sr=1-2-ent)

For Big Bucks Only
Moon Phase Deer Hunting
Moon Struck: Hunting Strategies that Revolve Around the Moon

Sigurd Olson (http://singingwilderness.net/wordpress/)

Listening Point
Lonely Land
Meaning Of Wilderness: Essential Articles and Speeches
Of Time And Place
Open Horizons
Reflections from the North Country
Runes Of The North
Spirit Of The North: The Quotable Sigurd F. Olson
The Hidden Forest
The Singing Wilderness
Wilderness Days

Dr. Leonard Lee Rue III (http://www.ruewildlifephotos.com/index/gallery/BOOKS)

Beavers
Cottontail
Deer Hunter's Illustrated Dictionary

Furbearing Animals of North America
How to Photograph Animals in the Wild
Leonard Lee Rue III's Deer Hunting Tips and Techniques
Leonard L. Rue III's Way of the Whitetail
Leonard L. Rue III's Whitetails
Meet the Opossum
New Jersey Out-of-Doors
Pictorial Guide to the Mammals of North America
The Deer Hunter's Encyclopedia
The Deer of North America
The Encyclopedia of Deer
Whitetail Savvy

Leo Somma http://www.amazon.com/s/ref=dp_byline_sr_book_2?ie=UTF8&field-author=Leo+Somma&search-alias=books&text=Leo+Somma&sort=relevancerank)

25 Projects for Outdoorsmen: Quick and Easy Plans for the Deer Camp, Home, Woods, and Backyard
Do-It-Yourself Projects for Bowhunters

John Trout, Jr. (www.amazon.com/John-Trout/e/B001JP29BI)

Ambushing Trophy Whitetails: Tactical Systems for Big-Buck Success
Finding Wounded Deer
Hunting Rutting Bucks: Secrets for Tagging the Biggest Buck of Your Life
Solving Coyote Problems: How to Coexist with North America's Most Persistent Predator
The Complete Book of Wild Turkey Hunting

Wayne Van Zwoll (http://highcountrywomen.com/)

America's Greatest Gunmakers
Bolt Action Rifles

Deer Rifles & Cartridges*
Hunter's Guide to Long-Range Shooting
Elk and Elk Hunting
Elk Rifles, Cartridges and Hunting Tactics
Leupold & Stevens… First Century
Mastering Mule Deer
Modern Sporting Rifle Cartridges
Shooter's Bible Guide to Rifle Ballistics*
The Complete Book of the .22
The Gun Digest Book of Sporting Optics
The Hunter's Guide to Accurate Shooting
The Hunter's Guide to Ballistics

John Weiss (http://www.amazon.com/John-Weiss/e/B001HMQ12Q)

Advanced Deerhunter's Bible
Planting Food Plots for Deer and Other Wildlife
Skinning, Aging, and Butchering Deer*
Sure-Fire Whitetail Tactics
The Bass Angler's Almanac: More Than 750 Tips & Tactics
The Whitetail Deer Hunter's Almanac
The Ultimate Guide to Butchering Deer: A Step-by-Step Guide to Field Dressing,

*A Skyhorse publication